Intercultural Communication

A READER

Larry A. Samovar
SAN DIEGO STATE UNIVERSITY,
EMERITUS

Richard E. Porter
CALIFORNIA STATE UNIVERSITY,
LONG BEACH, EMERITUS

Edwin R. McDaniel
AICHI SHUKUTOKU UNIVERSITY

WADSWORTH
CENGAGE Learning™

Australia • Brazil • Japan • Korea • Mexico • Singapore • Spain • United Kingdom • United States

WADSWORTH
CENGAGE Learning

**Intercultural Communication:
A Reader, Twelfth Edition**
Larry A. Samovar/Richard E. Porter/
Edwin R. McDaniel

Publisher: Lyn Uhl

Acquisitions Editor: Monica Eckman

Development Editor: Kimberly Gengler

Editorial Assistant: Kimberly Apfelbaum

Technology Project Manager: Stephanie
Gregoire

Executive Marketing Manager:
Erin Mitchell

Marketing Assistant: Mary Anne Payumo

Advertising Project Manager:
Shemika Britt

Senior Content Project Manager:
Karen Stocz

Creative Director: Rob Hugel

Art Director: Linda Helcher

Print Buyer: Sue Carroll

Permissions Editor: Sarah D'Stair

Production Service:
ICC Macmillan Inc.

Cover Images: Nevada Wier/Stone/
© Getty Images
Gavin Gough/The Image Bank/
© Getty Images © J Marshall—
Tribaleye Images/ Alamy

For product information and technology assistance, contact us at
Cengage Learning Academic Resource Center, 1-800-423-0563
For permission to use material from this text or product,
submit all requests online at **www.cengage.com/permissions.**
Further permissions questions can be e-mailed to
permissionrequest@cengage.com.

Library of Congress Control Number: 2008920144

ISBN-13: 978-0-495-55418-9

ISBN-10: 0-495-55418-9

Wadsworth Cengage Learning
25 Thomson Place
Boston, MA 02210
USA

Cengage Learning products are represented in Canada by Nelson Education, Ltd.

For your course and learning solutions, visit **academic.cengage.com.**

Purchase any of our products at your local college store or at our preferred online store **www.ichapters.com.**

Printed in the United States of America
2 3 4 5 6 7 12 11 10 09 08

Contents

Preface

The only person who is educated is the one who has learned how to learn and change.

CAROL ROGERS

A SIMPLE "THANK YOU"

We begin with simple a "thank you" to all those educators and students who have seen our book through eleven previous editions. We are not being pedestrian or trite when we say that it is indeed a special honor and distinction to be part of a book that has generated enough enthusiasm and interest to be published for the twelfth time. Hence, we trust you can understand why we are excited about this new edition and felt that we wanted to begin by expressing our appreciation to the thousands of individuals who have found something of value in our presentation.

BLENDING THE NEW AND THE OLD

We approached this new edition with the twin feelings of exhilaration and prudence. The excitement, as noted, was because the recognition we received warranted yet another new edition of our reader. Still, our sense of pride was moderated with a heavy dose of caution. As we proceeded, we wanted to preserve the basic framework and philosophy that has sustained us through the previous eleven editions, while at the same time we needed to include topics that are new to the field. Here then in our twelfth edition is that balance of these two complementary positions—the past and present.

First, the new treatment continues to reflect our belief that the basic core of the field should not be changed for the sake of being novel; such change would deprive the book of those fundamental concepts that have infused all of the previous editions. Second, a new book needs to reflect how intercultural theory has evolved since the last edition. We needed to present essays that mirror that change. We believe we have accomplished the blending of the old with new in this edition. We have, as is the case in all past editions, even staked out some new territory for the field.

A POINT OF VIEW

We commence this section with a somewhat obvious declaration—as a member of a multicultural world, the ability to successfully engage in intercultural communication may be one of the most important skills you will ever develop. If you believe that we offer that assertion because we are the editors of an intercultural book, you would be partially correct. However, you need only look around your immediate surroundings and the globe to see the validity of our conclusions. For now, more then ever before, you are being challenged by a future in which you will interact with people from a wide range of dissimilar cultural backgrounds. As we just noted, those people may include your neighbor who speaks with a foreign accent, someone a thousand miles away who considers you an enemy, or your new employer whose company is headquartered in another country. Regardless of the specifics, it behooves you to prepare to meet this new challenge brought by the mixing of cultures at home and abroad. This book is designed to assist you with that assignment. We begin by noting it will not be easy. First, because your view of the world is shaped by the perspective of your own culture, it is often difficult to understand and appreciate many of the actions originating in other people, groups, and nations. Your cultural perception tends to condition you to see people and events through a highly selective lens. Second, to be a successful intercultural communicator you must be open to new and different communication experiences, have empathy toward cultures different from your own, develop a universalistic, realistic worldview, and learn to be tolerant of views that differ from your own.

The communication characteristics are easy for you to read about, but let us assure you that translating them into action is a very difficult assignment. Yet training in intercultural communication does offer you an arena in which to work on these skills. In short, it is your ability to change, to make adjustments in your communication habits and behavior, that gives you the potential to engage in successful and effective intercultural contacts.

OUR APPROACH

The basic energizing motive for this book has remained the same since we became interested in the topic of intercultural communication over 40 years ago. We sincerely believe that the ability to communicate effectively with people from other cultures and co-cultures benefits each of us as individuals and has the potential to benefit the more than seven billion people with whom we share this planet. We have intentionally selected materials that will assist you in understanding those intercultural communication principles that are instrumental to success when you interact with people from diverse cultures. Fundamental to our approach is the conviction that *communication is a social activity; it is something people do to and with one another.* The activity might begin in our heads, but it is manifested in our behaviors, be they verbal or nonverbal. In both explicit and implicit ways, the information and the advice contained in this book are usable; the ideas presented can be translated into action.

NEW FEATURES

We have already noted that the study of intercultural communication is a vibrant and energetic discipline. As intercultural contacts became more intense and widespread the field has been forced to adapt to these new dynamics. As it has evolved we have attempted to mature and adapt with it. In 1972, the first edition contained 34 articles and essays. In this new edition we included 47 of which 30 are new to this volume. Of these, 25 were written exclusively for this edition. Also, six authors from earlier editions have made revisions to their selections for this new volume.

In one sense we would say that the tallying of 30 new essays constitutes "new features." But that count is obvious. There are however two other changes that are deserving of the title of "new features." First, in an attempt to broaden our theoretical base, we have incorporated the work of numerous international scholars from Germany, Korea, China, Japan, Kenya, Israel, and India who were able to compliment and counterbalance the research of the academic community in the United States. Second, because of our long held conviction that it is the deep structure of a culture that dictates how members of each culture view themselves and others, we have added a number of new essays that look at religion, world view, identity, and spiritually. These enduring deep structure elements carry a culture's most important beliefs, and are emotional, deeply felt concepts. They also have a profound influence on how perceptions are shaped and how people communicate. For these reasons we have added many new selections that examine the deep structure elements of culture. Finally, realizing we have been editing this book for nearly 40 years, we have chosen to include the voices of new, young scholars who have added a fresh perspective that we have been able to combine with the basic core of the field.

MAKE USE OF THE BOOK

As in the past, we intend this anthology to be for the general reader, so we have selected materials that are broadly based, comprehensive, and suitable for both undergraduate and graduate students. Although the level of difficulty varies from essay to essay, we have not gone beyond the level found in most textbooks directed toward college and university students.

Intercultural Communication: A Reader is designed to meet three specific needs. The first comes from a canon that maintains that successful intercultural communication is a matter of highest importance if humankind and society are to survive. Events during the past 40 years have created a world that sees us become increasingly linked together in a multitude of ways. From pollution to economics to health care, what happens to one culture potentially happens to all other cultures. This book, then, is designed to serve as a basic anthology for courses concerned with the issues associated with human interaction. Our intention is to make this book both theoretical and practical so that the issues associated with intercultural communication can be first understood and then acted upon.

Second, the book may be used as a supplemental text to existing service and basic communication skill courses and interpersonal communication courses. Third, the text provides resource material for courses in communication theory, small group communication, organizational and business communication, and mass communication, as well as for courses in anthropology, health care, sociology, social psychology, social welfare, social policy, business, and international relations. The long list of possible uses only underscores the increased level of intercultural interaction that is characteristic of what is often now called the "global village."

ORGANIZATION

The book is organized into eight closely related chapters. In Chapter 1, "Approaches to Understanding Intercultural Communication," our purpose is twofold: We hope to acquaint you with the basic concepts of intercultural communication while at the same time arousing your interest in the topic. Hence, the essays in this chapter are both theoretical and philosophical. The selections explain what intercultural communication is, why it is important, and how it operates. Chapter 2, "Cultural Identity: Issues of Belonging," has essays that demonstrate how different cultural and ethnic identities influence role expectations, perceptions, and intercultural interaction. Through various stories you will be able to get an appreciation of how a person's cultural identity helps shape his or her view of the world. Chapter 3, "International Cultures: Understanding Diversity," deals with the communication patterns of six specific cultures. We offer a sampling of cultures found in East Asia, India, Egypt, and Africa. We should add

that in many other chapters of the book we examine additional international cultures in the health care, business and educational setting. Chapter 4, "Co-Cultures: Living in Two Cultures," moves us from the international arena to co-cultures that exist within the United States. Here again space constraints have limited the total number of co-cultures we could include. Yet we believe that through the selection of groups such as Hawaiians, African Americans, Asian Americans, the disabled, and homosexuals, you will get an idea of the cultural diversity found in those groups with whom most of you have regular contact. As is the case with international cultures, many other co-cultures will appear in other chapters.

In Chapter 5, "Intercultural Messages: Verbal and Nonverbal Communication," we study how verbal and nonverbal symbols are used (and differ) in intercultural communication. We offer readings that will introduce you to some of the difficulties you might encounter when your intercultural partner uses a different verbal or nonverbal coding system. We will look at how verbal idiosyncrasies and distinctions influence problem solving, speaking, perception, and understanding. As noted, this chapter is also concerned with nonverbal symbols and explains some of the cultural differences in movement, facial expressions, eye contact, silence, space, time, and the like.

Chapter 6, "Cultural Contexts: The Influence of Setting," continues with the theme of how culture modifies interaction. This time, however, the interaction is examined within a specific context. The assumption is that rules which influence how members of a culture behave in certain settings will vary across cultures. To clarify this important issue, we have selected "places" where cultures often follow rules that differ from those found in North America. More specifically, we look at settings related to business, groups, negotiations, health care, and education. In Chapter 7, "Communicating Interculturally: Becoming Competent," readings are offered that highlight some problems inherent in intercultural communication. In addition, solutions are advanced that are intended to provide you with knowledge about and suggestions for improving intercultural communication.

Chapter 8, "Ethical Considerations: Prospects for the Future," presents essays that deal with ethical and moral issues as well as the future directions and challenges of intercultural communication. It is also the intent of this chapter to ask you not to conclude your study of intercultural communication with the reading of a single book or the completion of one course.

We believe that the study of intercultural communication is a lifetime endeavor. Each time we want to share an idea or feeling with someone from another culture, we face a new and exhilarating learning experience.

ASSISTANCE

As in the past, many people have helped us rethink and reshape this project. We express appreciation to our editors Jaime Perkins and Monica Eckman, who offered sound advice and positive direction as they guided our book from inception to completion. We also wish to thank Kimberly Gengler, who was always available to handle both major and minor problems. And, as we do with each edition, we must call attention to our first editor, Rebecca Hayden. Becky had enough courage and insight 38 years ago to decide that intercultural communication should and would become a viable discipline. We also need to recognize the contribution of Cengage Wadsworth Publishing Company. Although "corporate dynamics" have forced us to adapt to a never ending stream of new people and "philosophies," Cengage Wadsworth has nevertheless been consistent in their determination to produce and market a quality textbook that examines a topic of great importance to all college and university students who deem to call themselves "educated."

In a culture that values change, this anthology would not have survived for nearly 40 years if we had not been fortunate enough to have so many scholars willing to contribute original essays to each edition. Here in the twelfth edition, we acknowledge the work of Satoshi Ishii, Donald Klopf, Peggy Cooke, Yoshitaka Miike, Ronald Jackson, II, Jamie Moshin, John T. Warren, B. L. Zimmerman, Patricia Geist-Martin, Mei Zhong, Sabine Chai, Etsuko Kinefuchi, Chuka Onwumechili, Peter Nwuso, Mary Fong, Polly A. Begley, Ann Neville Miller, Young Yun Kim, Charmaine Ka'imikawa, Dawn Braithwaite, Charles Braithwaite, William F. Eadie, Justin Charlebois, Donald G. Ellis, Ifat Maoz, Carolyn Roy, Peter A. Andersen, Hua Wang, Kazuo Kishiyama, Michael B. Hinner, Patricia Parker, Jennifer Mease, Debbie A. Ockey, Karen Rasmussen, Jennifer Asenas, Eriko Katsumata, Brian H. Spitzberg, Summer Carnett, Katherine Slauta, Guo-Ming Chen, Marc D. Rich, Lucretia R. Robinson, Courtney Aherns, and José Rodriguez. We thank all of you for letting us share your voices with thousands of other people who share your commitment to intercultural matters.

Finally, we conclude the preface the way we started it. We again express our gratitude to the thousands of users of previous editions who have given the opportunity to "talk to them." Although the contact has been somewhat intangible, we nevertheless appreciate it all the same.

Approaches to Intercultural Communication

Every tale can be told in a different way.

GREEK PROVERB

The practice of intercultural communication is as old as humankind, coming into existence the first time people from different tribal cultures encountered one another and tried to communicate. History is filled with accounts of people endeavoring to learn other languages and understand different cultures. While the motives may have varied—to include travel, trade, intellectual exchange, religious proselytization, economic colonization, or political subjugation—the process of intercultural communication was similar. Despite such a long history and being so obviously critical to successful cross-cultural exchange, intercultural communication became a field of serious, systematic study only during the latter half of the twentieth century. Within the past 30 years or so, cultural diversity has been recognized as a critical factor when people from different cultural groups attempt to communicate.

Perhaps the major impetus for the ever-increasing effort to understand and explain the intercultural communication process is the realization that modern societies must learn to cooperate in order to prevent their mutual self-destruction. The history of intercultural communication has been largely characterized as a rhetoric of force rather than reason and understanding. People, however, are increasingly aware that the employment of force normally achieves only limited success. This is accompanied by a nearly unanimous consensus that saving the planet's ecology will require international cooperation on a scale previously unseen. An additional reason behind the importance of intercultural communication is more pragmatic. Rapid, affordable means of transportation have facilitated increased contact among cultures, giving rise to international economic interdependencies, transnational corporations, and culturally diverse workforces. The number of intercultural marriages continues to rise and immigration increases unabated. These developments have created a requirement for communication skills appropriate for life in a multicultural global village—regardless of whether we remain at home, visit another country, or sojourn abroad.

Prior to the mid-twentieth century, intercultural communication, while universal, was the province of only a select number of people. Government emissaries, merchants and traders, missionaries, geographical and archeological explorers, cultural anthropologists, military personnel, and wealthy tourists were the most common visitors to foreign cultures. Within the United States, intercultural contact was historically limited, restrained, and generally hierarchical in nature. Different ethnic groups tended to congregate into separate urban and rural communities. In the southern United States, members of nonwhite races were usually segregated until the mid-1960s, when laws were changed to mandate integrated schools, workforces, and to some extent, neighborhoods. Additionally, as a result of the cost, time, and rigors of international travel, most white Euro-Americans rarely left their own country. Technological advances have, of course, brought about marked changes in our ability to travel, and as a result, the United States is now a highly mobile society, both domestically and internationally.

At this juncture, we need to specify our approach to intercultural communication and recognize that other people investigate quite different perspectives. For example, some scholars who examine mass media are concerned with international broadcasting, worldwide freedom of expression, the premise of Western domination of media information, and the use of electronic technologies for instantaneous worldwide communication. Other groups study international communication with an emphasis on communication between national governments—the communication of diplomacy, economic assistance, disaster aid, and even political propaganda. Still others are interested in the communication needed to conduct business on a global basis. Their concerns include such issues as cross-cultural marketing, negotiation styles, management, and conflict resolution, as well as daily communication within multi- and transnational organizations.

Our concern, however, relates to the more personal aspects of communication: What happens when people from different cultures interact face-to-face? Thus, our approach explores the interpersonal dimensions of intercultural communication across different contexts. The essays we have selected for this edition focus on the variables of both culture and communication that are most likely to influence an intercultural communication encounter—those occasions when you attempt to exchange information, ideas, or feelings with someone from a different culture.

Intercultural communication research has revealed a variety of cross-cultural variations and produced a number of applicable theories. Despite these advances, the body of knowledge concerning intercultural communications is far from complete. Data relating to cultural diversity acquired from other disciplines has not yet been fully integrated. Much of the emergent information has been more a reaction to ongoing sociological, racial, and ethnic concerns than an attempt to define and explain intercultural communication. It is, however, clear that a facility with intercultural communication can mitigate, and sometimes even prevent, communication problems, often even before they arise.

An awareness of something as simple as cultural variations in eye contact can help teachers achieve greater communication effectiveness in their multicultural classroom. The international businessman who realizes that other cultures have different negotiation styles is more likely to acquire a contract satisfactory to both parties. Health care workers who understand that some people consider illness a curse may be able to provide better medical treatment. In a culturally diverse workforce, the manager who understands that there are variations in cultural values is more apt to be successful. A U.S. military patrol entering a home in Iraq or Afghanistan would be well served by a knowledge of local cultural etiquette. Succinctly, we believe that many problems can be resolved, or avoided, through an awareness and understanding of the components of intercultural communication. This book, by applying those components to numerous cultures and contexts, is an effort to promote that understanding.

Your exploration of intercultural communication begins with a series of varied articles designed to (1) introduce the philosophy underlying our concept of intercultural communication; (2) provide a general orientation to, and overview of, intercultural communication; (3) theorize about the analysis of intercultural transactions; (4) offer insight into different motivations underlying cultural variation; and (5) demonstrate the importance of intercultural communication in contemporary society. Our objective is to provide you an introduction to the diverse dimensions of intercultural communication that will help you to approach subsequent chapters with a mindset that makes further inquiry interesting, informative, and useful.

The initial essay, by the three editors of this text, is titled "Understanding Intercultural Communications: The Working Principles." This essay will introduce you to many of the specific subjects and issues associated with the study of intercultural communication. As a preface to the essay, we use the context of our rapidly integrating global community to demonstrate the importance of intercultural communication, both at home and aboard. Next, we discuss the purpose of communication, define it, and provide a review of its characteristics. Third, we offer an overview of culture—what it is and what it does. We then focus on the specific dimensions of culture that are most germane to human communication—those components that constitute the study of intercultural communication. We examine a number of major variables—perceptual elements, cognitive patterns, verbal and nonverbal behaviors, and social contexts—to help you better understand what happens when people of varying cultural backgrounds engage in communication. By understanding, at the outset of the book, what the study of intercultural communication entails, you will have a greater appreciation for the subsequent essays.

In the second essay, Harry C. Triandis introduces you to one way of approaching intercultural communication. Triandis begins by underscoring one of the propositions of this book—that culture and communication are linked. But, he goes on to show that cultural differences often lead to and cause miscommunication and conflict. This connection will become evident when he speaks of culture as including "the knowledge that people need to have in order to function effectively in their social environment."

To assist you in identifying what "knowledge" is most useful when interacting with another culture, Triandis examines what he calls *cultural syndromes*—"a shared pattern of beliefs, attitudes, self-definitions, norms, and values organized around a theme." In his discussion, Triandis defines, explains, and relates nine different syndromes, and reports that miscommunication can occur when people are not aware of these syndromes. Because effective intercultural communication is so dependent on mutual knowledge of the existing diversity, we ask you to learn about these syndromes as part of your intercultural communication training.

We extend our understanding of culture with the essay "Worldview in Intercultural Communication: A Religio-Cosmological Approach," which uses the concept of *worldview* as a window for looking at culture. The authors, Satoshi Ishii, Donald Klopf, and Peggy Cooke contend that worldview is a fundamental building block of culture that "permeates all other components of culture" and helps us to distinguish between cultures. A culture's worldview represents a collective description of how the cosmos and universe function and how each individual fits into that religious and philosophical scheme. Your worldview serves as a guide to answering questions related to pain, suffering, death, and the meaning of life. The authors' basic premise is that worldview shapes a culture's psyche and helps the members of that culture make sense of the world.

While worldview can take a variety of forms (scientific, metaphysical, and religious), it is generally agreed that religion exerts the greatest influence. Even a secular person is greatly affected by the writings, attitudes, beliefs, and ethics advanced by a culture's religious traditions. To help you appreciate the impact of religion on culture, the essay highlights the major dimensions of Eastern and Western religions, which collectively encompass some 80 percent of all people in the world. The authors also provide a discussion of some of the problems that might occur when Eastern and Western worldviews collide in the context of environmental communication. They conclude by recommending a "religio-cosmological approach" to investigating worldview, which can help to resolve and prevent intercultural communication problems.

"'Harmony without Uniformity': An Asiacentric Worldview and Its Communicative Implications," the fourth article in this chapter, continues our study of worldview. The author, Yoshitaka Miike, proposes that conflict and problems arise not from cultural difference itself but from the ignorance of that difference. Moreover, as global citizens, not only must we appreciate cultural diversity, we must *learn* from that diversity. According to Miike, all too often cultural difference is viewed through the lens of one's own worldview, but to truly understand and learn from another culture, "we must understand the worldview of the culture and its impact on the forms and functions of communication."

The essay contends that many intercultural studies have imposed the European worldview on other cultures, resulting in a critical examination rather than an investigation designed to gain "insight and inspiration." To begin the process of learning *from,* rather than merely *about,* other cultures, the author suggests that you need to (1) understand your own worldview, (2) understand other cultures' worldviews, and (3) understand how other cultures perceive your culture. This latter recommendation is particularly relevant on the stage of contemporary international relations.

In the second half of the essay, Miike discusses an "Asiancentric worldview and its communicative implications in local and global contexts." He proposes five Asiacentric communication propositions, which reflect his interpretation of the Asian worldview. These include (1) circularity, (2) harmony, (3) other-directedness, (4) reciprocity, and (5) relationality. Awareness and understanding of these propositions offers greater insight into Asian cultures and presents an alternative to the Eurocentric worldview. The essay concludes that the processes of globalization have increased the requirement to not just learn *about* other cultures but to find ways that promote and facilitate intercultural *learning.*

The next article, "Pathways of Human Understanding: An Inquiry into Western and North American Indian Worldview Structures," by Leo Schelbert, provides still another perspective on worldview. Schelbert examines "worldview structure," which he believes exists primarily in the subconscious and shapes one's understanding by serving as taken for granted, often unquestioned, "roads to be traveled." Western and Native American worldview structures are used to illustrate this concept.

The essay proposes that the original Western worldview structure, consisting of heaven, earth, and hell, has been largely subsumed by a duality consisting of "humans" and "nature." In this duality, nature is conceived as being subordinate to, and for the use of, humans. Following a discussion of four unique traits of the Western worldview structure, the essay examines the historical beginnings of the structure, which purportedly originated some 3,200 years ago in the southern steppes of Asia.

Schelbert then provides a contrasting example using the American Indian worldview structure, which differs radically from its Western counterpart. Rather than the dualistic individualism inherent in the Western perspective, American Indian worldview structure is characterized by a holistic understanding. In other words, all things, both animate and inanimate, are seen as "people" and all are considered sacred. In this view, sacred refers to an interdependence among things (or "people"), which are "enmeshed in a cosmic dance." The concept of a supreme being is said to be alien to the American Indian worldview structure. The conclusion provides a discussion of various paths that one may discover by closely examining varying worldview structures.

The final article in this chapter is "The Cultural Iceberg" by John Hooker, who argues that Westerners have historically assumed that their lifestyle was the only way to live. Hooker explains that international work and travel instilled in him the realization that people all over the world face similar problems in life but usually find quite different ways of dealing with those difficulties. The essay advocates a greater awareness of the influence of culture and how cultures vary. This will help people, in all walks of life, to more effectively interact in the globalized community.

Hooker likens culture to an iceberg, with the visible manifestations representing only a small portion of those ideals, behaviors, norms, etc., that constitute the culture's way of life. The majority of cultural variations lie beneath the surface, out of sight and awareness. He contends that most intercultural training programs tend to "reduce culture to matters of language, customs, and etiquette," more visible portions. These programs unfortunately fail to explicate the underlying cultural values, beliefs, and assumptions which actually shape the visible cultural manifestations. Culture can also be characterized as a language that gives meaning to a society's daily practices, much as language does to words. Continuing the metaphor, the author indicates that you need to be fluent in the "cultural grammar" in order to be truly competent in another culture.

The essay concludes with a clarion call for greater understanding of cultural differences, because culture is seen as the "theme of our age." Hooker warns, however, that living and working in a culture is much more demanding than a visit, even a lengthy sojourn, which provides only a limited and rather structured interaction with local inhabitants. To help overcome problems of adaptation, several suggestions are recommended.

Understanding Intercultural Communication: The Working Principles

EDWIN R. McDANIEL

LARRY A. SAMOVAR

RICHARD E. PORTER

INTERCULTURAL COMMUNICATION AND GLOBALIZATION

The primary objective of this chapter is to introduce and explain the basic elements of intercultural communication, which will assist you in understanding subsequent readings. Before addressing those fundamentals, however, we feel it necessary to provide a rationale for the growing importance of studying intercultural communication in a "globalized" society. In other words, we want to demonstrate how this subject is a factor in your everyday life.

By now, everyone has heard the term *globalization* so often, and in so many contexts it has become a cliché. It is commonly used to explain or justify almost any type of change. Google the term and you will get over 28 million suggested sites. According to some reports, the belief that the world is moving toward a "homogenized" culture is part of the reason for the rise in fundamentalist movements—be they Islamic, Zionist, Hindi, or Evangelical ("Globalization," 2003). In another view, globalization and the attendant

This original essay appears here in print for the first time. All rights reserved. Permission to reprint must be obtained from the authors and the publisher. Dr. Edwin R. McDaniel teaches in the Department of Language Communication at Aichi Shukutoku University, Nagoya, Japan; Dr. Larry A. Samovar is Professor Emeritus in the School of Communication at San Diego State University; and Dr. Richard E. Porter is Professor Emeritus in the Department of Communication Studies at California State University, Long Beach.

communication technology revolution are seen as a source of cultural divergence, leading to "a period of conflict, inequality, and segmentation" (Brooks, 2005, A-23).

Even though the word is overused and perceptions about the influence are varied, the phenomenon is real and it is producing profound changes in contemporary world society. Globalization is a seemingly unstoppable process that brings each of us into greater contact with the rest of the world and gives our daily lives an increasingly international orientation. The current world political order provides continuing examples of the need for enhanced intercultural communication skills, as security concerns, immigration issues, environmental challenges, disease control management, and economic change become more internationally interwoven.

In the arena of international security, concern over nuclear proliferation is bringing nations together in an effort to negotiate peaceful resolutions. For example, China, Japan, Russia, South Korea, and the United States are all engaged in discussions with North Korea over nuclear arms. Member nations of the United Nations have agreed to impose economic sanctions against Iran for their apparent efforts to develop nuclear arms. Achieving a mutually satisfactory resolution of these two problems will require considerable intercultural communication skill. In the Iraq and Afghanistan conflict, the role of culture has been recognized to such an extent that the U.S. Department of Defense has established a project called "Cultural Operations Research Human Terrain" (Parker, 2006), and the U.S. Marine Corps now requires "Corps-wide cultural training" (Higgins, Trusso, & Connable, 2005, p. 5).

Immigration is a problem that almost all developed nations must deal with as increasing numbers of immigrants leave their native country to seek better economic opportunities or escape political oppression. Many Western European nations are dealing with rising fundamentalism among Middle East minorities, who feel they are being disenfranchised. In the fall of 2005, inequities between the French dominant culture and children and grandchildren of North African immigrant minorities resulted in nationwide riots. Lack of a coherent immigration policy is creating division among segments of the U.S. population. Domestic relations in the United

States are also strained as immigrant minorities strive to assert their political will (Barboza, 2007). A primary source of friction between immigrants and native residents is cultural differences. It is an unfortunate fact that people continue to "find it easier to accept immigrants who look and behave as they do than those who are different" ("Immigrants," 2007, p. 74).

The multiple ecological challenges facing the world community will require extensive and prolonged cooperative interactions. Environmental issues that must be dealt with include such diverse problems as global warming, rain forest destruction, pelagic pollution, declining ocean fish stocks, desertification resulting from long droughts, and many more. There are also numerous predictions of a future crisis over the availability of enough fresh water. One report indicates that "two-fifths of the world's people already face serious shortages" (Kirby, 2003, p.1) and global warming is expected to exacerbate this scarcity (Borenstein, 2007). Intercultural communication will play a salient role in the mediation needed to find successful solutions to these varied problems.

Disease control across international borders is another area where effective intercultural communication is particularly critical. Western and Asian governments are engaged in extensive cooperation to thwart the potential of an avian influenza pandemic ("Coming," 2007). In 2006, the United States enacted the Pandemic Influenza Act, which is intended to promote "international health surveillance and containment efforts" (Osterholm, 2007, pp. 51-52). And of course the fight against AIDS and "Mad Cow" disease continues on a global scale.

Globalization's economic influence has been well documented. There is little doubt about the increasing role of international commercial interdependencies. The critical role this plays in our daily lives is illustrated by one simple example. "In the United States, approximately 80 percent of all prescription drugs come from offshore . . ." (Osterholm, 2007, p. 55). This means that if you get sick and need medication, there is an 80 percent chance the drug has been made by someone from another culture who lives and works in another country. The power of globalization on economics is demonstrated by the fact that today "foreign money finances about 32% of U.S. domestic investment, up from 7% in 1995" (Mandel, 2006, p. 58).

According to one economist, globalization has become so overwhelming that the domestic economy can no longer be controlled by the U.S. government, and we might need to establish "global institutions for governing the world economy" (Mandel, 2006, p. 60). Clearly this presents a compelling rationale for greater understanding on how to successfully communicate in a multicultural environment.

As demonstrated by the preceding discussions, globalization is forging a new, emerging world order. This new political alignment promises to be quite different from the immediate post-communism arrangement, which was heavily dominated by U.S. influence and, to a much lesser degree, Western Europe. Growing international interdependencies related to security, immigration, ecology, disease control, and the economy will require increased international cooperation. China and India are expected to gain great power status in the near future as they achieve economic, political, and perhaps military leverage. Certainly the United States will have to be more accommodating in many of the principal international organizations, such as the World Bank, International Monetary Fund (IMF), World Trade Organization (WTO), World Health Organization (WHO), United Nations (UN), and the like (Drezner, 2007).

As the global community continues to integrate, all of us, willingly or unwillingly, must learn to deal with a social order characterized by escalating levels of contact and communication with people of other cultures. To successfully live and work in this evolving multicultural society, we must become more culturally aware and learn how to be effective intercultural communicators. This book is filled with essays designed to help you achieve that skill.

As the first step on the path to learning how to employ effective intercultural communication, we begin with a fundamental definition: *Intercultural communication occurs whenever a person from one culture sends a message to be processed by a person from a different culture.* While this may seem simple and undemanding, it requires a thorough understanding of two key ingredients—communication and culture. Therefore, we start by examining communication and its various components. Then, culture is explained. Finally, we explore how these two concepts are fused into intercultural communication.

WHAT IS COMMUNICATION?

Your daily life is inundated with communication activities. The day usually begins with some type of alarm clock sending you a signal to "get up and get going." Often, you will turn on the TV or radio even before getting out of bed. Commuting to class, you are continually exposed to signs and billboards, often while continuing to listen to the car radio or your iPod. In the classroom, you are exposed to an array of communicative interactions such as lectures, group projects, reading a textbook, or even sitting in the back of the room talking to a classmate or checking for text messages. Time between classes is used for such activities as meeting with a study group, talking to friends, checking e-mail, reading in the library, or arranging plans for a weekend party. After class, many students have jobs where they must communicate with other employees or customers. Evenings are taken up with study, TV, catching a movie, hanging out, calling a friend, surfing the Net, or phoning home in hopes of getting help with the latest credit card bill. Finally, at day's end while lying in bed, you might spend a few moments with the TV or listening to music to relax before drifting off to sleep.

These are just a few of the instances of communication engaged in on a daily basis. To function normally in today's information-driven society, one cannot avoid communicating. Moreover, we seem to have an innate need to associate with, and connect to, other people through communication. Thus, the motives for entering into any communicative interaction can be classified into one of three broad categories. When we communicate, regardless of the situation or context, we are trying to persuade, inform, or entertain. In other words, people communicate for a purpose; they have an objective.

A Definition of Communication

It should be intuitively evident that communication is fundamental to contemporary daily life, something that cannot readily be avoided or escaped. But what exactly is communication? What happens when we communicate? In answering these questions, we will define and explain the phenomenon.

Communication has been defined in a variety of ways, often depending on the writer's objective or the specific setting. You could easily review a variety of communication textbooks and journal articles without discovering two identical definitions. Often the definitions are long and rather abstract, as the author attempts to include as many aspects of communication as possible. In other places, the definition is narrow and precise, designed to explain a specific type or instance of communication. For understanding the union of culture and communication, however, a succinct, clearly comprehensible definition best serves everyone's interests. Thus, for us, *communication is the management of messages with the objective of creating meaning* (Griffin, 2005). This definition is somewhat broad, yet is precise in specifying what takes place in every communicative episode. Nor does it attempt to establish what constitutes successful or unsuccessful communication, which is actually determined by the involved participants, can vary from one person to another, and is frequently scenario dependent. The only qualifiers we place on communication are intentionality and interaction. In other words, if communication is considered to be purposeful—to persuade, inform, or entertain—then we communicate with an intention, and we achieve these objectives only through interaction with others.

The Structure of Communication

Using our definition of communication, we are now ready to examine the eight major structural components used in managing messages to create meaning. The first and most obvious is the **sender**—the individual or group originating the message. A sender is someone with a need or desire, be it social, work, or information driven, to communicate with others. To fulfill this motivation, the sender formulates and transmits the message via a channel to the receiver(s).

The **message** consists of the information the sender wants understood—what is used to create meaning. Messages can take the form of verbal or nonverbal behaviors, which are encoded and transmitted via a **channel** to the receiver. The channel is any means that offers a path for moving the message from the sender to the receiver. For example, an oral message may be sent directly when in the immediate presence of the receiver or mediated through a cell phone. A visual, or nonverbal, message can be transmitted by waving good-bye to a friend as you drive away or mediated through a video camera or a picture. Today, websites such as YouTube and MySpace provide channels that offer senders a means to reach millions of receivers through mediated messages.

The **receiver(s)** is the intended recipient of the message and the locus where meaning is created. Because the receiver interprets the message and assigns a meaning, which may or may not be what the receiver intended, communication is often characterized as *receiver based*. You may send a friend a "tongue-in-cheek" text message, but for a variety of reasons, such as lack of nonverbal cues, the receiver may (mis)interpret the message and feel offended. After interpreting the message and assigning a meaning, the receiver will formulate a **response.** This is the action taken by the receiver as a result of the meaning he or she assigns to the message. A response can be benign, such as simply ignoring a provocative remark, or, at the other extreme, a physically aggressive act of violence.

Feedback is an important component of communication related to, yet separate from, the response. Feedback allows us to evaluate the effectiveness of a message. Perhaps the receiver smiles, or frowns, after decoding our message. This provides a clue as to how the message has been interpreted and helps us adjust our behavior to the developing situation. Depending on the feedback, we may rephrase or amplify our message to provide greater clarity, ask whether the message was understood, or perhaps even retract the statement.

Every communicative interaction takes place within a physical and contextual **environment**. The physical environment refers to the location where the communication occurs, such as a classroom, coffee shop, business office, or a nightclub. The contextual, or social, environment is more abstract and exerts a strong influence on the style of communication employed. Think about the different styles of communication you use during an interview or when applying for a student loan, asking a friend for a favor, visiting your professor's office, or apologizing for being late meeting a friend. We vary our communicative style in response to the occasion and the receiver—the contextual environment.

The final component of communication, **noise,** relates to the different types of interference or distractions that plague every communication event. *Physical noise* is separate from the communication participants and can take many forms, such as a squeaky air-conditioner fan in the classroom, someone talking loudly on their cell phone in Starbucks, the sounds of traffic coming through the window of an apartment, or feedback static from the instructor's microphone.

Noise that is inherent to the people participating in the communication episode can take a variety of forms. Suppose during a Friday afternoon class you find yourself concentrating more on plans for a Spring Break trip than on the lecture. Perhaps you are in a funk after learning your car needs an expensive brake job, or you might be worried about a term paper due next week. These are examples of *psychological noise* that can reduce your understanding of the classroom communication. *Physiological noise* relates to the physical well-being of the people engaged in the communication activity. Coming to class with too little sleep, feeling sleepy after a large lunch, or dealing with a head cold will interfere with the ability to fully comprehend the classroom activity.

The final type of noise frequently occurs during intercultural communication and can quickly produce misunderstandings. For effective communication in an intercultural interaction, participants must rely on a common language, which usually means that one or more individuals will not be using their native tongue. Native fluency in a second language is difficult, especially when nonverbal behaviors are considered. People who use another language will often have an accent or might misuse a word or phrase, which can adversely influence the receiver's understanding of the message. This type of distraction, referred to as *semantic noise*, also encompasses jargon, slang, and even specialized professional terminology (West & Turner, 2004).

Collectively, these eight components provide an overview of factors that can facilitate, shape, and impede communication encounters. But there is yet another influential factor that can play a role in communicative interactions. Our *culture* provides each of us with a set of standards that govern how, when, what, and even why we communicate. To appreciate culture's impact on communication, you must first have an understanding of culture itself.

WHAT IS CULTURE?

Culture is a popular and increasingly overused term in today's society. Expressions such as *cultural differences, cultural diversity, multiculturalism, corporate culture, cross-culture,* and other variations continually appear in the popular media. Culture has been linked to such fields as corporate management, health care, psychology, education, public relations, marketing, and advertising. We often hear about U.S. forces operating in Iraq and Afghanistan having insufficient knowledge and understanding of the local culture. The pervasive use of the term attests to the increased awareness of the role that culture plays in our everyday activities. Seldom, however, are we provided a definition of just what constitutes culture or exactly what it does. This section is intended to answer those questions for you.

A Definition of Culture

Similar to communication, culture has been subjected to numerous and often complex, abstract definitions as writers labored to incorporate and explain a broad array of cultural components and objectives. What is often considered the earliest definition of culture, and one still used today, was written in 1871 by British anthropologist Sir Edward Burnett Tylor, who said culture is "that complex whole which includes knowledge, belief, art, morals, law, custom, and any other capabilities and habits acquired by man as a member of society" ("Tylor," 2007).

Ruth Benedict offered a more succinct definition in 1934, when she wrote, "What really binds men together is their culture—the ideas and the standards they have in common" (1959, p.16). A more complex explanation was provided by Clifford Geertz, who said culture was "a historically transmitted pattern of meaning embodied in symbols, a system of inherited conceptions expressed in symbolic forms by means of which men communicate, perpetuate, and develop their knowledge about and attitudes toward life" (1973, p. 89). Definitions of culture commonly mention shared values, attitudes, beliefs, behaviors, norms, and material objects (e.g., Brislin, 1990;

Martin & Nakayama, 2005; Neuliep, 2003; Rogers & Steinfatt, 1999; Triandis, 1995), and all are quite correct. Indeed, the many and varied definitions attest to the complexity of this social concept called culture.

For our purposes, however, we offer a more applied, simplified definition. Stop for a minute and think about the word *football*. What mental picture comes to your mind? Most U.S. Americans will envision two teams of 11 men each in helmets and pads, but someone in Montréal, Canada, would imagine 12 men per team. A resident of Sidney, Australia, may think of two 18-man teams in shorts and jerseys competing to kick an oblong ball between two uprights, while a young woman in Sao Paulo, Brazil, would probably picture two opposing teams of 11 men, or women, attempting to kick a round ball into a net. In each case, the contest is referred to as "football," but the playing fields, equipment, and rules of each game are quite different.

Now try to remember your first visit to an ethnic restaurant that was completely different from any previous experience. When sitting down at the *sushi* counter, did you know what to order? At the South Indian vegetarian buffet, did you wonder why they provided a large tray and many small bowls of varying size and shape instead of plates? Were you surprised that there was no menu at the Chinese *dim sum* restaurant, where the different dishes were simply pushed around the dining area, from table to table, on a cart? Yet you probably saw Japanese, Indians, and Chinese ordering and eating in these respective establishments without hesitation or difficulty. They knew what to order and the appropriate social etiquettes for eating their native cuisine.

We use these two examples to illustrate our applied definition of culture. Simply stated, *culture is the rules for living and functioning in society.* In other words, culture provides the rules for playing the game of life (Gudykunst, 2004; Yamada, 1997). The rules will differ from culture to culture, and to function and be effective in a particular culture, you need to know how to apply the rules. We learn the rules of our own culture as a matter of course, beginning at birth and continuing throughout life. As a result, the rules are ingrained in our subconscious, enabling us to react to familiar situations without thinking. It is when we enter another culture, with different rules, that problems begin to arise.

The Function of Culture

If we accept the idea that culture can be viewed as a set of social rules, the purpose becomes self-evident. Cultural rules provide a framework that gives meaning to events, objects, and people. The rules enable us to make sense of our surroundings and reduce uncertainty about the social environment. Recall the first time you were introduced to someone you found attractive. You probably felt some level of nervousness because you wanted to make a positive impression. During the interaction you may have had a few thoughts about what to do and what not to do. Overall, however, you had a good idea of the proper courtesies, what to talk about, and generally how to behave. This is because you had learned the proper cultural rules of behavior by listening to and observing others. Now, take that same situation and imagine being introduced to a student from a different country, such as Jordan or Kenya. Would you know what to say and do? Would those cultural rules you had been learning since birth be effective, or even appropriate, in this new social situation?

Culture also provides us with an identity, or sense of self. From childhood, we are inculcated with the idea of belonging to a variety of groups—family, community, church, sports teams, and schools—and these memberships form our different identities. Our cultural identity is derived from our "sense of belonging to a particular cultural or ethnic group" (Lustig & Koester, 2006, p. 3), which may be Chinese, Mexican American, African American, Greek, Egyptian, Jewish, or one or more of many, many other possibilities. Growing up, we learn the rules of social conduct appropriate to our specific cultural group, or groups in the case of multicultural families such as Vietnamese American, Italian American, or Russian American. Cultural identity can become especially prominent during interactions between people from different cultural groups, such as a Pakistani Muslim and an Indian Hindu, who have been taught varied values, beliefs, and different sets of rules for social interaction. Thus, cultural identity can be a significant factor in the practice of intercultural communication.

Culture's Traits

While there are many different definitions of what culture is and does, there is a community of agreement on what constitutes the major characteristics. An examination of these characteristics will provide increased understanding of the amorphous, multi-faceted concept and also offer insight into how communication is influenced by culture.

Culture Is Learned. At birth, we have no knowledge of the many social rules we will ultimately need to function effectively in our culture, but we quickly begin to internalize this information. Through interactions, observations, and imitation, the proper ways of thinking and behaving are communicated to us. Being taught to eat with a fork, a pair of chopsticks, or even one's fingers is learning cultural behavior. Attending a Catholic mass on Sunday or praying at a Jewish Synagogue on Saturday is learning cultural behaviors and values. Celebrating Christmas, Kwanza, Ramadan, or Yon Kippur is learning cultural traditions. Culture is also acquired from art, proverbs, folklore, history, and a variety of other sources. This learning, commonly referred to as enculturation, is both conscious and subconscious and has the common objective of teaching us how to function properly within our cultural milieu.

Culture Is Transmitted Intergenerationally. The Spanish philosopher George Santayana wrote, "Those who cannot remember the past are condemned to repeat it." Clearly he was not referring to culture, which exists only if it is remembered and repeated by people. You learned your culture from family members, teachers, peers, books, personal observations, and a host of media sources. The appropriate way to act, what to say, and things to value were all communicated to the members of your generation by these many sources. You are also a source for passing these cultural expectations, usually with little or no variation, to succeeding generations. Culture represents our link to past and future generations, and communication is the critical factor in this equation.

Culture Is Symbolic. Words, gestures, and images are merely symbols used to convey meaning. It is the ability to use these symbols that allows us to engage in the many forms of social intercourse necessary for constructing and conveying culture. Our symbol-making ability enables learning and facilitates transmission from one person to another, group to group, and generation to generation. In addition to transmission, the portability of symbols creates the ability to store information, which allows cultures to preserve what is considered important, and to create a history. The preservation of culture provides each new generation with a road map to follow and a reference library to consult when unknown situations are encountered. Succeeding generations may introduce new behaviors or values, but the accumulation of past traditions is what we know as culture.

Culture Is Dynamic. Despite its historical nature, culture is never static. Within a culture, new ideas, inventions, and exposure to other cultures bring about change. One has only to look at discoveries such as the stirrup, gunpowder, the nautical compass, penicillin, or nuclear power to understand culture's susceptibility to innovation and new ideas. More recently, advances made by minority groups and the women's movement since the early 1970s have significantly altered the fabric of U.S. society. Invention of the computer chip, the Internet, and the discovery of DNA has brought profound changes not only to U.S. culture but to the rest of the world as well.

Diffusion, or cultural borrowing, is also a source of change. For example, in one episode of VH-1's *Hogan Knows Best* show, Hulk Hogan, the star, visited a Jewish kosher food market. After learning about the kosher process, he purchased a number of items, returned home, and proclaimed to the rest of the family that this was a healthy way to eat. This is how cultural practices become intermixed. Think about how common pizza (Italian), sushi (Japanese), tacos (Mexican), and tandoori chicken and naan bread (India) are to the U.S. American diet. The Internet has accelerated cultural diffusion by providing access to new knowledge and insights. Immigrants bring their own cultural practices, traditions, and artifacts, some of which become incorporated into the culture of their new homeland, for example, Vietnamese noodle shops in the United States, Indian restaurants in England, or Japanese foods in Brazil.

Cultural calamity, such as war, political upheaval, or large-scale natural disasters, can cause change. United States intervention in Afghanistan is bringing greater equality to the women of that nation. For better or worse, the invasion of Iraq has raised the influence of Shia cultural practices and lessened those of the Sunni. The ongoing strife in the Darfur region of western Sudan, largely between two ethnic groups, is pushing thousands of refugees into the neighboring nations of Chad and the Central African Republic. The refugees bring their own cultural beliefs, values, attitudes, and behaviors into the two countries, and become intermingled with the cultural practices of the native population.

Immigration is a major source of cultural diffusion. Many of the large U.S. urban centers now have places unofficially, or sometimes officially, called Little Italy, Little Saigon, Little Tokyo, Korea Town, China Town, Little India, etc. These areas are usually home to restaurants, markets, and stores catering to a specific ethnic group. However, they also serve to introduce different cultural practices to other segments of the population.

Most of the changes affecting culture, especially readily visible changes, are somewhat topical in nature, such as dress, food preference, modes of transportation, or housing. Values, ethics, morals, the importance of religion, or attitudes toward gender, age, and sexual orientation, which constitute the deep structures of culture, are far more resistant to major change and tend to endure from generation to generation. This resilience has been illustrated in recent political campaigns, when both sides continually promised a return to "traditional U.S. values."

Culture Is Ethnocentric. The strong sense of group identity, or attachment, produced by culture can also lead to ethnocentrism, the tendency to consider one's own culture as being superior to other cultures. Ethnocentrism can be a product of enculturation. Being continually told that that you live in the greatest country in the world or that your way of life is better than those of other nations or ethnic groups can lead to feelings of cultural superiority, especially among children. Ethnocentrism can also be a result of underexposure to other cultures. If exposed only to a U.S. cultural orientation, it is likely that you would develop the idea that your country is the center of the world, and you would tend to view the rest of the world from the perspective of U.S. culture.

An inability to understand or accept different ways and customs can also provoke feelings of ethnocentrism. It is quite natural to feel at ease with people who are like us and adhere to the same social norms and protocols. You know what to expect. It is also normal to feel uneasy when confronted with new and different social values, beliefs, and behaviors. You do not know what to expect. However, to view or evaluate those differences negatively simply because they are different from your expectations is a product of ethnocentrism. It should be self-evident that an ethnocentric disposition would be especially detrimental to effective intercultural communication.

THE INTEGRATION OF COMMUNICATION AND CULTURE

As we have tried to demonstrate, culture is an extremely complex, abstract concept that exerts a pervasive influence on every aspect of our lives. A number of cultural components are particularly relevant to the study of intercultural communication. These include (1) perception, (2) patterns of cognition, (3) verbal behaviors, (4) nonverbal behaviors, and (5) the influence of context. Although each of these components will be discussed separately, in an intercultural situation all become integrated and function at the same time.

Perception

We are bombarded daily with a wide variety of stimuli that we must cognitively process and assign a meaning. This process of selecting, organizing, and evaluating stimuli is referred to as perception. The volume of environmental stimuli is far too large for us to attend to everything, so we select only what is considered relevant or interesting. After determining what we will pay attention to, the next step is organizing the selected stimuli for evaluation. Just as in this book, the university library, or media news outlets, information must be given a structure before it can be interpreted. The third step of perception then becomes a process of evaluating and assigning meaning to the stimuli.

It is commonly assumed that people conduct their lives in accordance with how they perceive the world, and these perceptions are strongly influenced by culture. In other words, we see, hear, feel, taste, and even smell the world through the criteria that culture has placed on our perceptions. Thus, one's idea of beauty, attitude toward the elderly, concept of self in relation to others, and even what tastes good and bad are culturally influenced and can vary among social groups. For example, Vegemite is a yeast extract spread used on toast and sandwiches that is sometimes referred to as the "national food" of Australia. Yet, you will seldom find someone who is not from Australia or New Zealand who likes the taste, or even the smell, of this salty, dark paste spread.

As you would expect, perception is an important aspect of intercultural communication, because people from dissimilar cultures frequently perceive the world differently. Thus, it is important to be aware of the more relevant socio-cultural elements that have a significant and direct influence on the meanings we assign to stimuli. These elements represent our belief, value, and attitude systems and our worldview.

Beliefs, Values, and Attitudes. **Beliefs** can be defined as individually held subjective ideas about the nature of an object or event. These subjective ideas are, in large part, a product of culture, and they directly influence our behaviors. If you believe that horses are intended to be used only for work or pleasure, the thought of eating horsemeat may well be repulsive. The treatment of animals in the North American sport of rodeo is thought to be cruel and inhumane by some people, but clearly not by those who love the competition. In religion, many people believe there is only one god but others pay homage to multiple deities.

Values represent those things we hold important in life, such as morality, ethics, and aesthetics. We use values to distinguish between the desirable and the undesirable. Each person has a set of unique, personal values and a set of cultural values. The latter are a reflection of the rules a culture has established to reduce uncertainty, lessen the likelihood of conflict, help in decision making, and provide structure to social organization and interactions. Cultural values are a motivating force behind our behaviors. Someone from a culture that places a high value on harmonious social relations, such as Japan, will likely employ an indirect communication style. In contrast, a U.S. American can be expected to use a more direct style, because frankness, honesty, and openness are valued.

Our beliefs and values push us to hold certain **attitudes,** which are learned tendencies to act or respond in a specific way to events, objects, people, or orientations. Culturally instilled beliefs and values exert a strong influence on our attitudes. Thus, people tend to embrace what is liked and avoid what is disliked. Someone from a culture that considers cows sacred will take a negative attitude toward eating a Big Mac.

Worldview. Although the concept is quite abstract, worldview is among the most important elements of the perceptual attributes influencing intercultural communication. Stated simply, worldview is what forms people's orientation toward such philosophical concepts as God, the universe, nature, and the like. Normally, worldview is deeply imbedded in one's psyche and usually operates on a subconscious level. This can be problematic in an intercultural situation, where conflicting worldviews can come into play. As an example, many Asian and Native North American cultures hold a worldview that people should have a harmonious, symbiotic relationship with nature. In contrast, Euro-Americans are instilled with the concept that people must conquer and mold nature to conform to personal needs and desires. Individuals from nations possessing these two contrasting worldviews could well encounter difficulties when working to develop an international environmental protection plan. The concept of democracy, with everyone having an equal voice in government, is an integral part of the U.S. worldview. Contrast this with Iraq, where the worldview holds the tribal council as the appropriate form of government.

Cognitive Patterns

Another important consideration in intercultural communication is the influence of culture on cognitive thinking patterns, which includes reasoning and approaches to problem solving. Culture can often produce different ways of knowing and doing. Research by Nisbett (2003) has disclosed that Northeast Asians (Chinese, Japanese, and Koreans) employ a holistic thinking pattern, whereas Westerners use a linear, cause-and-effect model, which places considerable value on logical reasoning and rationality. Thus, problems can be best solved by a systematic, in-depth analysis of each component, progressing individually from the simple to the more difficult. Northeast Asians, however, see problems as much more complex and interrelated, requiring a greater understanding of, and emphasis on, the collective rather than focusing separately on individual parts.

Thought patterns common to a culture influence the way individuals communicate and interact with each other. However, what is common in one culture may be problematic in another culture. To illustrate the potential of this problem, in Japanese-U.S.

business negotiations, the Japanese have a tendency to reopen issues that the U.S. side considers resolved (McDaniel, 2000). United States negotiators find this practice to be frustrating and time-consuming, believing that once a point has been agreed upon, it is completed. From the Japanese perspective, however, new topics can have an influence on previously discussed points. This example demonstrates the importance of understanding that variant patterns of cognition exist and the need to learn how to accommodate them in an intercultural communication encounter.

Verbal Behavior

The role of language in intercultural communication is self-evident in that all of the participants must, to some degree, share a language, be it their first or second. What is not so self-evident is the symbiosis that exists between culture and language, because one cannot exist without the other. Without a common language, a group of people would not be able to establish and perpetuate a culture. They would be unable to share their beliefs, values, social norms, and worldview with one another or to transmit these cultural characteristics to succeeding generations. In turn, culture helps people to establish, evolve, and preserve their language. Like culture, language must be shared in order to exist.

Language itself is merely a set of symbols that a cultural group has arbitrarily agreed upon to help them bring meaning to objects, events, emotions, experiences, places, and the like. Different cultures have, of course, decided to use different sets of symbols. The use of symbol systems to construct and express meaning, however, is an inexact process, because the meanings for words are open to a variety of translations by both individuals and cultures. In an earlier example, the word *horse* was used to illustrate that someone from France or Japan may be stimulated to think of food, whereas someone from the United States or the United Kingdom may picture working or pleasure animals. The word *parallel* can be used to demonstrate how culture influences meaning and can lead to misunderstandings in intercultural exchanges. In the United States, telling someone they are on a "parallel" course implies agreement or similarity of views. In Japanese, however, "parallel" is used to indicate that the parties disagree, because parallel lines (*heikō-sen*) never converge.

Nonverbal Behavior

Another critical factor in intercultural communication is nonverbal behavior, which includes gestures, facial expressions, eye contact and gaze, posture and movement, touch, dress, silence, the use of space and time, objects and artifacts, and paralanguage. These nonverbal behaviors are inextricably intertwined with verbal behaviors and often communicate as much or more meaning than the actual spoken words. As with language, culture also directly influences the use of, and meanings assigned to, nonverbal behavior. In intercultural communication, inappropriate or misused nonverbal behaviors can easily lead to misunderstandings and sometimes result in insults. A comprehensive examination of all nonverbal behaviors is beyond the scope of this chapter, but we will draw on a few cultural-specific examples to demonstrate their importance in intercultural communication exchanges.

Nonverbal greeting behaviors show remarkable variance across cultures. In the United States, a firm handshake among men is the norm, but among some Middle Eastern cultures, a gentle grip is used. In Mexico, acquaintances will often embrace (*abrazo*) each other after shaking hands. Longtime Russian male friends may engage in a bear hug and kiss each other on both cheeks. People from Japan and India traditionally bow to greet each other. Japanese men will place their hands to the side of the body and bow from the waist, with the subordinate individual bowing before and lower than the other person. Indians will perform the *namaste,* which entails holding the hands together in a prayer-like fashion at mid-chest and slightly bowing the head and shoulders (Axtell, 1991).

Eye contact is another important culturally influenced nonverbal communication behavior. The following experience was told to one of your authors. A young Euro-American elementary school teacher, in her first year, was assigned a class of predominantly minority-culture students. One minority student, while being addressed by the teacher, continually averted his eyes downward. The teacher felt the student was being disrespectful for not maintaining eye contact with her. Only later did the she learn that avoiding eye contact was a demonstration of respect in the student's culture. Among some Native Americans, children are taught to show adults respect by avoiding eye contact. When giving a presentation in Japan, it is common to see people in the audience with their eyes shut, because this is thought to facilitate listening (try it . . . you maybe surprised).

Nonverbal expressions, like language, form a coding system for constructing and expressing meaning, and these expressions are culture bound. Through culture, we learn which nonverbal behavior is proper for different social interactions. But what is appropriate and polite in one culture may be disrespectful or even insulting in another culture. People engaging in intercultural communication, therefore, should try to maintain a continual awareness of how body behaviors may influence the interaction.

Contextual Influences

We have defined culture as a set of rules established and used by a group of people to conduct social interaction. These rules determine what is considered correct communicative behavior, including both verbal and nonverbal elements, for both physical and social (situational) contexts. For example, you would not normally attend a funeral wearing shorts and tennis shoes or talk on your cell phone during the service. Your culture has taught you that these behaviors are contextually inappropriate (i.e., disrespectful).

Context is also an important consideration in intercultural communication interactions, where the rules for specific situations usually vary. What is appropriate in one culture is not necessarily correct in another. As we said, in the United States, funerals are traditionally a solemn occasion, but an Irish wake can be a boisterous gathering of family and friends (Brislin, 2000). In a restaurant in Germany, the atmosphere is usually somewhat subdued, with customers engaging in quiet conversation. In Spain, however, the conversation will be much louder and more animated. In U.S. universities, students are expected to interactively engage the instructor, but in Japan the expectation is that the instructor will simply lecture, with very little or no interaction.

In these examples, we see the importance of having an awareness of the cultural rules governing the context of an intercultural communication exchange. Unless both parties in the exchange are sensitive to how culture affects the contextual aspects of communication, difficulties will most certainly arise and could negate effective interaction.

CONCLUSION

We began with a discussion of how the forces of contemporary geopolitics, technology, economics, immigration, and media have coalesced to produce an ever-shrinking world community, making interaction among people from different cultures more and more common and necessary. We will end with a reflection on the requirement and urgency for greater tolerance of cultural differences generated by this new multi-polar world order.

The world's population, as well as U.S. domestic demographics, continues to move toward a pluralistic, multicultural society at a quick-step pace. The social forces behind this movement will not easily or soon subside. The resulting cultural mixing requires that we, both individually and as a society, become more tolerant of the beliefs, worldviews, values, and behaviors of people from other cultures. Acceptance or tolerance may not be appropriate in every situation, nor is universal, unquestioning acquiescence to every difference advocated. We do, however, have to be willing to "live and let live" on a broader scale. That we do not yet seem able or prepared to do this is demonstrated by ongoing international and domestic struggles.

The international community is beleaguered with sectarian violence arising from ideological, cultural, and racial differences. As we write this chapter, religious sects in Iraq continue to kill and torture each other over religious differences. In the Darfur region of Sudan, people continue to be killed and driven from their homes as a result of cultural and racial differences. The long-standing Israeli-Palestinian conflict remains unresolved. The Kurdish minority in Turkey presently enjoys an uneasy peace with the dominant Turks. In the western region of China, some members of the indigenous Uygur ethnic minority have occasionally rioted against what they see as government policies favoring immigration into the region by other Chinese ethnic groups, especially the Han. The entire Horn of Africa is an extremely unstable region as a result of ethnic and religious conflict, made worse by drought, famine, overpopulation, and unchecked violence ("The Path," 2006). The ongoing war on terrorism, a product of variant ideological and cultural perspectives, promises to be protracted and violent.

Intolerance of differences is also an issue within the United States, where we are divided over such culturally based issues as stem cell research, same-sex marriage, school prayer, affirmative action, assisted suicide, and right to life versus freedom of choice. The demands of coping with diverse customs, values, views, and behaviors inherent in a multicultural society are producing increased levels of personal frustration, social stress, and often violence.

As the tides of immigrants and refugees continues to arrive in the United States and other developed nations, we will be confronted with increased cultural diversity. If we continue to assert that cultural diversity is a valuable, desirable asset and embrace the concept of a global village, we must quickly learn to accept and tolerate the resulting differences. Your authors do not profess to have the solution to these problems. However, as a means of better preparing you for life in the global village, we do hope to stimulate thought and discussion about the advantages and difficulties of multiculturalism and the need for effective intercultural communication.

References

Axtell, R. E. (1991). *Gestures*. New York: John Wiley & Sons.

Barboza, T. (2007, February 23). For some, Beverly Hills ballots went too Farsi. *Los Angeles Times,* pp. A1–A18.

Benedict, R. (1959). *Patterns of culture* (Sentry Edition). Boston: Houghton Mifflin.

Borenstine, S. (2007, March 11). Worldwide shortage of water predicted. *San Diego Union Tribune,* A-1.

Brislin, R. W. (Ed.). (1990). Applied cross-cultural psychology: An introduction. In R. W.

Brislin (Ed.), *Applied cross-cultural psychology* (pp. 9–33). Newbury Park, CA: Sage.

Brislin, R. W. (2000). *Understanding culture's influence on behavior* (2nd ed.). Fort Worth, TX: Harcourt.

Brooks, D. (2005, August 10). All cultures are not equal. *New York Times,* p. A. 23.

Coming home to roost?: Bird flu in Asia. (2007, January 27). *The Economist,* pp. 37–38.

Drezner, D. W. (2007). The new new world order. *Foreign Affairs, 86*(2), 34–46.

Geertz, C. (1973). *The interpretation of cultures*. New York: Basic Books.

Globalization and culture. (2003 May/June). *Cato Policy Report,* pp. 8–10, 16.

Griffin, E. (2005). *A first look at communication theory* (6th ed.). Boston: McGraw-Hill.

Gudykunst, W. B. (2004). *Bridging differences* (4th ed.). Thousand Oaks, CA: Sage.

Higgins, J. L., Trusso, M. L., & Connable, A. B. (2005). Marine Corps intelligence. *Marine Corps Gazette, 89*(12), 23–24

Immigrants: Waves of fear. (2007, January 13). *The Economist,* p. 74.

Kirby, A. (2003, June 20). Why world's taps are running dry. *BBC News.* Retrieved April 11, 2007, from BBC News: http://news.bbc.co.uk/1/hi/sci/tech/2943946.stm

Lustig, M. W., & Koester, J. (2006). The nature of cultural identity. In M. W. Lustig & J. Koester (Eds.), *Among us: Essays on identity, belonging, and intercultural competence* (2nd ed., pp. 3–8). New York: Longman.

Martin, J. N., & Nakayama, T. K. (2005). *Experiencing intercultural communication: An introduction* (2nd ed.). Boston: McGraw-Hill.

Mandel, M. (2006, November 20). Can anyone steer this economy? *Business Week,* 56–62.

McDaniel, E. R. (2000). *Japanese negotiation practices: Low-context communication in a high-context culture.* Unpublished doctoral dissertation, Arizona State University.

Neuliep, J. W. (2003). *Intercultural cultural communication: A contextual approach* (2nd ed.). Boston: Houghton Mifflin.

Nisbett, R. (2003). *The geography of thought.* New York: Free Press.

Osterholm, M. T. (2007). Unprepared for a pandemic. *Foreign Affairs, 86*(2), 47–57.

Parker, G. (2006). Knowing the enemy. *The New Yorker, 82*(42), 60–69.

The Path to Ruin. (2006, August 12). *The Economist,* pp. 18–20.

Rogers, E. M., & Steinfatt, T. M. (1999). *Intercultural communication.* Prospect Heights, IL: Waveland.

Sir Edward Burnett Tylor,. (2007). In *Encyclopædia Britannica.* Retrieved March 29, 2007, from Encyclopædia Britannica Online: http://www.britannica.com/eb/article-7484

Triandis, H. C. (1995). *Individualism and collectivism.* Boulder, CO: Westview Press.

West, R., & Turner, L. H. (2004). *Introducing communication theory: Analysis and application* (2nd ed.). Boston: McGraw-Hill.

Yamada, H. (1997). *Different games, different rules: Why Americans and Japanese misunderstand each other.* New York: Oxford University Press.

Concepts and Questions

1. Do you believe that most people are prepared to engage in intercultural communication?

2. How often do you find yourself in situations where increased facility in intercultural communication would be useful? What are some of these occasions?

3. How can knowledge of the basic principles of communication be useful in daily life?

4. How do the authors define culture? Can you think of other definitions of culture that might help you to better understand intercultural communication?

5. What is the purpose of culture? What do the authors mean by the statement that "culture is learned"?

6. What are some of the instances in your life that demonstrate how culture is learned?

7. What are cultural values? How do they relate to individual values?

8. Distinguish several ways in which verbal behavior might differ between cultures.

9. What role does context play in communication? How does context affect intercultural communication?

10. Think of five international situations where an understanding of culture and communication behaviors would be beneficial.

Culture and Conflict

HARRY C. TRIANDIS

A report that appeared in the *New York Times* claimed that on January 9, 1991, at a meeting where the Foreign Minister of Iraq, Tariq Aziz, met the Secretary of State of the United States, James Baker, they miscommunicated. According to the report, Baker was very clear that the United States would attack if Iraq did not leave Kuwait. But he said it calmly. The miscommunication occurred because next to Aziz was seated Saddam Hussein's brother, who paid attention only to *how* Baker talked, rather than to *what* he said. He reported back to Baghdad "the Americans will not attack. They are weak. They are calm. They are not angry. They are only talking."

We do know that Western individualist cultures sample mostly the *content* of communications, whereas Eastern collectivist cultures sample mostly the *context* of communication (Gudykunst, 1993; Triandis, 1994). Thus, it is plausible that Hussein's brother, who had little exposure to the West, did not sample the conversation correctly. Also, Baker did not throw anything at Aziz to show that he was angry. He acted calmly. It is doubtful that Baker could have thrown anything. People cannot change their behavior that drastically, just because they are interacting with members of other cultures. We do not know what report Aziz gave to Hussein, but it is plausible that Hussein paid special attention to his brother's assessment, because trust in collectivist cultures is much greater within the intimate in-group than within the outer in-group. In any case, we do know that a war took place after that meeting. Cultural differences often cause miscommunications and conflict.

Conflict is greater when the two cultures are very different than when they are similar. Technically this difference is called "cultural distance" (Triandis, 1994).

From *The International Journal of Psychology*. Copyright © 2000, 35(2), 1435–152, www.psypress.co.uk. Reprinted by permission. Dr. Harry C. Triandis is Professor Emeritus in the Department of Psychology at the University of Illinois, Urbana-Champaign.

CULTURAL DISTANCE

Cultural distance is greater when people speak different languages. Even speaking languages that are related can be a problem. For example, the ancient Greek root of *sympathetic* is "to feel together." That is fairly close to the English meaning. But modern Greek, Italian, Spanish, and French use terms that are derived from that root yet mean "a nice, pleasant person." So, "I am sympathetic" does not translate correctly into "Je suis sympathique!"

Triandis (1994) listed many funny examples of mistranslations. For instance, at the office of an Italian physician: "Specialist in women and other diseases." Of course, what happens when languages are members of the same language family (say, Indo-European) can be even more of a problem when the languages have very different structures (e.g., tonal or click languages).

Cultural distance is also greater when people have different social structures, such as family structures. Todd (1983) has identified eight types of family structure, and simple terms such as "aunt" may convey different meanings when the family structure is different.

Religion, of course, can be a great source of differences in points of view. Even when one knows that the other person believes something different, there is the problem that humans use themselves as the anchors for such judgments. The diplomat may not believe that it is possible for the other diplomat to have such "outlandish" beliefs. A well-established social psychological phenomenon is called the "false consensus" effect (Mullen et al., 1985). Even when people know about this bias, they cannot wipe it out (Krueger & Clement, 1994). The phenomenon is that if we agree with a particular position, we believe that most other people also agree with it; if we disagree with a particular position, we believe that most people disagree with it. The phenomenon is even stronger when we interact with people who are similar to us in dress, profession, and other characteristics.

Differences in standards of living can create cultural distance. When the cost of sending a letter is a substantial fraction of one's budget, one may not be as likely to send the letter as when the cost is trivial in relation to one's budget.

Values differ substantially between cultures (Schwartz, 1992, 1994). These values are related to the cultural syndromes that we will discuss here.

MEANING OF CULTURE

Culture is a shared meaning system found among those who speak a particular language dialect, during a specific historic period, in a definable geographic region (Triandis, 1994). It functions to improve the adaptation of members of the culture to a particular ecology, and it includes the knowledge that people need to have in order to function effectively in their social environment.

Cultures differ drastically in the amount of aggression that is found both within and between them. For example, the Lepcha of the Indian Himalayas had one murder two centuries ago (Segall, Ember, & Ember, 1997). Homicide rates in some segments of U.S. society are extremely high. There is evidence that the absence of fathers during socialization is a factor in high rates (Segall et al.). There is some evidence that high between-cultures aggression is related to high within-culture aggression (Segall et al.).Warfare is associated with the unpredictability of resources and conflicts over territory; it is found most usually in societies where aggression within the family is permitted, where the media of communication portray aggression, where there are warlike sports, and where wrongdoing is severely punished (Segall et al.). There is evidence that democracies do not fight with each other (Ember, Ember, & Russett, 1992), so much so that some analysts have argued that it is "counterproductive to support any undemocratic regimes, even if they happen to be enemies of our enemies" (Ember & Ember, 1994).

Shared patterns of elements of subjective culture constitute subjective cultural syndromes (Triandis, 1996). A cultural syndrome is a shared pattern of beliefs, attitudes, self-definitions, norms, roles, and values organized around a theme.

Cultural differences are best conceptualized as different patterns of sampling information found in the environment (Triandis, 1989). In collectivist cultures (most traditional cultures, most Asian and Latin American cultures), people are more likely (a) to sample the collective self (reflecting interdependence with others) and to think of themselves as interdependent with their groups (family, coworkers, tribe, coreligionists, country), rather than to sample the individual self (reflecting an independent self) and to see themselves as autonomous individuals who are independent of their groups (Markus & Kitayama, 1991); (b) to give more priority to the goals of their in-group than to their personal goals (Triandis, 1995); (c) to use in-group norms to shape their behavior more than personal attitudes (Abrams, Ando, & Hinkle, 1998; Suh, Diener, Oishi, & Triandis, 1998); and (d) to conceive of social relationships as communal (Mills & Clark, 1982) rather than in exchange theory terms (Triandis, 1995). That is, they pay attention to the needs of others and stay in relationships even when that is not maximally beneficial to them. There is evidence that these four aspects are interrelated (Triandis & Gelfand, 1998).

The sampling of collectivists focuses on groups, with people seen as appendages of groups; the sampling of individualists focuses on individuals. A recent example is the coverage of the Kosovo war: CNN and BBC cover the refugees (individuals) in great detail. The Russian and the Serbs present nothing about the refugees on their television. The *Times of London* (April 7, 1999) had a story about a member of the Russian Duma who was so upset that the Russian TV did not mention the refugees at all that he went on a hunger strike. Finally, 12 days into the war, an independent Russian station mentioned the refugees. We called a friend in Belgrade and asked her whether she knew why NATO was bombing her city. She did not! Of course, such control of information is part of the war effort, but when it is consistent with the culture, it is a natural bias.

Culture shapes us, so we pay more attention to individuals and to the internal processes of individuals (attitudes, beliefs) if we are raised in an individualist culture, and more attention to groups, roles, norms, duties, and intergroup relationships if we are raised in a collectivist culture. Collectivist cultures have languages that do not require the use of "I" and "you" (Kashima & Kashima, 1997, 1998). They also have many culture-specific relational terms that are not found in individualist cultures, such as *philotimo* in Greek (Triandis, 1972), which is a positive attribute of an individual who does what the in-group expects; *amae* in Japanese, which reflects tolerance of deviation from norms by a dependent person (Yamaguchi, 1998); and *simpatia* among Latin Americans (Triandis, Marin, Lisansky, & Betancourt, 1984), which reflects the expectation that social relationships will include mostly positive and very few negative behaviors.

Collectivists use action verbs (e.g., he offered to help) rather than state verbs (e.g., he is helpful). This is because they prefer to use context in their communications. Zwier (1997), in four studies, obtained support for this cultural difference. Specifically, she found that the accounts of events given by Turkish and Dutch students show this difference. She content-analyzed the radio commentaries of Turkish and Dutch radio personalities and found the same difference. She asked Turkish and Dutch students to write a letter requesting a favor, and content-analyzed the letters. She examined the writing of Turkish/Dutch bilinguals when writing in the two languages, and found the same pattern.

The contrasting cultural pattern is individualism. Here people tend to (a) sample the individual self—this pattern is very common in North and Western Europe, North America (except Mexico), Australia, and New Zealand, where the self is conceived as independent of in-groups; (b) give priority to personal goals; (c) use attitudes much more than norms as determinants of their social behavior; and (d) pay attention only to their own needs and abandon interpersonal relationships that are not optimally beneficial to them. Individualist cultures have languages that require the use of "I" and "you" (Kashima & Kashima, 1997, 1998). English is a good example. It would be difficult to write a letter in English without using these words. Individualists are very positive about "me" and "we," whereas collectivists are sometimes ambivalent about "me" but very positive about "we."

CULTURAL SYNDROMES

Complexity

Some cultures (e.g., hunters and gatherers) are relatively simple, and other cultures (e.g., information societies) are relatively complex. The organizing theme of the syndrome is complexity. For example, in complex societies one finds subgroups with different beliefs and attitudes, whereas in simple societies individuals are in considerable agreement about their beliefs and attitudes. In fact, cultural uniformity and conformity are higher in simple than in complex societies. Simple cultures have few jobs; if we take into account specialties such as urologist and general practitioner, complex cultures have a quarter of a million different jobs (see *Dictionary of Occupational Titles,* 1977). The size of settlements is one of the best ways to index cultural complexity (Chick, 1997).

Tightness

Tight cultures have many rules, norms, and ideas about what is correct behavior in each situation; loose cultures have fewer rules and norms. In tight cultures, people become quite upset when others do not follow the norms of the society, and may even kill those who do not behave as expected, whereas in loose cultures people are tolerant of many deviations from normative behaviors.

Thus, conformity is high in tight cultures. In Thailand, which is a loose culture, the expression *"mai bin rai"* (never mind) is used frequently. In Japan, which is a tight culture, people are sometimes criticized for minor deviations from norms, such as having too much suntan, or having curly hair (Kidder, 1992). Most Japanese live in fear that they will not act properly (Iwao, 1993).

Tightness is more likely when the culture is relatively isolated from other cultures, so that consensus about what is proper behavior can develop. It is also more likely that tightness will occur in situations where people are highly interdependent (when the other deviates from norms it hurts the relationship) and where there is a high population density (high density requires norms so that people will not hurt each other; also, when the other deviates one notices it).

When cultures are at the intersection of great cultures (e.g., Thailand is at the intersection of China and India), contradictory norms may be found, and people cannot be too strict in imposing norms. Also, when the population density is low, it may not even be known that a person who is miles away has behaved improperly. Cosmopolitan cities are loose, except when they have ethnic enclaves, which can be very tight, whereas small communities are relatively tight.

Individualism and Collectivism

Triandis (1994) has suggested that individualism emerges in societies that are both complex and loose; collectivism, in societies that are both simple and tight. For example, theocracies or monasteries are both tight and relatively poor; Hollywood stars live in a culture that is both complex and loose. This speculation has not been tested rigorously, but the data seem to hang together reasonably well. It may be the case, for instance, that contemporary Japan, which is now quite complex, is less collectivist than the Japan of the 19th century. In fact, reports of 19th-century travelers to Japan (see Edgerton, 1985) mentioned hundreds of rules for how to laugh, sit, and so on, that apparently no longer operate in modern Japan.

Bond and Smith (1996) did a meta-analysis of studies of conformity that used the Asch paradigm, and found that collectivist cultures were higher in conformity than individualist cultures. This is what we would expect if tightness and collectivism were closely linked.

Kim and Markus (1998) showed that in the West people see "uniqueness" as desirable, whereas in East Asia it is often seen as "deviance"; in the West "conformity" is sometimes seen as undesirable, but in East Asia it is seen as "harmony." For example, content analyses of advertisements from the United States and Korea show different frequencies of uniqueness and conformity themes. Conformity themes were used by 95% of the Korean and 65% of the American advertisements; uniqueness themes were used by 89% of the American and 49% of the Korean advertisements.

Vertical and Horizontal Cultures

Vertical cultures accept hierarchy as a given. People are different from each other. Hierarchy is a natural state.Those at the top "naturally" have more power and privileges than those at the bottom of the hierarchy. Horizontal cultures accept equality as a given. People are basically similar, and if one is to divide any resource it should be done equally (Triandis, 1995).

Active-Passive Cultures

In active cultures, individuals try to change the environment to fit them; in passive cultures, people change themselves to fit into the environment (Diaz-Guerrero, 1979). The active cultures are more competitive and action-oriented, and emphasize self-fulfillment; the passive ones are more cooperative, emphasize the experience of living, and are especially concerned with getting along with others. In general, individualist cultures are more active than collectivist cultures, though the relationship between the two cultural syndromes is not strong.

Universalism-Particularism

In universalist cultures, people try to treat others on the basis of universal criteria (e.g., all competent persons, regardless of who they are in terms of sex, age, race, etc., are acceptable employees); in particularist cultures, people treat others on the basis of who the other person is (e.g., I know Joe Blow and he is a good person, so he will be a good employee; Parsons, 1968). In general, individualists are universalists and collectivists are particularists.

Diffuse-Specific

Diffuse cultures respond to the environment in a holistic manner (e.g., I do not like your report means I do not like you). Specific cultures discriminate different aspects of the stimulus complex (e.g., I do not like your report says nothing about liking you; Foa & Chemers, 1967).

Instrumental-Expressive

People may sample more heavily attributes that are instrumental (e.g., get the job done) or expressive (e.g., enjoy the social relationship). In general, individualists are more instrumental and collectivists are more expressive. When Latin Americans meet a friend in the street, they are likely to stop and chat, even when they are late for an appointment. The importance of the social relationship eclipses the importance of the instrumental relationship (Levine & Norenzayan, 1999).

Emotional Expression or Suppression

People may express their emotions freely, no matter what the consequences, or they may control the expression of emotion. The free expression of negative emotions can disrupt relationships, so collectivists tend to control such emotions. Individualists are often high in emotional expression. For example, Stephan, Stephan, and de Vargas (1996) tested the hypothesis that people in collectivist cultures would feel less comfortable expressing negative emotions than people in individualist cultures, and found strong support for that hypothesis.

In addition, the instigation of emotion is often culture specific. Stipek, Weiner, and Li (1989) found that when Americans were asked to recall what made them angry, they remembered mostly events that happened to them personally; when Chinese were given that task, they remembered mostly events that occurred to other people. This self-focus versus other-focus is an important contrast between individualism and collectivism (Kagiteibasi, 1997).

The Weights Given to Different Attributes in Social Perception

In addition to sampling different attributes, members of different cultures give different weights to the attributes that they sample. For example, in a conflict situation, an individual might sample the ethnicity of the other person, his profession, and his competence. Members of some cultures will give most of the weight to ethnicity and react to the other person on the basis of ethnicity; members of other cultures will give most of the weight to competence and profession, and disregard ethnicity. Triandis (1967) reviewed many crosscultural studies showing differences in the weights used in social perception. In general, members of collectivist cultures tend to sample and weigh ascribed attributes more heavily, whereas members of individualist cultures sample and weigh achieved attributes more heavily.

One can identify many more syndromes, such as those reflected in the Kluckhohn and Strodtbeck (1961) value orientations, the culture of honor (Nisbett & Cohen, 1996), and others. This introduction is sufficient for our purposes.

CULTURAL SYNDROMES AND THE SITUATION

Humans have a predisposition to respond that can be traced to culture, but their behavior depends very much more on the situation. For example, all humans have both collectivist and individualist

cognitions, but they sample them with different probabilities depending on the situation. When the in-group is being attacked, for instance, most humans become collectivists.

The larger the in-group, the less effective it is likely to be in calling for individuals to do what the in-group authorities want done. A call to arms by a clan leader is more likely to be effective than a call to arms by a state, though penalties may make the latter effective in many countries.

Certain factors increase the probability that the collectivist cognitive system will be activated. This is most likely to happen when (a) the individual knows that most other people in the particular situation are collectivists, which makes the norm that one must act as a collectivist more salient; (b) the individual's membership in a collective is especially salient—for instance, the individual represents a country; (c) within an in-group, the situation emphasizes what people have in common—for instance, common goals; (d) within an in-group, the situation emphasizes that people are in the same collective—for instance, people wear the same uniforms; and (e) within an in-group, the task is cooperative.

Certain factors increase the probability that the individualistic cognitive system will be activated. This is most likely to happen when (a) others in the situation are and behave like individualists, which makes individualist norms more salient; (b) the situation makes the person focus on what makes him or her different from others (Trafimow, Triandis, & Goto, 1991)—for instance, the person is dressed very differently from the rest of the group; and (c) the task is competitive.

Culture is relevant for understanding conflict in at least two domains: how conflict starts and how conflict evolves. Problems of poor communication are the major causes of the first, and problems of the way members of different cultures treat out-groups are relevant for understanding the second of these domains.

CULTURAL SYNDROMES AND COMMUNICATION

When people come into contact with members of other cultures, they are often not aware of their miscommunications, because they think that the others are more or less like they are. This is the stage of *unconscious incompetence*. After some interpersonal difficulties, people realize that they are miscommunicating, but they do not know exactly what is wrong. That is the stage of *conscious incompetence*. As they get to know more and more about the culture of the other, they begin communicating correctly, but they have to make an effort to communicate in a different way. That is the stage of *conscious competence*. Finally, after they develop habits of correct communication with members of the other culture, they reach the stage of *unconscious competence* where the communication is effortless and correct.

A very serious problem in communication is that people do not perceive the same "causes" of behavior (Miller, 1984; Morris & Peng, 1994). We call these *attributions*. When the actor thinks that a behavior is due to one cause and the observer thinks that the behavior is due to a different cause, they each give a different meaning to the behavior. For instance, a diplomat may invite another diplomat to dinner. The inviter may do so because he likes the other diplomat.

The invitee, however, may use the cause "his boss told him to invite me." Obviously, the meaning of the invitation is different for the two diplomats.

There are training procedures called "culture assimilators" (Fiedler, Mitchell, & Triandis, 1971), which consist of 100 or so episodes involving interactions between members of the two relevant cultures, with each episode followed by four attributions. Usually three attributions are "incorrect" from the point of view of the culture the trainee is learning about, and one is "correct." The trainee selects one attribution, and gets feedback as to whether it is the correct one from the point of view of the culture the trainee is trying to learn about. People who go through this training gradually learn to make the correct attributions from the point of view of the other culture. This reduces miscommunications (Bhawuk, 1998).

There is a well-researched phenomenon regarding attributions. When two groups, A and B, are in conflict, if a member of group B does something "nice," members of group A attribute the behavior to external factors (e.g., he was forced to do it by the circumstances); when a member of group B does something "nasty," members of group A attribute it to internal factors (e.g., they are nasty "by nature"). The attributions that group B makes about the behavior of group A are exact mirror images; that is, when A does something nice it is due to external factors, and when A does something nasty it is due to internal factors. When a member of group A makes attributions about the actions of other members of group A, if the action is positive it is attributed to internal factors and if it is negative it is attributed to external factors.

In all cultures, when we ask actors why they did something, they report external causes, but observers of these actions tend to use causes internal to the actor. This is called the "fundamental attribution error." In short, people all over the world have a tendency to make attributions incorrectly. However, those from individualistic cultures are even worse in this bias than those from collectivist cultures.

Another factor in miscommunications is the tendency of collectivists to sample the context of communications more than individualists, which results in their paying more attention to gestures, eye contact, level of voice, the direction of the two bodies, touching, the distance between the bodies, and the like. There is a large opportunity for errors and misinterpretations in the way people interpret paralinguistic cues. Also, the way people use time can result in misunderstandings, because people from monochronic time cultures are used to carrying out one conversation at a time, whereas people who use polychronic time carry several conversations simultaneously, which confuses and frustrates the users of monochronic time.

The structure of messages can be another source of difficulties. Western people tend to organize their thoughts and messages in a linear fashion: fact 1, fact 2, and so on; generalization; and conclusion. In many other cultures, people start with the conclusion, then find facts that fit the conclusion, and permit deviations from a straight line. In some cases, the argument is like a spiral, starting from general ideological or mystical considerations and gradually zeroing to a conclusion (Triandis, 1994). The extent to which ideology versus pragmatic matters are sampled also varies with culture. Glenn (1981) gave an interesting example. At a UN conference, the Russians advocated the use of reinforced concrete structures (ideal for all), whereas the American delegates said that "it depends on what works best" (pragmatic). Delegates from the Third World interpreted the exchange in favor of the Russians. They thought that the Americans were saying that "we are not good enough to use what they are using."

When a universalist meets a particularist, there can be interpersonal difficulties. For example, when presenting a position, the universalist may expect that all the facts will "fit in" with the position, whereas the particularist may not consider this necessary. When such expectations are present, the particularist might need to start the presentation with a universalist position (e.g., "we are all in favor of peace") and then present the particularist view.

Another source of miscommunication is that in some cultures communication is "associative" and in others "abstractive." In the West, it is typically abstractive; that is, one abstracts the most important elements of the argument and organizes them for the presentation. An associative presentation can present anything that is vaguely related to the point, which can frustrate the Westerner (Szalay, 1993). For example, in 1932, the finance minister of Japan was assassinated after agreeing to a 17% revaluation of the yen. In 1971, the American Treasury Secretary Connaly, oblivious to Japanese history, demanded a 17% revaluation of the yen. His Japanese counterpart rejected it without explanation. When Connaly suggested a 16.9% upward revaluation, the Japanese minister accepted it (Cohen, 1991).

Examples of associative communications abound. The *Los Angeles Times,* on February 12, 1977, published a conversation between two Egyptians. One was Westernized, and the other was traditional. The communication of the traditional was not understood by the Westernized. Another example was the presentation of the Egyptian ambassador to the UN in 1967, in which he accused the Americans of actively helping the Israelis. The American ambassador asked for proof, but the Egyptian answered that no proof was needed because it was "obvious that the Americans had intervened. How else could one explain that three quarters of the Egyptian air force was destroyed in a few hours? Only a large, powerful country could do this."

In sum, cultural distance can result in miscommunications, which may lead to international conflict. We now turn to the way the conflict is carried out, and look at the role of cultural syndromes in this area.

CULTURAL SYNDROMES AND CONFLICT

We need to distinguish conflict within the in-group from conflict between groups. Individualism is associated with conflict inside a culture, such as crime or divorce. Collectivism is associated with conflict between groups, such as ethnic cleansing or war.

Factors that have been found to increase aggression (see Triandis, 1994) include biological factors (e.g., high levels of testosterone), social structural factors (such as low family cohesion, few intimate relationships, low father involvement in the upbringing of sons, isolation from kin, and anonymity, all of which are associated with individualism), high levels of arousal (because of frustration, competition), hot weather, modeling (aggressive models, aggressive people receive more status in the society), gender marking (men and women are seen as very different), retaliation, economic inequality, few resources (associated with collectivism), social stress (e.g., high levels of inflation), ease of being aggressive (e.g., availability of weapons), and low costs (aggression does not lead to punishment). Clearly there are many factors, many of which do not have much to do with cultural patterns. Yet culture is important for many of these factors (Segall et al., 1997). Some of the factors, such as weak families, are associated with individualism and lead to within-group aggression; others are associated with collectivism.

When interacting with in-group members, people from collectivist cultures tend to be unusually sensitive to the needs of the others, supportive, helpful, and even self-sacrificing. However, when interacting with out-group members, they are usually indifferent and, if the two groups have incompatible goals, even hostile.

Once the in-group has been called to action against an out-group by in-group authorities, vertical collectivists are especially likely to become aggressive. This pattern leads to especially high levels of hostility when a "culture of honor" is present. Such cultures are found in situations where there are no police (or other authorities that can resolve conflict), so that people have to protect themselves against intruders by means of their personal efforts (Nisbett & Cohen, 1996). To extrapolate to the international scene, conflict would be higher if international bodies such as the United Nations did not exist.

Certain combinations of cultural syndromes can lead to treating the out-group inhumanely. In simple cultures, the distinction between different kinds of "others" is unlikely to occur. In vertical cultures, there is likely to be a perception that "others" are very different, just as people at the top and bottom of a hierarchy are seen as very different. In active cultures, the elimination of out-groups (e.g., ethnic cleansing) is likely to be seen as an especially good way to change the sociopolitical environment. In universalist cultures, treating all out-group members the same fits the cultural pattern. If one enemy is to be killed, all should be killed. In diffuse cultures, making distinctions between different kinds of enemies is not likely, so that all out-group members are likely to be treated badly. Instrumental cultures may be particularly effective in eliminating their enemies. Thus, when a particular combination of cultural syndromes is found—namely active, universalistic, diffuse, instrumental, vertical collectivism—inhumane treatment of out-groups is likely to occur.

All humans are ethnocentric (Triandis, 1994). That means that they think of their in-group as the standard of what is good and proper, and of other groups as good only to the extent that they are similar to the in-group. Ethnocentrism also results in members of a culture seeing their own norms and behavior as "natural" and "correct" and those of members of other cultures as "unnatural" and "incorrect." Ethnocentrism leads people to see their norms as universally valid; to avoid questioning norms, role definitions, and values; and to help in-group members feel proud of the in-group and, simultaneously, to reject out-groups (Triandis, 1994).

The rejection of out-groups is especially likely to occur in collectivist cultures. In extreme collectivist cultures, out-groups are often seen as "not quite human" and "not deserving any rights." Although individualists are capable of dealing with out-groups in an inhuman way (e.g., the My Lai incident during the Vietnam War), collectivists are even more extreme in dealing with out-groups (e.g., the rape of Nanking, where an estimated 300,000 civilians were killed, Chang, 1997; the Holocaust). Fortunately, the particular combination of active, universalistic, diffuse, instrumental, vertical collectivism is rare, so that such incidents do not occur frequently.

Furthermore, as indicated earlier, typical collectivism is usually incompatible with the active, universalistic, and instrumental syndromes so that the above-mentioned combination is really rare. Nevertheless, in the twentieth century we have witnessed many cases of genocide and ethnic cleansing, so we cannot ignore the data.

One way to avoid these inhuman actions would be to monitor cultures that tend toward this undesirable combination of syndromes and to change them to reduce the probability of occurrence of the particular combination of syndromes. There is very little research about the factors that result in the various syndromes mentioned earlier, but we do know something about the occurrence of collectivism.

PREVALENCE OF COLLECTIVISM

Collectivism is found in societies that are not affluent (Hofstede, 1980), especially where there is only one normative system—that is, a single culture that is not cosmopolitan. There is a fair amount of evidence about the attributes of collectivism and the causes of the development of this cultural pattern (Triandis, 1990).

Collectivism is also high among the lower social classes of any society (Kohn, 1969; Marshall, 1997), among those who have not traveled (Gerganov, Dilova, Petkova, & Paspalanova, 1996) or been socially mobile, and among those who have not been exposed to the modern mass media (McBride, 1998). When the major economic activity is based on agriculture, rather than on hunting, fishing, industry, or service, collectivism is often high.

Collectivism is thus found in societies that are relatively homogeneous (so that in-group norms can be widely accepted); where population density and job interdependence are high (because they require the development of and adherence to many rules of behavior); among members of the society who are relatively old (Noricks et al., 1987) and who are members of large families (because it is not possible for every member to do his or her own thing); and in groups that are quite religious (Triandis & Singelis, 1998). When the in-group is under pressure from the outside, collectivism increases. Thus, one consideration in international relations is whether the advantages of putting pressure on a country outbalance the disadvantages of increasing the collectivism of the country.

CONCLUSION

We examined two major ways in which culture is related to conflict. One is that cultural distance increases the probability of miscommunication. There are training programs that can overcome this problem. The second is the way a combination of cultural syndromes results in the inhuman treatment of out-groups.

References

Abrams, D., Ando, K., & Hinkle, S. (1998). Psychological attachment to groups: Cross-cultural differences in organizational identification and subjective norms as predictors of workers' turnover intentions. *Personality and Social Psychology Bulletin, 24,* 1027–1039.

Bhawuk, D. P. S. (1998). The role of culture theory in crosscultural training: A multimethod study of culture specific, culture general, and culture theory-based assimilators. *Journal of Cross-Cultural Psychology, 29,* 630–655.

Bond, R., & Smith, P. B. (1996). Culture and conformity: A meta-analysis of studies using Asch's (1952b, 1956) line judgement task. *Psychological Bulletin, 119,* 111–137.

Chang, I. (1997). *The rape of Nanking: The forgotten holocaust of World War II.* New York: Basic Books.

Chick, G. (1997). Cultural complexity: The concept and its measurement. *Cross-Cultural Research, 31,* 275–307.

Cohen, R. (1991). *Negotiating across cultures.* Washington, DC: United States Institute of Peace.

Diaz-Guerrero, R. (1979). The development of coping style. *Human Development, 22,* 320–331.

Dictionary of Occupational Titles (4th ed.). (1977). [Supplements in 1986]. Washington, DC: U.S. Government Publications Office.

Edgerton, R. B. (1985). *Rules, exceptions, and social order.* Berkeley: University of California Press.

Ember, M., & Ember, C. R. (1994). Prescriptions for peace: Policy implications of cross-cultural research on war and interpersonal violence. *Cross-Cultural Research, 28,* 343–350.

Ember, C. R., Ember, M., & Russett, B. (1992). Peace between participatory polities: A cross-cultural test of the "Democracies rarely fight each other" hypothesis. *World Politics, 44,* 573–599.

Fiedler, F. E., Mitchell, T., & Triandis, H. C. (1971). The culture assimilator: An approach to cross-cultural training. *Journal of Applied Psychology, 55,* 95–102.

Foa, U., & Chemers, M. M. (1967). The significance of role behaviour differentiation for Cross-cultural interaction training. *International Journal of Psychology, 2,* 45–57.

Gerganov, E. N., Dilova, M. L., Petkova, K. G., & Paspalanova, E. P. (1996). Culture-specific approach to the study of individualism/collectivism. *European Journal of Social Psychology, 26,* 277–297.

Glenn, E. (1981). *Man and mankind: Conflicts and communication between cultures.* Norwood, NJ: Ablex.

Gudykunst, W. (Ed.). (1993). *Communication in Japan and the United States.* Albany: State University of New York Press.

Hofstede, G. (1980). *Culture's consequences.* Beverly Hills, CA: Sage.

Iwao, S. (1993). *The Japanese woman: Traditional image and changing reality.* New York: Free Press.

Kagiteibasi, C. (1997). Individualism and collectivism. In I. W. Berry, M. H. Segall, & C. Kagiteibasi (Eds.), *Handbook of cross-cultural psychology* (2nd ed., pp. 1–50). Boston: Allyn & Bacon.

Kashima, E. S., & Kashima, Y. (1997). Practice of the self in conversations: Pronoun drop, sentence co-production and contextualization of the self. In K. Leung, U. Kim, S. Yamaguchi, & Y. Kashima (Eds.), *Progress in Asian social psychology* (Vol. 1, pp. 165–180). Singapore: Wiley.

Kashima, E. S., & Kashima, Y. (1998). Culture and language: The case of cultural dimensions and personal pronoun use. *Journal of Cross-Cultural Psychology, 29,* 461–486.

Kidder, L. (1992). Requirements for being "Japanese": Stories of returnees. *International Journal of Intercultural Relations, 16,* 383–394.

Kim, H., & Markus, H. R. (1998). *Deviance or uniqueness, harmony or conformity? A cultural analysis.* Unpublished manuscript.

Kluckhohn, F., & Strodtbeck, F. (1961). *Variations in value orientation.* Evanston, IL: Row, Peterson.

Kohn, M. K. (1969). *Class and conformity.* Homewood, IL: Dorsey Press.

Krueger, I., & Clement, R. W. (1994). The truly false consensus effect: An ineradicable egocentric bias in social perception. *Journal of Personality and Social Psychology, 67,* 596–610.

Levine, R. V., & Norenzayan, A. (1999). The pace of life in 31 countries. *Journal of Cross-Cultural Psychology, 30,* 178–205.

Markus, H., & Kitayama, S. (1991). Culture and self: Implications for cognition, emotion and motivation. *Psychological Review, 98,* 224–253.

Marshall, R. (1997). Variances in levels of individualism across two cultures and three social classes. *Journal of Cross-Cultural Psychology, 28,* 490–495.

McBride, A. (1998). Television, individualism, and social capital. *Political Science and Politics, 31,* 542–555.

Miller, J. G. (1984). Culture and the development of everyday social explanation. *Journal of Personality and Social Psychology, 46,* 961–978.

Mills, J., & Clark, M. S. (1982). Exchange and communal relationships. In L. Wheeler (Ed.), *Review of personality and social psychology* (Vol. 3, pp. 121–144). Beverly Hills, CA: Sage.

Morris, M. W., & Peng, K. (1994). Culture and cause: American and Chinese attributions for social and physical events. *Journal of Personality and Social Psychology, 67,* 949–971.

Mullen, B., Atkins, J. L., Champion, D. S., Edwards, C., Handy, D., Story, J. E., & Venderklok, M. (1985). The false consensus effect: A meta-analysis of 115 hypothesis tests. *Journal of Experimental Social Psychology, 21,* 262–283.

Nisbett, R. E., & Cohen, D. (1996). *Culture of honor.* Boulder, CO: Westview Press.

Noricks, J. S., Agler, L. H., Bartholomew, M., Howard-Smith, S., Martin, D., Pyles, S., & Shapiro, W. (1987). Age, abstract things and the American concept of person. *American Anthropologist, 89,* 667–675.

Parsons, T. (1968). *The structure of social action.* New York: Free Press.

Schwartz, S. H. (1992). Universals in the content and structure of values: Theoretical advances and empirical tests in 20 countries. In M. Zanna (Ed.), *Advances in experimental social psychology* (Vol. 25, pp. 1–166). New York: Academic Press.

Schwartz, S. H. (1994). Beyond individualism and collectivism: New cultural dimensions of value. In U. Kirn, H. C. Triandis, C. Kagiteibasi, S. C. Choi, & O. Yoon (Eds.), *Individualism and collectivism: Theory, method and applications* (pp. 85–122). Newbury Park, CA: Sage.

Segall, M. H., Ember, C. R., & Ember, M. (1997). Aggression, crime, and warfare. In J. W. Berry, M. H. Segall, & C. Kagiteibasi (Eds.), *Handbook of cross-cultural psychology* (2nd ed., Vol. 3, pp. 213–254). Boston: Allyn & Bacon.

Stephan, W. G., Stephan, C. W., & de Vargas, M. C. (1996). Emotional expression in Costa Rica and United States. *Journal of Cross-Cultural Psychology, 27,* 147–160.

Stipek, D., Weiner, B., & Li, K. (1989). Testing some attribution-emotion relations in the People's Republic of China. *Journal of Personality and Social Psychology, 56,* 109–116.

Suh, E., Diener, E., Oishi, S., & Triandis, H. C. (1998). The shifting basis of life satisfaction judgements across cultures: Emotions versus norms. *Journal of Personality and Social Psychology, 74,* 482–493.

Szalay, L. B. (1993). The *subjective worlds of Russians and Americans: A guide for mutual understanding.* Chevy Chase, MD: Institute of Comparative Social and Cultural Studies.

Todd, E. (1983). *La troisième planète.* Paris: Editions du Scuil.

Trafimow, D., Triandis, H. C., & Goto, S. (1991). Some tests of the distinction between private and collective self. *Journal of Personality and Social Psychology, 60,* 649–655.

Triandis, H. C. (1967). Toward an analysis of the components of interpersonal attitudes. In C. Sherif & M. Sherif (Eds.), *Atitudes, ego-involvement, and change* (pp. 227–270). New York: Wiley.

Triandis, H. C. (1972). *The analysis of subjective culture.* New York: Wiley.

Triandis, H. C. (1989). The self and social behaviour in differing cultural contexts. *Psychological Review, 96,* 506–520.

Triandis, H. C. (1990). Crosscultural studies of individualism and collectivism. In I. Berman (Ed.), *Nebraska Symposium on Motivation* (pp. 41–133). Lincoln: University of Nebraska Press.

Triandis, H. C. (1994). *Culture and social behaviour.* New York: McGraw-Hill.

Triandis, H. C. (1995). *Individualism and collectivism.* Boulder, CO: Westview Press.

Triandis, H. C. (1996). The psychological measurement of cultural syndromes. *American Psychologist, 51,* 407–415.

Triandis, H. C., & Gelfand, M. (1998). Converging measurement of horizontal and vertical individualism and collectivism. *Journal of Personality and Social Psychology, 74,* 118–28.

Triandis, H. C., Marin, G., Lisansky, J., & Betancourt, (1984). *Simpatia* as a cultural script of Hispanics. *Journal of Personality and Social Psychology, 47,* 1363–1374.

Triandis, H. C., & Singelis, T. M. (1998). Training to recognize individual differences in collectivism and individualism within culture. *International Journal of Intercultural Relations, 22,* 35–48.

Yamaguchi, S. (1998, August). The *meaning of amae.* Paper presented at the Congress of the International Association of Cross-Cultural Psychology, Bellingham, WA.

Zwier, S. (1997). *Patterns of language use in individualistic and collectivist cultures.* Unpublished doctoral dissertation, Free University of Amsterdam, The Netherlands.

Concepts and Questions

1. Differentiate between message *content* and message *context.* How do different cultures react to content and context? How might cultural diversity in attending to content and context affect intercultural communication?

2. What does Triandis mean by cultural distance? How does language affect cultural distance?

3. What is Triandis referring to when he discusses different patterns of sampling information found in the environment? How might these differences affect intercultural communication between an individual from a collectivist culture and someone from an individualistic culture?

4. What differences may be found in the use of "I" and "you" in collectivistic and individualistic cultures?

5. What is cultural tightness? How might cultural diversity in tightness affect intercultural communication?
6. Differentiate between vertical and horizontal cultures.
7. How is culture relevant for understanding conflict?
8. Triandis holds that a very serious problem in communication is that people do not perceive the same "causes" of behavior. How does culture diversity affect the perception of causes?
9. How does culture affect interpersonal aggression? What cultures do you believe would be least prone to violence?
10. What are the characteristics of a collectivistic culture?

Worldview in Intercultural Communication: A Religio-Cosmological Approach

Satoshi Ishii

Donald Klopf

Peggy Cooke

Today we live in a world in which we are inescapably connected to each other, yet separated by divergent points of view that make it increasingly difficult to reach each other. How can we achieve understanding across the gulf of worldviews that separate and threaten us? (*Spectra,* December 2006, p. 10)

Worldview forms some of the most fundamental portions of culture and serves to distinguish one culture from another. Its importance stems from the role it plays in defining reality and truth or explaining the purposes of human life. Worldview thus represents one of the most essential qualities of culture impacting all aspects of how a culture perceives and recognizes the environment. Nurius (1994) reflects that the propensity for individuals to establish and sustain an image of a comprehensive, orderly, and predictable world fulfills one of the most fundamental human needs. Pennington (1985) proclaims that worldview must be given high, if not first, priority in the study of culture because it permeates all other components of culture. She further suggests that by understanding a culture's worldview, it is possible to attain reasonable accuracy in predicting behaviors and motivations in other dimensions. As such, worldview becomes a

This original essay appears here in print for the first time. All rights reserved. Permission to reprint must be obtained from the publisher and the authors. Dr. Satoshi Ishii is Professor Emeritus at Dokkyo University, Japan, Dr. Donald Klopf is Professor Emeritus at the University of Hawaii and West Virginia University, and Dr. Peggy Cooke is an intercultural communication consultant and manages a training program for the State of Washington.

critical element of successful intercultural and environmental communication.

Under such scholarly circumstances, this study attempts to delineate major qualities, types, and religio-cosmological perspectives of worldview.

WORLDVIEW DEFINED

Although the term *worldview* probably originated in German philosophy as *Weltanschauung,* literally *worldview,* it has come to represent a variety of approaches to help understand the underpinnings of cultural diversity. It consists of the most general and comprehensive concepts and unstated assumptions about human life.

Anthropologists Spradley and McCurdy (1980) define *worldview* as the way people characteristically look out on the universe. To communication educators Paige and Martin (1996), *worldview* is one of the lenses through which people view reality and the rest of the world. Sociologists Cosner, Nock, Steffan, and Rhea (1987) define it as a definition of reality. Psychologist Harriman (1947) relates the association of *worldview* with German *Weltanschauung* and considers it to be a total frame of reference.

Reflecting a religious perspective, Helve (1991) characterizes *worldview as* a systematized totality of beliefs about the world. In the same vein, Emerson (1996) conceives it as a set of assumptions about how the world is and ought to be organized. Nurius (1994), operating from a social work orientation, assumes a tack at odds with other worldview advocates. She uses the term *assumptive worlds* to describe clusters of fundamental assumptions that people hold about themselves and the world surrounding them. Samovar, Porter, and McDaniel (2007) report a more inclusive view that *worldview* is culture's orientation to supernatural, human, and natural entities in the cosmological universe and other philosophical issues influencing how its members see the world.

Klopf and McCroskey (2007) also offer an inclusive perspective in their definition of *worldview:*

> Worldview is a set of interrelated assumptions and beliefs about the nature of reality, the organization of the universe, the purposes of human life, God, and other philosophical matters that are concerned with the concept of being. Worldview relates to a culture's orientations toward ontological matters or the nature of being and serves to explain how and why things got to be as they are and why they continue that way. (p. 97)

ELEMENTS OF WORLDVIEW

What constitutes worldview? The definitions stated above include some of the essential elements of worldview. Other elements are to be added beginning with an anthropological analysis extended by Redfield (1953). He argues that the framework is the same for every culture's interpretation of worldview. His Cartesian-dualistic system includes twelve general conceptions of these elements:

1. The self or principal actor on humankind's stage
2. The others, those within the purview of the self
3. Other people—the unidentifiable mass
4. Differences between men and women
5. Distinctions between "we" (our own people) and "they" (other people)
6. Distinctions between what is human and what is not
7. Invisible beings, forces, and principles
8. Animals
9. Concepts of human nature
10. A spatial orientation
11. A temporal orientation
12. Ideas about birth and death

Pennington's (1985) cosmological conceptions of worldview elements appear in the form of ten statements. The salient characteristics of her statement list are:

1. The culture's dominant beliefs and attitudes about a human's place in nature and society
2. The general pattern of relationships between humans and nature
3. The relationship between humans and the culture's supreme being
4. The supreme being's power over life and events
5. Humans' competitive or cooperative nature
6. Humans' expressions of their beliefs
7. Humans' myths about the origins of people
8. Humans' beliefs in the supernatural

9. The living patterns as group practices
10. The ways a group uses rituals, prayers, and other ceremonies

Dodd (1987) categorizes worldview elements into nine groups, most of which tend to stereotypically contrast the East and the West.

Shame vs. Guilt. An Easterner bringing shame to a group is likely to be cast out of it. Westerners consider the individual more important than the group. Saving face is important in the East; not so in the West.

Task vs. People. The East accentuates people's relationships. The West stresses task accomplishment.

Secular vs. Spiritual. Eastern spiritual cultures rely on intuition and introspection. Secular Western cultures are analytical and logical.

Dead vs. Living. The East believes the dead can influence the living, bringing them luck or harm. The West is less prone to think that way.

Human vs. Nature. Humans are either subject to nature, in harmony with nature, or should control nature. The East favors harmony with nature; the West control.

Doing vs. Being. The East prefers harmonious relations, being rather than doing.

Linear vs. Cyclical. In the East, life is birth, life, death, and rebirth. In the West, birth, life, and death.

Fatalism vs. Control. To the fatalist, what happens is beyond a person's control, tending to be an Eastern view. In the control view, people are masters of their own destiny, tending to be a Western view. Worldview is thus closely connected with religious attitudes, beliefs, values, and practices.

FORMATION OF WORLDVIEWS

Worldview is implicit and symbolically implied but not explicitly expressed. Helve (1991) believes it is improbable that people would be aware of their latent worldview. How it is formed, therefore, is a significant matter of speculation.

Worldview evidently develops in early childhood. Helve (1991) determined through empirical research that its actual growth can be comprehended by applying one or all of the theories identified as *cognitive development, social learning,* or *socialization.* She concluded each extended a sensible explanation.

Rubin and Peplau (1975) credit the child's parents, religious instruction, and education in the schools attended as contributors to worldview formation. Each child's maturation, his or her experiences in the physical environment, and his or her activities in the social environment contribute to the formation of worldview. Then each child draws conclusions about what the world is like from his or her experiences and activities in the physical and social environment. In this respect, each child is an active product of the environment, and his or her way of viewing the world is shaped by shared images and constructions of his or her social group or class.

Children and young people view and conceptualize the world in various ways at different stages in their growth according to their own physical and mental development. Infancy, childhood, and adolescence involve distinct stages in behaving, learning, and thinking. The shaping of their needs, desires, beliefs, and values vary from stage to stage and so too does their worldview undergo change as they grow and mature.

Emerson (1996) places stress on religion in the development of worldview. By outlining what ought to be and by creating and reinforcing social group norms through interaction, religion has a substantial influence on a person's worldview. Religion not only shapes reasoning but also provides the meaning, importance, and properness of different social arrangements and institutions. Religion thus infuses all of these with universal, if not transcendent, significance.

Religious beliefs and practices greatly differ, of course: that is why, as Emerson (1996) contends, people hold different worldviews. Those with conservative worldviews base their moral and ethical authority in the transcendent. Those holding more liberal worldviews participate in the religious and secular cultures that root their moral and ethical norms in humans. They generally stress reason and logical thinking.

Even though Emerson (1996) emphasizes religion's role in worldview development, he recognizes a person's position in the social structure as significant. He perceives it, however, as only secondary. Reasonable people living in different cultures of the world are exposed to dissimilar realities in their everyday life. This dissimilar exposure leads them to arrive at distinct worldviews. Emerson's point is substantiated by Cooke (1992), who measured worldview among university students in Japan, Korea, Puerto Rico, and the United States. Her survey findings reveal significant differences among the four socio-cultural groups; each group arrived at different conceptions of worldview.

Although religion plays one of the most significant roles in the formation of worldview, it is inappropriate to constrain it to a purely religious dimension. Worldview stems from a variety of other sources.

TYPES OF WORLDVIEW

Helve (1991) classifies worldview into three major types. In doing so, she appears to endorse the Chamberlain and Zika (1992) position. Helve's types are *scientific, metaphysical,* and *religious.*

The *scientific* worldview is based on the rules laid down by the exact sciences. It is open and self-correcting in accordance with new systematic and methodological findings. Helve (1991) found it to appear most clearly among scientific scholars. A quasi-scientific worldview results from television, newspaper, and magazine influences, she notes, and it is more "information based" as a worldview than scientific. Those with a scientific bent do not harbor this quasi-scientific worldview.

A *metaphysical* worldview tends to be based on abstract general reasoning without an empirical base. For example, the metaphysical worldview of young children may contain beliefs in imaginary beings such as Santa Claus, ghosts, monsters, witches, and fairies. Older children may include elements of magic and superstition. Teenagers might construct their worldview around horoscopes and behave in accordance with the advice they give. The metaphysical worldview is apt to consist of certain types of unnatural beings, their characteristics, and their relationships. These beings originate partly in religious traditions and partly in folklore, some of which is created by the mass media.

The third type of worldview is *religious*. For most people, religion serves as the foundation of their worldview. The content of their beliefs will vary from person to person depending upon their religious perspectives. A Catholic's worldview undoubtedly will differ from that of a Jew, a Protestant's from a Buddhist's, a Muslim's from a Hindu's, and a Confucianist's from a Shintoist's.

THE RELIGIOUS PERSPECTIVE

Religion, as has been repeatedly stressed, is a deep and pervasive determinant of worldview. Even the most secular of people feel religion's influences. Those who reject religious faith still follow much of the religious heritage that influences their culture.

Dimensions of Religion

Religion, Emerson (1996) attests, is multidimensional. He conceptualizes it along two representative dimensions, religiosity and orthodoxy, each with two subdivisions, public and private. Religiosity refers to the intensity and consistency of religious practices. Orthodoxy is the degree to which a person's beliefs center on a guiding authority, for example, the scriptures of the church.

Public religiosity describes the religious activities practiced with other people. It is manifest in frequent church attendance and participation in membership functions. Private religiosity is a person's personal and undisclosed religious practice. Examples include the frequency of prayer and holy script reading as well as a doubt-free faith.

Public orthodoxy refers to the sharing of religious beliefs in the company of others. Private orthodoxy is the held beliefs that rely on a transcendent authority, a god, or a supernatural being.

EASTERN AND WESTERN RELIGIO-COSMOLOGICAL WORLDVIEWS

As a more manageable thinking about the world's diverse faiths, Smart (1988) groups them into two major divisions: Eastern and Western. Each division can help increase an understanding of the impact that religion has on the content and development of a person's worldview. Eastern and Western religious traditions may account for some 80 percent of the world's population. The remaining 20 percent will consist of animists, atheists, shamanists, and the like.

Religious Similarities

Although the two major divisions, Eastern and Western, have few common teachings, they do possess similarities typical of all religions. Samovar, Porter, and Stefani (1998) identify five such similarities, the most important being *sacred writings*. All of the world's major religions have sacred writings, such as the Holy Bible, the Qur'an, and Buddhist sutras, commonly revered by believers. These writings function as the means and vehicles for the propagation of the religion's knowledge and wisdom.

Another similarity is an *authority figure*. God, Allah, the Buddha, Jesus, and Muhammad are all representative authority figures who are believed to be far greater and more powerful than the religion's members.

Rituals are the third similarity. They are religious practices required of the membership or acts that are forbidden to the members. For example, believers must meditate regularly or be baptized. They must pray at special times and fast on designated days. They may not eat pork or beef. These acts embody humility, restraint, and behaviors of great religious significance.

Speculation, as another similarity, typifies all religions. Humans commonly seek answers to mysteries of life—what is life, death, suffering, or origins of the universe—and religions are believed to supply answers to such mysteries, speculative at best.

Religion also commonly includes *ethics*, a set of moral principles for the membership to observe. For most religions, the set contains moral items such as prohibiting killing, stealing, and lying, observing marital fidelity, paying honor to parents, and the like.

Eastern Religio-Cosmological Worldview

Eastern (Chinese, Indian, Japanese, Korean, and other) cultures commonly embrace religious traditions that feature relational harmony as the ultimate good (Smart, 1988). Relational harmony has been consistently believed to be the major tenet recognized in Eastern religions such as Buddhism, Confucianism, Hinduism, Shintoism, and Taoism. Further, although these religions differ considerably, their theological foundations are similar in that gods and deities are in every place and in every form, rather than a single place or form.

In Figure 1, Ishii (2001) has developed Contrastive Models of Eastern Poly-Pantheistic and Western Monotheistic Worldviews from religio-cosmological perspectives to graphically illustrate the respective positions and correlations of supernatural beings, human

Figure 1 *Contrastive Models of Eastern Poly-Pantheistic and Western Monotheistic Worldviews*

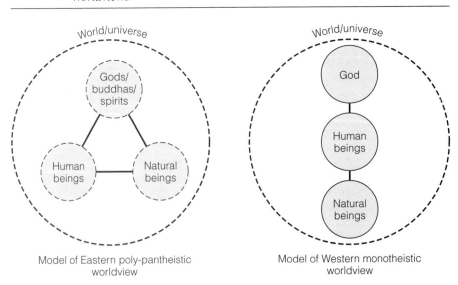

Model of Eastern poly-pantheistic worldview

Model of Western monotheistic worldview

beings, and natural beings. The outer broken circle of the left model of Eastern poly-pantheistic worldview signifies that the world/universe in which supernatural beings (e.g., buddhas, deities, gods, goddesses, spirits, etc.), human beings, and natural beings (e.g., animals, astronomical objects, mountains, plants, rivers, etc.) are believed to exist is a cosmologically open system, spatially and/or temporally limited or unlimited.

The three triangularly arranged broken circles, respectively, imply various supernatural beings' realm, human beings' realm, and natural beings' realm. Their triangular arrangement is not hierarchically predetermined and rigidly fixed but is relative, dynamic, and interchangeable according to contextual and situational changes. The brokenness of each circle indicates that the sovereignty of each existential realm is not decisively predetermined and closed to each other but is relative, flexibly open, and dynamically interchangeable.

These characteristics of Eastern religio-cosmological worldview have traditionally given extensive influences to Eastern people's cognitive, affective, and behavioral activities in not simply human-to-human but also human-to-supernatural and human-to-nature communication contexts.

Western Religio-Cosmological Worldview

The Western capsulation of religion, and hence worldview, is in sharp contrast to the Eastern one. Western religions represented by Judaism, Christianity, and Islam perceive the ultimate good as transformation and salvation, stressing that divine grace is the desired end, whether in this life or the next.

Differences among these religions are obvious, yet they have a common religio-cosmological foundation. The three religions are monotheistic, believing in one Almighty God, who is "out there" and everything else is here, with a great gulf in between. Smart (1988) states that in the Western religions everything is ultimately headed to one end—to the Kingdom of God or to heaven. At the end of a person's life will be an accounting or payoff, either eternal death or resurrection of his or her body. Further, the things that belong to Almighty God are highly sacred, to be treated with special awe and reverence. What is of particular importance in the Western

religions is felicity—happiness and bliss—beyond this earthly life.

In Figure 1, like the outer broken circle of the left model, the right model of Western monotheistic worldview is hypothetically believed to have an outer broken circle of the world/universe in which one Almighty God's realm, human beings' realm, and natural beings' realm exist. Their hierarchical positions and interrelations are absolute, rigidly predetermined, and unchangeable. Almighty God's realm is always placed at the top of the hierarchy, human beings' realm in the middle, and natural beings' realm at the bottom. The three solid circles respectively imply that the three realms are fixed and closed to each other, and not interchangeable.

In promoting the study of worldview in this age of interreligious conflicts, it is growingly essential to investigate the potential influences of Western monotheistic religious cosmology on Westerners' cognitive, affective, and behavioral activities in intercultural communication contexts.

Contrastive Summary of Eastern and Western Worldviews

Psychologists Gilgen and Cho (1979) perceive religio-cosmological worldview in an East-West dichotomy—the East based on Eastern poly-pantheistic religions and the West on European and North American monotheistic beliefs. They are contrastively summarized as follows:

Eastern Worldview	Western Worldview
Humans are one with nature and perceive the spiritual and personal physical as one.	Humans are separate from nature and overshadowed by a God.
Mind and body are one.	Humans consist of mind, body, and soul.
Humans should accept their basic oneness with nature rather than try to control it.	Humans have to manipulate and control nature to survive.
Humans are one with nature; they should feel comfortable with anyone.	Humans should reward actions competitive in spirit.

(Continued)

Eastern Worldview	Western Worldview
Science and technology create an illusion of progress.	Science and technology provide the good life.
Enlightenment causes differences to disappear and brings oneness with the universe, coming about through meditation.	No such belief.

In order to improve interreligious issues repeatedly breaking out in the contemporary world, intercultural communication scholars and educators are widely urged to conduct systematic studies of different religio-cosmological worldviews from ethnocentrism-free perspectives.

Colliding Worldviews and Environmental Communication

Unfortunately, fruitful intercultural encounters and relations are not always the norm even when highly educated men and women meet together. Misunderstandings, conflicts, and serious consequences occasionally result in their encounters and relations.

No less contentious are the frequent encounters and relations between developers and environmentalists, those who want to conquer and exploit nature and those who try to maintain that humans are one with nature and that destroying nature will lead to destroying humans. These conflicts and collisions are being fought at various levels: local, national, and international.

Clark (1998) warns us that environmental destruction is speedily accelerating in many parts of the world. At the local level, the loss of forests, soil erosion, and overdrafts of ground water are common occurrences. At the national level, increased yields of timber and food crops are now unsustainable. At the international level, people worldwide are mining natural resources, particularly fossil fuels. Human-induced global warming, overgrazing, and deforestation are compounding large-scale droughts, famines, storms, and floods. Pollution issues are multiplying as waters are poisoned, as forests, rivers, and lakes are decimated by acid rain, and as cities worldwide suffer from foul air.

Dodd (1987) reminds us about the appropriateness of humans' relations with nature—either humans are subject to nature, in harmony with it, or should control it. Today's environmental state suggests that harmony is absent, control is not working, and consequently humans will soon be subject to total natural disaster. Worldviews are thus colliding as we communicate closer and closer about environmental issues with our fellow humans throughout the world.

Clark (1989) points a finger at the Western worldview, placing blame for contemporary environmental conditions directly on the West. Although major polluters, soil eroders, and deforesters are prevalent in the East as well, Clark believes it is the Western nature-controlling worldview that is destroying the environment. She suggests that the Western worldview lacks proper values and goals, and has grown obsolete. All worldviews, she claims, require adjustment if humans are to survive. However, the most in need of critically rethinking and redoing is that of the Western civilization whose enormous military, science-technological, and economic power and hegemony increasingly impinge upon the entire globe.

Untying the Gordian Knot

Clark (1989) gives us a thread with which we might find our way out of the labyrinth created by colliding worldviews. Her way may help untie the Gordian knot in which disparate worldviews are enmeshed as they attempt to exist together in the twenty-first century.

In ages past, Clark (1989) argues, worldviews evolved gradually, often imperceptibly. With today's enormous powers unleashed by science and technology from the Western worldview creating excessive environmental change, humankind can no longer rely on the old, indiscernible thinking. Human goals need to be reordered.

All worldviews require some degree of adjustment if the species is to survive. Tracing the beliefs and assumptions underlying them is the first step in making social change possible. This first step is one that students of intercultural communication can undertake, learning to understand the differences in worldview globally, and to comprehend the beliefs and assumptions on which they are based.

Clark (1989) cautions that imposing a new worldview certainly will fail unless it comes from within the cultural context. People of a culture must actively participate in the change making. For a new worldview to evolve, everyone must participate in the change process.

In her 1998 article in *Zygon*, Clark (1998) expounds on her new worldview in detail. Her plan may appear too esoteric for students of intercultural communication to consider. Pennington (1985) believes, however, that reasonable preciseness can be reached in predicting behaviors and motivations in the social, economic, and political lives of cultures of the globe. As Smart (1988) prompts us, we tend to ignore at our peril the worldview dimensions of our communication across cultures.

SUMMARY AND CONCLUSION

This study has attempted to define *worldview*, describe its conceptual elements and structure, illustrate its hypothetical connection with religious cosmology, and finally make possible suggestions to improve, if not solve, contemporary worldview and environmental conflicts emerging in various parts of the world. The religio-cosmological approach to the study of worldview will serve as a new groundbreaking signpost for intercultural communication scholars and educators by providing new imminent scholarly tasks from a variety of interdisciplinary perspectives.

Tehranian and Chappell (2002), scholars of inter-religious and intercivilizational studies, contend

> The way to resolve these conflicts is not to pit one camp against another, . . . ; for the human race to survive, it is necessary to open up all channels of communication for dialogue, negotiation, and creation of values commensurate with the challenges of our own times. (p. xxix)

References

Chamberlain, K., & Zika, S. (1992). Religiosity, meaning in life, and psychological well being. In J. F. Schumacher (Ed.), *Religion and mental health*. New York: Oxford University Press.

Clark, M. E. (1989). *Ariadne's thread: The search for new modes of thinking*. New York: St. Martin's Press.

Clark, M. E. (1998). Human nature: What we need to know about ourselves in the twenty-first century. *Zygon, 333*, 645–659.

Cooke, P. (1992). *The relationship between culture and worldview: A cross-cultural comparison of Japan, Korea, Puerto Rico, and the United States*. Unpublished master's thesis, West Virginia University, Morgantown, W V.

Cosner, L., Nock, S., Steffan, P., & Rhea, B. (1987). *Introduction to sociology* (2nd ed.). San Diego, CA: Harcourt Brace.

Dodd, C. H. (1987). *Dynamics of intercultural communication* (2nd ed.). Dubuque, IA: W. C. Brown.

Emerson, M. O. (1996). Through tinted glasses: Religion, worldviews, and abortion attitudes. *Journal for the Scientific Study of Religion, 35*, 41–55.

Gilgen, A., & Cho, J. (1979). Questionnaire to measure Eastern and Western thought. *Psychological Report, 44*.

Helve, H. (1991). The formation of religious attitudes and worldviews: A longitudinal study of young Finns. *Social Compass, 38*, 373–392.

Ishii, S. (2001). An emerging rationale for triworld communication studies from Buddhist perspectives, *Human Communication, 4(1)*, 1–10.

Klopf, D. W., & McCroskey, J. C. (2007). *Intercultural communication encounters*. Boston: Pearson Education.

Nurius, P. S. (1994). Assumptive worlds, self-definition, and striving among women. *Basic and Applied Social Psychology, 15*, 311–327.

Paige, R. M., & Martin, J. N. (1996). Ethics in intercultural training. In D. Landis & R. S. Bhagat (Eds.), *Handbook of Intercultural Training* (2nd ed.). Thousand Oaks, CA: Sage.

Pennington, U. L. (1985). Intercultural communication. In L. Samovar & R. E. Porter (Eds.), *Intercultural Communication: A Reader* (4th ed.). Belmont, CA: Wadsworth.

Redfield, R. (1953). *The primitive world and its transformation*. Ithaca, NY: Cornell University Press.

Rubin, Z., & Peplau, L. A. (1975). Who believes in a just world? *Journal of Social Issues, 31*, 65–89.

Samovar, L., Porter, R. E., & McDaniel, E. R. (2007). *Communication between cultures* (6th ed.). Belmont, CA: Wadsworth.

Smart, R. (1988). Religion-caused complications in intercultural communication. In L. Samovar & R. E. Porter (Eds.), *Intercultural communication: A Reader* (5th ed.). Belmont, CA: Wadsworth.

Spectra (2006, December), *42*(12), p. 10.

Spradley, J. P., & McCurdy, U. W. (1980). *Anthropology: The cultural perspective* (2nd ed.). Prospect Heights, IL: Waveland.

Tehranian, M., & Chappell, D. W. (2002). Introduction: Civilization, terror, and dialogue. In M. Tehranian & D. W. Chappell (Eds.), *Dialogue of civilizations: A new agenda for a new millennium*. London: I. B. Tauris.

Concepts and Questions

1. According to Ishii, Klopf, and Cooke, how does worldview shape and represent culture?
2. What is the most significant aspect of worldview? How does cultural diversity lead to differing worldviews?
3. What are the major characteristics of *scientific, metaphysical,* and *religious* worldviews?
4. What are religiosity and orthodoxy? How do they contribute to shaping worldviews?
5. According to Samovar, Porter, and Stefani, what are the five similarities typical of all religions?
6. How does worldview generally differ between Eastern polytheistic and Western monotheistic cultures?
7. According to Dodd, what are the three types of humans' relationships with nature? How do they represent Eastern and Western worldviews?
8. How does Clark caution people of the highly industrialized nations about contemporary environmental crises?
9. How would you differentiate between Eastern and Western perspectives regarding ethics?
10. What should be done to rectify, if not resolve, today's worldwide interreligious conflicts, particularly from the perspective of worldview?

"Harmony without Uniformity": An Asiacentric Worldview and Its Communicative Implications

Yoshitaka Miike

In response to Samuel Huntington's (1993, 1996) proposition that the world would be divided by "the clash of civilizations," Tu Weiming (2006) tersely states, "Civilizations do not clash. Only ignorance does" (p. 12). Indeed, ignorance of cultural diversity, not cultural diversity itself, is a source of disharmony and conflict in the global village. To be sure, as Chesebro (1996) notes, "multiculturalism is a symbolic issue, a question of how we understand ourselves, how we understand our heritages, and how we understand our futures to be" (p. 13). As such, it does sometimes radically challenge our basic sense of identity, community, and humanity. And yet, we must learn to appreciate all cultural traditions as valuable resources for humanity because diversity is vital to human survival and flourishing (Tu, 2001b). It is counterproductive to see difference as an obstacle to "progress" in the age of intercultural encounters. Our task as global citizens is not to "liberate" different people from their "primitive" and "uncivilized" traditions, but to learn from different people *with* their respective traditions about alternative visions of humanity and communication.

In this essay, I will share my thoughts on the what and how of culture learning toward mutual understanding and dialogue and discuss, as an illustrative example, how Asians and non-Asians alike may be able to benefit from an Asiacentric worldview and its implications for communication. I will reinterpret

This original essay appears here in print for the first time. All rights reserved. Permission to reprint must be obtained from the author and the publisher. Dr. Yoshitaka Miike teaches in the Department of Communication at the University of Hawai'i at Hilo.

Molefi Kete Asante's (1993) idea of "multiculturalism without hierarchy" (i.e., the coexistence of many cultures alongside) in the global context and apply the Confucian ideal of "harmony without uniformity" (i.e., the balanced integration of different elements) to the contemporary world. Wisdom is a precious gift to humanity. Every continent, every community, and every culture has accumulated indigenous wisdom, from which we can learn a great deal about how we should relate to one another, nature, and the sprits in the universe (Miike, 2004). It is my argument in the succeeding discussion, therefore, that, if we are to remain hopeful for a prosperous and peaceful world and to realize unity in diversity in the global society, we ought to reflect earnestly on the question of humanity and the way of communication from different local knowledges in different cultures.

CULTURES IN HIERARCHY AND CULTURES ALONGSIDE

Asante (2003b) claims that difference alone does not create a problem, and that it is the assigning of hierarchical value to difference that creates a problem. His idea of "multiculturalism without hierarchy" thus pinpoints how cultures should relate to one another in the context of diversity. He implies that, if multiculturalism is defined as the coexistence of many cultures, there are two ways of cultural coexistence: (1) cultures in hierarchy and (2) cultures alongside. *Cultures in hierarchy* is the form of cultural coexistence in which we see one culture above others so that we learn a frame of reference from one culture and view others through the single cultural standpoint. *Cultures alongside* is the form of cultural coexistence in which we see all cultures equal so that we learn different outlooks from different cultures and view all cultures through their respective cultural lenses. Asante (1993) refers to the second form of cultural coexistence as pluralism without hierarchy and hegemony. He believes that when we bring together local knowledges from all cultures, we will have a truly global knowledge about people in the world and move toward a truly transcultural understanding of humanity, culture, and communication. In this section, using Satoshi Ishii's (1997) conceptualization of culture, I will envision the ideal of culture

learning that enhances "multiculturalism without hierarchy." My thesis here is that in order to appreciate any culture, we must understand the worldview of the culture and its impact on the forms and functions of communication.

Worldview as the Mental Layer of Culture

Ishii (1997) proposes a three-layer structure model of culture (see Figure 1). According to him, culture consists of three layers—material, behavioral, and mental. The most external, overt, and visible layer of culture is the material one, which is represented by various artifacts (e.g., food and clothing) produced, operated, and controlled by the behavioral layer. The semi-overt layer of culture is the behavioral one, which is comprised of verbal and nonverbal behaviors as symbols (e.g., words and gestures) and reflects the mental layer. The most internal, covert, and invisible layer of culture is the mental one, which functions in the form of values, beliefs, and attitudes. Ishii (1997) holds that "understanding the mental layer is the most important in intercultural communication situations because it is the core of culture which operates and controls the two outer behavioral and material layers" (p. 321). The mental layer of a culture is, in a nutshell, a cultural worldview that answers ultimate questions about humanity (e.g., Who are we? Where have we been? Where are we going? For what do we live?)

Figure 1 *Satoshi Ishii's Model of Culture*

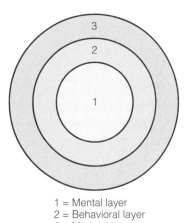

1 = Mental layer
2 = Behavioral layer
3 = Material layer

Samovar, Porter, and McDaniel (2007) define a worldview as "a culture's orientation toward God, humanity, nature, questions of existence, the universe, and the cosmos, life, moral and ethical reasoning, suffering, death, and other philosophical issues that influence how its members perceive their world" (p. 73). A worldview should be regarded as neither completely static nor completely fluid. It is always evolving and transforming and yet maintains the contours of the culture. Different portions of the worldview are instilled in the minds of different members of the culture. Given that it is the deep structure of communication (i.e., the mental layer), we may or may not be aware of its profound impact on the surface structure of communication (i.e., the behavioral and material layers). Because the mental layer of a culture is the most internal and invisible, we can only guess what it is like by comprehensively interpreting the linguistic, religious, philosophical, and historical foundations of the culture. As Ishii, Klopf, and Cooke (2006) comment, worldview is, more often than not, "implied but not verbally expressed. . . . How it is formed, therefore, is a matter of speculation" (p. 34).

Learning about and from Cultures

Learning *about* cultures is one thing. Learning *from* cultures is another. We can be very arrogant and ethnocentric, but we can still learn about other cultures. Learning from cultures, on the other hand, requires us to be humble and modest in order to understand and

appreciate other cultures (Miike, 2005). The former approach is an attempt to describe, interpret, and evaluate a different culture through the worldview that is *not* derived from the culture. In other words, we use the mental layer of our own culture to analyze the material, behavioral, and mental layers of other cultures. In this approach, cultural critique, rather than mutual learning, is prone to take place because we tend to treat other cultures like texts for criticism and their members like objects for analysis. I call such an approach "centrism." For example, if we use the mental layer of European cultures to understand African cultures, our Eurocentrism (*not* Eurocentricity) will most likely distort the cultural realities of the African world from an outsider's point of view (see Figure 2). When we consciously or unconsciously presume that independence, individualism, and freedom are better than interdependence, communalism, and obligation without reference to the African worldview, we are tempted to view African and European cultures in hierarchy, not alongside, and fail to acknowledge of the *ubuntu*-based humanity in the African context. Indeed, we relate only to African cultures in a *hierarchical* way.

The latter approach is an attempt to observe, describe, interpret, and evaluate a different culture through the worldview that is derived from the culture. To put it in another way, we use the mental layer of the culture to understand its material and behavioral layers. In this approach, culture learning and cross-cultural self-reflection are likely to take place because we tend to view other cultures as

Figure 2 *Eurocentrism*

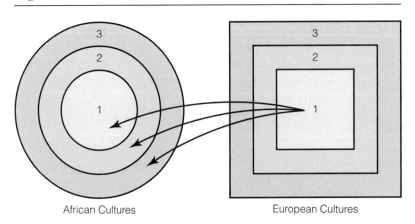

African Cultures   European Cultures

Figure 3 *Afrocentricity and Asiacentricity*

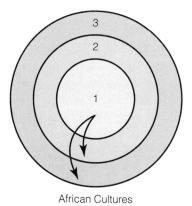

African Cultures

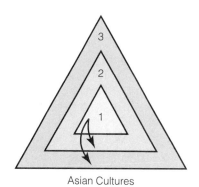

Asian Cultures

resources of insights and their members as agents. I call such an approach "centricity." For instance, if we use the mental layers of African and Asian cultures to understand the material and behavioral layers of African and Asian cultures, our Afrocentricity and Asiacentricity (*not* Afrocentrism and Asiacentrism) will more accurately capture the cultural realities of the African and Asian worlds from an insider's point of view (see Figure 3). It goes without saying that it is often difficult but critically important for us to engage in learning from, not about, cultures if we wish to broaden and deepen the understanding of culture-specific thought and action and to expand the notion of humanity in cultural context. This ideal form of culture learning undoubtedly helps us achieve multiculturalism without hierarchy and facilitate dialogue among civilizations (Miike, 2005).

HUMANISM AS AN EXPRESSION OF EUROCENTRISM

What is problematic in many intercultural studies is that the mental layer of European cultures is frequently used to analyze the behavioral and material layers of non-European cultures, which decontextualizes them and obscures their nexus with the mental layer of non-European cultures. Because it is the mental layer of culture that explains why these symbolic behaviors and material artifacts are of immense value, such analyses will not result in the deeper appreciation and better understanding of behavioral and material layers of non-European cultures.

Consequently, those descriptions present them as exoteric, irrational, and backward and, hence, ultimately create the image of "the Other" (Miike, 2004). In other words, they impose the Eurocentric vision of humanity on other versions of humanity. I contend that we should begin to rethink the role of non-Western worldviews in comprehending non-Western behaviors and in redefining and reconceptualizing humanity and communication. I reiterate that we must see all cultures as central resources of humanistic insight and inspiration, not peripheral targets of analysis and critique from someone else's point of view (Miike, 2006).

The nature and ideal of humanity has often been defined and delimited by the Eurocentric worldview. It is particularly indebted to, and intertwined with, the European Enlightenment mentality. Its core values are instrumental rationality, individual liberty, calculated self-interest, material progress, and rights consciousness (Tu, 2002). These values have served as Eurocentric criteria from which to scrutinize and judge non-European versions of humanity. They have shaped false dichotomies such as the civilized and the primitive, the modern and the traditional, the progressive and the backward, the developed and the developing, and the humane and the inhumane. In spite of criticisms of these invalid binaries, Eurocentric constructions of humanity have led to Eurocentric critiques of other centric views of humanity. They have also made oblivious to us the past and potential contributions of non-European cultures to human civilization. As Rogers (1976) cautions, therefore, it is very easy for us to "forget that India,

China, Persia, and Egypt were old, old centers of civilization, that their rich cultures had in fact provided the basis for contemporary Western cultures" (p. 216). Looking at the non-Western world only with a Eurocentric *critical* eye and looking at the West only with a Eurocentric *uncritical* eye, nonetheless, poses a serious problem in understanding humanity and communication. This is especially so when the Eurocentric vision of humanity, heavily influenced by the Enlightenment mentality, is undermining the human condition.

Being a Teacher and Being a Student

Asante (1998) posits that "Any interpretation of African culture must begin at once to dispense with the notion that, in all things, Europe is teacher and Africa is pupil" (p. 71). There is a persistent and pervasive tendency to approach European cultures from a student's perspective and non-European cultures from a teacher's perspective in the study of culture and communication. In fact, much intercultural research deals with non-European cultures as targets for analysis and critique, but not resources for insight and inspiration (Asante, Miike, & Yin, 2008). Therefore, it promotes a teacher's perspective on non-European cultures, which decenters and dislocates non-European people. It should be kept in mind, however, that we do not appreciate cultures when we always analyze and critique them. We appreciate cultures when we learn from them. We must be diligent students of non-Western learning and abandon the role of being teachers from the West at all times (Miike, 2006). Tu (2001a), for instance, duly insists on the value of seeing African cultures from a student's point of view:

> If we consider ethnic, cultural, linguistic, and religious diversity as a global asset, Africa should not be characterized by the HIV epidemic, poverty, unemployment, and social disintegration alone. It should also be recognized as a rich reservoir for human spirituality and the wisdom of elders. The African Renaissance, symbolized by the geological and biological diversity of the tiny area around Capetown (said to be comparable in richness to the vast area of Canada) ought to be a source of inspiration for a changed mindset that addresses social development as a global joint venture. (p. 257)

Three Steps to Cross-Cultural Dialogue

With "a global mindset by which we try to see things through the eyes of others and add their knowledge to our personal repertoires" (Chen & Starosta, 2000, p. 1), we can perhaps take three steps to cross-cultural dialogue. The first step is to understand the mental layer of our own culture and its impact on the behavioral and material layers. The second step is to understand the mental layer of other cultures and their impacts on the behavioral and material layers. The third step is to listen to others' perspectives on our culture and share our perspectives on other cultures in order to reflect on what it means to be human in both local and global contexts and how humans should relate to one another, nature, and the spirits. In this step, we must engage in dialogue among civilizations with Asante's (2006) spirit of mutual respect and learning: "As creators of our own societies, we have valuable experiences to share, not to impose, which might be examined and adapted in a sprit of sharing and dialogue. This is the real meaning of intercultural interaction" (p. 154). Tu (2001a) echoes Asante's position by saying that "the celebration of cultural diversity, without falling into the trap of pernicious relativism, is profoundly meaningful for global stewardship" (p. 257).

ASIACENTRIC WORLDVIEW AND COMMUNICATION

In this section, I will draw on my previous work based on the principle of Asiacentricity (Miike, 2003, 2004, 2006, 2007) and outline an Asiacentric worldview and its communicative implications in local and global contexts. More specifically, I will discuss five Asiacentric propositions on human communication. They are "propositions" (*not* truths) in the sense that they reflect my interpretation of the "invisible" mental layer of Asian cultures and my intent to tap into Asian cultural wisdom both for an Asiacentric understanding of Asian communication and for dialogue among civilizations. Hence, they do not capture the whole profile of the Asian communicator and the entire picture of Asian communication. My discussion here is based on the five elements of an Asiacentric worldview that I have identified from the existing literature on the psychology and practices of Asian cultures and communication (e.g., Chen & Miike, 2003; Dissanayake, 1988;

Kincaid, 1987; Miike & Chen, 2006, 2007; Nordstrom, 1983): (1) circularity, (2) harmony, (3) other-directedness, (4) reciprocity, and (5) relationality. These recurring themes altogether paint an Asiacentric picture of humanity and communication.

Asiacentric Communication Proposition #1

The first Asiacentric proposition is that communication is a process in which we remind ourselves of the interdependence and interrelatedness of the universe. This proposition can complement the Western dominant thinking that communication is a process in which we demonstrate our independence and express our individuality. Humans are prone to engage in a present-oriented and lifeworld-centered way of thinking. Therefore, according to the Asian worldview, it is necessary for us to constantly communicate with fellow humans, nature, and the world of spirits in order to escape from the illusion that we are independent individuals in a particular place at a particular time. Asian patterns of group communication more practically correspond to this ideal of communication as a reminder of the non-separateness. The Japanese *nemawashi* style, for example, allows group members not only to exchange ideas but also to increase the sense of interdependence and interrelatedness (Kume, 2007; Nishiyama, 1971).

The two Asiacentric themes of relationality and circularity have much to do with the ontological belief that the universe is a great whole in which everyone and everything are interrelated across space and time (Chen, 2006; Ishii, 1998; Miike, 2003). Asian religions and philosophies illuminate the interpenetrated nature of the self, family, community, society, nation, world, and cosmos. Confucius (551–479 BCE) remarks in the *Analects* (6:28) that "if you wish to establish yourself, you have to help others to establish themselves; if you wish to complete yourself, you have to help others to complete themselves." Similarly, in the words of Suzuki (2006), Buddhism teaches: "So to save oneself we have to save others. . . . By helping others, I may be able to save myself. My salvation and others' salvation are so intimately involved, connected together, that we can never save ourselves just by ourselves. We must always be saved together" (p. 19). More interestingly, the Hindu notion of *Virat Purusha* [Cosmic Person] views each individual as the manifestation of the cosmos itself; the universe is "a single body where each element lives for all and all live for one . . . [T]he weal and woe of one individual affect another" (Saral, 1983, p. 54). It is the teaching of Hinduism that "the world of distinct and separate objects and processes is a manifestation of a more fundamental reality that is undivided and unconditioned" (Jain, 1991, p. 80).

The Asian worldview essentially defines communication as an endless process in which we continuously locate and relocate ourselves in an ever-expanding network of relationships across space and time. This ancient yet radical Eastern idea of communication must be taken seriously now that the global village has never been so divided by wealth, influence, and power in world history, and that we have polluted the air we breathe and poisoned the water we drink to the extent that we risk our own lives (Tu, 2002). Social disintegration is also becoming a worldwide phenomenon in modern societies. As Asante (2005) observes, "The lack of connectedness creates insensitivity to others, harshness, abrasiveness, and arrogance" (p. 135). Yum (2000) further points out that "Although individualism has its own strength as a value, individualism that is not accompanied by commitments to large entities eventually forces people into a state of isolation, where life itself becomes meaningless" (p. 71). We must learn about communication as a way to realize that our well-being is inextricably and inescapably intertwined with those of other members of the human family, nature, and even the supernatural.

Asiacentric Communication Proposition #2

The second Asiacentric proposition is that communication is a process in which we reduce our selfishness and egocentrism. This Eastern viewpoint makes a sharp contrast to the Western presumption that communication is a process in which we prove ourselves and enhance our self-esteem. It may sound as if Asian traditions of thought discourage the values of autonomy and agency. That is not the case at all. Rather, Asian religious-philosophers, especially Buddhist thinkers, are critically aware that humans are by nature self-centered and egocentric (Ishii, 2004). Therefore, according to their teachings, humans ought to discipline and cultivate themselves in order to experience the oneness of the universe and harmoniously coexist with fellow humans, nature, and the world of spirits. In the Asian worldview, communication is conceptualized as central to this process of self-discipline, self-cultivation, self-development, and self-realization. The Asian way of knowing hence centers on the elimination of excessive and aggressive ego as a primary source of mental suffering and perceptual barriers (Ishii, 2004).

Dogen (1200–1253), the founder of the Soto Zen school in Japan, writes at the very beginning of his thirteenth-century book, Shobogenzo [Treasury of the Eye of the True Dharma]: "To study the Way is to study the self. To study the self is to forget the self. To forget the self is to be enlightened by all things." What he meant was that removing all the divisions and distinctions of self and other renders it possible to form an ultimate unity with everything. According to Dogen, intrapersonal communication, in which we reduce selfishness and egocentrism, can lead to ultimate communication with the whole universe (Saito, 1970). Likewise, the Confucian way of learning to be human is to engage in ceaseless self-cultivation and creative self-transformation by crafting the self as a center of myriad relationships. The point of departure in quest of our authentic identity is, paradoxically, to overcome selfishness and egocentrism (Tu, 2002). What is intriguing about Buddhist and Confucian epistemologies is that we need to reduce our selfishness and egocentrism through communication and then become better communicators as a result of self-discipline and self-cultivation.

Asian daily experiences also appear to concertedly indicate that interacting with other humans, nature, and the spirits facilitates the process of disciplining and cultivating ourselves. Asians may be truly touched and highly motivated to discipline themselves and work harder when they listen to, or simply observe, individuals who possess sophisticated skills through their years of practice or people who are struggling against all odds in their lives. Moreover, reducing selfishness and egocentrism means increasing connection and cooperation not only at the interpersonal level but also at other levels. From the perspective of Zen Buddhism, "An awareness of 'oneness' develops from emptying oneself and accepting the other" (Saito, 1970, p. 17). Encountering fellow humans, nature, and the spirits in a way that we reduce our selfishness and egocentrism enables us to rise above nepotism, parochialism, ethnocentrism, and anthropocentrism as well as egocentrism. In such a sense, this second communicative proposition is, once again, in consonance with the two Asian themes of relationality and circularity. In this increasing ego-driven world, the time is right to turn our attention to the role of interpersonal communication as an ego-reduction and self-decentering practice. For, as Chen (2005) understands, in order for us to fully unfold the potential as co-creators of the whole universe with heaven and earth, our "self must be ceaselessly edified, constantly liberated, and perpetually purified" (p. 7) in intercultural encounters with the other.

Asiacentric Communication Proposition #3

The third Asiacentric proposition is that communication is a process in which we feel the joy and suffering of all sentient beings. This proposition is linked particularly with the Asian theme of other-directedness. As the Chinese concept of renqing, the Japanese concept of ninjo, and the Korean concept of cheong imply, emotional sensitivity, not instrumental rationality, occupies a central place in being and becoming fully human in the Asian worldview. To feel through sensitivity rather than to analyze through rationality is one of the "habits of the heart" in Asian communication (Chen & Starosta, 2003). Such a feature manifests many trans-Asian premises and practices of communication. The Filipino practice of pahiwatig (Mendoza, 2004), the Japanese exercise of sasshi (Ishii & Bruneau, 1994), and the Korean performance of nunchi (Robinson, 2003), for instance, underscore and underline the importance of communicative sensitivity to the joy and suffering of fellow human beings. This preponderance toward affection rather than cognition does not mean that Asians are not rational and do not rely on reason (Chen, 2006), but feelings and emotions are equally, or even more, valued as essential qualities in the Asian version of humanity and communication.

Asian religions and philosophies also endorse this communicative proposition. Confucianism delimits the cardinal concept of ren [human-heartedness] in light of sympathy and empathy. Buddhism likewise emphasizes the development of compassion, which literally means "feelings in common." Tu (2001b) accounts for the centrality of emotional sensitivity in Buddhist and Confucian visions of humanity:

Both Confucianism and Buddhism maintain that sympathy, empathy, and compassion are at the same time the minimum requirement and the maximum realization of the human way. According to Confucian and Buddhist modes of thinking, human beings are sentient beings. Sensitivity, rather than rationality, is the distinctive feature of humanity. We feel; therefore we are. Through feeling, we realize our own existence and the coexistence of other human beings, indeed birds, animals, plants, and all the myriad things in the universe. Since this feeling of interconnectedness is not merely a private emotion but a sense of fellowship that is intersubjectively confirmable, it is a commonly shareable value. (pp. 83–84)

It is important to note that the Asian worldview does not encourage speaker-centered affective communication where individuals explicitly disclose emotions to one another. Because, as Kim (2001) notes, "Relational emotions that bind and bond individuals together, not the private and narcissistic emotions, are emphasized" (p. 67), according to the Asian experience, emotional convergence in communication is often possible when the listener, who is ego-decentered and other-directed, attempts to sense and read the speaker's emotional dynamics. To be communicatively active in the Asian sense thus is to be perceptive, receptive, and introspective to "feel together" with fellow humans, nature, and the spirits (Miike, 2007). Buddhist theories also postulate that the development of compassion parallels the increased degrees of the awareness of interdependent interrelatedness and egoless altruism. As the first and second Asiacentric propositions suggest, then, communication can augment such an awareness and egolessness, which, in turn, helps to develop empathic sensitivity to communicate and feel togetherness and interdependence. This Asian portrait of communication may be pressed into service so as to extend the affective and altruistic aspect of humanity in the global community.

Asiacentric Communication Proposition #4

The fourth Asiacentric proposition is that communication is a process in which we receive and return our debts to all sentient beings. Many Asian religious-philosophical teachings as well as everyday practices highlight the fact that our existence is dependent on all other beings. The Buddhist doctrine of *pratitya samutpada* [dependent co-arising] is a case in point (Chang & Holt, 1991;

Dissanayake, 1983; Ishii, 1998). It is the idea that "the existence of every being in the universe is made possible only by Buddhist *engi* or predetermined co-originations and corelationships with all other beings" (Ishii, 2001, p. 7). Implicit in this Asian worldview is that we must be grateful to our fellow humans, natural environments, and ancestral spirits for our blessings and have ethical obligations to return something to them. We owe our debts of gratitude to our ancestors, parents, neighbors, teachers, friends, animals, mountains, rivers, plants, and so forth and so on. Confucianism and Hinduism similarly accentuate the primacy of obligatory reciprocity in embodying supportive interdependence and loving relationships (Saral, 1983; Yum, 2000). Here, the Asian theme of reciprocity or mutuality comes into play.

Daisetsu Suzuki (1870–1966), perhaps the most renowned scholar of Zen Buddhism in the West, once advocated the importance of *shujo-no-on* [the debt of gratitude that we owe to the universe for our existence] for humanity (Sato, 1959). In traditional Japanese culture, people ought to feel obligated to remember and repay the *on* [debt of gratitude] that they had received from all contacts in the course of their life. In particular, four types of *on* were emphasized: *on* from parents as life givers, *on* from teachers and mentors, *on* from lords, and *shujo-no-on*. From a Buddhist viewpoint, *shujo-no-on* is the ultimate *on* of interdependence based on our awareness and appreciation of the support of the universe with which we are living on the earth. Suzuki in Sato (1959) explicates this concept as follows:

It rains and the ground becomes wet. It is the *on* of rain; it is the virtue of rain. The earth absorbs the rain, and sends it to the roots of trees and grasses, and then to their buds. This is the *on* of the great earth. They are helping each other, loving each other; it is *on*. I receive *on* from others, at the same time I extend *on* to others. . . . It is love and the action of love we feel as *on* for each other. To understand *shujo-no-on* means to get rid of the world of power-domination, to enter into the area of loving each other and helping each other. . . . "*Okage-sama*" means literally "appreciation of the protection of the tree under its shade," but the implication can be extended to our existence on the earth in the solar system, in this Universe. Indeed, true meaning of human existence lies in realizing this relationship. (p. 244)

Other Asian concepts in Asian languages such as the Filipino concept of *utang na loob* and the Thai concept of *bhunkun* also allude to communication as the process of reciprocating love and kindness. These cultural practices ideally enhance our deep affection and consideration toward others. It is noteworthy that this communication process of receiving and returning debts of gratitude often goes beyond here-and-now reciprocity. As Ho (1993) notices, the Asian worldview stresses an extended, circular perspective on space and time in the need to repay our debt of gratitude. That is, if we are unable to pay in our present life, the debt may be passed on to the next and future generations. Or it may also be assumed in our next life. As Yum (2000) writes, "In a sense, a person is forever indebted to others, who in turn are constrained by other debts" (p. 66). Such an Asian perspective on communication based on duty and responsibility may be perceived as a challenge to individual freedom, but it can project non-rights-centered character building and communication ethics in the age of global exploitation.

Asiacentric Communication Proposition #5

The fifth Asiacentric proposition is that communication is a process in which we moralize and harmonize the universe. This proposition concerns itself with the Asian axiological emphasis on the social order and, ultimately, the order of the universe. It also concerns itself with an Asian criterion by which to evaluate communicative conduct. In Asian cultures, generally speaking, communication is positively evaluated when it attempts to actualize the moral integrity and harmony of the universe, while it is negatively evaluated when it aims to pursue our own individual self-interest. Like the African worldview, "humaneness is characterized by how well people live in harmony with each other and nature. To be inhumane is to live poorly in relationship to your fellow human beings and nature" (Asante, 2005, p. 135). Hence, ethics and morality revolve around harmony from the intrapersonal level to the cosmological level. In the Asian worldview, harmony is the end rather than the means of communication (Chen, 2004, 2006). As Chen and Starosta (2003) clarify, harmony in Asian communication processes "represents a kind of ethical appeal that can induce a sense of duty for cooperation with the other party, not by the communicator's strategic words but by the sincere display of whole-hearted concern with the other" (p. 6).

The Asian de-emphasis on speech has been stereotypically exaggerated in the culture and communication literature to the extent that it gives the impression that Asians traditionally have not valued the act of speaking at all. But speaking for the benefit of others, not for the sake of self-interest, is much cherished in Asian traditions of thought. Dissanayake (2003), for instance, explores the Buddhist teaching of *samma vaca* [right speech] and its moral implications in human communication. There are four primary guidelines for right speech: (1) right speech should be de-linked with falsehoods of any sort; (2) right speech discourages slander and calumny leading to friction and hostility among people; (3) right speech presupposes the absence of, and refraining from, harsh language; and (4) right speech encourages speakers to desist from frivolous and idle chatter and to embrace purposeful and productive speech. There is also much to learn from Confucius's teaching of "humble talk and moral action" (Chang, 1997) and Gandhi's nonviolent philosophy of *Satyagraha* (Merriam, 1975; Starosta & Chaudhary, 1993) about moralizing and harmonizing styles and strategies of communication.

"An exemplary person seeks harmony but not uniformity," Confucius opines in the *Analects* (13:12). This ideal of "harmony without uniformity" can be an ultimate goal of communication both in Asian societies and in the global village. In Confucius's mind, a global citizen is a person who can fully recognize diversity as the basis for harmony and take the moral responsibility to make the best out of it. To such a citizen, intercultural communication is a means of integrating differences without creating sameness. Tu in UNESCO (2006) articulates the critical relationship between harmony and diversity:

> Harmony is predicated on diversity and difference. The opposite of harmony is sameness. The "great unity" is diametrically opposed to homogenized unity. The greatness of the "great unity" lies in its convergence, confluence, integration, and harmonization of different colors, sounds, tastes, and experiences. Harmony embraces difference. Without difference, harmony is impossible. If we do not mix spices, we

cannot make tasty soup. Without different sounds, there is no music. Without different colors, there are no paintings. Geodiversity and biodiversity are preconditions for human survival, and linguistic and cultural diversity is congenial to human flourishing. (p. 181)

Asiacentric Communication Ethics and Competence

Obviously, all Asians do not subscribe to the aforementioned propositions. They do not necessarily reflect the way Asians actually communicate in real-life situations. However, they serve as theoretical lenses from which to see an Asian version of humanity and to view Asian thought and action. They are designed to provide much food for thought in rethinking the nature and ideal of human communication in Asia and beyond from an alternative vantage point. For example, we can reexamine current conceptualizations of communication ethics and competence from these Asiacentric propositions. They suggest that an ethical communicator can (1) remind herself or himself and others of interrelatedness and interdependence through communication, (2) discipline and cultivate herself or himself without being overly self-centered through communication, (3) develop her or his altruistic sensitivity to the sufferings of others, (4) feel her or his obligation to remember the debts that she or he has received and to try to return them in one way or another, and (5) speak up for greater harmony and morality.

Just as many proponents of Asian values who are often misunderstood by Western conservative intellectuals (Mahbubani, 2002), I am *not* asserting that these Asiacentric viewpoints on humans communicating are superior to Eurocentric ones, but I am protesting that they are not inferior to them. They are rooted in the Asian worldview and yet may be sharable along with those rooted in, say, the African worldview toward what Tu (2006) calls "a dialogical civilization" or what Sitaram (1998) calls "a higher humanity." In Sitaram's (1998) view, such a truly human civilization "is not an extension of any one culture; rather it would be the essence of all cultures of the entire humanity" (p. 13). As such, there is room for Asiacentric, as well as Afrocentric and other non-Western, contributions. As Asante (1993) avers, there is also "space for Eurocentricity in a multicultural

enterprise so long as it does not parade as universal. No one wants to banish the Eurocentric view. It is a valid view of reality where it does not force its way" (p. 188).

CHERISHING THE OLD TO KNOW THE NEW

It was my intention in this essay to argue that learning from, not about, cultures for self-reflexivity is a *sine qua non* for cross-cultural dialogue and to illustrate how Asians and non-Asians can benefit from an Asiacentric worldview and its implications for communication in local and global contexts. Tu (2001b) propounds two propositions on globalization. First, globalization can be hegemonic homogenization without cultural diversity and sensitivity, but through dialogue it may lead to a genuine sense of global community. Second, the search for identity can degenerate into extreme ethnocentrism and exclusion, but through dialogue it may lead to an authentic way of intercultural communication and to a real respect for diversity. It is then up to us whether we will further risk our lifeboat by imposing the ethnocentric version of humanity on others and dividing the world with the clash of ignorance, or we will engage in mutual dialogue with the principle of "multiculturalism without hierarchy" toward "harmony without uniformity."

Asante (2003a) maintains that innovation and tradition are key to humanizing the world. He contends that "The generation of the new, the novel, is basic to the advancement of cultural ideas but also is the maintenance of the traditional" (p. 78). His contention is in perfect resonance with the Confucian spirit of "cherishing the old to know the new" (*Analects*, 2:11). It is indeed imperative for us to study and apply old wisdoms both locally and globally in order to respond to new situations in the changing world (Miike, 2004). Tu (1998) aptly describes where we stand in search of global ethics and humanistic values:

The problematique of the viability of the human race . . . is that having transformed ourselves into the most aggressive and self-destructive animal the evolutionary process has ever witnessed, we have now added ourselves to the long list of endangered species. This is the magnitude of the human dilemma today. We are urgently in need of a new way of perceiving, a new mode of thinking, even a new form of life, which is predicated on a radically transformed attitude and worldview. Paradoxically, our determined effort to move away from militarism, materialism, aggression, conflict, and destruction may be a new discovery, but it is also a return to the spiritual roots that have provided the ground for humans to survive and flourish for centuries. In this sense, our humanity is at a crossroads (p. 3).

References

Asante, M. K. (1993). Multiculturalism without hierarchy: An Afrocentric response to Diane Ravitch. In F. J. Beckwith & M. E. Bauman (Eds.), *Are you politically correct? Debating America's cultural standards* (pp. 185–193). Buffalo, NY: Prometheus Books.

Asante, M. K. (1998). *The Afrocentric idea* (1998), (Rev. ed.). Philadelphia: Temple University Press.

Asante, M. K. (2003a). *Afrocentricity: The theory of social change* (Rev. ed.). Chicago: African American Images.

Asante, M. K. (2003b). Education for liberation: On campus with a purpose. In V. L. Farmer (Ed.), *The black student's guide to graduate and professional school success* (pp. 162–169). Westport, CT: Greenwood Press.

Asante, M. K. (2005). *Race, rhetoric, and identity: The architecton of soul*. Amherst, NY: Humanity Books.

Asante, M. K. (2006). The rhetoric of globalization: The Europeanization of human ideas. *Journal of Multicultural Discourses, 1*(2), 152–158.

Asante, M. K., Miike, Y., & Yin, J. (Eds.). (2008). *The global intercultural communication reader*. New York: Routledge.

Chang, H.-C. (1997). Language and words: Communication in the *Analects* of Confucius. *Journal of Language and Social Psychology, 16*(2), 107–131.

Chang, H.-C., & Holt, G. R. (1991). The concept of *yuan* and Chinese interpersonal relationships. In S. Ting-Toomey & F. Korzenny (Eds.), *Cross-cultural interpersonal communication* (pp. 28–57). Newbury Park, CA: Sage.

Chen, G.-M. (2004). The two faces of Chinese communication. *Human Communication, 7*(1), 25–36.

Chen, G.-M. (2005). A model of global communication competence. *China Media Research, 1*(1), 3–11.

Chen, G.-M. (2006). Asian communication studies: What and where to now. *Review of Communication, 6*(4), 295–311.

Chen, G.-M., & Miike, Y. (Eds.). (2003). Asian approaches to human communication [Special issue]. *Intercultural Communication Studies, 12*(4), 1–218.

Chen, G.-M., & Starosta, W. J. (2000). Communication and global society: An introduction. In G.-M. Chen & W. J. Starosta (Eds.), *Communication and global society* (pp. 1–16). New York: Peter Lang.

Chen, G.-M., & Starosta, W. J. (2003). Asian approaches to human communication: A dialogue. *Intercultural Communication Studies, 12*(4), 1–15.

Chesebro, J. W. (1996, December). Unity in diversity: Multiculturalism, guilt/victimage, and a new scholarly orientation. *Spectra, 32*(12), 10–14.

Dissanayake, W. (1983). The communication significance of the Buddhist concept of dependent co-origination. *Communication, 8*(1), 29–45.

Dissanayake, W. (Ed.). (1988). *Communication theory: The Asian perspective*. Singapore: Asian Mass Communication Research and Information Center.

Dissanayake, W. (2003). Asian approaches to human communication: Retrospect and prospect. *Intercultural Communication Studies, 12*(4), 17–37.

Ho, D. Y. F. (1993). Relational orientation in Asian social psychology. In U. Kim & J. W. Berry (Eds.), *Indigenous psychologies: Research and experience in cultural context* (pp. 240–259). Newbury Park, CA: Sage.

Huntington, S. P. (1993). The clash of civilizations? *Foreign Affairs, 72*(3), 22–49.

Huntington, S. P. (1996). *The clash of civilizations and the remaking of world order*. New York: Simon & Schuster.

Ishii, S. (1997). Tasks for intercultural communication researchers in the Asia-Pacific region in the 21st century. *Dokkyo International Review, 10*, 313–326.

Ishii, S. (1998). Developing a Buddhist *en*-based systems paradigm for the study of Japanese human relationships. *Japan Review, 10*, 109–122.

Ishii, S. (2001). An emerging rationale for triworld communication studies from Buddhist perspectives. *Human Communication, 4*(1), 1–10.

Ishii, S. (2004). Proposing a Buddhist consciousness-only epistemological model for intrapersonal communication research. *Journal of Intercultural Communication Research, 33*(2), 63–76.

Ishii, S., & Bruneau, T. (1994). Silence and silences in cross-cultural perspective: Japan and the United States. In L. A. Samovar & R. E. Porter (Eds.), *Intercultural communication: A reader* (7th ed., pp. 246–251). Belmont, CA: Wadsworth.

Ishii, S., & Klopf, D., & Cooke, P. (2006). Our locus in the universe: Worldview and intercultural communication. In L. A. Samovar, R. E. Porter, & E. R. McDaniel (Eds.), *Intercultural communication: A reader* (11th ed., pp. 32–38). Belmont, CA: Thomson Wadsworth.

Jain, N. C. (1991). Worldview and cultural patterns of India. In L. A. Samovar & R. E. Porter (Eds.),

Intercultural communication: A reader (6th ed., pp. 78–87). Belmont, CA: Wadsworth.

Kim, U. (2001). Culture, science, and indigenous psychologies: An integrated analysis. In D. Matsumoto (Ed.), *Handbook of culture and psychology* (pp. 51–75). New York: Oxford University Press.

Kincaid, D. L. (Ed.). (1987). *Communication theory: Eastern and Western perspectives*. San Diego, CA: Academic Press.

Kume, T. (2007). Contrastive prototypes of communication styles in decision making: *Mawashi* style vs. *tooshi* style. In M. B. Hinner (Ed.), *The influence of culture in the world of business*. Berlin, Germany: Peter Lang Frankfurt.

Mahbubani, K. (2002). *Can Asians think? Understanding the divide between East and West*. South Royalton, VT: Steerforth Press.

Mendoza, S. L. (2004). *Pahiwatig*: The role of ambiguity in Filipino American communication patterns. In M. Fong & R. Chuang (Eds.), *Communicating ethnic and cultural identity* (pp. 151–164). Lanham, MD: Rowman & Littlefield.

Merriam, A. H. (1975). Symbolic action in India: Gandhi's nonverbal persuasion. *Quarterly Journal of Speech, 61*(3), 290–306.

Miike, Y. (2003). Beyond Eurocentrism in the intercultural field: Searching for an Asiacentric paradigm. In W. J. Starosta & G.-M. Chen (Eds.), *Ferment in the intercultural field: Axiology/value/praxis* (pp. 243–276). Thousand Oaks, CA: Sage.

Miike, Y. (2004). Rethinking humanity, culture, and communication: Asiacentric critiques and contributions. *Human Communication, 7*(1), 67–82.

Miike, Y. (2005). *The conceptual significance of centricity in intercultural communication research: Lessons from the metatheory of Afrocentricity*. Paper presented at the annual meeting of the National Communication Association, Boston, MA.

Miike, Y. (2006). Non-Western theory in Western research? An Asiacentric agenda for Asian communication studies. *Review of Communication, 6*(1/2), 4–31.

Miike, Y. (2007). An Asiacentric reflection on Eurocentric bias in communication theory. *Communication Monographs, 74*(2).

Miike, Y., & Chen, G.-M. (2006). Perspectives on Asian cultures and communication: An updated bibliography. *China Media Research, 2*(1), 98–106.

Miike, Y., & Chen, G.-M. (Eds.). (2007). Asian contributions to communication theory [Special issue]. *China Media Research, 3*(4).

Nishiyama, K. (1971). Interpersonal persuasion in a vertical society: The case of Japan. *Speech Monographs, 38*(2), 148–154.

Nordstrom, L. (Ed.). (1983). Communication—East and West [Special issue]. *Communication, 8*(1), 1–132.

Robinson, J. H. (2003). Communication in Korea: Playing things by eye. In L. A. Samovar & R. E. Porter (Eds.), *Intercultural communication: A reader* (10th ed., pp. 57–64). Belmont, CA: Wadsworth.

Rogers, E. M. (1976). Communication and development: The passing of the dominant paradigm. *Communication Research, 3*(2), 213–240.

Saito, M. (1970). Learning to communicate. *General Semantics Bulletin, 37*, 14–18.

Samovar, L. A., Porter, R. E., & McDaniel, E. R. (2007). *Communication between cultures*. Belmont, CA: Thomson Wadsworth.

Saral, T. B. (1983). Hindu philosophy of communication. *Communication, 8*(1), 47–58.

Sato, K. (1959). The concept of *on* in Ruth Benedict and D. T. Suzuki. *Psychologia, 2*(4), 243–245.

Starosta, W. J., & Chaudhary, A. G. (1993). "I can wait 40 or 400 years": Gandhian *Satyagraha* West and East. *International Philosophical Quarterly, 33*(2), 163–172.

Sitaram, K. S. (1998). Introduction: Multiculturalism for a higher humanity. In K. S. Sitaram & M. H. Prosser (Eds.), *Civic discourse: Multiculturalism, cultural diversity, and global communication* (pp. 1–14). Stamford, CT: Ablex.

Suzuki, D. (2006). *Daisetsu speaking on Zen: Three lectures in English that impressed the world* (Souiku Shigematsu, trans.). Tokyo: Art Days.

Tu, W. (1998). Mustering the conceptual resources to grasp a world in flux. In J. A. Kushigian (Ed.), *International studies in the next millennium: Meeting the challenge of globalization* (pp. 3–15). Westport, CT: Praeger.

Tu, W. (2001a). Mutual learning as an agenda for social development. In J. Baudot (Ed.), *Building a world community: Globalization and the common good* (pp. 253–260). Copenhagen, Demark: Royal Danish Ministry of Foreign Affairs.

Tu, W. (2001b). The context of dialogue: Globalization and diversity. In G. Picco (Ed.), *Crossing the divide: Dialogue among civilizations* (pp. 49–96). South Orange, NJ: School of Diplomacy and International Relations, Seton Hall University.

Tu, W. (2002). Beyond the Enlightenment mentality. In H. Y. Jung (Ed.), *Comparative political culture in the age of globalization: An introductory anthology* (pp. 251–266). Lanham, MD: Lexington Books.

Tu, W. (2006). The Confucian ethic and the spirit of East Asian modernity. In UNESCO (Ed.), *Cultural diversity and transversal values: East-West dialogue on spiritual and secular dynamics* (pp. 7–13). Paris, France: UNESCO.

UNESCO (Ed.). (2006). *The forum of reflexion: What UNESCO for the future?* Paris, France: UNESCO.

Yum, J. O. (2000). The impact of Confucianism on interpersonal relationships and communication patterns in East Asia. In L. A. Samovar & R. E. Porter (Eds.), *Intercultural communication: A reader* (9th ed., pp. 63–73). Belmont, CA: Wadsworth.

Concepts and Questions

1. How does the essay describe worldview? In what ways is this different from or similar to the previous and following essays?
2. Differentiate between learning *about* other cultures and learning *from* other cultures.
3. What is meant by "cultures in hierarchy"? Is this considered a negative or positive perspective? Why? Is there a better way of viewing cultures?
4. Describe and provide examples of the core values underlying the Eurocentric worldview.
5. Are there any dangers of exploring other cultures from a strictly descriptive perspective? Will simply analyzing and critiquing another culture help or hinder intercultural understanding and communication?
6. Describe and discuss the three steps to cross-cultural dialogue.
7. Summarize, with examples, the five Asiacentric communication propositions.
8. According to the essay, "the Asian worldview stresses an extended, circular perspective on space and time . . ." How is this similar or different from the American Indian worldview structure discussed in the next essay by Schelbert?
9. What are some ways that a culture's worldview could influence their communication style? How could these create difficulties during an intercultural communication interaction?
10. Do you think there are any benefits that Westerners can learn from the Asiacentric worldview? If not, why? If yes, what are they?

Pathways of Human Understanding: An Inquiry into Western and North American Indian Worldview Structures

LEO SCHELBERT

Human societies, large and small, in the past and in the present, were shaped by worldviews that not only gave shelter, but also led the individual and collective mind into captivity. Efforts to secure sustenance, to maintain bonds between peoples, to shape religious, technical, and artistic practice, such strivings have all been "in-formed," that is, have been shaped by worldviews that underlie systems of thought claiming intrinsic validity and normative meaning and show the imprint of mostly hidden structures.[1]

THE MEANING OF WORLDVIEW STRUCTURE

How may a worldview structure be understood? One must grasp what it is not. It is less than a worldview, although it shapes the arrangement of its contents. It is less than religion, although it forms its core, its rituals, theologies, and codes. It is less than ideology, understood as an ordered system of thought taken as normative and based on claimed self-evidence; although a worldview structure represents simultaneously its internal force and its distillation. A worldview

Reprinted from the *American Indian Culture and Research Journal,* volume 27, number 1, by permission of the American Indian Studies Center, UCLA. © 2003 Regents of the University of California. Dr. Leo Schelbert is professor emeritus at the University of Illinois at Chicago.

structure is less than philosophy, understood as an interpretative system of what is, of how humans understand, and of what humans ought to do and what not; yet it hides behind the numerous interpretative systems, often formed in the solitude of a self, but within thought styles dominant at a given time and place.

How do worldview structures differ from religions, philosophies, and ideologies? They are less a content than a form, less a visible entity than a hidden system, less a positive claim than a template employed as a matter of course.

A worldview structure lies buried behind the textured forms, like a skeleton composed of interrelated elements. Worldviews as structures mostly remain hidden, unseen, unperceived, and rarely emerge into the field of vision of a seeker's vision quest. They are taken for granted as the roads to be traveled and often escape the processes of questioning. Thus the realm of worldview structures is neither sacred practice nor embraced doctrine of what is true and normative, but the frame, the pattern, the paradigm that shapes understanding similar to language, explored as a system of signs.[2]

Two major forms of worldview structures shall be sketched here in order to illuminate their hidden forms and interpretative power: that of Western culture and that of the indigenous peoples of the preconquest northern western hemisphere.

THE WESTERN WORLDVIEW STRUCTURE

Tripartite and Dual Domains

The worldview structure that informs Western culture postulates fundamentally three domains: heaven, earth, and hell. Heaven is viewed as the realm of an ultimate reality, often perceived as a place, as that which is beyond the earth. The Copernican replacement of the Ptolemaic system has nearly dislodged this view in theoretical understanding, if not in everyday experience and among certain groups of faith.[3] The earth, and within it most radically the world of humans, is reduced to spatial and temporal irrelevance. Hell, originally too a specific place as the abode of a personal power of evil, has

also largely receded into a mere metaphor of a person's mental state.[4]

If that tripartite worldview geography—heaven, earth, and hell—has gradually disappeared from many circles, and if religious traditions strive hard at meaning-restoring reformulations, some even by simply brushing aside the view of astrophysics as the very invention of the devil, another aspect of the Western worldview structure has remained firmly in place throughout the Western cultural tradition, the foundational dichotomy between "nature" and "humans." Nature is viewed as a threefold entity: the world of inanimate forces of wind and rock and earth; the world of organic life, from micro-organisms such as viruses and bacteria to grasses, flowers, trees, and plants; the world of animals, those beings with *anima,* yet not a soul, and radically positioned below humans. In contrast to this tripartite "nature," humans, it is claimed, are radically different: they are animate beings endowed with reason, with self-consciousness, and with genuine decision-making power. Although the indisputable closeness between humans and animals especially within the mammalian species entails at times serious discomfort, since the proclaimed gap seems to be dangerously narrow, the special position of humans is firmly defended as unquestionable.[5]

In this duality, nature exists for humans who are charged to make use of it to maximize their food and energy supply and to realize their full potential as unique beings. Nature is to be used, if not abused; it is to be shaped and to be made subject in three powerful ways: in the inanimate world by technology, in the plant world by agriculture, from seed manipulation of some ten thousand years ago to today's genetic engineering; in the world of animals by animal husbandry, that is, the religiously and philosophically sanctioned keeping of animals in captivity, mainly as a supply of meat and milk for humans. If the tripartite structure of heaven, earth, and hell has faded into the background, the twopartite assumption that the world of humans is to be sharply distinguished from that of nature has become ever more enhanced by the increase of human manipulatory power derived from science, although concerned challenges have also emerged. Yet most do not question the dichotomy "humans-nature," but focus primarily on a specific reformulation of the relationship.

Traits of the Western Worldview

The Western worldview structure "Heaven-Earth-Hell" and within it "humans-nature" has several unique features. Four shall be mentioned. First, ultimate reality is viewed personalistically and predominantly in male terms. It is a He who is the creator, guide, judge of all that is; it is He—in some traditions of the West perceived tri-personally but in one essence—from which all ultimately derives and into whose radiant presence all returns. This personalism has been radicalized in Western culture by insisting that monotheism is a mark of unquestioned cultural superiority.[6]

Second, in the Western worldview structure the world is understood as hierarchically ordered: Ultimate reality is perceived as wholly separate from all else that is and in unlimited control; human reality is seen as separate from anything else within the earth; the reality of nature is understood as holistically gifted to humans by ultimate divine decree. This hierarchical worldview structure organically translates into economic, social, and political orders: the rule of the haves over the have-nots, men over women, the strong over the weak, the learned over the ignorant, the priesthood over the laity.[7]

Besides being personalistically and hierarchically oriented, the Western worldview claims, third, a radical historicity of the created world: "*En arche en ho logos,* in the beginning was the Word": It is all movement from a defined start to a defined finish when all the endless becoming and decaying will end in favor of eternal beingness.[8] All except ultimate reality is historical and, often adding a unique twist, is claimed to be in an ascent, if not without fallbacks and retrogression. Human history is declared to be a history of progress, to be upward-bound, ever more increasing human skill, knowledge, and, hopefully, also wisdom.[9]

To the claim of historicity a fourth trait is to be added, a mind-set of dualism which claims an all pervasive polarity of what is: the duality of positive and negative, of human and divine, of humans and nature, of right and wrong, of virtue and sin, of salvation and damnation. The duality is perhaps most decisively practiced in epistemology: by constructing the duality of subject and object, the latter assumed to be observable, measurable, and to be numerically weighted with reliable exactitude.[10]

Origins of the Western Worldview Structure

Where does this worldview structure come from? Its origins are clearly non-"Western." The West's main cultural tradition is "derived"—it is not original to Europe. The indigenous traditions of European peoples such as the Celtic, Germanic, Slavic, and Etruscan have vanished or have survived only in a fragmentary and submerged form which today some hope to revive in the so-called Wiccan movement.[11] Since the Roman invasions, Western Europe's indigenous traditions have been replaced with Middle Eastern traditions by violence or in a process of gradual persuasion. Some claim that the first recognizable formulation of the tripartite and dualistic view of reality which so decisively marks Western culture reaches back some 3,200 years when Zarathustra first formulated his creed in the southern Asian steppe lands: He proclaimed the heavens as Ahura Mazda's abode and that of the angels, the earth as the domain of humans and of their flocks, and hell as the place of Angra Mainyu and the devas. The Zoroastrian vision was gradually reformulated by Hebrew tribes and crystallized into Judaism, which in turn became reformulated into Christianity and then both Judaism and Christianity, into the faith of Islam.[12]

This is not to make light of the profound differences between these traditions, which evolved over three millennia, or to deny autonomous elements in each, but only to point to the sameness of their fundamental structure. These Middle Eastern traditions, which have shaped Western culture, view reality as composed—though in varying ways—of heaven, earth, and hell; all understand ultimate reality in personalist terms: Zarathustra as Ahura Mazda, Moses as Jahwe, Jesus as Abba (Father), Muhammad as Allah, all opposed by the antagonists of the divine, by Angra Mainyu, Satan, Beelzebub, or Iblis with their evil forces of varied names. All Middle Eastern traditions, furthermore, know of a central formulator, anchored in a particular historical moment: Zarathustra, Moses, Jesus, Muhammad. In all of these traditions and their numerous derivatives also the dualism "nature-humans" remains untouched as a reflection of the more radical duality "created-uncreated," from which derive the dualities virtue versus sin, good versus bad, what is of the spirit versus what is of the flesh.

Finally, directional historicity rules supreme: The events of the world, human and non-human, all move from a defined beginning to a cataclysmic end that includes not only a postulated eternal bliss for the saved—a beatitude sometimes expressed as pure beatific vision or in terms of sensual joy—but also an eternal world of excruciating torment for the damned.

These basic structural elements seem to lead to another shared trait, the stance of exclusivity. Except perhaps for the Baha'i, a creed derived from the Shi'ite Muslim tradition, the mainstream of the faithful is comforted by their respective faith's claim of exclusive validity: Zarathustra does not accommodate Moses, Moses does not accommodate Jesus, Jesus does not accommodate Muhammad.[13] Hostile incompatibility, furthermore, is intensified by textualization. The making of texts is indeed a magnificent gift to human memory: How rewarding to read in the Avesta, to savor David's Psalms of praise or the prophets' invectives against stubborn people, to ponder the claims of the Sermon of the Mount, or to study a Sura of the Holy Qur'an. Yet texts ossify what has been said or what has occurred: Gone (or perceivable from a faint distance only) is the vibrancy of the moment, the power of intonation, the subtlety of body language, and the mood pervading a given situation. But more importantly, texts fixate: If a statement is attributed to an ultimate authoritative voice—if a text pronounces in the name of Ahura Mazda or of Jahwe or of Abba or of Allah, if it is textualized as the authentic voice of Zarathustra or Moses or Jesus or Muhammad, then there is no recourse. Truth stands against falsehood and struggle emerges within a tradition over meaning: literal meaning, allegoric meaning, and spiritual meaning.

Is it too devious to view in these structural patterns a deep-seated pathology of the Middle Eastern and, by derivation, also of the Western mind, having emerged most powerfully after 1500 C.E. when Europeans and their descendants embarked on their partly successful world conquest? Although it seems that in all human societies religion and politics intertwined and on occasion entered each other's service, in the Middle Eastern, and by derivation in the Western cultural traditions, exclusivity, hostility, and persecution have remained endemic.[14] The West in its European as well as in its neo-European core that emerged since the sixteenth century, to use a Western chronological system, has been wedded to the principle of *cuius regio, eius religio,* that is, in whose region (I live), in whose religion or ideology (I need to dwell). How foreign is to the Middle Eastern and, by derivation, the Western tradition the spirit of the Twelfth Rock Edict of the Buddhist Emperor Ashoka, who had ruled large parts of India in the third century BCE (265–238 or 273–232). He had this message carved in stone, which reads in part: "His Majesty . . . gives praise to all religious teachers. . . . Other people's teachers should be given praise in every way. By doing so one profits one's own religion and benefits the other's religion. By doing otherwise one damages one's own religion and does harm to the other person's."[15]

To summarize: The Western worldview structure, which hides behind the numerous ideologies, religious persuasions, and philosophies of the West, is a derivative of Middle Eastern traditions. Although between them exist trenchant differences, they reflect a unity of a worldview structure that is rooted in rival authoritative texts of revelational claim that derived from mutually exclusive authoritative founders, but defined the structure of reality in similar terms.

THE WORLDVIEW STRUCTURE OF THE PEOPLES OF THE NORTHERN WESTERN HEMISPHERE

The Great Difference

If one enters the preconquest religio-philosophical world of the indigenous peoples of the northern western hemisphere as it has survived to this day, one faces not only numerous forms of alien rituals, sacred songs, and religio-philosophical expressions, but also a basic worldview structure that is radically different from that of the conquerors from across the Atlantic whose religio-philosophical outlook had been shaped by the traditions of the Middle East. Around 1600 CE some seven to nine million indigenous peoples were organized into over one hundred different nations which followed their unique religious practice, shaped their own set of sacred symbols, and devised their own rituals enveloping their economic seasonal activities as well as the stages of their personal lives.[16] Like the traditions of other peoples, theirs too have evolved, although since the conquest, under trying conditions of an all-encompassing alien domination. Among these peoples one searches in vain for canonical sacred texts,[17] for exclusive authoritative formulators, for a dualist division of the world that opposes the natural world to the human one, for a directional view of time, and for a personalistically conceived ultimate reality. To describe the indigenous worldview structure proves difficult. From the start Euro-American justification of conquest transformed the radical difference between the cultures of the invaders and those of the invaded into a claimed primitivity and savagery. Although today explicit savagist or primitivist views have nearly vanished, reductionist descriptions that view American Indian religions as devoid of a complex religio-philosophical foundation are still firmly in place.

What the invader peoples saw was indeed shocking to their sensibility: a buffalo bladder as a sacred ritual's centerpiece;[18] a first salmon caught in the spawning journey upriver brought to the expectant assembled people in a sacred manner, whose skeleton is given back to the river after ritual consumption to prove to all the salmon that they will be treated with the proper reverence and gratitude;[19] the leaving behind of half the kill in a harsh winter's hunt so that the other meat-eating beings such as the wolves and coyotes suffering from hunger might also find some relief, at the *very* time when the hunter's people faced famine due to white incursions and the concomitant destruction of the basis of their sustenance;[20] or, finally, after a successful hunt the giving of "thanks by offering tobacco to the thunders, trees, stars, and moon, thus nurturing these beings in return for their gift of meat" and thus acknowledging the animals' spiritual "masters."[21]

It is understandable that the conqueror peoples thought they had met up with incomprehensible primitivity. The indigenous peoples seemed not to grasp a most basic "fact" of reality, the duality "humans-nature," and especially the difference between humans and the animal world, those central features of the Middle East-derived Euro-American worldview structure. Furthermore, there was the absence of the duality "God" and "Satan" as well as the consequent duality of the "good" and the "sinful." The indigenous peoples' religio-philosophical outlook seemed to know neither divine transcendence nor a personalistically perceived absolute power, nor a need for salvation. Their invocation of sacred powers was (and remains) this-worldly, an activation of supportive mutuality since for them "the spirits are relatives rather than despots."[22]

The American Indian Worldview Structure

What kind of worldview structure hides behind such inconceivable unorthodoxy and its consequent religious practice as followed by peoples such as the Pequot, Narraganset, Iroquois, the Menominee, Anishinaabeg, Osakiwug, the Creek, Cherokee, Choctaw, the Lakota, Pueblo, or Tlingit? Some scholars claim that it is absurd to search for a common core in the numerous religious practices of the indigenous peoples of the northern western hemisphere. The forms were too different, they assert, and the various peoples had nothing substantive in common. Yet others disagree, and it seems possible to distill in the numerous externally different traditions a common worldview structure which has remained basic and may be sketched as follows:[23]

> At the center of whatever is or was lies an ineffable mystery named differently by different peoples with words such as Orenda, Manitou, Wakan Tanka, or Maek Awaetok. It is a view that has been pressed into the Middle East-derived mistranslation "Great Spirit" and has been misdirected by the talk of "animism" in the supposed indigenous view that everything had a "spirit" as something personalistic, separate, and independent from its manifestation.[24]

Yet the personalism that marks Western thought and is so central to Indo-European languages such as English is absent in the indigenous thought of the peoples of the northern western hemisphere. In their perception all that is represents interdependent formations of sacred forces which are in constant and complex interaction; some of these formations are viewed as of immense power such as the sun, storms, and rains; others are delicate such as the butterflies and the ants, or humble as the moles underground, yet knowledgeable of the world below that of humans.[25]

The indigenous mind perceives this all-encompassing set of formations of sacred forces as people—as four-legged people, as two-legged people, as crawling, swimming or winged people; as people that are green, or stony, or soft. Trees are called standing people and if their bark or sap is collected for human use, they are approached in a sense of ritually enhanced gratitude. Thus in the indigenous worldview there is no such entity as "nature"; all forms of being are on a similar plane, are interdependent, are "peoples," surely different, yet not hierarchically ordered in the Middle East-derived Western cultural sense. Neither is there a supreme creator being, although missionary and anthropological efforts as well as those of a respectful, but Western-shaped mentality have tried to press indigenous thought into such categories.[26] Not that the indigenous mind is not keenly aware of difference: The ant people are certainly different from the wolf people or the "standing people," the trees, from the two-legged people, yet it is a difference of degree in representing the primal force, not of essence. The two-legged people appear to the indigenous understanding as the most problematic because they seem to be the least attuned to the great interdependent play of forces, yet at the same time ritually charged to safeguard the interplay of cosmic energies from destructive disharmony for the benefit of all "peoples."[27]

Traits of the Indigenous Worldview Structure

Several features of the indigenous worldview structure may be touched upon. First, the indigenous view of the sacred does not root its religiosity in the postulate of a supreme transcendent being who is ontologically wholly different from all else that is. Terms such as theism, pantheism, or polytheism, therefore, have no place in an analysis of the indigenous worldview structure. Sacredness means radical kinship and interdependence, an ongoing "cosmic give-and-take"[28] among beings large and small, creative and destructive, visible, invisible, or dimly perceived, beneficent and dangerous, all interacting on a spectral scale of mutuality rather than in a dualistic opposition. The invocation of sacred power is "a call to friends rather than a supplication," and in the various ceremonies the "spirit peoples" are fed in reciprocity.[29] The earth is thus not perceived as the playground of good and evil, humankind is not seen as embedded in a divine plan, and no deity bestows its blessing or curse, its eternal reward or damnation. Instead numerous names such as the "thunder beings" or "the grandfathers" or the "corn mother" point to the great primal force that forms, permeates, and is the universe. Such names are powerful visualizations of what might best be named "the Ineffable Mystery."

As in other traditions, one also meets in American Indian visualizations of the sacred the ambivalent figure of the trickster, a being imagined as at once sacred, creative, mischievous, ingenious, funny, bawdy, and lazy. Often clothed in the garb of the coyote, yet capable of numerous impersonations and transformations at will, the trickster not only mirrors the radical ambivalence of all that is, but also highlights the two-legged peoples' propensity to foul up the this-wordily sacred order, and he metaphorically unmasks their all too easy ability to be out of tune with the great cosmic song.[30]

Second, the indigenous worldview structure postulates a radical immanent alertness. Although there is no divine sovereign, nor sin, nor a devil such as Angra Mainyu or Satan or Iblis as a divinity's antipode, there is the constant awareness of the danger of disjuncture and thus of the effort needed to safeguard and promote the interdependent harmony of all that is. Especially the guardians of the sacred, that is those charged with the welfare of their communities, constantly need to face impending trouble that is experienced by individuals, the human community, or the world. By ritually harnessing creative power, their "central object of work and prayer" becomes "the people's immortality on earth."[31]

The indigenous worldview perceives all beings enmeshed in a cosmic dance. This perception of the world is echoed in modern science. Has not quantum physics led the Western mind in a roundabout way toward a parallel understanding of the universe in which myriad forms of energy formations exist and act in a complex interplay of creativity and destruction? The physicist Werner Heisenberg declared: Western "science [now] classifies the world . . . not into different groups of objects but into different groups of connections. . . . The world thus appears to be a complicated tissue of events, in which connections of different kinds alternate or overlap or combine and thereby determine the texture of the whole."[32] In the indigenous worldview structure then the central dualisms of object and subject, of good and evil, and of redemptive suffering as payment for trespasses of the divine will are absent in favor of a view that reality needs a constant "retuning," necessary especially for the two-legged people in their dealings with all their relations, the other "peoples."

Third, absent in the indigenous worldview structure is directionality, the assumption of a linear flow of the world's history from a defined start to a defined finish. Human beginnings are certainly interpreted in numerous emergence (not creation) stories, but their intent is not to present events-bound facticity, but to reveal the inner workings of the world. For the mind of the indigenous peoples of the northern western hemisphere human perception is radically metaphorical and "The Metaphor Is the Message."[33] The history of the world and within it that of humans is neither linear nor moving towards a divinely set end, but circular, a flow of becoming, blossoming, withering, and re-becoming. As Chief Seattle (1788–1866) declared: "Tribe follows tribe, nation follows nation, like the waves of the sea."[34] History is symbolized in the rhythm of the seasons, labeled not in abstract names of lunar months, but in terms of recurring events surrounding the green peoples and the four-legged peoples. The world is understood in a rhythmic space-time continuum that is defined by the co-ordinates above and below, and especially east and west, north and south, and rooted in the landscape where a particular people belongs.[35]

Fourth, the indigenous people are not tied to orthodoxies, to patterns of correct thinking and believing in indisputable and divinely sanctioned claims, but are engaged in orthopraxis or ortho-ritualism, that is, the proper use of sacred items and the proper performance of sacred rites as the activation of life-preserving spiritual energies so that all "peoples" might live interacting with the "relatives," that is, all the "peoples" that exist, has to occur in a ritual manner in order to assure the proper interplay of creative forces and to ward off those that harm and destroy. Acquisitive agriculture, dominating animal husbandry, and a power-seeking technology were thus tamed by the assumption of a sacred interdependence of all beings that demands proper reverential distance.[36]

CONCLUSION

In order to put further relief into this comparative sketch, an outline of the worldview structure underlying the traditions of India or of the African Yoruba or Pacific Island peoples would be telling.[37] Yet the above given comparison perhaps demonstrates sufficiently the challenge of an attempt to historicize religio-philosophical traditions not in the richness of their outward and spiritual expressions, but in their underlying structure. One view claims that such efforts severely diminish the authoritative orienting power of the varied forms of creeds such as Judaism, Christianity, or Islam. Diminished, too, is the authority of secular forms derived from traditions rooted in the Enlightenment of the West such as the rationalism of Locke, the philosophical idealism of Hegel, the materialism of Marx, or of other play forms of Western thought systems proclaimed as philosophical truth. These traditions are unmasked as sharing the same structures, if in different outward garbs. The boat of human understanding, to shift metaphors, is thus being pushed out from the safe harbor of a given religious or philosophical tradition into the ocean of numerous ideological possibilities as pathways of human understanding of the world.

However, if historicizing worldview structures means losing the claimed self-evidence of the foundation of the various dominant systems of thought devised by humans, such an effort may also liberate. Wilhelm Dilthey observed joyfully: "These are the last consequences of historical consciousness. It breaks the last chains which philosophy and natural science have sustained. It wholly liberates the human being. But at the same time it gives this liberated person an immeasurable wealth and saves the soul's unity. Because now she may, comforted, venerate in every one of these worldviews a part of the total truth."[38] The radical Other comes into view as neither inferior, nor underdeveloped, nor savage. The stance of the Other becomes understood not as a wayward variation of the phenomenon of human culture, but as a structural Other whose traditions are not *equal* in the sense of sameness, but *equivalent* in their interpretative power and sophistication. That process demands a divesting of one's mind from conquest-derived ideologies such as explicit or implied primitivism and animism, as well as from well-meant but distorting attempts of reading the structural Other in terms of the Middle East-derived patterns that dominate the mind of the West.

An examination of the various worldview traditions may lead to several possible answers. Some will embrace their "cradle worldview," as one student aptly referred to the tradition one has been born into without choice, with ever greater appreciation as their proper way of understanding the world and its mysteries, and they will remain firmly rooted in what it has to offer to human understanding. If for others the cradle worldview should have ceased to be a useful guide to an understanding of the mysteries of life and death, of joy and pain, of the rise and fall of cultures and peoples, they may follow the Hindu path of *ishtadevata.* In the Hindu Bhakti tradition a person is encouraged to discover her or his very own *ishta,* the representation of sacred ultimate reality that seems to a person to be existentially right, be it the in-figuration of Kali, or Krishna, or Vishnu, or a non-personal Ultimate named Brahman. The choices of others are thereby neither denied nor slighted nor attacked, but given silent inner recognition. In exploring the pathways of human understanding one may, regardless of one's cradle worldview, similarly encounter a worldview that represents one's existentially proper *ishta* which may serve as a guide in the brief journey through life. Thus also the indigenous preconquest religio-philosophical traditions of the northern western hemisphere that today have gained renewed vitality may offer to many a powerful interpretation of the world and of the beings that people it, although that understanding is not easily grasped in its inherent interpretative power and even less easily properly practiced.

Finally, in contemplating different worldviews some may, instead of making a particular choice, opt to remain at sea, viewing with awe the numerous pathways of understanding human ingenuity has designed over the millennia. They may be nourished by the very plurality of worldviews they encounter in the global village. This does not mean indifferent relativism, but to remain suspended in inquiring effort and to live "in the question" rather than in a specific answer.

After the fall of cultural walls in the present age, all need to become aware of their radical *Ortung,* their bondage into a specific place and time by birth, or by their *ishta,* their existentially embraced choice. The immense landscapes of other traditions need not only to be recognized, but also to be given respectful contemplation. Perhaps recognizing this great challenge may be an integral part in the search for peace on the planet earth, a peace to which a conscious pluralistic effort that equivalently includes the traditions of the "Other" may significantly contribute.

Acknowledgments

This essay is a revised version of the annual Scholarship Association Lecture given on November 12, 2002, at the University of Illinois at Chicago.

Notes

1. A pioneering work on worldviews is Wilhelm Dilthey, *Weltanschauungslehre: Abhandlungen zur Philosphie der Philosophie. Gesammelte Shriften,* vol. 8 (Leipzig: B. G. Teubner, 1931); pages 75–118 of this work are translated into English in H. P. Rickman, ed. and transl., *W. Dilthey: Selected Writings* (Cambridge, England: Cambridge University Press. 1976), 133–154. Studies that address the aspect of Dilthey's wide-ranging ideas include: Michael Ermath, *Wilhelm Dilthey: The Crtiique of Historical Reason* (Chicago: University of Chicago Press, 1978), 323–338: H. P. Rickman, *Wilhelm Dilthey: Pioneer of Human Studies* (Berkeley: University of California Press, 1979), 41–51; and Theodore Plantinga, *Historical Understanding in the Thought of Wilhelm Dilthey* (Toronto: University of Toronto Press, 1980), 139–143. A concise overview of Dilthey's thought is Rudolf A. Makkreel, "Dilthey, Wilhelm, 1833–1911," *Routledge Enclopedia of Philosophy,* ed., Edward Craig (London: Routledge, 1998), 3: 77–83: also see Rudolf A. Makkreel and Frithjof Rodi, eds., *Selected Works/Dilthey,* 5 vols, (Princeton, NJ: Princeton University Press, 1985). Rickman aptly summarizes Dilthey's position: "The human metaphysical impulse craves a *Weltanschauung* (a world-view) which combines a coherent picture of reality with an ideal of life and principles of conduct," 47. Although Dilthey's suggestive *Weltanschauungslehre* is advanced for its time, the comment of Vine Deloria, Jr., applies: A major task is "to understand man's experiences . . . from a world viewpoint, not simply a Western one," *God Is Red* (New York: Grosset & Dunlap, 1973), 123. A valuable guide to such a task is Heinz Kimmerle, *Interkulturlle Philosphie: Zur Einfiührung* (Hamburg: Verlag Junius, 2002), with an international bibliography, 157–166. Quotations from foreign language sources are given in my translation.

2. In the section "The Structure of Worldview," in *Weltanschauungslehre,* Dilthey does not sharply distinguish between the content and the structure of a worldview, yet states suggestively: "Each life-condition (Lebensverhältnis) evolves into a system (Gefüge) in which the same forms of approach are structurally related. And thus also worldviews are ordered structures (regelmässige Gebilde)," 83. He declares, "The ultimate root of a worldview is life," ibid., 78.

3. The interpretative religio-philosophical struggles that the triumph or the Copernican system unleashed in Western Christendom are impressively documented in Dava Sobel, *Galileo's Daughter: A Historical Memoir of Science, Faith, and Love* (New York: Walker, 1999).

4. Markwart Herzog states: "In the mainline churches hell does not play a foundational (tragende) role anymore"; see *Metzler Lexicon Religion* (Stuttgart: J. B. Metzler, 1999), 64. The influential theologian Karl Rahner interprets hell as "a definitive state which man himself has achieved on his own behalf" and he dismisses Jesus' "images (fire, worm, darkness, etc.)" as part of "the mental furniture of [his] contemporary apocalyptic" tradition; see *Encyclopedia of Theology* (New York: Seabury Press, 1975), 602–604, quotation 604, 603. Fundamentalist groups, in contrast, insist that hell is a place and an eternal state of torment for the damned; see the numerous doctrinal statements in *The Encyclopedia of American Religions: Religious Creeds.* J. Gordon Melton and James Sauer, vol. 2 (Detroit: Gale Research, 1994), esp. 251–394.

5. These complex issues are discussed by Gary L. Francione, *Rain Without Thunder: The Ideology of the Animal Rights Movement* (Philadelphia: Temple University Press, 1996). The study contrasts the "Animal Rights and Animal Welfare" ideologies and concludes, "the animal protection movement will continue to march in one direction—backwards," 230. See also Erica Fudge, *Perceiving Animals: Humans and Beasts in Early Modern English Culture* (New York: St. Martin's Press, 2000). In what Richard Ryder called "speciesism" in 1971, three claims of Western ideology are at issue: the Jewish and Christian view that humans are created in God's image (a position anathema to Islam); the Aristotelian view that only humans are endowed with rationality; and the Augustinian position that original sin meant the descent of humans to the level of animals, especially as expressed in sexuality.

6. Stanley Walens formulates: "anthropologists . . . have been forced to revise their ideas about the course of human intellectual history . . . as a gradual progress from fantasy to rationality, that is "from animal worship, through a number of stages, to the worship of an anthropomorphic but invisible deity." He claims that "many of the spurious facts and interpretations of these schemes remain unquestioned"; see "Animals," in *The Encyclopedia of Religions*, ed. Mircea Eliade (New York: Macmillan, 1987). 1: 291–296; quotation. 292.

7. Joseph Bruchac III observes succinctly, "the Western view of the world . . . remains shaped by linear thinking, straight lines, and hierarchies"; see "The Circle of Stories," in *Buried Roots and Indestructible Seeds: The Survival of American Indian Life in Story, History, and Spirit* (Madison: University of Wisconsin Press. 1993), 14; Vine Deloria, Jr., *Singing for a Spirit: A Portrait of the Dakota Sioux* (Santa Fe: Clear Light Publishers, 1999) . . . "They always camped in a circle . . . so that they could remember that they were all equals," 155.

8. Western ideas about history as a directional flow are sketched by Karl Löwith, *Meaning in History* (Chicago: University of Chicago Press, 1949); however, see also the unique study of Michael Murray, *Modern Philosophy of History: Its Origin and Destination* (The Hague: Martinus Nijhoff, 1970). The study traces the main positions from Martin Heidegger over Hegel and Joachim of Flora to Augustine and it critically complements Löwith's book.

9. A keen critique is offered by Ali A. Mazrui, "'Progress': Illegitimate Child of Judeo Christian Universalism and Western Ethnocentrism—A Third World Critique in *Progress: Fact or Illusion?* eds. Marx and Bruce Mazlish (Ann Arbor: University or Michigan Press, 1996), 153–174: Mazrui claims, "The Jews taught the world about one universal God—and then identified *themselves* as the chosen people. Similarly the West told the world about the universalism of both science and the gospel of Jesus—and then the white man of the West put himself forward as . . . the role model of humanity," 154.

10. See Ugo Bianchi, "Dualism," in *Encyclopedia of Religion*, 4: 506–512, a summary of his *Dualismo Religioso: Saggio Storico e Etnologico*, 2nd. rev. ed. (Roma: Edizioni dell' Ateneo, 1952); Bianchi applies the term "to those religions, to those ideological systems whose mythology implies an original and substantial dichotomy in relation to superhuman and prehuman beings who rule the world . . . [and] who are viewed as antagonistic and evil on *the basis of intrinsic nature*," 7.

11. See Melton and Sauer, eds. *Religious Creeds*, 2: 447–451, for neo-pagan and Wiccan statements of faith.

12. Mary Boyce, *Zoroastrianism: Their Religious Beliefs and Practices* (London: Routledge and Kegan Paul, 1979), I, views "Zoroastrianism as the oldest of the revealed world religions" and claims that it probably had more influence on mankind, directly and indirectly, than any other single faith . . . and some of its leading doctrines were adopted by Judaism, Christianity, and Islam." See also her *Zoroastrianism: It's Antiquity and Constant Vigor* (Costa Mesa, CA: Biblioteca Persica. 1992), 62–82. Her observation resonates also for the later Middle Eastern traditions: "Zoroaster . . . concentrated his thought . . . and devotion on Mazda himself, the mightiest of Beings, whose Holy Spirit yet enters into everyone who is worthy to receive it," 71.

13. For the relationship of Islam to Moses see Brannon M. Wheeler, *Moses in the Qur'an and Islamic Exegesis* London: Routledge Courzon, 2002); for Islam's view of Jesus, see Tarif Khalidi, *The Muslim Jesusr: Sayings and Stories in Islamic' Literature* (Cambridge: Harvard University Press, 2001). Although Khalidi observes "certain broad atmospheric continuities between the Qur'an and certain books of the Old and New Testament, canonical and apocryphal," he finds that "The Quranic Jesus . . . has little in common with the Jesus of the Gospel" 16. See also Roger Arnaldez, "Three Messengers and Three Messages," in *Three Messengers for One God*, trans. Gerald w. Schlabach with Mary Louise Gude and David B. Burrell (Notre Dame: University of Notre Dame Press. 1994), 1–55.

14. Dilthey, *Welltanshauungslehre,* laments "the familiar, yet vexing fact that world-views vary so widely and conflict so sharply" and seem to be "at war with each other," 47.

15. Quoted by L. S. Cousins, "Buddhism," in *A New Handbook of Living Religions*, ed. John R. Hinnells (London: Penguin Book., 1997), 379.

16. Several encyclopedic works may be mentioned: Duane Champagne, ed., *The Native North Americann Almanac* (Detroit: Gale Research. 1994); Frederick R. Hoxie, ed., *Encyclopedia of North American Indians* (Boston: Houghton Miffiin. 1996); Sharon Malinowski and Anna Sheets, eds., *The Gale Encyclopedia of Native American Tribes.* 4 vols;. (Detroit: Gale, 1998); and Rayna Green, ed., *The British Museum Encyclopedia of Native North America* (Bloomington: Indiana University Press, 1999); this volume, designed for the general reader, combines impressively explanatory texts, primary sources, and pictorial material.

17. Vine Deloria, Jr., however, observes: "Neihardt's *Black Elk* and *When the Tree Flowered,* and *The Sacred Pipe* by Joseph Epes Brown, the basic works of the Black Elk theological tradition, now bid fair to become the canon or at least the central core of a North American theological canon which will someday challenge the Eastern and Western traditions as a *way* of looking at the world"; see the foreword to John G. Neihardt, *Black Elk Speaks,* Twenty-First Century Edition (Lincoln: University of Nebraska Press, 2000), xvi. See, however, the incisive critique by Julian Rice. *Black Elk's Story: Distinguishing Its Lakota Purpose* (Albuquerque: University of New Mexico Press, 1991), esp. 15–35; the author stresses the importance of the transcripts, published as *The Sixth Grandfather: Black Elk's Teachings Given to John G. Neihardt,* ed. Raymond J. DeMallie (Lincoln: University of Nebraska Press, 1984).

18. *The Sacred Pipe: Black Elk's Account of the Seven Rites of the Oglala Sioux,* recorded: and edited by Joseph Epes Brown (Norman: University of Oklahoma Press, 1989), 106–107.

19. See George M. Guilmet and David Lloyd Whited, "American Indian and Non-Indian Philosophies of Technology and Their Differential Impact on the Environment of the Southern Puget Sound," *American Indian Culture and Research Journal* 26, 1 (2002): 36–41.

20. *Black Elk Speaks,* 49–50.

21. Kenneth M. Morrison, "Native American Religions: Creating Through Cosmic Give-and-Take, in *Native North American Almanac,* ed. Champagne, 639; also see James; Wilson, *The Earth Shall Weep: A History of Native America* (New York: Grove Press, 1998), 25–26.

22. Rice, *Black Elk's Story,* 25.

23. Among numerous other valuable titles see Deloria, *God is Red;* Jamake Highwater, The *Primal Mind: Vision and Reality in American Indian America* (New York: Harper & Row, 1981); Joseph Epes Brown, *The Spiritual Legacy of the American Indian* (New York: Crossroads, 1982); Arthur Versluis, *The Elements of Native American Traditions* (Rockport, MA: Element, 1993); J. Donald Hughes, *American Indian Ecology* (El Paso: Texas Western Press, 1983; 1996).

24. Rice, *Black Elk's Story,* seems to suggest that "spirit" should be understood as a metaphor pointing to the process of activating power; he observes, "Embodiment is the culmination of the spiritual process," 28.

25. Rice, *Black Elk's Story,* 68–69, 71, 93–94.

26. The term "spirit," especially as used in the term "Great Spirit," is misleading, not the least on a linguistic basis since the English language seems to lack a proper word for the reality toward which indigenous terms point. Concerning the thought-shaping force of language see Benjamin Lee Whorf, "An American Indian Model of the Universe," in *Language Thought, and Reality: Selected Writings,* ed. John B. Carroll (New York: Technology Press of the Massachusetts Institute of Technology and John Wiley and Sons, 1956), 57–86.

27. Rice, *Black Elk's Story,* formulates it concisely: "Lakota religion enhances life on earth through ritual disciplines," 65, and "The ritualizing of physical necessity helps to create an existence of joy and meaning," 67, a principle that seems to apply also to other indigenous religio-philosphical traditions. Consequently, "neglecting or improperly performing rituals" was a major trespass, 65.

28. Morrison, "Native American Religions," 633.

29. Rice, *Black Elk's Story,* 28.

30. See Kimberly Blaeser, "Trickster: A Compendium," in *Buried Roots,* 47–66, with pertinent bibliographical titles.

31. Rice, *Black Elk's Story,* 39.

32. Quoted by Peter Matthiessen in *The Snow Leopard* (New York: Penguin, 1987), 64; an attempt to locate the passage in Heisenberg's publications remained unsuccessful.

33. Rice, *Black Elk's Story*. 148, title of "Conclusion."

34. Quoted in Deloria, *God Is Red*, 115; see the whole chapter "The Concept of History," 111–117. Deloria suggests a view that parallels the traditions of India.

35. Deloria, *God Is Red*. 75; and Arthur Versluis, *Earth: The Spiritual Landscape of Native America* (Rochester, VT: Inner Traditions, 1992), 102–112. John Loftin, "Traditional Practices Among Contemporary Indians," in *The Native North American Almanac*, ed. Duane Champagne (Detroit: Gale Research Inc., 1994), 649, states succinctly: ". . . space always has a sacred center."

36. William Cronon, *Changes in the Land: Indians, Colonists, and the Ecology of New England* (New York: Hill and Wang, 1983), describes in detail the incompatibility of the economic ideals and resulting economic systems of the indigenous peoples with those of the invader peoples, yet without probing the underlying divergent religio-philosophical positions. He shows that both peoples were shapers of their environments, but in radically different ways. Whereas the indigenous world approached their surroundings from the perspective of symbiosis, the Euro-Americans understood their task in the light of the biblical command to make the earth subject to them, if in proper stewardship. The article by Guilmet and Whited, "American Indian and Non-Indian Philosophies of Technology" relating to the Puget Sound is a superb case study of the issues involved (*American Indian Culture and Research Journal*, 26 [2002], 36–41).

37. See, for instance, Heinrich Zimmer, *Philosophies of India*, ed. Joseph Campbell (Princeton: Princeton University Press, 1969); on the Yoruba, see E. Thomas Lawson, *Religions of Africa* (New York: HarperSanFrancisco, 1985), 50–76; Michael Kioni Dudley, *Man, God, and Nature* (Honolulu: NaKane oka Malo Press, 1990), 9–29.

38. "Handschriftliche Zusätze . . . Zur Weltanschaungslehre," vol. 8, 218–224. Dilthey wrote the passage for an address titled "Traum" [Dream] which he gave on the occasion of his seventieth birthday, but did not use this passage.

Concepts and Questions

1. What does Schelbert mean when he says that worldview structures are often unquestioned?

2. Does the Western worldview structure consider humans part of nature or apart from nature? What do you think is the reason for this?

3. Describe and discuss the traits of the Western worldview structure. Can you provide examples from your daily life that conform to these structural traits?

4. The essay purports that the European drive to explore and colonize distant lands, beginning in the 1500s, was a product of the Western worldview structure. What aspects of this worldview structure do you think motivated this movement?

5. What are the different traits of the American Indian worldview structure? Provide an example for each.

6. What are the advantages or disadvantages of the "interdependent harmony" that is promoted by the American Indian worldview structure? Are there any contemporary situations where this could be beneficial?

7. What does the author mean when he says the indigenous worldview structure considers history as being "circular"? How does the essay describe this perspective?

8. In your own words, provide a summary of the two different worldview structures. What are the basic differences in the two?

9. How would these two different worldview structures affect an intercultural interaction? Give an example.

The Cultural Iceberg

JOHN HOOKER

A bishop from the United States stood before a congregation of African women in Mutare, Zimbabwe. Sermons run long in Zimbabwe, and he honored the custom. About an hour into his homily, he began to discuss the conflict between the Tutsis and Hutus in Rwanda. Refugees from the civil war fled their homes so quickly that they had to leave everything behind. The bishop told about their desperate need for the basics of life, such as food and clothing.

At this point many of the women in the congregation began to disrobe. They brought their garments to the front of the auditorium and piled them before the pulpit. A bystander explained to the startled bishop that they were donating their clothes to the refugees. Did he not say that they needed clothing? The following day, the bishop noticed that several women were wearing large plastic bags. They had given away their only piece of clothing.

Someone told me this story shortly before I arrived in Mutare to take a teaching job. Knowing what I now know about the Shona people of the region, I do not doubt its accuracy for an instant. This kind of generosity is part of the culture.

We Westerners find Shona generosity bewildering because our culture is universalist. Most of us want to believe that everyone is basically like us. Naturally there are surface differences in language, cuisine, and customs, but any other differences are explained by the level of development. Other peoples are simply less advanced. The problem is that the Shona do not fit into this scheme. It is difficult to put their largesse on the same level as cuisine or custom, because this level of selflessness is scarcely conceivable in the West. Yet it is even less reasonable to attribute saintly behavior to a lack of development. I suggest a third possibility: the Shona operate on a radically different worldview than we

do, one we cannot grasp unless we suspend some of our deepest assumptions about society and human nature.

We Westerners must change the way we think about other cultures. We must become aware of how our universalism narrows our perspective. In many ways it connects us with others, because it sustains our interest in the world and inspires us to give assistance and, perhaps all too often, advice. But this same universalism blocks our comprehension of what these cultures are all about, because we cannot acknowledge how fundamentally different they are.

The old analogy of the iceberg says it well. Culture lies primarily under the surface, beneath conscious awareness. This means that the most important cultural differences are invisible. It took me years to realize this, but when I did, my eyes began to open. I began to see different peoples as facing the same basic life problems but finding radically different solutions, solutions that challenge my deepest assumptions but that nonetheless have a logic of their own. Paradoxically, now that I recognize how different other peoples are, I am in a position to relate to them authentically and live and work among them successfully.

The purpose of this essay is to help prepare Western professionals for the otherness of other cultures. It is written for the growing number of business people, negotiators, social workers, lawyers, physicians, military personnel—and, of course, clergy—who work on the international scene or in multicultural settings. It draws on the insights of cultural anthropology to understand culture as a fascinating subject in its own right, but it simultaneously infers practical lessons. The two are in fact inseparable, because it is through everyday experience that we learn how culture works.

THE WESTERN MIND-SET

Western culture is so called because it originated in the western part of the Eurasian land mass. It might be defined as the dominant culture of Europe and its ethnic offspring, including Australia, Canada, New Zealand, and the United States. Latin American countries owe much to their Western roots, but they differ significantly enough that it is convenient to follow Samuel P. Huntington (1996) and classify them as non-Western.

We Westerners have always assumed that there is essentially one way to live: ours. Anyone who lives differently just needs some time, and perhaps some advice from us, to develop properly. This mind-set has shaped not only the West but also, to a great degree, the entire world. Half a millennium ago, European colonial powers began bringing the "three M's" to peoples around the globe: the military to subdue them, markets to realize a profit, and missionaries to tell them how to live and think like we do.

These habits persist. The global economic system, modeled after Western capitalism, propels "developing" countries down a path of rapidly rising resource consumption. The automobile fleet on Delhi streets doubles every few years, even though the air is already thick with pollutants. The World Bank and International Monetary Fund use unpaid debts as leverage: to obtain further Westernization of national economies, with mixed results. After the fall of the Soviet Union, Western consultants flocked into Russia to try to install an economic system that runs contrary to almost every aspect of Russian history and culture. Its total failure became a spectacle that humiliated the Russian people before the world. Even the recent Asian financial crisis was arguably less an Asian than a Western failure, because investors tried to impose Western financial practices in a part of the world with a very different tradition.

Why are we Westerners like this? We live in the age of CNN and the Internet. Air travel is cheap, and business is global. Given so much contact with the world, why can we not appreciate that others have their own very different and legitimate ways? Part of the answer is that our encounters with other cultures are often inauthentic. TV, movies, and English-language Web pages provide a highly filtered version of life elsewhere. If they are to hold our interest, they must be intelligible and must therefore reinterpret reality to fit our worldview. Tourism keeps us in a managed world of hotels, restaurants, and tourist attractions. The protective bubble lets in some of the sights, sounds, and flavors of a foreign country but insulates us as much as possible from the culture itself, which travelers tend to find confusing and upsetting. Because so many travelers view culture as consisting of little more than its surface features, they do not sense the loss.

Business, however, brings many Westerners into direct and intimate contact with other peoples, and it has not been without its effect. In the old days Western business made little concession to the host culture, due to its economic hegemony. But Japan changed everything. During the 1980s, Japan built a formidable economic machine that set the standard of quality for the world, and the hegemonic balance began to tip. Northwest Airlines scheduled direct "auto executive" flights between Detroit and Tokyo. Business leaders worldwide began taking Japan seriously, and later the entire Pacific Rim, as Japanese investment spawned highly competitive industry in that part of the world. Conscious of their economic power and wary of foreigners by nature, Japanese business people expected Western visitors to make cultural adjustments. Those who refused hit a brick wall.

Western business people absorbed some genuine cultural lessons during this period. A stream of books on cross-cultural management appeared, and continues unabated. Corporations and consulting firms organized workshops on the same topic, and MBA programs offered courses in Japanese and Chinese. But even here, the primary reaction was to reduce culture to matters of language, customs, and etiquette. The cross-cultural guides warn that in Latin America one should not be offended if kept waiting for forty-five minutes, or if one's host takes care of other business simultaneously. In Germany one should keep the office door shut. In parts of Africa one should greet associates in the hallway, even if this means saying hello to the same person several times a day. If someone offers a business card in Japan, one should receive it with both hands, study it, and perhaps place it on the table in front of oneself.

Business people are willing to observe rules of etiquette, but too often only because offensive behavior can distract attention from the business at hand. Too many regard the business itself as the same game whether played in Boston or Bangkok. In reality, deeply held cultural assumptions shape both etiquette and business. Latin Americans tend to be late because their underlying conception of time is different. Germans have their own sense of space that requires order and privacy. For many Africans, human existence is irreducibly communal; failing to acknowledge another person is subhuman. Japanese build their society on group harmony; whence the importance of respecting others through business card rituals and a thousand other courtesies.

Business is likewise grounded in culture. It owes its existence to the fact that people have certain attitudes toward commitments, authority, work, and community. Only something as deep and pervasive as culture can inculcate these behaviors, and business simply takes advantage of them. It is a ripple on an ocean of culture. The question remains: why do Westerners resist the fundamental differences between themselves and others, even others with whom they work closely in the business world? It is because our universalism is an essential component of our culture. It is inextricably related to our sense of time, the way we process information, our faith in reason, our reliance on technology, our belief in progress, our egalitarianism, our secularism, our romanticism, our neglect of courtesy, our missionary impulse, our exploitation of nature, our expansionism and colonialism, our respect for law, our guilt complex, our fascination with natural science, our mechanisms for dealing with stress, and even our peculiar sense of humor. These elements support one another, much as the organisms in an ecosystem do.

All cultures are systems of this sort, and I will undertake to describe some of them. Only this will, I believe, fully reveal how radically cultures differ and prepare us to deal with the differences.

CULTURE AND LANGUAGE

When I step off the plane in Guangzhou, I cannot understand a word of the Cantonese dialect spoken there. Yet the language is only part of the system of practices and institutions that make up Cantonese culture. Why should I expect everything else to be transparent? The whole culture is likely to be as strange as the language.

Cultures differ as radically as languages because they themselves are, in part, extended languages. The set of behaviors we call "language" is a subset of a larger set of meaningful behaviors that help to define a culture. A culture bestows meaning on all of its practices in the very same way that it gives meaning to words.

This view traces to the philosopher Ludwig Wittgenstein. Suppose I scratch my head. If someone just asked me a difficult question, this may mean I am perplexed. If I am sitting in a Sotheby's auction, I may have just bid £10,000. If I am driving alone, it may be nothing more than relieving an itch. The gesture obtains its meaning from the role it plays in a social practice and the way people respond to it. Its meaning may therefore vary from one situation to another, or it may have no meaning at all.

The meaning of a gesture can vary across cultures as well as within a culture. Pounding one's fist into one's hand emphasizes a point in the United States but is obscene in Singapore. A woman in the United States who wears a scarf may simply be protecting her hair from the wind. A woman in Germany who does the same identifies herself as Muslim.

Wittgenstein emphasized that words receive their meaning contextually, just as gestures do, rather than by dictionary definitions. The same principle applies to more complex behaviors and even institutions. Think about what it means to wear a white dress, say "I do," and receive a ring while standing in a church, versus what it means to do the same while standing on the stage of a playhouse. Marriage means what it does because of the practices and expectations that surround it. Culture gives them meaning in the same way it gives meaning to words, gestures, and attire. Culture is a maker of meaning. The meaning of the whole is likely to be no less obscure to an outsider than the meaning of the part we somewhat arbitrarily call "language."

I may protest that when I step into the culture of Guangzhou, Westerner though I be, I am quite well aware of how different it is. The traffic is chaotic and frightening, the sewers leak (or do not exist), and the high-rise flats are appallingly crowded. But the Westerner in me writes these off to a lack of development. Chinese are still basically like Americans, or least they will be once they learn better. This is why Bill Clinton can travel to Beijing and tell President Jiang how to run his country.

This is not to suggest that only Westerners have a sense of superiority. Most peoples regard others as inferior. The Chinese themselves call their country *Zhōngguó* (central kingdom), because they traditionally consider themselves the center of civilization and see Westerners, for example, as close to barbarism. The very word *barbaric* reflects the ancient Greek taunt that foreigners say nonsense syllables ("ba ba") because they are too ignorant to have a coherent language. The Western sense of superiority differs because of its universalist twist: it regards other cultures as less developed. It sees the nations of the world as more or less advanced on a single ladder of development (with Western nations obviously on the upper rungs), rather than as advancing in fundamentally different directions. Only Westerners would describe as "developing" a nation that was already ancient and highly developed when European civilization was still in diapers. This attitude reflects our own cultural needs more than arrogance, but it gets us into trouble. If I am in Guangzhou on business, for example, my failure to acknowledge how different it is can lead to increasing frustration and anxiety. I attend my first meeting, but no one seems to be serious about making a deal. Back home I can negotiate with people I met only yesterday, but here it is best to build a long-term relationship (*guānxi*) with my business partners. At home, agreements are based on a legal framework that presupposes the universality of rules and law. Westerners, bless their hearts, can believe in this, but Chinese ultimately cannot. For them a piece of legal paper is worthless, and deals are grounded in flesh and blood, that is, in personal relationships of trust and mutual obligation. I may eventually convince my partners to sign a Western-style contract, but the next day they want to renegotiate. To them, the idea of slavish adherence to what is written on paper, when the world changes daily, is perverse. As the business gets under way, my associates may want to put their relatives in key positions. To my mind nepotism is bad business and probably unethical, but here contractual obligation to a firm is a concept with little meaning, whereas loyalty to the extended family has powered a great civilization for five thousand years. My associates expect me to keep an eye on lower-level employees constantly, even though I am accustomed to giving instructions at the beginning of the day and checking on things occasionally. It has not occurred to me that internalized rules and guilt play a more important motivational role in my own culture than in China. Here in Guangzhou, employees are equally responsible, but they respond to people rather than guilt. I have concerns about how the business is run, but when the president of the firm is in the room, everyone simply agrees with what he says, and no one wants to bring up problems in the company.

Authority is conceived in a very different way here. In addition to these mounting frustrations, I seem to be unable to predict what my associates will say or do next. Sometimes they seem perfectly reasonable, but moments later they come up with irrational and inexplicable ideas. The irrationality of the system itself, as I see it, almost defies belief. Every company action requires approvals from layers of bureaucrats who seem to know little about the business and who sometimes want something in return. Worse, the process drags on interminably. I cannot understand why the Chinese people would do this to themselves. Yet the Chinese built a civilization that has flourished for eons. It also occurs to me that my own country might appear equally dysfunctional to a Chinese visitor. Every news broadcast is saturated with reports of crime and violence; poverty and despair persist amid incredible affluence; and perhaps most shockingly to Chinese sensibilities, elders often languish in institutions without financial or personal support from those who owe them their being. Yet one can see these as flaws in a greater system that has much to recommend it. One can presumably achieve a similar perspective in China, if one understands how the culture works.

Such is the purpose of this essay. It is a brief attempt to prepare you to understand and cope with a strange country by explaining how its system is put together, much as a grammar text prepares one to learn a language.

Cultural grammar can be viewed as the way people solve life's basic problems. One particularly thorny problem is stress, which results from our lack of control over what happens to us. Westerners turn to science and technology for a sense of control. This is why we have so much technology—not because we are smarter or more highly developed. Chinese organize themselves around strong families, respect for age and authority, *guāxnì*, superstition, and rituals. Chinese developed such key technologies as the compass and gunpowder, but only the West felt the need to use them to control their environment, for instance by colonizing much of the world. If we view cultures as stress-management mechanisms, incomprehensible behavior begins to make sense. Even better, we can use this understanding to cope with life as the locals do.

How does one learn a culture? Much as one learns its language. It is best done with a combination of intellectual preparation and immersion, as neither method alone seems optimal. One can learn a foreign language in orderly, intellectual fashion on home shores, but only with diligent study and much discipline. Alternatively, one can learn it by absorption, particularly when cast into an alien environment and survival demands it. There are teaching methods that eschew all intellectual treatment and try to duplicate the learning process of a child. But for adult learning, it seems better to use the intellectual resources that adults have and children do not. Systematic study can lay the groundwork for later learning by immersion.

WHY UNDERSTAND CULTURE?

Our age calls for cultural awareness at both the social and the professional levels. Socially, we sense that culture is somehow at the root of the major issues of the day. The reasons are evident enough. Immigrants of widely different backgrounds pour into Western countries in unprecedented numbers. At the same time, the Western economic system stretches its tentacles into every corner of the earth, restructuring economies and cultures.

The result is cultural change and disruption around the globe. One cannot pick up the daily newspaper without reading of ethnic struggle on several continents. The growing concentration of wealth exacerbates the tension between rich and poor. Resentment of cultural change and Western economic dominance inspires terrorism and the rise of militant fundamentalism. Western nations struggle with the task of holding their diverse populations together. People in the United States, the most multicultural of nations, talk of culture wars, fear resurgent racism, flee crime and violence, and come to blows over such social issues as abortion. Anyone who doubts the power of culture can think about how some ordinary, decent people in the Balkans became monsters overnight when ethnic hatred was unleashed. Culture is the theme of our age. Our most pressing issues are profoundly cultural in nature. We try to address them, but without an appreciation of how deeply culture determines our worldviews, we can only grope and fumble.

On a professional level, cultural understanding helps us adjust to unfamiliar environments in which we must work. The term *culture shock* is unfortunate, because it suggests that there is an initial shock when one gets off the plane, and it goes away after a few days. The initial shock may or may not happen. One who has always lived in an affluent nation and flies into Conakry, capital of Guinea, is in for a shock. However, one who flies into Beijing is more likely to be delighted and impressed than shocked during an initial period. The problem is adjusting over the longer term. Dealing with the stress of not understanding the language, never really knowing what is going on, and having to deal with behavior that seems strange, annoying, or downright insulting requires an enormous amount of energy. Initially one operates on an adrenaline high and can deal with it. But eventually one's body and psyche want to return to a more normal state. One begins looking for a way out.

If one intends to live or work in a new cultural environment, previous experience can be misleading. Long and extensive travel without adjustment problems is no indication of what it may be like actually to live or work in a strange culture. As already mentioned, the typical traveler is insulated from the indigenous society that supplies the cooks and the maids. Even the international backpacker may have no idea what it means to work in an unfamiliar country. Hitching rides in rural Kazakstan can be physically and emotionally demanding, but it is a different kind of challenge. A backpacker interacts with the locals primarily on the basic level of obtaining food, shelter, and transport. There is little real engagement with a culture. In fact, the backpacking experience is much less an encounter with other cultures than a rite of passage in the backpacker's own culture. It is no accident that almost all international backpackers are from northern Europe, North America, and Australia. By contrast, a person who lives and works in a culture, negotiates agreements, supervises employees, and develops a market must engage the culture at a sophisticated level.

One strategy for avoiding burnout is to seek out aspects of the culture one can learn to appreciate or enjoy, and then make the most of them. This obviously works best when one knows something about the culture. This is an obvious strategy in such matters as food, for instance in China, internationally known for its advanced cuisine. But it is important to know what one is doing. Not only are bad restaurants legion, but Chinese food can be different in China than elsewhere. I have eaten soup that is indistinguishable from newsprint and hot water ground to pulp in a blender. (I will forgo a description of the sea beetles and tendon sheath.) But food that is amenable to one's palate is almost certain to be better than the daily fare back home. This is something to which one can look forward every day to get past the rough spots.

This strategy can be generalized, and one can take it a certain distance without a deeper knowledge of the culture. In India there is a wide selection of English-language newspapers, written with eloquence and intelligence; one should not miss the letters to the editor, a favorite pastime for would-be writers. In Scandinavia cyclists can pursue their hobby on bicycle-friendly streets. Tokyo is a huge, crowded city, but one can explore without fear of crime. In Mexico a request for assistance in broken Spanish receives a friendly response. If one seeks them out, these small pleasures accumulate and help convert an overall negative experience to a positive one.

Small pleasures cannot, however, carry the full weight of cultural adjustment. Stress is ultimately generated by a feeling that one has no control over the situation. Knowledge of the culture helps create a sense of mastery that relieves much of the stress. Furthermore, every culture has its own distinctive mechanisms for dealing with stress. This is an aspect of culture so fundamental that it can serve as a principle around which one's understanding of a country is organized. It can be a great relief to plug into a society's management mechanism, particularly if one moves from the relatively, weak postindustrial mainstream culture of the United States, which provides little support in this area, to a strong, traditional culture. But doing so requires a rather deep knowledge of how the culture works.

A bonus of cultural knowledge is the favorable impression it makes on hosts. Most peoples are quite sensitive about perceived attitudes to their culture.

A lack of knowledge or enthusiasm may be interpreted as an insult, as a signal that their culture is not worth learning about. They are likely to respond warmly, on the other hand, to active interest and involvement. In most of the world, developing personal relationships is absolutely essential to getting anything done. If people sense respect for their culture, this is likely to go a long way toward building indispensable professional relationships.

Reference

Huntington, S. P. (1996). *The clash of civilizations and the remaking of world order.* New York: Simon and Schuster.

Concepts and Questions

1. What does Hooker mean when he says, "We must become aware of how our universalism narrows our perspective?" Do you disagree or disagree? Why?
2. The essay contends that Westerners live with the assumption that the Western way of life is the best and that with time and advice people from other cultures will adopt that way. What is the basis for this belief? What is your opinion? Why?
3. How and why do TV, movies, and English-language Web pages provide highly filtered versions of life in other cultures?
4. What problems can result from teaching cultural variance as merely differences in language, customs, and etiquette?
5. Hooker says that "Business is grounded in culture." What is meant by this?
6. How do culture and language complement each other?
7. Why do "most peoples regard others as inferior"?
8. What is meant by the term "cultural grammar"?
9. According to Hooker, what are the best ways to learn a culture?
10. Explain some of the major issues of today that are rooted in cultural differences.

Identity: Issues of Belonging

2

An identity world seems to be arrived
at by the way in which the person faces
and uses his experiences.

JAMES BALDWIN

Today, all of us are living in an especially dynamic era of social transformation—the old is being transformed by the new more rapidly than ever before. Globalization is exerting enormous social, political, and economic pressures on the existing nation-state geopolitical order. Institutions have fostered an environment where electronic labor, capital, and media content flow nearly seamlessly across national borders. Seemingly endless waves of immigrants are leaving their homelands to search for greater economic opportunity and personal freedom in other countries. International political and economic integration in the form of alliances and trade agreements have become common necessities. Multinational corporations are evolving into transnational organizations. Taken in aggregate, the continually changing social conditions arising from these forces create a powerful milieu influencing the construction and maintenance of one's self-identity. In fact, a frequently voiced critique of globalization is the concern that other nations and cultures will ultimately become mere homogenized representations of Western capitalism, forfeiting much of the uniqueness represented by their national and cultural identities. Therefore, it becomes both important and necessary to understand the role of identity and how culture works in forming and preserving your identity.

Probably the most important function of identity is to provide meaning by serving as a source of self-definition. In other words, we organize meaning around our self-identity (Castells, 1997). In part, identities provide a foundation for meaning due to their origins, which can stem from a variety of influences, such as geography, history, fantasies, religion, and many, many more. Identity also takes various time- and scenario-dependent forms, to include nation, state, region, religion, ethnic, gender, socioeconomic status, profession, and others.

A major influence of identity formation and maintenance is culture. Your identity is socially constructed through a cultural lens, employing the medium of communication. We identify with our initial cultural in-group as a function of enculturation and later, as a result of interaction, expand to other cultural groups or social institutions (Castells, 1997). This produces a culturally bound concept of the "socially appropriate" identity. Recruiting slogans used by the U.S. Army can provide you an example of this synergy between culture and identity. Beginning in the early 1990s, potential army recruits were enticed by the slogan "Be All You Can Be." In early 2001, this was changed to "Army of One." In late 2006, "Army Strong" became the recruitment mantra, which officials indicated was "meant to convey the idea that if you join the Army you will gain physical and emotional strength, as well as strength of character and purpose" ("New," 2006, p. 1). In all three instances, the slogans served to emphasize the importance of self-determination, independence, and individual achievement. This emphasis on the individual is quite in contrast to that of a collective culture, where identity is strongly tied to, and dependent on, in-group memberships.

Our ever-changing social environment is increasingly characterized by frequent and unavoidable multicultural interactions. Now, it is common for sojourners to live and work for extended periods in other cultures. As a result, the influence of culture on identity must be understood. For this reason, we offer five essays dealing with various aspects of culture and identity. We begin with an essay that demonstrates some of the complexities associated with the issue of self-identity. In "Constructing, Negotiating, and Communicating Jewishness in America," Jamie Moshin and Ronald Jackson examine how U.S. Jews view their identity, the historical evolution of Jewish identity in the United States, and how Jews have used humor to communicate their identity. They argue that contemporary Jewish identity is a product of "shared communal values, morality, rituals, and connection with other Jews." Religion may or may not play a role in their lives. Thus, in today's social order, there are multiple ways of being Jewish.

The authors then provide an overview of the historical evolution of Jewish identity in the United States. They begin in the early 1900s, when Jews were seen as "a non-white, undesirable race" and continue till today, when Jews are often considered a "model minority." This history is characterized by a continuing effort to endure and rise above discrimination. The problem of Jewish identity is explained as a struggle to be a part of, yet separate from, the white majority, a struggle that is ongoing.

Humor has served as a viable pathway for Jews to enact and communicate their Jewishness. But the authors warn that this humor should not be interpreted as self-deprecation, but should be viewed as "the primary means of self-protection and warding off anti-Semitism." Thus, Jews are seen to use humor as a protective measure to make themselves "less vulnerable to the laughter and hostility of the other" and more acceptable to the dominant culture.

In our second essay, John Warren looks at the issue of "whiteness" in the United States, which he casts as both a form of identity and a social structure, and the latter can either provide or deny access to social power. The author begins by explaining four broad categories used by communication scholars to examine whiteness. These are (1) whiteness as an anti-racist practice; (2) how whiteness is promoted in scholarship, film, TV, and other forms of text; (3) how whiteness influences our communicative behaviors; and (4) how whiteness is performed.

Warren sees identity as a product of communicative behaviors, in their entirety, arising from daily social interactions. Using an ordinary personal anecdote, he demonstrates how whiteness is both an identity and a social structure, completely intertwined and mutually supportive. The essay concludes with a forecast on future whiteness scholarship and a suggestion for a constructive approach.

Gender represents another influential factor in the formation of identity. At first blush, this seems rather simple and straightforward. If you are born a boy, you develop a male identity; if born a girl, you develop a female identity. But what happens when one's internal feelings of gender are in conflict with their body's external manifestations? Suddenly the world is not so simple or straightforward. To help you understand the dynamics in the construction of cultural identity, A. L. Zimmerman and Patricia Geist-Martin provide a narrative essay about Amber. "The Hybrid Identities of Gender Queer: Claiming Neither/Nor, Both/And," addresses the issues of how gender can affect the development of cultural identity. In the essay, you will follow the identity construction of Amber, a person born into a female body but who identifies more with being a male. By the age of seven, Amber's taste in dress was definitely that of a boy. By eight, she knew that people often assumed she was a male. At ten, she was sometimes an embarrassment to her family because people would ask questions like, "What is your son's name?" As Amber grew older, she continued to encounter social situations where her gender preferences produced negative reactions.

Following Amber's story, the authors discuss hybridity—the coming together of two or more cultural identities and the resulting opportunity for development of a third identity. However, the opportunity to communicate about this alternative identity is inhibited because it lies outside the boundaries of the common language. The concept of hybridity is applied to gender to produce what the authors call "queer gender." This, they claim, disrupts the binary of being either all male or all female. The authors then continue Amber's narrative, detailing how she adapts to her queer gender identity and finally finds peace in claiming the identity of "both/and" while also claiming to be "neither/nor."

The U.S. population is characterized by an overwhelming majority of people who came to this land from another country, and contemporary immigration continues to add to this patchwork quilt of ethnicities and cultures. Many, especially those of European ancestry, have become completely assimilated into what can be considered the dominant culture—Euro-American. For these people, ethnic identity often is not an active consideration, but something to reflect on during holidays, reunions, or when indulging in special foods. However, for many Americans, especially the recent arrivals, and those who have distinct physical characteristics that set them apart from the Euro-Americans, ethnic identity often carries much greater weight and importance. To help you understand this, our last two essays examine the role that ethnic identity can play in a person's life.

Sabine Chai and Mei Zhong believe that your ethnic history plays an important part in shaping your identity. Thus, they begin their essay, "Chinese American Ethnic and Cultural Identity" with an historical overview of the Chinese experience in the United States, which began with immigrant workers arriving in California during the first half of the nineteenth century. Beginning with the first arrivals until 1943, the Chinese were the target of discrimination and exploitation.

To determine how this history and other factors may influence contemporary Chinese American's sense of identity, the author's talked with ten U.S.-born Chinese. The objective was to let the Chinese Americans talk freely about how they defined themselves. The responses revealed four factors that were considered important in defining a Chinese American: (1) being Chinese and being born/raised in the United States; (2) growing up in a Chinese family; (3) growing up in the United States; (4) having a connection to other Chinese Americans. The essay provides you an in-depth discussion of each of these factors.

Although being raised in the United States may seem like merely a matter of geography, Chai and Zhong point out that this carries considerable significance for Chinese American ethnic identity. Specifically, many had to learn to deal with being a member of a minority group and endure traditional stereotypes, especially those presented by the mass media. What was especially important to the interviewees was "having friends of a similar background." This need to interact with people who share a common experience was determined to also be a way for the Chinese Americans to create their identity.

In our next essay, Etsuko Kinefuchi continues the examination of ethnic American identity. Her article, "What's (not) in a Label?: Understanding Korean American Adoptee Identity Through Self-Identified Labels" looks at the issue of ethnic labels, which Kinefuchi considers to be the principal means we use to "express, describe, and understand identities." While labels are considered necessary to our daily conversation, the author warns us that they can also be limiting.

The essay argues that for intercultural communication interactions to be successful, participants must understand each other's "avowed" identities and their reasons for the avowal. To illustrate this process, the identity experience of native Koreans adopted by white couples in the United States is explored through first-person accounts. Among her many discoveries, Kinefuchi relates that one's place of birth is a significant source of identity, even though they may have lived there for only a short time. As in the previous essay, some of the Korean Americans revealed that having other ethnic Korean American friends was an important source of self-identity. But other adoptees eschewed their biological appearance and cultural birthright in favor of their "white" upbringing. These individuals ascribed to the "white" identity label. Still others felt their identity was with multiple ethnic groups, rather than just one. And a few disdained all ethnic, racial, and adopted status labels in favor of their personal interests and activities.

The essay concludes with a discussion of how identity labels can be interpreted differently through ascription and avowal and disclosed that even personal understanding of the same label can vary from one person to another. Kinefuchi's work shows us, once again, just how complex the issue of identity can be.

A recent National Public Radio program carried an interview with a U.S. international businessman whose travels kept him away from home over 200 days each year. As the world community becomes more integrated, more and more sojourners are finding themselves continually moving across cultural borders. This movement has become so widespread that the phrase *cultural transient* has been coined to describe the phenomenon. The problems arising from this living in this cultural flux and how it impacts on one's identity is the theme of our next article—"Straddling Cultural Borders: Exploring Identity in Multiple Reacculturation," by Chuka Onwumechili, Peter O. Nwosu, and Ronald L. Jackson II.

The essay tells us that since the early 1950s scholars have been looking at the question of how people adjust to the problems associated with entering a new "host culture." Most of their findings indicate that the adjustment pattern begins with a period of euphoria and then often advances to culture shock, recovery, and eventually adjustment. Upon returning home the person is likely to go through a similar pattern, often called "re-entry shock." Recently, researchers have also become concerned with how the experience of traveling and living in a foreign culture influences cultural identity. In an attempt to update the research on cultural transients Onwumechili, Nwosu, and Jackson have added some new key variables to the challenges facing the person living in multiple cultures.

The authors believe not all acculturation and reacculturation situations are the same. They see four types of transient activity: (a) short-term socioeconomic/political transients, (b) long-term socioeconomic/political transients, (c) short-term service/

employment transients, and (d) long-term service/employment transients. In each instance the authors are concerned with the effects on the transient's cultural identity. Blending identity with the processes of moving in and out of two or more cultures demands that the transient, regardless of amount of time spent in the host culture, decide on a "contract" style that they are comfortable with. The authors suggest three of the most common strategies utilized by experienced transients. The first is called a *ready-to-sign* approach. In this case the transient has decided she/he is comfortable with their existing cultural identity and feels no need to make any adjustments. Second, the *quasi-completed* contract, often called the "middle ground", occurs when the transient is open to merging parts of the identity of both cultures. The third type of cultural adaptation is called the *co-created contract*. According to the authors, here "cultural identity is fully open to negotiation" and the transient is "committed to jointly negotiating a third culture with members of the host culture." What is important about this essay is not the details involved in each of the contact methods, but rather the realization that when you move from one culture to another you must be attentive to the fact that you will have to re-access your identity as part of the transient activity.

References

Castells, M. (1997). *The power of identity*. Malden, MA: Blackwell.
New Army Recruiting Slogan Unveiled. (2006, October 9). Retrieved May 7, 2007, from http://www.military.com/NewsContent/0,13319,116399,00.html

Constructing, Negotiating, and Communicating Jewish Identity in America

Jamie J. Moshin
Ronald L. Jackson II

INTRODUCTION: RACE, ETHNICITY, AND RELIGION

The religious precepts and deepest values of Judaism, the world's oldest monotheistic faith, have altered dramatically since its inception. Changes to dogmatic principles have led to the creation of many Judaic sects, including Reform, Conservative, Modern Orthodox, Chasidism, Reconstructionism, and Humanism, and have caused many within and outside of the faith to question what exactly constitutes a "good" Jew. In this chapter, we discuss the cultural creation, representation, and communication of American Jewish identity—or "Jewishness." In order to do so, we will discuss the social construction of Jewishness as race/ethnicity/religion, look at how people label and take on Jewish identities, and examine particularly "Jewish" ways of talking.

First, how do people "become" Jewish? Judaism has traditionally been determined through matrilineal descent. That is, if the mother is Jewish, then the child is Jewish—this is unlike the Christian faith, in which one is considered Christian *only* if one believes in the faith's dogma. While more traditional Orthodox Jews tend to assign Jewishness solely through this pattern of heredity, more modern Jews tend to be less concerned

with matrilineal descent. That is, one may be Jewish via conversion or by having a Jewish father. As you may be able to tell, this makes classifying people as Jewish or not Jewish somewhat confusing. That is, if Jewish identity—being Jewish or not being Jewish—is determined primarily through blood descent, doesn't that make Jewishness a race? Jewish individuals, however, have long felt extremely uncomfortable being classified as members of a "race," preferring to be seen as either an ethnicity or a religious group.

Some scholars give the analysis that while Jews must actively choose their Judaism, it is still inextricably tied to them through blood and matrilineal descent—which sounds a lot like Jewishness as a race (Cohen & Eisen, 2000). Most, however, tend to agree that Judaism is an ethnicity, and not a race (Amyot & Sigelman, 1996; Brodkin, 2004; Gilman, 1986; Hecht & Faulkner, 2000; Jackson, 1999; Medding, 1987; London & Chazan, 1990; Sorin, 1993). By "Jewish ethnicity," we mean "all other communal or collective aspects of being Jewish: all manner of attachment to Jewish family members, neighbors, secular institutions, and the Jewish people worldwide" (Cohen & Eisen, 2000, p. 102). Jews are distinctive in their ethnic identity; Jewish ethnicity is a unique blend of religious and national components so integrated that to pull them apart would totally distort Jewish identity (London & Chazan, 1990).

This talk of race and ethnicity surely begs the question, "but isn't Judaism just a religion?" As part of the flexible Jewish identity, Jewish Americans seem to be floating farther and farther away from a Jewish religious center, while keeping a certain sense of "Jewishness"—Jewish identity—intact. Jews are especially uncommon, in that they are the only American collectivity that is both a bona fide religious group and an ethnic group (Cohen & Eisen, 2000). Whereas Judaism was once predicated entirely on religion as defined by rabbinic and Talmudic law, Jews today now decide for themselves exactly how religious they want to be. Although Judaism can still be an integral part of Jewishness, the two constitute different aspects of a multi-faceted identity. Jews tend to characterize their behavior as either religious or non-religious (Hecht & Faulkner, 2000). Judaism is entirely voluntary and compartmentalized as only one part of Jewish identity: "Jewish identity has come to be understood in terms of feelings of Jewish affinity, on the one hand, and acts of Jewish affiliation, on the other" (Rosen, 1995, p. 15). Jewish identity can further be defined as "the inner experience of the self in relationship to the religious, political, ethnic, and/or cultural elements of Judaism, the Jewish people, and Israel" (Arnow, 1994, p. 30).

Unlike Christianity, Judaism is not dependent on any particular precepts of faith; one can be Jewish without believing in God. God is factoring less and less into modern-day Jewishness; Judaism is witnessing "secularization from within" and a "privatization of faith," and is newly focused on a self-expression that might be construed as damaging to organized faith (Wertheimer, 1993, p. 198). Judaism is now defined by religious individualism in which people make their own decisions regarding involvement—or lack thereof—in organized religion. Essentially, American Jews by and large are ambivalent to synagogues and God, yet have still decided to live as "Jewish selves" (Cohen & Eisen, 2000). Modern American Jews now tend to place greater importance on shared communal values, morality, rituals, and connection with other Jews, and it is these qualities that describe a "good Jew." The thrust has changed from Judaism to Jewishness, and from dogmatic religion to civil religion (Sorin, 1994). As Horace M. Kallen said, "The place and function of Judaism in Jewish life is like the place of any religion in any national life. It is an item in that life; only an item, no matter how important, in a whole which is determined by the ethnic character of the people that live it, by their history, their collective will and interest" (In Toll, 1997, p. 72).

Before we move on, one other concept is worth noting. In this piece, we do not consider "Jewish" to be static and unchanging. That is, there are many ways of being Jewish, and any Jewish individual might treat their Jewish identity differently depending on the context. This notion of multiple, competing and coexisting identities is very common within cultural studies. Stuart Hall notes that identity is an always incomplete production which undergoes constant transformation, varying with "the different ways in which we are positioned by, and position ourselves within, the narratives of the past" (1996, p. 213). Additionally, identity is not created and monitored only by that particular individual, but by society as a whole. We do not create our own identities ourselves; society, media, friends, and family are also responsible for structuring how identities are created and viewed: "Our identity is partly shaped by recognition or its absence, often by the *mis*recognition of others, and so a person or group of people can suffer real damage, real distortion, if the people or society around them mirror back to them a confining or demeaning or contemptible picture of themselves" (Taylor, 1994, p. 25). Because race is a social construct, not based in reality—yet, oddly, still has real societal implications—there are no set answers about identity.

Now that we better understand American Jewish identity as it is today, as well as the flexible and socially constructed nature of that identity, let us look at how it became this way. For instance, where did this still uncomfortable distinction between Jewishness as race, ethnicity, and religion come from? To answer this question, we must look at Jewish American identity at the turn of the twentieth century, when America was witnessing a large increase in Jewish immigration. As Stuart Hall notes, "One needs to know how different racial and ethnic groups were inserted historically, and the relations which have tended to erode and transform, or to preserve these distinctions through time—not simply as residues and traces of previous modes, but as active structuring principles of the present organization of society" (1996, p. 54).

White, Black, or Jewish? The History of Jews in America

In the early 1900s, Jewish Americans were struggling to assert and find their place in American society—hoping to mold themselves as white, and as a "model minority," but not meeting with much success in this regard. Jews in Europe were being racialized as non-white and non-Aryan by anti-Semitism; particularly virulent were the political seeds of Nazism in Germany, where this racialization was already taking place. It was this racialization of Jews that would eventually smooth the path to their attempted extermination during the Holocaust (Rogin, 1996). James Baldwin notes that, "Jews came here from countries where they were not white, and they came here in part *because* they were not white . . . the price of the ticket . . . was to become white" (1984, p. 90). This push for whiteness was not met with immediate success; Jews were considered to be racially Black, and thus hierarchically below white

America: "In time . . . 'inferior' religious cultures became inferior races" (Brodkin, 2004, p. 54).

In an 1893 *New York Times* article, the Jewish Lower East Side, where much of America's Jewish population lived, was described as "the eyesore of New York, and perhaps the filthiest place on the western continent. It is impossible for a Christian to live there because he [sic] will be driven out, either by blows or the dirt and stench. Cleanliness is an unknown quantity to these people" (In Brodkin, 2004, p. 24). These popular views were mirrored in the science of the time; Madison Grant's influential *The Passing of the Great Race* (1916) was instrumental in racializing Jews in America. Grant argued that there were three or four major European races; of these, the Nordics were superior, and the Jews were the worst of all (Brodkin, 2004). The racist testimony of "science" helps to set apart certain, disempowered races and ethnicities as "abnormal" (Bhabha, 1996). Grant's studies helped instill racism and support the call for eugenics for those who were not white Protestant elites.

In addition to Grant's testimony, there was a historically powerful association between Jews and tobacco, and the stereotype of Jews as smokers was a means of labeling the essential, racialized nature of Jews (Gilman, 2003). From the nineteenth century on, Jews were the face of the tobacco industry in Eastern Europe—an association that was initially positive, as tobacco was then seen as a luxury item. However, as the dangers of tobacco came to light, health reform became strongly linked with anti-Semitism, and the unhealthiness caused by tobacco was seen as a particular weakness of the racialized Jewish body. In a similar vein, much social significance was placed on the Jewish nose; as Sander Gilman puts it, "You can change your Moses, but you can't change your noses" (2003, p. 111). In the mid-nineteenth century, unattractive noses were seen as a sure sign of syphilis. Jews were equated with the disease because of their "distinguishing" noses. The noses were a clear sign of "racial" deformity. Science helped define Jews as easily distinguishable via physical characteristics. Nose jobs made it possible for Jews to pass as non-Jews and thus happily blend in with general society.

In 1924, a United States law made entering the country impossible for immigrants from Southern and Eastern Europe, the vast majority of whom were Jews; the Jewish percentage of net migration to the United States dropped from 21.2 percent in 1920 to almost zero in 1924. Jews were considered less than white, and were bound together with Asians and Blacks under the "orientalist" umbrella (Rogin, 1996).

How did this change? How did America progress from viewing Jews as a non-white, undesirable race, to viewing them as a "model minority"—or a group that is "different" and disempowered but still "accepted"—and as white? First, a disclaimer is in order: While Jews are seen as one of America's "model minorities"—because of their success in high-profile careers such as medicine and the law, family values, focus on education, and the like—this move has not been easy, and is still something of an overstatement. According to the Federal Bureau of Investigation, Jews are still the most persecuted religious minority in the United States (2004). As of 2004, 67.9 percent of the victims of crimes motivated by racial prejudice were Black, and 67.8 percent of the victims of crimes motivated by religious intolerance were Jewish. Additionally, the vestiges of Jewish racialization still remain; in fact, a 1987 Supreme Court ruling that Jews and Arabs could benefit from civil rights laws prohibiting discrimination did so on the grounds that neither group was racially white (Brodkin, 2004). This division persists; many Jewish Americans tend to see themselves as "others," and not as white (Hecht, 2002).

While the transition to "model minority" is an admittedly incomplete one, the story goes that "Jews gradually became Caucasians over the course of the twentieth century" (Jacobson, 1998, p. 172). Sadly, this ascension up the "racial" ladder was largely achieved as Jewish Americans distanced themselves from other minorities with whom they were associated: "The virtues and rewards that [Jews] claimed for themselves as good Jewish sons depended upon showing how similar Jewish culture was to bourgeois cultural ideals and upon differentiating Jewish culture from a depraved and unworthy African American culture" (Brodkin, 2004, p. 150). Further, the Jewish ethnicity was created as exemplary through "the invention of a deficient African American culture" (Brodkin, 2004, p. 151). Toni Morrison has pointed out that, "In race talk the move into mainstream America always means buying into the notion of American Blacks as the real aliens" (1993, p. 57).

The chasm between Blacks and Jews was high-lighted and accepted as fact within cinema, via the usage of blackface, or minstrelsy. Minstrelsy (the usage of Black face-paint to portray African Americans in a generally demeaning and stereotypical manner) originated in the United States in the late 1700s and gained widespread popularity when it made its way into films in the early 1900s (Jackson, 2006). Sadly, "The Black mask offered a way to play with the collective fears of a degraded and threatening—and male—Other while at the same time maintaining some symbolic control over them" (Lott, 1993, p. 25).

Blackface marked the separation of not only whites from Blacks, but also Jews-attempting-to-become-white from Blacks. By the turn of the twentieth century the most popular and noted blackface performers were Jewish. Blackface was the Jews' "stain of shame" (Rogin, 1998, p. 87). This blackface underscored the line between white and Black, and it helped *create* American ethnic identities that were not Black: "With blackface American Jews exposed the contrasting situations of Jews and Blacks that allowed Jews to rise above the people whose cause and whose music they made their own." (Rogin, 1996, p. 68). As demonstrated by Rogin's turn of phrase—"stain of shame," blackface left an indelible mark on American society, both on Jews and on Blacks: "It was not just that anti-black racism replaced anti-Semitism as the badge of belonging in the United States, but that the badge was worn as blackface, and often by Jews" (1996, p. 64). The minstrel film which has had the most significant and lasting impact on the American psyche was also the first talkie—a film in which the actors' dialogue was audible and no longer just conveyed by subtitles. *The Jazz Singer* (1927), which depicts Jewish star Al Jolson in blackface, "marks the beginning of the drift by which American Jews became racial Caucasians" (Jacobson, 1998, p. 187) and suggests that blackness should be characterized, mocked, and represented as despicable. It became the genesis of a new kind of scripting of Black bodies (Jackson, 2006).

It was largely through the usage of blackface that Jews became both white and American, but no longer Black. Two separate side points should be noted here, however. First, even in Hollywood where Jewish Americans were inordinately successful (Gabler, 1988), Jews were not allowed full entry into the public sphere. In fact, the word "Jew" was not even uttered in a film until 1940's *The Great Dictator,* and there was a significant backlash against Jewish control of the movie industry in the 1920s and 1930s. Second, while many American Jews were distancing themselves from African Americans and positioning themselves as "white," they continued to fight discrimination in all its forms: "Many Jews treated American freedom not as a given, however, but as something to be achieved in the struggle against all forms of discrimination. Jews opposed racial prejudice in greater numbers, proportionately, than did any other white ethnic group" (Rogin, 1996, p. 76). This struggle against the suffering of Blacks happens because "Jews and Blacks are a pariah people—a people who had to make and re-make themselves as outsiders on the margins of American society and culture . . . Both groups defined themselves as a people deeply shaped by America but never *fully* a part of America" (West & Lerner, 1995, p. 2). As Rogin argues, "Jews were the White ethnic group most identified with Blacks and most supportive of civil rights for racial minorities" (1996, p. 76).

Communicating Jewishness Today: Assimilation, Closeting, and Otherness

This struggle to be part of the majority, while always being cognizant of one's differences from the majority, has had tremendous influence in shaping how numerous Jewish individuals feel about their own identities today. For many more overtly and strongly religious Jews, the pressure of being in a culture, yet being different, is extremely difficult, prompting them to assimilate or acculturate and closet this Jewish identity.

We are witnessing an era of assimilation for American Jews. Assimilation occurs when a minority group takes on the practices and culture of the majority, losing their own culture in the process. This assimilation of American Jews has been made easier by the dwindling centrality of religiosity. As a white ethnicity, Jews have the freedom and luxury of blending in with the predominant culture—that is, because Jews do not look noticeably different than the white majority.

As part of their multi-faceted Jewish identity, Jews are also free to be Jewish within, yet American on the outside—known as acculturation. Acculturation occurs when a minority group takes on characteristics and practices of the majority, yet still retains those elements of their culture that makes them distinct. Acculturation allows Jews to be publicly American and privately Jewish. As they are no longer the ever-traveling nomads, Jews have moved from being sojourners to being Americans (Toll, 1997). American pluralism means that one is free to be Jewish, and free to be so in many ways. The pressure of assimilation, however, often makes it difficult to be Jewish in the United States (Schoem, 1988). Jewish identity is an ever-present struggle between embracing Jewish life and becoming assimilated (Kaufman & Raphael, 1987). Jewish philosopher Hannah Arendt was rather cynical on this point, arguing that Jews have only two choices: to be a "pariah," a conscious outsider who stands apart from both the majority and the minority and is thus able to act politically, or to be a "parvenu"—an assimilated Jew (1978). It is so easy to fade into the dominant, Christian culture that Judaism may become unnecessary (Gordis, 1995). This assimilation means that Judaism might be in danger of forever disappearing: "For those with a fundamental commitment to Jewish collective existence as a separate people, religion and culture, assimilation evokes profound anxiety, expressed in ever more highly charged phrases like internal erosion and corruption, spiritual Jewish genocide, and the end of American Jewish history" (Amyot & Sigelman, 1996, p. 177).

While Jews are blending in with the rest of society, and the external Jewish identity is being eroded away to display an American identity instead, there is still one role Jews refuse to adopt, and one way in which they are quite content to remain the "other"—namely, Jews are not Christian: "Jews are like a Russian doll. The outside is assimilated and fits into society. But the inner doll can never fit in totally because, quite simply, Jews are not Christians" (LA Times, 1998, p. A6). Christianity is "the boundary marker par excellence" (Cohen & Eisen, 2000, p. 99). This divide manifests itself in Jewish humor as well: "One of the purposes of Jewish jokes . . . is to help maintain boundaries, separating Jews from non-Jews" (Berger, 1997, p. 54).

Because modern American Jews maintain that core identity of "Jewishness" as they acculturate, and because they retain a definite sense of self as "not Christian," they retain the unpleasant sensation of being the "other"—a distinction traceable through history:

> In a culture which neither recognizes nor values individual differences, the awareness between self and other inevitably translates into an invidious comparison. The awareness of being a Jew in a predominantly non-Jewish society calls attention to the self, exposing it to view. To be different in a culture which prizes social conformity and popularity is to be marked as lesser. Hence, Jews frequently experience themselves as lesser in comparison to non-Jews. (Kaufman & Raphael, 1987, p. 35)

Jews are ascribed "good" and "bad" qualities in the form of stereotypes, and these stereotypes are eventually seen as real by Jews themselves: "As Jews react to the world by altering their sense of identity, what they wish themselves to be, so they become what the group labeling them as Other had determined them to be" (Gilman, 1986, p. 12). Many Jews accept a stereotyped mirage of themselves projected by the dominant society, realizing that try as they might, their core Jewishness will not change and they will thus never *not* be the "other."

This constant feeling of otherness and perpetual fear of anti-Semitism tends to put somewhat of a muzzle on Jewish communication, and helps to force the expression of Jewish identity back into their private lives. Jews' unique status as a white "other" (that is, not a part of the majority yet still appearing to be white) might enable them to blend in with White America (Hecht & Faulkner, 2002). One of the predominant ways in which Jewish individuals can do this is through "closeting." The term, borrowed from homosexual discourse, demonstrates that it is often difficult to tell whether someone else is Jewish, which means that Jewish identity can be hidden from society at large; it is hard to tell whether someone is Jewish unless that Jewish individual shares that information. Jews may let others know of their Jewishness through discourse, deciding to "out" themselves if the moment or recipient of the knowledge seems right. Closeting, and the silence that accompanies it, acts as its own sort of discourse. Jews will often remain "silent about their Jewish identity including being silent when someone asks about religion, not responding to anti-Semitic remarks, and being silent when others mention Christian holidays" (Hecht & Faulkner, 2000, p. 377).

Because Jews can often pass as members of the larger American Christian society, disclosing that one is Jewish becomes a large issue. If Jews disclose their core identities to the wrong person, they run the risk of stigma or bodily harm, and of feeling different—and thus, perhaps, inferior—in comparison to the norm. Due to the fear of how others will react to the disclosure of Jewish identity, a Jewish American individual "typically seeks to determine if the other person is Jewish or not, and uses various direct and indirect messages for communicating their own identities" (Hecht & Faulkner, 2000, p. 378). In order to make this determination, American Jews may resort to an extremely vague form of discourse, trying to find out whether their conversational partner is Jewish by dropping hints and references to Judaic customs, rather than just "outing" themselves. They may also pay attention to identity signs displayed by the other participant, including language use (such as the utterance of Yiddish), name, or appearance. Jews tend to closet themselves in order to ward off anti-Semitism, but stereotypical signs such as talking with one's hands or being argumentative might tip off the conversation partner (Hornstein, 2002).

One of the most frequent causes of disclosure is hearing an anti-Semitic remark, or a mention of the Holocaust, prompting Jewish individuals to defend themselves and their people (Hecht & Faulkner, 2000). At the same time, the same remark may also result in a further withdrawal into the closet: "The ownership and control of private information, in this case being Jewish, became salient for participants when they felt vulnerable to attack" (p. 385).

Part of being an "other" in American society means that one must participate in the discourse of the majority (Gilman, 1986). This increases the self-awareness—and awareness of difference—felt by the American Jew. Operating within the discourse of the reference group brings with it a perceived mockery of speaking differently (or Jewishly), and this mockery further leads to a sense of discomfort with one's differences, acceptance/acknowledgment of perceived stereotypes, and self-mockery. Operating within the discourse of the majority—as disempowered Others—means that Jews have long been associated with numerous, frequently damaging stereotypes. Among the many common negative—and not necessarily accurate or realistic—stereotypes associated with American Jews are "cunning," "unscrupulous,"

"money-hungry," "manipulating," "garish," "parasitic," "wimpy," "unethical," "neurotic," "unbalanced," "sexually insecure," "ostentatious," and fallibly "clever" (Desser & Friedman, 1993). As they put it, "This catalog of 'the Jew who' seems almost endless—and almost always in bad taste" (p. 149). It is very important to note here that being Jewish *in no way* means that Jewish individuals act this way in actuality. Jewish individuals are not more or less likely to be greedy or wimpy than individuals from any other racial or ethnic group. The very real problem is, however, that stereotypes act as an expectation; Jewish individuals are supposed or expected to act a certain way simply by dint of being Jewish, and any character flaw is magnified as being a signifier of this ethnicity.

One of the most common and well-known features of American Jewish discourse, and one that also seems to thrive on mockery and a lack of comfort in the larger society, is humor. Jewish Americans very frequently enact their identity through humorous discourse. Not only has humor become one of those signs associated with Jewishness, it has also been used for as long as Judaism has been in existence to ward off anti-Semitism.

Jewish Humor and More

Leo Rosten said that "In nothing is Jewish psychology so vividly recalled as in Jewish jokes" (In Harris & Rabinovitch, 1988, p. ix). From George Burns to Woody Allen, Billy Crystal to Sascha Baron-Cohen, Rodney Dangerfield to Jerry Seinfeld, Gilda Radner to Sarah Silverman, Judaism has defined, and been defined by humor. Jewish humor has become mainstream American humor, and "the Jewish style, with its heavy reliance upon Yiddish and Yiddishisms has emerged not only as *a* comic style, but as *the* prevailing comic style," adding new life to American culture (Bloom, 2001, p. 1). As Jewish humorists became popular, they spoke not only for Jewish Americans, but for *all* Americans. Their humor resulted in a mainstream embrace of characteristically Jewish speaking habits, such as "self parody" and "talking back" (Bloom, 2001, p. 4). Additionally, we have begun to witness the common inclusion of Yiddish (the non-religious language of Eastern European Jews) in common American vernacular, with words such as "schmuck," "chutzpah," and "klutz" being used by gentiles and

Jews alike. In the public mind, Judaism is frequently equated with funniness. Rabbi Joseph Telushkin confirms this, noting that "the long-standing Jewish prominence in American comedy—over the past forty years, some 80 percent of the country's leading comics have been Jews—suggests that Jewish humor has a broad-based appeal" (Telushkin, 1992, p. 19).

What, then, *is* Jewish humor? First, there is a sense that to be defined as true Jewish humor, it must come from Jews: "Jewish jokes are only those which are told by Jews to other Jews. Non-Jews tell jokes about Jews" (Silberman-Federman, 1995, p. 214). There is the discomforting feeling that any joke about Jews, but not *from* Jews is anti-Semitic: "A Jewish joke then is both developed and defined by Jews, while an anti-Semitic joke is manufactured and presented by non-Jews" (Silberman-Federman, 1995, p. 214). Like all ethnic jokes, there is a big difference between those told by insiders and those told by outsiders: in-group members tend to see jokes made by themselves as creating a sense of unity and solidarity, and stemming from shared experience, whereas those told by out-group members create a feeling as if they are spawned by fear or hatred: "What makes a joke Jewish? Obviously, it must apply to Jews, but more significantly, it must express a Jewish sensibility. Merely giving individuals in a joke Jewish names, or ascribing the joke to Jewish characters, does not a Jewish joke make" (Telushkin, 1992, p. 16). Ethnic humor toes the line between insight and prejudice, and should meet four general guidelines: one should be comfortable relating the humor to a member of the group of whom it makes fun; insiders should find it as funny as do outsiders; outsiders should be extremely careful relating ethnic jokes with scathing punch lines so as not to demean or hurt others; and members of ethnic groups should be treated as individuals, not stereotypes.

Given the Jews' unpleasant history (from the Spanish inquisition to the Holocaust, and beyond), it seems amazing that they are able to see the humor in anything, let alone be known as the masters of the genre: "The air is full of jokes and it is surprising how many of them have a vaguely Jewish flavour . . . Yet there is little in Jewish experience, and even less in Jewish tradition, to dispose one to laughter" (Bermant, 1986, p. 2). Absurd Jewish humor "often falls into the category of 'laughing in order not to cry'" (Telushkin, 1992, p. 56). The existence of Jewish humor defies

logic—but, then, so does the continued survival of the Jewish people. Every era has brought a new enemy hoping to blot out Judaism and the Jews. Sigmund Freud might have figured out how this history of pain could result in so much laughter; he posited that humor involves the transference of pain and suffering into a pleasant experience. He also noted that all Jewish humor involves self-deprecation in some form (Silberman-Federman, 1995).

Self-deprecating humor is one of the hallmarks of the Jews: "The simple fact is that Jews laugh at everything . . . but most of all they laugh at themselves . . . Jews may have extravagant expectations of everyone, but they have impossible expectations of themselves, and are fiercely, relentlessly, masochistically self-critical" (Bermant, 1986, p. 242). This tendency toward masochism can find its roots in the painful history (and modern "othering") of the Jews: "The seclusion, poverty, absence of opportunity, and bitterness of life in the ghetto certainly favored psychic masochism; so did the persecution and the bias encountered outside the ghetto" (Juni & Katz, 2001, p. 121).

While humor as a means of self-infliction seems to be one of the major purposes of humor as discourse for Jews, the main purpose is even more intertwined with the "othering" effect of Judaism. Humor is the primary means of self-protection and warding off anti-Semitism. Partially, humor might be seen as making the Jew more palatable to the reference group: "The clown, provided of course he is sufficiently amusing, is forgiven everything, even—when necessary—his Jewishness. Humour is not only an acceptable way of conveying unacceptable truths, it renders the conveyor himself acceptable" (Bermant, 1986, p. 3).

Modern American Jews use humor to protect themselves in a society in which they are the "other": "The joke thus reveals the truth of the language of the Jews, that it is a weapon they use to defend themselves against the attacks of the Christian world" (Bermant, in Silberman-Federman, 1995, p. 219). This tactic is analogous to the Abbot and Costello episode in which Abbot chases Costello with a bat, but when he is caught, Costello takes the bat and hits himself on the head. Then, lying prostrate on the floor, Costello looks up at Abbot and says, "What are you going to do to me now?" (Juni & Katz, 2001). Only by laughing at themselves do Jews become less vulnerable to the laughter and hostility of the other.

Self-directed humor is not only a discursive tactic for protecting oneself from one's aggressor, but it also may be used as a tactic for gaining the upper hand (Juni & Katz, 2001). As noted previously, Jews have gained a unique and privileged status as the funny "other." In addition, a victim who laughs instead of crying snatches victory from the attacker. Once Jews are able to laugh at themselves and, in so doing, ward off the blows of others, they can show up their attacker, and, indeed, mock the entire world.

The other aspect of intercultural communication in which Jews tend to stand apart—and through which they have established themselves as a model minority—is their concentration and emphasis on family and education. The family is the centerpiece of Jewish society (Donin, 1972), and it is no mistake that one of the Ten Commandments—a cornerstone of Jewish society throughout the ages—is to honor one's parents. Additionally, the Torah and the Talmud both place a great deal of emphasis on love between parents, and on passing that love down generation to generation (Telushkin, 1994). Indeed, having a family is seen as life's greatest accomplishment: "A good child is a great gift—and, for a Jew, all the vindication one's life ever needs" (Borowitz, 1984). Jewish parents—and mothers in particular—are known for showing extraordinary concern for their children, and for erring on the side of overprotection. This tendency to do the best by one's own children, unfortunately, has manifested itself in the negative stereotype of the over-protective, nagging, and self-effacing Jewish mother.

Part of family life in American Jewish society and communication is the concentration on education. As Rabbi Israel ben Joseph Alnakawa argued, "A man [sic] should honor his father and mother more for the moral instruction they gave him, than for their having brought him into this world" (in Telushkin, 1994, p. 153). For Jewish individuals and families, education is more about training a child for living, not just for a livelihood (Donin, 1972). Education is of top priority in Jewish American society. In fact, in Jewish society the rabbi has a larger obligation to teach his or her community than to be a religious leader. As a result of the extremely high importance placed on education, a disproportionately large number of Jewish Americans have prestigious jobs, such as doctor, lawyer, and politician. Again, however, because of this success, many stereotypes about Jews as money-hungry and ethically-questionable have

surfaced, and have fueled the Jewish humor noted earlier: "In humor about Jews, no area is more sensitive than jokes about business practices and ethics. Indeed, were it not for such jokes, there would be almost no humor offensive to Jews" (Telushkin, 2000, p. 64).

CONCLUSION

The history of Jews in America, and of Jews throughout the world, has not always been an easy one. For various reasons, Jews have often encountered hatred and prejudice. Finally, in America, Jews have become a respected minority. Even here, however, it is not always comfortable being Jewish; hate and ignorance often makes living as a Jewish individual uneasy.

Struggling to become both white and American has shaped how Jews view themselves, and how they are viewed by others. Depending on societal constructs, the situation in which they find themselves, and the perceptions of individuals, Jewishness can alternatively be racial, ethnic, or religious. Defining oneself as Jewish also necessarily means comparing and contrasting oneself to other religions, races, and ethnicities, and often setting up boundaries.

Becoming white and American has also involved the struggle between maintaining a sense of Jewishness and assimilating into the larger American, Christian culture. Part of retaining this Jewishness and communicating it often involves, ironically, silence. Jewish individuals often closet their Jewishness, choosing to acculturate into society as a whole; this closeting is often necessary to make differences less obvious, and make safety and comfort a possibility.

One of the common means of communication by which Jewish individuals have set themselves apart as distinct, yet imbued the larger society with Jewishness and become accepted is humor. Jewish humor serves to make uncomfortable experiences more pleasant, attack society-at-large in order to diffuse tension, and make Jews less worthy of assault. Attacking oneself makes one not only less vulnerable, but also—finally—more accepted.

References

Amyot, R., & Sigelman, L. (1996). Jews without Judaism? Assimilation and Jewish identity in the United States. *Social Science Quarterly, 77*(3), 176–189.

Arendt, H. (1978). *The Jew as pariah: Jewish identity and politics in the modern age.* New York: Grove Press.

Arnow, D. (1994, Fall). Toward a psychology of Jewish identity: A multidimensional approach. *Journal of Jewish Communal Service,* 29–36.

Baldwin, J. (1984, April) On being "white" and other lies. *Essence,* 90–92.

Berger, A. A. (1997). *The genius of the Jewish joke.* Northvale, NJ: Jason Aronson.

Bermant, C. *What's the joke?: A study of Jewish humour through the ages.* London: Weidenfeld and Nicolson.

Bhabha, H. K. (1996). "The other question: Difference, discrimination, and the discourse of colonialism." In H. A. Baker, Jr., M. Diawara, & R. H. Lindeborg (Eds.), *Black British cultural studies: A reader* (pp. 87–106). Chicago: The University of Chicago Press.

Bloom, J. D. (2000). *Gravity fails: The comic Jewish shaping of modern America.* Westport, CT: Praeger.

Borowitz, E. B. (1984). *Liberal Judaism.* New York: Union of American Hebrew Congregations.

Brodkin, K. (2004). *How Jews became white folks and what that says about race in America.* New Brunswick, NJ: Rutgers University Press.

Cohen, S. M., & Eisen, A. M. (2000). *The Jew within: Self, family and community in America.* Bloomington: Indiana University Press.

Desser, D., & Friedman, L. D. (1993). *American-Jewish filmmakers: Traditions and trends.* Urban: University of Illinois Press.

Donin, Rabbi H. H. (1972). *To be a Jew: A guide to Jewish observance in contemporary life.* New York: Basic Books.

Federal Bureau of Investigations, Department of Justice. (2004). Crime in the United States 2004. Retrieved June 21, 2006, from at http://www.fbi.gov/ucr/cius_04/

Gabler, N. (1988). *An empire of their own: How the Jews invented Hollywood.* New York: Crown Publishers.

Gilman, S. (1986). *Jewish self-hatred: Anti-Semitism and the secret language of the Jews.* Baltimore: Johns Hopkins University Press.

Gilman, S. (2003). *Jewish frontiers: Essays on bodies, histories, and identities.* New York: Palgrave Macmillan.

Gordis, D. (1995). Rethinking America's hospitality: New challenges to American Jewish identity. *Jewish Spectator, 60*(2), 5–11.

Hall, S. (1996). Race, articulation, and societies structure in discourse. In Houston A. Baker, Jr., Manthia Diawara, & Ruth H. Lindeborg (Eds.), *Black British cultural studies: A reader* (pp. 16–60). Chicago: University of Chicago Press.

Harris, D., & Rabinovitch, I. (1988). *The jokes of oppression: The humor of Soviet Jews.* Northvale, NJ: Jason Aronson.

Hecht, M., & Faulkner, S. (2000). Sometimes Jewish, sometimes not: The closeting of Jewish American identity. *Communication Studies, 51*(4), 372–387.

Hecht, M., Faulkner, S. , Meyer, C., Niles, T.A., Golden, D., & Cutler, M. (2002, December). Looking through *northern exposure* at Jewish American identity and the communication theory of identity. *Journal of Communication, 52*(4), 852–869.

Hornstein, G. (2002). The risks of silence, or how I went to England and disappeared in plain sight. *The Chronicle of Higher Education,* 17–22.

Jackson, R. L. (1999). *The negotiation of cultural identity.* Westport, CT: Praeger Press.

Jackson, R. L. (2006). *Scripting the Black masculine body: Identity, discourse and racial politics in popular media.* Albany, NY: SUNY Press.

Jacobson, M. F. (1998). *Whiteness of a different color: European immigrants and the alchemy of race.* Cambridge, MA: Harvard University Press.

Juni, S., & Katz, B. (2001). Self-effacing wit as a response to oppression: Dynamics in ethnic humor. *The Journal of General Psychology, 128*(2), 119–143.

Kauffman, G., & Raphael, L. (1987). Shame: A perspective on Jewish identity. *Journal of Psychology and Judaism, 11*(1), 30–40.

National Desk. (1998, April 30). *Los Angeles Times,* A6.

Lott, E. (1993). *Love and theft: Blackface minstrelsy and the American working class.* New York: Oxford University Press.

Medding, P. (1987). Segmented ethnicity and the new Jewish politics. In L. Frankel (Ed.), *Studies in contemporary Jewry* (vol. 7, pp. 26–39). Jerusalem: Institute of Contemporary Jewry, the Hebrew University Press.

Morrison, T. (1993). On the backs of Blacks. *Time, 142*(21), 57. Jerusalem: Institute of Contemporary Jewry, the Hebrew University Press.

Rogin, M. (1996). *Blackface, white noise: Jewish immigrants in the Hollywood melting pot.* Berkeley, CA: University of California Press.

Rogin, M. (1998). Black sacrifice, Jewish redemption: From Al Jolson's *Jazz Singer* to John Garfield's *Body and Soul.* In V.P. Franklin, N. L. Grant, H. M. Kletnick, & G. R. McNeil (Eds.), *African Americans and Jews in the twentieth century: Studies in convergence and conflict.* Columbia: University of Missouri Press.

Rosen, S. (1995). *Jewish identity and identity development.* New York: American Jewish Committee.

Schoem, D. (1998). Learning to be a part-time Jew. In W. P. Zenner, *Persistence and flexibility: Anthropological perspectives on the American Jewish experience.* New York: State University of New York Press.

Silberman-Federman, N. J. (1995, Spring). Jewish humor, self-hatred, or anti-Semitism: The sociology of Hanukkah cards in America. *Journal of Popular Culture, 28*(4), 211–238.

Sorin, G. (1993). Not by ethnicity alone: A search for meaning in American Jewish identity. *Reviews in American History, 21,* 190–194.

Taylor, C. (1994). The politics of recognition. In C. Taylor, K. A. Appiah, J. Habermas, S. C. Rockefeller, M. Walzer, & S. Wolf, *Multiculturalism: Examining the politics of recognition* (pp. 25–73). Princeton, NJ: Princeton University Press.

Telushkin, Rabbi J. (1992). *Jewish humor: What the best Jewish jokes say about the Jews.* New York: William Morrow. Telushkin, Rabbi J. (1994). *Jewish wisdom: Ethical, spiritual, and historical lessons from the great works and thinkers.* New York: William Morrow.

Toll, W. (1997). Horace M. Kallen: Pluralism and American Jewish identity. *American Jewish History,* 57–74.

Wertheimer, J. (1993). *A people divided: Judaism in contemporary America.* New York: BasicBooks.

West, C., & Lerner, M. (1995). *Jews and Blacks: Let the healing begin.* New York: Putnam Publishing.

Concepts and Questions

1. What is assimilation? Can you think of any examples in society, or in your own life?
2. What is acculturation? Can you think of any examples in society, or in your own life?
3. What qualifies as a Jewish joke?
4. How does humor serve to protect the Jews?
5. How does Jewishness connect to a label of "race?"
6. How did minstrelsy lead to the eventual acceptance of Jews as white, and as a model minority?
7. What are some ways in which being a minority in the United States might be different for Jewish Americans than for, for instance, Asian Americans or African Americans?
8. Can you think of ways in which ethnicity and/or race is flexible?
9. Christmas is often a difficult time for Jewish Americans. Why do you think this might be?
10. What are some ways in which positive aspects of Jewish life have fueled negative stereotypes?

Living Within Whiteness: A Project Aimed at Undermining Racism

JOHN T. WARREN

INTRODUCTION

In 1995, I took a feminist theory course at my undergraduate university. It was the final requirement in my women's studies minor, a set of courses I took primarily because as a man in this society I desired a more full understanding of how my gender worked to privilege me, even in ways not immediately apparent to me. In that course, I was introduced to Ruth Frankenberg's (1993) impressive book *White Women, Race Matters: The Social Construction of Whiteness.* While I found much of interest in that book for my study of feminism and my own male privilege, I discovered a question—a project—that would serve as the site for the first part of my research career (Warren, 2003). The idea of whiteness, much like the idea of my maleness, would force me to ask about how privilege worked in and through my body, even in ways that I couldn't readily see or imagine.

In this brief essay, I want to reflect on the whiteness project—to ask how this research frames white identity and white people's responsibility within conversations and debates on racism in the United States (and, as Raka Shome, 1999 reminds us, the majority of the Westernized world). Further, I want to highlight some major contributions communication scholars have provided to this project. This will provide an opportunity to examine the central question whiteness scholars are asking today: how do we keep in tension questions of the individual actor in culture and the cultural systems that constitute the individual actor? This

This original essay appears here in print for the first time. All rights reserved. Permission to reprint must be obtained from the author and the publisher. Dr. John T. Warren teaches communication pedagogy at Southern Illinois University, Carbondale, Illinois.

system-individual has been a major issue since Peggy McIntosh (1997) demanded we talk about it in her early essay "White Privilege, Male Privilege." Thus, the final portion of this essay asks about the future of the whiteness project and where students of intercultural communication might take this research in the future.

THE WHITENESS PROJECT: IDENTITY OR SOCIAL STRUCTURE

In the intercultural communication course I teach, I often begin class conversations with structure, asking students to see how communication functions to create structures that frame, and in some ways determine, how we live our lives. One need only look to grammar as a system to see how structures determine how we move through the world—random words without grammatical structure are nonsensical; they do not help us as we do our daily activities. Grammar is but one structure that rules, much like the subject-verb-object rules of grammar itself, our daily interactions. But grammar is not the only structure that rules our communication with others. Indeed, we live with and under all sorts of cultural and social rules. From how to talk to a professor to how one interacts with people who are different than us, we come to see communication as a rule-bound structure, taught to us from birth. Early on in my own childhood, I was carefully taught how to be a good person, how to be a man, and as I have come to understand, I was taught how to enact race, even if those rules were never stated as such. But how I was taught to walk down the street, understand my worth, and how to understand my relationship to others in a way that was highly marked and coded by race. My whiteness, my white skin in a world that privileges such things, was taught to me in very careful ways.

Yet, as I remind my students, to blame social structure alone—those multiple sites in which I was learning my whiteness—is to forget how social structure gets there in the first place. Indeed, it is in the minor moments (a comment from my mother, a television show, a news story, a novel in my English class) in which these structures are built. Like grains of sand, these moments build on top of one another and with pressure and time come to take on the appearance of rock. Looking at a rock outside of historical context, one sees only smooth surfaces, feels the hard textures, and senses the weight; however, seen in historical context, sedimentary rock is only the grains of sand under pressure and time. The rock is only what the individual grains had generated. And so is my whiteness, generated through my ancestors and repeated over time, an outcome of social norms and social practices. The acts themselves, the moments of entering a mall and not getting followed as an elementary example, build on top of those other grains and produce the rock of race, the appearance of something that somehow exists outside of everyday actions.

But making this case in class can be tough—race is both social structure and individual actions. It is both—and that is what makes talking about whiteness so hard, so difficult. As a teacher, my first response is to do two seemingly opposite things: tell people to change their everyday actions and at the same time tell them to understand that their individual actions are not the cause or end of racism in this country. It feels like a trap. And this is what makes whiteness—the idea of racial privilege—so hard to discuss. Whiteness, like any racial category, is slippery (Johnson, 2003). It shifts as soon as you think you have a grasp of what it can do.

Simply put: Whiteness is both an identity and a social structure—it is both who I am (or who I have been constituted as, in those moments of learning during my lifetime) and the structure of power which privileges me, makes me the benefactor of power in unseen (to me) ways. To talk about whiteness as only structure or only identity is to forget the complicated nature of how race works in the United States. The work on whiteness has a long history, chronicled at least in part by Roediger's (1998) collection *Black on White*, and can be traced to early conversations about skin politics and cultural power. White scholars, however, have recently taken up charges by bell hooks (1990) and others to investigate how whiteness marks our lives. Indeed, since that time, hundreds of articles, books, conference papers, and videos have been generated to tackle this thing called whiteness. By way of brief summary, I will return to a logic of organizing the literature that I created some time ago as I think it still offers a heuristic way of imagining the work being done in this field (Warren, 1999).

First, several scholars have engaged in what I call Whiteness as Anti-Racist Practice. In this set of writings, scholars seek to deconstruct whiteness, to see its logics and power, in an effort to undermine it. For instance, in Frankenberg's (1993) *White Women, Race Matters* we see an effort to locate in women's everyday talk the logics of racism, the ways people understand their whiteness. Also, in Peggy McIntosh's (1997) early work, she offered a listing of privileges that she receives as a result of her race privilege. In Christine Sleeter's (1996) work in education studies, she offers a way of thinking about multicultural education that works against white supremacy and dominance in the classroom. Each of these complicated and important studies offers a peek at how whiteness functions with the sole purpose of undermining, of calling it out, of asking readers to pause and reconsider our actions as implicated people in the world. While not necessarily citing Freire's (1992) oft quoted "Changing our language is part of the process of changing the world" (p. 74), this work asks us to understand how racism is perpetuated, while also providing the possibility and hope for change.

Second, multiple scholars have looked to various texts (film, television, and other textual cites like scholarship) to see how in our own writing and in our cultural/historical texts, we have perpetuated whiteness. Harris (1998), in a very powerful analysis of U.S. legal history, analyzes how whiteness was conceived in early U.S. law as property, as something a person could count on as a form of currency. Toni Morrison's (1992) *Playing in the Dark* is a masterful piece on the role of whiteness metaphors in literature. In her work, she reveals how major novels like *Moby Dick* have generated decades of cumulative power in the racial imagination, affecting how people even understand the terms "white" and "black." This was built on by Richard Dyer's (1988) work "White" which examines film texts and uncovers how metaphors of color have been played out in film. In all of these studies, the authors allow access to how race is repeated within these texts to recreate whiteness.

Third, rhetorical scholars have busily worked to establish an impressive body of literature examining whiteness as a rhetorical location. Here, the focus on discursive constructions of whiteness has generated a powerful way of seeing whiteness in and through our everyday talk. Most notable is Nakayama and Krizek's (1995) essay "Whiteness: A Strategic Rhetoric," in which the authors extract the major identifier labels white students use to describe themselves. In this work, they can see how the use of "majority" or

"American" works to recreate whiteness as a privileged location. From this work, Crenshaw (1997) and Shome (1996) each produced essays that worked with these ideas of racial privilege embedded in everyday talk. Nakayama and Martin's (1999) *Whiteness: The Communication of a Racial Identity* brought together multiple rhetoricians on the topic. In other fields, scholars like Staub (1997) and Chambers (1997) have added to this body of literature.

The fourth and final general trend in the literature is Whiteness as a Performative Accomplishment, seeking to uncover how whiteness is produced through discourse over time in ways that produce bodies—that is, asking how our communicative norms produce the rules and practices that govern how bodies are reproduced. This is where I have spent the majority of my time (Warren, 2001a, 2001b, 2003). In my work, I have tried to understand how race is not located in the body (in my white body)—but rather, my white body stands as a result of multiple racist practices. That is, the social norms that have produced my body were determined by the norms that produced my grandparents' and my parents' bodies. Those norms also produced the body of my son who is now implicated in a system he did not design but will nonetheless benefit from. Others in this area of study are Butler (1993), Cooks (2003), and several others who are featured in a new book on whiteness and performance (Cooks & Simpson, in press).

WHITENESS: MAJOR CONTRIBUTIONS FROM COMMUNICATION

It is probably best to ask someone who is not a communication scholar what communication truly offers to the study of whiteness. Perhaps, I and others in the field of intercultural communication might be biased when we (or I) say that communication research has changed the conversation in whiteness studies. We have done so by forcing a more complicated relationship between identity and bodies, between communication and the institutionalized nature of racial power in the United States. A good example of this is the debate between those who desire to divorce the discursive power of whiteness (norms of talk, language structures, and interaction styles) from white bodies (individuals who may or may not participate in racism). The principal author in this debate, for me, is Annlouise Keating (1995) who works diligently to separate whiteness from white people: "The fact that a person is born with 'white' skin does not necessarily mean that s/he will think, act, and write in the 'white' ways" (p. 907). Keating is, in many ways, correct—the structure of power in which her and my body lives within is not the same as our everyday practices. Certainly, I can look at my body of work and my interactions with students and friends and strangers and say that I've tried not to repeat the racism I know to be so embedded in me. I can do my best, knowing that I may not be aware of the many ways I do whiteness without knowing it. But conflating the two does not help our understanding of racism and power. In this way, Keating is correct.

Yet, one must never imagine the picture (clean divisions between systems of race and those who benefit from them) is so easy. In a powerful response, Dreama Moon (1999), a communication scholar, reminds us that while whiteness and white people are not the same, they are not so easily distinguishable either. Indeed, they are woven together in powerful ways:

> While I agree that it is important not to conflate [whiteness and white people], I would argue that it is politically unwise to pretend that white *people* somehow are not implicated in the everyday production and reproduction of 'whiteness.' (p. 179)

With Moon's correction, we have just a glance of how intercultural communication scholars have made a difference in this conversation.

In another important dialogue on whiteness, education and social activist authors have sought to create an abolitionist project for whiteness, calling on everyday (white) people to enact treason to whiteness, to deny those privileges that whiteness grants (see Ignatiev & Garvey, 1996; McLaren, 1999). These so-called "race traitors" advocate turning one's back to whiteness in solidarity with people of color who do not receive the same advantages. They call upon notions of performance, asking people to "do brownness" in an effort to reject the power of whiteness (McLaren, 1999). Communication scholars have retorted back, reminding us that we must be much more careful with such terms, for the logic of abolitionist projects is loaded (Moon & Flores, 2000)

and the use of performance is often offered without careful application and understanding of the term and its history (Warren, 2001b).

These are just two ways that communication scholars are working to contribute to the field. But the central addition to advancing debates on whiteness and anti-racism I would argue is the careful analysis and study of communication in everyday contexts. In so much of the literature on whiteness, the discussion reads as if one's identity (that is, their whiteness) is a given; they fail to see the major corrective that intercultural communication insists upon. That is, many scholars fail to note how identity is created in the first place. This is where communication scholars shine the brightest, for it is within the logic of communication—the idea that one's self is a product of their (and others') communication over time—where we even begin to understand how identity is formed. By analyzing communication (between people, over time, via multiple formats and venues), we are able to see the messages that form decisions that produce identity.

An example: consider the movie *Crash*, the blockbuster film set in Los Angeles that discusses prejudice and the effect of racism on the lives of a series of individuals. In this movie, Sandra Bullock, when faced with the presence of two black men on an open street, pulls her purse to her chest, probably unconsciously, to protect it. In this moment, one can see how communication constitutes identity—hers, as a possible victim, and the black men, as possible victimizers. Yet, that act alone is not sufficient to produce identity. Sandra Bullock's character did not invent this moment for it is widely available in a multitude of contexts. In media and everyday contexts, this moment is repeated, re-done, re-said through nonverbals (looks, expressions, movements, and adjustments of space). And in this moment, this remaking of potential victim and potential victimizer, race is recreated, for race (and racialized gender) is exactly the message that is produced, not only for the characters, but the millions of audience members who bought their tickets to see *Crash*. So this moment, if not examined in communication terms, can seem like an act of racism, these identities playing out their script. However, with communication as the center, we see that it is the script (and the repeating of the script) that makes the identities possible. For how can we understand race without the communicative cues that mark Sandra Bullock a white woman in need of protection and the two black men as raced figures in need of being protected against?

Communication, as shown previously, allows you to see how identities come to be and not take their status for granted. That is, within a communicative frame one sees that identity is produced through communication, made possible within our everyday interactions. The consideration of interaction as productive is not entirely new (we often note in communication classes that when we talk or when we gesture that meaning is made); what is new is that we often consider the self to be the maker of that communication and of that meaning. The radical shift that innovative communication theory allows for is that it is the communicators that are created in these moments.

WHITENESS: IDENTITY AND SOCIAL STRUCTURE

I began this essay by asking whether whiteness was an identity or social structure. I suggested that it is both—indeed, here I want to take that issue up to a larger extent. In this section, I want to draw greater connections between whiteness as an identity and whiteness as a social structure that guides and directs one's actions. My hope here is to explain how and in what ways they co-construct each other—that is, the way identity and structure occur and are made at the same time. In order to do so, I will examine a moment of my own life and try to unpack how whiteness was produced. To be clear, this moment is not an extreme example, though the analytical process would likely be the same if it were. Rather, I use a more mundane, everyday moment to show how communication need not be extraordinary to make a big difference.

The moment: I was in my office talking with a colleague and, like so many other professors have before, we covered the major things we always talk about: our latest faculty meeting, the new memo from the Dean's office, and, of course, our students. In our talk of our students, we begin talking about a favorite student of mine—he is a young black student of ours, a good student with a kind of dedication we both enjoy. He is in both of our classes and doing well, but we both note a weakness in his writing, a kind

of failure to understand the basic principles of constructing traditional argument. His form is off, as he struggles to get the principles of APA citation correct or build a traditional argument, or write the clear literature review we desire. We both note this and comment that we hope he finds his footing before the ground swallows him. After my fellow professor leaves my office I turn to the stack of papers on my desk and while I have to read them before class, I'm distracted, thinking of this student, his brilliant ideas, and my concerns about his writing. I also begin to wonder why I never find myself this distracted by my students who know the form and continue to repeat the same story over and over again. That is, here is this amazing student with these amazing ideas and I'm obsessed with the structure of his ideas, not the ideas themselves. And like so many of my students who turn in the most beautiful prose that says nothing in particular, I (many times) fail to wonder about the absence of ideas in light of easily readable writing.

This moment is not spectacular—it fails to capture the attention and does not really suggest the kind of drama that burning crosses and riots might create. This moment is more likely to be the kind of thing anyone can foster into his or her memory. It happens in multiple contexts, differently to be sure, but the script is repeated: questions about person X, a person of color (most often black) followed by questions of form over structure. They are often coded in the seemingly complimentary beginning ("she is so articulate") but closely followed by the hitch ("you'd never guess. . ."). So here is this moment—what does it say about the relationship between whiteness and the identity/structure conversation at hand?

I begin by noting that my colleague and I are both white—that is, we both identify as white people and our skin is marked by so many privileges. We both have enjoyed the invisibility of white skin, never having to account for race since it never mattered to us. Of course, this is juxtaposed to our student's body, which is not white and has never "enjoyed" the luxury of invisibility (most assuredly within this predominantly white university). During this conversation, in which we are basking in our institutional privilege that allows us to critique and discuss this student of color, we carefully work (with the best of intentions) to individualize this student—it is his inabilities we are noting, not (1) our own; (2) the institutions; or (3) the norms that have created the standards we are so vigorously trying to protect. That is, it is significant that our critique falls upon this student without any questions of the origins of the critique. Our position is clear—we are professors and we knowingly evaluate others. He, the student, is the one who fails or succeeds in meeting our expectations. This movement is not only about diverting attention away from us and our own location within social structures, but is really about individualizing this student, ripping him from this academic context. That is, he stands on his own. This is significant because it is quite powerful to remove a person from context. His writing, in this way, is not about failing to meet our expectations and assumptions about what writing should be like, but about failing to meet the institutional norms my colleague and I protect. It is complicated, this moment. We both want him to succeed, even as we hold up the norms that make his success questionable.

What does this say about whiteness? In this moment, whiteness can be seen as social structure. That is, whiteness serves as the overarching structure under which both my colleague and I operate, as well as the system of power this student understands he must negotiate. Whiteness guides my understandings of proper writing, undergirds my evaluative comments, and allows me to see this student outside any context and/or cultural tradition he might treasure. Whiteness structures the educational system that we all function within, even if our skin is not white. Whiteness is coded in the language choices we use and the academic language we use to try to communicate, even across our differences. Whiteness structures the larger world, the larger picture of government, entertainment, and education generally. Whiteness has created who I am, who I will become, and how I will see myself. It is the water that surrounds the fish, the air that surrounds the nose; whiteness serves as the social rules that permeate the way I move down the hallway or across the street. Whiteness is the structure.

Yet, whiteness is not a rulebook or an essential characteristic that we all "just have," regardless of how much it might seem like it. Rather, whiteness exists in the small repeated ways we do our lives, complete our speech, and live our lives. Whiteness is recreated as we move down the hallways or the street—the doing of it remakes the idea of whiteness.

It makes the identity of whiteness possible. We make ourselves, each of us, in the acts of our everyday interactions. In this way, whiteness is an identity—one created and recreated many times without our direct knowledge or consent. In the example earlier, it is not my colleague and I who invent whiteness—but we remake it in our talk, in our evaluation, and in our unreflective support of the system of whiteness. Whiteness is not ours alone, but we have done our part.

And so, whiteness is both. It is a structure, but one recreated through each of our everyday actions; on the other hand, whiteness is an identity recreated through each of our everyday actions. And because it is both, it makes it hard to pinpoint with any ease or reliability.

WHITENESS: THE FUTURE OF A QUESTION

I end here with a brief note on the future of the whiteness question. I'm often asked, "Where is this area of research going and how will communication lead the way?" I offer here three directions that I suspect will become the eventual outcomes of this work.

First, research in whiteness and cultural power will continue. Simply said, the studies that have been done thus far in the field of communication (as well as education, sociology, and cultural studies, to name a few) have only suggested the depth of the problem. We have yet to really grasp what is at stake in the whiteness research, much less really construct any coherent response to it. Like so many areas of research, whiteness research suffers from too much research too soon, leaving the field with too much scholarship on the topic—too much doing very similar work. However, this early period of writing is about trying to understand it, getting the basic idea of it, and trying to create a language for talking about it. We are not done with this work—much remains to be said. I think the next great movement in this research is probably going to be inspired (as the initial project was) by scholars of color, pushing white researchers to do better work on the topic. I have faith that when pushed, the research will advance.

Second, privilege research will continue to grow. One might locate whiteness research within the growing literature that examines privilege. Certainly, Peggy McIntosh's (1997) leading research article on white privilege was sparked by her work in women's studies, which has been asking about male privilege for decades. As research grows analyzing issues of class and sexuality, one can see a whole new growth in research from varying perspectives. This is good for us as both a discipline and a culture for, as bell hooks (1990) might ask us to do, we need to radically change how we understand issues of power and oppression. For too long we have allowed these questions to be about those who suffer the pains of oppression and have left the ones who benefit from systems of power unchallenged. By engaging in privilege studies, we might better understand the depths to which whiteness (and heterosexuality, class privilege, etc.) has inscribed how we live our lives.

Third, a critical approach to the changing nature of power will result in/through this research. That is, as we become more comfortable in asking questions about privilege, we will need to account for that comfort. This is to say, we will need to ask questions that go to the heart of our research, questioning the taken-for-granted in our research, and talk about privilege. For instance, in a recent article I co-wrote with Kathy Hytten (Warren & Hytten, 2005), we talk about various positions that individuals take up when faced with research and critical analyses of whiteness. We identified four problematic "faces" or relations to whiteness: The *Torpified* is a position characterized by guilt and fear, leaving the privileged individual paralyzed to act and imagine new ways of moving forward in the world. The *Missionary* is an individual who acts without the proper focus, believing that in his or her own privilege he or she is the one who knows how to "fix" the problem of racism. The *Cynic* is the person who, when faced with the question of racism, fails to see beyond the problem, denying any possibility for change. The final position we found was the *Intellectual*, that figure who turns questions of racism and the problem of privilege into an intellectual game that never allows the work to affect his or her own actions. Each of these shares a number of problems, even as they vary in how they get applied. At the heart of each is an effort to individualize problems of racism, never putting their own complicity and/or participation with racism on the line. Further, each position keeps whiteness and racism stable—even as these positions are *in relation to* whiteness research, they nevertheless remain quite distanced

from allowing that research to affect their actions in ways that are dialogic and progressive.

I end here in much the same way that Kathy and I do in the essay described above—I call for what we named the "Critical Democrat," a position that is reflexive (that is, deeply committed to understanding how racism has marked their lives) and critical (that is, dedicated to a balanced and careful examination that places one's actions and understandings next to the voices and understandings of others). Here, one never assumes their own vision of the world is correct or the only way to understand issues of racism, but rather a position that acknowledges that our understandings are cultural products and therefore always already tainted by our own lived histories and circumstances. To do this, we must understand that whiteness (like any privileged position) is both an identity—who we are (or may be)—as well as a social system that levies power and produces those/our identities. To understand power and privilege within this matrix is to see it as an active process imbued with history and embedded with subjective cultural knowledge.

References

Butler, J. (1993). *Bodies that matter: On the discursive limits of "sex."* NY: Routledge.

Chambers, R. (1997). The unexamined. In M. Hill (Ed.), *Whiteness: A critical reader,* (pp. 187–203). New York: New York University Press.

Cooks, L. (2003). Pedagogy, performance, and positionality: Teaching about whiteness in interracial communication. *Communication Education, 52,* 245–57.

Cooks, L., & Simpson, J. (Eds.) (2007). *Whiteness, pedagogy and performance: Displacing race.* Lanham, MD: Lexington

Crenshaw, C. (1997). Resisting whiteness' rhetorical silence. *Western Journal of Communication, 61,* 253–78.

Dyer, R. (1997). *White.* London: Routledge.

Frankenberg, R. (1993). *White women, race matters: The social construction of whiteness.* Minneapolis: University of Minnesota Press.

Freire, P. (1992). *Pedagogy of hope: Reliving pedagogy of the oppressed.* New York: Continuum.

Harris, C. (1998). Whiteness as property. In D. Roediger (Ed.), *Black on white: Black writers on what it means to be white* (pp. 103–118). New York: Schocken Books.

hooks, b. (1990). *Yearning: Race, gender, and cultural politics.* Boston: South End Press.

hooks, b. (1990). *Yearning: Race, gender, and cultural politics.* New York: Routledge.

Ignatiev, N. & John G. (1996). Abolish the white race: By any means necessary. In N. Ignatiev & John G. (Eds.), *Race traitor*, (pp. 9–14). New York: Routledge.

Johnson, E. P. (2003). *Appropriating Blackness: Performance and the politics of authenticity*. Durham: Duke University Press.

Keating, A. (1995). Interrogating "whiteness," (de)constructing "race." *College English, 57*, 901–18.

McIntosh, P. (1997). White privilege and male privilege: A personal account of coming to see correspondences through work in women's studies. In R. Delgado & J. Stepfanic (Eds.), *Critical white studies: Looking behind the mirror* (pp. 291–99). Philadelphia: Temple University Press.

McLaren, P. (1999). Unthinking whiteness, rethinking democracy: Critical citizenship in gringolandia. In C. Clark & J. O'Donnell (Eds.), *Becoming and unbecoming white: Owning and disowning a racial identity* (pp. 10–55). Westport: Bergin & Garvey.

Moon, D. (1999) White enculturation and bourgeois ideology: The discursive production of "good (white) girls." In T. K. Nakayama & J. Martin (Eds.), *Whiteness: The communication of social identity,* (pp. 177–97). Thousand Oaks, CA: Sage.

Moon, D., & Flores, L. A. (2000). Antiracism and the abolition of whiteness: Rhetorical strategies of domination among "race traitors." *Communication Studies, 5*, 97–115.

Morrison, T. (1992). *Playing in the dark: Whiteness and the literary imagination*. New York: Vintage.

Nakayama, T. K., & Krizek, R. L. (1995). Whiteness: A strategic rhetoric. *Quarterly Journal of Speech, 81*, 291–309.

Nakayama, T. K., & Martin, J. N. (Eds.) (1999). *Whiteness: The communication of social identity* (pp. 107–28). Thousand Oaks, CA: Sage.

Roediger, D. (1998). *Black on white: Black writers on what it means to be white*. New York: Schocken Books.

Shome, R. (1999). Whiteness and the politics of location: Postcolonial reflections. In T. K. Nakayama & J. N. Martin (Eds.), *Whiteness: The communication of social identity* (pp. 107–28). Thousand Oaks, CA: Sage.

Shome, Raka (1996). Race and popular cinema: The rhetorical strategies of whiteness in "City of Joy." *Communication Quarterly, 44*, 502–18.

Sleeter, C. (1996). *Multicultural education as activism*. Albany, NY: SUNY Press.

Staub, M. E. The whitest I: On reading the Hill-Thomas transcripts. In M. Hill (Ed.), *Whiteness: A critical reader,* (pp. 47–62). New York: New York University Press.

Warren, J. T., & Hytten, K. (2004). The faces of whiteness: Pitfalls and the critical democrat. *Communication Education, 53*, 321–339.

Warren, J. T. (1999). Whiteness and cultural theory: Perspectives on research and education. *The Urban Review, 31*, 185–203.

Warren, J. T. (2003). *Performing purity: Whiteness, pedagogy, and the reconstitution of power*. New York: Peter Lang.

Warren, J. T. (2001a). Doing whiteness: On the performative dimensions of race in the classroom. *Communication Education, 50*, 91–108.

Warren, J. T. (2001b). Performing whiteness differently: Rethinking the abolitionist project. *Educational Theory, 51*, 451–67.

Concepts and Questions

1. Do you agree with the author's statement that he is privileged as a result of his gender? Why?

2. What are some of the cultural and social "rules" that influence your daily life? Do they facilitate or hinder your daily activities? How?

3. What does the author mean when he considers his whiteness as "generated through my ancestors and repeated over time, an outcome of social norms and social practices"?

4. As discussed in this essay, how are white skin and the concept of whiteness different?

5. Warren provides an example of whiteness being enacted in the movie *Crash*. Can you think of some examples that you have seen or enacted?

6. How does communication work to produce, sustain, and even change identity?

7. Warren considers whiteness to be both an identity and a social structure. Explain this idea.

8. How does whiteness structure the "larger world, the larger picture of government, entertainment, and education generally".?

The Hybrid Identities of Gender Queer: Claiming Neither/Nor, Both/And

A. L. ZIMMERMAN

PATRICIA GEIST-MARTIN

I'm seven years old and I know what I want. I want my hair short. I want to buy blue corduroys in the boys' clothing department. I want to wear boys' sneakers. And I definitely do not care about the grass stains on my knees from playing ball with the boys at recess. I don't understand why my mother keeps asking me to "wear a dress" and care about how I look. I sit on my panda bear comforter as she stands in my doorway; we go around and around in an endless discussion about my wardrobe. She pleads with great desire. I indignantly resist. I'm perplexed by her troubled response to my choice of what feels comfortable. She leaves defeated.

I win the discussion. Content, I lay out my clothing choice on my small bed; a pair of purple corduroys, a long-sleeved white-buttoned oxford, brown loafers, and the best piece of all, a black clip-on bow tie. Article by article I put on the clothing, feeling victorious, feeling happy. As I finger the bow tie and carefully clip it to both sides of the collar, I feel myself becoming something more, a little bit bigger perhaps. I already know that people look at me and think I'm strange. I don't know why, but I just can't bring myself to wear a dress.

At eight years old I know that people assume I'm a boy. I know this as I contemplate walking into a bathroom with large letters MEN on the door. I'm at an amusement park with my family and I can't find the women's bathroom. I hesitate at the entrance as carnival music fills my ears. I wonder, if I go in, will men scream at me to get out? Will someone come up to me and tell me that I'm a bad girl? Will it be

obvious that I don't have a penis? I look around to make sure my family doesn't see me and walk in past the men standing at urinals to a bathroom stall. I'm afraid to sit down, believing I'll be found out if I do so. I stand in front of the toilet bowl trying to think of a way to urinate standing up without making a mess. I decide to sit down and go as fast as I can. Finished, I open the stall door. I stare at the floor as I walk, and then at my hands as I wash them. A few steps outside of the bathroom I remember to breathe again.

At ten years old, I look like the picture perfect Midwestern boy on the sidewalk waiting for a parade to start. I sit next to my dad in a pair of multicolored boys' swim trunks and a plain green T-shirt. A man he knows comes up to the two of us and starts talking. After a while he asks my dad, "What's your son's name?" My dad chuckles a response, "This is my daughter, Amber." Slightly embarrassed, I hug my knees. The man, trying to recover from what he believes is a wrong assessment, quickly adds, "Well, that won't happen once she gets breasts!" My body gets hot and I want to disappear.

It's four years later and I have breasts. Now, at 14, I am standing in a small, hot, and sweat-filled locker room with 20 other girls. The walls are covered in red, matching the color of our faces as we recover from the basketball game our teams just played against one another. I stand next to my teammates, across the room from the opposing team. As I take off my shorts, revealing a pair of spandex, I hear laughing from across the room. A girl with long dark curly hair scrunches up her face and throws her words at me, "Are those boxers? What are you? Some kind of girl boy?" The other team members continue laughing as I hurriedly grab clothing to cover up. One of my teammates shouts back, "Shut up. She's more of a girl than you'll ever be." Silence fills the room except for the shuffling of clothes and their whispers.

At 17, I stand in line with 70 other female soldiers waiting for a seamstress to measure my body for a dress uniform. Just yesterday we marched more than 12 miles in the early morning summer humidity of Missouri, weapons in hand and packs on our backs. Our line stretches around old office cubicle dividers, a strange kind of maze housed in an old warehouse with no windows. Fans big enough to fill up a double doorway, placed strategically around the maze, ease the scorch of the midday sun. The line moves

This original essay appeared here in print for the first time in the eleventh edition. All rights reserved. Permission to reprint must be obtained from the authors and the publisher. Dr. A. L. Zimmerman teaches in the Department of Speech Communication at Southern Illinois University, Carbondale. Dr. Patricia Geist-Martin teaches in the School of Communication at San Diego State University.

slowly as we all stand in our bras and underwear waiting our turn.

Pockets of women chatter around me as I stand silently, patiently, waiting for my measurements. From a pocket next to me, a woman breaks out of her conversation, suspiciously glancing at my stomach and inquires, "Are you sure you're not a man?" I manage a fatigued shrug, "Yes." The other women around her follow her gaze to my midsection. Baffled, they stand assessing me.

I stand confused by the question. I look down at my stomach, marked by ridges of tightly carved muscle, a result of thousands of basic training sit-ups and push-ups. I look up and then around me at the many women in line. Softer, rounder bodies stand next to my leaner, harder body. The line moves slightly as I continue to mull over myself as aberration.

At 22, my dark auburn hair hangs slightly above my shoulders and my closet is filled with more feminine clothing. I lie in bed with the shades drawn, fearful of the morning light. I consider my four-month depression resulting from my transition to a new city and a new academic graduate program. I want to break free and find my voice. So far, I'm still in the closet in this new place, along with the clothing that I wear in an attempt to "pass" as a "normal," heterosexual, "gender-appropriate" female. I run my fingers through the hair that continually bothers me, the hair that feels so apart from me. I want to cut it all off, be free of the strands that mask my queer movement. I know that if I cut it, the questions will come, and the looks will come. I also know if I cut it, I'll clean out my closet; it will be a kind of cleaning that brings me back to my body and my voice. I decide the time has come. I quickly dress in the dark. I drive to the nearest hair salon and nervously put down my name for a haircut. As I sit waiting, I waver in my decision. Maybe I'm being rash? Maybe I should reconsider? No. I need to cut it off.

A short woman with glasses and a thick Spanish accent calls my name, "Aumbear." I stand and hesitantly walk over to the swiveling seat. She casually asks, "Well, what are we doing today?" I puff up my chest and blurt, "Cutting it all off." With that I sit down, hoping that she does it without question, without trepidation. I can see in her face that she is concerned. After draping me with the hair cape, she selects a scissors from her drawer and worriedly asks me, "How much is cutting it all off?" Gaining steam in my

decision, I assert, "All of it." She winces behind her glasses and turns to a woman cutting hair next to her, "She wants to cut it all off." Losing patience, I want to scream, "Just cut it!" Instead we find middle ground.

She is more comfortable cutting my hair little by little, checking in with me periodically about the length. We start this game, and over and over I affirm, "Yes, shorter." She continues to cut nervously. I can feel myself gaining more and more confidence. I muse, contrary to the story about Sampson in the Bible, in which a man that derives strength from his hair, I gain strength as the hair falls. I do feel more strength as I exit the hair salon. I feel bare, clean to the world and to myself.

* * * * *

These narrative moments chronicle the journey of my gender queer body. It is a journey that offers insight into questions surrounding culture, communication, and identity. I focus my journey around three unfolding layers. First, I relate my gender queer experience to the concept of hybridity. Second, I offer two stories, highlighting my own questioning of identity, and how others question my identity. Lastly, I provide a final reflection on my journey of gender and hybridity.

DISCOVERING THE HYBRIDITY OF GENDER

As the world becomes increasingly globalized, identity becomes an increasingly complex site for understanding communicative interaction. It is in communication that identity is negotiated. Coover and Murphy (2000) find communication as "integral to the ongoing negotiation of self, a process during which individuals are defined by others as they, in turn, define and redefine themselves" (p. 125). When communicating identity, people make choices based on experiences of the body and how their bodies move in social environments (Eisenberg, 2001). Scholars like Bhabha (1994) and Hall (1990) indicate that identity crosses many borders and binaries. Shome and Hegde (2002) suggest that identity is "above all a performative expression of transnational change, an area of imminent concern to communication scholars" (p. 266). They write about the powerful possibilities of understanding the relationship between the hybrid of individual and collective identities.

The concept of hybridity is a fertile site to begin questioning identity. Kraidy (2002) describes the hybrid as "a communicative practice constitutive of, and constituted by, sociopolitical and economic arrangements" (p. 317). These arrangements are often written in and on the body within systems of hegemony. This writing in and on the body discursively situates bodies that exceed binary structures as the "other." It is within this "otherness" that the hybrid is most often explored. This is demonstrated throughout the previous stories: When people are unable to apply a gender language to the body of the person with whom they are communicating, they mark the person with the "other" label.

Hybridity is the coming together of two or more cultural identities and, in this process, offers a third or alternate identity that is often outside of language in that there is no prescriptive way to communicate about an alternate identity. Anzaldua (1987) writes about her experience of hybridity or mestiza, viewing her identity as one that breaks down the subject/object of the flesh, cultivating agency by moving away from dualisms. Bhabha (1994) also marks the hybrid identity as one that moves in a "third space," or beyond socio-cultural dualisms. In the third space, hybrid identity "exceeds the frame of the image, it eludes the eye, evacuates the self as a site of identity and autonomy and—most important—leaves a resistant trace, a stain of the subject, a sign of resistance" (p. 49). The hybrid body enacts resistance by remaining fluid, by challenging the fixity of prescribed identity roles. It is this image of the body that opens up possibilities for revolutionary self-assertiveness of identity (Dash, 1995). For example, in that moment of need when the men's restroom was the only one I could find, I enacted a tentative resistance that carried with it an ever-present feeling of surveillance. Yet I know now what I questioned then: My self-assertiveness to move into spaces limited to only the "appropriate" gender was a mini-revolution aimed at trying on one of my hybrid identities.

In our attempt to understand this idea of revolutionary self-assertiveness, we turn to examining the gender queer, materially marked female body. We extend this examination by locating a gender queer body as a form of hybrid body. Gender queer is a matter of passing through different identities. Bornstein (1998) views gender queering as "when all the mechanical or automatic ways I've developed for dealing with people simply fall aside, or reveal themselves as the bag of tricks I use to grease the social machinery of my interactions" (p. 179). Hybridity functions in a similar way; it is a meshing of identities that demands new ways of communicating about identity, resulting in a transformation of culture and communication. As with the women in the stomach story, when a body does not fit culturally, it is difficult to communicate about it, and offers a fissure in the act of normalizing.

A queer gender body, then, disrupts this binary of all male or all female, creating a dialectical tension that offers a space to explore the temporality of Bhabha's (1994) proposed third space. The tension is created in communicative interactions when assumed gender roles are fragmented or broken. If the queer body or hybrid body cannot be categorized or fixed, it also cannot be regulated. This elusory action, although problematic for many queer bodies, does function as resistance. As Kanneh (1995) points out, "Not only, then, does the representation of the body characteristically oscillate between, and confuse, natural and cultural attributes in discussions of race, but feminine and masculine—or feminist and non-feminist—agency becomes an issue" (p. 348). The story about being able to identify gender by markings such as breasts introduces interesting questions about the identities given to women based on biology, and the ways in which it is acceptable to talk about women's body in our culture.

Another reason for focusing on this kind of queer body is to highlight the beneficial relationship between queer theory and the concept of hybridity. Both theories are concerned with the in-between and resistance; both are concerned with giving voice to muted identities. Yep (2003) situates queer as a worldmaking, an "opening and creation of spaces without a map, the invention and proliferation of ideas without an unchanging and predetermined goal, and the expansion of individual freedom and collective possibilities without the constraints of suffocating identities and restrictive membership" (p. 35). The hybrid identity functions in much the same way within and across cultures.

It is important to recognize that writing about "the queer body" is a different matter from writing about "a queer body" (Gingrich-Philbrook, 2001). In other words, each body discursively moves in and through the world with its own understanding in relation to the larger socio-cultural context. One way to enter the relationship of self and culture in communication is expressing the hybrid body through personal narrative. Personal narratives, according to Langellier (1989), "participate in the ongoing rhythm of people's lives as a reflection of their social organization and cultural values" (p. 261). Engaging in personal narrative highlights the rhythm of stories, a rhythm that forms us, a rhythm we can embody to create new forms. Ellis and Bochner (2000) capture the role of narrative by suggesting that lived experience "both anticipates telling and draws meaning from it. Narrative is both about living and part of it" (p. 746). Personal narrative is a method of inquiry akin to hybridity as it seeks to illuminate the meanings found in the in-between spaces.

* * * * *

The personal narrative I share in this piece is my hybrid body, an experience of female gender queer movement in and through culture. In claiming hybrid status, I make a risky decision. I am a white, American, Western academic, identities that carry privilege in our current cultural structures. I am also a white, American, Western academic who is queer, inhabiting a space that continually works to deconstruct the oppression of my body, in terms of both gender and sexual identity. I desire to contribute to the dialogue surrounding culture, identity, and communication; speaking from my queer body is how I know to participate from an honest and reflective space. My personal queer narrative is how I come to understand the larger socio-cultural phenomenon of hybrid identity, culture, and communication.

GENDER QUEER TRACING

I stare into my small bathroom mirror with a pair of hair clippers in my hand. The night beyond my windows is dark, icy, and silent. Inside, the vapid glow of a bare bulb casts shadows across my reflected image—an image that is no longer familiar to me, an image that often appears unfamiliar to me. As I grip the clippers, I wrestle with the decision to shave off my hair. The length of my hair is already considered short, so shaving it wouldn't be drastic, or would it? I look over at the clock. It reads 2:36 a.m. I take a deep breath and reason that my urge to shave my head must be connected to some late-night delirium. I think about putting the clippers away and fading

into the dark of my apartment to sleep peacefully with a full head of hair.

Yet, even as my mind ponders this movement, my fingers clench tighter around the electric silver teeth. I take a step toward the mirror, trying to get a closer look at the self this mirror is presenting. My eyes, the pictures of sunflowers floating in pools of sea green, my face, light etchings of worn stories, and my hair, a lifeless brown stringed mop—images I don't recognize of a person I'm not quite sure actually exists. I push up on the power button with my thumb. An electric hum fills the small bathroom. I raise the clippers to my head and allow the teeth to chew my hair in methodical rows. Clumps of hair fall onto my shoulders, trail down my shirt, and collect in a garden of locks at my feet. I run the clippers across my head over and over again with fervent intensity. I can't bear to leave behind a stray hair to tell the story of the past—a past I am trying to shave away with each stroke. I want to take this person I don't recognize and start over. I want to strip myself down to zero and add from there. I want to make my own meaning of self, so I can recognize the image in the mirror.

The image confuses me because when my body moves in the world, I am often perceived as that which I am not. Biologically, I was born the female sex. Culturally, I was socialized with the norms of female gender. Coupled together, these two realities provide a script for my body to act according to the expectations of a heterosexual woman. In claiming my own identity, I don't exactly fit either of these categories. In relation to others, I am perceived in many different ways. Sometimes my identity is perceived as a young gay man. Sometimes it is a heterosexual man. Sometimes it is a dyke woman. Sometimes it is a heterosexual woman. Sometimes people can't decide. Sometimes I can't decide. Why is it so important to decide?

* * * * *

It is a Friday night, warm and inviting, and I am walking with three friends to the local queer dance bar. It is a special night of drag performance to raise money for breast cancer awareness. We enter the double doors, shuffle to the cash register, pay the cover charge, and step into the bar. To the left is a dance floor that leads to a small stage. To the right is multitier seating to watch the drag show, play pool, or sit at the bar. We select a small table near the dance floor.

The air is thick with smoke and chatter as we wait for the performance to begin. I notice both men and women watching our table. I am keenly aware that both men and women are watching me. I wonder: Am I being perceived as queer boy or queer girl? As I contemplate, the show begins and beautiful drag queens fill the stage performing Madonna, the Pointer Sisters, Christina Aguilera, and Britney Spears. After the show, I flirt with a woman near the dance stage who acknowledges me as a woman (what did she communicate that told me this?). I also talk with a gay man who thought I was a cute queer boy (what did he communicate that told me this?). Part of me enjoys the gender bending, but part of me is exhausted by the many questions I am asked by others. Did you know that you look like a cute boy? Did you know that I wasn't sure whether you were a boy or a girl?

I am also exhausted by the many awkward interactions I have in public spaces. Early one morning I wait in line to order a beverage at a coffee house. I stare up at the menu on the wall, trying to decide among the many options. As I approach the counter for service, I'm asked by the cashier, "How can I help you, sir?" I respond with my order, letting the label "sir" sit in the air between us. As I wait for my cup of hot coffee, I secretly hope that the cashier doesn't look at me more closely and then, with embarrassment, apologize for calling me sir. But this is what happens.

Flustered, the cashier looks away, ending our communication. I want to tell the cashier that I don't care, that it doesn't matter to me how I'm labeled as long as I'm not feared. But I don't say anything. I take my coffee and sit down at a small circular table under a colorful painting of fish dancing. As I take my first sip of the steaming liquid, I overhear the cashier talking about me, feeling embarrassed, still uncomfortable with the uncertainty. I want to scream, "*Let it go, I don't care!* What I care about is your inability to handle ambiguity."

I care when good friends tell me that they never view me as anything but a woman. As I drive up a curvy wooded road, my friend Sam stares out the window angrily recounting a moment when a server has again referred to me as a man. She can't understand the gender misappropriation. It makes her feel uncomfortable. She wants to clearly mark my body as female. I stare at the passing row of trees and try to make an argument for discontinuity. She's still angry.

In another moment, my friend Roy is perplexed. We are walking around a lake on a balmy spring day, and he crinkles his nose as he tries to understand that some people mark me as male. He's always seen me as feminine. I share stories with him about the gender confusion I create. He is quiet, only the rhythm of our feet marking time while the wind fills the silent space between us.

My friend Ashley tells me that I'm good at being a woman. We lie next to one another sharing intimate stories. I look at her closely, and confess that I disagree with her assessment. In a more forceful voice, she reiterates my excellent performance of woman. Inside I cringe, but do not tell her that it makes me feel extremely uncomfortable for her to fix that identity to my body.

* * * * *

The labels "man" and "woman" both feel foreign to my ears. Claiming either identity makes me feel uncomfortable. In one moment I champion a female body for the cause of reproductive rights of choice. In another moment I glean the privilege of male masculinity so that I'll be taken more seriously. When I do make a choice in these moments, am I reifying binary gender? Does living in a hybrid space mean I can choose to "pass" as either gender when it serves my best interest?

In the American culture in which I live, I'm well aware of how "my body" is associated with "the body" of female. I see the objectification of the female body for others' desires on flashy billboards, in glossy magazines, on dramatic television, and in blockbuster movies. I hear objectification through slang language of female body parts deployed to denigrate. Over and over I've been told that the worth of the female body is directly associated with its reproductive ability and consumable beauty. I am to wear long flowing hair, tastefully applied makeup, and worry about my weight. So when my body moves in the world, it communicates a resistance to the male gaze and ignores socially constructed gender imperatives. I leave a trail. The ambiguous hybrid I embrace leaves a resistive trail, challenging assumptions about the markings of gender.

For both hybrid and queer subjectivities, disruption, or marking of the third space, is indispensable in our efforts to illuminate the damage of oppressed bodies. By examining the issue of hybridity through my lens of lived experience, I have demonstrated the value of communicating hybrid identity across and through cultural experience. I hope that the sharing of my story offers a bridge toward understanding that all of our bodies carry stories that enhance our culture when we express them, and that these stories connect us.

I look into the mirror at my reflection. The image remains elusive to my understanding. My identity is fluid, exceeding the frame of the mirror. I rub my hands across the stubble on my head. I feel comforted by the neutral gender marking of a shaved head. I feel close to my body as in-between site. In this moment, I like not knowing, I like feeling lost in the gender continuum. Even if others view me as purely female or in the moment as male, I feel peace in claiming the identity of both/and while also claiming neither/nor.

References

Anzaldua, G. (1987). *Borderlands: The new mestiza—la frontera*. San Francisco: Spinsters/Aunt Lute.

Bhabha, H. K. (1994). *Location of culture*. London: Routledge.

Bornstein, K. (1998). *My gender workbook*. New York: Routledge.

Coover, G. E., & Murphy S. T. (2000). The communicated self: Exploring the interaction between self and social context. *Human Communication Research, 26*, 125–147.

Dash, M. (1995). In search of the lost body: Redefining the subject in Caribbean literature. In B. Ashcroft, G. Griffiths, & H. Tiffin (Eds.), *The postcolonial studies reader* (pp. 332–335). London: Routledge.

Eisenberg, E. M. (2001). Building a mystery: Toward a new theory of communication and identity. *Journal of Communication, 51*, 534–552.

Ellis, C., & Bochner, A. P. (2000). Autoethnography, personal narrative, reflexivity: Researcher as subject. In N. K. Denzin & Y. S. Lincoln (Eds.), *Handbook of qualitative research* (2nd ed., pp. 733–768). Thousand Oaks, CA: Sage.

Gingrich-Philbrook, C. (2001). Bite your tongue: Four songs of body and language. In L. C. Miller & R. J. Pelias (Eds.), *The green window: Proceedings of the Giant City Conference on performative writing* (pp. 1–7). Carbondale: Southern Illinois University.

Hall, S. (1990). Cultural identity and diaspora. In J. Rutherford (Ed.), *Identity: Community, culture, difference* (pp. 222–237). London: Lawrence & Wishart.

Kanneh, K. (1995). Feminism and the colonial body. In B. Ashcroft, G. Griffiths, & H. Tifflin (Eds.), *The postcolonial studies reader* (pp. 346–348). New York: Routledge.

Kraidy, M. M. (2002). Hybridity in cultural globalization. *Communication Theory, 123*, 316–339.

Langellier, K. M. (1989). Personal narratives: Perspectives on theory and research. *Text and Performance Quarterly, 9*, 243–276.

Loomba, A. (1998). *Colonialism/postcolonialism*. London: Routledge.

Shome, R., & Hedge, R. S. (2002). Postcolonial approaches to communication: Charting the terrain, engaging the intersections. *Communication Theory, 123*, 249–270.

Yep, G. A. (2003). The violence of heteronormativity in communication studies: Notes on injury, healing, and queer world-making. In G. A. Yep, K. E. Lovaas, & J. P. Elia (Eds.), *Queer theory and communication: From disciplining queers to queering the discipline(s)* (pp. 11–60). New York: Harrington.

Concepts and Questions

1. How might the experience of growing up in a "hybrid" body affect the process of establishing one's cultural identity?

2. Reflect on the feelings a youth in a hybrid existence would experience while interacting with others in a variety of social situations.

3. What is meant by the idea of negotiating a "self," and how does communication enter into that process?

4. Hybridity is defined as the coming together of two or more cultural identities. Specify a number of situations beyond gender where hybridity enters into the definition of cultural identity.

5. The authors state that a queer gender body disrupts the binary of being all male or all female. How might this disruption affect the intercultural communication process?

6. How can people learn to communicate more effectively with people who possess queer gender hybrid identities?

7. What lessons can be learned about effective intercultural communication from having read this essay?

Chinese American Ethnic and Cultural Identity

SABINE CHAI

MEI ZHONG

My new roommate Natalie[1] and I are walking through the sweltering heat toward our first morning of classes at Beijing Language and Culture University. "I am from New Jersey," she tells me, "but my parents are from Taiwan." She throws her brown hair with the blond highlights over her shoulder as we enter the air-conditioned building and find our way to a small classroom on the second floor. The teacher is all excited about getting to know us. We are doing introductions. "Ni shi na guo ren?" (Where are you from?) Natalie beams at him. "Wo shi zhongguo ren." (I am Chinese.), she says. The teacher is not flustered for a moment. "No, you are not," he responds. My roommate looks confused. "You are American, aren't you?" he says. I see her eyes filling with tears. Now the teacher looks confused too. "Ok, maybe a little Chinese, a very little bit Chinese," he says consolingly and moves on to the next student: "Where are you from?

What happened here? Why did Natalie expect to be accepted as Chinese? Why was it important to her? How does this fit together with her clear identification as a girl from New Jersey? Would this conversation have been different if it had taken place in the United States, with a teacher from the United States? Questions like these are all related to one topic: ethnic identity. Ethnic identity is defined as "a multidimensional construct that includes issues of group membership, self-image, ethnic affiliation and larger cultural affiliation, and ingroup and intergroup attitudes"(Ting-Toomey, Yee-Jung, Shapiro, Garcia, Wright, & Oetzel, 2000, p. 49). This essay

This original essay appears here in print for the first time. All rights reserved. Permission to reprint must be obtained from the authors and the publisher. Ms. Sabine Chai is a doctoral student in the Department of Communication at the University of Maryland/ College Park. Dr. Mei Zhong teaches in the School of Journalism and Media Studies at San Diego State University.

reflects a search for answers to the questions above. More broadly, it explores Chinese American ethnic identity as defined earlier, as an issue of how Chinese Americans define themselves as members of different groups, how others define them, and how discrepancies between definitions are lived and negotiated.

The purpose of this article is not to provide one answer. Rather, it is to lay out pieces of a patchwork blanket. Each piece of cloth contributes to the understanding of the whole. The narrative is built on three assumptions and consequently consists of three main parts. First, the authors believe that a person's history does not begin with birth but rather has roots that extend much further into the past. Knowing about these roots can contribute significantly to understanding the here-and-now. The first section of this article, therefore, offers a brief summary of Chinese American history. Second, although each individual has his or her own story, taking a few steps back to observe a larger number of people can contribute to understanding patterns we may not see when looking at individual cases. Therefore, the second section of this article presents an introduction to ethnic identity theory. Finally, the authors believe that one of the best paths toward learning is listening. To this end, a study was conducted using in-depth interviews with Chinese Americans who were willing to share the stories of their lives and their ideas on ethnic identity issues. The final part of this article presents the results of this study.

CHINESE IN THE UNITED STATES

The earliest Chinese recorded in America landed on the West Coast in the first half of the nineteenth century. Significant numbers, however, came with the Gold Rush that began in 1849. In 1851, 10,000 Chinese had arrived in California. A year later this number increased to 25,000 among a total population of 380,000 (Chen, 1981). Initially, the majority of them worked as miners. Large numbers left that profession however, when the state of California introduced a foreign miners' tax of $20 per month in 1850, an amount that is equivalent to $500 in 2006 (Sahr, 2007). This tax was lowered to $3 in 1852 (the equivalent of $75 in 2006) and remained the largest single source of state revenue until it was declared unconstitutional in 1870 (Chen, 1981).

In the 1860s, workers from China were hired to build the Western part of the Transcontinental Railroad. The Central Pacific Railroad Corporation appreciated Chinese workers particularly because they were reliable and cheaper than others. Apart from mining and the railroad, Chinese were also employed as farm laborers as well as in factories, such as wool mills, and in the shoe and garment production industries (Chen, 1981).

The initially welcoming atmosphere for the Chinese soon changed. The 1854 ruling that Chinese were colored people and therefore could not give evidence against white people in court opened the door to abuses of various kinds. In addition, Chinese were declared not eligible for naturalization, which denied them the right to permanent residency. In the economic crisis after the Civil War (1861–1865), a lot of the anger and frustration of the population unloaded on the Chinese who were thrown out of their jobs, driven from their homes, and often physically attacked or even killed. Expelled from work in the mines, fields, and factories, many Chinese turned to opening restaurants and laundries (Takaki, 1993). In 1882, the Exclusion Act was signed into law. This bill and its various extensions meant the end to free immigration of Chinese laborers.

The beginning of World War II brought a change of feeling toward the Chinese in the United States. As China was fighting the Japanese in Asia, the Chinese turned into allies and bolstering their morale became of interest to the United States. Therefore, while Japanese Americans were collected in internment camps, the Exclusion Act for the Chinese was repealed in 1943, they became eligible for naturalization, and a small quota of 105 Chinese immigrants per year was granted.

In 1949, the establishment of the People's Republic of China led to a wave of immigration, consisting of intellectuals and members of the upper class. Between 1961 and 2000, 1.3 million immigrants were admitted to the United States from China, Hong Kong, Macao, and Taiwan, resulting in a population of 2.9 million people of Chinese heritage in the United States by 2000 (Zhou, 2006).

BECOMING CHINESE AMERICAN

Who are these people who were ready to weather so many storms to settle in a new country? Who are their American-born children and grandchildren? Both China and the United States have been fast to answer these questions. For the Manchu emperors (1644–1911), the Chinese in America were traitors. Leaving China was illegal, so those who did could not truly be Chinese (Kung, 1973). The status of overseas Chinese rose when the Republic of China was established, in 1911, as Chinese abroad had made significant financial contributions to this effort. However, in spite of financial assistance Chinese in the United States were considered something like very remote relatives whose loyalties were doubtful. In the collective eye of the United States, the Chinese were at first a welcome source of cheap labor. Then, they quickly turned into unwanted competition, or aliens who could not be assimilated. World War II made the Chinese allies. Being allies may translate to being useful, but does not necessarily translate to being welcome, as indicated by the meager yearly quota of 105 which was established in 1943. Until today, many U.S. Americans seem to consider Chinese Americans as foreigners, whose loyalties are always doubtful (Chang, 2003).

Two dominant groups, Chinese and Americans, have defined the identity of Chinese Americans for them. Before presenting a third approach, the following paragraphs offer some ideas from ethnic identity theories and research on what may happen when people move from one culture into another or grow up as members of a minority group.

IDENTITY THEORY

The three main theories researchers have built on to look at ethnic identity are Erikson's ego identity formation theory (1968), social identity theory (Tajfel & Turner, 1979), and the acculturation framework (Berry, Trimble, & Olmedo, 1986). Although Erikson himself did not develop his theory with ethnic identity in mind but rather with the general identity development of adolescents, the theory was adopted by a number of researchers. Marcia (1980) suggested that ethnic identity development passes through four stages—a diffuse state, foreclosed status, moratorium, and achieved identity. An individual in the diffuse stage has neither explored his or her ethnic identity nor committed to one. Persons in the foreclosed status have made a commitment to an ethnic identity, usually based on parental or other authority figures' values, without individual exploration of other possibilities. An individual in the moratorium stage is exploring but has not made a commitment. Finally, an individual who went through exploration and reached a firm commitment is considered to have an achieved identity.

Atkinson, Morten, and Sue (1989) proposed the Minority Identity Development Model with five stages that lead from trying to adopt the cultural values and lifestyle of Euro-Americans through a stage of ambivalent feelings about both dominant and minority group, a stage of rejection of the dominant group and embracing of the minority group, a stage of questioning dogmatic beliefs, finally, to the "synergetic articulation and awareness stage" (Uba, 1994, p. 93), in which cultural values of both the dominant and the minority group are accepted or rejected on an objective basis. Although this model was proposed as a schema for therapists and not as a personality theory (Uba, 1994), a number of authors have applied these stages to individuals (Helms, 1994; Phinney, 1989).

More recent research (Yeh & Hwang, 2000; Ying, Coombs, & Lee, 1999) critiqued the ethnic identity development models for their inherent bias toward linear, unidirectional development toward independence and individualism. In all these models, for example, adapting other people's opinions is considered a lower developmental stage whereas independent, individualistic decision making is the highest level and goal of identity development. Yeh and Hwang (2000) proposed a reconceptualization of ethnic identity development to give room to the interdependent self, which is "defined by and understood in terms of the relational and social environment" (Yeh & Hwang, 2000, p. 424). A well-functioning interdependent self is flexible and able to adapt to various contexts. This reconceptualization is especially valuable for persons who need to function in diverse cultural contexts. The concept of the interdependent self allows for seeing them not as "spineless" as the old ethnic identity development models might, but as people with highly developed, mature and complex identities.

Another theoretical framework frequently used in ethnic identity research is social identity theory (Tajfel & Turner, 1979). The basic assumption of the theory is that humans are social beings that achieve a sense of belonging through membership of a group which in turn contributes to a positive self-concept. In the case of minority groups disparaged by society, the feeling of belonging can also be connected to a poorer self-concept. A lot of research in that area has been done with minority children (Aboud, 1987) and African Americans (Banks, 1976; Gordon, 1980). Findings are inconclusive. The finding that ethnic minority children frequently pick white dolls or pictures either as more similar to them or as more attractive has often been interpreted as low self-esteem and self-hatred. This interpretation has been criticized for assuming that children base their decisions on the same culturally influenced values as adults—an assumption that cannot be verified (Hutnik, 1986; Katz, 1987). Other studies found no support for low self-esteem in ethnic minority children (Ou & McAdoo, 1999; Phinney, 1989).

The acculturation literature differs from the older assimilation paradigm in that it assumes not a two-dimensional continuum leading immigrants and their descendants into the melting pot (Hutnik, 1986), but a more complex quadra-polar model (Berry, Trimble, & Olmedo, 1986). Individuals have to consider two questions: (1) Is it valuable to maintain relationships with other groups? (2) Is it valuable to maintain one's own cultural identity and characteristics? Depending on how these questions are answered, people fall into four categories. Answering "yes" to question one and "no" to question two shows that somebody is assimilating to the out-group. The contrary shows 'separation' from the larger cultural group and concentration on the in-group. Answering "no" to both questions shows that somebody is "marginal" to both groups. Finally, answering "yes" to both questions shows integration into both the minority group and the dominant group.

A study with both first- and second-generation Chinese Americans (Tsai, Ying, & Lee, 2000) found that a bipolar model fit the development of the first generation better: The more they identify with being American, the less they identify with being Chinese and vice versa. For the second generation, however, "being Chinese" and "being American" were not related—a sign that the quadra-polar model is more applicable to the descendants of immigrants than the bipolar model. A study with Asian Indian English girls (Hutnik, 1986) showed that in the second generation ethnic identity and everyday social functioning in diverse settings had become autonomous. This leads to another interesting model: Huang (1994) proposed that in the context of ethnic minority individuals' identity formation, both a personal internal identity and a social external identity work together to form an identity. Kwan and Sodowsky (1997) applied this idea to a study with Chinese American immigrants and found that the "observable social and cultural behaviors" (Kwan & Sodowsky, 1997, p. 53) of external ethnic identity could function independently from the cognitive, moral, and affective dimensions of internal ethnic identity.

Researchers have come up with widely diverging speculations on what will happen to today's minorities' ethnic identities in the future. One of the oldest ideas is Gans' (1979) theory of symbolic ethnicity. Other than the straight-line theorists, who proposed a "rapid decline and eventual extinction of ethnicity" (Gans, 1979, p. 3), Gans suggested that ethnicity would be kept alive by later generations in a modified form. Looking at descendants of early immigrant groups from Europe, he concluded that although they did not practice original customs and traditions they, nevertheless, felt attached to their ethnic identity and fostered a nostalgic allegiance to the culture of the immigrant generation (Gans, 1979). Some researchers have suggested that today's minorities will go through a similar process (Waters, 1990).

An alternative picture of the future of ethnic identity is presented by the Hansen hypothesis (Hansen, 1938; Isajiw, 1990), which was also derived from observing early European immigrants and their descendants. According to this hypothesis, the children of immigrants will rebel against the culture of their parents and distance themselves from their ethnic group. The third generation, then, returns to the group and wants to revive the connection. Some studies found support for this hypothesis—for example, Ting-Toomey's (1981) study on ethnic identity and friendship patterns in Chinese American college students. However, findings overall are inconclusive.

Finally, some researchers have suggested that descendants of Chinese, Japanese, Korean, Filipino, or other Asian groups will give up their particular ethnic identity to consider themselves Asian American (Kibria, 2002; Tuan, 1998). Whereas some see this as a necessary step toward gaining political power in the United States (Nagel, 1994), others consider this development possible but ascribe it to influences from the majority group aiming at "racializing" minority groups (Nagel, 1994; Tuan, 1998).

SEARCHING FOR A CHINESE AMERICAN IDENTITY: AN INTERVIEW STUDY

As stated above, both Chinese and Americans have defined Chinese Americans in various ways over the course of history. Research, too, has mostly considered how Chinese Americans fit into or relate to existing frameworks such as race and minority groups. Our interest was in finding out how Chinese Americans would define themselves. To achieve this objective, ten in-depth interviews were conducted with U.S. citizens whose parents or grandparents had immigrated from China, Hong Kong, Macao, or Taiwan. Interview responses, which used open-ended questions to give interviewees the freedom to develop their own ideas, were analyzed in terms of the following two broad topic areas.

1. What does it mean to Chinese Americans to be Chinese American?
2. What (if anything) holds Chinese Americans together as a group?

RESULTS AND ANALYSIS: BEING CHINESE AMERICAN

Answers to the first topic were derived mainly from interviewees' responses to two questions: *What makes you a Chinese American?* and *How would you describe somebody who is Chinese American?* Also included were stories told that were relevant to these questions. Interviewees' answers suggested four areas that are crucial to defining Chinese Americans: (a) a combination of *being Chinese* and being born and/or raised in the United States, (b) experiences connected to growing up in a Chinese family, (c) experiences connected to growing up in the United States, and (d) the connection to other Chinese Americans. In the following, each of these four points is discussed in depth in the format of a collection of narratives taken from the interviews. To protect interviewees' anonymity, their actual names were replaced with names of their choice.

Being Chinese and Born in the United States

When asked what made them Chinese Americans, the first response of a number of interviewees was similar to this one: "just being born Chinese, I guess, but then being born in the United States, which makes me American" (Astrid). This definition makes *being Chinese* qualitatively different from *being American*. *Being American* is related to a geographical location either at birth or where the majority of childhood was spent. *Being Chinese,* on the other hand, is a question of blood. Interviewees pointed to their parents saying that they both were Chinese, making it a necessity that their children would inherit *being Chinese*.

Others defined *being Chinese American* differently, as being part of a history. This history is, on the one hand, the "over 4,000 years of history recorded" (Mia) of the ancestral homeland. Being connected to this history was for many a cause of pride. On the other hand, being part of a history means sharing a history of immigration and struggle. As all interviewees were either 2nd generation (i.e., the parents immigrated) or 2.5 generation (i.e., one parent immigrated; one was born or grew up in the United States), immigration happened fairly recently. "My personal expectation would be that [a Chinese American] is someone who experiences, to some degree or another, the same kind of struggles that I struggle with in terms of being recognized as an American" (Sarah).

This struggle, however, is not only related to being accepted in the United States. "When I think Chinese American, I think of people of my generation, where the parents immigrated. There's something that my generation is aware of, like a culture clash, from conflict growing up" (Michelle). Here, the struggle is not only with the U.S. environment, but also between the Chinese parent generation and their American-born offspring. The children grow up with an awareness of difference and need to negotiate ways of dealing with demands from both their families and the larger environment.

Finally, being Chinese American was frequently defined as having a connection with both being Chinese and being American. For example, "What makes me Chinese American is in the connection that I feel when I am exposed to aspects of Chinese culture; where I can say 'OK, that's part of me and I accept that'" (Sarah). But on the other hand, "I feel very blessed that I was born in this country. Every time I go somewhere [i.e., in Europe or Asia] I am thankful that I live here. It feels like home here in America" (Karen).

In this context of being born Chinese and growing up in the United States, struggle and feelings of connection seem to lie close together. Therefore, the next two sections explore the two areas where the strongest feelings of connection meet the most intense struggles: the family home, and the U.S. home country.

Growing up in a Chinese Family

Five topics related to family life recurred throughout the interviews: (a) a focus on education and academic achievement, (b) the role of language acquisition, (c) values, (d) being *othered* by the first generation, and (e) *othering* the first generation.

The importance of achievement. "My parents were very strict about grades. They didn't like anything that wasn't an A" (Jenny). Almost all interviewees reported this or similar experiences. Parents expected their children to work hard to achieve high and often helped to choose their professional careers. Most interviewees also signaled some understanding for why the parents pressured them so much. "The parents had to work very hard to come to America in order for us to succeed, so I guess it's in a way understandable that they want to push us this way." (Michelle). Another reason for the pressure to achieve was that achievement was "a reflection of you and the family. You have to keep face for your family" (Mia). Indeed, seven out of ten interviewees held graduate degrees or were in the course of acquiring them and two more held bachelors degrees.

The role of language. An issue closely related to how interviewees defined themselves and other Chinese Americans was language. If both parents had immigrated, their children usually grew up speaking at least one Chinese language. "We were required to speak Mandarin at home and if we didn't we were punished" (Sarah). Although few showed excitement about having gone to Chinese School themselves, many nevertheless expressed a wish to send their own children.

The level of exposure to Chinese languages differed greatly between interviewees, from speaking several dialects fluently to not speaking any at all. Consequently, the role language played for them in defining Chinese Americans differed as well. The following three quotes are examples of the wide spectrum of possible views. "I'd expect a Chinese American to know some form of Chinese. When I hear that people are Chinese and they tell me that they're fifth generation, they don't understand any Chinese or speak any Chinese, . . . they could be white because they don't know any other language [than English] and they were raised in a very American way" (Jenny). "I think it [what can be expected of a Chinese American] depends on the region of the country, it depends on who they grew up with, it depends on whether they speak the language" (Sarah). "I can't speak Chinese . . . , and that's kind of sad. I definitely regret not learning. . . . That I can't speak Chinese probably makes me more Chinese American" (Astrid). So, attitudes about languages ranged all the way from knowledge being a *sine qua non* for being Chinese American, over a debatable issue, to a nice but unnecessary plus on the cake.

A possible reason for why the language was so important to those who spoke it was expressed like this: "A way of thinking is inherent in the language" (Frank). Others stated similar ideas. "Sometimes people joke around in Chinese, like with my roommate, and I appreciate that because I think maybe there is a little bit of bonding that occurs because of that" (Michelle). "To me, language is really important; it's the way to communicate. That's how I connect to the older generation" (Mia). Here, language seems to function not only as a tool to get messages across but also as a door to understanding how others think and to connecting with them on that level.

Values. Most interviewees agreed that keeping up traditions in regard to celebrating Chinese holidays or religious practices were not as important to their parents as instilling in their children the values they grew up with. Two topics related to values recurred through the interviews: the importance of being proud to be Chinese, and valuing the family.

To some degree, most parents attempted to impart pride in their heritage to their children. "My parents always told me that Chinese, your culture is very important. We do this because we're Chinese, and we don't

care what other people think but this is the way Chinese people do it" (Frank). Some adopted these feelings as their own. "To me culture is probably more history; it's so important for people to understand the struggles and be proud that they are Chinese" (Mia). Others expressed something like a feeling of connection or expected such a feeling of connection of other Chinese Americans. "A Chinese American is someone who owns up to the fact that they are Chinese, . . . someone who if not necessarily practices and celebrates Chinese customs and the culture and history, at least appreciates and understands that is a part of his or her life" (Karen). Still others did not feel connected to their background until college age but found an interest in it later on. "From my experience in elementary school, I think, for a long time I looked down, did not want to be Chinese" (Alison). "The first few years [of college] I was very turned off to my Chinese culture" but "I always compare myself to my brother. He has so many friends who are immigrants and he knows a lot of their culture. I think that would have been nice for me, if I had been able to experience that instead of not having knowledge of [my Chinese background]" (Astrid).

Of particular importance to most parents was to teach their children to value their family. As most did not have extended family networks around, valuing the family translated mostly to respecting their parents. Some learned to take comprehensive responsibility at least for their nuclear family. "Taking care of the family that's very important. For example, two of my brothers were supported because I made a good income and it was important for me to contribute to their education and help my parents out. They could afford sending my brothers to the best schools in the country" (Mia). Others expressed a basic commitment to caring for their parents but seemed to be unsure what form this care should take. "Yes, we would definitely [take care of the parents when they get older]. My mom wants me to move back to my old house where I grew up and take care of her but I have not crossed that bridge yet. I don't know if I, if it would be the best for us . . . but I definitely want to be able to take care of them" (Alison).

All interviewees mentioned that they had close relationships with their families. As most interviewees' parents were still relatively young, the question of caregiving was not relevant to many. However, another form that respect for parents could take was achieving in the areas important to the parents. For example, "They liked that I went back to Taiwan to learn language. I can tell from my mom that sort of [bragging], *Oh, but you know, my son, he went back to Taiwan to learn*" (Frank). As discussed above, the achievement of the children seemed to be an important part of the face of the parents, and achieving is a way to show respect to the family.

Being othered by the first generation. Being *othered* means to be treated as or made to feel like an *other*, like somebody who does not belong. A number of interviewees expressed having experienced or seen such treatment from the immigrant generation or other Chinese. "Their [i.e., Chinese American friends'] grandparents will tell it to your face, You're not Chinese. You don't even speak Chinese. How can you call yourself Chinese?" (Karen). Others who had traveled to China said, "They could definitely tell that I was American. I dress differently and I spoke Chinese with an accent and I just don't look Chinese" (Jenny). Some talked about being reluctant to even visit China for fear of not fitting in. "I'm really scared to go there because I feel I wouldn't fit in or I would be a disgrace to them [i.e., the relatives] because I can't speak the language and I'm so Americanized and it would just be humiliating" (Astrid).

On the other hand, interviewees also experienced being excluded by the parent generation in unexpected directions. "A lot of Chinese people will refer to Caucasian people as American, and I would always think to myself: Why are they saying that? It would bother me, you know, I would think: Well, I am American" (Alison).

Othering the first generation. Not only does the first generation see the later generations as different, the second and later generations may also distance themselves from the first generation. "When I was growing up, most of it [i.e., shared experiences with other Chinese Americans] tends to be around making fun of your parents. As a teenager, you sit around, make fun of their accent, or make fun of the funny things they do that were very different from your American counterparts that you grew up with, many things that you are embarrassed that your parents do because in mainstream American culture it's something that's very odd" (Frank).

Maybe this difference in background that interviewees saw between their parents and themselves is one of the reasons interviewees rarely had friends among first-generation peers. "At church, there would be a lot of immigrants. The people who are my generation, we called them FOBs [i.e., Fresh Off the Boat], which I don't know whether it's nice or not. They would form their own groups and we would form ours" (Michelle). Or at college, "Asian Americans and international students from Asia never really connected. I think some of the Asian Americans looked down on the international students because they didn't speak English well or because they had what Asian Americans might consider old fashioned ideas. Maybe the Asian American students saw the international students as representing what their parents believed and what they desperately tried to get away from" (Sarah).

Growing up in the United States

As stated above, being born and raised in the United States initially sounds mostly like a reference to geography. However, in the narratives of the interviewees growing up in the United States meant much more. Three topics stand out: (a) being othered, (b) learning to be a minority, and (c) being American 100%.

Being othered. Interviewees talked about being treated like an other in two ways: maliciously and due to ignorance. Almost all interviewees talked about being teased and taunted as children for being Chinese. "I remember the older teenagers in my [elementary] school, when I was walking home they would call me names, like Chinaman, ching chang Chinaman, something like that. So I would always dread going home because I would get harassed, not always, but when I ran across them" (Alison).

Apart from these direct attacks, interviewees talked about unintentional othering due to ignorance or stereotypes. "I had people talk to me in Chinese or Japanese hoping that I could speak it. I was on a bus in undergrad and this European American man was sitting next to me and kept talking to me about Japanese. I already told him "I am not Japanese, why would I know, I'm sorry" but he kept going on about it. It was just kind of annoying" (Astrid). Or, "When I walked into my chemistry class, I heard someone say, 'Great, there's a Chinese person in the class. There goes the curve'" (Karen), expressing the assumption that all Chinese are good in the sciences.

Learning to be a minority. Most interviewees reported being the only Chinese child in their elementary school class, often even in the whole school. For those who had grown up speaking Chinese at home, the beginning of school also meant a crash course in English. "I started learning English in kindergarten. So, you're the outsider, you're learning the language, this other thing everybody else is speaking." (Frank). Some interviewees suggested that while they were learning to fit in, they also learned to be embarrassed of their parents for staying foreigners.

Either later in school or in college classes, interviewees had more Chinese American or other Asian American classmates, but a consciousness of the ethnic or racial makeup of groups often remained. "In grad school, we hardly have any other Asian Americans. So, I definitely feel out of place a lot of times because I look around and think, oh yeah, I'm the only Asian here" (Astrid).

Being a minority was reflected in the under- and misrepresentation of Chinese Americans in the media. "Any time you look at the media there is always stereotyping that the only thing that Chinese know how to do is Kung Fu" (Mia). Others considered the Kung Fu focus an improvement over earlier representations. "I think this has expanded people's consciousness. All of a sudden it's not just because you're Asian you're a nerdy pre-engineer but you're also kick-ass and you can beat the bad guys because of your admittedly stereotypical martial arts skills" (Sarah). Nevertheless, roles represented by Chinese Americans are limited. One interviewee reflected on the influence the media had on her identity development: "The media show me what the majority finds acceptable, I think, and it also shows me that, I guess, my group is not really high on the list of what's important" (Astrid).

Male interviewees especially expressed anger at the representation of Chinese males in the media. "For a long time I was really mad that there are no Asian American guys on TV. If they are on TV or in film they are gay or into martial arts" (Frank). Or, "All the images that the media portray [of Chinese Americans] are very negative. They always make them buck toothed, slant eyes, nerds that get pushed around. The White Americans portray themselves as cool, nothing can go wrong, always the hero, always the knight in shining armor, always get the girl, the list just goes on and on and on" (David).

Some interviewees noticed that they had adopted some of the stereotypes that they saw in the environment about their own group or other Asian American groups. For example, "I saw a special about the Japanese internment camps and the Japanese Americans in the camp spoke perfect English. It seemed wrong to me. I expected them to have an accent" (Jenny).

Maybe because of the misrepresentation they saw, maybe because of the expectations of others, but many interviewees felt that they were or had to be ambassadors of their ethnic group. For example, "Right now we moved to a very rural, very Caucasian neighborhood that has a reputation for being racist and that makes me uncomfortable. It's also a sense of pressure that maybe none of these people have ever interacted with Asians before, so I better be a good example, because I don't want them to be like "She's a bitch" and then by extrapolation think that all Asians are bad" (Sarah). Others talked about their fear that the low performance of Asian American co-workers would reflect negatively on them. Several interviewees mentioned that spreading awareness and educating others about Chinese culture was important to them because they hoped it would lead to better integration.

Being American 100%. In spite of the various difficulties discussed earlier, interviewees strongly identified with being American and expected other Chinese Americans to feel the same way. "A Chinese American speaks fluent English, is more American than Chinese in terms of culture and loyalties, clothing, interest in politics, if we were to be in the military fighting for our country—America. If going to another country we would not necessarily identify ourselves as Chinese but as American. I think Chinese comes secondary" (Alison).

Being American was expressed through feeling connected to U.S. cultural icons, such as "Sesame Street and Elmo, Winnie the Pooh, and Coca Cola" (Karen). Interviewees identified with U.S. American values and ideals such as liberty, democracy, capitalism, freedom of speech, freedom of religion, and the pursuit of happiness. Finally, they expressed that they felt at home in the United States and were proud to be American. "I would call myself Chinese American with no hyphen because when you have Chinese space American, Chinese becomes an adjective that modifies American, so that we become like any other type of American. Being an American is very important to me" (Sarah).

Being Part of the Community

When discussing friendships, all interviewees pointed out that having friends of a similar background was particularly important to them. Although most had non-Chinese American friends as well, they felt a special connection with others whose parents had also immigrated from China or other East Asian countries. "It wasn't until seventh grade that I started meeting more American-born Chinese like myself and then started learning that they were going through all the same things I went through. We kind of learned, hey, we were all kind of brought up the same way. My closest girlfriends ultimately ended up being Chinese American" (Karen). This connection to others from similar background is influential in two ways: First, the similarity in experience helped interviewees make friends among other Chinese Americans. Second, many considered having those friends itself a definitional element of being Chinese American. For example, "[One part of] what makes me Chinese American is interacting with people who have the same background, experiences, being friends with them, spending time with them, seeing that there are many shared experiences that bind us together in a group" (Frank).

CHINESE AMERICANS: A DISTINCTIVE GROUP?

To gain insight into the second issue, we reexamined the interviewees' responses from the perspective of that topic—*What (if anything) holds Chinese Americans together as a group?* While we do not claim completeness, some of the ideas derived from the interviews are presented.

To varying degrees, the interview responses provide an outline of what Chinese Americans share with each other: the self-definition as both Chinese and American, similar personal histories from growing up in Chinese families in a U.S. environment, and the connection felt to others with a similar history. Although interviewees' views on some of the issues involved differed greatly, they nevertheless agreed that these were issues. For example, ideas about the role of language in Chinese American ethnic identity varied. However, all interviewees had reflected on the question and defined themselves in relation to it. Maybe one of the strongest but least discussed commonalities among interviewees was that they had all spent significant time reflecting on their identity and finding their own place in relation to two cultures.

Apart from reflection, interviewees also took a very active role in shaping their own ethnic identity. Looking at what was offered on both the Chinese and American side of the table, they, to differing degrees, took the initiative to decide for themselves which parts they wanted to adopt and which ones to discard. One interviewee, for example, reflected on his relationship to his parents' views on Chinese politics. "My parents are totally nationalistic, in terms of Taiwan. That type of thinking is a generation behind me. I haven't experienced it, so it doesn't really matter to me. I personally think that all these people are actually Chinese. I say I'm Chinese American, but I was born in Taiwan. That's as narrow as I get" (Frank).

Another way interviewees seemed to tailor *being Chinese* to their needs appeared to be by changing definitions and meanings of Chinese traditions and values. For example, "My family got together this weekend for Chinese New Year. To my family, now, it's more like a fun thing to get together, not because it's a tradition anymore but it's a theme to get together" (Mia). Here, traditions are kept but furnished with a new purpose and meaning.

Another area that seemed to have changed is family values. Most interviewees expressed that their family is very important to them and many felt responsible for taking care of the family financially. However, when they said *family,* they mostly meant parents and siblings only. This view departs from the traditional Chinese view which includes the extended family. One possible reason is that due to the family's immigration, no extended family was around that interviewees' could have learned to feel responsible for. Another possible reason, however, is that they have adopted the common American definition of a nuclear family.

A separate example for this phenomenon is the question of giving care to elderly parents. A number of interviewees stated that they felt responsible for that. However, when the issue became salient, some were not sure anymore that being their parents' caregivers would be "the best for us" (Alison). The meaning of filial piety seemed to be changing.

Considering the discussion above, interviewees shared not only the situation in life they were born into, but also a common way of creating their identity in this situation that includes defining themselves in relation to being both Chinese and American and actively redefining what it means to be both Chinese and American.

ETHNIC IDENTITY: QUO VADIS?

A number of interviewees reflected on the difficulty of finding a self-definition without being challenged by either Chinese or Americans. "People are labeling me *not American* and my family feels I'm not Chinese, then what does that leave me? What are we? Are we this new breed?" (Karen). Considering the theories on ethnic identity discussed earlier, the narratives emerging from the interviews seem to fit with some aspects of theory previously considered, but also defy definition in relation to existing frameworks.

Although an interview in adult age cannot really trace ethnic identity development, interviewees did mention ideas similar to the stages in Marcia's (1980) model. Some interviewees mentioned a time before they started thinking about their identity; most talked about at some point adopting the views of others, either of their parents or the mainstream environment, and, finally, how they struggled through questions of ethnic identity to arrive at their current views and ideas. Not for all did development take this course.

Signs that the second and later generations change traditions to better fit their new surrounding could also be early indicators of the development of symbolic ethnicity (Gans, 1979). Whether later generations will take this path remains to be seen. As long as the majority of Chinese in the United States are first generation, this issue can probably not truly be evaluated.

Very important to the interviewees' identity, however, was what social identity theory calls the need to be part of a group (Tajfel & Turner, 1979). In this regard, Chinese Americans challenge existing frameworks such as the quadra-polar model of acculturation (Berry, Trimble, & Olmedo, 1986). For them, the decision is not whether or not to value an in-group versus an out-group. Rather, both Chinese and American are in-groups for Chinese Americans. They define themselves as members of one group by blood and as members of the other group by birthright. The struggle rarely seemed to be about accepting or rejecting one or the other side rather than about being accepted as members in the groups to which interviewees felt they belonged.

In the United States, Chinese Americans are often told to rather identify as Chinese. However, interviewees of this study also experienced being told by Chinese to rather consider themselves American, as Natalie in the opening story of this article. When she expected to be welcomed home, she found herself in a foreign country that did not know her. So, who are Chinese Americans? Are they a new breed? Or maybe just another addition to the patchwork blanket that is America? We hope this study offers a small piece of insight into that puzzle.

Note

1. All names in this article, except for those of published authors, have been changed.

References

Aboud, F. E. (1987). The development of ethnic self-identification and attitudes. In J. S. Phinney & M. J. Rotheram, *Children's ethnic socialization: Pluralism and development* (pp. 32–55). Thousand Oaks, CA: Sage.

Atkinson, D., Morten, G., & Sue, D. W. (1989). A minority identity development model. In D. Atkinson, G. Morten, & D. W. Sue (Eds.), *Counseling American minorities* (pp. 35–52). Dubuque, IA: William C. Brown.

Banks, W. (1976). White preference in blacks: A paradigm in search of a phenomenon. *Psychological Bulletin, 83,* 1179–1186.

Berry, J. W., Trimble, J. E., & Olmedo, E. L. (1986). Assessment of acculturation. In W. J. Lonner & J. W. Berry (Eds.), *Field methods in cross-cultural research* (pp. 291–324). Beverly Hills, CA: Sage.

Chang, I. (2003). *The Chinese in America: A narrative history.* New York: Viking.

Chen, J. (1981). *The Chinese of America.* New York: Harper & Row.

Cheng, L.-R., L. (2004). The challenge of hyphenated identity. *Topics in Language Disorders, 24,* 216–224.

Erikson, E. H. (1968). *Identity: Youth and crisis.* New York: W. W. Norton.

Gans, H. J. (1979). Symbolic ethnicity: The future of ethnic groups and cultures in America. *Ethnic and Racial Studies, 2,* 1–20.

Hansen, M. L. (1983). *The problems of the third generation immigrants.* Rock Island, IL: Augustana Historical Society.

Helms, J. E. (1994). The conceptualization of racial identity and other racial constructs. In E. J. Trickett, R. J. Watts, & D. Birman (Eds.), *Human diversity: Perspectives on people in context* (pp. 285–311). San Francisco: Jossey-Bass.

Huang, L. N. (1994). An integrative view of identity formation: A model for Asian Americans. In E. P. Salett, & D. R. Koslow (Eds.), *Race, ethnicity, and self: Identity in multicultural perspective* (pp. 42–59). Washington, DC: National MultiCultural Institute.

Hutnik, N. (1986). Patterns of ethnic minority identification and modes of social adaptation. *Ethnic and Racial Studies, 9,* 150–167.

Isajiw, W. W. (1990). Ethnic-identity retention. In R. Breton, W. W. Isajiw, W. E. Kalbach, & J. G. Reitz (Eds.), *Ethnic identity: Varieties of experience in a Canadian city* (pp. 34–91). Toronto, Ontario, Canada: University of Toronto Press.

Katz, P. A. (1987). Developmental and social processes in ethnic attitudes and self-identification. In J. S. Phinney & M. J. Rotheram, *Children's ethnic socialization: Pluralism and development* (pp. 92–99). Thousand Oaks, CA: Sage.

Kibria, N. (2002). *Becoming Asian American: Second-generation Chinese and Korean American identities.* Baltimore, MD: Johns Hopkins University Press.

Kung, S. W. (1973). *Chinese in American life: Some aspects of their history, status, problems, and contributions.* Westport, CT: Greenwood Press.

Kwan, K.-L., K., & Sodowsky, G. R. (1997). Internal and external ethnic identity and their correlates: A study of Chinese American immigrants. *Journal of Multicultural Counseling and Development, 25,* 51–67.

Marcia, J. (1980). Identity in adolescence. In J. Adelson (Ed.), *Handbook of adolescent psychology* (pp. 159–187). New York: Wiley.

Nagel, J. (1994). Constructing ethnicity: Creating and recreating ethnic identity and culture. *Social Problems, 41,* 152–176.

Ou, Y. S., & McAdoo, H. P. (1999). The ethnic socialization of Chinese American children. In H. P. McAdoo (Ed.), *Family ethnicity: Strength in diversity* (2nd ed., pp. 252–276). Thousand Oaks, CA: Sage.

Phinney, J. S. (1989). Stages of ethnic identity development in minority group adolescents. *Journal of Early Adolescence, 9,* 34–49.

Sahr, R. (2007). *Inflation conversion factors for dollars 1665 to estimated 2017.* Retrieved March 24, 2007, from Oregon State University, Department of Political Science Web site: http://oregonstate.edu/cla/polisci/faculty/sahr/infcf16652007.xls

Tajfel, H., & Turner, J. (1979). An integrative theory of intergroup conflict. In W. Austin & S. Worchel (Eds.), *The social psychology of intergroup relations* (pp. 33–47). Monterey, CA: Brooks/Cole.

Takaki, R. (1993). *A different mirror: A history of multicultural America.* Boston: Little, Brown.

Ting-Toomey, S. (1981). Ethnic identity and close friendship in Chinese-American college students. *International Journal of Intercultural Relations, 5,* 383–405.

Ting-Toomey, S., Yee-Jung, K. K., Shapiro, R. B., Garcia, W., Wright, T. J., & Oetzel, J. G. (2000). Ethnic/cultural identity salience and conflict styles in four U.S. ethnic groups. *International Journal of Intercultural Relations, 24,* 47–81.

Tsai, J. L., Ying, Y.-W., & Lee, P. A. (2000). The meaning of "being Chinese" and "being American": Variation among Chinese American young adults. *Journal of Cross-Cultural Psychology, 31,* 302–332.

Tuan, M. (1998). *Forever foreigners or honorary whites? The Asian ethnic experience today.* Piscataway, NJ: Rutgers University Press.

Uba, L. (1994). *Asian Americans: Personality patterns, identity, and mental health.* New York: Guilford Press.

Waters, M. C. (1990). *Ethnic options: Choosing identities in America.* Berkeley: University of California Press.

Yeh, C. J., & Hwang, M. Y. (2000). Interdependence in ethnic identity and self: implications for theory and practice. *Journal of Counseling and Development, 78,* 420–429.

Ying, Y.-W., Coombs, M., & Lee, P. A. (1999). Family intergenerational relationship of Asian American adolescents. *Cultural Diversity and Ethnic Minority Psychology, 5,* 350–363.

Zhou, M. (2006). Negotiating culture and ethnicity: Intergenerational relations in Chinese immigrant families in the United States. In R. Mahalingam (Ed.), *Cultural psychology of immigrants* (pp. 315–336). Mahwah, NJ: Erlbaum.

APPENDIX–STRUGGLING TO BE HEARD (CHENG, 2004)

I am a child of the Chinese diaspora, born at the crossroads.

I am Chinese American,

A product of the city of Shanghai I have never known.

An immigrant and the daughter of Cantonese,

I speak Cantonese with love, the language of Dim Sum and Chinatown.

I speak English with passion, it's the tongue of my consciousness,

It is my crystal, my tool, my craft.

I am from Taiwan, island grown, Taiwanese is my dream,

Ripples from my tongue, rests in my heart,

I am from Pacific Asia, a stranger from a different shore, deeply rooted in history.

I am from California, I love the city of San Diego.

I am Asian, Asia is in me, but I cannot return.

I am Chinese, China lives in me but there's no way back;

I am Taiwanese. Taiwan remembers me, but I have no home there.

I am new. History made my hyphenated existence. I was born at the crossroads and I am whole.

Concepts and Questions

1. In your own words, provide a definition of "ethnic identity."
2. How does knowledge of one's ethnic history influence their identity? Do you think a lack of awareness of one's ethnic history would also influence identity? How?
3. What do the authors mean by the statement, "Two dominant groups, Chinese and Americans, have defined the identity of Chinese Americans"?
4. Zhong and Chai used interviews to let their Chinese American participants "Define themselves." Define your own ethnic identity to a classmate.
5. How is language a source of identity?
6. Why do you think most parents of Chinese American children thought it was important to teach the value of family to their children?
7. How do the authors define "being othered"? Can you describe a time or situation where you felt "othered"?
8. What are some reasons why a newly arrived immigrant from China (or another country) might want to associate with other new arrivals from that country?
9. How can the media create stereotypes of ethnic minorities? Give some examples of current minority stereotypes.
10. At the end of the essay, the authors ask " . . . who are Chinese Americans?" How would you answer that query?

What's (not) in a Label?: Multiplicity and the Dynamics of Identity Among Korean Americans

Etsuko Kinefuchi

TAKING IDENTITY LABELS SERIOUSLY

African American, Native American, Asian, Latino/a, Black, White, Arab American, Korean, Italian, Caucasian, Hispanic, Middle Eastern . . . . Those and many other ethnic and racial labels are an integral part of our everyday communication. Despite (or because of) the pervasive use of labels in our everyday discourse, we rarely take time to think about their meanings and the assumptions we hold about them. When I say, "Latino," what groups of individuals am I picturing? What do I assume about the identity of people I subsume under this label? I begin this essay with a premise that we need to take labels and the act of labeling seriously. I say this for several reasons. First, labeling is one of the primary ways by which we express, describe, and understand identities. Identity labels serve as an anchor that reflects how identity is maintained and evolved (Hecht, Collier, & Ribeau, 1993). Reflecting social realities and changing cultural, social, and political consciousness, cultural identity labels such as ethnic labels are a site for understanding communal identities (Collier & Thomas, 1988; Hecht et. al, 1993; Witteborn, 2004). Often, "labels" are thought of as only referring to negative stereotypes, but any descriptive and evaluative names we use for groups and individuals, including our own

This original essay appears here in print for the first time. All rights reserved. Permission to reprint must be obtained from the author and publisher. Dr. Etusko Kinefuchi teaches in the Department of Communication at The University of North Carolina at Greensboro.

groups and ourselves, are labels. Understood this way, it is virtually impossible to communicate without using labels.

Second, labels necessarily call attention to certain aspects of our (and our understanding of and attitudes toward others') social, cultural, and political experiences, standpoints, and relationships while leaving out other aspects. Labels are, thus, simultaneously useful and limiting. If we only focus on the aspect highlighted by a label, we may fail to understand the richness of multicultural identities within groups and even within individuals. Third, there are often differences between ascription and avowal (Collier & Thomas, 1988). That is, the labels we use for other groups and individuals may not be the labels they chose for themselves. Moreover, because a word can contain multiple meanings, the meaning that we attach to a label may not be the same meaning others attach to it. These concerns are particularly relevant in intercultural communication because discrepancies in meaning and preferred labels can pose challenges to and sometimes damage intercultural relationships.

Finally, labeling is intricately related to the relations of power. Discursive representations, including labels, and their meanings widely used in public discourses are most often created, defined and policed by those who have power to dominate such processes (Spencer, 1984). Thus, labeling not only defines inclusion and exclusion (Woodward, 1997) but also normalizes and naturalizes dominant groups' experiences and perspectives over others (Ono, 1998; Spencer, 1984). As a result, labels, particularly applied to ethnic and racial groups, are often decontexualized and used ahistorically for the purpose of expedient communication but without regards to the people to whom the labels are applied (Oboler, 1995).

All these reasons suggest that labels must not be taken as self-evident representations of identity. For intercultural communication to be a mutually satisfying experience, co-creation of identity must occur, and such co-creation is possible only when communicators are able to equally participate in the creation and negotiation of meanings (Yep, 2002). Understanding our intercultural communication partners' avowed identities and their reasons for the avowal is an important step toward this end. In what follows, I engage in this step by exploring identity experiences of Koreans who were adopted by white U.S. Americans.

Korean adoptees represent a rapidly growing population in the United States—internationally *and* interracially adopted children. International adoptees have been an integral part of U.S. family landscape for over a half century, and the number continues to grow every year. According to the U.S. Department of State, the number of visas issued to orphans coming to the United States every year increased from 7,093 in 1990 to 20,679 in 2006. Geographically and racially, Asian adoptees have always comprised the largest group among the international adoptees; for example, the immigration statistics by Department of Homeland Security shows that, out of the 22,710 foreign children adopted by U.S. American families in 2005, as many as 10,558 were from Asia. Initially started as a way to provide homes for orphans after the Korean War, adoptions from South Korea have the longest history in international adoptions and thus constitute a large group of adoptees who have grown up in the United States.

Adopted Koreans' identities are a particularly rich site for understanding and theorizing cultural identity in the United States because they have crossed multiple borders of identity units—family, race, ethnicity, and nation. Historically, Asians and Asian Americans have been portrayed by the mainstream U.S. society as perpetual foreigners who are *essentially* different from "American"—a label historically equated to being white (Foner, 1998). Such foreignness has been shown as not simply cultural and geographical, but as innate stemming from biological differences between the people in the "Orient" and their counterparts in the "Occident" (Lowe, 1996; Nakayama, 1998; Said, 1979; Takaki, 1988). Examination of Korean adoptees' identity experiences likely provide first-person accounts of how the existing identity boundaries may be negotiated by border-crossers.

MULTIVOCALITY IN IDENTITY EXPRESSIONS

The identity expressions that are examined here were derived from in-depth interviews with twenty adults who were born in Korea and were adopted by white U.S. American families. The interviews allowed me to understand their lived experience from their own perspectives (Kvale, 1996).

The adoptees' demographics were very diverse. The adopted age, for example, varied from a few weeks old to eleven years old. Their families came in different shapes and sizes; some families were multiracial with several adopted children, some only adopted from South Korea, some had both biological children and adopted children, and so forth. There were two aspects of their upbringing that the participants had in common in addition to the fact that they were adopted from Korea by white American parents. Their families were all middle-class to upper middle-class, and they grew up in predominantly white communities for the major part of their childhood and adolescence. A few participants had attended inner city schools at one point or another during their K-12 education, and therefore had contact with many racial minorities. Yet, they described the rest of their education as occurring in white majority schools. Most of them grew up in suburbs.

Many issues were discussed in those interviews including their relationships with their families, their experiences and struggles with identities during childhood and adolescence, significant events that contributed to the transformations in the ways they see their cultural identities, and their current views and expressions of their cultural identities. This essay focuses on the last issue—their current cultural identities as adults.

To gain insights into their views of their cultural identities, I asked them to tell me how they describe themselves culturally. Though the question was a broad one, most of the participants seemed to process the question within the overall interview theme of ethnicity, race, and adoption. All but three persons discussed their current identities in terms of ethnicity, nationality, race, and the adoption status, using such labels as "American," "Korean American," "Korean," "adopted Korean American." These labels, however, did not neatly represent coherent, unified, or constant voices across the interviewees and even within the interviewees. Moreover, some expressions revealed their resistance to one concrete label and other-imposed pre-existing labels. Such choices and resistances were explained in the context of the transformations they underwent to reach the current views of themselves. Below, I discuss Korean adoptees' self-identified identity labels, their subjective meanings that underlie the labels, followed by my reflections on the adoptees' use of these labels.

The adoptees' names used in this paper are all fictional.

"Korean American": Biculturality and Negotiation

The most popular identity expression given by the interviewees was "Korean American" or "Korean." Five adoptees used the two labels interchangeably during their interviews to stress the biculturality of their beings. When the label "Korean" was given, the fact that they are also "American" was assumed. In one of the interviewee's words, "I know that I'm American and stuff like that. I live an American life, but my roots are in Korea." Whether the interviewees used "Korean" or "Korean American," the word "Korean" was included largely for two reasons: identification with and pride in Korean culture as their roots, and existence of close, comfortable friendships with non-adopted Korean Americans. They feel that their perspectives and mannerisms are very Americanized, because they grew up in the U.S. society and their parents are white Americans and not of Korean ethnicity. However, they believe that they are equally Korean because Korea is their natal homeland, and they felt proud to have this heritage. For example, Mike, who was adopted at age five, gave the following analogy to illustrate his pride as a Korean:

> When the Olympic was in Korea, I had a pride. Hey, it's my home country. I was born there. And the World Cup is going to be there in 2002. It's a pride thing. Here is an example. I live in Minnesota, and I've been always a Vikings fan even when they are bad. Always loyal, you know. Same thing with Korea. That's me, I was born in Korea. I'm proud of it. If I moved away from Minnesota, I'll still be a Viking fan, because that's where I was raised. That's a pride thing.

In this articulation of Koreanness, ethnic identity is constructed as a primordial condition that is given by birth and is constant over time and place in one's life. The root was, is, and will always be a constitutive part of self, serving as a source of self-worth. Interestingly, Mike has never been to Korea since adoption, while all others who chose this identity term have visited the country—an event that significantly contributed to the salience they now place on their Korean background. Mike attributes his strong identification as Korean to his adoptive parents who encouraged him to be proud of his Korean heritage. His parents were part of the founders of a Korean cultural camp for adopted Korean children in his city.

Although Mike has always thought of himself as Korean American and has been proud to be Korean as long as he can remember, other interviewees who now view themselves Korean Americans have gone through significant transformations in the ways they felt about their Korean roots and identifying themselves as "Korean." During their childhood and adolescence, they consciously and subconsciously distanced themselves from Asians, including adopted Koreans, due to various reasons including a desire to dissociate themselves from stereotypes of Asians and a desire to be included in the "popular" crowd of white students who constituted the majority in school. This changed, however, through significant events such as meeting other Korean Americans, visiting Korea, and going to racially and ethnically diverse colleges. More often, a combination of several events helped to transform other adoptees to feel positive and strong about their Korean background. Bethany, a mid-twenties social worker, for example, visited Korea twice and attended an international conference of adopted Koreans several years ago. She explained how the meaning of the label, "Korean American," changed for her after she befriended Korean Americans in college.

> I always would have said "I'm Korean American," but with not much pride. Now I can talk about Korea, and my experiences there, with my Caucasian friends. I wasn't able to do that before because I was embarrassed or I just didn't know how they would take it. But now I have a lot of pride about being Korean because of the influence of my [Korean American] friends and learning more about the culture. I have more interest in it than I ever have before.

Like Bethany, having close non-adopted Korean American friends was an important reason for the adoptees' self-identification as Korean American. Their close friends consist of many, if not only, 1.5- and second-generation Korean Americans who are not adoptees, and they feel very comfortable around them. Most often, those friendships were formed during their college years when they find themselves in the company of students with various backgrounds

including Korean Americans, whereas their earlier schooling was among white students. One of these adoptees is Mollie, a recent college graduate, whose primary friends now consist of non-adopted Korean Americans. She expressed her identification with her non-adopted friends in the following words:

> I think growing up in a white family, you are not white enough to hang out with white kids, because of your physical characteristics. But at the same time, you can't just go to Korea and fit in. With the friends I have, they are pretty much all second generation Korean, and they are pretty much half and half. They have just enough Korean pride and they are also just as Americanized, too.

This sense of identification, however, did not come instantly; it gradually happened through her acquisition of Koreanness by spending time with the second-generation friends and by learning the Korean language. As Mollie became more competent in the language, she has not only come to understand Korean mannerisms but also use them in her communication with her non-adopted Korean friends. Her transformation, in turn, was affirmed when her friends accepted her into their community:

> My friends have told me that I've changed a lot from the time they first met me to the point I am today. They don't consider me as Korean adopted. They don't look at me as an adopted person. They look at me like the second generation, because of how Koreanized I am.

If Mollie's words represent someone who views Korean mannerisms as an important criterion of claiming the label of Korean American, others thought of it as a site that they can and should negotiate. For example, three adoptees who self-identified as Korean American mentioned their selective adaptation to Korean mannerisms, and they all referred to the cultural rules involved in cross-age communication as examples of the negotiated site. One of them, Bethany, gave the following account to explain the difference between her 1.5-generation friend and herself:

> . . . everybody that's older to her is *appa*. Like older brother. So even if they are two years older than me, even if they are a year older than you, you are supposed to. And to me the only people I call *appa* is like the people I really respect. If I feel that they deserve

the respect, I'll give it to them. In that way, my mentality is more Americanized, whereas she is very Koreanized.

Other adoptees' examples resonated with Bethany's. While they identify closely with non-adopted friends and felt that these friendships are comfortable and invaluable sources of Korean culture, they believed that they did not have to conform to all Korean norms to claim the identity label of Korean American. They felt that they could choose what and how much of cultural norms they accept and practice.

"Adopted Korean American": Salience of "Adopted" Part of Self

> I'm adopted Korean American, because being an adopted Korean is so much part of who I am, not just being Korean, but being adopted Korean. [Emily, college junior]

Four adoptees, including Emily, a college student, felt that their adopted background is a salient aspect of who they are and thus needs to be part of their self-definition. One reason given by three adoptees was the uncertainty and resulting incompetence they felt about performing Korean cultural norms. Matt, a mid-twenties Internet consultant, for example, talked about differences between himself and non-adopted Korean Americans. He previously believed that Korean American and adopted Korean were the same because the two groups share the same ethnic heritage. After spending some time in Korea, however, he came to realize how "un-Korean" he was as compared to non-adopted Korean Americans and how oblivious he was to Korean cultural nuances. This awareness, in turn, led to uncertainty about his Korean cultural competence. He explained this newfound challenge as follows:

> If I speak Korean, is my Korean good? Am I Korean enough? Am I acting Korean? Did I bow enough? Did I shake two hands? Am I supposed to shake one hand? If you are Korean American or Korean, you don't have all those issues, because you just know that you are doing it right. And the friction is even amplified by the fact that other persons look at you and say, "Gosh, this person is Korean. How come you are not acting correct?" And that's a source of friction.

The sense of uncertainty and incompetence resulting from perceived lack of authenticity, therefore, facilitated

Matt to assert his adopted aspect of identity. He feels very comfortable around other adopted Koreans, because he does not have to worry about violating cultural norms. Like Mollie, a self-identified Korean American, Matt views competent performance of Korean mannerisms and interaction norms as an important criterion of the label, Korean American. This contrasted the adoptees who identified themselves as Korean American and expressed their right to negotiate such norms.

For another person, David, a late-twenties investment broker, his choice of including the word "adopted" was not a matter of perceived cultural inadequacy, because, adopted at age 11, Korean mannerisms come naturally to him. Being surrounded by 1.5- and second-generation Korean American friends and being married to a second-generation woman, his life, in his words, "revolves around Korean Americans." However, he feels that his adopted status equally defines him, because it has contributed to the psychological distance he feels toward his family. He expressed the salience of this issue as follows:

> I'm still very close to my family. But I always felt like I was kind of a charity case. I always did things so I would please my parents here. And even though my parents never said that, I was old enough to realize that's what my Korean mom would want me to do, and that was kind of my role to be the best child because I owed them my life. So, I never did things that other regular teenager growing up would do without thinking first "Oh, are they gonna like that?" I always second-guessed before doing something that I wanted to do myself. So I always had this barrier to my family. They don't know that, or they don't think that, but I think that. I always wonder what would it be like to be in a family that doesn't have kids, so they want a kid to be part of their family.

His view of himself, thus, has been influenced by his parents' reason for adopting him; he was adopted because his adoptive parents wanted to help a special needs child, and not because they were unable to have children. They already had five biological children before adopting David. The idea that he was a "charity" adoption case has been deeply internalized and has had a significant effect on his self-concept and behavioral choices while growing up and even today. This was in fact a recurrent theme during my interview with him across various topics we covered.

In sum, as Emily's words in the beginning of this section illustrates, the adopted aspect of identity was too important for these adoptees to exclude from their identity expressions. It has defined a large part of their experiences and consciousness thus far if not more than being a person of Korean descent and being a U.S. American.

"American": Unexamined to Examined

Three adoptees who self-identified themselves as "American" generally agreed on their Americanized upbringing and thus their Americanized worldviews and mannerisms. When asked to elaborate on the meaning of "Americanized," they all referred to the fact that they were raised by white parents and that they grew up in the U.S. society. Beyond this, their reasons for claiming the label varied. Sandy, a mid-thirties hair dresser, felt that she was American because she neither knows many people of Asian or Korean descent nor does she see commonalities with Asians, and because a majority of her friends are white. She had no particular interest in seeking Asian friends and is more comfortable being the only or one of few Asians among whites than being one of many Asians. Thus, "culturelessness" (Perry, 2001), or lack of cultural ties to other Koreans and Asians in general, coupled with her immersion among white Americans, prompted her choice of the label "American." This way, much like other adoptees mentioned earlier, Sandy defined her identity in terms of her circle of friends, and "American" represented to her a lack of interest and connection to an ethnic or a racially defined minority culture.

In comparison, Jill, a late-twenties university employee, has friends of Asian backgrounds and is eager to get to know more. Though she used to pay little attention to racial or ethnic differences, several recent events such as going to Japan and meeting other people of Asian descent propelled her to examine her ethnic and racial identities. At the time of interview, Jill was beginning to see her connection to other Asian Americans, though she did not particularly identify with Korean Americans because she felt rather ignorant about Korean traditions, customs, and mannerisms. Yet, her first identification is with "American" because of her Americanized upbringing.

Different from the first two, the third adoptee who identified herself as "American" has interrogated her Korean identity and immersed herself in Korean culture. For Stephanie, a mid-twenties college student, Korean culture and people are part of her everyday life, but she has come full circle to see herself as "American" because she recognizes her difference from both adopted-Koreans and non-adopted Koreans. She explained her identity journey as follows:

> Initially I was American, and when I started to become involved in Korean [culture], I wanted to be like 100% Korean culture. And after being in for two years, and coming back, I think I'm American. Obviously I look Korean and stuff, but really my way of thinking is mostly American, and that's how pretty much I identify myself. I mean I eat Korean food, and I watch Korean videos, and even my fiancé is Korean. But my way of thinking is really American.

Her intense absorption of Korean culture brought Stephanie, on one hand, an appreciation of the culture, and, on the other hand, realizations of her disagreement with some aspects of Korean culture. Unlike Matt, who struggles with Korean authenticity, Stephanie feels OK if others think she is rude or strange because she does not have certain Korean mannerisms; she is the one who decides who she is, and not others.

As shown, the adoptees who identified themselves as "American" agreed upon the prevalence of the generalized, white, mainstream socialization as Americans. When their reasons were further explored, it became clear that the three individuals underwent very different identity processes and held very different ideas about the same label, "American"; it may represent a void of ethnic or racial culture; it may be an unexamined, casual choice; or it may be a choice resulting from extensive identity exploration.

"I'm White": Race as Socialization

Two adoptees described themselves as "Asian, but I am really white." They shared common reasons for claiming the label. First, they both recognize that others see them as Asians but emphasized their non-Asian upbringing and mannerisms. Second, like Sandy, both adoptees expressed comfort with being the only Asian among whites and other racial groups. Neither of them identify with "Korean" or "Korean American" because they have little interest in Korean culture and they know very few Korean Americans. One of them, Amy, a mid-twenties college student, emphasized: "I'm Asian, but at the same time I'm white. I'm whiter than anyone here, because I'm adopted." She quoted her white friend's words as a testimony of her non-Asianness.

> Most of my friends are Caucasian. And I don't think they view me as Korean or Asian. They just know me as Amy, as who I am. They like me for who I am, and even though I'm Korean, they would never be like, "This is my Korean friend." They don't introduce me like that. My best friend said a while ago, "You know, you don't even seem like you are Asian." She would forget that I was Asian. She wouldn't look at me as Asian. Most of my friends don't. It's just who I am, not what I look like.

By defying the dominant use of physical traits as racial markers and emphasizing her white upbringing and affirmation by her white friends, Amy constructs her identity as white and asserts her right to the label "white."

Michelle, a mid-twenties public relations professional, agrees with Amy. She jokingly described herself as "possibly a whitest Asian anybody ever met." This was not because she was deprived of opportunities to learn about her Korean heritage. On the contrary, growing up, her adoptive parents encouraged the cultivation of her ethnic identity and enrolled her to Korean cultural camps when she was younger. While she is grateful for her parents' efforts, she never developed interest in exploring ethnic background and racial identity. As she describes below, this lack of interest in her ethnic background became a site of challenge while attending a college that stressed multiculturalism:

> In the college kind of atmosphere where everyone is kind of getting back to their roots, figuring out who they are, there was so much pressure on me to explore that part of who I am, and I just wasn't interested. And I was really put down by the student core population because of it. I really feel like for minorities, it's almost like a necessity to find that part of yourself, and for everyone else that is white, it's a luxury. If they are Irish, and they want to know more about Ireland, their lineage, then that's really neat, that's great. But for me, well, what's wrong with her. She is not doing it. You are just in denial of who you are. I'm not in denial of who I am. Who I am is I've grown up here since six months old. And that is one of my biggest issues. If I

don't want to find out about it, it's fine with me, and I don't understand why it's the big issue with other people.

While she claims to be "white," this excerpt shows that Michelle is well aware of the dominant racial discourses that interpret her as Asian and a person of color. She recognizes that she does not have the same options as white persons have with respect to exploring their ethnicities (Waters, 1990). A large part of Michelle's non-identification with Asian and Korean stemmed from her multiracial family background. Growing up with seven siblings of different racial backgrounds (black, Korean, and white), she felt that she understood multiple perspectives. Particularly, she is close to her black siblings who have gone through many instances of blatant racism. Seeing their struggles, Michelle sometimes feels that she understands and identifies with black Americans' experiences, mannerisms, and perspectives far better than she does Asian Americans'.

In sum, the expression, "I'm white," signified the adoptees' resistance to be subsumed in the category of "Asian" or "Korean" solely based on their racial markers or ethnic background. They emphasized the centrality of their socialization among white Americans and other non-Asian Americans through their families and friends in the development of their cultural identity. White, mainstream upbringing in the U.S. society—the same reason that led some adoptees to self-identify as "American"—served as the reason for claiming whiteness for these two adoptees.

Asian and White: In-Between and Neither

Two adoptees, Brandi and Sally, felt that no one label can express their identities because they were situated in the space between Asian and white. Though they see themselves as Koreans by their ethnicity, this ethnic background has not been prominent in their lives due to the little connection they have had thus far with Koreans, Korean Americans, and other Korean adoptees. Rather, they felt ties to other Asian Americans in general because they both have evolving friendships with people of Asian descent and because it is how society classifies them. They also identify with "white" because of their parents and because of their predominantly white upbringing. Despite their identification with both groups, they do not feel that they completely belong to either group. Sally, a college senior, noted that it was probably close to how biracial persons feel, because "you are in the middle. You don't know really who you could identify with." For Sally, her identification with other people of Asian descent is a recent development due to her encounters with more Asians and Asian Americans at her college. Now she feels that she is "getting close to being Asian and being more accepting of being Asian." She shared her experience at a Chinese New Year celebration with her Asian friends as an example of this emerging identity:

> Certain people think "Oh, Asian people look the same," but you see all the differences and like freckles, Asian girls with freckles and everything. And I've seen attractive Asian men. It was different to me. It opened my eyes more than what I had thought before.

Much of her "Asian" dimension is yet to be explored, and the in-between space, though it can be frustrating, is an exciting space that allows her to discover more about herself and her changing attitudes toward people of Asian descent.

Like Sally, Brandi, a college sophomore, felt that she is in the middle of Asian and white. Different from Sally, however, Brandi has immersed herself among Asian American friends for quite some time now, and her sense of in-betweenness is characterized more by "stuck-ness" than fluidity. She lives among two racially defined worlds that see little commonalties with each other. Her boyfriend is Hmong, and her social circle in her hometown consists of a variety of friends of Asian descent. In contrast, when school is in session, she is away from her hometown and associates with a crowd from her small, private college where the majority of the students are white. She hears from both sides about negative stereotypes and prejudices they have about the other group, and she found it mentally and emotionally exhausting having to navigate herself between the two groups. At the time of the interview, Brandi was seeking a therapist to deal with her identity struggle.

Resisting Identity Labels

The adoptees' identity expressions that I discussed thus far focused on ethnicity or race, whether they felt strongly about one label, resisting an ascribed label, felt stuck in between groups, or being in the state of flux. There were four interviewees, however, who felt that no ethnic, racial, or any other cultural identity label accurately represents who they are.

One of these adoptees, Kristen, a full-time mother of two young children, has gone through phases of identity development where she identified herself one way or another in ethnic or racial terms. Growing up without the influence of other Koreans and Asians in general, she used to simply think of herself as an American. However, her encounter with people of various Asian backgrounds at work during her college years led her to identify more with Asian Americans. She also went through a phase where she was fixated by her identity as an adopted Korean; a few years ago, she and several other adoptees took a trip to Korea in hope of finding their pre-adoption information. The trip unfortunately proved futile and was emotionally draining. Nevertheless, this experience served as a closure for her preoccupation with Korea and her adopted self. When she came back from the trip, she craved balanced and inclusive relationships with her family and friends. Now she feels that her identification is with multiple groups and not with any particular group:

> Now I'm not sure what I would classify myself. I still regard myself as far as living in the United States as being an Asian American overall. And I'm a little bit more involved in Korean adoptee groups, and I have a lot more Korean adoptee friends. But I also have friends that are other nationalities, so I don't necessarily categorize myself totally as a Korean American, either. I guess I'd like to think of it more globally.

Though Kristen chose not to identify with any group, she still referred to ethnic and racial groups as well as her adopted status in describing her identity. Her resistance to an ethnic, racial, or any cultural label was motivated by her desire to embrace multiplicity in herself. Three remaining adoptees, on the other hand, preferred to describe themselves without using any racial or ethnic labels. They emphasized that identity is more of an individual matter. One of these adoptees, Paul, a graphic designer in his early-twenties, emphasized that his identity is defined by his interests and personality and not his ethnicity or race. Though his parents always made it clear to him that they were supportive of him if he wished to learn about his

Korean heritage, he was never interested in taking up this offer. He felt that his lack of interest in his ethnic background stems from his desire to be simply "normal": "When you are growing up, when you are child, you don't really want to be different. You don't want to call attention to yourself."

Another adoptee, Joan, a college senior on her way to graduate school, said, "I'm totally not involved in adoptee things." She had no exposure to Korean culture or people while growing up, and she attended predominantly white schools. Her parents stressed education, and that is how she identifies herself if she must define herself by something. Education and career are what consume her current life. Both Paul and Joan find it odd when people are drawn to others only because they share common ethnicity, race, or adoptive background. Joan made the following comment on this point:

> They always do that to me, but not vice versa, because I don't see them as adopted first. I see their personality. But whenever I meet someone or most of the time, we've known each other only maybe a week or even an hour, and they'd be inviting me to like picnic of Korean adoptees or this social gathering or whatever. I always thought that was kind of funny.

The third adoptee who resisted ethnic and racial labels was Jay, a mid-twenties man in sales. Jay grew up in a multiracial family with five adopted children including himself. Growing up, he had little exposure to Korean culture, nor did he talk with his family about being a racial minority. He did not have open communication with his parents, but it was the way he preferred. He described himself as a very independent person who is able to relate to many people as individuals. Different from Paul and Joan, Jay took Korean language classes in college, and his primary group of friends consists of the 1.5- and second-generation Korean Americans. Nevertheless, he finds the label "Korean American" too constraining. When asked about why he mainly socializes with the Korean American friends, he gave me common interests as examples (e.g., like to drink and golf), rather than commonalities due to the same ethnic background. He articulated his resistance to group-based labels as follows:

> People feel so much more comfortable when there is a label attached. They can identify through some type of

common bond. I prefer not to think in terms of that, because when you put a label on something, it's more black and white. I prefer to think that there is a lot of gray area. That's how I view it. So, I really wouldn't want to identify myself as Korean American or Korean adoptee, or something else. I'm just another person, you know. That's how I look at it.

In sum, though in different words, these three adoptees' responses demonstrated that ethnicity, race, and adopted status may constitute a part of adopted Koreans' identities but they may or may not be central to Korean adoptees' lived experiences. The lack of identification with these aspects, however, is not meant to be a fixed reality. Joan, for example, noted that she may go to Seoul in the future and that the need to do so will come to her when she is ready.

MULTIVOCALITY, RELATIONALITY, AND FLUIDITY OF IDENTITY

As shown, a variety of self-chosen identity expressions and their meanings were articulated by young adult Korean adoptees. Some reflective conclusions may be drawn from the analysis. First, the adoptees' self-chosen labels were largely motivated by a number of relational reasons including emerging, existing, or lack of friendships with ethnic and racial groups and knowledge and behavioral adequacy in communicating with people of referenced ethnic and racial cultures. For instance, those who chose "Korean American" stressed their close socialization with Korean Americans. Thus, favorable interactions with the people whom the adoptees see as the members of the identity category seem to partly validate the appropriateness of the labels (Huang, 1994; Tajfel, 1978). This relational validation of identity label resonates with Kich's (1992) study about biracial Americans whose identification as "interracial, biracial, international citizen, hapa, Amerasian, or whatever, is often amplified by a mutual process of identification and connection with others who are also biracial" (p. 313). On the other hand, many interviewees also accentuated their differences from non-adopted Koreans, other Asians, or white Americans in explaining their choices of identity labels. Such relational articulations of their identities—similarities, validations, and differences—illustrate that identity is neither pre-given nor individual creation; it is rather created relationally (Gergen, 1991; Lowe; 1996; Martin & Nakayama, 1999).

The variety of emergent identity labels suggest varying degrees of saliency and intensity (Collier & Thomas, 1988) with which adoptees approach their ethnic roots, race, socialization, personhood, or interest. On this point, this study contrasted with previous studies; many of the adoptees in this study expressed strong connection to their ethnic heritage, whereas past studies agreed that Korean adoptees have relatively weak identification with their ethnic origin (Evan B. Donaldson Adoption Institute, 1999; Feigelman & Silverman, 1983; Huh & Reid, 2000; Kim, 1977). The literature suggested that this tendency originated from lack of adoptees' early ethnic and racial exposures. In my study, however, some adoptees expressed little identification with their Korean roots *despite* their early exposure to Korean culture, while other adoptees developed strong identification with their Korean ethnicity *despite* little cultural exposure earlier in their lives. For many, the experiences with positive triggering events in late adolescence and early adulthood played important roles in their identification with their ethnic and/or racial backgrounds.

Multivocality among the participants was also demonstrated through the diverse meanings behind the same identity label. They may have chosen the same label, but they have undergone different paths and are at different phases in their identity journeys. Thus, labels such as "American" and "Korean American" had both shared and personal definitions across several participants who self-identified by the label. Personal definitions reflect the adoptees' subjectivities and hold important meanings for them, and yet such personal definitions are not likely to be understood from the identity label alone. Moreover, some adoptees have come to define the same label differently after a series of events that challenged their past understanding of what "Korean Americans" or "Asian" mean to them. The multiple, subjective, and shifting meanings call for a more complex understanding of the relationship between identity label and identity. Identity labels should not be assumed self-evident, nor should they be thought as constant and containing one meaning. They must be understood as a temporary, incomplete, and situated discursive representations of identity—identity that is in itself a "positioning" and is subject to constant transformation (Hall, 1994, 1996).

The emergent themes of multivocality, fluidity, and relationality were further articulated in the ways the adoptees resisted and redefined identity labels. Some of them resisted identification with any one ethnic or racial label, and others resisted ethnic or racial labels altogether and emphasized the importance of personal identity. Yet other adoptees contested the dominant, essentialist construction of race. Notably, no adoptee chose "Asian American" as their primary mode of identification. Some adoptees expressed their rejections of the label due to its lack of cultural specificity. Others rejected it because it represents racial lumping. This partly reflected their early experiences with Asianness; almost all adoptees experienced racist incidents while growing up, and, as a result, they distanced themselves from the label "Asian" or "Asian American." Now as young adults, many adoptees expressed connections to people of Asian descent and recognized racialized shared experiences. Nonetheless, "Asian American" took a backseat in the adoptees' identity experiences.

Transracial adoption literature is often concerned with whether adoptees *correctly* identify with their ethnic and racial backgrounds (Feigelman & Silverman, 1983; Huh & Reid, 2000; Kim, 1977; McRoy & Zurcher, 1983; Simon & Altstein, 1992; Volkman, 2005). *Incorrect* identification, the literature reasons, is a sign of identity *confusion* and is problematic because such confusion may affect ethnic and racial minority adoptees' psychological health. However, a question that must be asked here is: By *whose* standard? As Yep (1998) argued, co-creation of identity is possible only when interactants can equally participate in identity negotiation. Then, insisting that ethnic and racial minority individuals identify with *their* groups could silence the voices of individuals who feel otherwise. If we are to account for lived experiences of a racially and ethnically defined group (Delgado, 1998)—which the increasing postmodern and postcolonial sensibilities demand—then, multivocality within the group must be affirmed.

INVITATION TO EXPLORATION OF MULTIVOCALITY

If you meet the Korean adoptees that I had a pleasure of interviewing for this study, you may see "Asian" persons or you may think of them as simply "Asian

Americans." Further, if you learned that they are of Korean descent, then you may conclude that they are "Korean American." Though these identity labels may *correctly* reflect the mainstream U.S. discourse of race and ethnicity, they may or may not represent the adoptees' avowed identities. Or they may be the labels the adoptees choose but for very different reasons.

The identity labels and meanings discussed in this chapter are not meant to be exhaustive nor constant. Any insights that are drawn about identity and discursive representations of identity must be regarded as tentative. Multivocality and dynamics of Korean adoptees' identities are, on one hand, articulated in their identity labels, and, on the other hand, impossible to be contained in the labels. Hall's (1994) view of cultural identity is most relevant here:

> Cultural identity . . . [i]s a matter of "becoming" as well as of "being." It belongs to the future as much as to the past. It is not something which already exists, transcending place, time, history and culture. Cultural identities come from somewhere, have histories. But like everything which is historical, they undergo constant transformation. (Hall, 1994, p. 394)

Even for those who feel comfortable with the cultural identity location they currently inhabit, their "positioning" remains in the process of constant transformation. Matt who described himself as "adopted Korean American" reminded me of this at the end of his interview: "If you come back in ten years from now, I'd give you a different answer."

I would like to end this essay with a caution and an invitation. The diversity of labels and multiplicity of meanings behind labels should not be taken as a reason for withdrawal from intercultural interactions. On the contrary, they are all the more reasons why such interactions are necessary. Only through engaging the other, we can begin to examine our assumptions and appreciate the complexity and many forms of identity. Diverse ways in which transnational, transracial adoptees negotiate their identities suggest that we as society need to reevaluate commonly held ideas about race, ethnicity, family, and belonging. I hope you take this essay as an invitation to share with others personal experiences with and meanings of various identity labels so that we can develop more situated, inclusive understandings of identity.

References

Collier, M. J., & Thomas, M. (1988). Cultural identity: An interpretive perspective. In Y. Y. Kim & W. B. Gudykunst (Eds.), *Theories in intercultural communication*. Thousand Oaks, CA: Sage, pp. 99–120.

Delgado, F. P. (1998). When the silenced speak. *Western Journal of Communication, 62*(4), 420–438.

Department of Homeland Security. *Immigration Statistics, 2005.* Retrieved March 13, 2007, from http://www.dhs.gov/ximgtn/statistics/publications/LPR05.shtm

Evan B. Donaldson Adoption Institute. (1999). *Survey of adult Korean adoptees: Report on the findings.* New York: Evan B. Donaldson Adoption Institute.

Feigelman, W., & Silverman, A. (1983). *Chosen children: New patterns of adoptive relationships.* New York: Praeger.

Foner, E. (1998). Who is an American? In P. S. Rothenberg (Ed.), *Race, class, and gender in the United States* (pp. 84–91). New York: St. Martin's.

Gergen, K. J. (1991). *The saturated self: Dilemmas of identity in contemporary life.* New York: BasicBooks.

Hall, S. (1994). Cultural identity and diaspora. In P. Williams & L. Chrisman (Eds.), *Colonial discourse and post-colonial theory: A reader* (pp. 392–403). New York: Columbia University Press.

Hall, S. (1996). Introduction: Who needs identity? In S. Hall & P. D. Gay (Eds.), *Questions of cultural identity* (pp. 1–17). London: Sage.

Hecht, M. L., Collier, M. J., & Ribeau, S. A. (1993). *African American communication: Ethnic identity and cultural interpretation.* Newbury Park, CA: Sage.

Huang, L. N. (1994). An integrative view of identity formation: A model for Asian Americans. In E. P. Salett & D. R. Koslow (Eds.), *Race, ethnicity, and self* (pp. 42–62). Washington, D. C.: National MultiCultural Institute.

Huh, N. S., & Reid, W. J. (2000). Intercountry, transracial adoption and ethnic identity: A Korean example. *International Social Work, 43*(1), 75–87.

Kich, G. K. (1992). The developmental process of asserting a biracial, bicultural identity. In M. P. P. Root (Ed.), *Racially mixed people in America* (pp. 304–317). Newbury Park, CA: Sage.

Kim, D. S. (1977). How they fared in American homes: A follow-up study of adopted Korean children in the United States. *Children Today, 6*, 2–6, 36.

Kvale, S. (1996). *InterViews: An introduction to qualitative research interviewing.* Thousand Oaks, CA: Sage.

Lowe, L. (1996). *Immigrant acts.* Durham: Duke University Press.

Martin, J. N., & Nakayama, T. K. (1999). Thinking dialectically about culture and communication. *Communication Theory, 9*(1), 1–25.

McRoy, R., & Zurcher, L. (1983). *Transracial and inracial adoptees: The adolescent years*. Springfield, IL: Charles C. Thomas.

Oboler, S. (1995). *Ethnic labels, Latino lives: Identity and the politics of (re)presentation in the United States*. Minneapolis: University of Minnesota.

Perry, P. (2001). White means never having to say you're ethnic. *Journal of Contemporary Ethnography, 30*(1), 56–91.

Said, E. W. (1979). *Orientalism*. New York: Vintage Books.

Simon, R. J., & Altstein, H. (1992). *Adoption, race, and identity*. New York: Praeger.

Spencer, D. (1984). Defining reality: A powerful tool. In C. Kramarae, M. Schulz, & M. M. O"Barr (Eds.), *Language and power* (pp. 194–205). Beverly Hills: Sage.

Tajfel, H. (1978). *The social psychology of minorities*. New York: Minority Right Group.

Takaki, R. (1989). *Strangers from a different shore: A History of Asian Americans*. Boston: Little, Brown and Company.

U.S. Department of State. *Immigrant Visas Issued to Orphans coming to the U.S.* Retrieved March 13, 2007, from http://travel.state.gov/family/adoption/stats/stats_451.html

Yep, G. A. (2002). My three cultures: Navigating the multicultural identity landscape. In J. N. Martin, T. K. Nakayama, & L. A. Flores (Eds.), *Readings in intercultural communication* (2nd ed., pp. 60–66). Boston: McGraw Hill.

Volkman, T. A. (2005). Embodying Chinese culture: Transnational adoption in North America. In T. A. Volkman (Ed.), *Cultures of transnational adoption* (pp. 81–113). Durham, NC: Duke University Press.

Waters, M. C. (1990). *Ethnic options: Choosing identities in America*. Berkeley, CA: University of California Press.

Witteborn, S. (2004). Of being an Arab woman before and after September 11: The enactment of communal identities in talk. *The Howard Journal of Communication, 15,* 83–98.

Woodward, K. (1997). Concepts of identity and difference. In K. Woodward (Ed.), *Identity and difference* (pp. 7–61). London: Sage.

Concepts and Questions

1. How would you define the term "ethnic label"? What ethnic labels would apply to yourself?

2. Explain the statement, "Labels are . . . simultaneously useful and limiting."

3. What is meant when the author says that adopted Koreans "Have crossed multiple borders of identity units—family, race, ethnicity, and nation"?

4. Do you agree with the essay's assertion that one's place of birth is a significant source of identity? Why? Does your place of birth influence your identity? How?

5. How could learning about your ethnic culture increase pride in your ethnic identity?

6. How can learning the language and mannerisms of your ethnic homeland influence identity and communication?

7. One of the interviewees in the essay stated: "But my way of thinking is really American." What do you think was meant by this statement? Can you connect it to the essay in Chapter 3 by Richard E Nisbett?

8. Explain how one's "socialization" can be a salient source of identity?

9. What does it mean to identify with multiple ethnic groups? What are some of the problems and advantages that might come from this?

10. What factors, such as race, ethnicity, interest, personality, etc., do you consider as part of your identity?

Straddling Cultural Borders: Exploring Identity in Multiple Reacculturation

CHUKA ONWUMECHILI
PETER O. NWOSU
RONALD L. JACKSON II

INTRODUCTION

The study of multiple reacculturation is very sparse in the intercultural adjustment field. Sussman (2005) suggests that this is so because "the number of Americans or other Westerners re-migrating to their home countries is negligible so no research has examined this phenomenon. But Western return sojourners are plentiful (business executives, students and teachers, missionaries, government and military personnel) and much research has investigated these populations" (p. 30). In essence, because most of intercultural adjustment studies are conducted by Western researchers, most research has focused attention on those incidences common to Westerners. This skewing of research has resulted in the absence of studies on the lives of those who move back and forth across cultures. These rarely studied individuals are better known as cultural transients.

Some scholars such as Onwumechili, Nwosu, Jackson, and James-Hughes (2003), Kim (2001), and Berry (1999) point out that the lack of accurate global data makes it difficult to track the trend of these

transients. The number of transients, however, is likely to be significant because of factors such as large economic gaps between nations and improved and relatively less expensive global transportation. These factors, for instance, have promoted the increase in movement of labor across international borders. For instance, the phenomenon tagged *Taai Hung Yahn*[1] or "astronauts" in Hong Kong describes husbands and single men who shuttle between their new immigrant country in the West where their family now resides and their new businesses in their home country Hong Kong. Other examples include Africans who work in the United States but return frequently to Africa for significant periods in the year, and the frequent border crossings (back and forth) by Mexicans into the United States. Sussman (2005) also points out the rise of another group of transients: "the new Hong Kong immigrant is that of the manager whose work takes him to Shenzhen or Dongguan or Shanghai for a week or month at a time and whose family remains in Hong Kong" (pp. 33–34). Therefore, the incidence of transiency is not only apparent but it is perhaps increasing and driven largely by economics, ease of transportation, and search for respect and status as demonstrated in Onwumechili et al. (2003).

It is because of the importance of transients and the scarcity of research on their lives that this paper focuses on theorizing about their negotiation of cultural identity as they move from one culture to the other. The essay begins with a review of acculturation research. Then it provides details about the types of intercultural transients. The remainder of the paper applies several cultural identity theories, with particular focus on cultural contracts theory, to the negotiation of transients' identity.

ACCULTURATION RESEARCH

Acculturation studies have been with us for almost a century. Persons (1987) cited Park as one of the earliest researchers in the area. Park carried out a 1914 study of immigrants coming in contact with a host culture and concluded that such immigrants follow a progressive and linear process that began with contact, went through accommodation, and culminated in assimilation. Communication scholars, however, often cite studies in the 1950s as the harbinger of research in acculturation in the field of intercultural communication. One of such early 1950s studies was by Sven Lysgaard (1955) who investigated the cultural adjustment patterns of Norwegian Fulbright scholars to the United States. Lysgaard's study became historical as it provided the field with a model of cultural adjustment pattern of foreigners in a host culture. That model known as the U-curve hypothesized that the adjustment patterns began with a period of euphoria and then advanced to culture shock, recovery, and eventual adjustment (Figure 1).

The U-curve hypothesis was eventually extended to a W-curve by Gullahorn and Gullahorn (1963) who hypothesized that those who had experienced U-curve pattern are likely to go through a similar pattern upon their return home (Figure 2). Today, both the U-curve and W-curve are no longer considered valid descriptors of cultural adjustment patterns (Onwumechili & Okereke-Arungwa, 2001). The primary reason for this is that several scholars have not found research support for any of the two hypotheses (Anderson, 1994; Berry, 1999; Brislin, 1981; Sussman, 2001; Ward, Okura, & Kojima, 1998). Berry (1999), for instance, noted that there is more than one possible outcome for individuals who come into contact with a foreign culture. Both the U and W curves failed to acknowledge the possibility of different outcomes for different individuals and instead theorized that all

persons are bound to adjust to the host culture. Berry's work, as well as Navas et al. (2005, 2007) and Bourhis (1997), showed that individuals do not always adjust successfully to a host foreign culture. Instead, they may assimilate, become separated from the host culture, or become deviant depending on their response to the culture shock, their choices for coping, and the relationship between their adjustment ideal and reality. Padilla and Perez (2003) also note that there are numerous factors including skin color, accented speech, religious dressing, and gender that may affect choices that persons make on whether to assimilate, adjust, or separate from a host culture. Furthermore, other studies showed that reacculturation for those who return to their home culture after stay in a foreign culture were not a mere extension of the U curve. Instead, the returning sojourners had significantly different problems, which included a fixed perception of the homeland, unawareness of own and other's changes, unexpectedness of reentry problems, among a host of other factors (see Berry, 2005; Cox, 2004; Sussman, 1986; and Uehara, 1986). The U and W curves, however, remain significant at least because of their illustrative value in describing patterns of acculturation for those who eventually adjust to a foreign culture (Onwumechili et al., 2003). The figures below provide graphic descriptions of both curves.

Figure 1 *The U-Curve Indicating a Process of Euphoria upon Entry, Shock and Depression before Recovery and Adjustment*

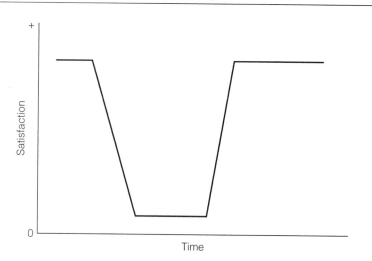

Figure 2 *The W-Curve Which Extended the U-Curve Hypothesis to the Sojourners Return to the Homeland*

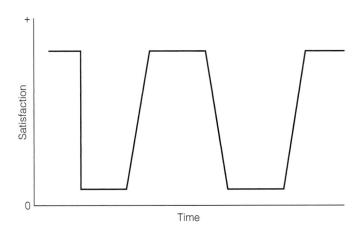

Acculturation and reacculturation studies, including those reviewed here, have contributed several important concepts in the first 40 years of the field. These include an understanding of culture shock, patterns of adjustment, and communication competence, among others. The field, however, has shifted in the last 15 years to a new focus on discovering the effect on cultural identity for individuals who come in contact with foreign cultures (Kim, 2001; Sussman, 2000). This new focus, for example, has included studies in the area of third culture building (Casmir, 1993; Chen & Starosta, 1998) and multiculturalism (Adler, 1982).

It is surprising that in spite of over 50 years of research in the field, the study of a growing group of transients has been largely ignored. Onwumechili et al (2003) provide a graphic description, called *cyclical curves,* of the adjustment pattern for transients (see Figure 3). Of course, the figure merely provides an illustrative example of the process for a transient who successfully adjusts across cultures back and forth but the graph does not reflect outcomes for all transients.

Figure 3 *The Cyclical Curve Which Provides a Further Extension of the W-Curve to Depict the Process that Some Transients Experience in Several Encounters with Entries and Reentries*

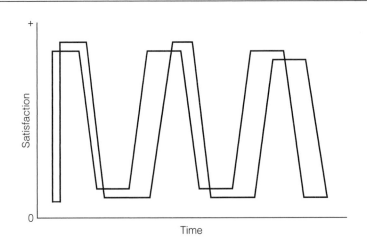

Table 1 *Transient Typologies*

Function of Transient Activity	Length of Stay	
	Short Term (6 months or less in multiple locations)	**Long Term** (More than 6 months in one locations)
Socioeconomic/Political	Brief-staying "astronauts," Nigerian transients	Long-staying "astronauts"
Service-Employment	Agricultural guest workers	Armed Force personnel

TYPOLOGIES OF CULTURAL TRANSIENTS

Onwumechili et al. (2003) provide taxonomy of cultural transients using two key variables to describe categories of cultural transients. The variables—length of stay in a culture and function of transient activity—were used to create (a) short-term socioeconomic/political transients, (b) long-term socioeconomic/political transients, (c) short-term service/employment transients, and (d) long-term service/employment transients.

Socioeconomic/political categorizes those situations where the decision to maintain a link with the transient's country of birth is based on social and/or business reasons. One of the most important differences between the socioeconomic transient and the service/employment transient is that the former is often a citizen of both cultures or at least has permanent residency status. Another important difference between the socioeconomic transient and the service/employment dimension is that for the former, one of the cultural abodes is not used as a place of employment. For the socioeconomic dimension, the place of employment in the home country, if with a large organization, is often with one that does not necessarily seek to hire someone with an international link. Furthermore, the decision to seek a home country employment is socioculturally influenced by the person's affinity with his homeland.

The service/employment category refers to transients whose move is often to seek employment in a foreign continent but whose primary residence is often the country of birth. Transients who are classified under the service/employment category often enter one of the cultures in order to work on a periodic basis. These transients may often keep working in both cultural locations. Their employment away

from home is essentially temporary or seasonal. Their contact with the non-homeland culture has very little to do with social reasons and more to do with employment. We describe each of the categories in detail in the subsequent subsections and Table 1 (above) also shows each typology.

Short-Term Socioeconomic/ Political Transients

These transients are those whose reasons for moving repeatedly between two or more cultures are often socioeconomic or political. The short term identifies these transients as those who spend perhaps six months or less in one culture before moving to the next culture to spend a similar amount of time, back and forth. These types of transients have been in existence as far back as the nineteenth century. Rossler (1995) reported that German craftsmen and artisans denoted such travel patterns in Europe to fill needs for such skills in certain geographical areas.

The length of time is critical in differentiating this group of travelers from the usual vacationers who spend less than a month in visiting a foreign country or place that is culturally different. It is also important to note that because of the short stay of six months or less, transients are often individuals that are self employed or those working in low-paying jobs where the turnover is immense. Such a situation allows them to leave the job and easily return to a similar job upon return. Among Nigerians who are involved in this type of intercultural travel are those whose employment is in the hospitality, transportation (e.g., taxicab business), tax accounting (largely seasonal), or low-paying occupations.

The Hong Kong "astronauts" have been a widely reported group of transients in recent times. Some astronauts can be classified as short-term transients in the socioeconomic category. Chen (1990) reported that one of Hong Kong's "astronauts," Stanley Tam, had flown from Hong Kong to Toronto seven times in 30 months as he shuttled between his job in Hong Kong and his family in Toronto.

Chen points out that sometimes these "astronauts" could earn three times in Hong Kong the income that they could earn in the United States. They felt more secure in the United States and Canada, however, because the social life and schooling were preferred and they had no fear of communist life and policy that could be introduced in Hong Kong by China. Chen added that "Between 30 percent and 60 percent of emigrants are coming back to Hong Kong (after they fled following the handover of Hong Kong to China in 1984) filling important posts left behind by the departure of skilled professionals."

It was a similar situation that drove Nigerians to transiency. Most Nigerians initially traveled to the West before the early 1980s with the plan for a temporary stay after which they would return home to Nigeria for a permanent stay. However, Nigeria's economy collapsed in the early 1980s, a consequence of decades of neglect from military rule, forcing the sojourners to rethink about a permanent return. A large number of those who had a rethink decided to stay permanently in a foreign country, in many cases taking up citizenship. Those who chose to return did not want to take the chance of making a permanent return. Instead, they chose the option of becoming transients (see case in Onwumechili et al.'s report, 2003, pp. 47–48).

Long-Term Socioeconomic/ Political Transients

These transients share similar characteristics with their short-term colleagues. We describe them as long term, however, because they spend a longer period of time in one of the cultures they encounter. In essence, these persons may spend a couple of years in one culture and then sojourn in another country and repeat the process. They do not move from one culture to the other as frequently as do their short-term colleagues.

Some of the Hong Kong "astronauts" also fit into this category. Chen (1990) describes one of such "astronauts" who had returned to Hong Kong after settling in the United States for four years. Chen cited the

"astronaut" as stating "I earn about $6,400 a month here (Hong Kong) but couldn't make more than $2,000 if I worked for someone in the United States." Chen also found that in the case of Hong Kong returnees, factors like "language barriers, cultural differences, and the challenge of building a new life" were instrumental in making a decision to become transient. In the same report, Chen described another "astronaut" who immigrated to Australia and stayed for two years to satisfy residency requirements before returning to Hong Kong. The transient at the time of Chen's report in 1990 planned to stay in Hong Kong to save money until 1995 before returning once again to Australia. There are other examples such as the case of Andres Bermudez who rose from a foreign farm worker to a large farm contractor in California earning over $300,000 a year (Bakker & Smith, n.d.; Mena, 2001). Bermudez later traveled back and forth between the United States and Mexico at least once every three years, staying for significant lengths of time, before deciding to run for mayor of Jerez, Mexico.

Onwumechili et al. (2003) reported that immigration laws are often critical in determining whether a transient would be short or long term. Citizenship provides for travelers to become long-term transients with easy entry and reentry after long absences from a country. The authors also report that several countries, including Ecuador, have recognized the transients' needs by legalizing dual citizenship.

Short-Term Service/ Employment Transients

The short-term service/employment transient is one who primarily moves across cultural borders because of the demand of work and not because of social considerations. They may choose to work in both cultures and are often in the employ of a large organization that is allowed to hire international labor on a temporary or short-term basis. They are short term because they spend perhaps six months or less in one culture before moving to the next culture to spend a similar amount of time, back and forth.

Seasonal migrant labor groups represent this category of short term transients. The United States has used these labor groups for years. *The Bracero Program*, for instance, was implemented from 1942 to 1964 and it was used to hire agricultural workers from Mexico to work on farms in the United States (Martins, 1994). Martins adds that some of these workers "returned year after year" (p. 877). These returnees often had employment in their home country and only worked seasonally in the United States. By the time the program was completed, over four million Mexican farm workers had entered the United States. Several countries including Germany, the United Arab Emirates, Qatar, Kuwait, and Luxembourg also utilize guest workers (Castles, 2006; Jones, 1996; Rudolph, 1996). The German guest worker system also known as *Gastarbeiter* was initially used after World War II when there was a shortage of industrial workers. The program attracted workers from Turkey, Italy, Greece, and Portugal, among other countries. Several of these workers did not return permanently to their home states but began to move transnationally across two countries. The *Gastarbeiter* is still alive today as Turkish citizens stream across the border to Germany to meet shortages in the lower-skilled jobs (Castles, 2006; Rudolph, 1996).

Long-Term Service/Employment Transients

This category of transients shares similar characteristics with their short-term counterparts. They are considered to be long-term transients because they spend a longer period of time in one of the cultures that they encounter. In essence, these persons may spend a couple of years in employment in one culture and then sojourn in another country and then repeat the process. Onwumechili, Nwosu, Jackson, and James-Hughes (2003) identified some sailors and other military personnel who are on oversea tour of military duty as being part of this category of transients. A significant point about military personnel who are on oversea duty is that, unlike their civilian colleagues who frequently encounter foreign culture while oversea, the military personnel are often situated among a network of familiar co-military personnel and friends. They could spend much or all of their time in a foreign land isolated from the host foreign culture by being resident on a military base and surrounding themselves with on-base activities. However, no matter how isolated they may wish to be they will, at least for brief periods, encounter the host culture when they venture outside the base or come in contact with locals who work on base.

Military personnel on oversea tours are not the only people that can be classified as being members of this category of long-term transients. Foreign employees who are contracted for the long term away from their homeland, for instance, also fit into this category. Several nations, including the United States, Canada, and Germany, have programs that advance the importation of foreign workers to fill shortages of labor in specific employment areas. The United States introduced the H1-B visa which attracts foreigners to the country to fill shortages in several employment areas, but they are not offered citizenship or permanent residence and their stay in the country is dependent on their continued attachment to their employer. These transients may travel back and forth between their homeland and the United States during their period of employment in the United States. In 2000, Germany introduced five-year visas that are designed to attract information technology experts to the country. The German visas have been relatively successful but, like their U.S. equivalent, they do not offer permanent stay or citizenship. Again, however, like the U.S. equivalent, it allows those with such visas to become cultural transients straddling the borders of their homeland and Germany.

CULTURAL IDENTITY SHIFTING

Cultural transients are affected by constant challenges to their identities as they move from one culture to the other. There are several theories of cultural identity that allow us to analyze probable cultural effects on the identity of transients. These theories include the *Cultural Identity Model of Cultural Transitions* (CIM), *mindful identity shifting*, *multicultural personhood* (intercultural person), *I-Other dialectic* (e.g., stranger-host), *network theory*, *community builder*, and the *cultural identity model of cultural transitions* (CIM). Some of these theories are subsumed in Jackson's (1999) cultural contracts theory.

In this section, we shall begin our discussion by reviewing the applicability of Cultural Identity Model which has been used by Sussman (2005) to explain the cultural identity of Hong Kong returnees including "astronauts." We will also review Jackson's cultural contracts theory which is an appropriate theory that is used in explaining the cultural identity struggles of transients.

The typologies of cultural transients, which we discussed earlier, are also salient in the negotiation of a transient's identity. It is difficult, however, to discuss all variables that may affect the transients' negotiation of identity because they are simply too numerous. A transient, for instance, may become demotivated in the process of seeking bi-cultural identity because his or her time in one cultural environment is brief. The opposite will be true for a transient in a long-term cultural environment. Additionally, Padilla's work indicates that a transient's acculturation goal may also be frustrated by local reactions that may include stigmatization, language differentiation, and other types of discriminations. These reactions may force the transient to re-assess his or her cultural identity goal. Furthermore, the transient's cultural value dimension (e.g., collectivism or individualism) may affect how and the type of identity that he or she may prefer to negotiate. In essence, the negotiation of cultural identity is complex and is difficult to categorize precisely because the process of negotiating cultural identity is affected by numerous variables and characteristics. Thus, it is better and more efficient to describe transients' cultural identity effects independent of transient typologies. We will, therefore, discuss briefly some of those cultural identity effects in the subsequent sections.

The Cultural Identity Model (CIM)

Sussman (2005) introduced the CIM in order to understand the consequences of the sojourner's return home, but she has also used it to investigate remigration in Hong Kong. Sussman (2005) notes that an individual's cultural identity may change during an intercultural encounter, but it remains latent and only becomes "salient upon commencement of repatriation" (p. 5). The cultural encounter after repatriation leads to optional cultural identity shifts. These shifts are labeled as subtractive, additive, affirmative, or intercultural. Those who experience subtractive cultural identity outcome (discomfort with home culture upon return) are those who had left home with low cultural identity with their homeland but with the capability for moderate cultural flexibility. They also had high adaptation with the foreign culture. Those who experience additive cultural identity outcome (discomfort with home culture upon return) are those who had left home with moderate cultural

identity with their homeland and had high cultural flexibility, which led to high adaptation with the foreign culture. Those who experience affirmative cultural identity outcome (comfort with home culture upon return) are those who had left home with high cultural identity with their homeland but had low cultural flexibility and, thus, they had low adaptation with the foreign culture. Those who experience intercultural identity outcome (comfort with home culture upon return) are those who had left home with low cultural identity with their homeland but had high cultural flexibility and, thus, had high adaptation with the foreign culture. It is this later group, intercultural identity, that appears to describe individuals who are more likely to be comfortable with the life of a transient as they have very high cultural flexibility that allows them to adapt to several cultures in their back and forth movement. Sussman's (2005) research, however, found that only few of the Hong Kong remigrants fell into that category.

Other Effects of Identity Shifting

Several other theories of cultural identity shifting require discussion at this point, for instance Langer's (1989) discussion of *Mindfulness and Identity Shifting* which is based on three explicit criteria that include creation of new categories, openness to new information, and the awareness of more than one cultural perspective. Langer posits that individuals are active, or mindful, in seeking to negotiate a cultural identity when they come into contact with a new cultural environment. The opposite is an individual who engages in mindless communication where the person is oblivious of cultural events around him or herself and instead is largely "intransigent." Langer's discussion of the creation of a new cultural identity category is consistent with the discussions of *Third Culture Building* (TCB) by Chen and Starosta (1998) and Casmir (1993, 1999). Here, Casmir argues that a person builds a third cultural identity by using interpersonal, mass media, and the desire to acculturate. This person then develops a beneficial and cooperative culture with the host environment.

Additionally, Langer's first criterion for creation of a new cultural category is also largely consistent with Sussman's CIM and the conceptions of *Multicultural Personhood* by several scholars (see Kim, 2001; Kim &

Ruben, 1988; Milhouse, Asante, & Nwosu, 2001; Adler, 1982). Multicultural personhood, however, is somewhat different from TCB in subtle ways. TCB argues that the individual interacts with a host to build a third culture that melds some aspects of the individual's culture with aspects of the host culture. Whereas, multicultural personhood, which has also been referred to as both "intercultural" (Sussman, 2001, 2005; Kim, 2001) and "transcultural" (Milhouse et al., 2001), is more than merely building a third culture from the contact between two or more cultures. Instead, Sussman (2005) describes it as an identity that allows the individual to "hold multiple cultural identities simultaneously and draw on each as the need requires. . . . This identity shift paradigm is neither the integration of home and host culture values (hybridization) nor the bicultural strategy which result from the acculturation experience but rather an identity in which the repatriates define themselves as world citizens and are able to interact appropriately or effectively in many countries or regions switching cultural frames as needed" (p. 9). Milhouse et al. suggest further that being transcultural requires one to free oneself from the obsessions of one's culture—to free oneself from one's cultural prison, and to be able to see things from varying and multiple perspectives, and to act out in such ways.

Networks Upon Reentry

Network analysis is critical to the understanding of the transient's relationships with others. Network analysis, however, has been rarely used in the discussion of cultural identity among intercultural communication scholars. Network is best understood as a set of relationships. It contains a set of objects and a description of relationships between or among the objects (Boissevain, 1974; Kadushin, n.d.; Weimann, 1989). Network analysis is important in understanding the transient's negotiation of cultural identity because identity is not created in isolation but it is only understood, developed, changed, or modified in the process of interacting and relating with others.

Two key network principles help explain problems that transients encounter and, thus, those principles are important in predicting how a transient's cultural identity might shift over time. One of those principles is that of propinquity. Propinquity proposes that network relationships are strengthened by

geographical proximity. The other principle is that of homophily which predicts that the more the members of a network share in common the stronger the relationships. Abdelhady (2006), McCarthy (2005), and Jenkins (2005) have all cited networks as assisting cultural travelers, in the long term, with alleviating feelings of dislocation in the economic, cultural, religious, and political spheres. For the transient, however, his or her relationship with a network may develop a pathology over time because the transient often severs geographical proximity and fails to share events and acts with his friends for a significant amount of time because of his or her travels to the "other" culture. The travels end up disrupting the network which repairs itself by developing a modified network of relationship that excludes the "absentee" transient. In essence, the transient will struggle to reenter the network upon reentry. This type of network pathology is significant in determining how the transient creates his or her cultural identity. More detailed discussion can be found in Weimann's (1989) discussion of networks and strengths of friendship ties and Boissevain's (1974) analysis of the relationship between personal networks and the social environment.

Transients and Cultural Contracts

Jackson's (1999, 2002) conception of cultural contracts explains an implied but mindful agreement between cultural interacts to coordinate a relationship. Onwumechili et al. (2003) note that the theory stands out because "it recognizes the possibility of intracultural contract negotiations among friends, acquaintances, family, and strangers" (p. 55). While they agree that most of the theories discussed earlier are useful in understanding several aspects of negotiating cultural identity, they stress that cultural contracts theory appears to be the appropriate theory for predicting how transients might shift their cultural identity.

Jackson (1999, 2002) argues that cultural contracts theory is particularly important and essential in answering the question "What is it that is negotiated?" The answer to this significant question is muted in theories of identity negotiation but the use of the metaphor "contracts" brings to the fore the answer to the question. Invariably, not only does Jackson's theory provide an illuminating answer, it also for the first time brings together the concepts of

Table 2 *Cultural Identity Contracts and Transients*

	Ready-To-Sign	Quasi-Completed	Co-Created
Description	Cultural identity is predetermined. There is no room for negotiations during multiple reentry interaction.	Cultural identity is a mixture of predetermined identity and a result of some openness to negotiation during multiple reentry interaction.	Cultural identify is fully open to negotiation during multiple reentry interaction.
Purpose	To avoid stress that may be caused by multiple adjustments.	Careful choice of when to adjust in order to achieve predetermined goals.	Seeks full acceptance by hosts. Transient works towards full competence.
Drawbacks	Culture shock. There could also be lack of ongoing competence in at least one cultural location.	There is possible cultural marginalization in each cultural system.	Stressful. Transients must be socially active during each reentry. Each host feels unfulfilled by relationship with transient because each host seeks the transient's assimilation to the local culture and not a co-created cultural outcome.

identity and intercultural negotiation in simple to understand terms.

The theory points out that everyone has negotiated at least one cultural contract over their lifetime and that each contract has an impact on the person's identity. It denies the existence of a "noncultural" or culturally generic contract. Thus, all contracts are "cultural." This point has implications for our understanding of identity negotiation of transients. In essence, it raises the question as to whether a transient can be "intercultural" as defined by Sussman's CIM theory. Can a transient who has traveled to a few European and East African countries and has achieved cultural competence in each of those claim to be have developed an intercultural/global identity (as conceived by Sussman) when he or she comes into contact with Senegal for the very first time? The cultural contracts theory would say "No." She or he cannot claim that such contracts are "generic" and, thus, applicable to Senegal even though the individual signed several cultural contracts in those various visits. If that someone was to use that supposedly "generic" culture, then the cultural contracts theory will describe it as intent to use a prenegotiated contract.

This brings us to a discussion of the types of cultural contracts that can be negotiated and how they apply to transients. They are *ready-to-sign*, *quasi-completed*, and *co-created* contracts (see Table 2). Each type of contract demonstrates the following salient premises—that identities require affirmation, they are in flux, they are only understood interactively, and they are indubitably contractual.

Ready-to-sign contracts describe situations where the transient has already made a determination on his/her cultural identity and feels little need to adjust that decision. This fits the example of Senegal that we had previously discussed. In essence, the transient has negotiated with the self and shows little or no interest in constantly adjusting to the culture that he or she enters and reenters repeatedly. Onwumechili et al. (2003) point out that "over time, it is fairly common for a reacculturating transient to take routine trips to the same location and become less and less mindful of subtle differences among the hosts upon reentry. They have changed very little of themselves in the process" (p. 56). They go on to cite the works of Kim (2001) and Sussman (2001) by noting that "naturally, the stress of multiple reacculturation can be exhausting and one means of lessening such stress is to avoid major adjustments to behaviors, attitudes and perspectives" (p. 56). On the face of it, a ready-to-sign contract may seem the appropriate option for a transient to use in developing a cultural identity. The acculturation literature, however, is steeped in warnings against the development of a cultural identity that is based on a ready-to-sign contract. Cross (1995) warns of possible shock and stress because culture is always in flux (never static) and, thus, identities should not be static. Moreover, no one is an island to himself or herself. Thus, in order to ensure ongoing cultural competence it seems that transients must remain open, to a certain degree, as advised by Ting-Toomey (1999).

The *Quasi-completed contract* is preferred by a transient who is neither fixed in his or her ways nor fully committed to co-creating a cultural system. Instead, the transient is in a "cultural limbo" or middle ground where full reacculturation is not an acceptable option. In a sense, this type of cultural contract is somewhat prenegotiated and, at the same time, partially open for negotiation. Transients who choose this cultural contract option may do so based on their reentry purpose as predicted by Onwumechili et al. (2003). For instance, a Nigerian transient who initially migrated to the United States and has assumed a new cultural identity that is largely influenced by his stay in the United States may decide to apply a quasi-completed cultural contract upon reentries to Nigeria. The transient realizes that he or she has changed and that some cultural distance now exists between what he or she used to be and what he or she is now. To bridge this gap, the transient may consciously seek situations where he/she demonstrates competence with the local Nigerian culture. The transient, in this example, is not fully committed to opening himself or herself to changing a cultural identity that had been largely influenced by stay in the United States. Instead, the transient shows some willingness to negotiate an "accommodation" of the Nigerian culture, it is never an openness to co-create nor is it ever an intention to entirely reject the Nigerian culture to which he or she reenters repeatedly in travels.

The third type of cultural contract is the *co-created contract*. Here, cultural identity is fully open to negotiation. Little is held back. The co-created contract is one in which the transient is fully committed to jointly negotiating a third culture with members of the host culture. Several scholars point to this type of cultural contract as desirable (Langer, 1989; Ting-Toomey, 1999). The transient's choice of this contract, however, is not always met with acceptance by family and friends (Onwumechili et al., 2003), and one's own local culture or community. The family and friends of a transient who reenters his initial home culture always expect the returnee transient to be unchanged. Thus, they are more likely than not to frown at the transient's attempt to co-create a different culture, a different identity from what the family and friends, and the local culture or community are familiar with.

A cultural contract is a metaphorical theory that helps us to better understand how transients negotiate cultural identity. It does not, however, inform us on how this group of international travelers copes with the obvious stress that is associated with straddling cultures and negotiating identity. To learn about what transients do for coping we have to refer to the work of Cross and Strauss (1998). Both authors point to the use of buffering, bonding, bridging, and code switching to ameliorate the stress of negotiating identity. The first strategy—buffering—is a defensive strategy used to soften or block out the stress. In essence, the transient may rationalize his or her resistance to cultural influence or seek other persons with similar identity. The latter three strategies are strategies that reach out to the host culture to seek ways to assist in adjusting to a new identity. For instance, the transient may seek to renew membership in a social network (bonding), verbal demonstration of an understanding of a cultural ritual (bridging), or switching to host cultural behavior in certain contexts (code switching).

CONCLUSION

In this essay, we have attempted to re-capture several issues that we previously raised in a 2003 published article (see Onwumechili et al.). We have also added germane literature from more recent sources in an attempt to better understand multiple reacculturation which generates the cyclical curves that is experienced by some transients. We have also focused much of our writing on an important aspect of the lives of transients, which is the process of negotiating cultural contracts in order to develop cultural identities during their travels.

It is important to understand that while we advance the cultural contracts theory as an appropriate framework for understanding how transients negotiate their identity, we do not deny the importance of the other theoretical frameworks. In fact, we have shown how other theoretical frameworks might provide us with insights on the lives of transients, particularly as they seek to define their cultural identity. The task ahead is still enormous as scholars attempt to understand this group of sojourners.

Note

1. While the Chinese words refer to "astronauts" they also can loosely mean "man without wife."

References

Abdelhady, D. (2006). Beyond home/host networks: Forms of solidarity among Lebanese immigrants in a global era. *Identities: Global Studies in Culture and Power, 13,* 427–453.

Adler, P. (1982). Beyond cultural identity: Reflections on cultural and multicultural man. In L. Samovar & R. Porter (Eds.), *Intercultural communication: A reader.* Belmont, CA: Wadsworth.

Anderson, L. (1994). A new look at an old construct: Cross-cultural adaptation. *International Journal of Intercultural Relations, 18,* 293–328.

Bakker, M., & Smith, M. (n.d.). El rey del tomate: Migrant political transnationalism in Mexico. Retrieved from http://www. hcd.ucdavis.edu/facultysmith/

Berry, J. (2005). Acculturation: Living successfully in two cultures. *International Journal of Intercultural Relations, 29*(6), 697–712.

Berry, J. (1999). Intercultural relations in plural societies. *Canadian Psychology, 40,* 12–21.

Boissevain, J. (1974). *Friends of friends: Networks, manipulators, and coalitions.* New York: St. Martin's Press.

Bourhis, R., Moise L., Perreaut, S., & Senecal, S. (1997). Toward an interactive acculturation model: A social psychological approach. *International Journal of Psychology, 32*(6), 369–386.

Brislin, R. (1981). *Cross-cultural encounters.* New York: Pergamon Press.

Casmir, F. (1993). Third culture building: A paradigm shift for international and intercultural communication. *Communication Yearbook, 16,* 407–428.

Casmir, F. (1999). Foundations for the study of intercultural communication based on a third culture building model. *International Journal of Intercultural Relations, 23,* 91–116.

Castles, S. (2006). Guestworkers in Europe: A resurrection? *International Migration Review, XL*(4), 741–766.

Chen, K. (1990, January 6). Hong Kong's frequent-flyer "Astronauts." *San Francisco Examiner.*

Chen, G., & Starosta, W. (1998). *Foundations of intercultural communication.* Needham Heights, MA: Allyn & Bacon.

Cox, B. (2004). The role of communication, technology, and cultural identity in repatriation adjustment. *International Journal of Intercultural Relations, 28*(3/4), 201–219.

Cross, S. (1995). Self-construals, coping and stress in cross-cultural adaptation. *Journal of Cross-Cultural Psychology, 26*(6), 673–697.

Cross, W., & Strauss, L. (1998). The everyday functions of African American identity. In J. Swim & C. Stangor (Eds.), *Prejudice: The target's perspective.* New York: Academic Press.

Gullahorn, J. T., & Gullahorn, J. E. (1963). An extension of the U-curve hypothesis. *Journal of Social Issues, 19*(3), 33–47.

Jackson, R. L. (1999). *The negotiation of cultural identity.* Westport, CT: Praeger Press.

Jackson, R. L. (2002). Exploring African American identity negotiation in the academy: Toward a transformative vision of African American communication scholarship. *Howard Journal of Communication, 12*(4), 43–57.

Jenkins, W. (2005). Deconstructing diasporas: Networks and identities among the Irish in Buffalo and Toronto. *Immigrants and Minorities, 23*(2/3), 1870–1910.

Jones, P. (1996). Immigrants, Germans and national identity in the new Germany: Some policy issues. *International Journal of Popular Geography, 2*(2), 119–131.

Kadushin, C. (n.d.). Introduction to social network theory. http://www.home.eathlink.net/~ckadushin/

Kim, Y. (2001). *Becoming intercultural: An integrative theory of communication and cross-cultural adaptation.* Newbury Park, CA: Sage Publications.

Kim, Y., & Ruben, B. (1998). Intercultural transformation: A systems theory. In Y. Kim & W. Gudykunst. (Eds.), *Theories in intercultural communication* (pp. 299–321). Newbury Park, CA: Sage Publications.

Langer, E. (1989). *Mindfulness.* Reading, MA: Addison-Wesley.

Lysgaard, S. (1955). Adjustment in a foreign society: Norwegian Fulbright grantees visiting the United States. *International Social Science Bulletin, VII,* 145–151.

Martin, P. (1994). *The endless quest: Helping America's farm workers.* Boulder, CO: Westview Press.

McCarthy, A. (2005). "Bands of fellowship": The role of personal relationships and social networks among Irish migrants in New Zealand, 1861–1911. *Immigrants and Minorities, 23*(2/3), 339–358.

Mena, J. (2001, June 30). Three men, two nations, one dream. *Los Angeles Times,* p. A1.

Milhouse, V., Asante, M., & Nwosu, P. (2001). Introduction. In V. Milhouse, M. Asante, & P. Nwosu. (Eds.), *Transcultural realities: Interdisciplinary perspectives on cross-cultural relations.* Newbury Park, CA: Sage Publications.

Mora, M. (2006). Self-employed Mexican immigrants residing along the United States-Mexico border: The earnings effect of working in the United States versus Mexico. *International Migration Review, XL*(4), 885–898.

Navas, M., Rojas, A., Garcia, M., & Pumares, P. (2007). Acculturation strategies and attitudes according to the relative acculturation extended model (RAEM): The perspectives of natives versus immigrants. *International Journal of Intercultural Relations, 31*(1), 67–86.

Navas, M., Garcia, M., Sanchez, J., Rojas, A., Pumares, P., & Fernandez, J. (2005). Relative acculturation extended model (RAEM): New contributions with regard to the study of acculturation. *International Journal of Intercultural Relations, 29*(1), 21–37.

Onwumechili, C., Nwosu, P., Jackson, R., II, & James-Hughes, J. (2003). In the deep valley with mountains to climb: Exploring identity and multiple reacculturation. *International Journal of Intercultural Relations, 27*, 41–62.

Onwumechili, C., & Okereke-Arungwa, J. (2001). Research and training in cross-cultural readjustment: Recommendations for advancements. In V. Milhouse, M. K. Asante, & P. Nwosu, (Eds.), *Transcultural realities: Interdisciplinary perspectives on cross-cultural relations* (pp. 267–279). Thousand Oaks, CA: Sage Publications.

Padilla, A., & Perez, W. (2003). Acculturation, social identity, and social cognition: A new perspective. *Hispanic Journal of Behavioral Sciences, 25*(1), 35–55.

Persons, S. (1987). *Ethnic studies at Chicago: 1905–45.* Urbana: University of Illinois Press.

Rossler, H. (1995). Traveling workers and the German labor movement. In D. Hoerder & J. Nagler (Eds.), *People in transit: German migrations in comparative perspective, 1820–1930* (pp. 127–146). Washington, DC: German Historical Institute.

Rudolph, H. (1996). The new gastarbeiter system in Germany. *New Community, 22*(2), 287–300.

Sussman, N. (2005). People on the move: The transnational flow of Chinese human capital. Paper presented at the Hong Kong University of Science and Technology, October 20–22.

Sussman, N. (2001). Repatriation transitions: Psychological preparedness, cultural identity, and attributions among American managers. *International Journal of Intercultural Relations, 25*(2), 109–123.

Sussman, N. (2000). The dynamic nature of cultural identity throughout cultural transitions: Why home is not so sweet. *Personality and Social Psychological Review, 4*, 355–373.

Sussman, N. (1986). Reentry research and training: Methods and implications. *International Journal of Intercultural Relations, 10*(2), 235–253.

Ting-Toomey, S. (1999). *Communicating across cultures.* New York: Guilford Publications.

Uehara, A. (1986). The nature of American student reentry adjustment and perception of the sojourn adjustment. *International Journal of Intercultural Relations, 10*(4), 415–438.

Ward, C., Okura, Y., Kennedy, A., & Kojima, T. (1998). The U-curve on trial: A longitudinal study of psychological and sociocultural adjustment during cross-cultural transition. *International Journal of Intercultural Relations, 22*(3), 277–291.

Weimann, G. (1989). Social networks and communication. In M. Asante & W.Gudykunst (Eds.), *Handbook of international and intercultural communication* (pp. 186–203). Newbury Park, CA: Sage Publications.

Concepts and Questions

1. Why has there been an increase in the movement across borders?
2. What are some of the reasons people are moving across borders?
3. What is the U-curve hypothesis? What are its stages? Why does Chuka, Nwosu, and Jackson believe it is no longer an accurate tool for analyzing culture shock?
4. What are some factors that can influence the reentry process?
5. How does cultural identity influence the reentry process?
6. What are the key variables that can mediate transient activity?
7. What are the three types of cultural contracts that can be negotiated and how do they apply to transients?
8. Which of the three types of cultural contracts would be most useful if you were in the role of a cultural transient?

3

International Cultures: Understanding Diversity

It is not the language but the speaker that we want to understand.

INDIAN SAYING FROM VEDAUPANISHADS

One important self-evident truism about human behavior is that your past experiences affect your behavior in both subtle and manifest ways. This maxim is so transparent that we fear people often overlook its impact on personal patterns of social perception and interaction. Think for a moment about some of those situations in which you and some of your friends shared what you believed to be the *same experience*, yet later when you discussed the event you soon discovered there were differences in your perceptions of that experience. We offer a simple example to make our point. If you and your friends were walking through a park and a large dog came bounding up to you, that event could be perceived quite differently depending upon each person's *prior experiences* with dogs. You might have had a pet dog as a child and, therefore, perceived the dog as friendly and bent down to pet it. As a child, however, one of your friends might have been bitten by a dog and, therefore, have a very different perception of the event. He or she might have reacted to the dog by moving away or even running. Although this example may seem basic, it nevertheless focuses your attention on the fundamental idea that the stimuli you received from the environment were the same, yet because everyone has a unique personality and background, each of you experienced an individually unique set of feelings, sensations, and responses.

When the element of culture is added to the perceptual process, individual, past histories take on added significance. For you are not only a product of your individual experiences, you are also a product of your culture.

As we have already discussed, culture affects your ways of perceiving and acting. Culture has instilled in you the accepted societal behaviors and values that have been passed from generation to generation. Yet, because these behaviors are so much a part of your persona, you might forget that behaviors are culturally engendered and vary among cultures. This is why someone from Japan, for example, might remain silent if disturbed by another's actions, whereas an Israeli or an Italian would more likely vigorously verbalize their displeasure. Whatever the culture, you can better understand your behavior and the reactions of others during an interaction if you realize that what you are hearing and seeing is a reflection of the other's culture. As you might predict, cultural understanding comes more easily when your cultural experiences are similar to those of the people with whom you are interacting. Conversely, when different and diverse backgrounds are brought to a communication encounter, it is often difficult to share internal states and feelings. In this chapter, we will focus on these difficulties by examining some of the experiences and perceptual backgrounds found among a sampling of international cultures.

We begin with this question: How do you learn to interact with and understand people who come from very different areas of the global village? This answer is not simple, yet it is at the core of this book. The need for such understanding is obvious. If you look around the world at any particular moment, you will find people from diverse cultures in constant interaction with one another. The nightly news makes it abundantly clear that all cultures, including those that are quite different from yours, are linked together in the global community. Events that happen in one part of the world can and do influence events all over the world. Whether they are concerns about the global economy, concerns about food, water, energy, global warming, or major differences in sociopolitical philosophies, no culture can remain completely isolated from nor unaffected by the rest of the world.

Two things are crucial if you are to relate effectively with people from diverse international cultures: (1) you must be knowledgeable about the diversity of people from other cultures; and (2) you must respect their diversity. This chapter presents five essays that will assist you with both of these assignments. Through these essays, you will explore the rich diversity found in several international cultures. Although these cultures represent only a small portion of the countless cultures found throughout the world, they are somewhat representative and should help you discover how people in other cultures develop their view of the world. To a very great extent, a culture's worldview determines how its members perceive themselves, each other, and their place in the universe; it serves as an underlying pattern for interaction within a culture. We begin with a glimpse of worldview diversity by detailing the inherent differences between cultures holding an individualistic orientation and those that subscribe to collectivistism.

Of the many social psychological variables that describe cultures, one of the most significant is the individualism—collectivism continuum. People who live primarily in northern Europe, the present and former British Commonwealth, and the United States tend toward individualism. In most Asian cultures, and particularly in East Asia, however, a social prejudice against individuality is common. In "Living Together vs. Going It Alone," Richard E. Nisbett discusses these cultural characteristics and the impact they have on individual and collective behavior. Members of independence-oriented cultures tend to value personal distinctiveness, whereas Asians are more likely to value sameness and blending in with others. Individual choices and personal preferences are characteristic of individualistic cultures, whereas in interdependent societies available choices favor the group rather than the individual. In the same vein, individualistic-oriented people tend to seek goals of personal accomplishment, whereas interdependence-oriented individuals prefer group accomplishment. Feelings of self-worth in independent cultures derive from individual success. In interdependent cultures, these feelings are usually aligned with feelings of being in harmony with one's group.

Nisbett focuses on the independent versus the interdependent aspects of Western and Asian cultures. He shows, for example, that training for independence or interdependence begins very early. For Westerners, it is common for children to sleep in their own beds—quite often in separate rooms—promoting independence. Among Asians, it is much more common for children to sleep in the same bed as their parents—and perhaps other siblings—fostering an interdependent relationship. As children mature, the nature of their family and peer interactions fosters the development of independence or interdependence. Thus, independent and interdependent orientations become ingrained in children's personalities at a very early age. Independent orientations lead to insistence on freedom of individual action, desires for distinctiveness, a preference for egalitarianism and achieved status, and a belief in universal rules of proper behavior. For the interdependent personality, orientations include a preference for collective action, a desire to blend harmoniously with the group, acceptance of hierarchy and ascribed status, and variable rules of behavior that take into account the context and the nature of the relationships involved.

Nisbett ends his essay with a discussion of the Japanese notions of *erabi* and *awase*—the styles of conflict reduction and negotiation favored by independent and interdependent personalities. The Western *erabi* orientation involves a belief that the environment can be manipulated for individual goals and accomplishment. Debate is a major form of communicative behavior leading to the resolution of conflict. The Asian *awase* style assumes that the environment cannot be manipulated and that people must adjust themselves to it. Negotiations do not involve debate but are based on mutual trust and cooperation, which leads to a mutually satisfying outcome for all.

Spirituality is a dimension of your psyche that helps you extend yourself to others and of course influences how you perceive the world. And, like so many other dimensions of personality, spirituality has its roots in your culture. Understanding the diverse cultural bases of spirituality is important because it can facilitate understanding and strengthen intercultural relationships. In the next essay, "The Spirituality of 'Being,' Grace and Tao in Intercultural Communication," Mary Fong introduces you to a comparison of U.S. and Chinese spiritual perspectives and their applications to intercultural communication.

She begins with a discussion of two spiritual concepts and their related key components to assist you in developing a wider, deeper, and richer understanding of your intercultural counterparts. The first perspective is *grace*. Found in Christianity, grace is considered a significant attribute of God that promotes kindness without regard to worth or merit of the individual to whom it is directed. In her explanation, Fong traces the historical roots of grace as found in the teachings of Jesus. Ideally, one receives grace by incorporating it into everyday life and extending the act of grace to others in daily interactions.

The second perspective is the notion of the *Tao* which originated in China during the fourth and third centuries B.C. Taoists pursued individual perfection, deeper understanding into the life force workings of nature, and a union with the cosmic principle they believed existed in all entities. To this end, Taoists were opposed to man-made institutions, elaborate ceremonies, social conventions, and rules of behavior they believed formed a cover for hypocrisy and self-seeking, scheming, reaching for power, enslavement of peasants, and wasteful destructive wars.

Fong traces the development of Taoist teachings through the writings of Chuang-tze, and Lao-tzu. Taoist philosophy was derived through a profound contemplation of nature and the variety of human experience and conditions. Taoism believes that the only freedom worth pursuing and preserving is the perfect harmony with the power or principle that is embodied in the heart of all that is, which is the *Tao*, or the Way. From this point of view, "all things are in process and intertwined and interdependent."

In continuing her dialogue, Fong introduces you to the concepts of *yin* and *yang* forces, which are the dynamic dualistic interaction that creates all of reality. She also discusses the principle of *Te,* which is the power, effect, or vital force of the *Tao. Te* is seen as an inner quality of the individual that is effective in influencing people and events without conscious effort.

After she outlines the basic characteristics of Grace and the *Tao,* Fong presents a comparison of the two perspectives revealing some of their major differences. For example, Christians have a personal relationship with their God. On the other hand, Chuang-tzu held that people have no closer relationship to the ultimate principle of the universe than an ant or a rock. Thus, from the Taoist perspective, all things are of equal worth. She continues by pointing out how the Christian and Taoist approaches lead to differences in spiritual worldviews that can influence intercultural communication. These differences then lead Fong into a discussion of the practice of spiritual ways in which she outlines some ideas from both Taoism and Christianity and how they are put into practice.

Fong ends her essay with an illustration of intercultural communication differences by presenting two scenarios where varied spiritual worldviews led to differences in the interpretation of events. In these situations, Fong relates how the situations developed and how they might be handled from a perspective of Grace and from a perspective of Tao.

The first two selections in the chapter deal with comparisons of the East and West in rather general terms. The next three essays deal with specific and very important cultures: India, Egypt, and sub-Saharan Africa.

Like China, the nation of India has a population of over one billion. The impact of globalization has led Americans and Indians into greater contact with one another resulting in an ever-increasing need for effective intercultural communication. From the outsourcing of manufacturing and service elements by American businesses to India and the need to conduct serious international negotiations, both countries now must learn about the perceptions and communication styles of the other. Rajesh Kumar and Anand Kumar Sethi, in their article "Communicating with Indians," are concerned with how Western managers, dealing with their counterparts from India, might respond to behaviors that are very different from those found in their own culture. Although the authors focus on the business setting, their assumptions and suggestions apply to any interaction involving India and the West.

To better understand how these interactions might occur, Kumar and Sethi begin with a detailed analysis of four general communication dimensions: (a) high context versus low context, (b) ideological versus pragmatism, (c) associative versus abstractive, and (d) verbal versus nonverbal communication. Once these dimensions are explained the authors compare how these characteristics are revealed differently in India and in the West. Using the four communication dimensions as a template, the authors offer some concrete steps that "Western expatriates can undertake to enhance effective communication with Indians." Specifically, they believe your chances for successful communication with Indians increase if you are aware of Indian communication styles and learn to deal with your emotional responses so that they do not become negative, avoid ideological debates, and also manifest a positive attitude toward the Indian culture. As noted earlier, even though their examples are drawn from the business context, their four suggestions can applied to any face-to-face interaction involving Indians and Westerners.

Egypt is one of the world's most ancient civilizations with a history that dates back to at least 3,000 B.C.E. And while it is relatively small in land size (192 square miles), and has a population of approximately seventy-eight million people, its significant and enduring history has produced a culture whose impact on the world remains as important today as it was in earlier times. In her essay titled "Dismantling Misconceptions About Islam in Egypt" Polly Begley looks at this important culture. Although Begley's focus is primarily on Egypt, her analysis on Islamic religion can be useful to all of those who seek to understand the world's fastest growing religion—regardless of the location.

To this end, Begley examines some of the perceptual and communication misconceptions regarding the Islamic faith. These misunderstandings in turn can impede interactions among Egyptians and non-Egyptians. She begins with a concise summary of the origins of the Egyptian worldview. According to Begley the core of this worldview may lie in the simple belief that to find peace one must be willing to surrender his or her life to God. Once this "surrender" takes place, Islam becomes a way of life that in one form or another dominates every moment of a Muslim's existence—from birth, to death—and even beyond. When one concedes his or her life to the total and complete control of God, it then behooves him or her to obey the decrees and cannons of Islam. It is in the carrying out of these behaviors that you find many of the misconceptions held by Westerners. In her essay Begley identifies some of those misperceptions and stereotypes that can "deepen hostility and mistrust among societies."

First, Begley explains how "outsiders" are often confused by the manner in which Muslims assemble themselves to pray. For example, when prostrating to pray, even in public, non-Muslims frequently find this behavior strange and out of place when carried out in a location other than a Mosque. Second, Begley maintains misinterpretations regarding the "four tenets" and "five pillars" of Islam also add to the negative apprehensions Westerners have toward Muslims. To help relieve those apprehensions Begley, in just a few pages, concisely summarizes these two important hallmarks of Islam. Because of the current perceptions and misunderstandings associated with the idea of *jihad* Begley "dismantles" the false information linked to this Pillar. In this section of her essay she also discusses how the "depiction of terrorism should not be applied to Egypt." Third, in the next section of her essay Begley discusses many of the misconceptions associated with Muslim women. She concludes her paper by offering four recommendations that will help create a comprehensive understanding between Muslims and non-Muslims: (1) educate young people about Muslims, (2) use the Internet as an educational tool to bridge cultures, (3) promote media literacy for young people, and (4) have people learn about the Arabic language.

The final essay in this chapter by Ann Neville Miller is titled "When Face-to-Face Won't Work: Use of Informal Intermediaries to Communicate Interpersonally in Sub-Saharan Africa." This essay is unique on two counts. First, it looks at a region of the world that is un-familiar to most Westerners. Although nearly 400 million people live in this part of Africa, it nevertheless remains obscure to most of us. Second, Miller looks at a type of interpersonal communication that employs informal intermediaries—a practice that is not very common in the United States. Yet, as Miller points out, "third parties to communicate certain interpersonal messages is a phenomenon that appears with regularity in a variety of cultures."

In most instances intermediaries are used to mediate disputes or to convey sensitive information. Usually this third person is not directly involved with the dispute or topic under question. Topics "carried" by the intermediary from person to person frequently deal with issues related to conflicts with supervisors or co-workers, sensitive situations between friends and family, or marital and financial problems. Another common use of the personal "conduit" is the transmission of bad news. Information concerning terminal illness and death is a frequent intermediated topic.

As a means of presenting her analysis within a theoretical context Miller uses two theoretical constructs that apply to collective cultures—*face negotiation theory* and *politeness theory*. Both theories emphasize minimal face-to-face conflict as part of the cultural value system. If, for example, someone has an "outsider" carry negative, poignant, or emotional messages they can avoid the trauma often associated with delivering such messages while at the same time they can maintain group harmony. This process helps keep the originator of the message from suffering a loss of face. And, when unequal social relationships are involved, it also permits intermediaries to help the parties "keep their distance." Maintaining ones' relational position is an important component of politeness theory.

By reading Miller's discussion of intermediaries you should be better able to appreciate that not all cultures solve problems or deal with interpersonal conflicts in the same manner. Cultures may develop very different processes for resolving social problems and interpersonal conflicts. Lacking an appreciation of how these processes are carried out could lead you into a difficult interpersonal situation if you violate or fail to use appropriate third-party intermediaries.

Living Together versus Going It Alone

Richard E. Nisbett

Most Westerners, or at any rate most Americans, are confident that the following generalizations apply to pretty much everyone:

- Each individual has a set of characteristic, distinctive attributes. Moreover, people *want* to be distinctive—different from other individuals in important ways.
- People are largely in control of their own behavior; they feel better when they are in situations in which choice and personal preference determine outcomes.
- People are oriented toward personal goals of success and achievement; they find that relationships and group memberships sometimes get in the way of attaining these goals.
- People strive to feel good about themselves; personal successes and assurances that they have positive qualities are important to their sense of well-being.
- People prefer equality in personal relations, or when relationships are hierarchical, they prefer a superior position.
- People believe the same rules should apply to everyone.
- Individuals should not be singled out for special treatment because of their personal attributes or connections to important people. Justice should be blind.

There are indeed hundreds of millions of such people, but they are to be found primarily in Europe, especially northern Europe, and in the present and

former nations of the British Commonwealth, including the United States. The social-psychological characteristics of most of the rest of the world's people, especially those of East Asia, tend to be different to one degree or another (see Fiske, Kitayama, Markus, & Nisbett, 1998; Hsu, 1983; Markus & Kitayama, 1991b; Triandis, 1995).

THE NON-WESTERN SELF

There is an Asian expression that reflects a cultural prejudice against individuality: "The peg that stands out is pounded down." In general, East Asians are supposed to be less concerned with personal goals or self-aggrandizement than are Westerners. Group goals and coordinated action are more often the concerns. Maintaining harmonious social relations is likely to take precedence over achieving personal success. Success is often sought as a group goal rather than as a personal badge of merit. Individual distinctiveness is not particularly desirable. For Asians, feeling good about themselves is likely to be tied to the sense that they are in harmony with the wishes of the groups to which they belong and are meeting the group's expectations. Equality of treatment is not assumed, nor is it necessarily regarded as desirable.

The rules that apply to relationships in East Asia are presumed to be local, particular, and well specified by roles rather than universals. An Asian friend told me the most remarkable thing about visiting American households is that everyone is always thanking everyone else: "Thank you for setting the table"; "Thank you for getting the car washed." In her country, everyone has clear obligations in a given context, and you don't thank people for carrying out their obligations. Choice is not a high priority for most of the world's people. (An East Asian friend once asked me why Americans found it necessary to have a choice among 40 breakfast cereals in the supermarket.) And Asians do not necessarily feel that their competence as a decision maker is on the line when they do have to make a choice.

Most Americans over a certain age well remember their primer, called *Dick and Jane*. Dick and Jane and their dog, Spot, were quite the active individualists. The first page of an early edition from the 1930s (the primer was widely used until the 1960s) depicts a little boy running across a lawn. The first sentences are "See Dick run. See Dick play. See Dick run and play." This would seem the most natural sort of basic information to convey about kids—to the Western mentality. But the first page of the Chinese primer of the same era shows a little boy sitting on the shoulders of a bigger boy. "Big brother takes care of little brother. Big brother loves little brother. Little brother loves big brother." It is not individual action but relationships between people that seem important to convey in a child's first encounter with the printed word. Indeed, the Western-style self is virtually a figment of the imagination to the East Asian. As philosopher Hu Shih writes, "In the Confucian human-centered philosophy man cannot exist alone; all action must be in the form of interaction between man and man" (Shiu, 1919, p. 116, cited in King, 1991). The person always exists within particular situations where there are particular people with whom one has relationships of a particular kind—and the notion that there can be attributes or actions that are not conditioned on social circumstances is foreign to the Asian mentality. Anthropologist Edward T. Hall introduced the notion of "low-context" versus "high-context" societies to capture differences in self-understanding (Hall, 1976). To the Westerner, it makes sense to speak of a person as having attributes that are independent of circumstances or particular personal relations. This self—this bounded, impermeable free agent—can move from group to group and setting without significant alteration. But for the Easterner (and for many other peoples, to one degree or another), the person is connected, fluid, and conditional. As philosopher Donald Munro (1985) put it, "East Asians understand themselves in terms of their relation to the whole, such as the family, society, *Tao* Principle, or Pure Consciousness." The person participates in a set of relationships that make it possible to act; purely independent behavior is usually not possible or really even desirable.

Since all action is in concert with others, or at the very least affects others, harmony in relationships becomes a chief goal of social life. I have presented a schematic illustration intended to capture the different types of sense of self in relation to in-group, or close circle of friends and family; the illustration also conveys relative distance between in-group and out-group, or people who are mere acquaintances at most (Iyengar, Lepper, & Ross, 1999). Easterners feel embedded in their in-groups and distant from their out-groups. They tend to feel they are very similar to in-group members, and they are much more trusting of them than of out-group members. Westerners feel relatively detached from their in-groups and tend not to make as great distinctions between in-group and out-group.

Some linguistic facts illustrate the social-psychological gap between the East and the West. In Chinese, there is no word for "individualism." The closest one can come is the word for "selfishness." The Chinese character *jen*—benevolence—means two men. In Japanese, the word "I"—meaning the trans-situational, unconditional, generalized self with all its attributes, goals, abilities, and preferences—is not often used in conversation. Instead, Japanese has many words for "I," depending on audience and context. When a Japanese woman gives an official speech, she customarily uses *Watashi*, which is the closest Japanese comes to the trans-situational "I." When a man refers to himself in relation to his college chums, he might say *Boku* or *Ore*. When a father talks to his child, he says *Otosan* (Dad). A young girl might refer to herself by her nickname when talking to a family member: "Tomo is going to school today." The Japanese often call themselves *Jibun*, the etymology of which leads to a term meaning "my portion."

Figure 1 *Eastern and Western Views of the Relations Among Self, In-Group, and Out-Group*

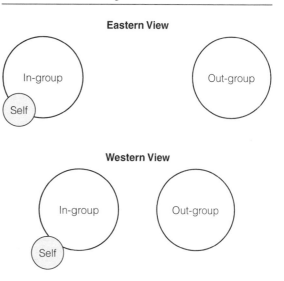

In Korean, the sentence "Could you come to dinner?" requires different words for "you," which is common in many languages, but also for "dinner," depending on whether one is inviting a student or a professor. Such practices reflect not mere politeness or self-effacement, but rather the Eastern conviction that one is a different person when interacting with different people.[1]

"Tell me about yourself" seems a straightforward enough question to ask of someone, but the kind of answer you get very much depends on what society you ask it in. North Americans will tell you about their personality traits ("friendly, hardworking"), role categories ("teacher," "I work for a company that makes microchips"), and activities ("I go camping a lot"). Americans don't condition their self-descriptions much on context (Holmberg, Markus, Herzog, & Franks, 1997). The Chinese, Japanese, and Korean self, on the other hand, very much depends on context ("I am serious at work," "I am fun-loving with my friends"). A study asking Japanese and Americans to describe themselves either in particular contexts or without specifying a particular kind of situation showed that Japanese found it very difficult to describe themselves without specifying a particular kind of situation—for example, at work, at home, or with friends (Cousins, 1989). Americans, in contrast, tended to be stumped when the investigator specified a context—"I am what I am." When describing themselves, Asians make reference to social roles ("I am Joan's friend") to a much greater extent than Americans do (Ip & Bond, 1995). Another study (Markus & Kitayama, 1991b) found that twice as many Japanese as American self-descriptions referred to other people ("I cook dinner with my sister").

When North Americans are surveyed about their attributes and preferences, they characteristically overestimate their distinctiveness. On question after question, North Americans report themselves to be more unique than they really are, whereas Asians are much less likely to make this error (Markus & Kitayama, 1991b). Westerners also prefer uniqueness in the environment and in their possessions. Social psychologists Heejung Kim and Hazel Markus asked Koreans and Americans to choose which object in a pictured array of objects they preferred. Americans chose the rarest object, whereas Koreans chose the most common object (Kim & Markus, 1999). Asked to choose a pen as a gift, Americans chose the least common color offered and East Asians the most common.

It's revealing that the word for "self-esteem" in Japanese is *serufu esutiimu*. There is no indigenous term that captures the concept of feeling good about oneself. Westerners are more concerned with enhancing themselves in their own and others' eyes than are Easterners. Americans are much more likely to make spontaneous favorable comments about themselves than are Japanese (Holmberg, Markus, Herzog, & Franks, 1997). When self-appraisal measures are administered to Americans and Canadians, it turns out that, like the children of Lake Wobegon, they are pretty much all above average. Asians rate themselves much lower on most dimensions, not only endorsing fewer positive statements but being more likely to insist that they have negative qualities (Kitayama, Markus, & Lieberman, 1995). It's not likely that the Asian ratings merely reflect a requirement for greater modesty than exists for North Americans. Asians are in fact under greater compunction to appear modest, but the difference in self-ratings exists even when participants think their answers are completely anonymous.

It isn't that Asians feel bad about their own attributes. Rather, there is no strong cultural obligation to feel that they are special or unusually talented. The goal for the self in relation to society is not so much to establish superiority or uniqueness, but to achieve harmony within a network of supportive social relationships and to play one's part in achieving collective ends. These goals require a certain amount of self-criticism—the opposite of tooting one's own horn. If I am to fit in with the group, I must root out those aspects of myself that annoy others or make their tasks more difficult. In contrast to the Asian practice of teaching children to blend harmoniously with others, some American children go to schools in which each child gets to be a "VIP" for a day.

Japanese schoolchildren are taught how to practice self-criticism, both to improve their relations with others and to become more skilled in solving problems. This stance of perfectionism through self-criticism continues throughout life. Sushi chefs and math teachers are not regarded as coming into their own until they have been at their jobs for a decade. Throughout their careers, in fact, Japanese teachers are observed and helped by their peers to become better at their jobs. Contrast this with the American practice of putting teachers' college graduates into the classroom after a few months of training and then leaving them alone to succeed or not, to the good or ill fortune of a generation of students (see Heine, Lehman, Markus, & Kitayama, 1999).

An experiment by Steven Heine and his colleagues captures the difference between the Western push to feel good about the self and the Asian drive for self-improvement (Heine et al, 2001). The experimenters asked Canadian and Japanese students to take a bogus "creativity" test and then gave the students "feedback" indicating that they had done very well or very badly. The experimenters then secretly observed how long the participants worked on a similar task. The Canadians worked longer on the task if they had succeeded; the Japanese worked longer if they failed. The Japanese were not being masochistic. They simply saw an opportunity for self-improvement and took it. The study has intriguing implications for skill development in both the East and the West. Westerners are likely to get very good at a "few things they start out doing well to begin with. Easterners seem more likely to become Jacks and Jills" of all trades.

Independence vs. Interdependence

Training for independence or interdependence starts quite literally in the crib. Whereas it is common for American babies to sleep in a bed separate from their parents, or even in a separate room, this is rare for East Asian babies—and, for that matter, babies pretty much everywhere else. Instead, sleeping in the same bed is far more common (Shweder, Balle-Jensen, & Goldstein, 1995). The differences are intensified in waking life. Adoring adults from several generations often surround the Chinese baby (even before the one-child policy began producing "little emperors"). The Japanese baby is almost always with its mother. The close association with mother is a condition that some Japanese apparently would like to continue indefinitely. Investigators at the University of Michigan's Institute for Social Research recently conducted a study requiring creation of a scale comparing the degree to which adult Japanese and American respondents want to be with their mothers. The task proved very difficult, because the Japanese investigators insisted that a reasonable endpoint on the scale would be "I want to be with my mother almost all the time." The Americans, of course, insisted that this would be uproariously funny to American respondents and would cause them to cease taking the interview seriously.

Independence for Western children is often encouraged in rather explicit ways. Western parents constantly require their children to do things on their own and ask them to make their own choices. "Would you like to go to bed now or would you like to have a snack first?" The Asian parent makes the decision for the child on the assumption that the parent knows best what is good for the child.

An emphasis on relationships encourages a concern with the feelings of others. When American mothers play with their toddlers, they tend to ask questions about objects and supply information about them. But when Japanese mothers play with their toddlers, their questions are more likely to concern feelings. Japanese mothers are particularly likely to use feeling-related words when their children misbehave: "The farmer feels bad if you did not eat everything your mom cooked for you." "The toy is crying because you threw it." "The wall says 'ouch'" (Azuma, 1994; Fernald & Morikawa, 1993). Concentrating attention on objects, as American parents tend to do, helps to prepare children for a world in which they are expected to act independently. Focusing on feelings and social relations, as Asian parents tend to do, helps children to anticipate the reactions of other people with whom they will have to coordinate their behavior.

The consequences of this differential focus on the emotional states of others can be seen in adulthood. There is evidence that Asians are more accurately aware of the feelings and attitudes of others than are Westerners. For example, Jeffrey Sanchez-Burks and his colleagues (2002) showed to Koreans and Americans evaluations that employers had made on rating scales. The Koreans were better able to infer from the ratings just what the employers felt about their employees than were the Americans, who tended to simply take the ratings at face value. This focus on others' emotions extends even to perceptions of the animal world. Taka Masuda and I showed underwater video scenes to Japanese and American students and asked them to report what they saw. The Japanese students reported "seeing" more feelings and motivations on the part of fish than did Americans; for example, "The red fish must be angry because its scales were hurt" (Masuda & Nisbett, 2001). Similarly, Kaiping Peng and Phoebe

Ellsworth (2002) showed Chinese and American students animated pictures of fish moving in various patterns in relation to one another. For example, a group might appear to chase an individual fish or to scoot away when the individual fish approached. The investigators asked the students what both the individual fish and the groups of fish were feeling. The Chinese readily complied with the requests. The Americans had difficulty with both tasks and were literally baffled when asked to report what the group emotions might be.

The relative degree of sensitivity to others' emotions is reflected in tacit assumptions about the nature of communication. Westerners teach their children to communicate their ideas clearly and to adopt a "transmitter" orientation; that is, the speaker is responsible for uttering sentences that can be clearly understood by the hearer—and understood, in fact, more or less independently of the context. It's the speaker's fault if there is a miscommunication. Asians, in contrast, teach their children a "receiver" orientation, meaning that it is the hearer's responsibility to understand what is being said. If a child's loud singing annoys an American parent, the parent would be likely just to tell the kid to pipe down. No ambiguity there. The Asian parent would be more likely to say, "How well you sing a song." At first the child might feel pleased, but it would likely dawn on the child that something else might have been meant, and the child would try being quieter or not singing at all (Kojima, 1984).

Westerners—and perhaps especially Americans—are apt to find Asians hard to read because Asians are likely to assume that their point has been made indirectly and with finesse. Meanwhile, the Westerner is in fact very much in the dark. Asians, in turn, are apt to find Westerners—perhaps especially Americans—direct to the point of condescension or even rudeness.

There are many ways of parsing the distinction between relatively independent and relatively interdependent societies (see Doi, 1971/1981; Hampden-Turner & Trompenaars, 1993; Hofstede, 1980; Hsu, 1983; Markus & Kitayama, 1991a; Triandis, 1994, 1995), but in illustrating these it may be helpful to focus on four related but somewhat distinct dimensions:

- Insistence on freedom of individual action versus a preference for collective action
- Desire for individual distinctiveness versus a preference for blending harmoniously with the group

- A preference for egalitarianism and achieved status versus acceptance of hierarchy and ascribed status
- A belief that the rules governing proper behavior should be universal versus a preference for particularistic approaches that take into account the context and the nature of the relationships involved

These dimensions are correlated with one another, but it is possible, for example, for a given society to be quite independent in terms of some dimensions and much less so in terms of others. Social scientists have attempted to measure each of these dimensions, and other associated ones, in a variety of ways, including value surveys, studies of archived material, and experiments.

To examine the value of individual distinction versus harmonious relations with the group, Hampden-Turner and Trompenaars (1993) asked managers to indicate which of the following types of job they preferred: (a) jobs in which personal initiatives are encouraged and individual initiatives are achieved, or (b) jobs in which no one is singled out for personal honor but in which everyone works together.

More than 90 percent of American, Canadian, Australian, British, Dutch, and Swedish respondents endorsed the first choice—the individual freedom alternative—compared with fewer than 50 percent of Japanese and Singaporeans. Preferences of the Germans, Italians, Belgians, and French were intermediate.

The United States is sometimes described as a place where, if you claim to amount to much, you should be able to show that you change your area code every five years or so. (This was before the phone company started changing people's area codes without waiting for them to move.) In some other countries, the relationship with the corporation where one is employed and the connection with one's colleagues there are more highly valued than in the United States, and are presumed to be more or less permanent. To assess this difference among cultures, Hampden-Turner and Trompenaars asked their participants to choose between the following expectations: If I apply for a job in a company, (a) I will almost certainly work there for the rest of my life, or (b) I am almost sure the relationship will have a limited duration.

More than 90 percent of Americans, Canadians, Australians, British, and Dutch thought a limited job duration was likely. This was true for only about

40 percent of Japanese (though it would doubtless be substantially higher today after "downsizing" has come even to Japan). The French, Germans, Italians, and Belgians were again intermediate, though closer to the other Europeans than to the Asians.

To examine the relative value placed on achieved versus ascribed status, Hampden-Turner and Trompenaars asked their participants whether or not they shared the following view: Becoming successful and respected is a matter of hard work. It is important for a manager to be older than his subordinates. Older people should be more respected than younger people.

More than 60 percent of American, Canadian, Australian, Swedish, and British respondents rejected the idea of status being based in any way on age. About 60 percent of Japanese, Korean, and Singapore respondents accepted hierarchy based in part on age. French, Italians, Germans, and Belgians were again intermediate, though closer to the other Europeans than to the Asians.

Needless to say, there is great potential for conflict when people from cultures having different orientations must deal with one another. This is particularly true when people who value universal rules deal with people who think each particular situation should be examined on its merits and that different rules might be appropriate for different people. Westerners prefer to live by abstract principles and like to believe these principles are applicable to everyone. To set aside universal rules in order to accommodate particular cases seems immoral to the Westerner. To insist on the same rules for every case can seem at best obtuse and rigid, and at worst cruel, to the Easterner. Many of Hampden-Turner and Trompenaars's questions reveal what a marked difference exists among cultures in their preference for universally applicable rules versus special consideration of cases based on their distinctive aspects. One of their questions deals with how to handle the case of an employee whose work for a company, though excellent for 15 years, has been unsatisfactory for a year. If there is no reason to expect that performance will improve, (a) should the employee be dismissed on the grounds that job performance should remain the grounds for dismissal, regardless of the age of the person and his previous record; or (b) is it wrong to disregard the 15 years the employee has been working for the company, and does one have to take into account the company's responsibility for his life?

More than 75 percent of Americans and Canadians felt the employee should be let go. About 20 percent of Koreans and Singaporeans agreed with that view. About 30 percent of Japanese, French, Italians, and Germans agreed, and about 40 percent of British, Australians, Dutch, and Belgians agreed. (Atypically, on this question, the British and the Australians were closer to the continental Europeans than to the North Americans.)

As these results show, Westerners' commitment to universally applied rules influences their understanding of the nature of agreements between individuals and between corporations. By extension, in the Western view, once a contract has been agreed to, it is binding regardless of circumstances that might make the arrangement much less attractive to one of the parties than it was initially. But to people from interdependent, high-context cultures, changing circumstances dictate alterations in the agreement.

An important business implication of the differences between independent and interdependent societies is that advertising needs to be modified for particular cultural audiences. Marketing experts Sang-pil Han and Sharon Shavitt (1994) analyzed American and Korean advertisements in popular news magazines and women's magazines. They found that American advertisements emphasize individual benefits and preferences ("Make your way through the crowd"; "Alive with pleasure"), whereas Korean advertisements are more likely to emphasize collective ones ("We have a way of bringing people closer together"; "Ringing out the news of business friendships that really work"). When Han and Shavitt performed experiments, showing people different kinds of advertisements, they found that the individualist advertisements were more effective with Americans and the collectivist ones with Koreans.

Independence versus interdependence is of course not an either/or matter. Every society—and every individual—is a blend of both. It turns out that it is remarkably easy to bring one or another orientation to the fore. Psychologists Wendi Gardner, Shira Gabriel, and Angela Lee (1999) "primed" American college students to think either independently or interdependently. They did this in two different ways. In one experiment, participants were asked to read a story about a general who had to choose a warrior to send to the king. In an "independent" version, the king had to choose the best individual for the job. In an "interdependent" version, the general wanted to make a choice that would benefit his family (Trafimow, Triandis, & Goto, 1991). In another priming method, participants were asked to search for words in a paragraph describing a trip to a city. The words were either independent in nature (e.g., "I," "mine") or interdependent (e.g., "we," "ours").

After reading the story or searching for words in the paragraph, participants were asked to fill out a value survey that assessed the importance they placed on individualist values (such as freedom and living a varied life) and collectivist values (such as belongingness and respect for elders). They also read a story in which "Lisa" refused to give her friend "Amy" directions to an art store because she was engrossed in reading a book; they were then asked whether Lisa's behavior was inappropriately selfish. Students who had been exposed to an independence prime rated individualist values higher and collectivist values lower than did students exposed to an interdependence prime. The independence-primed participants were also more forgiving of the book-engrossed Lisa. Gardner and her colleagues repeated their study adding Hong Kong students to their American sample and also added an unprimed control condition. American students rated individualist values higher than collectivist values—unless they had been exposed to an interdependence prime. Hong Kong students rated collectivist values higher than individualist values—unless they had been exposed to an independence prime.

Of course, Easterners are constantly being "primed" with interdependence cues and Westerners with independence cues. This raises the possibility that even if their upbringing had not made them inclined in one direction or another, the cues that surround them should make people living in interdependent societies behave in generally interdependent ways and those living in independent societies behave in generally independent ways. In fact, this is a common report of people who live in the "other" culture for a while. My favorite example concerns a young Canadian psychologist who lived for several years in Japan. He then applied for jobs at North American universities. His adviser was horrified to discover that his letter began with apologies about his unworthiness for the jobs in question. Other evidence shows that self-esteem is highly malleable (Heine &

Lehman, 1997). Japanese who live in the West for a while show a notable increase in self-esteem, probably because the situations they encounter are in general more esteem-enhancing than those typical in Japan (Kitayama, Markus, Matsumoto, & Norasakkunit, 1997). The social psychological characteristics of people raised in very different cultures are far from completely immutable.

Variants of Viewpoint

The work of Hampden-Turner and Trompenaars makes clear that the West is no monolith concerning issues of independence versus interdependence. There are also substantial regularities to the differences found in Western countries. In general, the Mediterranean countries plus Belgium and Germany are intermediate between the East Asian countries, on the one hand, and the countries most heavily influenced by Protestant, Anglo-Saxon culture, on the other. There is more regularity even than that. Someone has said, "The Idea moves west," meaning that the values of individuality, freedom, rationality, and universalism became progressively more dominant and articulated as civilization moved westward from its origins in the Fertile Crescent. The Babylonians codified and universalized the law. The Israelites emphasized individual distinctiveness. The Greeks valued individuality even more and added a commitment to personal freedom, the spirit of debate, and formal logic. The Romans brought a gift for rational organization and something resembling the Chinese genius for technological achievement, and—after a trough lasting almost a millennium—their successors, the Italians, rediscovered these values and built on the accomplishments of the Greek and Roman eras. The Protestant Reformation, beginning in Germany and Switzerland and largely bypassing France and Belgium, added individual responsibility and a definition of work as a sacred activity. The Reformation also brought a weakened commitment to the family and other in-groups coupled with a greater willingness to trust out-groups and have dealings with their members. These values were all intensified in the Calvinist subcultures of Britain, including the Puritans and Presbyterians, whose egalitarian ideology laid the groundwork for the government of the United States. (Thomas Jefferson was merely paraphrasing the Puritan sympathizer

John Locke when he wrote, "We hold these truths to be self-evident, that all men are created equal . . . with certain inalienable rights, that among these are life, liberty . . .")

There are also major differences among Eastern cultures in all sorts of important social behavior and values, some of which are related to independence versus interdependence.

I was in China in 1982 at the tail end of the Cultural Revolution. The country seemed extremely exotic—in both its traditional aspects and its Communist-imposed aspects. (This was well before a Starbucks was installed in the Forbidden City!) The first Western play to be performed in Beijing since the revolution was mounted while I was there. It was Arthur Miller's *Death of a Salesman*. The choice seemed very strange. I regarded the play as being not merely highly Western in character but distinctly American. Its central figure is a salesman, "a man way out there in the blue riding on a smile and a shoeshine." To my astonishment, the play was a tremendous success. But Arthur Miller, who had come to China to collaborate on production of the play, provided a satisfactory reason for its reception. "The play is about family," he said, "and the Chinese invented family." He might have added that the play is also about *face*, or the need to have the respect of the community, and the Chinese also invented face.

The Japanese have perhaps as much concern with face as do the Chinese, but probably less involvement with the immediate family and more commitment to the corporation. There are other marked differences between the Japanese and Chinese. The sociologist Robert Bellah, the philosopher Hajime Nakamura, the psychologist Dora Dien, and the social philosopher Lin Yutang, among many others, have detailed some of these differences (Bellah, 1957/1985; Dien, 1997, 1999; Lin, 1936; Nakamura, 1964/1985). Though social constraints are in general greater on both Chinese and Japanese than on Westerners, the constraints come primarily from authorities in the case of the Chinese and chiefly from peers in the case of the Japanese. Control in Chinese classrooms, for example, is achieved by the teacher, but by classmates in Japan. Dora Dien has written that the "Chinese emphasize particular dyadic [two-person] relationships while retaining their individuality, whereas the Japanese tend to submerge themselves in the group" (Dien, 1999, p. 377). Though both Chinese and Japanese are required to conform to move smoothly through their daily lives, the Chinese are said to chafe under the requirements and the Japanese actually to enjoy them. The Japanese are held to share with the Germans and the Dutch a need for order in all spheres of their lives; the Chinese share with Mediterraneans a more relaxed approach to life.

It is sometimes argued that one particular type of social relationship is unique to the Japanese. This is *amae*, a concept discussed at length by the Japanese psychoanalyst Takeo Doi (1971/1981, 1974). *Amae* describes a relationship in which an inferior, a child or employee, for example, is allowed to engage in inappropriate behavior—to ask for an expensive toy or to request a promotion at a time not justified by company policy—as an expression of confidence that the relationship is sufficiently close that the superior will be indulgent. *Amae* facilitates the relationship, enhancing trust between the two parties and cementing bonds, though these results come at some cost to the autonomy of the inferior.

The very real differences among Eastern cultures and among Western cultures, however, shouldn't blind us to the fact that the East and the West are in general quite different from each other with respect to a great many centrally important values and social-psychological attributes.

AWASE AND ERABI: STYLES OF CONFLICT AND NEGOTIATION

Debate is almost as uncommon in modern Asia as in ancient China. In fact, the whole rhetoric of argumentation that is second nature to Westerners is largely absent in Asia. North Americans begin to express opinions and justify them as early as the show-and-tell sessions of nursery school ("This is my robot; he's fun to play with because . . ."). In contrast, there is not much argumentation or trafficking in opinions in Asian life. A Japanese friend has told me that the concept of a "lively discussion" does not exist in Japan—because of the risk to group harmony. It is this fact that likely undermined an attempt he once made to have an American-style dinner party in Japan, inviting only Japanese guests who expressed a fondness for the institution—from the martinis through the steak to the apple pie. The effort fell flat for want of opinions and people willing to defend them.

The absence of a tradition of debate has particularly dramatic implications for the conduct of political life. Very recently, South Korea installed its first democratic government. Prior to that, it had been illegal to discuss North Korea. Westerners find this hard to comprehend, inasmuch as South Korea has performed one of the world's most impressive economic miracles of the past 40 years and North Korea is a failed state in every respect. But because of the absence of a tradition of debate, Koreans have no faith that correct ideas will win in the marketplace of ideas, and previous governments "protected" their citizens by preventing discussion of Communist ideas and North Korean practices.

The tradition of debate goes hand in hand with a certain style of rhetoric in the law and in science. The rhetoric of scientific papers consists of an overview of the ideas to be considered, a description of the relevant basic theories, a specific hypothesis, a statement of the methods and justification of them, a presentation of the evidence produced by the methods, an argument as to why the evidence supports the hypothesis, a refutation of possible counterarguments, a reference back to the basic theory, and a comment on the larger territory of which the article is a part. For Americans, this rhetoric is constructed bit by bit from nursery school through college. By the time they are graduate students, it is second nature. But for the most part, the rhetoric is new to the Asian student, and learning it can be a slow and painful process. It is not uncommon for American science professors to be impressed by their hardworking, highly selected Asian students and then to be disappointed by their first major paper—not because of their incomplete command of English, but because of their lack of mastery of the rhetoric common in the professor's field. In my experience, it is also not uncommon for professors to fail to recognize that it is the lack of the Western rhetoric style they are objecting to, rather than some deeper lack of comprehension of the enterprise in which they're engaged.

The combative, rhetorical form is also absent from Asian law. In Asia the law does not consist, as it does in the West for the most part, of a contest between opponents. More typically, the disputants take their case to a middleman whose goal is not fairness but animosity reduction—by seeking a middle way through the claims of the opponents (Leung, 1987). There is no attempt to derive a resolution to a legal conflict from a universal principle. On the contrary, Asians are likely to consider justice in the abstract, by-the-book Western sense to be rigid and unfeeling.

Negotiation also has a different character in the high-context societies of the East than in the low-context societies of the West (see Cohen, 1997). Political scientist Mushakoji Kinhide characterizes the Western *erabi* (active, agentic) style as being grounded in the belief that "man can freely manipulate his environment for his own purposes. This view implies a behavioral sequence whereby a person sets his objective, develops a plan designed to reach that objective, and then acts to change the environment in accordance with that plan" (Kinhide, 1976, pp. 45–46, cited in Cohen, 1997). To a person having such a style, there is not much point in concentrating on relationships. It is the results that count. Proposals and decisions tend to be of the either/or variety because the Westerner knows what he wants and has a clear idea what is appropriate to give and to take in order to have an acceptable deal. Negotiations should be short and to the point, so as not to waste time reaching the goal.

The Japanese *awase* (harmonious, fitting-in) style, "rejects the idea that man can manipulate the environment and assumes instead that he adjusts himself to it" (Kinhide, 1976, p. 40, cited in Cohen, 1997). Negotiations are not thought of as "ballistic," one-shot efforts never to be revisited, and relationships are presumed to be long-term. Either/or choices are avoided. There is a belief that "short-term wisdom may be long-term folly" (Cohen, 1997, p. 37). A Japanese negotiator may yield more in negotiations for a first deal than a similarly placed Westerner might, expecting that this will lay the groundwork for future trust and cooperation. Issues are presumed to be complex, subjective, and intertwined, unlike the simplicity, objectivity, and "fragmentability" that the American with the *erabi* style assumes.

So, there are very dramatic social-psychological differences between East Asians as a group and people of European culture as a group. East Asians live in an interdependent world in which the self is part of a larger whole; Westerners live in a world in which the self is a unitary free agent. Easterners value success and achievement in good part because they reflect well on the groups they belong to; Westerners value these things because they are badges of personal merit. Easterners value fitting in and engage in self-criticism to make sure that they do so; Westerners value individuality and strive to make themselves look good. Easterners are highly attuned to the feelings of others and strive for interpersonal harmony; Westerners are more concerned with knowing themselves and are prepared to sacrifice harmony for fairness. Easterners are accepting of hierarchy and group control; Westerners are more likely to prefer equality and scope for personal action. Asians avoid controversy and debate; Westerners have faith in the rhetoric of argumentation in arenas from the law to politics to science.

None of these generalizations applies to all members of their respective groups, of course. Every society has individuals who more nearly resemble those of other, quite different societies than they do those of their own society; and every individual within a given society moves quite a bit between the independent and interdependent poles over the course of a lifetime—over the course of a day, in fact. But the variations between and within societies, as well as within individuals, should not blind us to the fact that there are very real differences, substantial on the average, between East Asians and people of European culture.

As nearly as we can tell, these social differences are much the same as the differences that characterized the ancient Chinese and Greeks. And if it was the social circumstances that produced the cognitive differences between ancient Chinese and Greeks, then we might expect to find cognitive differences between modern East Asians and Westerners that map onto the differences between the ancient Chinese and Greeks.[2]

Notes

1. The generic "I" is commonly used in China today, but this is a recent development following the Sun Yat-sen revolution in the early twentieth century.
2. This is not to imply that marked differences have been present continuously. For example, no one would say that the eleventh-century European peasant was much of an individualist, and both China and Japan have passed through periods in which individualism was highly valued, at least for artists and intellectuals.

References

Azuma, H. (1994). *Education and socialization in Japan.* Tokyo: University of Tokyo Press.

Bellah, R. (1985). *Tokagawa religion: The cultural roots of modern Japan.* New York: Free Press. (Original work published 1957.)

Cohen, R. (1997). *Negotiating across cultures: International communication in an interdependent world.* Washington, DC: United States Institute of Peace Press.

Cousins, S. D. (1989). Culture and self-perception in Japan and the United States. *Journal of Personality and Social Psychology, 56,* 124–131.

Dien, D. S.-F. (1997). *Confucianism and cultural psychology: Comparing the Chinese and the Japanese.* Hayward: California State University.

Dien, D. S.-F. (1999). Chinese authority-directed orientation and Japanese peer-group orientation: Questioning the notion of collectivism. *Review of General Psychology, 3,* 372–385.

Doi, L. T. (1974). *Amae:* A key concept for understanding Japanese personality structure. In R. J. Smith & R. K. Beardsley (Eds.), *Japanese culture: Its development and characteristics.* Chicago: Aldine.

Doi, L. T. (1981). *The anatomy of dependence* (2nd ed.). Tokyo: Kodansha. (Original work published 1971.)

Fernald, A., & Morikawa, H. (1993). Common themes and cultural variations in Japanese and American mothers' speech to infants. *Child Development, 64,* 637–656.

Fiske, A. P., Kitayama, S., Markus, H. R., & Nisbett, R. E. (1998). The cultural matrix of social psychology. In D.T. Gilbert, S. T. Fiske, & G. Lindzey (Eds.), *Handbook of social psychology* (4th ed., pp. 915–981). Boston: McGraw-Hill.

Gardner, W. L., Gabriel, S., & Lee, A. Y. (1999). "I" value freedom, but "we" value relationships: Self-construal priming mirrors cultural differences in judgment. *Psychological Science, 10,* 321–326.

Hall, E. T. (1976). *Beyond culture.* New York: Anchor Books.

Hampden-Turner, C., & Trompenaars, A. (1993). *The seven cultures of capitalism: Value systems for creating wealth in the United States, Japan, Germany, France, Britain, Sweden, and the Netherlands.* New York: Doubleday.

Han, S., & Shavitt, S. (1994). Persuasion and culture: Advertising appeals in individualistic and collective societies. *Journal of Experimental Social Psychology, 30,* 326–350.

Heine, S. J., Kitayama, S., Lehman, D. R., Takata, T., Ide, E., Leung, C., & Matsumoto, H. (2001). Divergent consequences of success and failure in Japan and North America: An investigation of self-improving motivation. *Journal of Personality and Social Psychology, 81,* 599–615.

Heine, S. J., & Lehman, D. R. (1997). *Acculturation and self-esteem change: Evidence for a Western cultural foundation in the construct of self-esteem.* Paper presented at the second meeting of the Asian Association of Social Psychology, Kyoto, Japan.

Heine, S. J., Lehman, D. R., Markus, H. R., & Kitayama, S. (1999). Is there a universal need for positive self-regard? *Psychological Review, 106,* 766–794.

Hofstede, G. (1980). *Culture's consequences.* Beverly Hills, CA: Sage.

Holmberg, D., Markus, H., Herzog, A. R., & Franks, M. (1997). *Self-making in American adults: Content, structure and function.* Unpublished manuscript, University of Michigan, Ann Arbor.

Hsu, F. L. K. (1983). The self in cross-cultural perspective. In A. J. Marsella, B. D. Vos, & F. L. K. Hsu (Eds.), *Culture and self* (pp. 24–55). London: Tavistock.

Ip, G. W. M., & Bond, M. H. (1995). Culture, values, and the spontaneous self-concept. *Asian Journal of Psychology, 1,* 29–35.

Iyengar, S. S., Lepper, M. R., & Ross, L. (1999). Independence from whom? Interdependence from whom? Cultural perspectives on ingroups versus outgroups. In D. A. Prentice & D. T. Miller (Eds.), *Cultural divides: Understanding and overcoming group conflict.* New York: Russell Sage Foundation.

Kim, H., & Markus, H. R. (1999). Deviance or uniqueness, harmony or conformity? A cultural analysis. *Journal of Personality and Social Psychology, 77,* 785–800.

King, A. Y.-c. (1991). Kuan—his and network building: A sociological interpretation. *Daedalus, 120,* 60–84.

Kinhide, M. (1976). The cultural premises of Japanese diplomacy. In J. C. f. I. Exchange (Ed.), *The silent power: Japan's identity and world role.* Tokyo: Simul Press.

Kitayama, S., Markus, H. R., & Lieberman, C. (1995). The collective construction of self-esteem: Implications for culture, self, and emotion. In J. Russell, J. Fernandez-Dols, T. Manstead, & J. Wellenkamp (Eds.), *Everyday conceptions of emotion: An introduction to the psychology, anthropology, and linguistics of emotion.* Dordrecht: Kluwer.

Kitayama, S., Markus, H. R., Matsumoto, H., & Norasakkunit, V. (1997). Individual and collective processes in the construction of the self: Self-enhancement in the United States and self-depreciation in Japan. *Journal of Personality and Social Psychology, 72,* 1245–1267.

Kojima, H. (1984). A significant stride toward the comparative study of control. *American Psychologist, 39,* 972–973.

Leung, K. (1987). Some determinants of reactions to procedural models for conflict resolution: A cross-national study. *Journal of Personality and Social Psychology, 53,* 898–908.

Lin, Y. (1936). *My country and my people.* London: Heinemann.

Markus, H., & Kitayama, S. (1991a). Cultural variation in the self-concept. In J. Strauss & G. R. Goethals (Eds.), *The self: Interdisciplinary approaches.* New York: Springer-Verlag.

Markus, H., & Kitayama, S. (1991b). Culture and the self: Implications for cognition, emotion, and motivation. *Psychological Review, 98,* 224–253.

Masuda, T., & Nisbett, R. E. (2001). Attending holistically vs. analytically: Comparing the context sensitivity of Japanese and Americans. *Journal of Personality and Social Psychology, 81,* 922–934.

Munro, D. J. (1985). *The concept of man in early China.* Stanford, CA: Stanford University Press.

Nakammura, H. (1985). *Ways of thinking of Eastern peoples.* Honolulu: University of Hawaii Press. (Original work published 1964)

Sanchez-Burks, J., Lee, F., Choi, I., Nisbett, R. E., Zhao, S., & Koo, J. (2002). *Conversing across cultural ideologies: East-West communication styles in work and non-work contexts.* Unpublished manuscript, University of Southern California.

Shiu, H. (1919). *Chung-kuo che-hsueh shi ta-kang* [An outline of the history of Chinese philosophy]. Shanghai: Commercial Press.

Shweder, R., Balle-Jensen, L., & Goldstein, W. (1995). Who sleeps by whom revisited: A method for extracting the moral goods implicit in praxis. In P. J. Miller, J. J. Goodnow, & F. Kessell (Eds.), *Cultural practices as contexts for development.* San Francisco: Jossey-Bass.

Trafimow, D., Triandis, H. C., & Goto, S. G. (1991). Some tests of the distinction between the private self and the collective self. *Journal of Personality and Social Psychology, 60,* 649–655.

Triandis, H. C. (1994). *Culture and social behavior.* New York: McGraw-Hill.

Triandis, H. C. (1995). *Individualism and collectivism.* Boulder, CO: Westview Press.

Concepts and Questions

1. Compare and contrast the beliefs and values of independent and interdependent persons.

2. What are some of the child-rearing dynamics that lead to the development of the independent person? The interdependent person?

3. Why is harmony a chief goal among interdependent people?

4. How do schools contribute to the development of an independent person? An interdependent person?

5. How do independent and interdependent people differ in their degree of sensitivity to others' emotional states?

6. How might American and Asian managers describe the kind of jobs they prefer?

7. How is product advertising affected when the target audience is composed of independent people? Of interdependent people?

8. Describe the *awase* and *erabi* forms or styles of conflict and negotiation.
9. What kinds of problems might arise during a contract negotiation if one team of negotiators subscribed to an *awase* style of negotiation and the other team subscribed to an *erabi* style?
10. How do time frames affect negotiations between Asians and Westerners?

The Spirituality of "Being" Grace and Tao in Intercultural Communication

Mary Fong

ommunication scholars have studied various aspects of intercultural communication such as adaptation (Adler, 1975; Furnham, 1987; Furnham and Bochner, 1982; Hammer, Gudykunst, and Wiseman, 1978; Kim; 1988), intercultural communication competence (Bennett, 1986; Chen, 1989; Gudykunst & Hammer, 1987), relationship development (Chen, 1995; Nakanishi, 1987; Ogawa, 1979, Casmir & Asuncion-Lande, 1989), differences across cultures in terms of values (Kluckhohn & Strodbeck, 1961), language (Hoijer, 1994), nonverbal (Andersen, 1994; Ricard, 1993), conflict management (Ting-Toomey, 1988), and so forth. Little attention has been written on the spirituality of intercultural communication.

When intercultural differences and conflicts arise because of differing cultural ways of communicating, intercultural interactants may or may not always have the knowledge of the differing meanings and intent behind the cultural acts. I believe that our practice of spirituality can be a way to extend ourselves to one another to facilitate understanding and strengthening intercultural relationships. With this in mind, I believe our spiritual practices can help promote humanistic insights and adaptations that can transcend our cultural differences because we are simply human beings who share common emotions, desires, hopes, and dreams.

In this essay, I introduce two spiritual perspectives and select key concepts that may be edifying to people who encounter differences and conflicts in their intercultural communications. I will not be able to provide an in-depth elaboration and discussion of

This original essay appears here in print for the first time. All rights reserved. Permission to reprint must be obtained from the author and the publisher. Dr. Mary Fong teaches in the Department of Communication Studies at California State University, San Bernardino.

these selected concepts in comparison to books that provide a wider, deeper, and richer development of understanding for their readers. I will begin discussing the concept of grace, commonly known in the Christian faith. Next, I will introduce *Tao* (pronounced as Dao), a central precept in Eastern spirituality of Taoism. In understanding some aspects of Taoism, some discussion of *yin* and *yang, te,* and *wu wei* will be unraveled. Lastly, I will cover the fruits of the spirit in Christianity. Although the aforementioned precepts from both spiritual perspectives may differ in some respects, there are some aspects that are shared, and some concepts that are plausible in their existence in spite of the differing spiritual emphasis.

TWO SPIRITUAL WAYS OF "BEING"

Grace

Grace is a significant attribute of God in the Christian faith. God in one respect is described in the Bible as merciful, gracious, long-suffering, and abounding in goodness and truth (New International Version, Exodus 34:6). The term grace is defined as, "favor or kindness shown without regard to the worth or merit of the one who receives it and in spite of what that person deserves" (Youngblood, 1995, p. 522). Terms such as mercy, love, compassion, and patience are almost always related to the concept of grace. In the Christian faith, the grace of God is manifested in Jesus Christ's teachings, his act of salvation for human beings, the gift of the holy spirit, and spiritual blessings (Youngblood, 1995).

The Christian faith believes that Jesus Christ is the incarnation of God into human form to come to earth to spread truth and love to people; and to help them to realize the fallible aspects of their life, to have them turn away from weak living, and to receive God's grace. Jesus Christ's act of salvation for human beings involved his persecution and dying on the cross to save humankind by laying down his life, an ultimate act of love, in order to triumph over Satan. That is, the act of Jesus Christ dying on the cross and not giving into temptation and hatred toward his persecutors, but rather asking for his Heavenly Father to forgive the persecutors for their wrongful acts. Jesus Christ died, but rose from the dead by

revealing his holy spirit to witnesses. Jesus' act of salvation showed God's love and power over Satan, rather than succumbing to the power of Satan. Days prior to Jesus' death, he said,

> I will ask the Father, and he will give you another Counselor to be with you forever—the Spirit of truth. The world cannot accept him (heavenly God), because it neither sees him nor knows him. But you know him, for he lives with you and will be in you. I will not leave you as orphans; I will come to you. Before long, the world will not see me anymore, but you will see me. Because I live, you also will live. On that day you will realize that I am in my Father, and you are in me, and I am in you. (NIV, John 14:16–20, p. 1625)

> All this I have spoken while still with you. But the Counselor, the Holy Spirit, whom the Father will send in my name, will teach you all things and will remind you of everything I have said to you. Peace I leave with you; my peace I give you. I do not give to you as the world gives. Do not let your hearts be troubled and do not be afraid. (NIV, John 14:25–27, p. 1626)

When a person receives God's grace, we come to experience and acknowledge this phenomenon of grace in our everyday life. There is the act of giving and receiving grace to one another. Do you recall a time when someone did a kind or generous act toward you and you felt you did nothing to deserve it? For instance, when I was researching for this essay, I spent hours in a Christian bookstore reading and typing notes from books on this topic. As I was reading, I kept thinking that I want to experience the sense of God's grace so that I would have a better grasp of this concept in my life that I have heard about. The sun had just set and I packed my belongings.

As I approached my car in the parking lot, I saw a dime on the ground next to the driver's door. I smiled and happily picked up the coin, tucking it in my jean pocket, knowing that for more than 20 years, I have countless stories of repeatedly experiencing this path of God's grace in my life. Virtually every time I have come across a coin on the floor, I am typically thinking about something important at the time. I get this sense of validation of my thoughts and also that I am moving in the right direction. I was joyful about receiving the coin because I felt my efforts working on this essay and wanting to sense this concept of grace were being validated.

I buckled up, turned the ignition key, and my entire dashboard lit up, flickered, and died along with my motor that refused to turn over. I was shocked and tried the ignition key again. No luck, my car battery was dead. I was stuck, some 25 miles from home. "Oh, no, what should I do?" I thought to myself. I was not an "AAA member."

I got out of the car and walked back to the bookstore and asked several women and men if they had jumper cables. Finally, a man had some and I followed him to his SUV, which was parked next to mine. We both were hoping that it was just my car battery, since my car was just over two years old. He connected the jumper cables on to both of our car batteries. I turned my ignition key and my car started! I was so pleased and relieved that I could drive home. I thanked the man and said, "You're a life saver!" He smiled and said, "Drive safely."

As I was driving on the freeway, I realized that I just had experienced God's grace. A kind stranger gave me grace through his giving of his time, efforts, and sharing of his jumper cables to help start my car when I had done nothing to deserve or earn his assistance. He received nothing in return, and I was someone who took time away from his family who was visiting the Christian bookstore. He did it cheerfully and graciously.

With this stranger, I had to take a leap of faith to trust his character and that he would help me get my car started. With a similar thought, people take a leap of faith to trust and to receive grace from a total stranger, that is, a heavenly God, Jesus Christ's teachings and his act of salvation for human beings to bring goodness in their lives. This concept of receiving grace from God extends to the act of people giving grace to others in our everyday interactions and, for the purposes of this essay, in our intercultural communications. This leads us to the Taoist spiritual perspective, discussing the *tao*.

Tao

Taoism flourished in China in the period identified as the Warring States during the fourth and third centuries B.C. (401–221 B.C.). During this era, there was much political and social unrest and great intellectual developments. Confucians were primarily concerned with creating an acceptable political and social system.

The Taoist pursued individual perfection, a deeper understanding into the life force and workings of nature, and union with the cosmic principle that they believed exist in all entities (Smith, 1980).

The Taoist were against artificialities of man-made institutions, elaborate ceremonial and moral social conventions, detailed rules of behavior that formed a cover for hypocrisy and self-seeking, scheming, positioning for power, enslavement of peasantry, and wasteful destructive wars. Instead, the Taoist believed that people ought to learn to conform to spontaneous and natural processes of natural phenomena such as birth, growth, decay, and death. Freedom, peace, and happiness for all human beings can only be attained by conformity to the natural cosmic laws, and not man-made laws (Smith, 1980).

The Taoist teachings of Chuang-tzu and the famous Chinese anthology classic attributed to Lao-tzu called the *Tao Te Ching* are often referred to in understanding Taoism. Chuang-tzu, a famous Taoist philosopher, profoundly contemplated nature and the variety of human experience and conditions. The Taoists expounded on two fundamental precepts: the Way (Tao) and its efficacy (Te). Chuang-tzu's Taoist teachings were predicated on the fundamental principle that a person's life and one's spiritual integrity are to be most valued and devoted. Further, the only freedom worth pursuing and preserving is the perfect harmony with the power or principle which is embodied in the heart of all that is, which is the *tao* (Smith, 1980).

Ni (1997) describes the Tao as integral truth, a truth that does not emphasize any point of view and that it is neutral, like zero. There is an avoidance of extremes, which maintains a standpoint that creates no prejudicial tendency. Zero doctrine means returning to stillness, purity, nothing, or zero in order to be at a point of clarity. If a person holds a doctrine, one does not have a mind that is open and flexible because one is fixed on that doctrine.

Based on an analysis of some of the passages in Lao Tzu's classic book, *Tao Te Ching,* the *Tao* is creative, giving rise to a world of rich diversity and also maintaining its comprehensive harmony (Cheng, 2004). "The natural constant Way (Tao) gives birth to beings but does not possess them, it produces evolution but does not rule it. All beings are born depending on it, yet none know to thank it, all die because of it, yet none can resent it (Clearly, 1991). The constancy of *tao,* for example, is "not enriched by storage and accumulation, nor is it impoverished by disbursement and enjoyment" (Clearly, 1991, p. 4). The constancy of the *tao* is only a reference for discussion. *Tao* can only be experienced internally and perceived in indirect ways that involve subtle observations and prudent focusing of the mind which activities are not explicitly and easily expressible in language. The famous Taoist philosopher, Laozi, describes the constant *Tao* as non-spoken, something independent of any finite or definite object or event, and beyond our phenomenal world of things. Tao as Ultimate truth cannot be defined because language has its limitations and truth is defined by one's viewpoint (Ni, 1997). Language, however, can be used to express the human experience and the perception of the *Tao* (Cheng, 2004).

Laozi stated, "One needs a mind of emptiness in order to see the subtleties of the dao; one needs a mind of distinctions to see the boundaries of the dao." (Cheng, 2004, p. 146). To "be with the Tao," or to be on the wavelength of the natural workings of the cosmic universe, involves a person moving with the rhythm of the oneness and the many interacting components as smoothly as water flowing down a stream (Combs, 2004). Everything is in a state of constant change and transition. All things are in process and are intertwined and interdependent. The true way consists of right conduct, to strive to act as heaven had ordained for humankind.

Yin and Yang. Two opposite modalities, *yin* and *yang* represent the dynamic dualistic interaction that creates all of reality. These two equal opposite forces work together in a harmonious perpetual transformation that occurs within everything. The *yin* force has characteristics such as passive, female, receptive, night, cold, soft, wet, winter, shadow, and negative. The *yang* force has characteristics such as active, male, creative, day, heat, hard, dry, summer, sun, and positive. For the Taoist, yin and yang are opposite, but equal complementary forces that are independent of any concept of morality. These forces sustain an evolving process in everything in the universe where completion and unity exist in the Tao (Smith, 1980; Wing, 1979). In the center of the white and black fields of the Yin and Yang are dots that represent the seeds of change as polar reversals (Wing, 1979). For

example, the sun reaches its peak at noon (yang), thereafter, the sun slowly begins to wane and the day increasingly becomes darker as the sun sets (yin), and then becomes night evolving slowly to the break of the day. There are myriad differences as the Tao fosters life: it harmonizes dark and light, regulates the four seasons, and tunes the forces of nature (Clearly, 1991).

Te. The power, effect, or vital force of the Tao is *te.* It is also described to be the form or character of an entity and its potentiality to become. *Te* is an inner quality of character of a person that is powerfully effective in influencing people and shaping events without conscious effort. The Taoist believes that *te* is the spontaneous unfolding of the *tao* of their own nature and a person can exercise one's *te* by being his or her true self. A person who has kingly *te* is one who is able to see light in total darkness, penetrate to the spiritual essence of entities, and takes care of the needs of all who seek his help (Smith, 1980).

Wu Wei. The concept of *wu wei* refers to the avoidance of action or nonaction that is hostile or aggressive in nature. To treat a person in an inferior way is the essence of aggression. Aggressive action may be direct or indirect in nature. Verbal insults, lying, hatred, harmful actions with malice intent, and violence are direct aggressive action. Indirect aggressive action may come in the form of ignoring, sneering, excluding others intentionally, passive aggressive behaviors, and so on. By practicing *wu wei,* a person avoids starting new vicious cycles of indirect aggressive behaviors and direct aggressive behaviors (e.g., lying, hatred, and violence) and thus interrupts the cycles. Instead, a person returns to the roots of one's nature, that is, being natural and spontaneous (Welch, 1966). Moreover, by doing nonaction that is not aggressive is simply letting the nature of Tao take its own course and there is no subject to claim action, whether effortless or effortful (Cheng, 2004).

CHRISTIANITY AND TAOISM

Some Differences

The Christian and Taoist approaches have areas of marked contrast. Followers of the Christian faith believe in a personal, creative, and redemptive God. In contrast, Taoist followers believe there is no God, but that Tao is represented as being devoid of action, thought, feeling, and desire. It is nonpurposive (Smith, 1980).

Christians have a personal relationship with God. Christians see themselves as children of God and through their faith they receive the promise of the Holy Spirit (NIV, Galatians 4:7). In Taoism, however, Chuang-tzu believed that people hold no closer relation to the ultimate principle of the universe than does a lowly insect as the ant or an inanimate object. From the standpoint of Tao, all things are of equal worth. To attain to a human form is a source of joy. However, a person's life on earth is only a passing moment in an eternal process of transformation in which there are myriad forms equally good (Smith, 1980).

In Christianity, there is a realization that there are conflicting powers of good and evil, truth and lies, spiritual light and darkness that are opposed to one another with the intent on the destruction of the other (Smith, 1980). Believers of Christ believe that in all things, good and bad, God works for the good of those who love him (NIV, Romans 8:28). In Taoism, *yin* and *yang* are not conceived as good or bad. Rather, *yin* and *yang* are seen as two opposing and equally complementary forces that work together in harmony that are in constant transformation within the Tao.

The Christian and Taoist approaches, along with other spiritual faiths, ethnic, and cultural groups have some differences in terms of spiritual worldviews and ways of communicating. In the midst of cultural differences, how can people manage their intercultural interactions? As human beings socialized in their faiths and cultural communities, we have learned principles of life and rules of what is considered appropriate and inappropriate communications. When our social expectations are not met, or when we perceive inappropriate behavior, or where there are differences in communication styles based on our spiritual and cultural systems, we respond in either a functional or a dysfunctional manner (Fong, 2004). A person who uses dysfunctional behaviors is negative or hostile with an attitude of suspicion, fear, prejudice, or ethnocentrism. Dysfunctional strategies such as criticizing, withdrawing, and ignoring are most likely to result in alienation, isolation, and chaos in intercultural interactions. Instead we can practice our communication skills of functional behavior which are positive and nurturing with an attitude of openness, acceptance, trust, and respect while choosing adaptive communication strategies such as explaining, observing, listening, and inquiring. All of these are likely to result in building rapport, understanding, and harmony in our intercultural relations (Fong, 2004).

Sometimes, however, when cultural differences or conflicts arise or expectations are not met in our intercultural interactions, we may focus our perception on our own cultural upbringing as "right" or "wrong" ideas or what is appropriate, inappropriate, offensive, or rude behavior of the other interactant. I believe our spirituality can enhance and foster our intercultural relations and our communications toward one another by looking beyond our differences and conflicts, by looking beyond our immediate judgments of the other, and by looking beyond ourselves to have a spiritual disposition toward the other interactant, thus creating and increasing the likelihood of satisfying intercultural interactions that bridge differences through spiritual communication.

PRACTICING SPIRITUAL WAYS

Although both spiritual approaches have differing perspectives and ways, they have the commonality of pursuing the truth, freedom from unhealthy binds, development of one's spirituality, and having the right conduct. All of these commonalities bring positive energy of attitude, intent, values, and the striving for goodness that can transcend differences and conflicts that might arise in intercultural interactions where differing patterns of communication exist. I will briefly present some ideas from both spiritual teachings of Taoism and Christianity in developing people's spirituality and what is considered good conduct in communicating with people.

Tao

The original meaning of the Chinese character, *tao*, is a road, a path, a way. Extending the concept of *tao*, it came to mean the way in which a person acts, the method one uses, the principle that directs what a person does in relationships and situations. This way is of the heaven or nature in which people handle themselves with right conduct to bring peace, happiness, and welfare to themselves and to others (Smith, 1980).

The Mo-tzu school of Ancient Taoism taught that all people return to the faith of impartial heaven by following the Heavenly Way. This Heavenly Way is a good spiritual life listening to one's own spiritual wisdom or internal energy awareness or conscience. Mo-tzu emphasized that one should treat everyone fairly in every circumstance and to avoid favoritism and biases (Ni, 1997).

Chuang-tzu's text taught that wise people seek for harmony in relationships. In order to accomplish this, one needs to make a conscious and persistent effort to pursue the Tao or Way. In pursuit of the Tao the sages of olden times practiced four virtues: love, righteousness, propriety, and wisdom. The Chuang-tzu text taught that goodness is not something external from oneself that one must pursue to attain. In the lives of humans, just as in the natural world, there are no absolute norms of virtue, justice, or happiness that function at all times and in all situations. The Chuang-tzu also taught that people can attune themselves to the rhythm of life. People ought to relinquish their anxieties, fretfulness, and conscious striving for power, glory, wealth, or fame. The Chuang-tzu held that there is an eternal principle that is contained within and beyond all that exists (Smith, 1980).

The book, Wen-Tzu: Understanding the Mysteries, is filled with Lao-tzu's teachings that are translated into English by Thomas Cleary. In this book, Lao-tzu said, "Virtue is in what you give, not in what you get. Therefore when sages want to be valued by others, first they value others, when they want to be respected by others, first they respect others. When they want to overcome others, first they overcome themselves, when they want to humble others, first they humble themselves. So they are both noble and lowly, using the Way to adjust and control this" (Clearly, 1991, p. 59).

Lao-tzu also wrote, "Great people are peaceful and have no longings, they are calm and have no worries" (Clearly, 1991 p. 4). "Sages cultivate the basis within and do not adorn themselves outwardly with superficialities. They activate their vital spirit and lay to rest their learned opinions. Therefore they are open and uncontrived, yet there is nothing they do not do, they have no rule, yet there is no unruliness" (Clearly, 1991, p. 5).

According to Lao-tzu, "Those who serve life adapt to changes as they act. Changes arise from the times, those who know the times do not behave in fixed ways. Therefore, I say, "Ways can be guides, but not fixed paths, names can be designated, but not fixed labels" (Clearly, 1991, p. 8). Sages do "what is appropriate without scheming, they are trusted without speaking. They succeed without thinking about it, achieve without contriving to do so." (Clearly, 1991, p. 9).

Lao-tzu also spoke of the Way as "empty and un-reified, even and easy, clear and calm, flexible and yielding, unadulterated and pure, plain and simple. These are concrete images of the Way" (Clearly, 1991, p. 5). Moreover, achieving a state of empti-ness means there is no burden within. Evenness refers to the state of a person's mind as unrestrained. When desires do not burden a person, this is the consummation of emptiness. When a person has no likes or dislikes, this is the consummation of even-ness. When a person is unified and unchanging, this is the consummation of calmness. When a per-son is not mixed up in things, this is the consumma-tion of purity. When a person neither grieves nor delights, this is the consummation of virtue (Clearly, 1991). Real people embody the tao through "open emptiness, even easiness, clear cleanness, flexible yielding, unadulterated purity, and plain simplicity, not getting mixed up in things" (Clearly, 1991, p. 7).

For Lao-tzu, the Classic Taoist moved in a state of emptiness, meandering in the great nothingness. They go beyond convention and are not constrained or bound by society. Lao-tzu further said, "When people are caught up in social customs, they are in-evitably bound physically and drained mentally, therefore they cannot avoid being burdened. Those who allow themselves to be tied down are always those whose lives are directed from outside" (Clearly, 1991, p. 24–25).

"Clear serenity is the consummation of virtue. Flexible yielding is the function of the Way. Empty calm is the ancestor of all beings. When these three are put into practice, you enter into formlessness. Formlessness is a term for oneness, oneness means mindlessly merging with the world" (Clearly, 1991, p. 11). . . . "Spiritual light is attainment of the inward. When people attain the inward, their internal organs are calm, their thoughts are even, their eyes and ears are clear, and their sinews and bones are strong. They are mas-terful but not contentious, firm and strong yet never ex-hausted. They are not too excessive in anything, nor are they inadequate in anything" (Clearly, 1991, p. 12).

Taoist followers are encouraged to practice meditation, yoga, and fasting in order to purify the mind and body. The purpose of doing these practices also helps the follower to develop calmness, stillness, and emptiness within as a way to relinquish desires, constraints, and burdens of one's life in order to return to one's true self and achieve clarity.

Fruits of the Spirit

In the Christian faith, believers are taught to develop and strive for qualities known as the fruits of the spirit for the purpose of developing one's spiritual character and also how we ought to conduct ourselves and treat others. "Let your conversation be always full of grace," said Apostle Paul (NIV, Colossians 4:6, p. 1817). The Christian faith teaches that people ought to manifest the fruit of the Spirit in giving grace to others in our conversations and behavior. The "fruit of the Spirit is love, joy, peace, patience, kindness, goodness, faithfulness, gentleness and self-control" (NIV, Galatians 5:22, p. 1787). "Joy is love enjoying, peace (or long-suffering) is love waiting . . . faithfulness is love keeping its word" (Stanley, 1996, p. 377).

The Bible defines "Love is patient, love is kind. It does not envy, it does not boast, it is not proud. It is not rude, it is not self-seeking, it is not easily angered, it keeps no record of wrongs. Love does not delight in evil but rejoices with the truth. It always protects, always trusts, always hopes, always perseveres. Love never fails" (NIV, 1 Corinthians 13:1–8, p. 1752).

Joy is referred to as a positive attitude or pleasant emotion or a feeling of delight. There are many levels of joy that are referred to in the Bible including gladness, contentment, and cheerfulness. The highest joy is one that is holy and pure. This kind of joy rises above circumstances and focuses on the very character of God. For instance, the Psalmist rejoices over God's righteousness (NIV, Psalm, 71:14–16); salvation (NIV, Psalm, 21:1; 71:23); mercy (NIV, Psalms, 31:7); creation (NIV, Psalms, 148:5); word (NIV, Psalm, 199:14, 162); and faithfulness (NIV, Psalm, 33:1–6). Christians rejoice because of God's characteristics and his acts (Youngblood, 1995). This joy is required of the righteous person (NIV, Psalm 150; NIV, Philippians 4:4) that is produced by the Spirit of God (NIV, Galatians 5:22). This kind of joy is possible, even in the midst of sorrow (NIV, 1 Corinthians 12:26; 2 Corinthians 6:10; 7:4), looking to our sovereign

God, who works out all good and bad things for our ultimate good to achieve the character of Christ (NIV, Romans 8:28–30).

Peace, patience, and kindness are also the fruits of the spirit. Jesus Christ spoke of peace involving inner tranquility, hope, trust, faith, and quietness in the mind and soul of a person through a relationship with God. Peace sometimes had a physical meaning, suggesting security (NIV, Psalm 4:8); contentment (NIV, Isaiah 26:3); prosperity (NIV, Psalm 122:6-7); and the absence of war (NIV, 1Samuel 7:14). Patience is defined as a quality that a person is encouraged to have that is Christ-like by having "forebearance under suffering and endurance in the face of adversity" (Youngblood, 1995, p. 950). In the New Testament of the Bible, the Greek word translated as "grace" best represents the idea of God's kindness or loving kindness. That is, God's graciousness toward believers, in turn, encourages people to treat all with kindness or grace (NIV, Luke 6:35).

The final fruits of the spirit include goodness, gentleness, and self-control. Goodness has the quality of praiseworthy character, of moral excellence. God's goodness consists of righteousness, holiness, justice, kindness, grace, mercy, and love (NIV, Exodus 33:19; NIV, Romans 2:4). Faithfulness refers to dependability, loyalty, and stability, particularly as it describes God in his relationship to human believers. And Christians are expected to develop this quality in their lives and way they conduct themselves. Gentleness is defined in Nelson's New Illustrated Bible Dictionary (1995) as "kindness, consideration, a spirit of fairness, and compassion" (p. 488). Apostle Paul declared that Christians should have a spirit of gentleness toward all people (NIV, Philippians 4:5; 2 Corinthians 10:1). Self-control involves the control of one's actions and emotions by human will which is governed by the Holy Spirit within oneself.

There are other spiritual qualities and proper conduct that Christians are encouraged to develop. In the Bible, the Apostle Paul spoke of clothing "yourselves with compassion, kindness, humility, gentleness, and patience. Bear with each other and forgive whatever grievances you may have against one another. Forgive as the Lord forgave you. And over all these virtues put on love, which binds the all together in perfect unity. Let the peace of Christ rule in your hearts, since as members of one body you were called to peace" (NIV, Colossians 3:12–15, p. 1816).

Humility and compassion are two more important spiritual qualities that are encouraged in the Bible that are worthy of discussion. Humility is a "freedom from arrogance that grows out of the recognition that all we have and are comes from God. . . . True humility does not produce pride but gratitude" (Youngblood, 1995, p. 586). We have infinite worth and dignity because of our relationship with God (1 Corinthians 4:6–7; 1 Peter 1:18–19).

Nouwen, McNeill, and Morrison (1982) discuss the compassion act of "self-emptying for others," which involves the process of paying

> attention to others with the desire to make them the center and to make their interests our own . . . . When someone listens to us with real concentration and expresses sincere care for our struggles and our pains, we feel that something very deep is happening to us. Slowly, fears melt away, tensions dissolve, anxieties retreat, and we discover that we carry within us something we can trust and offer as a gift to others. The simple experience of being valuable and important to someone else has a tremendous re-creative power. (p. 81)

As Nouwen, McNeill, and Morrison (1982) have said, "Compassion is not just a feeling, it is an act of doing something for another who is in need." The Bible teaches doing good to all (NIV, Galatians 6:10); loving both your neighbors and enemies (NIV, Matthew 5:43); showing respect (NIV, 1 Peter 2:17) and brotherly kindness to everyone (NIV, 2 Peter 1:5-7); and being considerate, impartial, and sincere (NIV, James 3:17).

Fisher (2005) states, "Jesus plants a seed in our hearts for a desire to really know the Holy Spirit. What we do with this challenge is totally up to us" (p. 64). Moreover, Fisher (2005), who is a theologian, explains if we are open to receiving his messages of ideas and learning from the Holy Spirit, it would require being a good listener.

The Apostle Paul said, "But now you must rid yourselves of all such things as these: anger, rage, malice, slander, and filthy language from your lips. Do not lie to each other, since you have taken off your old self with its practices and have put on the new self, which is being renewed in knowledge in the image of its Creator" (Colossians 3: 8–10, p. 1816). Elsewhere in the Bible, the Apostle Paul said, ". . . whatever is true, whatever is noble, whatever is right, whatever is pure, whatever is lovely, whatever is admirable—if anything is excellent or praiseworthy—think about such things. Whatever you have learned or received or heard from me, or seen in me—put it into practice. And the God of peace will be with you" (Philippians 4: 8–9, p. 1809).

In developing their spirituality and learning proper conduct, Christian believers learn by attending church, fellowship groups, prayers to God, reading the Bible, and from their experiences and interactions with people. All of these practices are done for the purpose of learning more about God's character, spiritual wisdom, and development of one's spirituality and Godly conduct toward people.

Some Similarities between Christianity and Taoism

Although the Christian faith and Taoism differ in their respectful ways, I will only mention some similarities between them. Both spiritual approaches believe that their followers ought to have liberation. The Chuang-tzu taught the need to be free and unfettered. He taught that the only freedom worth obtaining is the freedom that is aligned in perfect harmony with the power or principle which lies at the center of all, which he refers to as the Tao (Smith, 1980). For Christians, liberation comes through the act of praying to and receiving Jesus Christ as their Savior and God who saved them from the bondage of evil and sin. Jesus said, "If you hold to my teaching, you are really my disciples. Then you will know the truth, and the truth will set you free (NIV, John 8:32, p. 1613).

Another commonality that both spiritual approaches have is the belief that God and Tao have a constant or unchanging quality about them. Both are believed to have inherently supreme or absolute goodness, and this goodness can thus be found in believers who follow and practice the Tao (Cheng, 2004) or adhere to Jesus Christ's teachings, the Holy Spirit and God. Both spiritual approaches encourage people to develop their spiritual qualities of peace, kindness, harmony, compassion, patience, love, humility, practicing moral conduct, and so on. In the next section, let us take a look at two intercultural interactions and see how both spiritual approaches are displayed.

Intercultural Communication Differences

Both scenarios come from my intercultural interactions. The first scenario was with a former housemate and student who was from Mainland China. One day she was in the kitchen and I was elsewhere in the house. Suddenly I heard this tremendous scream, "Oh, my goodness! Aauugghh! Aauugghh!" I ran to the kitchen saw her in a terrible panic, and said urgently, "What's the matter?" I saw her hands on her face, trembling, and pointing over at the counter. I said, "Oh ants. We can just clean it up." She shook her head frantically and said that she cannot kill ants. She said that she can not kill anything because of her beliefs. I said, "OK, then I'll just clean it up." She saw me cleaning up the ants, and she would scream now and then. From the Taoist approach, all living beings are of equal existence. From the Christian view, there is no saying that we cannot kill ants. From my Christian view, I did not judge her for her beliefs. I only was concerned about cleaning up the ants. I was a bit surprised that she was acting so hysterical by screaming, covering her face, and trembling. Otherwise, I just accepted the situation and communicated with a spirit of patience, kindness, gentleness, and self-control.

The second scenario involved having some people over at my home one evening at 6:00 pm to work on a campus-community project. A Caucasian American 25-year-old male graduate student had arrived five to ten minutes early. I was getting out of the shower just a few minutes prior to 6:00 p.m. What made matters worse was that my bathroom electrical outlet had blown a fuse and I could not blow-dry my hair. So I quickly went to the hallway to blow-dry my hair. I heard pounding on my front door and someone ringing my doorbell several times—back and forth, pound, pound, pound, ding-dong, ding-dong. I dried my hair a bit more and ran downstairs to open the door. My student walks in my home upset and said, "You are always late!" I said, "Oh, how long were you waiting?" He said, "I was waiting some five minutes. You're always late!" I said, "I'm sorry about that." I told him that he was the first to arrive and I had only shortly before arrived home from running errands. I changed the subject and asked him whether he could connect my VCR to my television. As he was working on that, I noticed the time on the cable box on the television and asked the student to read the time. He said, 6:03. I said, "Alex, it's 6:03, what do you mean I'm late?" Alex was culturally brought up to either arrive early or to be on time. For a small group meeting I considered it acceptable to be fashionably late since people were getting off work and had to fight traffic. The other group members trickled in 10 to 15 minutes after six o'clock, as they were coming from work. The point of this illustration is to show that Alex handled the cultural differences of time in a dysfunctional manner. Alex chose to react in a demanding and rude manner by pounding on the door and ringing the doorbell several times when his expectations were not met. He lacked self-control, gentleness, and patience among other spiritual qualities. A Taoist would have also observed that Alex lacked humbleness and self-constraint. "A person who is humble, always has others' interests in mind, and practices self-emptying and self constraint would be like a nourishing and soothing water and thus can be said to embody the *dao* and be considered a good person" (Cheng, 2004, p. 171).

A Taoist might offer Alex the number eight saying from the Lao-tzu's classic book, *Tao Te Ching*, that reads:

The highest good is like water.

Water gives life to the ten-thousand things and does not strive.

It flows in places men reject and so is like the Tao.

In dwelling, be close to the land.

In meditation, go deep in the heart.

In dealing with others, be gentle and kind.

In speech, be true.

In ruling, be just.

In business, be competent.

In action, watch the timing.

No fight: No blame.

References

Adler, P. S. (1975). The transitional experience: An alternative view of culture shock. *Journal of Humanistic Psychology, 15,* 13–23.

Andersen, P. A. (1994). Explaining intercultural differences in nonverbal communication. In L. A. Samovar & R. E. Porter (Eds.), *Intercultural Communication: A Reader* (pp. 229–239). Belmont, CA: Wadsworth.

Barker, K. (1985). *The NIV study bible.* Grand Rapids, MI: Zondervan.

Bennett, M. J. (1986). A developmental approach to training for intercultural sensitivity. *International Journal of Intercultural Relations, 10,* 179–196.

Casmir, F. L., & Asuncion-Lande, N. (1989). Intercultural communication revisited: Conceptualization, paradigm building, and methodological approaches. *Communication Yearbook, 12,* 278–309.

Chen, G. M. (1989). Relationships of the dimensions of intercultural communication competence. *Communication Quarterly, 37,* 118–133.

Chen, G. M. (1995). Differences in self-disclosure patterns among Americans versus Chinese: A comparative study. *Journal of Cross-Cultural Psychology, 26,* 84–91.

Cheng, C. Y. (2004). Dimensions of the dao and onto-ethics in light of the DDJ. *Journal of Chinese Philosophy, 31*(2), 143–182.

Clearly, T. (1991). Wen-*Tzu: Understanding the mysteries: Further teachings of Lao-tzu.* Boston: Shambhala.

Combs, S. C. (2004). The useless/usefulness of argumentation: The dao of disputation. *Argumentation and Advocacy, 41,* 58–70.

Feng, G-F., & English, J. (1972). *Tao Te Ching: Lao-tzu.* New York: Vintage Books.

Fisher, E. (2005). *Embraced by the Holy Spirit.* Sheppensburg, PA: Destiny Image.

Fong, M. (2004). Identity and the speech community. In M. Fong & R. Chuang (Eds.), *Communicating ethnic and cultural identity* (pp. 3–18). Lanham, MD: Rowman & Littlefield.

Furnham, A. (1987). The adjustment of sojourners. In Y. Y. Kim & W. B. Gudykunst (Eds.), *Cross-cultural adaptation: Current approaches* (pp. 42–61). Beverly Hills, CA: Sage Publications.

Furnham, A., & Bochner, S. (1982). Social difficulty in a foreign culture: An empirical analysis of culture shock. In S. Bochner (Ed.), *Culture in contact: Studies in cross-cultural interaction* (pp. 161–198). New York: Pergamon.

Furnham, A., & Bochner, S. (1986). Culture shock: *Psychological reactions to unfamiliar environments.* London: Methuen.

Gudykunst, W. B., & Hammer, M. R. (1987). Strangers and hosts: An uncertainty reduction-based theory of intercultural adaptation. In Y. Y. Kim & W. B. Gudykunst (Eds.), *Cross-cultural adaptation: Current approaches* (pp. 106–139).Newbury Park, CA: Sage.

Hammer, M. R., Gudykunst, W. B., & Wiseman, R. L. (1978). Dimensions of intercultural effectiveness: An exploratory study. *International Journal of Intercultural Relations, 2,* 382–392.

Hoijer, H. (1994). The Sapir-Whorf hypothesis. In L. A. Samovar & R. E. Porter (Eds.), *Intercultural communication: A reader* (pp. 194–200). Belmont, CA: Wadsworth.

Kim, Y. Y. (1988). *Communication and cross-cultural adaptation: An integrative theory.* Philadelphia: Multilingual Matter.

Kluckhohn, C., & Strodbeck, F. (1961). *Variations in value orientations.* Evanston, IL: Row, Peterson.

Nakanishi, M. (1987). Perceptions of self-disclosure in initial interaction: A Japanese sample. *Human Communication Research, 13,* 305–318.

Ni, Hua-Ching (1997). *Entering the Tao.* Boston: Shambhala.

Nouwen, H. J. M., McNeill, D. P., & Morrison, D. A. (1966). *Compassion: A reflection on the Christian life.* New York: Image Books Doubleday.

Ogawa, D. (1979). Communication characteristics of Asian Americans in urban settings: The case of Honolulu Japanese. In M. K. Asante, E. Newark, & C. A. Blake (Eds.), *Handbook of intercultural communication* (pp. 321–339). Beverly Hills, CA: Sage.

Ricard, V. B. (1993). *Developing intercultural communication skills.* Malabar, FL: Krieger.

Smith, D. H. (1980). *The wisdom of the Taoists.* New York: New Directions.

Stanley, C. (1996). *Charles Stanley's handbook for Christian living.* Nashville, TN: Thomas Nelson.

Ting-Toomey, S. (1988). Intercultural conflict styles: A face-negotiation theory. In R. Wiseman (Ed.), *Intercultural communication theory* (pp. 115–147). Thousand Oaks, CA: Sage.

Welch, Holmes (1966). *Taoism: The parting of the way.* Boston: Beacon Press.

Wing, R. L. (1979). *The I Ching workbook.* Garden City, NY: Doubleday.

Youngblood, R. F. (1995). *New illustrated bible dictionary.* Nashville, TN: Thomas Nelson.

Concepts and Questions

1. How may understanding the spirituality prevalent in another person facilitate intercultural communication between you and a member of that culture?

2. Compare and contrast the Christian concept of grace with the Taoist concept of Tao.

3. What are the sources of grace and of Tao? How do these sources differ?

4. How does the concept of harmony between being and nature compare to the concept of grace?

5. In what ways does the Tao act as a guide to proper conduct?

6. In what ways do the Taoist forces of *yin* and *yang* relate to the Christian force of grace?

7. How can the Christian and Taoist spiritual worldviews affect intercultural communication?

8. In what ways are the spiritual approaches of Christianity and Taoism similar? How do they differ?

Communicating with Indians

Rajesh Kumar
Anand Kumar Sethi

Human beings draw close to one another by their common nature, but habits and customs keep them apart.

Confucian Saying

Now it is not good for the Christians health to hustle the Asian brown for the Christian riles and the Aryan smiles and he weareth the Christian down. At the end of the fight is a tomb-stone white with the name of the late deceased and the epitaph drear "A fool lies here who tried to hustle the East."

Rudyard Kipling

"What kind of a bird are you, if you can't sing?" chirped the bird "What kind of a bird are you, if you can't swim?" quacked the duck.

Prokofiev in "Peter and the Wolf"

the great common door through which most forms of negativity enter is premature expectation. . . . All expectations are a judgment.

Communication is a fundamental aspect of human interaction in that individuals cannot but not communicate.[1] One may be effective or ineffective in accurately conveying what one wishes to say to the other party, but without question whenever we interact with another individual one does convey some message, whether or not we intended to convey that message to the other party. Above all, communication is a goal-driven activity in which one is either conveying some information to the other party to get them to do something or are trying to extract information from another person to further one's own objectives. Whether it is setting up a business meeting, or making an offer to buy or sell a particular commodity, communication

serves as the medium to help accomplish these goals.

Even within the confines of a particular culture communication is not necessarily problem free. Individual differences in personality, age, gender, social skills, and socioeconomic background are all likely contributors to communicative difficulties.[2] That said, communicative difficulties increase when one crosses cultural boundaries. As the cultural distance increases, so do the *assumptions* on the basis of which individuals communicate. Individuals socializing in different cultures communicate on the basis of *radically different assumptions* without necessarily being acutely aware of the assumptions that are shaping their behavior.[3]

The aim here is to assess the causes and the consequences of the communicative difficulties between the Indians and the Western expatriate manager. We will begin with a discussion of the communicative style common to India and then outline ways by which the Western expatriate manager might handle these challenges both efficiently as well as effectively.

THE INDIAN COMMUNICATIVE STYLE

The communicative style of a particular cultural group can be analyzed on the basis of different dimensions.[3a] The four dimensions that have garnered a lot of attention in the literature are: (a) high context versus low context; (b) ideologism versus pragmatism; (c) associative versus abstractive communication; and (d) verbal versus nonverbal communication.[4] We outline the salient characteristics of each of them and then indicate how the Indian culture maps on to them.

High-Context versus Low-Context Communicative Patterns

This is one of the most influential characterizations of different types of communicative styles and it draws attention to the fact that members of different cultural groups are more or less sensitive to the context of the message.[5] As Hall and Hall note, "*Context* is the information that surrounds an event; it is inextricably bound up with the meaning of that event. The elements that combine to produce a given meaning—events and contexts—are in different proportions

From *Doing Business in India: A Guide for Western Managers* (New York: Palgrave Macmillan, 2005, pp. 103, 107–114, 150–152.) Reprinted by permission.

depending on the culture."[6] *Context* has a powerful impact on how people choose to convey information, and in particular, it influences the communication mode that people choose to employ. Scholars have drawn a distinction between indirect versus direct, succinct versus elaborate, contextual versus personal, and affective versus instrumental modes of communicating.[7] In an indirect communicative mode, messages are conveyed implicitly rather than directly whereas in a direct communicative mode people state their intentions as clearly as they possibly can.

The distinction between a succinct and an elaborate communicative mode rests on the fact that in the former, people rely less on words and more on non-verbal nuances whereas in the elaborative mode, verbal expression is clearly prized. A contextual style is accommodative of the relationship among the parties whereas in a personal style people try to lessen the barriers among themselves. The affective mode of communication is more concerned with the "how" of communication whereas the instrumental mode of communication is intimately related to the issue of goal attainment. In high context cultures, communication is more often than not likely to be indirect, often elaborate, contextual, and affective rather than instrumental.[8]

In practical terms what this means is that in these cultures people will not overtly express their wishes and/or express rejection of any terms/conditions regarding a proposal. It also has the implication that in these cultures individuals may state the same thing in so many different ways. Likewise, the communicative tone and the content of the message will be heavily dependent on the hierarchical quality of the relationship among the parties. Finally, the communicative patterns in this context are not likely to be intimately related to the issue of goal attainment.

Many have pointed out that the Indian communicative style is indirect in nature.[9] The Indians often do not like to say "no" directly to the other party for fear of offending. As Girish Paranjpe, President (Finance) of Wipro Technologies states, "Indians do not speak up in meetings and do not like confronting the client, which sometimes leads to awkward situations like project delays and cost overruns."[10] Similar comments have been made by others as well.

Wendell Jones, Vice President Worldwide Service Delivery at DEC who managed the outsourcing relationship between NASDAQ and Tata Consultancy Services, noted that communicative difficulties stemming from differences in cultures was one of the major problems that he had to deal with.[11] Commenting on the interactions between the Germans and the Indians, Sujata Banerjee notes, "Well, it is difficult for Germans when an Indian says 'no problem' as the German *suspects* that the real *challenges* are not being admitted. For the Indian, 'no problem' simply means, 'I know there will be problems, but I am doing the best I can *at my end*.'"[12]

The Indian communicative style is also characterized by elaborateness rather than succinctness. The Indians like to talk and express their viewpoint in multiple ways. This behavioral tendency is most likely reinforced by the fact that Indians are context sensitive. Context sensitivity has the implication that all possible contingencies must be outlined and their implications clearly delineated. As Araoz points out, "The Indian engineer is often unaware that verbosity is very hard on Americans, who generally like co-workers to be succinct and logical in their business communication."[13]

The Indian communicative style is also very contextual, in that what individuals communicate, and how they communicate is shaped by the nature of the relationship between the individuals. For example, the Indian culture is hierarchical and this affects the pattern of communication between employees at different organizational levels. The Indian employee may adopt a very deferential attitude toward his superior and for this reason may be reluctant to initiate communication, much less convey information that may not be palatable to his or her superior.

As an Indian manager working in the subsidiary of a Danish company, noted, "We Indians cannot say 'no' to our boss. The boss will get angry."[14] The director of British American Corporation, a company studied by Sinha, noted, "Indians wasted their time talking too much. They rarely stick to the agenda in a meeting. There is a wide gap between what Indians professed and what they actually did. They were more concerned about what other people would say than what was the 'right' thing to do."[15]

Finally, it would be fair to say that the Indian communicative style is more affective rather than instrumental. This is a style that "requires the listener to carefully note what is being said and to observe how the sender is presenting the message. . . . The part of the message that is being left out may be just as important as the part that is being included."[16] A good example of this may be gleaned in the interactions between the U.S. Ambassador Allen and India's first Prime Minister, Jawaharlal Nehru. When the United States decided to give military aid to Pakistan in 1954, President Eisenhower instructed the American ambassador in India to meet Nehru and convey the message that this action was not directed against India. During the meeting Nehru was calm and restrained, leading the American ambassador, Allen, to conclude that Nehru was not offended by this action. However, as Cohen points out, this represented complete misjudgment by the American ambassador. He failed to understand the real meaning behind Nehru's reaction.[17]

Ideological versus Pragmatic Communicative Style

An ideological communicative style utilizes the dominant ideology extant in that culture at a particular point in time to structure communication, and as Triandis has pointed out this "assumes that the other person has the same view."[18] By contrast, a pragmatic communicative style utilizes a mode of communication that achieves the intended goal. The Indian communicative style is often ideological, shaped as it is both by an idealistic mode of thinking, and more recently by a resurgence in Indian nationalism. Indeed as Perry points out, "Washington D.C. based Pew Research Center's 2003 Global Attitude Survey found India was the most nationalistic place on earth with 74% of the respondents 'completely agreeing' that Indian culture is superior."[19] An ideological mode of communication uses one particular point of view to look at all types of problems. This has the implication that "When the universalistic person communicates with a particularistic, pragmatic opponent, the universalistic is likely to see the pragmatist as dealing with trivialities and as not having great thoughts, while the pragmatist is likely to see the 'universalists' as theoretical, fuzzy thinking, and dealing with generalities."[20] A related problem is that it may be hard to find common ground between the ideologist and the pragmatist, given that they are operating on the basis of radically different philosophies.

Historically, the ideological mode of thinking was dominant in India, and especially insofar as multinational firms were concerned. Even with the onset of liberalization in 1991, foreign investors, at least initially, were greeted with some degree of skepticism. The high-profile disputes involving many independent power producers and the likes of Cargill are a testimony to this fact. However, with the rapid rise of India's software industry, and the recognition that international firms have played a positive role in its development, is, to be sure, altering the way in which foreign investors are being viewed in India. That said, there is without question an upsurge in Indian nationalism, with a strong desire for India to be recognized and accorded its due status in the world as a major power. This of course, has the implication that all communication has to be viewed from the prism of Indian pride and greatness.

Associative versus Abstractive Communication Style

Scholars have also drawn a distinction between an associative and an abstractive communication style.[21] An associative style of communication does not engage in sharp differentiations between who the person is and what the person does. By contrast, an abstractive communication style makes such differentiations. This difference has important implications for the way messages are transmitted and how they are decoded in different cultures. If, for example, there is no sharp differentiation between whom the person is and what the person does, it may be difficult to give negative feedback to the other person without offending him or her.

It may also make it difficult to discuss the merits or demerits of any policy action in the abstract without assessing its implications for the individual or individuals concerned. It would be fair to say that while the Indian culture comprises both the associative as well as an abstract mode of communication, the associative style may be somewhat more dominant. This follows from the fact that the Indians are highly sensitive to criticism and may find it hard to follow the well-known precept of Fisher and Ury to "separate the people from the problem."[22] Although the issue of saving face may be less important in India compared to the Confucian cultures of China, Korea, Taiwan, and Japan, there is no question that face-related concerns are important. When one considers the fact that status, caste, age, and hierarchy are important, it is inevitable that issues of face become important. Communication designed to give feedback, elicit task-related compliance, and motivate employees, must therefore be sensitive to these concerns.

A good example is that of Tata Steel, a company that was actively trying to reshape its corporate culture. As Sinha points out, many senior managers resisted the change to an alternative system that was more egalitarian. He cites the comments of a young officer who noted, "There are senior managers who are power hungry; I mean those who are brought up in the old culture. For them this change is erroneous and obnoxious. They feel they should be informed, their consent should be solicited, and all the files must be routed through them."[23] The interpretation of their behavior is that the senior Indian managers would have lost face as a consequence of the alternative system, even though the system may have increased the efficiency of the organization.

Nonverbal Communication

Scholars are often at pains to point out that while individuals often pay attention to words, much of the most important communication often occurs nonverbally.[24] As Copeland and Griggs note, "On a very unconscious level many of us abroad can turn people off even when we are on good behavior."[25] This may occur for a number of different reasons such as making inappropriate gestures, or maintaining an inappropriate personal distance with the other party. Likewise, eye contact may make individuals in some cultures uncomfortable just as touching or informality may make others unhappy. Nonverbal behavior has four main components to which managers must pay attention. These are the issues of (a) distance; (b) touching; (c) eye contact; and (d) body movement.[26]

The North American or western European expatriate manager may find that the typical Indian manager or employee may have a very different style of nonverbal communication than what he or she might be used to do. One such example is provided by Gesteland who, when working in India, was taken out for lunch by his Indian business partner. As they went for lunch, the Indian held the hand of Gesteland, and at least initially, it made him a trifle

uncomfortable. In the European or American environment handholding is clearly indicative of sexual interest, but in the Indian environment, it only signifies friendship. Fortunately, Gesteland was "able to recognize this aspect of the Indian culture soon enough, and this prevented any behavior on his part that may have been considered to be a cultural faux pas.[27] The personal space or distance among individuals is dependent on the status of the individual one is interacting with. In general, this distance increases when one is talking with one's superior or when one is relating to someone who comes from a lower rung of the hierarchy. It has also been pointed out that while in the past Indians preferred to maintain eye contact only with a person of equal status, it is no longer true in contemporary India. As a manual prepared by the Canadian International Development Agency notes, "As middle to high ranking women employees in the public and private sectors look directly at a person while addressing them, they expect the same from their male colleagues."[28] Practitioners have also pointed out differences in the use of gestures, with the reference often being made to the fact that Indians often say "yes" by shaking their heads sideways, a gesture that would signify a "no" in the Western cultural tradition.

It is important to point out that nonverbal communication is unconscious and for that reason not very easy to control. That said, it makes it even more important that European and American managers pay attention to it, for otherwise they will end up communicating a message which they never intended to. This can lead to an unsuccessful negotiation, demotivation of an employee, or an overall climate in which people fail to communicate effectively and in a timely way.

COMMUNICATING WITH INDIANS: IMPLICATIONS FOR WESTERN MANAGERS

What can Western managers do to enhance their effectiveness in communicating with the Indians? At the outset, it should be stated that there is no magical solution that will help Western managers improve the effectiveness of their communication with Indians overnight. It is also important to point out that Indian companies have now increasingly become cognizant of the cultural gap and are instituting training programs to enhance the cross-cultural skills of their employees in interacting with their European and North American counterparts.[29]

For example, the Bangalore-based company Wipro Technologies is training their Indian employees to interact more effectively with the Americans. They have brought in American trainers and have hired consultants from companies such as McKinsey & Co. to provide training both in India as well as overseas. Infosys Technologies is also reportedly developing a program of change management for its employees.[30] One can reasonably surmise that one of its likely consequences would be a decrease in communication barriers over time. It is also important to point out that Indian professionals find it easier to communicate and work in the North American context vis-à-vis the European context for a wide variety of reasons, ranging from country-specific differences in language and culture in Europe, to a greater sense of conservatism in the European environment.[31]

That said, what concrete steps can the Western expatriate undertake to enhance his effectiveness in communication with the Indians? The Western expatriate needs to (a) have a better awareness about Indian communicative patterns; (b) be able to deal with his or her emotions more effectively; (c) avoid ideological debates; (d) be able to create the perception of an individual who enjoys working in the Indian subcultural milieu. The following paragraphs elaborate these steps.

Better Awareness about Indian Communicative Style

This is a truism but that does not lessen its importance. If Western managers lack an appreciation of how Indians communicate, they may find themselves in all sorts of difficulties and may lose their motivation to effectively conclude their assignment. Although this recommendation has a commonsensical quality to it, it is extremely important for a number of different reasons. First, and foremost, heightened awareness has the implication that the Western manager is likely to have more realistic or accurate expectations about his interactions with the Indian counterpart.

When expectations are realistic and accurate, the manager may learn to recognize, for example, that the unwillingness on part of the Indians to say "no" does not imply that the Indian is in perfect agreement on the specific issue or subject under discussion. He or she may have to probe further to get the answer he or she is looking for. In other words, a heightened sense of awareness will minimize misunderstandings or miscommunication. Similarly, when expectations are accurate, the manager is unlikely to experience negative emotions like frustration, anger, or anxiety, and this is surely beneficial for the interaction at hand. Not only are the manager's attentions not diverted from the task at hand; he or she is also unlikely to act in ways that may jeopardize future interaction. Accurate expectations may also convey to the Indian counterpart that the Western manager is truly interested in India, in that he or she has taken the time to learn about the local culture. This can only have positive effects on the interaction among the parties.

Better Equipped to Deal with Negative Emotions

Negative emotions are often inevitable in intercultural interactions. As mentioned earlier, these emotions are a product of conflicting expectations. Although heightened awareness of another culture does limit the emergence and the intensity of these emotions, it cannot prevent them entirely for a variety of reasons. First, the expectations of Western managers doing business in India are not going to change overnight. It takes a while before managers can both fully appreciate an alternative way by which people live, and most importantly, internalize these new expectations in their daily interactions with the Indian colleagues. Second, even with the best of preparation, no Western manager can hope to fully or completely grasp the Indian cultural nuances, with the implication that sometimes they may experience these emotions notwithstanding their prior preparation or understanding about the Indian culture.

How, then, can the Western manager hope to deal with these emotions effectively? It must be said at the outset that in managing emotions there are important personality differences, with some individuals being more capable of handling these emotions well. That said, the Western manager can clearly take steps that will minimize their occurrence. One of the things that may help the manager deal with these emotions in a positive way may come from the recognition that *he or she is not alone*. In other words, he or she must consider the possibility that there may be other

Western expatriates who may be experiencing the same emotions. This recognition may not only bolster his or her self-confidence but may also induce him or her to network with other expatriates in the area. Most importantly, this will lead him or her to the invaluable insight that he or she has not been dealt with in a unique way by the Indians. This, in turn, is likely to prevent him or her from developing a negative attitude about the Indians and that can surely be considered to be a positive development.

Second, even if the expatriate experiences negative emotions, he or she must resist the urge to express them. As Ambrose Bierce once remarked, "Speak when you are angry and you will make the best speech you will ever regret."[32] Emotions like anger, if expressed openly, will damage the relationship and make it that much harder to put the relationship back on track. This does not imply that the expatriate should not express his or her concerns about any issue or issues over which he or she has reservation; the argument is only that these concerns should be expressed in a culturally sensitive way. The Western manager may express his concerns calmly, may seek to revisit the issue later, or use the services of a key informant who may serve as a culturally adept mediator.

Third, the Western expatriate manager could seek to reframe the situation. He or she may want to look for the positive in an admittedly negative situation. This is not easy, but that is not to say that one should not attempt it. Maybe there is something in what the Indians have said, that at the very least, may be worth thinking about. This does not by any means exhaust all that the Western manager could do, but it does provide a broad overview of the strategies that the expatriate managers may use in bridging the cultural divide with their Indian counterpart.

Avoid Ideological Debates

It is very easy to fall in this trap, and exiting from it is likely to be difficult. The Indian mind-set is both nationalistic and idealistic, and while the latter may be changing as India integrates itself in the world economy, nationalism is unlikely to disappear any time soon. The Western mind-set is for the most part pragmatic (although there may well be differences across countries) and this sets the stage for a clash of conflicting ideologies. In a business-related context, ideological debates on the rapidity of the economic reform process in India and how open India should be for the transnational corporation have emerged.

These debates have also carried over to the issue or issues of protecting intellectual property, privatization, and the role of the government in the economy. Ideological debates brook no room for compromise, and if anything, may harden the position of the parties further. They may also detract from effective problem solving and may be counterproductive in the extreme. What is interesting about India is that ideological conflicts notwithstanding, transnational corporations can function effectively and profitably in the Indian context (though the energy sector may be an exception).

Creating the Perception of a Positive Attitude toward India

It is important that Western expatriates demonstrate a positive attitude toward India. This is a proposition that would be equally true for any culture one wishes to operate in, but this is likely to have a particular resonance in the Indian cultural context. The Indian mind-set has, fortunately or unfortunately, been deeply shaped by the colonial experience, and this has the implication that there is, at least initially, a certain degree of suspicion toward the foreign investor.

Clearly this suspicion may not be equally targeted toward all foreign investors, but it does mean that the foreign investor has to create a certain sense of reassurance in the Indian mind. This reassurance is best demonstrated by creating the perception that the expatriate has a positive view about India. A good example is provided in a study of the BAC Corporation in India conducted by Sinha. Mr. Wilson, a British national, who was the Managing Director of the company, had adapted and felt comfortable with the Indian mores. As Sinha notes, "He freely mixed with employees, often took lunch with them, attended their marriage ceremonies, spoke broken Hindi and Punjabi, and seemed to love the Indian curry. Employees found in him a great listener."[33] This may indeed be one of the reasons as to why the Indian employees had positive views of British expatriates.

Communicating cross-culturally is neither easy nor predictable. Each party seeks to communicate on the basis of its own sets of assumptions and this is without a doubt the starting point of any conflict. This essay has attempted to outline the cultural divide separating the Western manager from his or her Indian counterpart. In years to come, this divide may be lessened, but in the interim some suggestions as to how best this divide can be mediated have been provided.

References

The epigraphs in this essay are drawn from: W. B. Gudykunst and Y. Y: Kim (1992). *Communicating with Strangers: An Approach to Intercultural Communication,* pp. 41, 89; C. Storti (1990). *The Art of Crossing Cultures.* Maine: Intercultural Press; and D.C. Thomas (2002). *Essentials of International Management: A Cross Cultural Perspective.* Thousand Oaks, CA: Sage.

1. Cited in W. B. Gudykunst and Y. Y. Kim (1992). *Communicating with Strangers: An Approach to Intercultural Communication.* New York: McGraw Hill (p. 41).
2. M. Guirdham (1999). *Communicating across Cultures.* Hampshire, UK: Palgrave Macmillan.
3. H. W Lane, J. J. DiStefano, and M. L. Maznevski (1998). *International Management Behavior.* Oxford, UK: Blackwell Publishers.
3a H.C. Triandis (1995). *Culture and Social Behavior.* New York: McGraw Hill.
4. Ibid.
5. E. T. Hall and M. R. Hall (1995). *Understanding Cultural Differences: Germans, French, and Americans.* Yarmouth, ME: Intercultural Press.
6. Ibid., p. 6.
7. R. M. Hodgetts and F. Luthans (2000). *International Management: Culture, Strategy, and Behavior.* New York: McGraw Hill.
8. A. M. Francesco and B. A. Gold (1998). *International Organizational Behavior.* Upper Saddle River, NJ: Prentice Hall.
9. Canadian International Development Agency (1994). "Working With An Indian Partner: A Cross Cultural Guide for Effective Working Relationships"; P. Hobbs (2002). "The Complexity of India," *New Zealand Business,* November, pp. 12–13; R. Gopalakrishnan (2002). "If only India Knew what Indians Know." www.tara.com/rata_sons/articles/20020426_palkrishnan_2.htm
10. M. Jayashankar. "Building Outsourcing Bridges: Change Management Teams Help US Clients and Indian Firms Understand how to Work Together." www.businessworldindia.com/june21st,2004./indepth02.asp
11. Kramer and Messick. "Little Help from Our Enemies."
12. R. Gibson. "Intercultural Communication: A Passage to India." Interview with Sujara Bannerjee. www.business-spodight.de/dod13053?PHPSESSID, May 2003.
13. Araoz. "When Cultures Collide." Cited in J. B. P. Sinha (2003). *Multinationals in India: Interface of Culture.* New Delhi: Sage.
14. Cited in J. B. P. Sinha (2003). *Multinationals in India: Interface of Cultures.* New Delhi: Sage.
15. Cited in Ibid., p. 144.
16. Hodgetts and Luthans. *International Management.*
17. R. Cohen (1997). *Negotiating across Cultures: Communication Obstacles in International Diplomacy.* Washington, DC: United States Institute of Peace.
18. H. C. Triandis (1995). *Culture and Social Behavior* (p.193). New York: McGraw Hill.
19. A. Perry. "An Eternally Faltering Flame: Despite Its Billion-Plus Population, India is Always an Also-Ran at the Olympics." www.time.com/asia/magazine/article/0,13673,501040823-682346,00.html, February 9, 2004.
20. Triandis. *Culture and Social Behavior.*
21. Ibid.
22. R. Fisher and W. Ury (1991). *Getting to Yes.* Boston: Houghton Mifflin.
23. Cited in J. B. P. Sinha (2003). *Tata Steel: Becoming World Class.* New Delhi: Sri Ram Center for Industrial Relations and Human Resources.
24. L. Beamer and I Varner (2001). *Intercultural Communication in the Workplace.* New York: McGraw Hill.
25. L. Copeland and L. Griggs (1985). *Going International: How to Make Friends and Deal Effectively in the Global Marketplace.* New York: Random House.
26. R. R. Gesteland (1999). *Cross Cultural Business Behavior: Marketing, Negotiating, and Managing across Cultures.* Copenhagen: Copenhagen Business School Press.
27. Ibid., p. 71.
28. Canadian International Development Agency (1994). "Working with an Indian Partner: A Cross Cultural Guide for Effective Working Relationships," p. 16.
29. A. Viswanathan. "Indian Companies are Adding Western Flavour." www.wipro.com/newsroomn/newsitem/newstory288.htm, July 28, 2004.
30. Jayashankar. "Building Outsourcing Bridges."
31. P. Jasrotia. "IT Pros Find it Harder to Work in Europe." www.expressitpeople.com/20011029/cover1.htm, October 29, 2001.
32. Cited in A. Ben Ze-'ev (2000). The Subtlety of Emotions. Cambridge, MA: MIT Press.
33. Sinha. *Multinationals in India,* p. 139.

Concepts and Questions

1. Why do Kumar and Sethi assert that communication problems increase in difficulty when you include the dimension of cross-cultural differences?
2. Compare high-context to low-context communication patterns as they apply to India and the United States.
3. Compare ideological versus pragmatic communication styles as they apply to India and the United States.
4. Compare associative versus abstractive communication styles as they apply to India and the United States.
5. What are some major difference between India and the dominant culture of North America as it applies to nonverbal communication?
6. What advice do Kumar and Sethi offer to Western managers attempting to improve the manner in which they do business with the members of the Indian culture?

Dismantling Misconceptions About Islam in Egypt

POLLY A. BEGLEY

Just as the Nile runs through Egypt for almost eight hundred miles, giving it life, so also the Straight Way, the way of Allah, runs through it, beckoning its people. The search by Egypt's Muslim for a modern understanding of the Straight Way is the essence of today's passion for Islam.

C. MURPHY, 2002

Denmark's daily newspaper, *Jyllands-Posten*, published twelve cartoon drawings of the Prophet Mohammed on September 30th, 2005. The drawings, one depicting the Prophet with a bomb shaped turban, were considered blasphemous by Muslims and incited protests across the globe. Some of the demonstrations became violent. The media described the violence as a clash of civilizations and pointed to a divide or even a chasm between the Western world and the Muslim world. Is there a West-East chasm? A chasm denotes a broad difference of opinion or loyalty. A division reflects disagreement or discord between factions. In a world where peace is ideally negotiated through accurate and specific communication, these terms—divide and chasm—may prevent critical reasoning and hinder dialogue. In fact, if there are disagreements and differences of opinion, then they are likely rooted in a lack of education rather than a perceived insurmountable distance between the East and the West.

One young Muslim on www.Amrkhaled.net sent an apology and explanation to the Danes when he said, "We are sorry if some Muslims lost their senses and turned violent but you just don't know how dear Prophet Mohamed is to our hearts. Our Holy

This original essay appears here in print for the first time. All rights reserved. Permission to reprint must be obtained from the author and publisher. Polly A. Begley teaches in the Department of Communication Arts at Fresno City College, Fresno, California.

Qur'an ordained us to interact with different nations and now we do. All we need from you, Danes, is to know Prophet Mohamed first" (Shahine, 2006). Islamophobia has raged across the Western world in the wake of the attacks on the World Trade Center and the Pentagon, the cartoon debacle in Denmark, Pope Benedict XVI's comments about Islam at the University of Regensburg in Germany, and armed conflicts in the Middle East. What many have not realized is that the violent responses of a minority have been splashed across every headline, but the *umma* (Muslim world) have softly cried out for understanding and educational campaigns. A popular Egyptian preacher, Amr Khaled, sent out his plea for "Every single Muslim, every man and woman and even children . . . send it [messages] in any form you like, and in any language you prefer, and we will deliver it to the world." He further explained that this, "would be more in line with the teachings of the Holy Qur'an which says that people were created from different civilizations and cultures in order to merge and get mutually acquainted" (Shahine, 2006). An Islamic revival and movements for mutual interfaith understanding and enlightenment have sprung from the ancient land of the Pharaohs, where the Nile River flows and where Cairo, the largest Islamic city in the world, is located.

Cairenes call their beloved city, Cairo, the "Mother of the World." This sprawling city and surrounding suburbs of almost 16 million people is where the thousand-year-old Al Azhar University has produced numerous influential Islamic scholars. In fact, Murphy (2002) claims that, "Egypt is center stage in the drama of Islam's contemporary revival" (p. 10). Regrettably, there are misconceptions, stereotypes, and myths that haunt the followers of the Prophet, and the media and politicians have done little to alleviate unfamiliarity or misdirection about Islam. "The Prophet Mohammed maintained that there were two principal 'mercies' in life, water for the thirsty and education for the ignorant" (Beattie, 2005, p. 102). Thus, this chapter will provide illumination by dismantling some common misconceptions regarding Islam that obstruct interactions among Egyptians and non-Egyptians. Specifically, this essay examines the origins of the Egyptian worldview and misconceptions related to religious beliefs, violent intent, terrorism, and Muslim women. Finally, other recommendations

for improving interfaith understanding and dialogue will be presented.

ORIGINS OF EGYPTIAN WORLDVIEW

The Egyptian worldview developed thousands of years ago as a culmination of various African civilizations and beliefs. When the Sahara dried up and became a desert, several African groups migrated to the Nile Valley. Religion was an important part of everyday life because it provided a framework for an orderly existence and explained the unexplainable for the people who struggled through cycles of harsh famine and floods along the mighty waters of the Nile. There were as many as 2,000 deities and a myriad of complicated rituals associated with ancient Egyptian beliefs. Every action in life was the earthly symbol of divine activity as there was no distinction between science, art, and religious philosophy.

Nomadic Arabs invaded Egypt in 619 A.D., and eventually Islam replaced other religions to become the prevailing worldview in modern Egypt. Today, Pharaonic-era beliefs are confined to museums and tourist sites. Of course, traces of the antediluvian ideas of the Pharaohs could never truly be erased from the Nile, the sand, and the people of Egypt, but ancient beliefs and philosophies are not taught in Egyptian schools. Ancient history is considered to be anti-Islamic and has been replaced in Egyptian classrooms with Islamic history (Gershoni & Jankowski, 1995). Christianity is the only other significant religious minority and has dwindled to 12 to 15 percent of the population. Small enclaves of Christians live in central Egypt and in Old Cairo.

The historical roots of Islam are important to intercultural communication because this religion influences every part of life for 85 to 90 percent of Egypt's population. Islam began with Mohammed, who was the last of God's prophets. God spoke to Mohammed through the angel Gabriel about 609 A.D., and the messages were recorded in the Qur'an. The Qur'an, the book of Islam, is the miracle claimed by Mohammed and considered to be the exact words of God. This holy book contains 114 chapters (or *suras*) and outlines the will of God for the loyal followers of Islam (Waines, 1993).

Mohammed received the divine revelations of God in the city of Mecca, located in what is now known as Saudi Arabia, but he had a great impact on all of Arabia, including Egypt. Historically, the Middle East was turbulent. Vast areas, harsh deserts, warring tribes, and a precarious value placed on human life contributed to turmoil in the region. A number of leaders attempted to create a consolidated empire, but it was Mohammed and his followers who united all of Arabia under their control. Islam's appeal to Egyptians, and more than 1 billion Muslims worldwide, may lie in the pure simplicity and the ability to find "peace that comes when one's life is surrendered to God" (Smith, 1991, p. 222). Islamic beliefs dominate every moment from birth to death and beyond. This worldview reflects one of the youngest and fastest growing major religions in the world.

MISCONCEPTIONS

Misconceptions related to Islam have ranged from minor misunderstandings to major conflicts in which many lives have been lost. The Secretary-General of the United Nations along with the co-sponsorship of the Prime Ministers of Spain and Turkey launched the Alliance of Civilizations in 2005 with a comprehensive report completed in 2006 in order to promote understanding and improve communication between Muslims and non-Muslims. This report pointed to the desperate need to "counter the stereotypes and misconceptions that deepen patterns of hostility and mistrust among societies" (p. 3).

There Is no God but God

Should the sight of a group praying in an airport provoke suspicion and fear among bystanders? An incident that occurred in November of 2006 at the Minneapolis-St. Paul International Airport illustrates a general lack of knowledge and misconceptions about Islamic religious beliefs. A gate agent witnessed three of a group of six Middle Eastern men praying in Arabic near the boarding gate. The agent stated later, "I was suspicious by the way they were praying very loud" (Sternberg & Miller, 2006). A passenger also reported to the police feeling alarmed because the men were chanting "Allah, Allah, and Allah," and discussing politics as they boarded. After boarding the plane, a flight attendant received a note from another passenger, "pointing out [the] 'Arabic men'" in the cabin (Lohn, 2006; Sternberg & Miller, 2006). The six men were *imams* (religious leaders) returning home from a North American Imams Federation conference. They were eventually escorted off the plane, subjected to a search, and held for questioning by the U.S. Marshals Service, the FBI, the Secret Service, and the Transportation Security Administration. One of the *imams* commented that, "We were never bothering anyone, not saying anything loudly. We were prostrating ourselves, the normal way we pray" (Sternberg & Miller, 2006). Terrorist attacks in the United States and other countries have led to stricter airport security measures, but many questioned whether the airline employees had valid reasons for removing these men from the plane.

Perhaps the problem was that those observing the *imams'* behavior were not familiar with normal Muslim prayer routines. Fadel Soliman, recently appointed National Chaplain of the World Assembly of Muslim Youth in North and Central Americas and the founder of the Bridges Foundation, commented that, "Many Westerners view Muslims as creatures from the outer space . . . worshipping a different God named Allah." Soliman, through the Bridges Foundation, specializes in introducing Islam to non-Muslims and also trains Muslims on how to present their faith to others. He explained that Allah is the same God worshiped by Christians and Jews and that "We give different attributes to the same God" (Shahine, 2006). Ultimately, the above incident might not have occurred if more people understood the tenets and pillars of the Islam faith.

Four tenets are central to understanding Islam: (1) it is a monotheistic religion; (2) God created the world; (3) humans are fundamentally good from birth because they are God's creations and without "original sin." Muslims believe in the innate goodness of humanity, but contemporary societies "forget" their divine origins; and (4) for each Muslim there will be a day of judgment when God decides whether each person will go to heaven or be condemned to hell (Smith, 1991).

Islam outlines five pillars for Muslims. First, *shahada* (creed) is the confession of faith: *"La ilaha illa 'llah"* which translates as "There is no God but God, and Muhammed is his prophet" (Smith, 1991, p. 244).

Second, *salat* (prayer) is an important part of everyday life. Muslims are required to stop for prayer five times a day (*fajr, dhuhr, asr, maghrib, isha 'a*—dawn, after midday, afternoon, sunset, and nighttime) facing in the direction of the holy city of Mecca. Beattie (2005) described the call for the faithful to prayer, "'God is great,' the *muezzins* call: 'Allahu Akbar. There is no God but Allah and Mohammed is his Prophet.' At sundown, in particular, the amplified sound of dozens of *muezzins* sounding simultaneously is a distinctive and ethereal reminder that Cairo is first and foremost an Islamic city" (p. 91). Third, *zakat* (giving alms) to the poor is expected of each person. Fourth, *sawm* (fasting) during the month of Ramadan is required. This fast prompts Muslims to be disciplined and reminds them to be more charitable to the hungry and the poor within their societies. Finally, the *hajj* (pilgrimage) to Mecca is a requisite trip for those who are able to make the journey (Nigosian, 1987).

Islam does not require complicated rituals or sacrifices. Some experts argue that ancient Egyptian beliefs in countless deities and complicated rituals lost out over the appeal of monotheism and less complicated religious customs. Beattie (2005) disputes these claims because the polytheistic systems of the Pharaohs lasted intact for two and a half thousand years which is longer than other major world religions. The allure of Islam in Egypt may be that sincere faith unites and strengthens the people, and that this belief, similar to Pharaonic-era religions, provides a comforting framework for everyday existence in a turbulent world. If one repeats the shahada creed, then he or she is a Muslim. Good Muslims follow the five pillars. Monotheism has become the dominant worldview, but there are still misunderstandings and misrepresentations evident among the world's major philosophies.

Spreading the Faith by the Sword

Pope Benedict XVI delivered a speech in September 2006 at the University of Regensburg in Germany in which he made references to Islam and "holy war." In his speech entitled, "Faith, Reason and the University—Memories and Reflections," he quoted the Byzantine emperor Manuel II Paleologus as saying, "Show me just what Muhammad brought that was new and there you will find things only evil and in-

human, such as his command to spread by the sword the faith he preached" (Libreria Editrice Vaticana, 2006). Angry reactions ensued throughout the Muslim populations of the world. The Organization of the Islamic Conference released a statement in reference to the Pope's speech that stated, "The attribution of the spread of Islam around the world to the shedding of blood and violence . . . is a complete distortion of facts" ("Press Release," 2006). The Pope issued an apology after his speech and explained that the Byzantine emperor's quote did not reflect his personal opinion and in fact it was an invitation for interfaith dialogue.

Apology aside, the Pope's speech brought up another common misconception about Islam related to compulsion in religion and the term *jihad*. Fadel Soliman, who has addressed audiences regarding Islam, including members of the U.S. Congress and Pentagon officials, says that, "*Daawa* [advocacy] is not about converting people to Islam, the way many people assume it is. Allah said to Prophet Mohammed that his only mission is to deliver the message perfectly and that it is up to people to believe or not to believe" (Shahine, 2006). Mohamed El-Moctar El-Shinqiti (2006), a Mauritanian writer living in the United States, points out that historically Muslims subjugated populations to the empire as did other conquerors in the past, but religious writings do not advocate conversion to Islam. In fact, he references religious tolerance in Islam, "Let there be no compulsion in religion . . . (Al-Baqarah 2:256) . . . Moreover, Prophet Mohammed (peace be upon him) is told in the Qur'an that his mission is to teach and preach, not to impose or compel" (Playing the Empire Game section, para. 3).

But the media continues to attribute the concept of compulsion and more specifically, "holy war" to Islam. *Jihad* is an Arabic word from the Qur'an that has often been mistranslated as "holy war." The mere mention of an Islamic *jihad* has been depicted within Western literature and media as religious fanatics on a killing rampage. In contrast, Muslims remember "holy war" in terms of the Crusades of the twelfth and thirteenth centuries when Christian soldiers, sanctioned by the Pope, led military campaigns in the Holy Land. The literal meaning of *jihad* in Arabic is, "'Utmost effort' in promotion and defense of Islam" (Lippman, 1995, p. 113). In fact, El-Shinqiti (2006) states that the term "holy war" does not appear in the Qur'an. Even the terms of "defense of Islam" are limited as it is said, "Fight in the way of Allah against those who fight against you, but begin not hostilities. Lo! Allah loves not aggressors (Al-Baqarah 2:190)" (Sometimes Just but Never Holy section, para. 6).

Terrorism Associated with Islam

Moderate Muslims, the vast majority of the followers of the Prophet, espouse nonviolent change in Egypt and other Muslim countries. According to the United Nation's Alliance of Civilizations report (2006), "the exploitation of religion by ideologues intent on swaying people to their causes has led to the misguided perception that religion itself is a root cause of intercultural conflict" (p. 9). There is a powerful Islamic revival taking place in Egypt and other parts of the Middle East, but an entire religion and its adherents cannot be held responsible for the violent actions of a fringe minority. In order to understand how Islam and Muslims came to be associated with terrorism, we need to examine the common use of inflammatory labels and some of the reasons for this revival.

First, the terms and labels utilized by some media and political or religious leaders contribute to misconceptions and fan the fires of hatred against the followers of Islam. "Fundamentalism" is a term once used for Protestant Christians who sought to reestablish religious values in secular society. Recently, the term "fundamentalist" has been "used indiscriminately in the popular press and in Western political discourse to refer to any Islamist, no matter whether his aim is violent revolution or peaceful transformation. . . . Its current usage to describe activist Muslims is almost always pejorative and obscures their thoroughly modern views on society and religion" (Abdo, 2000, p. 11). Other terms implying the innate violent nature of Islam is "Islamic terrorism," "Islamic fascism," or Islamic radicals (United Nations, 2006, p. 13). The use of such terms creates the impression that Islamic activism leads to militancy and violent confrontation. Redefining words such as fundamentalist may help to change perceptions about Islam. Some scholars prefer the term "Islamists" which refers to Muslim activists who wish to reestablish Islamic values in society and does not carry the negativity of other group labels (Abdo, 2000).

Second, the reasons for the Islamic revival in Egypt and other parts of the Middle East are varied and complex. One such reason may stem from what Egyptians call *Al Naqsa* or "The Setback," which was the war with Israel in 1967. Egypt, Jordan, and Syria all lost large amounts of territory to Israel during this six-day war and some "Egyptians interpreted their disgrace as divine 'punishment' for straying from God" (Murphy, 2002, p. 30–31). Egyptian feelings of disgrace are further exacerbated by societal ills that continue to plague the people. Specifically, many experts point to poverty and corruption as a contributing factor of the Islamic revival, but it is interesting to note that Egyptians view the secularist rule of recent decades as an anomaly. So the reason for the return to Islam may in part be a return to religious values inundating every part of everyday life from as far back as the Pharaonic era through the establishment of Islam in the seventh century.

Living standards, however, are a pressing everyday concern in modern Egypt. "An estimated sixteen million Egyptians live below the poverty line, over half of them in the countryside. Nearly 50 percent of the country's population is illiterate. With 500,000 new jobseekers entering the job market annually, unemployment has long been a natural catastrophe" (Murphy, 2002, p. 14). Many of those living without their basic needs being met blame governmental mismanagement and widespread corruption. *Kossa* (literally translated as zucchini) is slang in Egypt for corrupt practices such as bribery and favoritism. If a person needs a job or a permit, he or she needs plenty of *kossa* and *wasta* (connections). An Egyptian attorney, Ahmed Sharaf Al Din, believes that most people see "this country as not their country, but the country of rich people and thieves . . . they love Egypt. But they hate the government" (Murphy, 2002, p. 20). Thus, Islamists see a return to Islamic values of social justice as one of the best solutions for societal problems. These societal problems have led to a grassroots Islamist movement to transform Egyptian society. This stirring of transformative change is coming from the streets and the middle and lower classes, which are producing their own bottom-up ideas for improved living standards through what has been described as "Popular Islam." The word is being spread by "popular sheikhs" preaching on the streets and whose "lives reflect the tragedies and hardships experienced by their followers . . . [and have] . . . become an antidote to official preachers co-opted by the state" (Abdo, 2000, p. 31).

Part of the solution for poor living conditions has been to organize community-funded projects such as the construction or improvement of mosques, clinics, hospitals, libraries, and museums. Mustafa Mahmoud, the host of a television show called "Science and Faith," and a fund raiser for multiple community projects says, "I have a deep faith in Islam. But it's a pity Islam is misunderstood in the West. They understand Islam through Khomeini and extremist groups. They remember the hostages and car bombs. Islam is a religion of mercy and love and beliefs" (Murphy, 2002, p. 30).

Islamic activists advocating for societal changes, building hospitals, and preaching mercy also disdained the violence perpetrated by the radical minority within their midst and mourned with the rest of the world the lives lost on September 11, 2001, in New York and Washington, D.C. These sentiments were reflected in an opinion poll conducted by a weekly English-language newspaper, al-Ahram. The poll found that "86 percent of Egyptians surveyed declared that Islamic groups that resort to violence do not work to the benefit of the country. Conversely, 73 percent of the respondents said nonviolent Muslim groups did benefit society" (Murphy, 2002, p. 14).

Perceptions of Muslim Women

A discussion of misconceptions related to Islam is not complete without raising the issue of the roles of Muslim women in Islam. A forum focusing on women in business took place in Cairo in 2005. Among other issues, the forum addressed ways of increasing investments in order to encourage Egyptian women in business and fiscal independence (Nafie, 2005). The 16th annual Global Summit for Women also took place in Cairo in June 2006. The summit president, Irene Natividad, said, "My hope was to break some of the stereotypes of Arab women as veiled, silent and passive . . . by presenting examples of women who have broken through, as well as efforts by those from the lower and middle ranks to get more involved in business" (United Nation Office for the Coordination of Humanitarian Affairs, 2006).

As Muslim women seek economic development, they are also active in religious scholarship. The Islamic

revival has not only been initiated by men, but Muslim women have also been instrumental as " 'bearers of culture,' the key to the perpetuation of the faith" (Abdo, 2000, p. 147). In Syria, women are becoming sheikhas, religious scholars. Fatima Ghayeh, a 16-year-old studying at a religious *madrasa* (school) in Damascus, Syria, says that "Today, girls are saying, 'We want to do something with Islam, and for Islam.' We're more active, and we ask questions" (Zoepf, 2006, p. A10). Zeinab al-Ghazali, the founder of the Egyptian Muslim Women's Association in 1937, sees women's role within Islam as a powerful one and sees the young people leading the way to Islamic revival. She stated, "It is important for women to be religious. It is through them that men find Islam and this influences the family to be religious" (Abdo, 2000, p. 149).

One sign of Muslim women's religious devotion is the veil, one of the most misunderstood elements of Islam by non-Muslims. The youth of Western societies are often concerned with having the latest fashions, and outward displays of spiritualism are dismissed as being as passé as last year's bell-bottom pants. But clothing choices for Muslims, specifically Muslim women, have a different focus. Farazi (2006) wrote about faith and fashion for www. AlJazeera.net and reported that female religious garments may be a matter of convenience, a way to avoid male stares, or to assert that a woman's clothing choices are only one part of her identity. Muneera Rashida and Sukina Abdul Noor of Poetic Pilgrimage, a popular U.K. hip-hop group who wear headscarves, defy the stereotype of the rap artist as being obsessed with material possessions. They say that, "We try to make hijab appear the coolest thing in the world to our young fans . . . . We tell them in our music that hijab is cool and they should not be ashamed of it" (Mumisa, 2006).

Understanding the different types of modest dress for Muslim women may help to dispel some misconceptions about veiling. Abdo (2000) describes the different styles:

> The head veil, or *hijab*, which literally means "curtain,"
> is essentially a headscarf. The *khimar*, a step up in
> the veiling process, is a headscarf that covers the hair
> completely and extends down to the waist, fully
> disguising the breasts. And the *niqab*, usually a black
> wrap that resembles a cape, extending from the head
> to the floor and covering everything except the eyes,

is the final stage. The *hijab* is considered by many Islamists to be obligatory for Muslim women, while those who wear or advocate the *niqab* tend to exist outside mainstream Egyptian society. (p. 143)

In fact, the Qu'ran does not specify the shape or color of women's coverings and does not ask women to cover their faces, so the *khimar* and *niqab* are from Arab cultures. The *hijab* is accompanied by loose clothing that covers the body's curves and may be one of the most conspicuous signs of Islamic intent to embrace spiritual above secular values. An Egyptian Web site, www.hamasna.com, launched in 2006, fights against television's sexually explicit music videos and programming by encouraging modesty through "The International Campaign for Defending Hijab." The site also "offers female singers and actresses alternative jobs should they decide to quit show biz and take the veil" (El-Jesri & Awad, 2006). In fact, Muslim men and women both have a responsibility to dress modestly, but the veil has been a source of stereotypes and misunderstandings regarding the roles of women in Islam.

Other Muslim women are taking the spotlight while maintaining their spiritual focus. Sukina, one of the members of the hip-hop group, Poetic Pilgrimage, breaks down stereotypes of women in Islam through her lyrics in the song "Definition of a Pilgrim" (personal communication, February 8, 2007):

evoking the name of Allah before I start roaming

desperately seeking something

cloaked in garments flowing

memorizing sacred hymns now my souls glowing

I write these hip-hop poems

in praise of the All Knowing

Poetic Pilgrimage, Miss Undastood, and Sister Haera are all female Muslim hip-hop artists who are educating and reeducating their audiences about women's roles and status in Islam.

FURTHER RECOMMENDATIONS

Youth Education

Overall, understanding of Muslims was found to be inadequate in a December 2005 Gallup poll in America which "found that, when asked what they admire most about Muslim societies, the most frequent response among respondents (32%) was 'nothing' and the second most frequent (25%) was 'I don't know'" (as cited in United Nations, 2006). In order to inform and dismantle misconceptions about Islam and Muslim societies, educational campaigns could be implemented in schools. These educational campaigns could come in the form of world religion classes offered in schools or increasing the number of youth exchange programs between America or Europe and Muslim communities in the Middle East. These programs would provide young people with the opportunity to get to know and communicate with peers who have religious values, cultural beliefs, and customs different than their own.

As mentioned in a previous section, another way to reach many of the young people of the world would be through music. Some hip-hop artists are Muslim, such as Mos Def, Mecca2Medina, Miss Undastood, Blind Alphabetz, Jurassic 5, Sister Haero, Prophets of the City, Reddy D, and Poetic Pilgrimage. The flowing rhythmic quality of classical Arabic may have made it easier for these artists to write poetry and raps in a variety of languages. Muneera, one of the singers from Poetic Pilgrimage, sends a message of piety and strength in a song called "Definition of a Pilgrim" in when she intones (personal communication, February 8, 2007):

To get away from painted street scenes of crack and cocaine but everyday remains the same of the same

Time to fix up readjust my frames life's just a spectacle

Looking at life from a more metaphysical

As I adhere to the call of my Lord fall on all fours

I arise as a Pilgrim Samurai with thumping sound systems in my headphones

These artists educate Muslims and non-Muslims about everyday life and Islam through their words and rhymes.

The Internet as an Educational Tool

Technological advances have changed the way we communicate, educate, and persuade. Groups fixated on promoting violence have been cognizant of the power of the Internet to persuade target audiences for quite some time. Kepel (2004) contended that "the war for Muslim minds entered the global jungle of the Internet" as graphic pictures of torture, be-headings, and wartime atrocities were made available online (p. 7). Fortunately, the *umma* have also begun to utilize the power of the Internet to counter information sent out by violent factions. Their messages focus on peace and invitations for dialogue between Muslims and non-Muslims. For example, the Web site www.IslamOnline.net was launched in early 2006 after the cartoons were published in Denmark's *Jyllands-Posten,* and was designed to educate about the Prophet and Islam. The Web sites www.Beliefnet .com and www.MuslimHeritage.com are also good sites to increase *ilm* (knowledge) about Islam (United Nations, 2006). Another online site is www.Soliya.net, which is for university students from the United States and Arab and Muslim countries to meet and discuss global issues.

Promoting Media Literacy for Youth

Educational campaigns would be ineffectual without also promoting critical thinking skills such as media literacy. Shaheen's 2001 analysis of nine hundred films containing Arab characters found that the majority were unrealistic and even racist (as cited in United Nations, 2006). Global populations are constantly exposed to unrealistic images and messages on television, films, and the Internet, but the logical skills to distinguish fact from fiction in the media are rarely part of educational plans. A 2003 study conducted by the Media Awareness Network researched Internet use by young Canadians and explored solutions to media illiteracy. These young people were frustrated by the adults attempting to control or limit their Internet access. They felt that the Internet was not about "censorship and control," but about "the principle of responsible decision making" (as cited in Möller & Amouroux, 2004, p. 168). The world's youth are increasingly becoming technologically proficient, so these decision-making skills should be taught through schools and public service messages and in various languages in order for them to make well-informed decisions and improve interfaith dialogue.

Language Choices

In every culture, the choices people make regarding language are vital to understanding and clear communication. Egyptians know well the beauty and power of language. Ancient hieroglyphs used the same word to signify both writing and art. Arabic replaced hieroglyphs in the seventh century, but this written language is also an art form in Egypt. Mosques are decorated with calligraphy and Egyptian homes commonly have scrolls written in exquisite script depicting the 99 names of God from the holy book in exquisite script. This classical language was preserved because it is the sacred dialect of the Qur'an (Hall, 1977). Other major languages branched out into various dialects, or became obsolete, but classical Arabic is still widely spoken among Muslims of every region. Egyptian children learn only in Arabic. Public prayers and ceremonies worldwide are conducted in Arabic even if the Muslim adherents are not Middle Eastern Arabs. Readers of the Qur'an have reported that the holy book is repetitive, confusing, and lacks compelling features when it is translated into other languages (Nigosian, 1987). In fact, the linguistic style of the Qur'an serves as a model for literature and speech throughout Islamic communities because the original verses in Arabic have a timeless beauty and rhythmic quality. The mastery of spoken and written classical Arabic is indicative of education and rank in Egypt. Arabic is a language that pleases the eyes, ears, and spirits of the people of Egypt. Visitors will find that a well-timed *Mish muskella* (no problem) or *Insha'allah* (if God wills it) will elicit approval and might improve relations with Egyptians. Regrettably, few American middle and high schools offer classes in Arabic, so individuals must find alternative ways to learn this language.

The importance and power of Arabic in Egypt makes the use of inflammatory words, in any language, by some politicians, religious leaders, and in the media a significant issue for many Muslims. According to the U.N. report, Alliance of Civilizations (2006), "such language fuels the spread of hatred and mistrust resulting in Islamophobia" (p. 20). Images and words help to shape our understanding of each other and the world around us, and a person who chooses words of violence is one step closer to committing a violent act. Unfortunately, backlash hate crimes against Arabs, Muslims, and even those who were thought to be Arab or Muslim (Sikhs and South Asians were also victims) increased by seventeen-fold across America after September 11, 2001 (Singh, 2002). The ability to choose the best words for the occasion or audience may be a *baraka* (blessing) and leads to productive interfaith interactions.

CONCLUSION

As the *khamaseen*, the destructive seasonal sandstorms from the desert, blows through Cairo, so do the misconceptions of Islam move through the communities of the world leaving misunderstandings and devastation. This essay sought to sweep away some common misconceptions regarding the Islamic faith that hinder interfaith communication. These misconceptions pertained to Islamic beliefs, violent intent, terrorism, and perceptions of Muslim women. It is unreasonable to assume that this short chronicle of Islam in Egypt will change the world in any significant manner, but *Insha'allah* (if God wills it), the readers of these words will have attained some additional understanding of the followers of the Prophet. Knowledge of the earth's major worldviews, especially the world's fastest growing religion, Islam, is the bridge that spans any distance between the East and the West. What was once considered to be an insurmountable chasm becomes the opportunity for an exchange of ideas, an invitation for dialogue, or even just a friendly chat over cups of *shay* or *ahwa* (coffee or tea) with a neighbor. And if you are fortunate enough to travel to Egypt and experience the phenomenal hospitality of the people, then they may share with you the following words: *Asslam o alikum wa rahmato Allah wa barakatoh*—Peace and Allah's mercy and blessings be upon you.

References

Abdo, G. (2000). *No God but God: Egypt and the triumph of Islam*. New York: Oxford University Press.

Beattie, A. (2005). *Cityscapes: Cairo*. New York: Oxford University Press.

El-Jesri, M., & Awad, S. (2006, August). Culture 101: The latest in news and gossip from cultural circles. *Egypt Today*. Retrieved August 25, 2006, from http://www.egypttoday.com/article.aspx?ArticleID=6866

El-Shinqiti, M. E. (2006, September 3). From holy war to holy peace. *www.IslamOnline.net*. Retrieved December 16, 2006, from http://www.islamonline.net/English/Living_Shariah/ContemporaryIssues/Interfaith/2006/08/01.shtml

Farazi, I. (2006, March 29). Following faith and fashion. *Aljazeera.net*. Retrieved August 25, 2006, from http://english.aljazeera.net/NR/exeres/CC89DE2B-E038-48E9-8178-F23181008CB4.htm

Gershoni, I., & Jankowski, J. P. (1995). *Redefining the Egyptian nation, 1930–1945*. New York: Cambridge University.

Hall, E. T. (1977). *Beyond culture*. Garden City, NY: Anchor Books.

Kepel, G. (2004). *The war for Muslim minds: Islam and the West*. Cambridge, MA: The Belknap Press of Harvard University Press.

Libreria Editrice Vaticana. (2006, September 12). *Meeting with the representatives of science at the University of Regensburg*. Retrieved January 31, 2007, from http://www.vatican.va/holy_father/benedict_xvi/speeches/2006/september/documents/hf_ben-xvi_spe_20060912_university-regensburg_en.html

Lippman, T. W. (1995). *Understanding Islam: An introduction to the Muslim world* (2nd ed.). New York: Meridian.

Lohn, M. (2006, November 21). 6 imams removed from Twin cities flight. *Washington Post*. Retrieved January 31, 2007, from http://www.washingtonpost.com/wp-dyn/content/article/2006/11/21/AR2006112100336.html

Möller, C., & Amouroux A. (Eds.). (2004). *The media freedom Internet cookbook*. Vienna: Organization for Security and Co-operation in Europe Publication. Retrieved February 8, 2007, from http://www.osce.org/item/13570.html

Mumisa, M. (2006, August 17–23). Sacred tunes. *Al-Ahram Weekly On-Line, 808*. Retrieved August 25, 2006, from http://weekly.ahram.org.eg/ 2006/808/feature.htm

Murphy, C. (2002). *Passion for Islam shaping the modern Middle East: The Egyptian experience*. New York: Scribner.

Nafie, R. (2005, November 24–30). Cornerstones of Peace. *Al-Ahram Weekly On-Line, 770*. Retrieved November 29, 2006, from http://weekly.ahram.org.eg/2005/770/ eg11.htm

Nigosian, S. (1987). *Islam: The way of submission*. Great Britain: Crucible.

Organization of the Islamic Conference. (2006, September 14). *Press release on the pope's recent statements on Islam*. Retrieved January 31, 2007, from http://www.oic-oci.org/press/English/2006/september%202006/pope.htm

Shahine, G. (2006, February 23–March 1). We introduce ourselves. *Al-Ahram Weekly On-Line, 783*. Retrieved August 25, 2006, from http://weekly.ahram.org.eg/2006/783/eg4.htm

Shahine, G. (2006, September 7–13). Fadel Soliman: Faces of Islam. *Al-Ahram Weekly On-Line, 811*. Retrieved December 16, 2006, from http://weekly.ahram.org.eg/2006/811/profile.htm

Singh, A. (2002, November). We are not the enemy: Hate crimes against Arabs, Muslims, and those perceived to be Arab or Muslim after September 11. *Human Rights Watch, 14*(6). Retrieved February 1, 2007, from http://www.hrw.org/reports/2002/usahate/

Smith, H. (1991). *The world's religions: Our great wisdom traditions.* San Francisco: Harper Collins.

United Nations. (2006, November 13). *Alliance of civilizations: Report of the high-level group.* Retrieved January 19, 2007, from http://www.unaoc.org/repository/HLG_Report.pdf

United Nation Office for the Coordination of Humanitarian Affairs. (2006, June 13). *Egypt: Arab businesswomen meet counterparts at "Davos for women."* Retrieved March 3, 2007, from http://www.irinnews.org/report.aspx?reportid=27005

Von Sternberg, B., & Miller, P. (2006, November 21). Uproar follows imams' detention. *Star Tribune.* Retrieved January 31, 2007, from http://www.startribune.com/462/story/826056.html

Waines, D. (1995). *An introduction to Islam.* Great Britain: Cambridge University.

Zoepf, K. (2006, August 29). Women lead an Islamic revival in Syria, testing its secularism. *The New York Times,* pp. A1, A10.

Concepts and Questions

1. What do you think Begley meant when she used the phrase "dismantling" while writing about some common misconceptions regarding the Islamic faith that might impede interactions among Egyptians and non-Egyptians?

2. Why does Begley believe that the notion of surrendering one's life to God is at the heart of Islam?

3. According to Begley, what are the four tenets of Islam that are central to understanding that religion?

4. How do the five pillars of Islam differ from the four tenets of Islam?

5. Why is the Islamic idea of *jihad* often misinterpreted by people from the West? What is the meaning of the word as it is used by much of American media? Do you believe that meaning is accurate?

6. Why, according to Begley, have Islam and Muslims come to be associated with terrorism?

7. What were your perceptions of Muslim women before reading the essay by Begley? Have you changed your perceptions now that you have read her analysis?

8. What recommendations does Begley suggest that might encourage cultural understanding between Muslims and non-Muslims? Can you think of any other recommendations?

When Face-to-Face Won't Work: Use of Informal Intermediaries to Communicate Interpersonally in Sub-Saharan Africa

ANN NEVILLE MILLER

INTRODUCTION

The young suitor doesn't wake up one fine day and walk up to his future father-in-law to tell him he intends to marry the daughter. Even facing the father-in-law alone is considered disrespectful. So he has to send a male relative of his father-in-law's age who will present the request by saying, "There is a cow in this home we are interested in buying." That puts the message across politely and if they are agreeable then the negotiations start (Sang, 2006, p. 1). The use of go-betweens, both formal versus informal, was mentioned as a cultural trait early in the history of the field of intercultural communication (Condon & Yousef, 1975), but the idea has attracted little attention in communication literature in the three decades since. Scattered evidence does exist that the use of third parties to communicate certain interpersonal messages is a phenomenon that appears with regularity in a variety of cultures (e.g., Kenen, Arden-Jones, & Eeles, 2004; Muira, 2000; Ting-Toomey & Kurogi, 1998). Marriage brokering, for example, is not uncommon in many parts of the world, especially South Asia. The broker may be entrusted not only with locating the prospective mate, but also with "testing the waters" to ensure that a family will not be embarrassed by undertaking an unsuccessful suit (Jaimon, 2005). The concept of third party disclosure of information has also been raised occasionally in U.S.-based health communication research, but almost always with reference to the violation of an individual's privacy through unauthorized leaking of a diagnosis by a confidante (see Greene, Derlega, Yep, & Petronio, 2003). Aside from these tidbits, a would-be sojourner culling communication literature for advice on the circumstances in which to expect this sort of interaction would not find much in the way of guidance. The informal use of uninvolved persons to mediate disputes or to convey information—what this chapter will term "intermediated communication"—is distinctly understudied.

In many sub-Saharan African cultures, on the other hand, intermediaries are used frequently and intentionally to accomplish a range of relational tasks. Conflicts with supervisors or coworkers, requests by children to parents or elders, sensitive situations between friends, and marital problems, all may at times be more gracefully handled by bringing in a third party to assist with communication. Bad news such as terminal illness as well as death and bereavement may also be communicated in an intermediated fashion. In some of these circumstances use of an intermediary is just one among several options legitimately available to a communicator. Siblings might discuss how to inform their mother about the serious road accident in which their brother had been involved; neighbors might strategize how to reveal concerns about the behavior of an errant child. In other situations third party communication is almost or fully institutionalized. During marriage negotiations, for example, the groom-to-be is often accompanied to his prospective bride's home by his uncles and clan elders, or family friends. These people speak on his behalf as the bride-price is agreed upon, while the young man himself and even his parents are expected to remain silent. In years past intermediation could begin even earlier in the courtship process as uncles, aunts, or other relatives were called upon to arrange an initial meeting between a young man and the young woman who had caught his eye. A similarly intermediated system of introduction has recently been described in Uganda, in which younger siblings or friends assist with the arrangement of adolescent sexual liaisons (Morrow, Sweat, & Morrow, 2004.)

Intermediaries can be relatives, friends, pastors, or co-workers, and the appropriate intermediary for one issue might not be selected to assist with another. But in all cases such individuals are chosen to carry an interpersonal message that for any of a number of reasons would not be possible or comfortable for the initiator to deliver in person. This essay explores intermediated communication in one sub-Saharan context, describing patterns of third party communication in various cultural groups in Kenya. First, however, I will briefly discuss two possible theoretical frameworks for consideration of use of intermediaries in interpersonal communication.

FACE NEGOTIATION THEORY AND POLITENESS THEORY APPLIED TO INTERMEDIATED COMMUNICATION

Although there is a paucity of material that specifically addresses intermediated communication, the practice is undoubtedly connected to a number of more regularly researched cultural and communicative constructs. Two models that claim to be valid across cultural groups—face negotiation theory and politeness theory—offer schemes by which this type of communication might be analyzed. Both give a central role to the concept of "face," or the sense of social self-image claimed by an individual in his or her relational network (see Domenici & Littlejohn, 2006). Both propose variables that should predict the type of "facework" that is likely to be used in a given situation," that is, the communicative behavior that individuals use to manage their own face and to uphold or threaten the face of others.

Ting-Toomey's (1988) face negotiation theory identifies individualism–collectivism along with high-power–low-power distance as the primary value orientations explaining understandings of face across cultures. Collectivism is defined as "the broad value tendencies of a culture in emphasizing the importance of the 'we' identity over the 'I' identity, in-group interests over individual interests, and mutual-face concerns over self-face concerns" (Ting-Toomey & Kurogi, 1998, p. 189). Individualism, on the other hand, stresses self-interest over other-interest; the "I" of personal identity over the "we." Both individualism and collectivism are assumed to exist to some degree in every culture, and for that matter in every individual, but one or the other tends to predominate in a given society. Most of sub-Saharan Africa is classified as collectivist in orientation (Gudykunst, 1998; Gyekye, 1997; Hofstede, 1991; Triandis, 1995).

Although the constructs of individualism and collectivism lack certain nuances needed for emic understandings of group-oriented thinking and values in some cultures, they are still important heuristics for at least beginning explorations of cultural contrasts. For instance, numerous studies have indicated that members of collectivist cultures (or individuals with interdependent self-construals (Markus & Kitayama, 1991) are more inclined than persons from more individualistic societies (or individuals with independent self-construals) to make use of indirect means of communication (e.g., Gudykunst, Matsumoto, Ting-Toomey, Nishida, Kim, et al., 1996; Holtgraves, 1997; Singelis & Brown, 1995; Triandis, 1995).

Collectivism has also, though much less commonly, been connected with intermediated communication. In a comparative study of conflict styles among four cultures, Ting-Toomey and associates (1999) found that Latino and Asian Americans were more likely to use avoiding and third party conflict styles than were European Americans. Third party intermediaries tended to be of high status, possess a credible reputation, and have a good relationship with both parties. Chinese participants in Leung's (1987) study preferred use of third parties for bargaining and mediation as a means of resolving conflict because it was deemed to be more likely to reduce animosity. In contrast, Americans preferred adversary adjudication, viewing it as more objective and fair. Leung also cited the status of the intermediary and his or her relationship to disputants as factors affecting preference for intermediated communication. African collectivism has been connected to intermediated communication by Moemeka (1996), who observed, "If what a person has to say is not in the best interest of the community, the person would be bound by custom to 'swallow his (or her) words.' Of course, the affected individual may whisper complaints into the ears of those who may be able to help in such other ways that would not conflict with community interest" (pp. 202–203).

Face negotiation theory further claims that the value dimension of power distance is also associated with cultural patterns of face negotiation. Hofstede (1991) defined power distance as the view that differences in status among community members are natural and desirable. This vertical power orientation is manifest in hierarchical roles, asymmetrical relationships, and rewards and punishments on the basis of rank, status, and sometimes age and gender. Individuals in high-power distance cultures are concerned with maximizing the distance between higher and lower power parties as a means of displaying deference. Thus conflict, the major communicative goal with which the theory is concerned, is often managed in such cultures with avoidance or indirectness. It may also be negotiated by informal third party mediation. Moemeka (1996) described the implication of this orientation for African communication:

> In Africa, vertical communication follows the hierarchical sociopolitical ranks within the community. What a person says is as important as who he or she is. In other words, social statuses within the community carry with them certain cultural limitations as to what to say, to whom to say it, how to say it, and when to say it. On the other hand, horizontal communication is relatively open and usually occurs among people of the same age (sometimes, only of the same sex), those who work together, live in proximity, or belong to the same ethnic group. (pp. 200–201)

In comparison to face negotiation theory, politeness theory has a narrower area of concern and has not, to the author's knowledge, been specifically applied to intermediated communication. Brown and Levinson's well-known model (1978, 1987) cites a close relative of intermediated communication—conversational indirectness—as the major sociolinguistic feature indicative of tending to matters of face. It suggests that culturally appropriate levels of indirectness can be predicted by the relational variables of power and social distance, plus the situational variable of magnitude of interpersonal imposition. All other factors being equal, the closer the relationship between two persons, the less the power differential between them, and smaller the magnitude of imposition the less likely it is that they will employ conversational indirectness. Although the weights of these factors in determining levels of indirectness in different cultures might vary, once those weights are taken into account a speaker's social cognitions may be revealed through how he or she chooses to communicate the same information to different individuals (Gonzales, Manning, & Haugen, 1992; Holtgraves & Yang, 1992).

Most investigations of politeness theory have been limited to the speech acts of requesting, inviting, or complimenting (Craig, Tracy, & Spissak, 1986; Pan, 2000; Wilson, Kim, & Meischke, 1991), but a model in the tradition of politeness theory that addresses politeness phenomena across interaction types is available in Scollon and Scollon's (1995) analysis of Athabaskan communication. The authors locate three overarching politeness systems: solidarity (used among persons who see themselves as equal in power and close in social relations and therefore comprised of direct communication with one another), deference (used when persons are equal in power but want to emphasize differences using indirectness) and hierarchical (used in asymmetrical relationships where persons on the top use direct communication and subordinates use indirect). The appropriateness of this framework to African contexts cannot, of course, be assumed (in fact, Gough, 1995, raised questions about the applicability of certain aspects of politeness theory to some African cultures). It does, however, raise the possibility that indirectness may operate across speech acts within certain relational systems, and it is at least feasible to consider that factors posited by the theory as determining levels of indirectness might also impact the choice to engage in intermediated communication.

APPLICATION TO INTERMEDIATED COMMUNICATION IN KENYA

These theories suggest that a major impetus for incorporating third parties into communication of interpersonal information might be concern over loss of face for one or the other party. Face negotiation theory proposes that third parties are more likely to be called in to assist with conflict resolution in collectivistic as opposed to individualistic cultures, and in high-power distance in comparison with low-power distance societies. Politeness theory suggests that within those environments indirect communication, and by extension intermediated communication, is most

likely when magnitude of imposition and power differential between parties are large and when the level of relational closeness is low.

Using these last three factors to structure the discussion, I now turn to a description of everyday use of intermediated communication in Kenyan society, or, more accurately, Kenyan societies. Kenya has not one, but somewhere between 40 and 50 distinct indigenous cultural and linguistic groups, each with its own rules, values, and traditions. To complicate matters further, many of these cultures are in a state of rapid but uneven westernization. Traditional practices in some cultures have scarcely changed for decades, especially in the rural areas. Other cultural patterns, especially in urban settings, have undergone massive metamorphosis. Although common themes run across ethnic groups and span the rural-urban divide, any comments made about Kenyan use of intermediated communication must be recognized as generalizations about a vastly diverse cultural landscape.

Magnitude of Threat to Face

Based on politeness theory we might anticipate that a high degree of threat to the face of either the communicator or the other party could prompt persons to engage in intermediated communication. Indeed, in the Kenyan environment disastrous family news such as the pregnancy of an unwed daughter can be communicated via an intermediary, particularly to the father. The girl's mother, or perhaps an aunt, would traditionally be the bearer of the bad tidings, and in such cases intermediation might be combined with indirectness. A father who was thus informed that one of the family cows had broken its leg would recognize from the metaphorical reference to incapacitation of a valued animal that the forthcoming news would be severe, and that an attempt was being made to soften its impact.

Communication about marital difficulties by nature also involves loss of face to various parties. Because harmony in marriage is one of the chief cornerstones on which harmony throughout Kenyan society in general is built, any conflict that arises between husband and wife must be handled carefully. Traditionally if a couple had serious disagreements to the point that the wife left and returned to her birth family, the husband could not expect to be reconciled to her unless he went to her family's home accompanied by his uncles and the clan elders. These intermediaries would make apologies to the family of the woman on behalf of her husband and often present a gift by way of appeasement for any wrongs she had suffered.

In the contemporary urban environment the role of the uncles and clan elders is often reassigned to the "best couple" or even a pastor. A participant in Golding and associates' (2007) study of couples communication among the Kamba ethnic group described how the best couple might become involved. "The best couple in our wedding is very close friends of ours. My wife can tell her all the problems. Then the best maid would tell the husband who would come and tell me what my wife is complaining about. If I have a problem I will explain to my best man who will tell the wife who in turn will tell my wife" (p. 20).

Whatever the identity of the intermediary, the sense that serious marital issues cannot and should not be addressed by the couple alone remains very current in Kenyan society. For example, a couple with whom I am acquainted had an argument that resulted in the wife's storming out and spending the night at the house of a relative. Because he felt that something very disturbing had happened in their marriage, something that had hurt him badly, the husband was shocked when his wife returned alone to their home the next day. It was only after two other couples were brought into the situation as intermediaries that he was able to believe that she was sincere in seeking reconciliation.

Power Differential between Parties

Politeness theory suggests that power differential within relationships plays a major role in determining the degree to which communication in a given situation is indirect. Use of intermediated communication in the Kenyan context also seems to be heavily influenced by power concerns. The societal structure of many Kenyan ethnic groups has traditionally been composed of nested hierarchies of relationships, with authority and submission based on age, marital status, wealth, and gender. In the millennial generation the hierarchy has to some degree been redefined, with education gaining importance as a sign of social status in certain communities such as the Luo, and wealth trumping other qualifications in some communities such as the Kikuyu. Nevertheless, the centrality of respect for, and proper submission to, authority as a cultural value remains to a great extent intact.

Power hierarchy in the family, too, was clearly delineated in past years. Although the position of father as supreme and unquestioned authority has eroded among some groups, even urban children still understand for the most part that interaction with their fathers must display a certain respectful deference. As a result of the outworking of this system, mothers may play an intermediary role between children and fathers. It has already been noted that in traditionally oriented families if a daughter becomes pregnant out of wedlock responsibility to make the father aware of the situation and to absorb some of his wrath on behalf of the child may fall to the mother or to an aunt. Intermediation may also be undertaken by mothers for children in more mundane matters. As one of my students recalled, "When I grew up and especially during my primary and secondary school, I never used to ask my father to buy me new school uniforms or inform him when I was sick. For the uniform, I could tell my mother who would in turn report to my father." Even when they are adults, children may have difficulty addressing their fathers directly until they themselves have attained a certain status either by virtue of being married and having children or because they have begun to display recognizable leadership qualities within the extended family circle.

Gender-based power differential is a defining component in the husband–wife relationship. Spousal power may have equalized to some degree in recent years, but many wives still find they must on occasion add to the credibility of their own status by bringing in a third party to carry messages to their husbands. When it comes to selecting an intermediary from within the family it is more common for women to approach their husband's family than their own for assistance (Golding et al., 2007). This is in part because a man's family may be assumed to know him well, but it is also because in many Kenyan kinship systems, once a woman marries she is no longer considered to be a member of her own family but is presumed to have transferred her membership to the family of her husband (see Ndeti, 1972). In polygamous families mothers may even use children to mediate communication with their husbands, anticipating that requests carried by such charming envoys will be difficult to resist. A child might be asked to carry a meal the mother had cooked over to the father in his hut, delivering the mother's message along with the food.

It is also common for women to enlist friends to enact intermediated communication with their husbands. A personal anecdote may serve as an example. Some time ago during a gathering that my husband and I attended, a Kenyan wife jokingly told a group of friends that she was trying to convince her husband to have another child, but without much success. "Yes, I keep telling him he needs a daughter to spoil!" she teased. The wife was, in fact, indirectly appealing to the men in the group to undertake intermediated communication for her. Her husband was fully aware of her strategy, and when two or three of the men present picked up the thread of conversation and encouraged him to have a third child he took notice. A year later, cradling his new daughter in his arms, he traced his change of mind explicitly to that conversation, "I thought, if these *wazee* [older men] are telling me to do this, I need to reconsider." My husband, who in true American style had viewed the entire conversation as good-natured ribbing of a friend, was surprised to be singled out among the *wazee* for the effectiveness of his (unwitting) part in the persuasive effort.

Because of their more powerful relational position men engage in intermediated communication less frequently than women. However, exceptions to this rule do occur. Research on disclosure of HIV positivity within couples has indicated that men are less likely than women to reveal their diagnosis directly to their spouse or partner (Miller & Rubin, in press). It appears that when they discover they are HIV-positive a substantial number of men persuade their wives that both should be tested for the virus and thereafter sit together to receive their test results. By withholding from their wives the fact that they already know their own diagnosis, husbands and boyfriends are able to maneuver clinic personnel into the position of intermediaries. A possible explanation of this finding may be that being HIV-positive dramatically lowers men's relational status. Because they have a stigmatized condition that they might very well have contracted through the socially unacceptable behavior of marital unfaithfulness, they may find themselves in the sort of low-power position normally occupied by their wives. To make matters worse, the message they know they need to convey is of the most sensitive and negative sort imaginable. As a result they turn, uncharacteristically, to intermediated communication.

Social Distance between Interactants

The level of indirectness in a specific conversational exchange is also predicted in politeness theory by the relational closeness of the individuals involved. In unequal relationships, social distance as a determining factor for intermediated communication is likely to be eclipsed by the effect of discrepancies in power. Even so, and especially within horizontal relationships, having a close relationship can render intermediated communication less necessary. Close friends can often speak frankly about sensitive issues.

Relational closeness is also a key to the special place that grandparents often hold in family conflict resolution. Among the Kikuyu, for example, it is traditional to name each succeeding child after a specified grandparent. Grandparents maintain a singular relationship with their namesakes, and with the namesakes of their spouses, to the extent that a grandmother may refer to the grandson who is named after her spouse as "my husband," and a grandfather may similarly refer to a granddaughter as "my wife." By virtue of this close relationship grandparents may play a key intermediary role in conflicts between parents and children.

The following incident, told to me by an urban Kenyan woman, illustrates the interaction of all three predictive factors described above and gives something of a sense of the careful attention required for effecting intermediation in a sensitive situation. Carole, a young urban resident in an ethnically mixed marriage, came to her friend Jane for advice on what to do about increasingly severe marital problems. The two had known one another for many years, so Carole felt free to be completely honest and open with Jane about her situation. After a long discussion they agreed that Carole needed to let her mother know what was happening. They also determined that the best means of doing so would be for Carole to send Jane as an emissary to Carole's mother's younger sister. The aunt, although of the same generation as Carole's mother, was closer in age to Carole and Jane, and could serve as a bridge between mother and daughter.

Carole knew her aunt was at the moment getting her hair done just minutes from downtown Nairobi where she and Jane were talking, so she contacted her aunt via cell phone to tell her that Jane wanted to drop by to say hi. This tactic was intended to alert the aunt that there was an issue that needed to be discussed, which it did. Jane then went alone to see the aunt on behalf of her friend.

Upon arrival at the beauty parlor Jane spent some minutes discussing a wide range of generalities until the aunt finally asked pointedly, "So, how is Carole's husband these days?" Having received the expected cue, Jane then unfolded the entire story. The conversation closed with Jane and the aunt's agreeing in principle that Carole's mother ought to know about her daughter's difficulties. Even though it was not explicitly stated, Carole's aunt correctly inferred from that comment that she herself was being requested to broach the subject with her sister.

This story presents a fascinating combination of direct, indirect, face-to-face (f2f), and intermediated communication. Four different combinations are evident: (1) f2f-direct communication (Carole tells Jane that she is having marital problems); (2) f2f-indirect communication (at the beauty parlor Jane hints to Carole's aunt that there is an important issue she needs to discuss with her); (3) intermediated-direct communication (Carole directly requests Jane to talk to her aunt about the problem); and (4) intermediated-indirect communication (Jane hints to Carole's aunt that Carole's mother needs to know about the situation and the aunt understands this to be a request for her to serve as intermediary.)

The direct and face-to-face communication in the incident occurred primarily between Jane and Carole, whose close relationship made it unnecessary for them to use intermediated communication even when the issue was extremely sensitive and embarrassing. At the same time intermediated communication was the method of choice for approaching Carole's mother, despite the fact that there is no indication in the story (or in real life) that their relationship was not a close one. Their difference in generational status in combination with the sensitive and face-threatening nature of the information was apparently the determining factor in that decision. The aunt was an appropriate choice for intermediary because she had a foot in both generations and she and Carole were emotionally close. Nevertheless, due to the face-threatening nature of the information she herself was initially approached in an intermediated manner. Carole's selection of the best means of accomplishing her communicative and relational goals, therefore, was a result of the relational factors of social distance and power, in combination with the situational factor of the nature of the information.

INTERMEDIATION BEYOND FACEWORK

Politeness theory and face negotiation theory privilege the concept of face as an explanation of certain types of communication, but defense against shame and management of a face threat are not the only motivations for sending messages via third parties in the Kenyan context. Another critical determining factor in the decision to seek an intermediary appears to be the degree to which the message contains distressing or negative news. For example, instead of communicating news of death directly to close kin of the deceased, concerned friends may request an intermediary, often an elderly or respected relative, to bear the ill tidings. It is assumed that because of this person's age and experience he or she will know how to gently or gradually break the news and afterward how best to comfort the individual. During the time I was writing this essay, one of my students came to excuse herself from class explaining that a relative had called her and told her that she needed to go home immediately. After giving her permission to miss class I said that I hoped nothing bad had happened. "So do I," she responded. The intermediary had purposefully given her just enough information for her to infer that the problem might be serious, but apparently had judged it best to let her find out the specifics upon arrival so that she would not be upset while she was traveling home.

There is a sense in which the distance achieved through intermediated and indirect communication expresses respectful appreciation. The explanation by one of my students of traditional Luo wedding negotiations is revealing in that regard:

> During negotiations, the young man would be accompanied by clan elders and uncles to the lady's home and these people would talk on his behalf since he wasn't meant to talk, out of respect for his future in-laws. The young lady's uncles and aunties would also receive them on behalf of her parents who were not meant to take part verbally in negotiations to maintain respect between the two parties.

Directness, in traditional environments at least, can be rude. This is perhaps not surprising when considered in conjunction with the requirements in many Kenyan cultures for keeping not only figurative but also physical distance within certain relationships. A man or woman who saw his or her parents-in-law—or among some groups, any elderly person—approaching on a path would step aside to give them a wide space in which to pass. Even now in the city some spatial prohibitions designed to show respect are still in force. For example, when visiting a friend in the hospital recently I ran into a male colleague who was seated on a bench outside the entrance waiting for his wife to emerge. He explained that she was visiting a female relative whose relationship to him made it culturally inappropriate for him as a man to enter the hospital room. From such a perspective the American penchant for talkativeness and direct expression can be unappealing and, when employed with authority figures, disrespectful (see Hastings, 2000). A full explanation of the use of intermediated communication would have to make provision not only for embarrassing or face-threatening situations but also for non-face related instances like these.

CLOSING THOUGHTS

First, it must be mentioned that there is a downside to intermediated communication. If the practice serves to reinforce values of hierarchy within society (see Piot, 1993) then it is to be expected that persons on the lower rungs of the ladder might at times feel that the requirement that authority figures be approached through third parties serves to petrify inefficient or even unjust systems. Creative but frustrated lower- and middle-level employees can be heard bemoaning the fact that no mechanism exists for them to give constructive input into corporate or institutional policies. Within the family, too, the expectation of intermediated communication between husbands and wives can perpetuate an inequitable relational power balance. In years past the distance between spousal statuses was so dramatic that within some cultural groups, such as the Baganda in neighboring Uganda, women could not even inform their husbands face-to-face that they were pregnant. Such extreme examples are few nowadays, but the fact remains that in a majority of African marriages wives are still the lower power partner, and the practice of intermediated communication by spouses is a confirmation of, if not a contributor to, that reality.

Second, intermediated communication is not confined to sub-Saharan societies. As evidence, I urge North American readers to recall a time in elementary or middle school when they sent or were sent by friends to inquire of a pre-adolescent heartthrob, "So-and-so likes you. Do you like her?" Intermediated communication is present in American life as well, and it does not entirely stop when we crossed the threshold into high school. In fact, United States history contains one of the most famous instances of intermediation for purposes of courtship, that of Miles Standish, whose intermediary turned out to be singularly ill suited for the communicative task with which Standish entrusted him. Thus although this chapter has focused on describing distinctively Kenyan approaches to intermediated communication, the recognition that third party communication plays a pivotal role in some African cultures should also motivate Western scholars to examine the role of informal intermediaries in their own backyards.

Third, Westerners must take care not to project their own (or Miles Standish's) cultural experiences onto the Kenyan situation and to assume that careful orchestration of third party involvement means that persons who engage in this type of communication suffer from chronic communication apprehension or lack of assertive communication skills (see Hara & Kim, 2004). Kenyans are as capable of being as direct and face-to-face in their communications as are Americans or Europeans. Stating a message indirectly and using intermediaries are more often signs of strength, self-control, and communicative sophistication than indications of lack of competence.

Intermediated communication as practiced in Kenyan interpersonal relationships, then, involves intricate, subtly choreographed interpersonal maneuvering, and provides a fascinating topic for observation. Unfortunately, like African communication patterns in general (Miller, 2005), it has been infrequently engaged in scholarly work. Yet from a practical standpoint, any sojourner in much of sub-Saharan Africa who hopes to be culturally alert, any aid worker who intends to be culturally effective, must on occasion be either the sender or recipient of such third party communication. In the age of AIDS, when a fuller understanding of interpersonal communication in the sub-Sahara has become critical, it is to be hoped that future scholarship will take up the challenge.

Acknowledgement

The author expresses appreciation to Daystar University M.A. students and faculty as well as numerous friends for sharing their thoughts on this topic, both oral and written, with her.

References

Brown, P., & Levinson, S. (1978). Universals in language usage: Politeness phenomena. In E. Goody (Ed.), *Questions and politeness* (pp. 56–389). London: Cambridge University Press.

Brown, P., & Levinson, S. (1987). *Politeness: Some universals in language usage.* Cambridge, MA: Cambridge University Press.

Condon, J., & Yousef, F. S. (1975). *An introduction to intercultural communication.* Indianapolis: Bobbs-Merrill.

Craig, R. T., Tracy, K., & Spissak, F. (1986). The discourse of requests: Assessment of a politeness approach. *Human Communication Research, 12,* 437–268.

Domenici, K., & Littlejohn, S. W. (2006). *Facework: Bridging theory and practice.* Thousand Oaks, CA: Sage Publications.

Golding, L., Miller, A. N., Ngula, K., Wambua, M. A., Rubin, D., Mutua, J., et al. (2007). Couples communication about sexual issues in Machakos District, Kenya. Paper submitted to the 2007 National Communication Association Convention, Chicago.

Gonzales, M. H., Manning, D. J., & Haugen, J. A. (1992). Explaining our sins: Factors influencing offender accounts and anticipated victim responses. *Journal of Personality and Social Psychology, 62,* 958–971.

Gough, D. H. (1995). Some problems for politeness theory: Deference and directness in Xhosa performative requests. *South African Journal of African Languages, 15,* 123–125.

Greene, K., Derlega, V. J., Yep, G. A., & Petronio, S. (2003). *Privacy and disclosure of HIV in interpersonal relationships: A sourcebook for researchers and practitioners.* Mahwah, NJ: Lawrence Erlbaum.

Gudykunst, W. (1998). Individualistic and collectivistic perspectives on communication: An introduction. *International Journal of Intercultural Relations, 22,* 107–134.

Gudykunst, W. B., Matsumoto, Y., Ting-Toomey, S., Nishida, T., Kim, K., & Heyman, S. (1996). The influence of cultural individualism-collectivism, self-construals, and individual values on communication styles across cultures. *Human Communication Research, 22,* 510–543.

Gyekye, K. (1997). *Tradition and modernity: Philosophical reflections on the African experience.* New York: Doubleday.

Hara, K., & Kim, M.-S. (2004). The effect of self-construals on conversational indirectness. *International Journal of Intercultural Relations, 28,* 1–18.

Hastings, S. (2000). Asian Indian "self-suppression" and self-disclosure: Enactment and adaptation of cultural identity. *Journal of Language and Social Psychology, 19,* 85–109.

Hofstede, G. (1991). *Cultures and organizations: Software of the mind.* London: McGraw-Hill.

Holtgraves, T. (1997). Styles of language use: Individual and cultural variability in conversational indirectness. *Journal of Personality and Social Psychology, 78,* 624–647.

Holtgraves, T., & Yang, J.-N. (1992). Interpersonal underpinnings of request strategies: Principles and differences due to culture and gender. *Journal of Personality and Social Psychology, 62,* 246–256.

Jaimon, R. S. (2005, May 7). The case of the vanishing matchmaker. *The Hindu: Online edition of India's National Newspaper.* Retrieved May 16, 2007, from http://www.hinuonnet.com/thehindu/mp/2005/05/07/stories.htm

Kenen, R., Arden-Jones, A., & Eeles, R. (2004). We are talking but are they listening? Communication patterns in families with a history of breast/ovarian cancer. *Psycho-oncology, 13,* 335–345.

Leung, K. (1987). Some determinants of reactions to procedural models for conflict resolution: A cross-national study. *Journal of Personality and Social Psychology, 53,* 898–908.

Markus, H., & Kitayama, S. (1991). Culture and the self: Implications for cognition, emotion, and motivation. *Psychological Review, 98,* 224–253.

Miller, A. N. (2005). Keeping up with cartography: A call to study African communication. *International and intercultural communication annual, 28,* 214–236. Washington DC: NCA.

Miller, A. N., & Rubin, D. L. (in press). Motivations and methods for self-disclosure of HIV seropositivity in Nairobi, Kenya. *AIDS and Behavior.*

Moemeka, A. (1996). Interpersonal communication in communalistic societies in Africa. In W. B. Gudykunst, S. Ting-Toomey, & T. Nishida (Eds.), *Communication in personal relationships across cultures* (pp. 217–236). Thousand Oaks, CA: Sage.

Morrow, O. I., Sweat, M. D., & Morrow, R. H. (2004). The *matalisi:* Pathway to early sexual initiation among the youth of Mpigi, Uganda. *AIDS and Behavior, 8,* 365–378.

Muira, S. (2000). The mediation of conflict in the traditional Hawaiian family: A collectivist approach. *Qualitative Research Reports in Communication, 1,* 19–25.

Ndeti, K. (1972). *Elements of Akamba life.* Nairobi: East African Publishing.

Pan, Y. (2000). *Politeness in Chinese face-to-face interaction.* Stamford, CT: Ablex.

Piot, C. D. (1993). Secrecy, ambiguity, and the everyday in Kabre culture. *American Anthropologist, 95,* 353–370.

Sang, N. (2006). *Reflections on politeness theory.* Unpublished paper.

Scollon, R., & Scollon, S. W. (1995). *Intercultural communication: A discourse approach.* Cambridge, MA: Blackwell.

Singelis, T. M., & Brown, W. J. (1995). Culture, self, and collectivist communication: Linking culture to individual behavior. *Human Communication Research, 21,* 354–389.

Ting-Toomey, S. (1988). Intercultural conflict styles: A face-negotiation theory. In Y. Y. Kim & W. B. Gudykunst (Eds.), *Theories in intercultural communication.* Newbury Park, CA: Sage Publications.

Ting-Toomey, S., & Kurogi, A. (1998). Facework competence in intercultural conflict: An updated face-negotiation theory. *International Journal of Intercultural Relations, 22,* 187–225.

Ting-Toomey, S., Yee-Jung, K., Shapiro, R., Garcia, W., Wright, T., & Oetzel, J. (2000). Ethnic/cultural identify salience and conflict styles in four U.S. ethnic groups. *International Journal of Intercultural Relations, 24,* 47–81.

Triandis, H. C. (1995). *Individualism and collectivism.* Boulder, CO: Westview.

Wilson, S. R., Kim, M.-S., & Meischke, H. (1991). Evaluating Brown and Levinson's politeness theory: A revised analysis of directives and face. *Research on Language and Social Interaction, 25,* 215–252.

Concepts and Questions

1. What are some tasks intermediaries are asked to carry out in parts of sub-Saharan Africa? Do you see a need for similar tasks to be carried out in North America? Why or why not?

2. Why is the concept of saving face used in other cultures more than in the United States?

3. Do you see saving face as a tool you would like to employ in your interpersonal relationships?

4. Why do collective cultures employ intermediaries with greater regularity than do individualistic cultures?

5. Explain why polite theory is related to the concept of intermediaries.

6. In what situations in your life would you find the use of intermediaries a useful interpersonal tool?

7. What does Miller mean when she writes about conversational indirectness and intermediaries?

8. Why do certain power hierarchy relationships lend themselves to intermediaries?

9. What is the "downside" to the use of intermediaries that Miller mentions in her essay?

Co-Cultures: Multiculturalism in the United States

4

No culture can live if it attempts to be exclusive.

MAHATMA GANDHI

In the previous chapter, we looked at international cultures—those cultures located outside the immediate borders of the United States—and generally focused on a single cultural group. In this chapter, we turn to the United States, where cultural diversity is commonly recognized as an important part of our history and future. Therefore, we now examine the dynamics of domestic multiculturalism by investigating some *co-cultures*—those diverse cultural groups that reside inside the United States. The co-cultures often have many of the defining characteristics found in any culture—a specialized language system, shared values, a collective worldview, common communication patterns, and often a common history. Also, members of a co-culture usually share a number of similar characteristics, such as religion, economic status, ethnic background, age, gender, or sexual preference. And with growing frequency, people residing in the United States may hold dual or even multiple co-cultural memberships. A gay African American man would be considered as a member of two co-cultures. A lesbian Jewish American woman over 65 would be a member of multiple co-cultural groups.

These diverse co-cultures bring new experiences and ways of interacting to an intercultural encounter. Their unique communicative behaviors may sometimes be confusing and baffling to members of the dominant culture. This diversity can be particularly salient when, for instance, members of a collectivistic co-culture, such as Vietnamese Americans, interact with someone from the highly individualistic Euro-American dominant culture. For example, a Vietnamese American, with strong extended family ties, might feel it important to ask for time off from work to help celebrate his uncle's birthday. But a Euro-American, more focused on the nuclear family, may view such a request as an inappropriate excuse for a day off.

Because the United States is a pluralistic, multicultural society, there is a vital need for competent communication between the dominant culture and the numerous co-cultures, as well as between the co-cultures themselves. You cannot communicate effectively with a member of a co-culture until you learn to appreciate the unique and rich opportunity offered by that co-culture. Insufficient knowledge about, stereotypes of, and prejudices toward people from co-cultures often lead to incorrect, hurtful, and even insulting assumptions. An awareness and understanding of the unique experiences of these co-cultures will help you overcome many communication problems.

The rich cultural diversity and complexity of U.S. society flows from an almost overwhelming number of co-cultures. As a result, we are obviously unable to examine each co-culture in this chapter. Thus, our selections are based on three considerations: (1) we need to make efficient use of limited space; (2) we want to include some social groups that are often in conflict with the dominant culture; and (3) we want to emphasize the range of different co-cultures. To this end, we selected representations from both the major co-cultures and from those less often encountered. You will also encounter additional co-cultures in subsequent chapters.

We begin this chapter with an essay that presents an ideological position informing intercultural communication among co-cultures. According to the author, Young Yun Kim, the theme of individualism is central to this ideology. In "*Unum* and *Pluribus*: Ideological Underpinnings of Interethnic Communication in the United States," Kim examines the historical development of American social institutions that were based on such liberal themes as equal rights and equal opportunity, which form the cornerstone of the Declaration of Independence, the Constitution, and the Bill of Rights.

Even with the historical tradition of equality, as Kim quickly points out, "Americans today are far from being of a same mind about various social issues" such as interethnic and interracial relations. As she notes, "interethnic relations have become a perpetual sore spot in the American consciousness" in which many Americans are galvanized into an "us-against-them" posture in the form of "identity politics," which can also be considered as "politics-of-difference" and "politics of recognition."

After providing an overview of the current U.S. domestic social dilemma, Kim uses the issues of race, ethnicity, and interethnic relations to examine interethnic communication. She then offers an in-depth discussion of four types of interethnic messages—*assimilation, pluralism, reconciliation,* and *extremism*—that we frequently hear in the media. Kim follows this discussion with a synthesis of the messages and concludes that interethnic relations remain salient in U.S. society, but the future remains unclear as Americans continue to "struggle with competing visions of *Unum* and *Pluribus* . . . and what it means to be Americans." She concludes with a note of optimism in that "the very fact that interethnic issues continue to engage American passion is itself an affirmation, and a hallmark, of the American liberal tradition. This tradition contributes to the stability of the American democracy."

Conflict is an inescapable part of any relationship and if managed improperly can lead to irreparable breakdowns—alienation at the interpersonal level or war in the international arena. As you might suspect, how conflict is viewed, managed, and resolved within a society is a function of cultural values. For the dominant U.S. culture, differences are considered inevitable, healthy, and valuable. Thus conflict is viewed as a natural part of social intercourse and resolution is usually accomplished through a dialectic process. In other cultures, particularly those with a group orientation, conflict represents a threat to good social order and is something that should be avoided. As a result, cultures, including U.S. co-cultures, often have dissimilar means of managing and resolving conflicts. This is illustrated in Charmaine I. Ka'imikaua's essay, "*Ho'oponopono*: A Hawaiian Cultural Process to Conflict Resolution."

The essay begins by explaining that *ho'oponopono* is a traditional form of communication used by Hawaiians to resolve conflicts and maintain harmonious interpersonal relations. The process is carried out using communal interaction and incorporates five distinct steps—problem identification, confession, restituting, forgiveness and release, or closure—which are discussed separately. Ka'imikaua's tells us that this process, rooted in ancient cultural traditions, continues to be practiced among Hawaiians and has been used to resolve conflicts in a variety of contemporary contexts. The essay demonstrates that culture has devised different ways of managing conflict to sustain positive relations.

Conflict is also a central theme in our next essay, "America in Black and Brown: Exploring Sources of Intercultural Tensions between Blacks and Latinos in the United States," by Peter Ogom Nwosu, which looks at existing tensions between two U.S. co-cultures. Nwosu examines the often contentious relationship between Black and Latino Americans from historical, cultural, and political perspectives. Arguing that neither group has a good understanding of the other, he provides a comprehensive comparison of their different historical experiences. The essay then uses these varied historical backgrounds as a foundation to explain how and why the psychological, cultural, and political perspectives of each group differ. Nwosu contents that although Latinos are generally aware of the *Black experience,* there is little understanding of *Black culture.* Equally problematic is the lack of awareness among Blacks about Latino culture. A particularly salient problem that tends to exacerbate the schism is the culturally based, contrasting communication styles employed by Blacks and Latinos. The essay concludes with a call for greater understanding and cooperation between Blacks and Latinos and for the need to view efforts to gain greater representation and opportunity not as an ethnic struggle but as one for human rights for everyone.

The next co-cultural group we consider is the disabled community. For many people, the disabled are not recognized as a distinct co-culture. There are, however, approximately 14 million disabled Americans between the ages of 16 and 64, and that number is increasing rapidly with the return of injured veterans from Iraq and Afghanistan. In 2007, there were over 150,000 Iraq war veterans receiving Veterans Administration disability benefits, and that number will continue to increase as the VA processes the flow of new applications. These veterans may suffer not only from physical wounds that may have resulted in lost limbs, paralysis, blindness, or dementia, but also from posttraumatic distress disorder (PTSD) which in essence can be a disabling dysfunctional emotional condition.

The disabled, including war veterans, often find themselves misunderstood, marginalized, or even cut off from the dominant nondisabled culture. Dawn O. Braithwaite and Charles A. Braithwaite look at some of the reasons for this isolation in "'Which Is My Good Leg?': Cultural Communication of Persons with Disabilities." They specifically examine how disabled persons view their communicative relationships with nondisabled persons. Reviewing research consisting of more than 100 in-depth interviews with physically disabled adults, the Braithwaites discovered that disabled people go through a process of redefinition involving three steps: (1) redefining the self as a part of the "new" culture, (2) redefining disability, and (3) redefining disability for the dominant culture. Being familiar with these steps will help you improve your ability to communicate effectively with members of the disabled co-culture.

The final essay in this chapter will introduce you to the communicative behaviors and dynamics associated with the gay and lesbian co-culture. In his article, "In Plain Sight: Gay and Lesbian Communication and Culture," William F. Eadie acknowledges that there is a disparity of views, ranging from hostility to acceptance, regarding the gay and lesbian community. Nevertheless, he challenges you to become acquainted with the cultural characteristics and communication style of the gay and lesbian members in our society.

In his essay, Eadie specifies three general statements about lesbian and gay culture: (1) being open about sexual orientation is a political statement; (2) lesbian and gay culture must deal with tensions relating to how open to be about one's sexuality; and (3) although lesbian and gay culture is generally characterized as being about sexual attraction and desire, being lesbian or gay is about much, much more than sex. The essay also provides insight into lesbian and gay communication behaviors and how sexual attraction and intimacy are negotiated. Eadie's essay provides first-hand insight into the lesbian and gay community and offers you a much greater understanding of this co-culture.

Unum and Pluribus: Ideological Underpinnings of Interethnic Communication in the United States

Young Yun Kim

The United States was founded as a construction organized by the ideology of classical liberalism in the Enlightenment tradition—a tradition rooted in the theories of European and Anglo-American philosophers such as John Locke, Adam Smith, and John Dewey. Central to this ideology is the theme of *individualism,* "the social priority of the individual vis-à-vis the State, the established Church, social classes . . . or other social groups" (Abercrombie, 1980, p. 56). While recognizing the existence of infinite individual differences, classical liberalism also stresses *universalism* that sees human nature presupposing and transcending social group categories such as ethnicity and race. As Michael Billig et al. (1988) have noted: "The assertions 'we are all human' and 'We are all individuals' are both equally and self-evidently 'true'" (p. 124). The liberal themes of individualism and universalism are further linked to the theme of *procedural equality,* that is, "equal rights" and "equal opportunities" afforded to all individuals in the form of "human rights"—the basic requisite of a free and democratic society. Enshrined in the Declaration of Independence, the Constitution, the Bill of Rights, and democratic and capitalistic institutions, these and related liberal principles constitute the core

of the American cultural ethos, projecting a vision of American society that seeks to transcend a monolithic tribal ancestral and territorial condition. Essayist Henry Grunwald captured this liberal tradition in a bicentennial essay (*Time,* July 5, 1976):

> The U.S. was not born in a tribal conflict, like so many other nations, but in a conflict over principles. Those principles were thought to be universal, which was part of the reason for the unprecedented policy of throwing the new country open to all comers. (p. 35)

Given these traditional ideals, however, Americans today are far from being of a same mind about various social issues. In fact, the opposite is true when it comes to "interethnic" (or "interracial") relations. Ever since the Reconstruction era of the late nineteenth century when "civil rights" debates began (Wilson, 1998), American society has experienced an extraordinary degree of unease, conflict, self-criticism, and mutual-criticism as it struggled to reconcile the ideals of individualism, universalism, and procedural equality with the reality of inequality, real or perceived, along particular ethnic/racial group lines. In recent decades, the traditional primacy of the individual has been increasingly challenged by the claims of the primacy of ethnic group identity over individual identity, particularistic group grievances that are historically and institutionally rooted, and the necessity to redress such grievances so as to achieve equal group status.

This American dilemma continues to stir heated public debates. Indeed, interethnic relations have become a perpetual sore spot in the American consciousness. It galvanizes Americans into "us-against-them" posturing in the form of "identity politics"—also described as "politics of difference" and "politics of recognition." Essayist Russell Baker (*The New York Times,* May 5, 1994) laments this situation in an essay entitled "Gone with the Unum":

> I have always been an *"E Pluribus Unum"* person myself, but the future does not look bright for an *"E Pluribus Unum"* America. The melting pot in which the Pluribus were to be combined into the Unum was not the success its advertisers had promised. . . . What is new these days is the passion with which we now pursue our tribal identities. . . . 0, Unum, what misery we courted when we forsook thee for Pluribus. (p. A15)

This original essay appears here in print for the first time. All rights reserved. Permission to reprint must be obtained from the author and the publisher. Earlier versions of this essay have appeared in previous editions. Dr. Young Yun Kim teaches in the Department of Communication at the University of Oklahoma, Norman, Oklahoma.

ANALYSIS

This author has sought to better understand the often-contentious landscape of interethnic communication in the contemporary United States (Kim, 1999, 2005). To this end, the present analysis scrutinizes differing views and opinions of American people in order to identify multiple ways in which the tradition of classical liberalism plays out in the contemporary American interethnic communication messages. The term, "ideology," is employed here in terms of what Billig (1991) refers to as "lived ideology," "a latent consciousness or philosophy" (pp. 27–29). In this sense, ideology refers to a set of social forces that stimulate, substantiate, and constrain the intellectual beliefs and expressions of thinking individuals. Individuals formulate and express their opinions by invoking socially shared beliefs *as their own,* rather than passively following the dictates of the mental schema within a given ideological tradition. Even in making remarks that are self-serving or even contradictory, they tend to consider their argument reasonable or even persuasive in the eyes of a rational audience. Communication messages are, thus, more than mere expressions of a communicator's own independent thoughts. That is, to say something is very often to "fight"—in the sense that messages serve as strategy and tactics for advocating a given communicator's own version of what he or she believes to be "common sense." In Billig's (1991) words:

> To maximize their chances of being persuasive, speakers should make appeal to the *sensus comunis,* which they share with their audience. Particularly useful were commonplaces, or the sort of moral maxims, which are laden with clichéd appeals to values. Thus, orators' discourse, which seeks to create new movements of opinion towards a position not commonly shared, will rehearse old commonly shared stereotypes. (p. 21)

Based on this social-psychological conception of ideology, a variety of data have been analyzed including messages communicated by political and civic leaders, activists, academicians, and ordinary citizens. Almost all of the data utilized in this analysis have been found in sources available since 1990. The data types range from trade books written for general readers, news magazine articles, articles in national and local newspapers, and transcripts of interviews and talk shows broadcast on radio and television. Some of these data are captured in naturally occurring events, whereas others were expressed in the form of personal reflections and testimonials. The data have been analyzed through a qualitative-interpretive exercise to surface the ideological themes underlying the publicly communicated messages pertaining to issues of ethnicity, race, and interethnic relations. This method of analysis shares features with other qualitative investigations such as discourse (or rhetorical) analysis designed to elucidate social-psychological processes through understanding spoken and unspoken messages (e.g., Billig, 1991; Billig et al., 1988; Van Dijk, 1997). In addition, systematic data from recent public opinion polls based on representative samples are utilized to complement the primarily episodic data.

The analysis has revealed four types of interethnic communication messages: (a) assimilationism; (2) pluralism; (3) reconciliation; and (4) extremism. Each of these message types is described in the following discussion. Commonly rooted in the ideology of classical liberalism, these message types capture the differing sets of beliefs and moral visions being voiced by Americans today. Together, they represent a full spectrum of ongoing debates and arguments about what American society is, should be, and should be doing, with respect to issues of ethnicity, race, and interethnic relations.

MESSAGES OF ASSIMILATIONISM

Three core principles of classical liberalism-individualism, universalism, and procedural equality continue to directly and powerfully underpin the mainstream thinking of Americans about interethnic relations. These liberal ideals shape the arguments commonly referred to as *assimilationism.* Employing such metaphors as "melting pot" and "color-blind society," assimilationist messages project a societal vision in which immigrants and indigenous ethnic minorities are mainstreamed into the normative culture and institutions. In this vision, the government is responsible for universally applying societal rules to all its citizens irrespective of skin color and religious creed. Immigrants and ethnic minorities, in turn, are expected to assimilate themselves socially and culturally, so as to become fully functional in the American society.

Assimilationist messages celebrate personal achievement and self-reliance. These messages place individual identity over and above group identity and question the validity and morality of categorical thought. Although each person is unique, all humans are also endowed with the same set of universal human needs, rights, and responsibilities. Prejudice directed for or against individuals simply based on group membership is morally wrong, not only because it is irrational but also because its focus on social categories contravenes the intellectual or moral prescription to value the unique qualities of every individual. The primacy of the individual over the group hinges on the value of equality as it pertains to the premise of common human nature and basic human rights that call for equal applications of laws and rules to all people regardless of their group categories. A fair society is one in which all individuals, regardless of their backgrounds, are granted equal rights and equal opportunity. Equality in this view means "fair play"—a notion rooted in a biopsychological (or naturalistic) worldview and the notion of "equity." This view accepts and appreciates differential individual merits in the allocation of resources and status based on the presumption that "there is a natural distribution of human talent, ranging from the few individuals of genius and talent to the defective and delinquent" (Rossides, 1976, p. 9).

As columnist David Brooks puts it, "when achievement and equality clash in America, achievement wins" (*The New York Times*, January 14, 2007, p. WK12). Each person, and each person alone, is seen as ultimately responsible for his or her own achievement of status. Everyone is expected to "play by the rules." Insistence on group-based policies such as affirmative action in college admissions and employment practices is "un-American"—one that endangers the larger fraternity of all Americans and obscures differential individual merits that must be *earned* individually. Emphasis on group identity over individual identity is deemed wrong because it renders itself to what essayist Pico Iyer (1990) calls "state-sponsored favoritism" that mandates racial or ethnic "preferences" or "quotas" and "reverse discrimination." Iyer, himself an Indian-born immigrant and world traveler, expresses his objection to such practices as follows:

> As an alien from India, I choose to live in America precisely because it is a place where aliens from India are, in principle, treated no better (and no worse) than anyone else. . . . The problem with people who keep raising the cry of "racism" is that they would have us see everything in terms of race. They treat minorities as emblems, and everyone as typecast. . . . As an Asian minority myself, I know of nothing more demeaning than being chosen for a job, or even a role, on the basis of my race. Nor is the accompanying assumption—that I need a helping hand because my ancestors were born outside Europe—very comforting. . . . Are we, in fact, to cling to a state of childlike dependency? (p. 86)

The assimilationist emphasis on individualism, universalism, and procedural equality has been repeatedly promoted in presidential inauguration addresses. Presidents, regardless of their party affiliations, have exalted the assimilationist values as the very heart of the American identity—a common identity constituted by individual identities and one that transcends category-based distinctions. Former President William Jefferson Clinton, for example, spoke of American citizens' "primary allegiance to the values America stands for and values we really live by" and stated: "Long before we were so diverse, our nation's motto was *E Pluribus Unum*—out of many, we are one. We must be one's neighbors; as fellow citizens; not separate camps, but family" (*Weekly Compilation of Presidential Documents*, 31, October 23, 1996, p. 851). The universal principles of individual identity and procedural equality are amply echoed in remarks of many other Americans. A newspaper reader wrote to the editor of *The New York Times Magazine* (April 29, 1992), objecting to an earlier article "Cultural Baggage" on the significance of ethnic group identity:

> I've been fighting ethnic labels since I was 12 or 13, and decided that only I had a right to define myself. . . . I am not almost WASP. I am African-American. I'm also part Cherokee from both sides of my family. But so what? . . . I've taken risks with my life that only I am

responsible for, and I have reaped substantial rewards for daring to be myself and not just different. (p. 10)

Stanley Crouch, an African American essayist, speaks to the common humanity of all races in arguing against racial politics in his book, *Always in Pursuit* (1998): "We . . . observe ourselves functioning in almost every capacity and exhibiting every inclination from the grand to the gaudy, from the idealistic to the shallow ethnic con" (p. 268). Likewise, Richard Lacayo, in an essay entitled "Whose Peers?" in a special issue of *Time* magazine (1993), disagreed with those who have argued for a guarantee of minority representation in jury composition in courtroom trials:

> [Some] advocates argue that just such a guarantee of minority representation should be part of the law. . . . If that is so, is the only solution an outright racial-quota system? And how finely would the jury need to be divided? Could Latinos in general judge other Latinos? Or would Cuban Americans be needed for the trial of Cuban Americans, Mexican Americans for other Mexican Americans, and so on? If the goal is better justice and greater legitimacy, American juries certainly need to be more representative. But in a just society, the process of creating a true assembly of peers need not be reduced to a systematic gathering of the tribes. (p. 61)

Perhaps one of the most compelling articulations of the traditional liberal ideals and of disapproval of identity politics was offered by Glenn C. Loury (1993), a prominent economic theorist and a public intellectual. In the following excerpt from one of his earlier writings, Loury reflects on his own social identity as an African American and his individual identity as a human being as follows.

> The most important challenges and opportunities that confront me derive not from my racial condition, but rather from my human condition. I am a husband, a father, a son, a teacher, an intellectual, a Christian, a citizen. In none of these roles is my race irrelevant, but neither can racial identity alone provide much guidance for my quest to adequately discharge these responsibilities. . . . The expression of my individual personality is to be found in the blueprint that I employ to guide this project of construction. The problem of devising such a plan for one's life is a

universal problem, which confronts all people, whatever their race, class, or ethnicity. (pp. 7–10)

MESSAGES OF PLURALISM

Directly challenging the aforementioned assimilationist messages are the messages of *pluralism*. Prominent in pluralist messages is the idea of the sanctity of the group. This notion is traceable to the experiences of unequal treatment, perceived or real, of certain individuals along ethnic lines. To varying degrees, pluralist messages replace the old "melting pot" metaphor with newer ones such as "mosaic," "quilt," and "salad bowl" that emphasize the distinctiveness of ethnic groups. As such, pluralist messages uphold *group identity* as a vital, if not primary, construct of a personhood, highlighting a fact of life that we are different "types" of persons defined by social categories such as race, ethnicity, language, culture, and national origin. Rooted in the worldview of *relativism* that classifies humanity into categories of distinct qualities, pluralist messages emphasize in-group sameness and point to the existence of a "natural attitude" (cf. Garfinkel, 1967) for their moral and intellectual claims for group distinctiveness.

Pluralist messages are predicated on the persistent reality of racial and ethnic prejudice—a reality in which the old liberal ideal of procedural equality is seen as not working well when it comes to serving the needs of certain minority groups. The sense of systematic mistreatment along ethnic and racial lines has given way to a new demand for a new politics of resentment and victimization. Instead of defining equality procedurally in terms of fairness of rules, pluralist messages advocate the contrary belief in *status equality* (in place of procedural equality), a demand for equal results in the interest of "emancipation" of specific groups that are historically oppressed or presently in need of institutional support through remedial laws and public policies. This outcome-based conception of equality is opposed to the procedure-based, universalistic view of equality, in that it allows for differential procedural treatments relative to different groups. Along this line, arguments have been made for a redistribution of power and resources to overcome racial inequalities (e.g., Hacker, 1992). Some pluralists advocate such an action as a remedy for status inequalities between and among ethnic and racial groups.

This pluralist position rejects the biopsychological explanation of inequality and replaces it with a sociocultural (or structural) explanation. That is, human beings are inherently equal in their original states, but their original natures become distorted and corrupted in the process of interaction with others in society and through the development of institutions such as language, culture, property, law, and social stratification among people (Tsuda, 1986). The traditional liberal notions of individual identity; universalistic application of laws, rules, rights, and responsibilities to everyone; and procedural equality without respect to equal outcomes are deemed a false ideology in that it serves only the end of legitimizing the capitalist system of "winners" and "losers" in society. In seeking group identity, relativism, and status equality, pluralist messages present race and ethnicity not merely as a basis for claiming cultural and social distinctiveness, but also as a central rallying point, a focal means to combat unjust practices such as "institutional racism." Prominent in these messages, accordingly, are terms such as ethnic "empowerment," "pride," "dignity," and "justice." Debunking the important liberal values of American life such as intellectual freedom and "free speech," pluralist messages demand suppression of "hate speech," loosely defined as words that a minority group finds offensive.

Specifically, schools and universities have sought to bring about a greater diversity of the university curriculum by replacing it with one "that would focus on the achievements of marginalized peoples and on the sins of the nation's founders" (Traub, 1998, p. 25). In San Francisco, for instance, the school board was reported to be developing a plan to require every high school student in the district to read works by authors of color (*The New York Times,* March 11, 1998, p. A21). Many university campuses have rejected the idea of an immutable canon of indispensable Western classics in favor of recognizing the reality of ethnic diversity in the United States. Curriculum changes like these have become commonplace, reflecting the emergence of pluralism in national consciousness at the end of the 1980s advocating the normative rights of minority groups. Some advocates of pluralism have even attempted to extend the pluralist messages to arguing for a guarantee of minority representation as part of the law. Believing that race influences not only prominent cases such as the Rodney King trial but also most cases involving minority defendants, Sheri

Lynn Johnson, a law professor, believes defendants should be guaranteed three members of their own racial group of a 12-member jury (cited in Lacayo, 1993, p. 61).

Also expressing the pluralist themes is the following reaction to the court decision which found the practice of race-based affirmative action programs in admission decisions at the University of Michigan (*The New York Times,* Editorials/Letters, March 30, 2001):

> Even with affirmative action in place, law school classes here at the University of Michigan are overwhelmingly dominated by White men. The compelling interest in maintaining such programs applies not just to minority students, but to all students who will now see even fewer non White faces and law school classes become even more homogeneous. Our legal system has produced yet another significantly disappointing decision, and many of us here fear that America is on the verge of taking one giant leap backward. (p. A22)

Molefi K. Asante, a prominent scholar of African-American studies, offers an eloquent argument against the "old" assimilationist ideals. In its place, Asante advocates the pluralist counter-ideals of group identity and status equality based on a particularistic view of human nature. In an essay entitled "Racism, Consciousness, and Afrocentricity," Asante (1993) reflects on his experience of growing up in a racist society and explains how he came to reject W. E. B. Du Bois' notion of "double consciousness" as a tragic outcome inescapable in the "Eurocentric" society. Asante, thus, proposes "Afrocentricity" as an alternative intellectual model based on which African Americans can claim an equal identity and status as a distinct people:

> The feeling that you are in quicksand is inescapable in the quagmire of a racist society. You think that you can make progress in the interpretation of what's happening now only to discover that every step you take sinks the possibility of escaping. You are a victim despite your best efforts to educate those around you to the obvious intellectual mud stuck in their minds. . . . Even from my young adult years I thought a precondition of my fullness, a necessary and natural part of my maturity, was the commitment to be who I am, to be Afrocentric. . . . Afrocentricity is the active centering of the African

in subject place in our historical landscape. This has always been my search; it has been a quest for sanity. (pp. 142–143)

The pluralistic insistence on a distinct group identity has drawn critical reactions from many for fostering division, "political correctness," and "self-segregation." In *The Disuniting of America* (1992), for example, historian Arthur M. Schlesinger, Jr., warned that pressing ethnic awareness too far poses the danger of the "disintegration of the national community, apartheid, Balkanization, tribalization" (p. 118). In *The Twilight of Common Dreams* (1995), sociologist Todd Gitlin maintained that America would be lost unless its obsession with cultural differences could be transcended in the name of the common good. More recently, Orland Patterson (2006), an African American sociologist at Harvard University, has characterized the phenomenon of self-segregation "the last major race problem" in the United States. Patterson finds it paradoxical that voluntary segregation on the part of ethnic minorities has been rising precisely as the decades of civil rights struggle to tear down racial barriers. Acknowledging that African Americans mention ethnic pride and White hostility as their main reasons for not moving to White neighborhoods, Patterson argues that "the disadvantages [of self-segregation], especially for youth, far outweigh the psychic gains" (p. A19).

MESSAGES OF RECONCILIATION

Straddled between the aforementioned ideological poles of assimilationism and pluralism are the voices of ideological reconciliation. These voices are what sociologist Alan Wolfe in *One Nation, After All* (1998) asserts as occupying "the vital center"—the "middle" America. Based on 200 in-depth interviews conducted in Boston, Atlanta, Tulsa, and San Diego metropolitan areas, Wolfe (1998) found "little support for the notion that middle-class Americans are engaged in bitter cultural conflict with one another" (p. 278). Instead, according to Wolfe, they are "struggling to find ways in which their core beliefs can be reconciled with experiences that seem to contradict them" (p. 281), while insisting on a set of values "capacious enough to be inclusive but demanding enough to uphold standards of personal responsibility" (p. 322).

The messages of reconciliation reflect the struggle of many Americans seeking moderation, tolerance, accommodation, integration, and balance. They are expressions of both hopes and difficulties in doing so. As such, reconciliation messages indicate a great deal of ambivalence, and even contradiction in the way many Americans think about the issues of race, ethnicity, and interethnic relations. They may, for example, support bilingual programs, but only if they are short-lived and not used as a political goal or instrument of power demanded by every group for its own separate slice of the political pie. They may support multiculturalism, but only to the extent that ethnic identity is subsumed under the common "American identity" that emphasizes individualism. They may support affirmative action programs based on group identity, but consider "quota" systems as unfair, divisive, and ultimately counterproductive. Or they may accept and even appreciate *Hanukkahs* and *Kwanzaas*, but they may also find that some people have gone too far when insisting on avoiding traditional phrases such as "Merry Christmas" in favor of "mushy" phrases such as "Happy Holidays" (Haberman, 2006). William A. Donohue, President of the Catholic League for Religious and Civil Rights, made just such a case as follows.

> The United States is 85 percent Christian, which means we are more Christian than India is Hindu and Israel is Jewish. Moreover, 96 percent of Americans celebrate Christmas. So why do we have to tippy-toe around the religious meaning of Christmas every December? There is something sick about Friendship Trees, Winter Solstice Concerts, Holiday Parades and Holly Day Festivals. . . . Diversity means respect for the traditions and heritages of all groups, not just those which have been cherry-picked by the multicultural gurus. . . . To be excluded is normal. Mother's Day, Father' Day, Veteran's Day, Black History Month, Gay Pride Parades—they all exclude someone. . . . By celebrating Christmas we are celebrating diversity. (*The New York Times*, Op-Ed, November 28, 2006, p. A23)

An attempt at ideological reconciliation was voiced in a remark former President Clinton made during a roundtable discussion on race televised on PBS (Public Broadcasting System) on July 9, 1998: "I believe there is an independent value to having young people learn in an environment where they're with people of many different racial and ethnic backgrounds. And the question is, How can you balance that with our devotion to merit?" (*The New York Times,* July 9, 1998, p. A21). A similar stance of reconciliation was taken by late former President Gerald Ford's Op-Ed article in 1999 titled "Inclusive America, Under Attack," according to columnist Jeffrey Toobin (2006). Ford wrote this article in support of affirmative action at the University of Michigan to argue that a pair of pending lawsuits would prohibit Michigan and other universities "from even considering race as one of many factors weighed by admission counselors," and that such a move would "condemn future college students to suffer the cultural and social impoverishment that afflicted my generation."

Reconciliatory views have been voiced by leaders of ethnic minorities, as well. Hugh Price, in his keynote address as the President of the National Urban League at the League's 1998 annual conference, shared his belief that the current conditions in the United States offer Blacks the "best shot we have ever had to shove ourselves the rest of the way into the American mainstream" (*The New York Times,* August 13, 1998). Racial discrimination still exists, Price pointed out, but African American parents must take greater responsibility for the education of their children:

> With unemployment so low, employers are gobbling up almost every willing and able worker with a pulse. Shame on us if we don't seize this historic opening in the economy. . . . I think we are moving rapidly toward the day when if you've got something to put on the table, employers aren't going to care what color you are. (p. A23)

Likewise, on Columbus Day in 1992, Niles Bird Runningwater, then president of the Indian student association at the University of Oklahoma, communicated a message of reconciliation:

> We don't choose to protest this fallacy of American history, but rather to celebrate the survival and continuance of Indian peoples . . . By doing this we can fully acknowledge 500 years of coexistence of Indian and non-Indian peoples in America. . . . We're trying to do our part in togetherness and participation by eliciting communication and excitement concerning the respect of others' cultures. (*The Oklahoma Daily,* March 24, 1992, p, 3)

Messages of reconciliation such as these can be traced to the mainstream, integrationist civil rights movement led by Martin Luther King, Jr. The traditional liberal ideals of individualism, universalism, and procedural equality have been largely upheld in the struggle to eliminate systematic discrimination against African Americans as a group. In an address titled "A Realistic Look at Race Relations," delivered on May 17, 1956, in New York City at the second anniversary of the National Association for the Advancement of Colored People, King stated, "We honor our country and ourselves by being here. Contrary to all we have been hearing about the wisdom of our being here, we know that we are here in the noblest tradition of our Judeo-Christian tradition and our democratic heritage. (www.CNN.com/specials/2007/king.papers, January 14, 2007). In the widely quoted "I Have a Dream" speech delivered before the Lincoln Memorial on August 28, 1963, King upheld the classical liberal ideals of individualism, universalism, and procedural equality:

> So I say to you, my friends, that even though we must face the difficulties of today and tomorrow, I still have a dream. It is a dream deeply rooted in the American dream that one day this nation will rise up and live out the true meaning of its creed—we hold these truths to be self-evident, that all men are created equal . . . I have a dream my four little children will one day live in a nation where they will not be judged by the color of their skin but by the content of their character. I have a dream today. (C. S. King, 1993, p. 101)

Voices of ideological reconciliation and ethnic integration often escape media attention or get lost in the midst of loud and conspicuous voices of committed ideologues from the left and the right. Yet messages of reconciliation are all around us when we look for them. In his autobiography *Walking with the Wind* (1998), John Lewis, a leader of the civil rights movement since the 1960s and a Democratic Congressman from Georgia, articulated his abiding faith in the "Beloved Community," a vision of what society could become were people of all class and ethnic backgrounds to reach across the barriers that divide them. Richard Rorty, in *Achieving Our Country* (1998), argued for ideological moderation and objects to intransigent "leftists" and "conservatives." In *Someone Else's House* (1998), Tamar Jacoby professed her faith in interethnic integration and called for realism of appreciating the real progress between Blacks and Whites that had taken place in American society and insisting on the need for both Blacks and Whites to stay on the long and slow course of integration. With respect to higher education, Gerald Graff in *Beyond the Culture Wars* (1992) and Alan Ryan in *Liberal Anxieties and Liberal Education* (1998) insisted that category-based ideas of cultural diversity in the academe must be moderated and put in dialogue with traditional courses to avoid continuation of a disconnected curriculum and mutual resentment.

Economist Glenn Loury, whose words were quoted earlier in this essay as an expression of assimilationism, has moved away from his earlier stance toward a more balanced position of reconciliation in recent years. In *The Anatomy of Racial Inequality* (2003), Loury argues that what keeps African Americans from achieving their goals is not simply racial discrimination ("discrimination in contract"), but the more complex reality of "racial stigma" (or "discrimination in contact"). Loury agreed with some of the pluralist views on racial inequality and points out the moral and logical limitations of "color-blind" liberal individualism. At the same time, he critiques the intellectual complacency of the conventional pluralists who would explain any and all problems with the dated cry of racism and racial discrimination.

MESSAGES OF EXTREMISM

The full spectrum of American public discourse on interethnic relations further includes the marginal voices of separatism, often characterized as "extremist" views. Whereas the aforementioned messages of assimilationism, pluralism, and reconciliation commonly adhere to the societal goal of interethnic *integration* (while disagreeing on specific visions as to how to achieve this goal), extremist messages often express a preference for a maximum in-group and out-group *separation*. Some of the most unambiguous separatist messages come from those identified with "extreme right" groups including the Ku Klux Klan, Neo Nazi, Skinheads, and those of the so-called Patriot movements. According to recent issues of *Intelligence Report,* the quarterly magazine of the Southern Poverty Law Center, such extremist groups are known for their commitment to racial purism, the supremacy of the White race, and, in some cases, even arms training and preparation for a race war.

George Bundi (a.k.a. Eric Hawthorne), who reportedly has worked to revitalize the neo-Nazi movement through a newly powerful network, the Internet, states his separatist view toward Blacks: "To put Black men and women in American society, which is traditionally and essentially established on European traditions, and to say, 'Here you go, you're an equal, now compete,' is just as ridiculous as assuming that you could move White people to the Congo and have them effectively compete"(*The New York Times Magazine,* February 25, 1996, pp. 40–41). Separatist messages also come from the "extreme left" including contemporary ethnic nationalist groups such as the New Black Panthers and the Nation of Islam. Among such messages are Leonard Jefferies' description of White Americans as "ice people" and Louis Farrakhan's call for Black nationalism and economic reparations, his assertion of Black racial superiority, and his condemnation of Jews as "bloodsuckers," which have been widely reported (e.g., *Time,* February 28, 1994, pp. 21–25).

Extreme separatist messages are sometimes voiced by those who are unaffiliated with a recognized extremist group. Although not always explicit, separatist views can be inferred from the inflammatory rhetorical devices employed to condemn or scapegoat an out-group or position the in-group as "victims." Among such messages is the phrase "culture war" Patrick Buchanan used in a speech he delivered during the 1992 Republican convention, during his run for president in 2000 under the banner of the Reform Party, and more recently in his book, *State of Emergency: The Third World Invasion and Conquest of America* (2006). His messages connoted an unmistakable line drawn to "defend" what is believed to be the authentic American culture. Indeed, separatist messages appear to be becoming increasingly louder: Robert Kimball (1990) characterizing Black studies in universities as "this war against Western culture" (p. xi); minority student protesters at Stanford University chanting "Down with racism, Western culture's got to go" (*The New York Times,* October 25, 1995, pp. AI, B8); a Black student leader at Northwestern University insisting that no Black people could be racists "because racism is a function of power" (*The New York Times,* October 25, 1995, p. B8); a group of Hispanic students at Cornell University occupying a building to demand separate Hispanic housing (*The New York Times,* April 20, 1994, p. B8).

Thus, *the extremes meet.* As much as separatist messages of the extreme right and the extreme left differ dramatically in specific claims, they converge in rigid in-group–out-group distinction, characterization of the in-group as "victims," full-blown confrontational rhetorical posturing, and fortification of mutually intransigent moral claims. Separatist messages of both kinds violate the rationality and civility normally expected by most Americans in public discourse. As such, extremist messages are deemed to be beyond the realms most Americans consider "reasonable." As Billig et al. (1988) observe, "the extreme bigot is free to play consistently and unambiguously in an area which is beyond reality but which taunts reality. There is no need to hedge and qualify statements in order not to pass a seemingly unreasonable judgment" (p. 118).

It is not surprising, then, that separatist arguments do not resonate with the American public at large. Although mainstream Americans diverge in their views on the *locus* of American life (individual vs. group identity); the nature, rights, and responsibilities of humans (universalism vs. relativism); and the meaning of equality (procedural equality vs. status equality), they join in their objection to the separatist vision of the United States and in their shared condemnation of "hate" messages as fundamentally un-American. Exemplifying such common rejections of separatist messages are the responses of several readers to a *Time* magazine cover story featuring Farrakhan, entitled "Pride and Prejudice" (February 28, 1994, pp. 21–34). Their letters to the magazine editor characterize Farrakhan in such unflattering terms as "a wild, hate-mongering preacher," "the Minister of Rage," and "a streetwise hipster who shrewdly plays to the emotions of the most miserable and hopeless of his own people." One reader admonishes the editor for even featuring the story in the magazine: "As an African American, I find it very upsetting that every time Farrakhan speaks the media give him a microphone and an amplifier. . . . We should stop pointing fingers and making excuses that seem to confuse and anger more than unite our community. We can't continue at this level."

Others have responded to Farrakhan's separatist messages by warning against putting group identity over individual identity. Shelby Steel, an African American professor at San Jose State University,

points to the danger of excessive claims of group identity in an opinion column in *The New York Times* (March 13, 1994):

> Louis Farrakhan personifies a specific territory in the collective imagination of Black America. (Only this place in the imagination explains the vast disparity between his prominence and his rather small following.) It is the territory where the group ceases to be a mere identity or culture and becomes a value in itself. Here the group becomes synonymous with truth, and no longer needs approval from others. . . . It is precisely their break from universal truths-tolerance, brotherhood, fair-mindedness—that enables them to assert the supremacy of their group. (p. E17)

IDEOLOGICAL CIRCLE: A SYNTHESIS

The present analysis has revealed varied renditions of the liberal ideological tradition. Classical liberalism is reproduced by individual Americans not so much in terms of a set of universally commonsensical values, as in the form of often dilemmatic and sometimes embattled conflicting values. Communication messages addressing issues of race, ethnicity, and interethnic relations do not automatically mirror the traditional liberal themes of individualism, universalism, and procedural equality. Rather, they are dynamically challenged by the contrary themes of group identity, relativism, and equal group status.

This ideological dialectic undergirds messages of assimilationism and pluralism, along with messages of reconciliation and separatism. These themes and counter-themes of classical liberalism broadly help us understand the full spectrum of messages we hear today. The traditional individualistic and universalistic ideals and the principle of procedural equality are most closely aligned with messages of assimilationism, generally identified as the position of the mainstream political right. On the other hand, messages of pluralism, often associated with the mainstream political left, advocate the primacy of group identity and application of laws and public policies relative to historical and institutional conditions particular to a group, so as to close the existing unequal status between groups. Struggling between these two ideological views are the moderating, balancing, integrating, and often-conflicted messages

Figure 1 *Ideological Circle Linking Four Types of Interethnic Communication Messages*

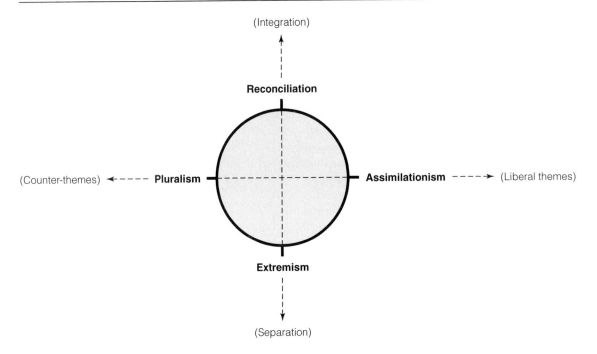

of reconciliation representing Middle America. In contrast, messages of extremism are commonly identified with the views of the extreme right and the extreme left—messages that emphasize in-group victimhood and moral superiority and maximum in-group–out-group separation.

Together, these four ideological positions constitute an *ideological circle* described in Figure 1. In this circle, the four positions are differentiated based on two bipolar dimensions: (1) the horizontal dimension of classical liberal and contrary themes, and (2) the vertical dimension of integrationist and separatist visions for the American society. The oppositional relationship between the assimilationist messages of liberal themes and pluralist messages of counter-themes is indicated by their respective positions of three o'clock and nine o'clock. Linking these two message types are the integrationist messages of reconciliation placed at the twelve o'clock position. The separatist messages of extremism (from both the extreme political right and the extreme political left) are merged into the six o'clock position, opposite from the position of the integrationist messages of reconciliation.

Even while being rigorously challenged by the voices advocating pluralism and extremism, the classical liberal ideals continue to occupy the mainstay of American consciousness on interethnic relations in the form of assimilationism and integrationism. The classical liberal tradition contains its own contrary themes, unresolved tensions, a dialectic—an ideological push-and-pull that often gives rise to heated debates and, in some cases, even acts of violence. These debates are not confined to the level of intellectual analysis; both themes and counter-themes have arisen from, and passed into, everyday consciousness of Americans who reflect on, and speak to, various issues of ethnicity and race. Indeed, we do not blindly follow the dictates of classical liberalism. Rather, we exercise a degree of freedom in making our own individual interpretations and judgments within the constraints of the liberal tradition.

This conclusion is largely supported by findings from public opinion polls. In a 1997 Time/CNN poll of more than 1,100 Americans, 96 percent of the respondents agreed with the assimilationist statement, "It should be the duty of all immigrants to learn English if they plan to stay in this country." In response to the question, "Which comes closest to your view on bilingual education in public schools?" only 11 percent agreed with the pluralist view that that "children of immigrants should be taught in their native language indefinitely." This is in sharp contrast with the 48 percent of the respondents who indicated "children of immigrants should be taught in their native language only until they know enough English to join regular classes," and with the remaining 40 percent who said "all children should be taught in English" (Gray, 1998, p. 70). Similar sentiments underlie the decisive passage of Proposition 227 in 1998 by California voters, thereby eliminating all bilingual education programs and replacing them with intensive English language instructions.

When "Ebonics" ("Black English") was endorsed by the Oakland Unified School District Board of Education at the end of 1996 as a legitimate language program, many public leaders who often diverge ideologically with respect to interethnic relations converged in denouncing and rejecting it as an "extremist," "dangerous," and "divisive" idea. From the camp commonly known as the "political right," Republican Senator Lauch Faircloth of North Carolina persisted in stating what had become the common view: "But I think Ebonics is absurd. This is a political correctness that has simply gone out of control." Similar voices were heard from the "political left" as well. Jesse Jackson stated: "I understand the attempt to reach out to these children, but this is an unacceptable surrender, bordering on disgrace" (cited in Lewis, 1998). Senior *Wall Street Journal* editor Joseph N. Boyce was even more indignant: "As a Black person and father of four, I find such notions insulting and, yes, racist" (cited in Palmeri, 1997). Poet Maya Angelou was also quoted to have been "incensed" by the plan, while Oakland writer Ishmael Reed labeled it a "travesty" (cited in Palmeri, 1997).

Indeed, the assimilationist-integrationist ideological stances continue to prevail in the American political landscape today. Some observers (e.g., Suarez-Orozco & Paez, 2002) foresee a continuing trend of pluralism. In *The Latino Wave* (2004), Jorge Ramos, news anchor of Univision, predicted this trend by highlighting the rapidly increasing numbers of Hispanic Americans who tend to maintain a strong allegiance to their countries of origin. Yet, other signs have been showing a continuing assimilative-integrative trend. The results of Gallop polls taken over the recent decades (1972 through 1997) show a dramatic increase in the percentage of White Americans who are willing to vote for a Black candidate for president (from 35 percent to 93 percent) and who approve of marriage between Blacks and Whites (25 percent to 61 percent) (*USA Today,* August 8, 1995, p. A11). In a more recent CNN opinion poll, 62 percent of the participants in a CNN poll responded that the country was ready for a Black president (*The New York Times,* December 19, 2006, p. 26). Furthermore, according to a USA Today/Gallup poll reported in early 2007, 95 percent of the participants reported that they themselves would consider voting for a Black presidential candidate (www.USAToday.com/news/Washington/2007-02-13-2008-campaign-poll_x.htm). The continuing efficacy of liberal ideals blurring and transcending ethnic categories is further reflected in the increase in the percentage of Americans who approve of marriage between Blacks and Whites increased from 25 percent in 1972 to 61 percent in 1995 (*USA Today,* August 8, 1995, p. A11). In terms of actual intermarriages in the United States, the number has escalated roughly from 310,000 in the 1960s to more than 1.1 million in the 1990s. Correspondingly, the incidence of births of mixed-race babies has multiplied 26 times as fast as that of any other group. As of the early 1990s, 52 percent of Jewish Americans, 65 percent of Japanese Americans, and 70 percent of Native Americans are reported to have married out of their faith, race, or ethnic heritage (Smolowe, 1993, pp. 64–65). In 2005, more than 7 percent of America's 59 million married couples are reported to be interracial, compared to less than 2 percent in 1970, factoring in all racial combinations (Crary, 2007).

Exactly how the nature of American interethnic relations and the underlying forces of differing ideological perspectives will unfold remains to be seen. Undoubtedly, debates will continue as Americans struggle with competing visions of *Unum* and *Pluribus*—visions of "We the People" and what it means to be Americans. Free and public debates, indeed, are essential for American society to guard itself against stagnation, disintegration, and entropy. The very fact that interethnic issues continue to engage American passion is itself an affirmation, and a hallmark, of the American liberal tradition. This tradition contributes to the stability of the American democracy, one that most Americans recognize, cherish, and celebrate. In the essayist Grunwald's (1976) words:

> So one must love America, most of all and most deeply for its constant, difficult, confused, gallant, and never-finished struggle to make freedom possible. One loves America for its accomplishments as well as for its unfinished business—and especially for its knowledge that its business is indeed unfinished. . . . One ultimately loves America for not what it is, or what it does, but for what it promises. . . . we must deeply believe, and we must prove, that after 200 years the American promise is still only in its beginning. (p. 36)

References

Abercrombie, N. (1980). *Class, structure, and knowledge.* Oxford: Basil Blackwell.

Asante, M. (1993). Racism, consciousness, and Afrocentricity. In G. Early (Ed.), *Lure and loathing: Essays on race, identity, and the ambivalence of assimilation* (pp. 127–148). New York: Penguin.

Baker, R. (1994, May 5). Gone with the Unum. *The New York Times*, p. A15.

Billig, M. (1991). *Ideology and opinions: Studies in rhetorical psychology.* London: Sage.

Billig, M., Condor, S., Edwards, D., Gane, M., Middleton, D., & Radley, A. (1988). *Ideological dilemmas: A social psychology of everyday thinking.* London: Sage.

Brooks, D. (2007, January 14). The American way of equality. *The New York Times*, Op-Ed Section, p. wk12.

Buchanan, P. (2006). *State of emergency: The Third World invasion and conquest of America.* New York: Thomas Dunne.

Crary, D. (2007, April 12). Interracial marriages surge across U.S. *USA Today*. Retrieved April 12, 2007, from http://www.usatoday.com/news/health/2007-04-12-interracial-marriage_N.htm

Crouch, S. (1998). *Always in pursuit: Fresh American perspective, 1995–1997.* New York: Pantheon.

Donohue, W. A. (2006, November 28). Celebrate diversity: Celebrate Christmas. *The New York Times*, Op-Ed Section, p. A23.

Garfinkel, H. (1967). *Studies in ethnomethodology.* Englewood Cliffs, NJ: Prentice-Hall.

Gitlin, T. (1995). *The twilight of common dreams: Why America is wracked by culture wars.* New York: Metropolitan.

Graff, G. (1992). *Beyond the culture wars: How teaching the conflicts can revitalize American education.* New York: Norton.

Gray, P. (1998). Teach your children well. *Time*, 69–71.

Grunwald, H. (1976, July 5). Loving America. *Time*, 35–36.

Hacker, A. (1992). *Two nations: Black and White, separate, hostile, unequal.* New York: Charles Scribner's Sons.

Haberman, C. (2006, December 19). "Happy holidays" to peace on earth? It's a tortured path. *The New York Times*, pp. B1, B3.

Iyer, P. (1990, September 3). The masks of minority terrorism. *Time*, 86.

Jacoby, T. (1998). *Someone else's house: America's unfinished struggle for integration.* New York: The Free Press.

Kim, Y. Y. (1999). *Unum and Pluribus:* Ideological underpinnings of interethnic communication in the United States. *International Journal of Intercultural Relations,* 23(4), 591–611.

Kim, Y. Y. (2005). Association and dissociation: A contextual theory of interethnic communication. In W. B. Gudykunst (Ed.), *Theorizing about intercultural communication* (pp. 323–349). Thousand Oaks, CA: Sage.

Kimball, R. (1990). *Tenured radicals: How politics has corrupted higher education.* New York: Harper & Row.

King, C. S. (1993). *The Martin Luther King, Jr., companion: Quotations from the speeches, essays, and books of Martin Luther King, Jr.* (selected by Coretta Scott King). New York: St. Martin.

Lacayo, R. (1993, Fall). Whose peers? *Time* (Special Issue, The New Faces of America), 60–61.

Lewis, J. (1998). *Walking with the wind: A memoir of the movement.* New York: Simon & Shuster.

Loury, G. (1993). Free at last? A personal perspective on race and identity in America. In G. Early (Ed.), *Lure and loathing: Essays on race, identity, and the ambivalence of assimilation* (pp.1–12). New York: Allen Lane:Penguin.

Loury, G. (2003). *The anatomy of racial inequality.* Cambridge, MA: Harvard University Press.

Palmeri, A. (1997, October). *Ebonics and politics: A Burkian analysis.* Paper presented at the annual meeting of the National Communication Association, Chicago.

Patterson, O. (2006, December 30). The last race problem. *The New York Times*, Op-Ed Section, p. A19.

Ramos, J. (2004). *The Latino wave: How Hispanics will elect the next American president.* New York: Rayo.

Rorty, R. (1998). *Achieving our country: Leftist thought in twentieth-century America.* Cambridge, MA: Harvard University Press.

Rossides, D. (1976). *The American class system: An introduction to social stratification.* Washington, DC: University Press of America.

Ryan, A. (1998). *Liberal anxieties and liberal education.* New York: Hill & Wang.

Schlesinger, A. M., Jr. (1992). *The disuniting of America: Reflections on a multicultural society.* New York: W. W. Norton.

Smolowe, J. (1993, Fall). Intermarried . . . with children. *Time* (Special issue: *The New Faces of America*), 64–65.

Suarez-Orozco, M., & Paez, M. (Eds.). (2002). *Latinos: Remaking America*. Berkeley, CA: University of California Press.

Toobin, J. (2006, December 30). Gerald Ford's affirmative action. *The New York Times*, Op-Ed Section, p. A19.

Traub, J. (1998, June 28). Nathan Glazer changes his mind, again. *The New York Times Magazine*, 22–25.

Tsuda, Y. (1986). *Language inequality and distortion*. Philadelphia: John Benjamin.

Van Dijk, T. A. (Ed.). (1997). *Discourse as social interaction*. Thousand Oaks, CA: Sage.

Ward, Arvil (1993). Which side are you on? *Amerasia Journal, 19*(2), 109–112.

Wilson, K. (1998, May). The contested space of prudence in the 1874–1875 civil rights debate. *Quarterly Journal of Speech, 84*(2), 131–149.

Wolfe, A. (1998). *One nation, after all*. New York: Viking.

Concepts and Questions

1. Why has the *E Pluribus Unum* concept of a "melting pot" society failed to materialize in contemporary American society?

2. How do "tribal identities" contribute to interethnic conflict?

3. What characterizes messages of assimilation? From whom are messages of assimilation most likely to emerge?

4. Can or do messages of assimilation lend themselves to improved interethnic communication?

5. Give an example of a message of pluralism. How do messages of pluralism differ from messages of assimilation?

6. What are messages of reconciliation? How do they relate to messages of assimilation and of pluralism?

7. From whom are messages of reconciliation most likely to emanate?

8. What are messages of extremism? Which groups of American society are most likely to promulgate messages of extremism?

9. How can an understanding of the philosophical underpinnings of the messages of assimilation, plurality, reconciliation, and extremism lead to better interethnic communication?

10. How can the American struggle between *Unum* and *Pluribus* be resolved?

Hoʻoponopono: A Hawaiian Cultural Process to Conflict Resolution

CHARMAINE I. KAʻIMIKAUA

In the Hawaiian culture, *hoʻoponopono* is a complex communication process that is used to maintain family relations or friendships. Usually, if a conflict occurs or a problem arises that strains interpersonal relationships among Hawaiian peoples the practice of *hoʻoponopono* is used to restore peace and harmony. According to Hawaiian historian Mary Kawena Pukui, the historic significance and meaning of *hoʻoponopono* (Pukui, 1972) means *"to set right"* or to find resolve for any wrongdoings. Although this practice may continue in contemporary times, *hoʻoponopono* is rooted historically in ancestral and spiritual identifications as *ʻaumākua* or deified ancestors of Hawaiians who also feel the painful presence of discord among the peoples. Any miscommunication, therefore, must be addressed for improving connectivity between sentient beings. It is important to understand that Hawaiian ideology utilizes a systems theory approach in which all living things are interrelated and connected to one another. Any disharmony, therefore, affects and is felt among animist beings and in all personal relationships. *Hoʻoponopono* seeks *"to make right"* any wrongdoings inflicted upon family members or friends through a communal conference of problem solving and conflict resolution.

The *hoʻoponopono* process is usually conducted in five stages that begins with identifying the problem. This is then followed by discussions that lead toward confession, restitution, and finally, forgiveness and release (Shook, 2002). *Hoʻoponopono* is usually

This original essay appears here in print for the first time. All rights reserved. Permission to reprint must be obtained from the author and publisher. Ms. Charmaine I. Kaʻimikaua teaches at Cypress College, Cypress, California.

conducted by a senior family member or respected outside elder.

The first stage is opened with *pule* or prayer asking *'aumākua* (ancestral spirits) for assisting guidance as well as their blessings to solve the problem. The second stage consists of identifying the problem or what is called *kūkulu kumuhana* as efforts are made to understand the discord. In this phase, if there is any resistance from family members or other relations, the senior family member or elder will reach out to that person in order to engage them more fully in the *ho'oponopono* process.

In the next stage, the focus specifically centers on the wrongdoing or *hala*, as this stage indicates that an entangled negative relationship exists between the intended victim and perpetrator. This means the troubled twosome are bound together not in one conflict but in a complex web of intricate layerings of problems or what is described as *hihia* (Pukui, 1972; Shook, 2002). It is during this phase that feelings of hurt and misunderstanding may arise between the involved persons. The leader chooses one particular problem to be discussed or what is known as *mahiki*, and as one conflict is resolved there may be an unraveling of other problematic layers to be solved in succession. If the conflict or discussion becomes too heated, a cooling off or silent period defined as *ho'omalu* is enacted.

Once the problem has been identified and openly discussed another stage of confessing any wrongdoing and forgiveness takes place or what is described in Hawaiian as *mihi*. It is important that forgiveness is included in the process and is usually expected as part of the resolution. In addition, this is also the stage where needed restitution is arranged and agreed upon. Also in this phase, an intense discussion or *kala*, may result between parties in order to achieve a loosening of any negative entanglement. Confession of wrongfulness and forgiveness are brought to the surface and begin an unraveling of the enmeshed web of hurt and anger. This is an important phase because tensions are released through the act of forgiveness or some type of restitution is paid to the victim or family.

The final stage known as *pani* is a summary of what has been discussed to reconfirm closure and the strengthening of family ties. Thereafter, the problem is never discussed or mentioned again among family or friends. Basically, a restatement of what has occurred within the problematic discussion between all members transpires and everyone moves forward as it is no longer necessary to restate the past. *Pani* is also the conclusive stage that includes a closing prayer or *pule ho'opau* to signify completion and that harmony is thus restored to the relationship. *Ho'oponopono* is often followed by a traditional meal or snack demonstrating commitment to familial bonding of love and friendship. The act of sharing a meal together establishes movement away from the conflict and there is a return to normalcy (Shook, 2002). Because *ho'oponopono* is a very complex communication process, it may take several sessions to restore harmony among family members and close friends.

Cultural traditions that are deeply ingrained and practiced in the daily lives of the Hawaiian people may be perceptive, intuitive, and natural processes that are culturally appropriate. The ancient tradition of *ho'oponopono* continues to be a praxis among the Hawaiian peoples that extends into modern times and may be employed to resolve conflict in various settings that fall within the Hawaiian cultural context. This is a significant cultural dynamic because Westernized approaches to conflict and problem solving sometimes fail to recognize that appropriate resolution techniques can be found within the cultural imagination.

The application of *ho'oponopono* has long-range capabilities that provide hope and possibility in imagining peaceful conclusions while keeping cultural pride and traditions intact. *Ho'oponopono* has been successfully applied among Hawaiians in social work, psychiatry, drug abuse treatment, prison reform, and other related areas in which social problems arise. *Ho'oponopono* provids a vehicle by which these problems can be discussed with the goal of possible resolution that can transcend the problem or conflict.

References

Pukui, M. K., Haertig, E. W., M.D., & Lee, C. A. (1972). *Nāna i ke Kumu: Look to the source.* Honolulu, HI: Hui Hānai Press.

Shook, V. E. (2002). *Ho'oponopono: Contemporary uses of a Hawaiian problem-solving process.* Honolulu, HI: University of Hawai'i Press.

Concepts and Questions

1. Ka'imikaua writes that the *ho'oponopono* process involves a "communal conference." Reflecting on the Triandis essay in Chapter 1, what kind of cultural syndrome would be used to characterize the Hawaiian culture?
2. Why do you think this type of conflict resolution process evolved in the Hawaiian culture?
3. What does Ka'imikaua mean that for Hawaiians "all living things are interrelated and connected to one another"? How might this influence their worldview?
4. What are the primary differences between the Euro-American and traditional Hawaiian methods of conflict resolution?
5. Can you think of situations in your personal or work life where *ho'oponopono* could have been used to resolve a conflict?

America in Black and Brown: Exploring Sources of Intercultural Tensions between Blacks and Latinos in the United States

PETER OGOM NWOSU

INTRODUCTION

More than fifteen years ago, in a 1990 issue of *Time* magazine, William Henry III, a staff writer with *Time*, commented about the uneasiness among American Blacks regarding the rising Latino population in the United States.[1] Black uneasiness according to Henry stemmed from three factors: first, Blacks believe they have waited the longest and endured the most in the fight for equality and justice and the presence of Latinos weakens their prospects for more Black access to resources in a nation that has not treated them fairly; second, Blacks fear being supplanted by Latinos as the nation's most influential minority group; and third, Blacks fear being outstripped in wealth, and consequently in status by, in their view, this new group to America.

The last few years have witnessed a significant rise in the Latino population, thus making them the nation's largest and fastest growing minority population, exacerbating Black fears as identified above, and consequently increasing the tension in Black-Latino relations. Indeed, if ever there was any doubt about the fragile and albeit competitive nature of

Black-Latino relations, it can be seen in the racial skirmishes between students from both groups in our nation's public schools, in the shifting alliances among both groups in the direction of where there is the largest gain for each group, and in voting booths across the nation. The 2001 mayoral election in Los Angeles, for example, revealed, to some degree, the nature of the fragile and competitive relationship between both groups. The election—a contest between the former speaker of the State Assembly, Antonio Villaraigosa, a Latino, and White city attorney James Hahn, both Democrats—ended in defeat for the once-powerful speaker. Villaraigosa lost to an unusual amalgam of Whites and Blacks. In fact, 80 percent of the Black vote went to Hahn, who also won 59 percent of the White vote. Villaraigosa secured 82 percent of the Latino vote, and as much as 54 percent of the Jewish vote, not enough to install him as the first Latino mayor of Los Angeles in over a century. In 2005, Villaraigosa ran again, this time with support of the Black community. He defeated Hahn in a run-off election to become the first Latino to govern Angelinos in more than 100 years. Villaraigosa won nearly 60 percent of the Black votes, a huge contrast to the less than 20 percent of the Black electorate that voted for him four years earlier. Political scientist Raphael Sonenshein has noted that the really interesting question is "what happens to relations between Latinos and Blacks now." Sonenshein's question is worth exploring in full because Black support for a Latino candidate is by no means "the sign of a full-scale coalition" given the fragile and purely competitive relationship between the two groups.[2]

This essay examines the nature of the fragile and competitive relationship between both groups from a historical, cultural, and political perspective. First, we begin with an examination of the history of both the African American and Latino experiences in the United States. Second, we examine both communities' perceptions of each other focusing on psychological, cultural, and political factors that shape these perceptions. Third, we explore some consequences for both groups of a strain in Black-Latino relations, and fourth, we offer suggestions for moving beyond the politics and the narrow vision of ethnicity that threatens to widen the relational chasm between both ethnic groups.

BLACK-LATINO RELATIONS: TWO HISTORIES

Any attempt to understand the growing tension in Black-Latino relations must begin first with a discussion of the historical experiences of both groups in the United States. Much is well known about the African American experience in the United States. Much has been written about slavery and the quest for free labor as the driving engine of the Black presence in America. Nearly 400 years since the first set of Africans arrived on the shores of Jamestown, Virginia, much continues to be written about the institution of slavery and state-church complicity in the denial of basic rights that officially defined the nature of Black-White relations in America. Even today, nearly 200 years after slavery was abolished, more than 140 years after the emancipation proclamation, and more than 40 years after the historic Civil Rights Act of 1964 and the momentous Voting Rights Act of 1965, Black freedom struggle remains fundamental to the existence of Black America.

However, because American Blacks have been consumed by their long personal and collective struggles for freedom, few have paid attention to the historical struggles for those same rights reflected in the Latino experience in America. Moreover, the paucity of research on the Hispanic experience in the United States further complicates any knowledge or understanding among American Blacks regarding the Latino freedom struggle. Most Americans, including Blacks, as reflected in Black fears noted earlier, tend to associate Latino history with immigration, and believe that most Spanish speakers are immigrants. This is not the case. Most Americans, including Blacks, in fact are unaware that Americans of Hispanic heritage have a varied history and a complicated ancestry that dates back more than 400 years. Americans of Hispanic origin are from birth "the result of the encounter of diverse people such as the Spaniards and the Portuguese with the diverse Indian nations of the Americas such as the Incas, Aztecs, Quechuas, Mayas, Tainos, Siboneyes, and others."[3] Americans of Hispanic origin are also the result of encounters with African peoples who were brought as slaves by force to the Americas. From these encounters emerged the different Latino people of Peru, Bolivia, Colombia, El Salvador, Mexico, Cuba,

Puerto Rico, Dominican Republic, Brazil, and other Latin American countries.[4]

Indeed contrary to popular opinion, "there are Spanish-speaking Californians, New Mexicans, and Texans whose ancestors lived in the Southwest long before their respective states became part of the United States."[5] In their authoritative account titled *The Hispanics in the United States: A History,* Stanford University scholars L.H. Gann and Peter Duignan note that Hispanics, like the vast majority of other Americans, trace their original homes to different countries including Mexico, Puerto Rico, Cuba, Nicaragua, El Salvador, Honduras, Spain, and Argentina.

> Some of them are proficient in Spanish, although others have lost the use of their ancestral tongue. Some are indifferent to their cultural inheritance and regard themselves as un-hyphenated Americans: others have a strong commitment to their Hispanic legacy. Some are rich and some are poor; some are conservative and some are radical; some are fair-skinned and some are swarthy or black.[6]

LATINOS AND SLAVERY

What is also significant in the context of Black-Latino relations is that few Blacks recognize the historic opposition to slavery by Latinos in the 1800s. The emerging historical account suggests that it was the opposition to American engagement in slavery that aroused a bitter debate in the United States over war with Mexico. L.H. Gann and Peter Duignan write that those who were the principal advocates of war with Mexico were Southerners who wanted to safeguard slavery as an institution within the United States through the creation of a new (possibly several) slave state(s). This desire became the imperative that shaped the discourse between those who were for war and those against war. The anti-war movement, already opposed to slavery, believed that the annexation of Texas was a conspiracy led by slave owners to essentially undermine American freedom and basic human rights. Given the charged atmosphere, James Polk, U.S. president at the time, decided on what seemed to be a middle-course solution to "satisfy both the slave states and the 'free soil' states: he

would acquire not only Texas but also Oregon and California, thus extending America's boundaries to the Pacific ocean."[7] President Polk not only made good on his quest by acquiring Texas and California, but he also acquired New Mexico and purchased Oregon from the British. Indeed all of the western and southwestern states of the United States—California, New Mexico, Arizona, Nevada, Utah, Colorado, Wyoming, and Texas—were all Mexican territories until 1848 when the Mexican-American war ended.

The Story of Texas

The story of Texas is particularly unique because the immediate cause for the Mexican-American war that began in 1846 derived from disputes over the territory and what behaviors were permissible within it. As English and German settlers from the United States flooded the province to engage in plantation agriculture with the aid of slave labor, the Mexican government began to insist that the newcomers abide by Mexican laws. One such law outlawed slavery. The position of the Mexican government incensed the newcomers, most of them from the American south, who argued that Mexican laws undermined their inalienable rights, and their professed notion of "manifest destiny." In 1836, the newcomers, taking advantage of the weaknesses in the Mexican leadership, declared Texas an independent sovereign state. The Mexican government under President Antonio López de Santa Anna tried to crush the rebellion, but failed due to the political problems Santa Anna was facing at home.

The next ten years saw strong political debates in the United States on whether the country should go to war to acquire Texas, and the rich territories of California and New Mexico, also at the time belonging to Mexico. The British, who were no friends of the Americans at the time, also had interests in these territories. While Mexico was willing to let Texas remain an independent sovereign state, and was being pressured by the British to recognize it as such, the Mexican government feared that the annexation of Texas by the United States might lead to the loss of other Mexican territories. The United States, on its own, feared that any failure to act might give advantage over these vast territories and the Pacific to the

British, who already had a controlling presence in Australia and New Zealand. In 1846, following months of wrangling, finger pointing, counter-accusations, and the admission of Texas as the 28th state, Mexico and the United States went to war, with the United States defeating the Mexican army, forcing Mexico to sign a peace treaty with the Americans on February 2, 1848. The treaty signed at Guadalupe Hidalgo, near Mexico City, surrendered control of California and New Mexico to the United States.

Although Mexico lost the war, the Treaty of Guadalupe Hidalgo provided guarantees that while these territories no longer belonged to Mexico, the U.S. government would respect the property, religious, and cultural rights (including language rights) of citizens of the conquered territories. In fact, as part of the treaty and to prevent any future claims, the U.S. government paid Mexico 15 million dollars in cash in exchange for the territories, and another 3.25 million dollars for claims made by American citizens on the Mexican government as a result of the war.

The propensity to expand the American frontier through the acquisition of land held by Latinos (especially Mexico) in the heydays of the American experiment has been a defining fissure in Latino-White relations. Each conquered territory resulted in the subjugation of Latinos into second-class citizens. The Hispanic struggles for justice have therefore been with respect to these rights, and the Treaty of Guadalupe Hidalgo provides the basis for the struggles, and thus is seen by many Latinos as the most important document for American Hispanics.

The Latino Population

While the Latino community in the United States has been around for well over 400 years, the rapid growth in its population began in the late 1960s as a result of refugee movements, immigration reform, and illegal immigration from several Latin American countries. By 1970, the U.S. government coined the term "Hispanic" to refer to people who were born in any of the Spanish-speaking countries of the Americas or people who could trace their ancestry to Spain or former colonial territories of Spain. Few Latinos, however, refer to themselves as Hispanics.

By 1980, Americans witnessed large Latino migrant populations settling in such places as Washington, DC,

New York, Trenton, Newark, Buffalo, and Providence in the Northeast; Miami, Houston, and Atlanta in the South; Las Vegas, Sacramento, San Jose, Santa Rosa, Anaheim, San Diego, and Los Angeles in the West; and Chicago and Lake County, Illinois, in the Midwest. In the last two decades, in some of the areas mentioned, Latinos have become a part of fully multi-ethnic neighborhoods, while in other areas ethnic Latino enclaves have emerged.

The latest Bureau of the Census numbers show that across the country, Latinos are now the nation's largest minority group, numbering about 37 million, compared with approximately 36.2 million Blacks. These numbers represent a 4.7 percent rise in the Latino population since April 2000, compared with a 1.5 percent rise in the Black population; and 0.8 percent increase for Americans of European background, whose population currently stands at 196 million. The current surge in Latino population, which has made American Blacks uncomfortable, is due essentially to higher birthrates and a huge wave of immigration, including illegal immigration. By the end of the 1990s, more than 50 percent of new immigrants who came to the United States came from Latin America, compared to 1970 when only 19 percent of new immigrants came from the region.[8] Given current trends, demographers project that by 2050, the U.S. population will be 52.8 percent European American, 24.5 percent Latino, 13.6 percent African American, 8.2 percent Asian American, and 1.0 percent Native American.[9] These numbers are important in assessing how each group jockeys for a fair share of the national cake.

DIFFERENT HISTORIES, DIFFERENT PERCEPTIONS

The differing historical experiences of American Blacks and American Hispanics provide an important framework for examining the differing perceptions of each other in both communities. Such examination must draw from three explanations: *a psychological explanation, a cultural explanation, and a political explanation*. The psychological explanation is crucial because it provides a prism to understanding the *how* and the *why* of the fragile nature of Black-Latino relations in America. The cultural explanation offers a window for understanding the nature and the consequences of the culture gap between the two ethnic minorities, and the political explanation provides a framework for exploring the basis for the emerging political divide between Hispanic America and Black America.

A Psychological Explanation

Communication scholars, whose discipline has been informed a great deal by psychology, make the case that human interactions are motivated by certain needs and desires. When people affiliate with others, they do so because such affiliation satisfies a particular need. Black-Latino relations can be likened to the sort of relations developed by two battered women who experience a low point in their lives because of abuse from their spouses or friends. The parallel experience of both women, an experience grounded in victimization, is precisely the basis or the reason for the *functional* relationship. Thus they become friends only because they have something in common. They see themselves as victims. They perform the mutually satisfying function of comforting each other. But once they get past the psychological feeling of pain and helplessness, they see no more need for the function.

One of the major crises of meaning in Black-Latino relations in America lies in this type of functional relationship. Black America and Hispanic America see each other as victims of an oppressive regime. The common enemy is White America. They come together to share a common feeling or attitude toward a perceived enemy, in this case, a negative attitude. Once the attitude is gone, the temporary friendship is gone. The friendship, after all, is based on the psychological need to find succor in others who share common problems. Without appearing simplistic, what binds the two groups together is the common enemy, nothing substantive, and nothing tangible. Here is a typical conversation overheard between two angry members of both ethnic groups over their failure to secure admission into a university graduate program:

BLACK MALE: Man, I can't believe they wouldn't let me into the program . . .

LATINO MALE: Me too, that sucks.

BLACK MALE: That department is so racist.

LATINO MALE: I was so qualified. I have been trying to get in since last year. And I hear there are no Mexicans in that program.

BLACK MALE: You know, that's right, you're right, I never thought about that.

LATINO MALE: I'm tired of being put down by White people. Those racist m—f—-!

BLACK MALE: Yeah, me too. I have had enough of being put down.

As you might guess, these two men both walked out together bonded by their common experience—a shared history of victimization, so to speak—without knowing anything about each other. What brings them together is that they are victims, and the relationship ends there—at the contact stage. The tragedy in the type of dialogue reflected by the two gentlemen is that the reliance on a common set of negative feelings toward a problem does nothing to enhance the relationship between both individuals. If Black-Latino relations are to improve, the relations must move beyond this type of casual contact. What is needed is a new kind of involvement and social bonding between both groups, where a sense of mutuality of being connected is present, and both groups learn more about each other and make a commitment to further each other's purpose. Real friendships and alliances begin with the desire to build lasting and sustained friendships.

A Cultural Explanation

Real friendships do not grow and flourish in an environment where participants do not know one another. The cultural explanation for the differing perceptions between American Blacks and Latinos draws fundamentally from this lack of knowledge about each other. Indeed, a culture gap does exist between Hispanic America and Black America. Both ethnic groups understand little of each other. The negative cultural stereotypes and the subterranean current of animosity between both groups further exemplify this gap. In truth, most Latinos are aware of *the Black experience,* but few understand *Black culture.* The distinction between the *Black experience* and *Black culture* is important here, because the former reflects the African American experience with slavery and its legacy of racism (of which most Latinos are aware), while the latter speaks to African American cultural patterns and communication style (which few Latinos understand).

Few Latinos recognize that the majority of Blacks who came to the United States brought with them a strong cultural heritage, which later became grounded in the spirituality of the Baptist faith. Under the weight of European oppression and exploitation however, American Blacks lost a great deal of their true cultural and ethnic identities. This is why Alex Haley's compelling book *Roots,* and its subsequent documentary as a series on national television, provided a spiritual lift in the cultural psyche of American Blacks. *Roots* also transformed Blacks in terms of their self-esteem, and spurred a new movement that placed Africa as central in the cultural lives of American Blacks.

While accounts of Africanisms or African cultural retentions in America have been provided in the numerous volumes on African history stored in various libraries across America, it is clear that not one major African language of the more than 250 languages spoken by Blacks, brought in chains to the Americas, survived the onslaught. What we know today, as Black language in America, is a patchwork of West African languages and English that most linguists and scholars now refer to as *Ebonics.* Ebonics has its own structure, syntax, and pragmatics, and various dialects of the language are spoken by Black people in many parts of the United States, especially in the South. A much more original strand of this language is used by the Black people of Gullah who inhabit parts of Georgia, South Carolina, Florida, and the Sea Islands off the coast of those three states. Although Ebonics is looked down upon as incorrect English (which it is not), most educated and middle-class Blacks clearly identify with it. They find great comfort and pleasure in the use of this language, and have developed the capacity to alternate between their native tongue and Standard American English—to code switch. What governs a person's desire to switch linguistic codes is the subject of conversation, the context of the conversation, and the gender of conversational partners. While Spanish is the *lingua franca* of many Latinos in the United States, a new language, *Spanglish*—a patchwork of Spanish and English, is emerging as the third most important language for Latinos. Like most Blacks, many Latinos are also able to alternate between these languages depending on the subject, the context, and the gender of conversational partners. But as Richard Rodriguez notes, Español (or Spanish) is "my family's language . . .

A family member would say something to me (in Español) and I would feel myself specially recognized.

My parents would say something to me and I would feel embraced by the sounds of their words. Those sounds said: I am speaking with ease in Spanish. I am addressing you in words I never use with los gringos (Europeans). I recognize you as someone special, close, like no one outside. You belong to us. In the family.[10]

In a sense, the use of these languages in both Black and Hispanic America suggest a particular comfort level and a strong feeling of belonging that one does not necessary have when one uses a language outside of one's cultural experience. Language therefore is an important instrument for maintaining group identity.

Black cultural patterns and communication styles are also a patchwork of Africanisms and some (not all) European American ways. The European ways present in African American cultural patterns and communication styles reflect the historical experience of American Blacks in the context of slavery. For example, inherent in Ebonics or Black English is a communication style that values animation or excitement, is loud, colorful, very direct, overt, and very straightforward. This approach to communication, which draws from both African (animation, loud, and colorful) and European ways (direct, overt, and straightforward), flies in the face of what is considered appropriate communication style among Hispanics. In comparison to American Blacks, Latino communication style is less animated, less direct, and has a much greater focus on face-saving. Since few Latinos understand Black communication style, most of them generally perceive Blacks as rude and disrespectful.

An almost similar cultural ignorance about Latinos is equally present in Black America, where many Blacks are both unaware of the Latino struggle for justice in America, but more importantly, do not understand Latino cultural patterns and communication styles. Latinos, for example, place a great deal of emphasis on respect for the elderly, and this respect is reflected in how language is used. There is also a relationship between one's status or hierarchy and the level of respect one receives from subordinates. Furthermore, there is a strong religious faith in Latino culture shaped by a Catholic tradition. The common phrase *Uno nunca se olvida de Dios,* "One should never forget about God," guides how one relates to self and to others. The loud, outspoken person, and the one who talks about his or her accomplishments and how good the individual looks, is looked down upon in Latino culture. Modesty then is the *soul* of communication in Latino culture. Few Blacks recognize and understand this fundamental cultural pattern and communication style of Latinos, and sometimes view Latinos as too cagey to be trusted.

Misconceptions and Stereotypes

Under the present dispensation, ethnic misconceptions and negative stereotypes about each group have found expression and welcome in candid conversations in both communities. Anti-Black and anti-Latino sentiments and prejudices, including the use of racial slurs, now abound on both sides of the ethnic divide. It is not uncommon in the Latino community (especially in California) to hear such racial slurs as *may-ate* (the Spanish term for the *n* word) hurled around in reference to the Black community. The racial skirmishes in our nation's public schools among young Blacks and Latinos reflect the increasing level of distrust in both communities. And while most Blacks supported Villaraigosa in his 2005 mayoral election, such support for a Latino candidate is by no means "the sign of a full-scale coalition" given the purely competitive relationship between the two groups.[11] At the hub of the growing pain in Black-Latino relations is the political explanation.

A Political Explanation

In the last two decades, Blacks have perceived the tremendous growth in Latino population as a threat to Black political power. This may explain why many Blacks voted against Villaraigosa in 2001. Even more startling was Black opposition to unchecked or unregulated immigration when many Blacks in California voted for the famous Proposition 187. Exit polls showed that 56 percent of African Americans and 64 percent of Whites voted in favor of Proposition 187. About 31 percent of Latinos, according to exit polls, also voted, surprisingly, for the proposition. Proposition 187 barred illegal immigrants from receiving public support throughout California's public education system, and required public educational institutions to verify the legal status of both immigrant students and their parents. Proposition 187 also required all providers of publicly funded, non-emergency health care services to verify the legal status of persons seeking services in order to be reimbursed by the state. In addition, Proposition 187 made the production and use of false documents a state felony, and required all service providers to report suspected illegal immigrants to law enforcement authorities and to the Immigration and Naturalization Service (INS).

Proposition 187 was based on the simple premise that denying public services to illegal immigrants would discourage them from coming to the United States. We know that most of the illegal immigrants to California that were to be affected by Proposition 187 were Latinos. Most came from Mexico, and many of them worked as migrants in farms and garment shops. That many Blacks ironically voted for Proposition 187 was not so much because they were, in principle, opposed to the goals of the proposition—(that illegal immigrants were draining state resources needed for other areas of governance), but they voted for Proposition 187 merely because of anti-Latino feelings on what was perceived as the emerging threat to Black political strength posed by a growing Latino population in California. The feelings are the same in several southern and midwestern states where there is a growing Latino population. Thus the politics of numbers have outweighed any serious effort at controlling or managing the complexities of illegal immigration in the country.

As we have seen since the passage of Proposition 187 in California, denying public services to illegal or undocumented immigrants has not been an easy proposition. Many public agencies refused to comply with its verification requirements, fearing that Proposition 187 affected innocent people. How does one, for example, deal with the U.S.-born child, children, or family members, all U.S. citizens by law, of a so-called illegal immigrant now living in the United States? While Proposition 187 was presented as an honest attempt to address a serious federal problem, the motivations became muddied in accusations that the proposition was racially or ethnically tainted.

There is a deep-seated feeling in Black America today that Hispanics (and other groups) have benefited too much from the spoils of the freedom struggle without making any substantive contribution to the struggle. While Blacks have fought hard, more than any other group in America, for affirmative action, public housing, and desegregation in public schools, they worry that groups whose history and experience do not compare to the Black experience are now benefiting at the same level from the gains won in these areas. Any growth in Latino population is therefore viewed in the context of what it means to the Black share of the national cake.

Syndicated columnist Julianne Malveaux, an African American, captured this feeling well in a series of questions she posed in her analysis of the election of Assemblyman Cruz Bustamante as the Lt. Governor of California, the first Latino to hold this position in more than a hundred years. "What happens," she asked, "when demographic shifts suggest that gains African Americans fought hard for must now be shared? Are we interested in offering the same affirmative action for which we have long fought? Or will we emulate Whites in forcing our Latino brothers and sisters to wrest gains from us."[12] There is an undercurrent of feeling in Black America that these gains cannot be shared. There is also a perception in Black America that Latinos think that they are next to White because of their fair skin. Related to this perception is the politics of race in America that had historically (rightly or wrongly) classified Latinos as White because of their skin color. The consequence of this is the emergence of the feeling in Black America that Latino light skin has provided certain White-skin privileges to American Hispanics that have been denied to Blacks. But this argument is illogical because it ignores the fact that light-skin Blacks have also benefited from certain White-skin privileges, and they have not been denied access to the gains of the freedom struggle.

The root of some of the anti-Black sentiments in the Latino community can be found in this sad state of affairs. Writes Malveaux: "I'll never forget sitting on a panel with a Latino brother who excoriated African American leadership for taking all of the political spoils and leaving 'crumbs' for Latinos. Strident and angry, the man went down a list of our best and brightest, pronouncing them all insensitive and corrupt. 'Wait until we get our turn,' he spat."[13]

be the most genuine pathway for progress in America and for creating a new vision of community in America. First, both groups must transcend the narrow vision about their common historical struggle. The vision of a common feeling about "the enemy," without anything substantive for sustained and lasting friendship, must end. Second, both communities must begin to build a culture of respect for each other. Building a culture of respect begins with closing the culture gap between both groups and removing long-standing negative cultural stereotypes that have become the perceptual lens through which each community has filtered the other for years. Third, genuine cooperation and partnership must guide Black-Latino relations.

In point of fact, there have been a few examples in which both groups have come together over common problems. In 1988, for example, when Cesar Chavez, the charismatic labor leader, went on a 36-day fast to fight for migrant farm workers rights, the Reverend Jesse Jackson and several activists came on board to participate. But the struggles for justice in both communities are often narrowly perceived in ethnic terms, rather than in terms of a broad-based coalition for change. The sentiment present but often not expressed is that "It's not really my problem, I'm only here to help you." In this context, the farm workers' struggle for justice is seen solely as a Latino struggle. The struggle for civil rights is seen solely as a Black struggle. Sadly, when Blacks or Latinos or other groups become involved in these causes, they do so because they simply want to help. There is not a feeling of *ownership* in the involvement.

The fact of the matter is that a farm worker's right is not just a Latino struggle, and civil rights should not to be seen as a Black struggle either. The origins of the struggles are certainly ethnic. But ethnic claims to ownership for these causes do serious damage to the struggles for justice. These struggles are purely struggles for human rights. We must cease to view them with ethnic lenses.

CONCLUSION: COMMON PROBLEMS, COMMON SOLUTIONS

Black America and Hispanic America cannot afford to wait until each gets its turn to hurt the other. Black and Latino historical struggles for freedom and justice are so intertwined that separation and divorce cannot

Notes

1. William Henry III (1990). Beyond the melting pot. *Time,* April 9.
2. Michael Finnegan and Mark Z. Baraback (2005). Villaraigosa's support goes beyond Latinos. *Los Angeles Times,* May 19, 2005.

3. Edwin Aldarondo (2003). Hispanics have a long and rich history in the United States. *The Standard-Times,* New Bedford, CT, January 29, p. A13.
4. Ibid.
5. L. H. Gann and Peter J. Duignan (1986). The Hispanics in the United States: A History. Boulder, CO; Westview Press, p. xi.
6. Ibid.
7. Ibid., p. 16.
8. U.S. Census Bureau (1999). *Coming to America: A Profile of the nation's foreign-born.*
9. U.S. Census Bureau (1996). *Statistical Abstract of the United States,* 116th edition.
10. Richard Rodriguez (1982). *Hunger of Memory: The Education of Richard Rodriguez.* Toronto, Canada: Bantam Books.
11. Finnegan and Baraback (2005).
12. Julianne Malveaux (1998). Black and brown people: Coalition or competition? *Black Issues in Higher Education,* 15(20), November 26, p. 42.
13. Ibid.

Concepts and Questions

1. What are some of the reasons behind the rise in the U.S. Latino population? Why has this rise created tensions with Black Americans?
2. What does the term "Hispanic" mean to you? Do you think this term generalizes or specifies people's cultural origins?
3. How can different historical experiences create different worldviews? What is the American historical experience of your ethnic group and how has it shaped your worldview?
4. What do you see as the major differences and the major similarities between the Black American and Latino American historical experiences?
5. Do you agree or disagree with Nwosu's assertion that one's native language can provide a feeling of comfort and belonging? Why?
6. How does language serve as a means of maintaining group identity?
7. Discuss and contrast the communication styles of Black Americans, Latinos, and Euro-Americans. What areas carry the greatest potential to create misunderstanding and produce conflict?
8. What measures can you think of to alleviate the fear of many Black Americans that the gains they have made in civil rights can not be shared with other minorities?
9. Nwosu suggests that one way to lessen tensions between Blacks and Latinos is to "close the culture gap." What does he mean by this? Can you think of other "culture gaps"?

"Which Is My Good Leg?": Cultural Communication of Persons with Disabilities

Dawn O. Braithwaite

Charles A. Braithwaite

UNDERSTANDING COMMUNICATION OF PERSONS WITH DISABILITIES AS CULTURAL COMMUNICATION

Jonathan is an articulate, intelligent, 35-year-old professional man who has used a wheelchair since he became paraplegic when he was 20 years old. He recalls inviting a nondisabled woman out to dinner at a nice restaurant. When the waitperson came to take their order, she looked only at his date and asked, in a condescending tone, "And what would *he* like to eat for dinner?" At the end of the meal the waitperson presented Jonathan's date with the check and thanked her for her patronage.[1]

Kim describes her recent experience at the airport: "A lot of people always come up and ask can they push my wheelchair. And, I can do it myself. They were invading my space, concentration, doing what I wanted to do, which I enjoy doing; doing what I was doing *on my own*. . . . And each time I said, 'No, I'm doing fine!' People looked at me like I was strange, you know, crazy or something. One person started pushing my chair anyway. I said [in an angry tone], 'Don't touch the wheelchair.' And then she just looked at me like I'd slapped her in the face."

This original article first appeared in the eleventh edition. All rights reserved. Permission to reprint must be obtained from the authors and the publisher. Dr. Dawn O. Braithwaite is Willa Cather Professor and Professor of Communication Studies at the University of Nebraska-Lincoln. Dr. Charles A. Braithwaite is Director of International Studies at the University of Nebraska-Lincoln.

Jeff, a nondisabled student, was working on a group project for class that included Helen, who uses a wheelchair. He related an incident that really embarrassed him. "I wasn't thinking and I said to the group, 'Let's run over to the student union and get some coffee.' I was mortified when I looked over at Helen and remembered that she can't walk. I felt like a real jerk." Helen later described the incident with Jeff, recalling,

> At yesterday's meeting, Jeff said, "Let's run over to the union" and then he looked over at me and I thought he would die. It didn't bother me at all; in fact, I use that phrase myself. I felt bad that Jeff was so embarrassed, but I didn't know what to say. Later in the group meeting I made it a point to say, "I've got to be running along now." I hope that Jeff noticed and felt OK about what he said."

Although it may seem hard for some of us to believe, these scenarios represent common experiences for many people with physical disabilities and are indicative of what often happens when people with disabilities and nondisabled others communicate.

The passage of the Americans with Disabilities Act of 1990 (ADA), a "bill of rights" for persons with disabilities, highlighted the fact that they are now a large, vocal, and dynamic group within the United States (Braithwaite & Labrecque, 1994; Braithwaite & Thompson, 2000). People with disabilities constitute a large segment of the American population that has increased over the years; estimates of how many people in the United States have disabilities run as high as one in five (Cunningham & Coombs, 1997; Pardek, 1998).

There are two reasons for increases in the numbers of persons with disabilities. First, as the American population ages and has a longer life expectancy, more people will live long enough to develop disabilities, some of them related to age. Second, advances in medical technologies now allow persons with disabilities to survive life-threatening illnesses and injuries where survival was not possible in earlier times. For example, when actor Christopher Reeve became quadriplegic after a horse-riding accident in May 1995, advances in medical technology allowed him to survive his injuries and to live with a severe disability.

In the past, most people with disabilities were sheltered, and many spent their lives at home or living in institutions; today, they are very much a part of the American mainstream. Each of us will have contact with people who have disabilities within our families, among our friends, or in the workplace. Some of us will develop disabilities ourselves. Marie, a college student who was paralyzed after diving into a swimming pool, remarked:

> I knew there were disabled people around, but I never thought this would happen to me. I never even *knew* a disabled person before *I* became one. If before this happened, I saw a person in a wheelchair, I would have been uncomfortable and not known what to say.

Marie's comment highlights the fact that many nondisabled people feel uncomfortable, some extremely so, interacting with people who are disabled. As people with disabilities continue to live, work, and study in American culture, there is a need for people with and without disabilities to know how to communicate effectively.

DISABILITY AND CULTURAL COMMUNICATION

Our goal in this essay is to focus on communication between nondisabled persons and persons with disabilities as *intercultural communication* (Carbaugh, 1990). People with disabilities use a distinctive speech code that implies specific models of personhood, society, and strategic action that differ from those of nondisabled people. People with disabilities develop distinctive meanings, rules, and ways of speaking that act as a powerful resource for creating and reinforcing perceptions of cultural differences between people with and without disabilities. The distinctive verbal and nonverbal communication used by people with disabilities creates a sense of cultural identity that constitutes a unique social reality.

Several researchers have described the communication of disabled and nondisabled persons as intercultural communication (Braithwaite, 1990, 1996; Emry & Wiseman, 1987; Fox, Giles, Orbe, & Bourhis, 2000; Padden & Humphries, 1988). That is, we recognize that people with disabilities develop certain unique communicative characteristics that are not shared by the majority of nondisabled individuals. In fact, except for individuals who are born with disabilities, becoming disabled is similar to assimilating from being a member of the nondisabled majority to being a member of a minority culture (Braithwaite, 1990, 1996). The onset of a physical disability requires learning new ways of thinking and talking about oneself, and developing new ways of communicating with others.

Adopting a cultural view of disability in this chapter, we start by introducing communication problems that can arise between persons in the nondisabled culture and those in the disabled culture. Second, we discuss some of the weaknesses of the earlier approaches researchers used to understand communication between nondisabled and disabled persons. Third, we discuss research findings from interviews with people who have physical disabilities that show them engaged in a process of re-definition; that is, they critique the prevailing stereotypes about disability, and they communicate in order to redefine what it means to be part of the disabled culture. Last, we talk about important contributions both scholars and students of intercultural communication can make to improve relations between people with and without disabilities.

Challenges for Communicators Who Are Disabled

As we adopt a cultural view and attempt to understand the communicative challenges faced by people with disabilities, it is useful to understand what a disability is. We start by distinguishing between "disability" and "handicap." Even though people often use these two terms interchangeably in everyday conversation, their meanings are quite different. The two terms imply different relationships between persons with disabilities and the larger society. The term *disability* describes those limitations that a person can overcome or compensate for by some means. Crewe and Athelstan (1985) identify five "key life functions" that may be affected by disability: (a) mobility, (b) employment, (c) self-care, (d) social relationships, and (e) communication. Many individuals are able to compensate for physical challenges associated with the first three key life functions through assistive devices (e.g., using a wheelchair or cane or using hand controls to drive a car), through training (e.g., physical therapy or training on how to take care of one's personal needs), through assistance (e.g., hiring a personal care assistant), or through occupational therapy to find suitable employment.

A disability becomes a *handicap* when the physical or social environment interacts with it to impede a person in some aspect of his or her life (Crewe & Athelstan, 1985). For example, a disabled individual with paraplegia can function well in the physical environment using a wheelchair, ramps, and curb cuts, but he or she is handicapped when buildings and/or public transportation are not accessible to wheelchair users. When a society is willing and/or able to create adaptations, people with disabilities are able to lead increasingly independent lives, which is very important to their self-esteem and health (Braithwaite & Harter, 2000; DeLoach & Greer, 1981). For people with disabilities, personal control and independence are vitally important, and "maintenance of identity and self-worth are tied to the perceived ability to control the illness, minimize its intrusiveness, and be independent" (Lyons, Sullivan, Ritvo, & Coyne, 1995, p. 134). This does not mean that people with disabilities deny their physical condition, but rather that they find ways to manage it, to obtain whatever help they need, and to lead their lives (Braithwaite & Eckstein, 2003).

It is important to realize that the practical and technological accommodations that are made to adapt the physical environment for people with disabilities are useful for nondisabled people as well. Most of us are unaware of just how handicapped we would be without these physical adaptations. For example, the authors' offices are located on the upper floors of our respective office buildings, and we often get to our office via elevator. We know that stairs take up a significant amount of space in a building. Space used for the stairwell on each level takes the place of at least one office per floor. The most space-efficient way to get people to the second floor would be a climbing rope, which would necessitate only a relatively small opening on each floor. However, how many of us could climb a rope to reach our offices? Clearly, we would be handicapped without stairs or elevators. When a student is walking with a heavy load of library books, automatic door openers, ramps, curb cuts, elevators, and larger doorways become important environmental adaptations that everyone can use and appreciate.

Physical limitations become handicaps for all of us when the physical environment cannot be adapted to meet our shortcomings.

Challenges to Relationships of People with Disabilities

Although it is possible to identify and find accommodations for physical challenges associated with mobility, self-care, and employment, the two key life functions of social relationships and communication often present much more formidable challenges. It is often less difficult to detect and correct physical barriers than it is to deal with the insidious social barriers facing people with disabilities. Coleman and DePaulo (1991) label these social barriers as "psychological disabling," which is common in Western culture where "much value is placed on physical bodies and physical attractiveness" (p. 64).

When people with disabilities begin relationships with nondisabled people, the challenges associated with forming any new relationship are often greater. For nondisabled people, this may be due to lack of experience interacting with people who are disabled, which leads to high uncertainty about how to interact with a person who is disabled (Braithwaite & Labrecque, 1994). Nondisabled persons may be uncertain about what to say or how to act. They are afraid of saying or doing the wrong thing or of hurting the feelings of the person with the disability, much as Jeff was with his group member, Helen, in the example at the beginning of this chapter. As a result, nondisabled persons may feel overly self-conscious, and their actions may be constrained, self-controlled, and rigid because they feel uncomfortable and uncertain (Belgrave & Mills, 1981; Braithwaite 1990; Dahnke, 1983; Higgins, 1992). Their behaviors, in turn, will appear uninterested or unaccepting to the person who is disabled. The nondisabled person will need to figure out how to communicate appropriately. Higgins (1992) pointed out that sometimes these communication attempts are not successful: "Wishing to act in a way acceptable to those with disabilities, they may unknowingly act offensively, patronizing disabled people with unwanted sympathy" (Higgins, 1992, p. 105).

High levels of uncertainty can negatively affect interaction and relationship development between people. It becomes easier to avoid that person rather than deal with not knowing what to do or say. Interestingly, researchers have found that the type of disability a person possesses does not change the way nondisabled persons react to them (Fichten, Robillard, Tagalakis, & Amsel, 1991). Although uncertainty reduction theory can be overly simplistic, especially when applied to ongoing relationships, this theory is useful in understanding some of the initial discomfort nondisabled people may feel when interacting with a stranger or early acquaintance who is disabled. Understanding the effects of uncertainty, people with disabilities work to devise ways to help nondisabled others reduce their discomfort (Braithwaite, 1990, 1996; Braithwaite & Labrecque, 1994).

Even when a nondisabled person tries to "say the right thing" and wants to communicate acceptance to the person with the disability, his or her nonverbal behavior may communicate rejection and avoidance instead (Thompson, 1982). For example, people with disabilities have observed that many nondisabled persons may keep a greater physical distance, avoid eye contact, avoid mentioning the disability, or cut the conversation short (Braithwaite, 1990, 1991, 1996). These nondisabled persons may be doing their best not to show their discomfort or not crowd the person with the disability. However, the outcome may be that the person with the disability perceives they do not want to interact. In this case, a person's disability becomes a handicap in the social environment as it can block the development of a relationship with a nondisabled person, who finds the interaction too uncomfortable.

Complicating matters, many nondisabled people hold stereotypes of people from the disabled culture. Coleman and DePaulo (1991) discuss some of these stereotypes concerning disabled people:

> For example, they often perceive them as dependent, socially introverted, emotionally unstable, depressed, hypersensitive, and easily offended, especially with regard to their disability. In addition, disabled people are often presumed to differ from nondisabled people in moral character, social skills, and political orientation. (p. 69)

Stereotypes like these do nothing but raise the level of uncertainty and discomfort the nondisabled person is experiencing.

When nondisabled persons make the effort to overcome discomfort and stereotypes to interact with people from the disabled culture, they often find themselves with conflicting expectations. On the one hand, Americans are taught to "help the handicapped." At the same time, Americans conceptualize persons as "individuals" who "have rights" and "make their own choices" (Carbaugh, 1988) and thus are taught to treat all people equally. However, when nondisabled persons encounter a person with a disability, this model of personhood creates a real dilemma. How can you both help a person and treat that person equally? For example, should you help a person with a disability open a door or try to help him up if he falls? If you are working with a blind person, should you help her find a doorway or get her lunch at the cafeteria? These dilemmas often result in high uncertainty for nondisabled people, who often end up trying to give more help than people with disabilities want or need (Braithwaite & Eckstein, 2003). In the end, it may simply seem easier to avoid situations in which you might have to interact with a disabled person rather than face feelings of discomfort and uncertainty (this is how many people react to communicating with people from other cultures). However, avoidance is not a very good solution in the end, especially if this person is to be a member of your work group or family, for example.

It should not be surprising to learn that most people with disabilities are well aware of the feelings and fears many nondisabled persons have. In fact, in research interviews, people with disabilities tell us they believe they "can just tell" who is uncomfortable around them or not. They are able to provide a great amount of detail on both the verbal and nonverbal signals of discomfort and avoidance of nondisabled persons (Braithwaite, 1990, 1996; Braithwaite & Eckstein, 2003), and they develop communication strategies to help them interact in these situations. For example, people with disabilities tell us that when they meet nondisabled persons, they will communicate in ways designed to get the discomfort "out of the way." They want the nondisabled person to treat them as a "person like anyone else," rather than focus solely on their disability (Braithwaite, 1991, 1996). For example, they may talk about topics they believe they have in common with the nondisabled person, such as cooking, sports, or music.

People with disabilities develop strategies to help them handle situations in which they may need help from nondisabled others in order to help reduce the uncertainty and discomfort of the nondisabled person (Braithwaite & Eckstein, 2003). For example, two men who are wheelchair users who need help getting out of their van in parking lots described how they plan ahead to get the help they need:

> Well, I have a mobile phone. . . . I will call into the store and let the store manager or whoever know, "Hey, we're in a White minivan and if you look out your window, you can see us! We're two guys in wheelchairs; can you come out and help us get out of the van?"

These men plan ahead to avoid having to ask for help and putting nondisabled strangers in potentially uncomfortable communication situations. Other people described situations in which they might accept help that they did not need because they understood that refusing help might increase the discomfort and uncertainty of the nondisabled person.

CHANGING THE FOCUS OF RESEARCHERS

When we first began looking at the research on communication between nondisabled and disabled persons, three problems came clearly to the forefront (for a recent summary, see Thompson, 2000). First, very little was known about the communication behavior of disabled people. Although a few researchers have studied disabled persons' communication, most of them have studied nondisabled persons' *reactions* to disabled others. These studies on "attitudes toward disabled persons" are analogous to the many studies that look at majority members' attitudes toward other "minority groups." A look at the intercultural communication literature as a whole reveals few studies from the perspective of persons representing minority groups. Although there has been some improvement over the years, there is still relatively little information on communication from the perspective of people with disabilities.

A second, related problem is that many researchers talk *about* people with disabilities, not *with* them. People with disabilities have rarely been represented in survey data. Most often these studies consist of nondisabled people reporting their impressions of disabled people. In experimental studies, the disabled person is most often "played" by a nondisabled person using a wheelchair (and not surprisingly, most people can tell that this is not a disabled person!). There are still too few studies that give us a sense of how people with and without disabilities communicate in actual conversations.

Third, and most significant, the research has most often taken the perspective of the nondisabled person; that is, researchers tend to focus on what people with disabilities should do to make nondisabled others feel more comfortable. Coming from this perspective, researchers do not consider the effects of communication on the person with the disability. For example, several studies have found that nondisabled persons are more comfortable when people with disabilities disclose about their disability, so the researchers suggest that disabled people should self-disclose to make nondisabled others more comfortable. Braithwaite (1991) points out that these researchers have forgotten to look at how self-disclosing might affect people who are disabled. Therefore, what we see coming from much of the nondisabled-oriented research is an *ethnocentric bias* that ignores the perspective of people from the disabled culture. Although there has been more research from the perspective of disabled interactants in recent years, there are still too few empirical studies, and we are left with a very incomplete picture of the communication of people who are disabled.

In the remainder of this essay, we will present selected findings from ongoing studies conducted from the perspective of people with disabilities that help us understand the communication of people with and without disabilities from a cultural perspective. These research findings come from more than 100 in-depth interviews completed by the first author with adults who are physically disabled. All of these people have disabilities that are visible to an observer, and none of them has significant communication-related disabilities (e.g., blindness, deafness, speech impairments). The goal of the research has been to describe communication with nondisabled people from the frame of reference of people who are disabled. Doing research by talking *with* people who are disabled helps to bring out information important to them and allows people with disabilities to describe experiences from their own cultural framework.

PROCESS OF REDEFINITION

A central theme emerging from the interviews is what we call *redefinition;* that is, people who are disabled critique the prevailing stereotypes about being disabled, they create new ways of perceiving themselves and their disability, and they develop ways of communicating as a result. We were able to see three types of redefinition: (a) redefining the self as part of a "new" culture, (b) redefining the concept of disability, and (c) redefining disability for the dominant culture.

Redefining the Self as Part of the Disabled Culture

In research interviews, many people with disabilities talk about themselves as part of a minority group or a culture. For some of the interviewees, this definition crosses disability lines; that is, their definition of "disabled" includes all those who have disabilities. For others, the definition is not as broad; when they think of disability, they are thinking about others with the same type of disability they have. For example, some of the people with mobility-related disabilities also included blind and deaf people with the discussed disability, and others talked only about other wheelchair users. However narrowly or broadly they define it, many do see themselves as part of a minority culture. For example, one of the interviewees said that being disabled "is like *West Side Story*. Tony and Maria; White and Puerto Rican. They were afraid of each other; ignorant of each other's cultures. People are people." Another man explained his view:

> First of all, I belong to a subculture [of disability] because of the way I have to deal with things, being in the medical system, welfare. There is the subculture. . . . I keep one foot in the nondisabled culture and one foot in my own culture. One of the reasons I do that is so that I don't go nuts.

This man's description of the "balancing act" between cultures demonstrates that membership in the disabled culture has several similarities to the experiences of other American cultural groups. Many of the interviewees have likened their own experiences to those of other cultural groups, particularly to the experiences of American people of color. Interviewees describe the loss of status and power that comes from being disabled, and they perceive that many people are uncomfortable with them simply because they are different.

When taking a cultural view, it is important to recognize that not everyone comes to the culture the same way. Some people are born with disabilities, and others acquire them later. For those people who are not born with a disability, membership in the culture is a process that emerges over time. For some, the process is an incremental one, as in the case of a person with a degenerative disease such as multiple sclerosis that develops over many years. For a person who has a sudden-onset disability, such as breaking one's neck in an accident and "waking up a quadriplegic," moving from the majority (a "normal" person) to the minority (a person who is disabled) may happen in a matter of seconds. This sudden transition into the disabled culture presents many significant challenges of redefinition and readjustment in all facets of an individual's life (Braithwaite, 1990, 1996; Goffman, 1963).

If disability is a culture, when does one become part of that culture? Even though a person is physically disabled, how one redefines oneself, from "normal" or nondisabled to disabled, is a process that develops over time. It is important to understand that becoming physically disabled does not mean one immediately has an awareness of being part of the disabled culture (Braithwaite, 1990, 1996). In fact, for most people, adjusting to disability happens in a series of stages or phases (Braithwaite, 1990; DeLoach & Greer, 1981; Padden & Humphries, 1988). DeLoach and Greer (1981) describe three phases of an individual's adjustment to disability: (1) stigma isolation, (2) stigma recognition, and (3) stigma incorporation. Their model helps us understand what is occurring in the process of adjustment to disability as acculturation. During this process, persons with disabilities progress from the onset of their disability to membership in the disabled culture.

Imagine the experience of Mark, a college student majoring in physical education who has a car accident and wakes up to find he is paralyzed. Mark enters the first phase, *stigma isolation,* upon becoming disabled. At this point, he is focusing on rehabilitation and all of the physical changes and challenges he is experiencing. It is likely that Mark has not yet noticed the changes in his social relationships and communication with nondisabled others.

The second phase, *stigma recognition,* begins when Mark realizes that his life and relationships have changed dramatically and he will need to find ways to minimize the effects of his disability as much as possible. Mark may try to return to normal routines and old relationships; for example, he may return to college. This can be a frustrating phase, because often things have changed more than the person at first realizes. Mark may try to reestablish his old relationships, only to find that his friends are no longer comfortable with him or that they can no longer share activities they had in common. For example, Mark may find it hard to maintain relationships with his friends from his softball team. Mark's friends, who were visiting him around the clock in the hospital, may not know what to do or say around him and may even start to avoid him. It is at this point that individuals who are disabled start to become aware that they are now interacting as members of a different culture than they were before, and they begin to assimilate the new culture into their identity and behavior (Braithwaite, 1990, 1996). Mark may notice how his friends are treating him, and he may not enjoy their company much at this point either.

This begins the third phase, what DeLoach and Greer (1981) call *stigma incorporation.* At this point, persons with a disability begin to integrate being disabled into their identity, their definition of self. The person begins to understand both the positive and negative aspects of being disabled and begins to develop ways to overcome and cope with the negative aspects of disability (DeLoach & Greer, 1981). In this stage of adjustment, people with disabilities develop ways of behaving and communicating so that they are able to function successfully in the nondisabled culture (Braithwaite, 1990, 1996). For example, after all he has experienced, Mark may find he now has an interest in psychology and sees more career opportunities there. When he switches his major, he finds he has a knack for statistics that he never knew he had, organizes a study group for his statistics class, and starts to make new friends.

Braithwaite (1996) argues that stigma incorporation represents what Morse and Johnson (1991) have labeled "regaining wellness," which occurs when individuals begin to take back control of their own lives and relationships, live as independently as possible, and adapt to new ways of doing things in their lives. Individuals develop ways of communicating with nondisabled others that help them live successfully as part of the disabled and nondisabled cultures simultaneously (Braithwaite, 1990, 1991, 1996; Braithwaite & Labrecque, 1994; Emry & Wiseman, 1987). This is what researchers call interability, intergroup communication (see Fox et al., 2000).

In this third phase, then, the person incorporates the role of disability into his or her identity and into his or her life. One man said, "You're the same person you were. You just don't do the same things you did before." Another put it this way: "If anyone refers to me as an amputee, that is guaranteed to get me madder than hell! I don't deny the leg amputation, but I am *me*. I am a whole person. *One*." It is during this phase that people can come to terms with both the negative and positive changes in their lives. One woman expressed it this way:

> I find myself telling people that this has been the worst thing that has happened to me. It has also been one of the best things. It forced me to examine what I felt about myself . . . my confidence is grounded in me, not in other people. As a woman, I am not as dependent on clothes, measurements, but what's inside me.

The late actor Christopher Reeve demonstrated the concept of stigma incorporation in an interview with Barbara Walters, four months after his devastating accident:

> You also gradually discover, as I'm discovering, that your body is not you. The mind and the spirit must take over. And that's the challenge as you move from obsessing about "Why me?" and "It's not fair" and move into "Well, what is the potential?" And, now, four months down the line I see opportunities and potential I wasn't capable of seeing back in Virginia in June . . . genuine joy and being alive means more. Every moment is more intense than it ever was.

One implication of this example is that stigma incorporation, becoming part of the disabled culture, is a process that develops over time.

Redefining Disability

A second type of redefinition discussed by interviewees is redefining the concept of disability. For example, one interviewee explained, "People will say, 'Thank God I'm not handicapped.' And I'll say, 'Let's see, how tall are you? Tell me how you get something off that shelf up there!'" His goal in this interchange is to force others to see disability as one of many *characteristics* of a person. From this perspective, everyone is handicapped in one way or another by our height, weight, sex, ethnicity, or physical attributes, and people must work to overcome those characteristics that are handicapping. Short people may need a stool to reach something on a high shelf, and people who are very tall may be stared at and certainly will not be able to drive small, economy-size cars. Most middle-aged professors cannot climb a rope to their office and need the accommodation of stairs. Similarly, people with disabilities must adapt to the physical and social challenges presented to them. One interviewee, who conducts workshops on disability awareness, talked about how he helps nondisabled people redefine disability:

> I will say to people, "How many of you made the clothes that you're wearing?" "How many of you grew the food that you ate yesterday?" "How many of you built the house that you live in?" Nobody raises their hand. Then after maybe five of those, I'll say, "And I bet you think you're independent." And I'll say, "I'll bet you, if we could measure how independent you feel in your life versus how independent I feel in mine, then I would rate just as high you do. And yet here I am 'depending' on people to get me dressed, undressed, on and off the john, etc. It's all in our heads, folks. Nobody is really independent." I can see them kind of go "Yeah, I never thought of it that way." And they begin to understand how it is that somebody living with this situation can feel independent. That independence really is a feeling and an attitude. It's not a physical reality.

It is also important to remember that, like any characteristic that we have, disability is context-specific. For example, a blind person will function better in a dark room than sighted persons, who will find themselves handicapped in that environment. The first author of this chapter spent several days at Gallaudet University in Washington, DC. At Gallaudet, where most students are deaf, it was the *author* who was disabled, as she needed interpreters to talk with the students there. At Gallaudet, people talk about being part of Deaf culture, but not about being disabled.

Redefining disability can also be reflected through changing the language we use to talk about disability.

One interviewee objected to the label "handicapped person," preferring the label "persons with a handicapping condition." He explained why: "You emphasize that person's identity and then you do something about the condition." The goal is to speak in ways that emphasize the *person*, rather than the disability. One interviewee, who had polio as a child, rejected the term "polio victim" and preferred to label herself as "a person whose arms and legs do not function very well." Talking with disability activists around the nation, we find many different approaches to language and labels about disability. One way we have found to accentuate the person is to talk about "*people* with disabilities" rather than "disabled people." The goal is to emphasize the person first, before introducing the disability, much like using the label "people of color." These are all forms of strategic action that help to create and maintain a sense of unique cultural identity among persons with disabilities (Braithwaite, 1996; Braithwaite & Thompson, 2000).

Redefining disability is also reflected in sensitizing oneself to commonly used labels for being disabled, such as being a "polio victim" or an "arthritis sufferer," or being "confined to a wheelchair" or "wheelchair bound." When trying to redefine disability as a characteristic of the person, one can change these phrases to a "person with polio," a "person who has arthritis," or a "wheelchair user." Some researchers suggest that we avoid talking about the communication of disabled and nondisabled people and instead use the phrase "interability communication" (see Fox et al., 2000). At first glance, it may be tempting to think this is no more than an attempt at political correctness, but those who understand language and culture know how strongly the words we use influence our perception of others, and theirs of us. The way people with disabilities are labeled will affect how they are seen by others and how they perceive themselves.

One of the more humorous and, at the same time, powerful examples of language regarding disability is the use of "TABs" to refer to nondisabled people. "TAB" is short for "temporarily able-bodied." One interviewee joked, "Everyone is a TAB. . . . I just got mine earlier than you!" Being called a TAB serves to remind nondisabled persons that no one is immune from disability. From this perspective, everyone is becoming disabled! It certainly does challenge our perspective to think about that. To end our discussion of disability and language, whatever labels we choose to use, it is clear that the language both creates and reflects the view of people with disabilities and disabled culture.

In addition to redefining disability, the interviewees also redefined "assisting devices" such as wheelchairs or canes. For example, one man told the following story about redefining his prosthetic leg:

> Now there were two girls about eight playing and I was in my shorts. And I'll play games with them and say "Which is my good leg?" And that gets them to thinking. Well, this one [he pats his artificial leg] is not nearly as old as the other one!

Another interviewee redefined assisting devices this way: "Do you know what a cane is? It's a portable railing! The essence of a wheelchair is a seat and wheels. Now, I don't know that a tricycle is not doing the exact same thing." Redefining assisting devices helps us see how they might mean different things to disabled and nondisabled persons. For example, several interviewees expressed frustration with people who played with their wheelchairs. One interviewee exclaimed, "This chair is not a toy, it is *part of me*. When you touch my chair, you are touching *me*." Another woman, a business executive, expanded on this by saying, "I don't know why people who push my chair feel compelled to make car sounds as they do it." In these examples, then, the problem is not the disability or the assisting device, but how one perceives the person using them.

Redefining Disability within Nondisabled Culture

Last, as people with disabilities redefine themselves as members of a culture, they also define what it means to have a disabling condition. Our experience is that people with disabilities are concerned with changing the view of disability within the larger culture (Braithwaite, 1990, 1996). Most people with disabilities we have encountered view themselves as public educators on disability issues. People told stories about taking the time to educate children and adults on what it means to be disabled. They are actively working to change the view of themselves as helpless, as victims, or as ill, and the ensuing treatment such a view brings. One wheelchair user said:

> People do not consider you, they consider the chair first. I was in a store with my purchases on my lap and

money on my lap. The clerk looked at my companion and not at me and said, "Cash or charge?"

This incident with the clerk represents a story we heard from *every* person in some form or another, just as it happened to Jonathan and his date at the beginning of this chapter. One woman, who has multiple sclerosis and uses a wheelchair, told of shopping for lingerie with her husband accompanying her. When they were in front of the lingerie counter, the clerk repeatedly talked only to her husband, saying, "And what size does she want?" The woman told her the size, and the clerk looked at the husband and said, "And what color does she want?"

Persons with disabilities recognize that nondisabled persons often see them as disabled first and as a person second (if at all). The most common theme expressed by people with disabilities in all of the interviews is that they want to be *seen and treated as a person first.* One man explained what he thought was important to remember: "A lot of people think that handicapped people are 'less than' and I find that it's not true at all. . . . Abling people, giving them their power back, empowering them." The interviewees rejected those situations or behaviors that would not lead them to be seen. A man with muscular dystrophy talked about the popular Labor Day telethon:

> I do not believe in those goddamned telethons . . . they're horrible, absolutely horrible. They get into the self-pity, you know, and disabled folk do not need that. Hit people in terms of their attitudes then try to deal with and process their feelings. And the telethons just go for the heart and leave it there.

One man suggested what he thought was a more useful approach:

> What I am concerned with is anything that can do away with the "us" versus "them" distinction. Well, you and I are anatomically different, but we're two human beings! And at the point, we can sit down and communicate eyeball to eyeball; the quicker you do that, the better!

Individually and collectively, people with disabilities do identify themselves as part of a culture. They are involved in a process of redefinition of themselves, and of disability. They desire to help nondisabled people understand and internalize a redefinition of people of the disabled culture as "persons first."

CONCLUSION

The research we have discussed highlights the usefulness of viewing disability from a cultural perspective. People with disabilities do recognize themselves as part of a culture, and understanding communication and relationships from this perspective sheds new light on the communication challenges that exist. Some time ago, Emry and Wiseman (1987) first argued for the usefulness of intercultural training about disability issues. They called for unfreezing old attitudes about disability and refreezing new ones. Our experience indicates that people with disabilities would agree with this goal.

We have asked people with disabilities whether they had training in communication during or after their rehabilitation. We anticipated that they would have received information and training to prepare them for changes in their communication and relationships after becoming disabled. We speculated that this education would be especially critical for those who experience sudden-onset disabilities because their self-concepts and all of their relationships would undergo such radical changes. Surprisingly, we found that less than 30 percent of the interviewees received disability-related communication training.

We believe intercultural communication scholars can help design research and training that could help make the transition from majority to minority an easier one (Braithwaite, 1990; Emry & Wiseman, 1987). We are encouraged by some advances that are taking place in educational and organizational settings (e.g., Colvert & Smith, 2000; Herold, 2000; Worley, 2000). We also see the need for research that expands to different types of disabilities—for example, for those with invisible disabilities (e.g., emphysema, diabetes) and socially stigmatized disabilities such as HIV. Overall, we see important contributions for communication scholars to make. When Braithwaite and Thompson (2000) published their *Handbook of Communication and People with Disabilities,* they were struck by how many researchers in communication studies are now studying disability communication and how many of these scholars are disabled. Clearly, the future does look brighter than when we began our work in disability and communication some years back. However, we still have a long way to go.

We do believe that students of intercultural communication should have an advantage in being able to better understand the perspective of people with disabilities, as presented in this chapter. We hope that you will be able to adapt and apply intercultural communication concepts and skills to interactions with persons in the disabled culture. We believe that people with disabilities themselves will better understand their own experience if they study intercultural communication and come to understand the cultural aspects of disability.

In closing, taking an intercultural perspective on communication and disability culture leads us to suggest the following practical proscriptions and prescriptions.

DON'T:

- *Avoid* communication with people who are disabled simply because you are uncomfortable or unsure.
- *Assume* that people with disabilities cannot speak for themselves or do things for themselves.
- *Force* your help on people with disabilities.
- *Use terms* such as "handicapped," "physically challenged," "crippled," "victim," and the like, unless requested to do so by people with disabilities.
- *Assume* that a disability defines who a person is.

DO:

- *Remember* that people with disabilities have experienced others' discomfort before and likely understand how you might be feeling.
- *Assume* that people with disabilities can do something unless they communicate otherwise.
- *Let people with disabilities tell you* if they want something, what they want, and when they want it. If a person with a disability refuses your help, don't go ahead and help anyway.
- *Use terms* such as "*people* with disabilities" rather than "disabled people." The goal is to stress the *person first*, before the disability.
- *Treat* people with disabilities as *persons first*, recognizing that you are not dealing with a disabled person but with a *person* who *has* a disability. This means actively seeking the humanity of the person with whom you are speaking, and focusing on individual characteristics instead of superficial physical appearance. Without diminishing the

significance of a person's physical disability, make a real effort to focus on all the many other aspects of that person as you communicate.

Note

1. The quotes and anecdotes in this chapter come from in-depth interviews with people who have visible physical disabilities. The names of the participants in these interviews have been changed to protect their privacy.

References

Belgrave, F. Z., & Mills, J. (1981). Effect upon desire for social interaction with a physically disabled person of mentioning the disability in different contexts. *Journal of Applied Social Psychology, 11*, 44–57.

Braithwaite, D. O. (1990). From majority to minority: An analysis of cultural change from nondisabled to disabled. *International Journal of Intercultural Relations, 14*, 465–483.

Braithwaite, D. O. (1991). "Just how much did that wheelchair cost?": Management of privacy boundaries by persons with disabilities. *Western Journal of Speech Communication, 55*, 254–274.

Braithwaite, D. O. (1996). "Persons first": Expanding communicative choices by persons with disabilities. In E. B. Ray (Ed.), *Communication and disenfranchisement: Social health issues and implications* (pp. 449–464). Mahwah, NJ: Erlbaum.

Braithwaite, D. O., & Eckstein, N. (2003). Reconceptualizing supportive interactions: How persons with disabilities communicatively manage assistance. *Journal of Applied Communication Research, 31*, 1–26.

Braithwaite, D. O., & Harter, L. (2000). Communication and the management of dialectical tensions in the personal relationships of people with disabilities. In D. O. Braithwaite & T. L. Thompson (Eds.), *Handbook of communication and people with disabilities: Research and application* (pp. 17–36). Mahwah, NJ: Erlbaum.

Braithwaite, D. O., & Labrecque, D. (1994). Responding to the Americans with Disabilities Act: Contributions of interpersonal communication research and training. *Journal of Applied Communication Research, 22*, 287–294.

Braithwaite, D. O., & Thompson, T. L. (Eds.). (2000). *Handbook of communication and people with disabilities: Research and application*. Mahwah, NJ: Erlbaum.

Carbaugh, D. (1988). *Talking American*. Norwood, NJ: Ablex.

Carbaugh, D. (Ed.). (1990). *Cultural communication and intercultural contact*. Hillsdale, NJ: Erlbaum.

Coleman, L. M., & DePaulo, B. M. (1991). Uncovering the human spirit: Moving beyond disability and "missed" communications. In N. Coupland, H. Giles, &

J. M. Wiemann (Eds.), *Miscommunication and problematic talk* (pp. 61–84). Newbury Park, CA: Sage.

Covert, A. L., & Smith, J. W. (2000). What is reasonable: Workplace communication and people who are disabled. In D. O. Braithwaite & T. L. Thompson (Eds.), *Handbook of communication and people with disabilities: Research and application* (pp. 141–158). Mahwah, NJ: Erlbaum.

Crewe, N., & Athelstan, G. (1985). *Social and psychological aspects of physical disability.* Minneapolis: University of Minnesota, Department of Independent Study and University Resources.

Cunningham, C., & Coombs, N. (1997). *Information access and adaptive technology.* Phoenix, AZ: Oryx Press.

Dahnke, G. L. (1983). Communication and handicapped and nonhandicapped persons: Toward a deductive theory. In M. Burgoon (Ed.), *Communication yearbook 6* (pp. 92–135). Beverly Hills, CA: Sage.

DeLoach, C., & Greer, B. G. (1981). *Adjustment to severe physical disability: A metamorphosis.* New York: McGraw-Hill.

Emry, R., & Wiseman, R. L. (1987). An intercultural understanding of nondisabled and disabled persons' communication. *International Journal of Intercultural Relations, 11,* 7–27.

Fichten, C. S., Robillard, K., Tagalakis, V., & Amsel, R. (1991). Casual interaction between college students with various disabilities and their nondisabled peers: The internal dialogue. *Rehabilitation Psychology, 36,* 3–20.

Fox, S. A., Giles, H., Orbe, M., & Bourhis, R. (2000). Interability communication: Theoretical perspectives. In D. O. Braithwaite & T. L. Thompson (Eds.), *Handbook of communication and people with disabilities: Research and application* (pp. 193–222). Mahwah, NJ: Erlbaum.

Goffman, E. (1963). *Stigma: Notes on the management of spoiled identity.* New York: Simon & Schuster.

Herold, K. P. (2000). Communication strategies in employment interviews for applicants with disabilities. In D. O. Braithwaite & T. L. Thompson (Eds.), *Handbook of communication and people with disabilities: Research and application* (pp. 159–175). Mahwah, NJ: Erlbaum.

Higgins, P. C. (1992). *Making disability: Exploring the social transformation of human variation.* Springfield, IL: Charles C. Thomas.

Lyons, R. F., Sullivan, M. J. L., Ritvo, P. G., & Coyne, J. C. (1995). *Relationships in chronic illness and disability.* Thousand Oaks, CA: Sage.

Morse, J. M., & Johnson, J. L. (1991). *The illness experience: Dimensions of suffering.* Newbury Park, CA: Sage.

Padden, C., & Humphries, T. (1988). *Deaf in America: Voices from a culture.* Cambridge, MA: Harvard University Press.

Pardeck, J. T. (1998). *Social work after the Americans with Disabilities Act: New challenges and opportunities for social service professionals.* Westport, CT: Auburn House.

Thompson, T. L. (1982). Disclosure as a disability management strategy: A review and conclusions. *Communication Quarterly, 30,* 196–202.

Thompson, T. L. (2000). A history of communication and disability research: The way we were. In D. O. Braithwaite & T. L. Thompson (Eds.), *Handbook of communication and people with disabilities: Research and application* (pp. 1–14). Mahwah, NJ: Erlbaum.

Worley, D. W. (2000). Communication and students with disabilities on college campuses. In D. O. Braithwaite & T. L. Thompson (Eds.), *Handbook of communication and people with disabilities: Research and application* (pp. 125–139). Mahwah, NJ: Erlbaum.

Concepts and Questions

1. In what ways does becoming disabled lead to changes in a person's communication patterns?

2. What are some of the cultural problems inherent in communication between nondisabled and disabled persons?

3. Why do Braithwaite and Braithwaite believe you should learn about the communication patterns of disabled persons? What purpose will be served by your knowing this information?

4. Give examples of what Braithwaite and Braithwaite mean when they say that "the distinctive verbal and nonverbal communication used by persons with disabilities creates a sense of cultural identity that constitutes a unique social reality"?

5. How would you distinguish between *disability* and *handicap*?

6. Why is nonverbal communication a factor when nondisabled persons and persons with disabilities engage in communication?

7. Enumerate the problems Braithwaite and Braithwaite describe relating to the current research being conducted on persons with disabilities.

8. What is meant by the term *redefinition*?

9. How would you answer the following question: If disability is a culture, then when does one become part of that culture?

In Plain Sight: Gay and Lesbian Communication and Culture

WILLIAM F. EADIE

Some of you will be eager to read this chapter, and others will want to avoid it. That is how strong are people's feelings about lesbian and gay culture in the United States today. Many college students see anyone who seems to exhibit same-sex attraction as people who are somehow threatening. Some may think that lesbians and gays rock the boat too much; others may believe that lesbians and gays are simply strange and thus are to be avoided. Students committed to their religious beliefs may see their lesbian and gay classmates as people who need to be saved—to be rescued from their sinful ways. Some students may see classmates they consider to be lesbian or gay to be easy targets for bullying or even abuse. Some students and their parents may worry that lesbian and gay faculty members will attempt to "recruit" students who are in their classes. Students who know that they are lesbian or gay may find that this chapter does not express their experiences and views in strong-enough terms. Lesbian women may be uncomfortable with a male author's attempt to summarize what is common about the lesbian and gay male experience. Students who are questioning their sexuality may find that reading this chapter helps them, or they may find that it confuses them all the more. In short, there are so many different potential mindsets that readers will have when beginning this essay that it will be impossible to address all of them.

That said, I am going to present some viewpoints on how communication, in its various forms, works to create lesbian and gay culture in the United States. I use the term "viewpoints" because there is no precise way to define, measure, and track developments in lesbian and gay culture, so we have to rely on observers to analyze and present what they see. Most of those viewpoints will be backed by data collected through systematic research, but some will reflect general observations of societal trends. And, as I selected and organized the information that appears in this chapter, my own viewpoint will predominate. It is thus only fair that you know something about the personal history and perspective I bring to writing the chapter.

I am a gay man who recently turned 60. My youth was "pre-Stonewall;" that is, I finished my undergraduate degree a year before a group of drag queens, who were being hassled by undercover police officers, began a demonstration in front of the Stonewall Bar in the Greenwich Village section of New York City on June 28, 1969. The demonstration attracted scores of gays and lesbians to the scene, and what came to be known as the Stonewall Riots began the Gay Liberation movement.

I was raised in a comfortable but conservative environment, and in elementary school I was branded as a "sissy." As I was not terribly coordinated, I was among the last picked for teams on the playground, and I was more interested in the performing arts than I was in sports. My parents insisted, however, that I should be engaged in doing "boy" things, so I tried every imaginable sport, and I became a very active participant in Scouting (Cub Scouts, Boy Scouts, Explorers). Some gay men report feeling more affinity and comfort with women, but I was not one of those. I was happiest being with one best male friend, and I have always had a male best friend, and sometimes more than one close male friend, throughout my life.

As an undergraduate, my best male friend was openly gay. Going to college had been a liberating experience for me, but I was still very emotionally tied to my parents, who on more than one occasion had said negative things about gays. Secretly, I was pleased to be able to rebel against my parents' authority by having a gay friend, though I never told them about his sexual orientation. For his part, my friend became convinced over the several years we were in school together, that I, too, was gay. He started taking me to gay bars, hoping I would take the hint, and when I didn't he decided to seduce me. I enjoyed the experience, but the thought of rebelling *that* much against my parents' hopes and dreams frightened me. I promptly declared that I was not gay and proceeded to stay in the closet for twenty more years.

After I finally did come out, to myself and to others, I began to reflect on those years. I realized that I knew all along that I was gay but was not willing to admit it to myself for fear that being open about my sexuality would ruin my relationships with my family and my prospects for success in life. In retrospect, I understood that being honest probably would have made my life even better than I imagined at the time. I was not ready to come out before my father died. I came out to my mother, and she was not at all happy about it. Over time, though, she decided that I was still the son she knew and loved; only now she knew a little more about me. As she aged and dementia set in, however, she took to asking me how my wife and children were doing. I always replied, "Everyone is just fine, Mom."

Today, I am quite comfortable with my sexuality. I don't mind if people know that I am gay, but I don't make a big deal of it, either. If you met me, you probably would not be surprised to learn that I was gay, but neither would you want to pin a huge "GAY" button on my shirt. I still love the performing arts, and I sing with two choruses, one of them a gay chorus. I'm still not very proficient at competitive sports, but I enjoy noncompetitive activities such as walking, bicycling, and recreational skiing. I'm not nearly as uncomfortable around women as I was when I was younger. And, it pains me that Scouting, an organization from which I benefited a great deal, has chosen to discriminate openly against boys who are or who might be gay.

My experience has helped me to see that the major issue facing lesbians and gays in U.S. society is that it is easy to hide. Defying societal pressures and choosing to live openly as a lesbian or gay man is thus a political act, one that has ramifications, both positive and negative, for many of our everyday interactions. And, it is from those everyday interactions that cultural differences are created.

Soon, I will elaborate how this personal information becomes political. I will include material on the "outsider" status that lesbians and gay men feel in society, the media's role in creating and perpetuating stereotypes, and the processes by which those stereotypes have been changing. I will discuss the coming-out process, the role of communication in that process, and how gay men and lesbians eventually are able to achieve intimacy and find themselves a community. I will discuss how people manage the tensions of displaying their sexuality to others, how public spaces are made safe for communication, how same-sex partners negotiate sexual attraction, and the problems entailed in achieving and maintaining intimacy in same-sex relationships.

WHEN THE PERSONAL IS POLITICAL

The Not-So Hidden Outsiders

More than other minority groups, lesbians and gay men have a better chance of living undetected by individuals within mainstream society. While ethnicity and national origin are often relatively easy to discern merely by looking at an individual, sexual orientation is not readily apparent.

Of course, there are plenty of people who think that they can tell otherwise. When I was in high school, students called Thursday "Queersday" and passed around the story that those who wore green on Thursday would be saying to all that they were queer (a term that had a negative meaning in those days). A group of lesbian and gay college students later turned that kind of thinking on its head when they declared that all students who wore jeans to school on Thursday would be telling their classmates that they were gay.

Pranks aside, why would students focus on clothing as an indicator that a classmate was gay? Perhaps it is because children from an early age are made very aware of differences between them and others, and by adolescence there is tremendous pressure to conform. A person who dresses differently enough to be beyond the boundaries of conformity communicates "outsider" status. So, a man who wears colors that are brighter than the norm or a female who dresses down all the time but who otherwise does not seem to be making another identity statement (such as being a "stoner" or a "skater") may be judged by others to be gay or lesbian.

Lesbian, gay, bisexual, transgendered, and questioning youth also feel their outsider status intensely. One of the most eloquently written descriptions of these feelings comes from Paul Monette's award-winning memoir, *Becoming a Man*:

> Everyone else had a childhood, for one thing—where they were coaxed and coached and taught all the short-hand . . . And every year they leaped further ahead, leaving me in the dust with all my doors closed . . . Until I was twenty-five, I was the only man I knew who had no story at all . . . That's how the closet feels, once you've made your nest in it and learned to call it home. Self-pity becomes your oxygen. (1992, p. 1)

Of course, what is in fashion changes rapidly and probably is not a good indicator of sexuality over time. In urban areas, one can easily find male "metrosexuals" and gay men who dress alike. *The New York Times* discovered that a lesbian style not only exists but influences the clothing choices of heterosexual women in a piece provocatively headlined, "The Secret Power of Lesbian Style" (Trebay, 2004). On the other hand, Sender (2004) has noted that if there is such a thing as "lesbian style," marketers feel at a loss to sell it to the lesbian community.

If clothing is becoming less and less of a giveaway, then what clues do people use to judge sexuality? In all likelihood, the first thing people will judge is any behavior that does not correspond with the individual's apparent gender. So, if men act "feminine" or women act "masculine" they are likely to be assumed to be gay. As a study by Gowen and Britt (2006) found that college students negatively judged male peers who they were told were "straight" but whose taped voice sounded stereotypically gay. Indeed, some gay men and lesbians may incorporate aspects of opposite-gender behavior in order to be noticed by other gay men and lesbians. However, the adoption of these behaviors does not necessarily mean that the individual would rather *be* the opposite gender. Most lesbians and gays are happy being women or men; they are simply emotionally and sexually attracted to members of the same gender.

Media and Stereotypes

Media portrayals of lesbians and gays have helped both to perpetuate stereotypes and, more recently, to promote tolerance and acceptance. According to Fejes and Petrich (1993), who reviewed a large number of studies on how lesbians and gays had been portrayed in films, on television, and in the news, gay characters in entertainment were often cast as farcical, weak, or menacing.

Smyth (2004), in a more recent study of gay male portrayals in news magazine stories, identified four classic stereotypes of gay men: (1) gay males are effeminate, (2) gay males are "sick" or mentally ill, (3) gay males are sexual predators, and (4) gay males are "violent, libido-driven monsters." Smyth studied stories that appeared in *Time* and *Newsweek* between 1946 and 2002, and he found that there were three distinct periods reflecting differences in how these periodicals covered gays. From 1946 to 1969, the newsmagazines portrayed gay men almost exclusively from a dark point of view, as sexually deviant, predatory, and sick. From 1969, following the Stonewall Riots, to 1980, coverage focused mostly on the emerging Gay Liberation movement, and reactions to that movement, mostly from religious or quasi-religious groups. While the articles themselves often focused on an emerging gay male identity and political agenda, there were still mentions of the old stereotypes in many of the articles. It was also during this period that the American Psychiatric Association removed homosexuality from its list of mental illnesses. From 1980 to 2002, the number of articles about gays surged dramatically. Portrayals of gay men as effeminate dropped sharply, though the news magazines still were interested in gay serial killers and unusual sexual practices. The prevalence of HIV and AIDS among gay men helped to perpetuate the "sick" stereotype, and coverage of the spread of AIDS perpetuated the stereotype of the sexual predator.

Similarly, Branchik (2007) analyzed representations of gay men in print advertising from 1917 to 2004 and found that these representations passed through four stages that were roughly equivalent to changes in societal views of gay men. These stages were (a) recognizing the men as being homosexual, (b) ridiculing them, (c) accepting them as "cutting edge," and (d) portraying them with respect.

Even though stereotypes have been dissipating in media coverage, they persist in many people's thinking. And, like all stereotypes, they have some basis in fact. There are certainly gay men who are effeminate, sick, predatory, or prone to sex-related criminal acts, but to characterize all or even most gay men as having one or more of these qualities would miss the mark completely. Some scholars would characterize these stereotypes as being products of *heterosexism*. That is, they arise from an assumption that behavior of heterosexual individuals is "normal" and behavior of homosexual individuals is "deviant," as opposed to merely "different." In fact, there are probably more heterosexual men who are effeminate, sick, predatory, or prone to sex-related criminal acts than there are gay men, because same-sex orientation is statistically still very much the exception (independent estimates range anywhere from 2 to 10 percent of the population).

Of course, I have been discussing twentieth century ideas about same-sex orientation. It has not always been thus, and in fact there is considerable historical evidence that sexuality with others of the same gender has in the past been honored instead of looked on with suspicion (see, for example, Boswell, 1994; Crompton, 2003; Greenberg, 1988).

Overcoming Stereotypes

One method many people seem to have for letting go of their stereotypes is to meet someone who does not fit them. A survey of San Diegans conducted during the time when Massachusetts started to marry lesbian and gay couples legally found that respondents who claimed to know at least one lesbian or gay person held more favorable attitudes toward lesbians and gays generally than did those who claimed to know no lesbians or gays. Income seemed to be a factor in associating with known lesbians and gays, as the largest number of people who said they knew no gay individuals were those who made under $20,000 annually. And, the more you know the better. People with the most favorable attitudes knew the largest number of gay people, and *vice versa*. Other factors also influenced people's attitudes. Those with liberal political ideologies held the most favorable attitudes, though even those describing themselves as very conservative split about evenly in feeling positively and negatively about gay people generally. Those who were not regular churchgoers also held more favorable attitudes, though churchgoers, like conservatives, split about evenly in their attitudes. Women were more likely to hold favorable attitudes than men, and younger people's attitudes were far more favorable than were those of older people. Overall, in this poll 60 percent of respondents said

that they viewed lesbians and gays favorably, while 26 percent viewed these groups unfavorably and 14 percent were unsure of how they felt ("Poll Analysis," 2004). A study of viewers of the television show, *Will and Grace,* which featured gay characters in leading roles, found that they held more positive attitudes toward lesbians and gays than did people who did not watch the show (Schiappa, Gregg, & Hewes, 2006). While one might expect that people seek out television programming that fits with their attitudes, positive attitudes toward lesbians and gays persisted even among those viewers who did not claim to have lesbian or gay friends.

Even though these numbers indicate that attitudes are changing, there is still danger associated with being openly lesbian or gay. In particular, this danger seems to affect people under 21 to the greatest degree. In a study published in the *American Journal of Public Health,* researchers reported on a survey of 1,248 gay and bisexual men aged 18 to 27 who lived in Austin, Texas; Albuquerque, New Mexico; or Phoenix, Arizona. Overall 5 percent of those surveyed reported that they had been the victims of anti-gay violence, while 11 percent indicated that they had been discriminated against because they were gay. But, of those under 21, the numbers jumped to 10 percent as having experienced anti-gay violence, while half reported that they had been discriminated against because they were gay (Huebner, Rebchook, & Kegeles, 2004). Horn (2006) found that adolescents aged 14 to 16 are most likely to exhibit hostility toward lesbian and gay peers and open displays of hostility decline as adolescents age into young adulthood. Nevertheless, the possibility of being reviled for being open about one's sexuality remains throughout one's life.

These data bring us back to the main point of this section, that being openly lesbian or gay is a political statement. When the odds are only 60:40 that others will have a favorable attitude toward you as a lesbian or gay man and when the odds are even greater that your openness at a young age may result in negative, even violent, consequences, no wonder many non-heterosexual individuals keep that information to themselves. They may date members of the opposite sex and may also marry and have families. Men in this situation may seek anonymous same-sex encounters outside of marriage, because the means for having such encounters are often readily (though, not always legally) available. These men may also deny that they have any same-sex attraction and claim that these encounters are necessary for a variety of reasons (e.g., "I don't get enough sex at home," "My wife won't do things sexually for me that other men will do," "I get a thrill out of anonymous encounters."). Public health workers call these individuals MSMs, or "Men who have Sex with Men." People in the African-American and Latino communities call this practice "dl," or being "on the down low" (Wolitski et al., 2006). These groups of people, along with intravenous drug users, have the highest risk for contracting HIV/AIDS.

The Process of Coming Out

So, despite the potential for negative consequences, it is healthier for people to be open about their same-sex attraction. But, getting to that point is not always easy. D'Augelli (1994) theorized that there are what he called "six interactive stages that non-heterosexual" individuals pass through as they develop an identity. The stages are:

1. Recognizing that one's attractions and feelings are not heterosexual, as well as telling others that one is not heterosexual.
2. Summarizing self-concepts, emotions, and desires into a personal identity as gay/lesbian/bisexual.
3. Developing a non-heterosexual social identity.
4. Disclosing one's identity to parents and redefining familial relationships afterward.
5. Developing capabilities to have intimate gay/lesbian/bisexual relationships.
6. Becoming a member of a gay/lesbian/bisexual community.

It is possible that these stages can be passed through quickly, but it is equally as likely that these stages will progress slowly if at all (and, individuals may work on multiple stages at once or may double back to previous stages). Each stage requires some degree of change to how one talks and each stage requires the ability to share with others what heretofore one considered to be private information. As people search for new ways of talking and for what they might consider to be the "right words" to say, they look to the examples of others. This process of learning to communicate differently helps lesbian and gay individuals to assimilate into the lesbian/gay/bisexual community.

The fact that disclosure of information about one's sexuality may evoke responses ranging from "that's wonderful," to spews of hateful words makes such disclosure a political one. "Political" communication, in this case, is constituted by messages that have the potential for promoting controversy. "Political" also means that such a disclosure tends to carry with it an assumption that the speaker holds a set of attitudes and beliefs that may be at odds with those of the listener. Such assumptions may not be correct. For example, lesbians and gays may be seen as being antagonistic to organized religion, while many consider themselves to be quite devout. Lesbians and gays may also be seen as holding liberal views about other political matters, while their views mostly may be quite conservative.

Communication and Identity Formation

D'Augelli's stages of identity formation are called "interactive" because they rely on communication with others to occur. As same-sex attraction is controversial information, lesbians and gays beginning on D'Augelli's stages need to find strategies for disclosing this information. These initial disclosures will usually be tentative and told to a confidant, often a trusted friend or an adult who is not a parent (e.g., a teacher, counselor, neighbor, clergyperson, or an aunt or uncle). The initial messages may not be in the form of "I am lesbian," but may be more general statements such as, "I'm having trouble with starting to date. My friends are dating, but I'm not," or even a statement such as, "I'm not sure that people like me; I don't fit in very well." The realization that one is attracted to members of the same sex may be present, but the individual may be choosing to hide that information behind what is often legitimate confusion. Depending on the response, the individual may finally say that they think they are more attracted to members of the same sex than to members of the opposite sex, or they may label themselves lesbian, gay, or bisexual. In many cases, the first formulation of sexual identity might be "I'm bisexual," because the speaker may believe that this statement is more socially acceptable than "I'm gay."

Once some form of admission that "I am different" is made, the gay or lesbian person will begin to look for information that will help her to figure out what is going on. Sometimes this information search is confined to books, magazines, or informational Web sites. Other times the information may come from pornography or erotica or from seeking out places where gays or lesbians gather. Sometimes, these places will be ones where anonymous sex might be had. Males in particular will try to experiment with gay sex to see if they find it to be exciting. The fact that sex in public places is usually against the law may add to the thrill of the experience.

As the lesbian or gay individual has contact with other lesbians and gays and compares themselves favorably to those other individuals, the idea that "I am different" should eventually become, "I am lesbian," or "I am gay." At that point, the dilemma becomes whether and how to let others know of one's sexual identity.

Coming Out as an Event

The process of "coming out of the closet" is actually described by all of D'Augelli's stages, taken collectively. The moments when the lesbian or gay individual actually tells the people closest to them of their sexual identity should ideally be (1) when that individual is ready and prepared to make the disclosure, and (2) when the other members are ready to hear what this individual has to say. In many cases, however, these scenes are not nearly so clean and well planned. Parents may learn about their child's sexuality, for example, by catching them with same-sex pornography, by reading their diaries, or by discovering them with a same-sex partner. Initial sexual experimentation may lead to trouble with the law or with delinquency, or the individual may burst out with the information at an emotional, but unplanned, moment.

Reactions to this information will be varied. The ideal reaction, from the lesbian or gay person's point of view, is described in advice available on the Web site of the support organizations, Parents and Friends of Lesbians and Gays (PFLAG) and Human Rights Campaign (HRC).

- Ask respectful questions to show you are interested.
- Be honest. If you feel awkward, say so. Ask the "dumb" questions.
- Laugh a little, but do it gently and respectfully. Do not use slang terms that could be considered derogatory.

- Send gentle signals that it is all right to continue to talk with you about being lesbian or gay.[1]

Still, there are many families where parents and siblings do not process this news in nearly as supportive a manner. Some family members will immediately cut off contact with the lesbian or gay member. Some families will try to persuade the lesbian or gay person that "this is a phase" or that "you can change." In the larger community, coming out as lesbian or gay is grounds for ex-communication in some religious denominations, and lesbian or gay individuals who work for some organizations may well find themselves out of a job after their same-sex attraction becomes known. Disclosure of same-sex attraction is grounds for dismissal from the U.S. Armed Forces.

No wonder that individuals who are questioning their sexuality are reluctant to talk to others about it until they are sure of a lesbian or gay identity. And no wonder that some people stay in the closet for years, as I did! Many lesbian and gay individuals feel tensions in their relationships with family, work, and social and religious institutions. Lesbians and gays may resolve these tensions in a variety of ways. They may decide to create alternative support institutions, such as "families of choice," as opposed to "families of origin." They may strive to achieve at work or in another area where they can gain recognition. They may become part of alternative social and religious structures. They may also become politically active, seeking to root out and eliminate discrimination wherever they find it. If they join political groups, these groups may employ tactics ranging from traditional lobbying to attention-grabbing demonstrations such as same-sex "kiss-ins," where same-sex couples deliberately engage in public displays of affection. (For an analysis of the political dimensions of two men kissing in public, see Morris & Sloop, 2006.)

Achieving Intimacy

It is usually difficult for a lesbian or gay person to progress to D'Augelli's fifth stage, learning how to develop intimate same-sex relationships, without having completed at least some of the fourth stage, allowing the people who matter to them to know them as sexual beings. Intimacy, by its very nature, demands a degree of honesty that is usually suppressed by the need to hide a major portion of one's self. In addition, fear of being discovered, fear of what others will think, or fear of losing one's job can keep people in hiding and afraid of their own sexuality. But, sometimes finding another person to trust and love can help an individual to be more open about same-sex attraction. Of course, intimate relationships can and do happen between people who cannot be open with others. Sometimes, these relationships are described to others as "roommates" or "friends," which is how a neighbor of mine described his living arrangement with his partner of seventeen years when I first met him. As soon as he realized that I was sympathetic to his situation, however, he began talking to me in much more open terms. The ability to be openly a part of an intimate relationship in the community at large is a test of not only how accepting the person has become of her own sexuality but how interactions with the community can create a climate where the couple are accepted and included by those around them.

Building Community

D'Augelli's final stage entails becoming a part of a lesbian/gay/bisexual community. This stage, too, does not necessarily wait for the other stages to finish, but can occur even while completing the earliest stages of the process. High school gay-straight alliance clubs can provide a supportive place to be different in an environment that puts a high premium on conformity. Universities may provide both a means for "out" lesbians and gays to gather but also often private groups, typically run by a counseling center, where questioning students can explore their sexuality. Lesbian and gay community centers also provide "coming out" workshops and other social services designed to assist people in finding a community and to feel as though they belong there.

Being in a community typically involves having a concentration of like-minded people with whom to interact on a daily basis. The U.S. census of 2000 was the first to allow individuals to identify themselves as same-sex couples, and Gates and Ost (2004) have compiled the census data to learn about lesbian and gay living patterns. They found that gay male and lesbian women couples tend to live on the east or west coasts of the United States, though not necessarily in the same locales. The ten most popular spots for gay male couples to live were San Francisco, California; Fort Lauderdale, Florida; Santa Rosa, California; Seattle-Bellevue-Everett, Washington; New York City, New York; Jersey City, New Jersey; Los Angeles-Long Beach, California; Santa Fe, New Mexico; Oakland, California; and Miami, Florida. Gay male couples tended to live in places that had higher concentrations of other gay couples, and they tended to live in more urban areas. For lesbian couples, the most popular places were often in college towns: Santa Rosa, California; Santa Cruz-Watsonville, California; Santa Fe, New Mexico; San Francisco, California; Oakland, California; Burlington, Vermont; Portland, Maine; Springfield, Massachusetts; Corvallis, Oregon; and Madison, Wisconsin. Gates and Ost also reported that 99 percent of U.S. counties had at least one same-sex couple living there.[2] Once in a community, gays and lesbians will often become involved in social organizations, such as square dancing or choral singing, business and networking groups such as a lesbian and gay Chamber of Commerce, and causes that benefit the community as a whole. There are even retirement communities created for lesbians and gays (Neville, 2007). Since lesbian and gay communities can be controversial, however, many of these organizations will have political ramifications, if not be overtly political. Over time, gay men have been involved in prevention of HIV/AIDS transmission and in raising funds for research on this disease, which began in the gay community but now affects far more heterosexual people worldwide. Lesbians have actively been involved in raising awareness about breast cancer and in funding breast cancer research. Both groups have campaigned against laws that allow discrimination in hiring and housing or which criminalize private and consensual sexual practices commonly engaged in by lesbian and gay couples. These campaigns culminated in the U.S. Supreme Court's 2003 decision in *Lawrence* v. *Texas,* where Justice Anthony Kennedy, writing for the Court majority, declared that two gay men could engage in consensual sexual activity in the privacy of one's home and "still retain their dignity as free persons." Most recently, the lesbian and gay community has been galvanized by a drive to legalize marriage for same-sex couples. This drive created a fair amount of national debate, as well as spawning legal attempts to restrict the term *marriage* to recognizing relationships among opposite-sex couples. However, *The New York Times'* decision to print announcements of the unions of same-sex couples in its wedding announcements pages did much for increasing the social acceptability of those relationships.

Communication and the Tensions of Being Open

In U.S. culture, gays and lesbians needed to remain hidden yet visible for so long that they developed ways of signaling their sexual orientation to like-minded people that would remain oblique to society as a whole. They also could choose to be so flamboyant that their sexuality could not be ignored.

The author and playwright Oscar Wilde proved to be a masterful practitioner of hiding a gay subtext in his stories and plays, work that was acclaimed by mainstream critics and audiences alike. For example, in his novella, *The Picture of Dorian Gray,* Wilde concocted a tale about a man who finds the secret to staying eternally beautiful and youthful. The secret is a portrait of himself that he has hidden in his attic. The portrait, not the man, is the one that ages. Ultimately, the story ends in horror, and the man receives his comeuppance, but its central fantasy appealed to the soul of every gay man who read it. Wilde himself was married to a woman but had many dalliances with young men, which included at least one long-term lover. Tried in court for being a homosexual, a crime in Victorian England, Wilde defended himself by claiming that he merely enjoyed the company and energy of younger men. Wilde was convicted and jailed, however, and the experience left him sick and defeated, unable to produce the kind of tales that had once made him the toast of London.

Camp as Gay Sensibility

Wilde has been credited not only as being the person around which our modern ideas about same-sex love were conceived but also as being the first practitioner of "camp." Camp has evolved into a central concept in understanding gay culture. In her famous 1964 essay, "Notes on 'Camp,'" critic Susan Sontag defined camp as a "sensibility," as opposed to an idea or a thing. Sensibilities, according to Sontag, are difficult to describe, but she argued that camp is a sensibility that requires aesthetic appreciation, because it is a style or taste. Since styles and tastes change frequently, however, one must be nimble and not given to set ways of seeing the world. Indeed, camp often turns the world on its ear, relying on exaggeration and a tendency to see double meaning in words and acts. Camp is theatrical, an attempt to be and do extraordinary things. Camp is "fabulous" (Sontag, 1964).

In a later essay, Meyer (1994) extended Sontag's analysis to argue that camp encompasses how lesbians and gays perform their lives in front of others. Camp is the embodiment of how gay individuals manage the tensions of being open about their sexuality in a society that brands them as deviant. Rather than hide one's difference, camp helps the gay or lesbian person to find an alternative way of being in the world, a "queer" reality that does not have to rely on the norms of mainstream society, a reality that, in fact, often mocks those norms.

A good example of this alternate reality is the concept of drag. Drag not only bends the idea of gender by allowing men to dress up as women and women as men, but it requires that the "drag queen" or "drag king" play with the character in some way. Puns are a commonly used form of verbal play. For example, "Anita Mann" has undoubtedly been used more than once as a drag name.

Perhaps a good way of explaining drag would be to compare it to female impersonation. Let's say that both a drag queen and a female impersonator are portraying actress and pop star Madonna. The female impersonator will attempt to look and sound as much like Madonna as possible, to create the illusion of Madonna as a tribute to her talent. The drag queen, on the other hand, will portray an exaggerated version of Madonna, playing with her persona to distort it in humorous or ironic ways.

Drag also allows an individual to be "someone else," at least for a while. One acquaintance of mine confided to me, "When I go to a bar in drag, all of the cute boys want to talk to me. I have a quick mouth, and they love my comebacks. But, out of drag I'm a large, older man, and if I went into the same bar as that person those boys wouldn't have anything to do with me. In drag, I'm fun and safe, but out of drag I'm someone to be avoided."

While camp originated as an integral part of gay life, Whitney (2006) has recently argued that it has been co-opted by the heterosexual world and as such may become a subtle means of oppressing the gay community while disguising itself as a liberating experience for all. Time and experience will tell whether this argument, while provocative, turns out to be valid, however.

It's about Sex, but Not Only about Sex

Of course, the point of same-sex attraction is that gays and lesbians want to find someone of the same gender with whom to be physically, emotionally, and spiritually intimate. Recall, however, that while D'Augelli's (1994) stages of developing a non-heterosexual identity included the capacity to form and maintain intimate same-sex relationships, D'Augelli placed this capacity low on his list, after coming out to family and friends. Clearly, a lot of developing a lesbian and gay identity involves exploring one's same-sex attraction and learning to flirt with and meet people who might be candidates for intimate relationships. Many, if not most, lesbians and gays do not wait until they have found their "soul mate" before having sex. Gay men often talk about finding Mr. Right, as opposed to finding Mr. Right-Now. But, as you might imagine, the latter is much easier to locate.

Making Public Communication Safe

Meeting other lesbian and gay people is not an easy task, however. If one is in a "safe" space, where everyone is gay or accepting of same-sex attraction, then conversing openly is not a problem. Bars have traditionally filled this role, though to a greater extent for men than for women. San Diego, for example, supports more than twenty bars catering primarily to gay men but no known exclusively lesbian bars at the time this essay was written. Coffee houses and some community-based restaurants have also emerged as bar alternatives, especially for gay and lesbian youth who are not of legal drinking age, and for those who may want a less pressured atmosphere. Social and volunteer organizations also serve as safe spaces for lesbians and gays to meet.

Meeting someone outside of these spaces can be tricky, especially if one is not sure that the other person shares one's same-sex attraction. Most lesbians and gay males develop some degree of sense of who around them might also be lesbian or gay (and this intuitive ability is referred to as "gaydar"). In public places, contact is usually established by exchanging gazes, typically more than once. Holding another's gaze is generally interpreted as a sign that the other

person might be interested. A conversation will often ensue, and an early task in that conversation will be to say something socially acceptable but that the other person can identify as a gay reference. Leap (1996), who has studied how gay men talk, both in the United States and internationally, provided an example of a conversation between a clothing sales clerk and a customer:

C: What are you asking for these? *[Points to one set of gray sweatshirts]*

S: Oh, I'm afraid they're not on sale today. But that colored shirt would look nice on you. *[Points to a pile of lavender sweatshirts, which are on sale]*

C: Yeah, I know. I own a few of them already. *[Grins]*

S: *[Grins back, no verbal comment]* (1996, p. 13)

Undoubtedly, these men walked away from this conversation with the knowledge that they were both gay. They understood that fact by (a) the reference to "lavender" a color generally associated with being gay, (b) the exaggerated response to the suggestion that the lavender shirt would look good on the customer, and (c) the fact that both men had exchanged mutual glances prior to beginning the conversation and they both grinned at the end of it. The conversational space was thus "safe," though still public, and if the two had been interested in pursuing each other's company further they could have exchanged contact information.

Negotiating Sexual Attraction

The above example involved two men who might have been interested in each other as potential friends or potential dates ("Mr. Right"). When gay men are looking for sex partners ("Mr. Right-Now"), however, they will tend to use mostly nonverbal signals to do so. What gay men call "cruising," typically starts with making eye contact with someone as the two pass each other. If one is interested, that person will typically slow down and look back. If the other person also looks back, one person may begin to follow the other person. The two might stop and begin a conversation, or they might silently look for a place to have sex (there is a classic set of photographs that illustrates this sequence online at http://phillipsdepury. liveauctioneers.com/lot2509621 .html). Generally, when men engage in an anonymous sexual encounter the less they know about the other person the better. Many choose to avoid the danger of sex in public by going to any of several Internet sites that feature ads from gays or lesbians looking for a "hook-up" in a particular geographical area (Ashford, 2006). Of course, cruising is not limited to gay men, and using the Internet to find partners for dating or sex is a pretty pervasive activity for people of all sexualities. And, like a lot of relational communication activity, the interaction patterns on the Internet do not seem to be terribly different whether one is straight or gay.

Part of the reason that HIV/AIDS was transmitted so quickly among gay men in the 1980s was that, by then, cruising in what were known as "gay ghettos" did not have to be carefully hidden and peer pressure to have a lot of anonymous sex was strong. One of the principal obstacles that had to be overcome in safer-sex campaigns within the gay community was to encourage gay men to avoid risky behaviors in an environment where talking was discouraged. Early HIV prevention campaigns focused on talking to your partner about your HIV status, which was, and still is, a good idea for couples that were dating or in a relationship. The solution seemed to be to teach gay men to regard every sex partner as being HIV-positive until proven otherwise.

Negotiating Intimacy

Most lesbians and gay men put a high premium on dating and forming intimate relationships, however. In this way, we are quite a bit like the rest of the populace, and our courtship communication patterns in many ways resemble those of our heterosexual counterparts in similar age groups. One exception, noted in a review of research on same-sex close relationships, is that both lesbians and gay men are more likely to remain in touch with their former partners after the relationship ends (Peplau & Fingerhut, 2007). Lesbian and gay couples do have unique issues to negotiate on their way to achieving intimacy at the physical, emotional, and spiritual levels, however (Tan, 2005). For one thing, the issue of "who does what" in the relationship has to be worked out bit by bit. In heterosexual relationships, societal expectations for the roles that men and women play can either be followed or reversed by the couple's decision. In lesbian and gay relationships, couples generally reject the notion that one of them plays the "man"

and the other plays the "woman." So, each physical or emotional task has to be worked out, either consciously, or by one person taking on that task and having it become part of who that person is in the relationship. Many lesbians and gay men also reject that their relationships should have to conform to the normative expectations of the heterosexual community. These issues often revolve around setting rules for how much physical, emotional, or spiritual attraction is allowed to each member of the couple outside of the relationship: lesbian and gay couples may not conform to heterosexual definitions of "cheating" in their relationships. This work is hard, and if it becomes too hard or leads to major conflict before the couple has committed to each other there will be a tendency to break off the relationship, rather than to work through the conflicts.

The fact that same-sex couples have no legal standing in many parts of the United States also means that couples either have to keep their finances and other matters separate, or they have to draft legal documents spelling out their agreements, knowing that the validity of those documents may be challenged successfully, perhaps by members of one individual's family, at some future date. While some lesbians and gay men may reject the idea of "marriage" as a religious institution, the legal institution of "marriage" provides a shortcut for allocating benefits and privileges to one's partner that a legal contract finds hard-pressed to provide. The emotional and ceremonial institution of "marriage" as a public commitment of two people to each other also would surely help couples to cement their partnerships. No wonder so many lesbians and gays have been energized to work for ways of providing legal marriage for same-sex couples.

SOME CLOSING THOUGHTS

In writing this essay, the readers I was keeping in mind were traditional-aged university sophomores and juniors. So, I tried to select and emphasize material that I thought might be most relevant to both the intellectual and emotional journeys of 19- or 20-year-olds. Clearly, not every second or third year college student is 19 or 20 years old, and if you fall into that category my examples may not fit where you are in your life.

I also tried to emphasize material that might be common to both lesbians and gay men. Because there has been much more research on the communication and relationship patterns of gay men than on lesbians, and because I am a gay man, this choice probably means that readers interested in lesbians as a group may feel disappointed in what they learned from this chapter. For example, research indicating that lesbians are less likely to be "out" at work (McDermott, 2006) is interesting but exceeds the scope of what I wanted to cover. There is also a significant body of scientific and social scientific knowledge building (for a summary, see Wade, 2007) that much of our sexuality, whether opposite-sex or same-sex, is strongly influenced by genetics, though men and women seemed to be programmed differently when it comes to their sexuality. This topic is one of those where "stay tuned" is the best advice. If you would like to understand more about the psychology of lesbians and gay men, I refer you to book-length works such as Coyle & Kitzinger (2002).

I have also ignored almost completely the "BT"—bisexual and transgender—part of the "LGBT" formulation. Both of these groups are more hidden, even within the lesbian and gay community. Men who call themselves bisexual are oftentimes MSMs; that is, they are in a relationship with a woman but seek out sex with men as well. Wade's (2007) summary of recent scientific and social scientific research on sexuality indicated that while some women may have very strong preferences for either the opposite or the same sex, others find their sexuality to be more fluid. Some women may be genuinely attracted to either men or women but find that their attractions change as they grow older. Bisexuals may have good reason to remain hidden; Herek (2002) found that heterosexuals' attitudes toward bisexuals were generally more negative than they were toward lesbians and gays.

Earlier in this essay, I wrote that exhibiting the behavior of the other gender does not necessarily identify one as a lesbian woman or gay man, and I commented that many, if not most, of us were quite happy being men or women. Transgendered individuals, on the other hand, do sense that they ought to be the opposite gender from what they are, physically. Much of the research on transgendered individuals is still quite new (see Papoulias, 2006, for a summary), so checking an advocacy Web site, such as that of the National Transgender Advocacy Coalition

(http://www.ntac.org/) should provide up-to-date information on this topic.

Finally, I have not written about many of the issues about which many lesbians and gay men care deeply, as well as about several of the tensions that exist within the lesbian and gay community. These tensions include poverty and homelessness among lesbians and gays; racism and sexism; concerns about how to foster healthy communication among lesbians and gay men of different ages (Hajek & Giles, 2002) or between gays and straights (Hajek & Giles, 2005); and worries that lesbian and gay culture is becoming too mainstream, resulting in the possible loss of the community's identity (Hattersley, 2004; McNamara, 2004).

Despite these shortcomings, I hope that I have provided you with some insight about communication among gay men and lesbians and how that communication manifests itself in the United States as a "culture." It used to be said that the members of the lesbian and gay community were "hiding in plain sight." Now that so many of us are no longer hiding, I hope that this information will help you to understand the ways in which members of this community may be different and the ways we are the same.

Notes

1. From the *Straight Guide to GLBT Americans.* Reprinted by permission. Information may be obtained from http://www.hrc.org/about_us/7177.hmt.
2. I am unable to determine if the survey question specifically asked respondents to identify themselves as lesbian or gay. If it did not, there is the possibility of the question being interpreted as two same-sex people who were cohabiting but not members of the lesbian and gay community.

References

Ashford, C. (2006). The only gay in the village: Sexuality and the Net. *Information & Communications Technology Law, 15,* 275–289.

Boswell, J. (1994). *Same-sex unions in premodern Europe.* New York: Villard.

Branchik, B. J. (2007). Pansies to parents: Gay male images in American print advertising. *Journal of Macromarketing, 27,* 38–50.

Crompton, L. (2003). *Homosexuality and civilization.* Cambridge: Harvard University Press.

Coyle, A., & Kitzinger, C. (Eds.) (2002). *Lesbian and gay psychology: New perspectives.* Oxford: Blackwell.

D'Augelli, A. R. (1994). Identity development and sexual orientation: Toward a model of lesbian, gay, and bisexual development. In E. J. Trickett, R. J. Watts, & D.

Birmans (Eds.), *Human diversity: Perspectives on people in context* (pp. 312–333). New York: Oxford University Press.

Gates, G. J., & Ost, J. (2004). *The gay and lesbian atlas.* Washington, DC: The Urban Institute Press.

Gowen, C. W., & Britt, T. W. (2006). The interactive effects of homosexual speech and sexual orientation on the stigmatization of men. *Journal of Language & Social Psychology, 25,* 437–456.

Greenberg, D. (1988). *The construction of homosexuality.* Chicago: University of Chicago Press.

Hajek, C. & Giles, H. (2002). The old man out: An intergroup analysis of intergenerational communication among gay men. *Journal of Communication, 30,* 698–714.

Hajek, C., & Giles, H. (2005). Intergroup communication schemas: Cognitive representations of talk with gay men. *Language & Communication 25,* 161–181.

Hattersley, M. (2004, January-February). Will success spoil gay culture? *Gay and Lesbian Review Worldwide, 11,* 33–34.

Herek, G. M. (2002). Heterosexuals' attitudes toward bisexual men and women in the United States. *Journal of Sex Research, 39,* 264–274.

Horn, S. S. (2006). Heterosexual adolescents' and young adults' beliefs and attitudes about homosexuality and gay and lesbian peers. *Cognitive Development, 21,* 420–440.

Huebner, D. M., Rebchook, G. M., & Kegeles, S. M. (2004). Experiences of harassment, discrimination, and physical violence among young gay and bisexual men. *American Journal of Public Health, 94,* 1200–1203.

Human Rights Watch & Parents and Friends of Lesbians and Gays. (n.d.). A straight guide to GLBT Americans. Retrieved April 12, 2007, from http://www.pflag.org/fileadmin/user_upload/Support/straightguideWEB.pdf

Leap, W. L. (1996). *Word's out: Gay men's English.* Minneapolis: University of Minnesota Press.

McDermott, E. (2006). Surviving in dangerous places: Lesbian identity performances in the workplace, social class and psychological health. *Feminism & Psychology, 16,* 193–211.

McNamara, M. (2004, April 25). When gay lost its outré. *Los Angeles Times.* Retrieved April 25, 2004, from http://www.latimes.com/features/lifestyle/la-ca-mcnamara25apr25,1,6298374.story

Meyer, M. (Ed.) (1994). *The politics and poetics of camp.* London: Routledge.

Monette, P. (1992). *Becoming a man: Half a life story.* New York: Harcourt Brace Jovanovich.

Morris, C. E., & Sloop, J. M. (2006). "What lips these lips have kissed": Refiguring the politics of queer public kissing. *Communication & Critical/Cultural Studies, 3,* 1–26.

Neville, T. (2007, April 6). Birds of a feather. *New York Times,* Retrieved April 6, 2007, from http://www.nytimes.com/2007/04/06/travel/escapes/06retire.html?ex=1334116800&en=5c1bf7a5b0bf7bbb&ei=5124&partner=permalink&exprod=permalink

Papoulias, C. (2006). Transgender. *Theory Culture & Society, 23,* 231–233.

Peplau, L. A., & Fingerhut, A.W. (2007). The close relationships of lesbians and gay men. *Annual Review of Psychology, 58,* 405–424.

"Poll Analysis." (2004). Retrieved April 25, 2004, from http://www.kpbs.org/Other/DynPage.php?id=1108

Schiappa, E., Gregg, P., & Hewes, D. (2006). Can one TV show make a difference? *Will & Grace* and the parasocial contact hypothesis. *Journal of Homosexuality, 51,* 15–38.

Sender, K. (2004). Neither fish nor fowl: Feminism desire, and the lesbian consumer market. *The Communication Review, 7,* 407–432.

Smyth, M. (2004, May). *(Mis-)Shaping gay, lesbian, and bisexual representations in popular discourse: historical analyses.* Paper presented to the International Communication Association, New Orleans, Louisiana.

Sontag, S. (1964, Autumn). On "Camp." *The Partisan Review, 30.*

Tan, P. P. (2005). The importance of spirituality among gay and lesbian individuals. *Journal of Homosexuality, 49,* 135–144.

Trebay, G. (2004, June 27). The secret power of lesbian style. *New York Times,* sec. 9, p. 1.

Wade, N. (2007, April 10). Pas de deux of sexuality is written in the genes. *New York Times.* Retrieved April 10, 2007, from http://www.nytimes.com/2007/04/10/health/10gene.html?ex=1333857600&en=87d00a870b9db178&ei=5124&partner=permalink&exprod=permalink

Whitney, E. (2006). Capitalizing on camp: Greed and the queer marketplace. *Text & Performance Quarterly, 26,* 36–46.

Wolitski, R. J., Jones, K. T., Wasserman, J. L., & Smith, J. C. (2006). Self-identifications: "Down low" among men who have sex with men (MSM) from 12 U.S. cities. *IDS Behavior, 10,* 519–529.

Concepts and Questions

1. Why would some readers be eager to read Eadie's article while other would prefer to avoid it?
2. Does Eadie's personal history affect your attitudes toward the lesbian and gay culture? How?

3. How does revealing one's lesbian or gay sexuality become a political statement? What specific behaviors might be interpreted as a political statement?
4. How do media portrayals of lesbians and gays perpetuate stereotypes? And how do the media foster positive images toward gays and lesbians?
5. What are the six interactive stages through which nonheterosexual individuals pass as they develop their identity?
6. How does Eadie describe the process by which gays and lesbians deal with the tensions associated with being open about sexuality?
7. What is the role of "camp" in the lesbian and gay culture? How would you explain "camp"?
8. What does Eadie mean when he refers to being in a "safe" space when meeting other lesbian and gay people?
9. What are some of the unique gay communication patterns Eadie describes? How do these forms of communication serve the gay culture?
10. What are some of the "societal expectations" that men and women are expected to adhere to in the "straight" community?
11. What are some of the benefits that lesbians and gays would gain by legalizing gay and lesbian relationships?

5

Intercultural Messages: Verbal and Nonverbal Communication

If we speak a different language, we would perceive a different world.

LUDWIG WITTGENSTEIN

As a member of the human species, one of your distinguishing features is your ability to utilize language, both verbal and nonverbal. You can receive, store, retrieve, manipulate, and generate symbols that stand for something else. By simply making certain sounds, marks on paper, and body movements, you can relate to and interact with others by showing them and telling them what you are thinking about and what you want to know. At first blush, verbal and nonverbal language appears rather simple—you create an action (linguistic or non-linguistic) and other people respond. Yet, as you know from personal experience, accurately sharing your ideas and feelings is not a trouble-free matter. In short, as we pointed out in Chapter 1, communication is a complex activity. The series of readings in this chapter seeks to explain some of those complexities—especially as they apply to culture, language, and intercultural communication.

This chapter contends that a culture's use of verbal and nonverbal symbols involves much more than sounds and meanings. It also involves forms of reasoning, how discourse is performed, specialized linguistic devices such as analogies and idioms, the use of time and space, unique ways of moving, and behaviors that display emotions. Hence, understanding the verbal and nonverbal language of any culture means viewing symbol sharing from this larger perspective. This eclectic outlook toward verbal and nonverbal language will help you understand the interaction patterns of cultures and co-cultures that are different from your own.

All of the selections in this chapter are predicated on two truisms: First, *verbal and nonverbal meanings are learned as part of a person's cultural affiliation*. Second, *these meanings reside within the individual*. For each culture there is a very elaborate set of verbal and nonverbal symbols to which people within that culture have learned to attach meaning. Although we consider verbal and nonverbal forms of symbolic interaction separately for convenience, we hasten to point out they are interrelated. Both involve very elaborate symbol systems where writing, speaking, or some other action represents an idea or feeling contained inside the person. They are also interrelated because nonverbal behavior usually accompanies verbal behavior. Verbal messages often rely on their nonverbal accompaniment for cues that aid the receiver in decoding the verbal symbols. Nonverbal behaviors not only serve to amplify and clarify verbal messages but can also serve as forms of symbolic interaction without verbal counterparts.

When you communicate with other members of your own culture you do so with relative ease. Your experiential backgrounds are similar enough that you share approximately the same meanings for most of the words and actions used in everyday living. Notice we used the word "approximately" in the last sentence. For even within your culture, people still sometimes disagree about the meanings of many of the verbal and nonverbal symbols being used. As words and actions move further from the reality of sensory data and become more abstract, there is far less agreement about appropriate meanings. In the use of words, for example, what do highly abstract words such as *worship, freedom, mental illness, equal opportunity, democracy, terrorism,* and *civil liberties* mean to you? Do they mean the same things to everyone? If you are in doubt, ask some friends; take a poll. You will surely find that people have different notions of these concepts and consequently different meanings for these words. Their experiences have been different, and they hold different beliefs, attitudes, values, concepts, and expectations. Yet all, or perhaps most, of these people are from the same culture. In most instances, educational backgrounds, experiences, and concepts of the universe are somewhat uniform.

The same ambiguity that we just mentioned can be applied to nonverbal messages. You notice two people talking and one has a clenched fist. You need to decide if they are agreeing, are about to get into a fight, or expressing exhilaration and enthusiasm over what just transpired. Even perceiving someone in tears can produce a variety of responses. Are these tears of joy or sorrow? Remember in all of our examples so far, we are talking about people from the same culture. When cultural diversity is introduced to the process of decoding words and actions, much larger differences in meanings and usage are found. A very simple yet vivid example can be seen in the unadorned word *dog.* To Americans, the word usually represents a furry, friendly, domesticated pet—a pet that is often treated like a member of the family. Yet, in some Asian cultures the meaning is very different. The "pet" often ends up on the dinner plate instead of on the family couch. What is true of the often ambiguous nature of words can also be seen in your use of nonverbal actions— particularly as when applied to culture. First, culture tends to determine the specific nonverbal behaviors that represent specific thoughts, feelings, or states of the communicator. Thus, what might be a sign of greeting in one culture might very well be an obscene gesture in another; or, what is considered a symbol of affirmation in one culture could be meaningless or even signify negation in another. Second, culture determines when it is appropriate to display or communicate various thoughts, feelings, or internal states; this is particularly evident in the display of emotions. Although there seems to be little cross-cultural difference in the nonverbal behaviors that express emotional states, there can be significant cultural differences in the specification of *which* emotions should be displayed, the degree to which they may be displayed, who may display them, and when or where they may be displayed. Think for a moment of all the different interpretations that can be attached to touch, gaze, attire, movement, space, and the like when you send and receive messages. Successful intercultural communication therefore requires that you recognize and understand culture's influence on both verbal and nonverbal interaction. It is the purpose of this chapter to assist you in that understanding. Reflect for a moment about all the potential meanings for the word *Jihad.* Does it mean a holy war or a war within oneself (i.e., an internal struggle)?

The first essay in this chapter begins with a pronouncement that we have stressed throughout this book—intercultural competence is indispensable for anyone who intends to compete in the global marketplace. Part of that competence means understanding the dual relationship between language and culture. That specific relationship serves as the nucleus of an essay by Justin Charlebois titled "Language, Culture, and Social Interaction." Charlebois is interested in more than the obvious notion that words mean different things to different people. Instead, he examines language from the perspective of the "social rules of speaking." These "rules," often referred to as pragmatic knowledge, deal with the ways in which members of a "speech community actually use language." What makes pragmatic knowledge so difficult for "outsiders" to understand is that this knowledge, like much of culture itself, is for the most part unconscious. Drawing on the research of Gumperz, Bateson, Goffman, and Tannen, the author examines how language, speech communities, and cultures are linked. As we already mentioned, Charlebois is primarily concerned with how cultural rules and practices of language are used in everyday conversation. Employing a host of real world examples, he demonstrates "culture bound" interactions as diverse as greetings, requests, politeness, "yes" and "no" responses, topic selection, uses of humor, and the like. All of these can influence the interpretations of certain interactions.

Conflict in the Middle East between Israeli-Jews and Palestinians has a long, sad, and bloody history. Antecedents of today's conflicts extend over thousands of years. Traditional discord notwithstanding, there might be ways in which the negative stereotypes, mutual distrust, and severe miscommunication, which highlight today's relationships, could be managed through an understanding of transformative dialogues. In their essay "Dialogue, Argument, and Cultural Communication Codes between Israeli-Jews and Palestinians," Donald G. Ellis and Ifat Maoz analyze cultural communication codes in order to establish dialogue between the opposing sides. Ellis and Maoz posit that the Israeli-Jewish and Arab cultures, because of the special circumstances of their histories, have developed unique speech codes that reflect their nearly polar-opposite cultural differences.

Ellis and Maoz suggest that the Arab language employs speech codes that seek to "accommodate" or "go along with," which orients speakers toward harmonious relationships. On the other hand, they assert that the Israeli-Jewish speech code is direct, pragmatic, assertive, explicit, and clear. These speech code differences are essentially the opposite of one another and, according to Ellis and Maoz, are partially responsible for the failure of dialogue to resolve the conflict between the two cultures. The authors believe that by studying these speech codes, you can better understand the linguistic bases of cultural conflict and be better prepared to help mediate that conflict.

One of the major premises of this chapter is the idea that culture influences nearly every aspect of how people use language. Our next selection illustrates how the reach of culture affects public speaking. That is to say, the common components of public speaking, such as organization, evidence, credibility, and argumentation, have a cultural dimension inherent in them. Ann Neville Miller, in her essay "Public Speaking Patterns in Kenya," describes how public speaking in the East African nation of Kenya is influenced, guided, and shaped by the Kenyan culture. Miller begins with a brief summary of the major cultural dimensions advanced by Geert Hofstede (individualism-collectivism, power distance) and Edward T. Hall (monochronic and polychronic time, high- and low-context communication). With these two theoretical perspectives as a backdrop, she then moves to a comparison of United States and

Kenyan public speaking patterns as they apply to (1) speaking purposes, (2) supporting material, (3) credibility, and (4) speech structure.

In the United States, most public speaking situations call for an informative or persuasive speech. Such is not the case in Kenya. As Miller notes, the average Kenyan, in contrast, makes abundant use of ceremonial speeches. The popularity of these speeches over those preferred by Americans is a reflection of cultural values. For example, in the United States, with its long history of argumentation and debate, persuading others to one's point of view is commonplace. In Kenya, where community, proper protocol, formal greetings, and tribute are important, the ceremonial speech is widely used.

For supporting material, people trained in public speaking in the United States learn to use evidence such as statistics to try to persuade an audience. However, Miller suggests, "The most convincing type of supporting material for a Kenyan public speech is a narrative." Part of employing narratives also has Kenyan speakers choosing proverbs over statistics. Miller makes comparisons between the United States and Kenya with regard to organizational patterns. In the United States, successful speakers are those who organize their speeches in a highly structured, logical, linear pattern. For many Kenyan speakers, the pattern is best seen as a bicycle wheel with the spokes wandering out to the rim. Miller adds, "The speaker gives illustrations, proverbs, and tells stories and then returns back to the thesis at the center, though not exactly at the place from which they departed." Again, when compared to the organization used by a Western speaker, such a pattern would seem aimless and without a logical configuration. All of Miller's examples and comparisons make it clear that people who give speeches call on their culture when selecting the rhetorical devices they deem most appropriate and effective.

Possibly one of the most important areas of intercultural communication—both internationally and domestically—is between U.S. Americans and Mexicans. Not only does Mexico share a common border with the United States, but it continues to be the largest source of new immigrants entering the United States—both legally and illegally. The fusion of the two cultures was highlighted in a special issue of *Time* magazine that detailed the unique culture developing along both sides of the United States–Mexican border. The new culture evolving is a combination of Euro-American, native Mexican, and Spanish-influenced Mexican backgrounds. To help you better understand the nature of this culture and the Mexican values that contribute to it, our next essay, "Mexican *Dichos:* Lessons Through Language" by Carolyn Roy, explores Mexican values as expressed by *dichos. Dichos* are popular proverbs, adages, and sayings that pass on many of the values that are important to Mexicans. The proverbs and adages shine a light on what the particular culture deems important. For example, Roy discusses how key values such as the cheerful acceptance of the "will of God," the need to place trust in others with great care, the significance of appearances, the necessity to guard one's privacy and not breach the privacy of others, prescribed gender roles, a communal spirit, and the importance of family are expressed and reinforced through use of Mexican *dichos.*

As noted in the introduction to this chapter, nonverbal messages, and the responses they produce, are culture bound. Peter A. Andersen and Hua Wang, in their essay "Beyond Language: Nonverbal Communication Across Cultures" make the same point in the following manner: "Culture shapes the display rules of when, how, what, and with whom certain nonverbal expressions should be revealed or suppressed and dictates which displays are appropriate in which specific situations." To help us appreciate and understand these codes, Andersen and Wang begin by offering a synopsis of nonverbal communication and its relevance to culture. This summary is followed by a brief discussion of the eight basic codes of nonverbal communication: physical appearance (attire), proxemics (space and distance), chronemics (time), kinesics (facial expressions, movements, gestures), haptics (touch), oculesics (eye contact and gaze), vocalics (paralanguage), and olfactics (smell). After a description of the eight codes, the authors move to an analysis of how these codes can differ from one culture to another. Andersen and Wang organize their comparative study around six key intercultural dimensions based on the seminal works of Edward T. Hall and Geert Hofstede. These dimensions include (a) high and low context—the degree to which communication is explicit and verbal or implicit and nonverbal, (b) identity—a culture's degree of individualism versus collectivism, (c) power distance—the degree to which power, prestige, and wealth are unequally distributed in a culture, (d) gender—the degree of traditional gender role achievement, control, and power, (e) uncertainty—the degree to which a culture values risk and ambiguity, and (f) immediacy—the degree of closeness, intimacy, and availability for communication. While explaining the six dimensions Andersen and Wang offer numerous examples of culturally diverse nonverbal behavior.

Turning to an examination of nonverbal behavior that is unique to a particular culture, we now look at some of the nonverbal behaviors often found in Mexican culture. Specifically, Ned Crouch, in his essay titled "Mexicans and Americans: A Different Sense of Space," examines how Mexicans employ space in a manner that can be quite dissimilar to how space is employed in most Western cultures. The use of space, like other aspects of human behavior, is deeply embedded in the core of a culture. For example, Crouch links the notion of personal space to cultural values related to collectivism versus individualism. In Mexico, with its group orientation, people are much more tolerant of sharing their space with others. In the West most people "carry a protective shell around them." Crouch notes that you can even see this "protective shell" in how homes are arranged. In the United States people speak of "my room" and "my privacy." This is not the case in Mexico. Employing numerous examples, Crouch shows how Mexicans share their space with others. He ties that "sharing of space" to a variety of Mexican perceptions and values. At the conclusion of his essay, Crouch offers some excellent examples on how Americans can adapt their views of space to the Mexican business setting.

Language, Culture, and Social Interaction

JUSTIN CHARLEBOIS

INTRODUCTION

Imagine a situation where John, an exchange student living in Japan, wants to postpone his return date to the United States. He needs to ask the staff in the international student exchange office to change his airline ticket. John speaks Japanese fluently and is frequently mistaken for a native speaker on the telephone. In response to his request, Mr. Matsuzaki hesitates and says, *"That's going to be a little bit difficult."* John leaves the conversation feeling very happy and starts making his summer plans. You can imagine his surprise when he discovers that his ticket cannot be changed. What happened?

Pragmatic knowledge is information of how to use language. It is sometimes referred to as the "social rules of speaking" (Wolfson, 1989). While an American might leave the above situation expecting that his or her request is going to be fulfilled, a Japanese, on the other hand, would classify "that's going to be a little bit difficult" as a refusal. John's misinterpretation of this situation resulted from a lack of pragmatic knowledge. This pragmatic knowledge, however, is an important part of "communicative competence" (Hymes, 1974) or what a speaker needs to know to communicate effectively within a particular "speech community" (Hymes, 1974). This is a group of people who share both the same variety of a language and the pragmatic rules of use that govern that variety. Forces such as globalization and information technology are making this term more difficult to define, yet it still remains useful as a lens through which to view how

groups of people understand language. Pragmatic knowledge is often unconscious, yet it can drastically affect communication.

Although culture is not always the root of intercultural misunderstandings (Scollon & Scollon, 1996), it does influence language and communicative situations. This knowledge provides the basis for cultural scripts that influence our understandings of various speech events. For example, in Saudi Arabia the common response to the greeting "How's your health?" is "Praise to God." While a response such as "fine" does not indicate a misunderstanding at the semantic or meaning level, it marks the person as an outsider of that particular speech community.

This essay focuses on culture's influence on speakers' understandings of language and communicative events. It will explore the intimate relationship between language and culture using a framework laid out by Gumperz (1982a, 1982b). Gumperz developed a theory of communication, incorporating concepts from both anthropology and sociology, which he terms "interactional sociolinguistics." In this essay, I will address the interrelationship between language and culture and how it affects communication. In a time of increasing globalization, an understanding of the intimate relationship between language and culture is essential.

INTERACTIONAL SOCIOLINGUISTICS

Imagine you are in the audience listening to a talk by a Japanese professor. She begins her speech with, *"My English is not that good, but today I would like to speak about . . ."* An American would most likely experience astonishment, perhaps even anger, upon hearing this. Why would someone who is not proficient in English be asked to give a public lecture? Most likely, however, her English would be extremely proficient which would cause Western members of the audience even more astonishment. Was she being hypocritical or fishing for a compliment? The reason for her remark is that humility is a treasured virtue in Japanese society; thus, her statement marked her as a member of the Japanese speech community. This contrasts sharply with a society such as the United States where expressing ability is a crucial part of success. It is quite conceivable, then, that Japanese who cannot speak with confidence about their accomplishments face additional barriers when interacting in a speech community such as that found in the United States.

It is precisely for this reason that anthropological linguist John Gumperz set out to study interethnic communication and detail the features of language that while seemingly marginal in nature have an important communicative function. Interactional sociolinguistics (Gumperz, 1982a, 1982b) is an approach to discourse analysis that seeks to make explicit the features of language that affect speakers' interpretation of meaning. Before discussing interactional sociolinguistics, I need to distinguish the concepts of "speech community" and "community of practice."

Speech Community

The term *speech community* refers to a community sharing the rules of conduct and interpretation of at least one linguistic variety (Hymes, 1974). Therefore, the United States and Canada can be seen as two separate speech communities. The distinction, however, is much more complicated than this simple categorization.

The problem with "speech community" is where to draw boundaries around particular communities. For example, speakers of American English and British English can be characterized as one speech community of English speakers or as two separate communities because they speak different varieties. They can be even further divided by geographic region. The point is that both countries are made up of many different speech communities. This leads to speakers of the same language having trouble communicating with each other because the pragmatic norms that govern each respective variety diverge.

The situation becomes even more complex when we consider multilingual speech communities. Boston and New York are prime examples of this. Within each of these cities there are separate Chinese American and European American speech communities. Even within the speech community of Chinese speakers, for example, speakers of Mandarin and Cantonese can be further divided. It is unclear, then, where one speech community begins and another one ends. The conceptualization of speech community thus needs to be seen as flexible. A term that better captures

the linguistic and social practices of actual people in lieu of the more abstract "speech community" is "community of practice."

Community of Practice (CofP)

A community of practice (CofP) is a group of people who over time share in the same set of social practices with a common purpose (Wenger, 1998). This group develops activities and ways of engaging in them. This might be as simple as a group of people gathering weekly to play soccer in order to relieve stress. People simultaneously belong to various CofPs. Examples include a club, sports team, family, or group of students who regularly meet for coffee after class. To further elaborate on the student example, this group probably has ritualized patterns or routines the members engage in. For example, one student might hold their favorite table while the others buy the coffee. Once they have their coffee, there is probably some consistency regarding what they talk about, yet there is also variation. What might appear to an onlooker as an arbitrary gathering is actually a group of people with a common purpose and ritualized patterns of behavior they engage in each week.

The degree to which one participates in a CofP varies as well. In the student group, there might be one member who only joins occasionally or another who leaves early. This also varies based on factors such as the amount of free time one has or level of social investment in the group. Of course some CofPs such as fraternities, sororities, and sports teams have strict rules about participation. The CofPs in which people participate and the level of their participation change over the course of their lifetimes as well. While a child's or teenager's central CofPs might be school and a school-related club or sport, an adult's is likely to be the workplace and family.

Community of practice is useful because it focuses on the linguistic and social practices of actual groups of people. It helps to avoid making generalizations about abstract categories such as age, ethnicity, gender, and social class. A focus on CofPs allows us to see how people experience and decipher the social order on a personal basis. For these reasons, I will be using CofP rather than speech community. In the next section, Gumperz's theory of verbal communication will be discussed.

Language and Culture: Gumperz

Gumperz has shown that while people may share grammatical knowledge of a language, the assumptions they bring to a communicative encounter are culturally bound. Whereas some ethnic groups, such as the Japanese, prize group harmony and avoid both direct conflict and explicit disagreement (Lebra, 1978), disagreement is an important part of socialization for people of Greek (Kakava, 2002) and Jewish descent (Schiffrin, 1984). When different ethnic groups engage in communication, they are often unconscious of the assumptions about language and culture that they bring to the encounter.

The first important concept in Gumperz's (1982a) framework is the notion of "contextual presuppositions." These are a type of assumed background knowledge or cultural scripts through which speakers interpret a situation. These include assumptions related both to certain utterances and social situations. Thus, an American speaker knows that "what's up?" or "how's it going?" are formulaic greetings that act as social lubricant and typically not conversation starters. Similarly, speakers have contextual presuppositions about specific social encounters. In undergraduate classrooms, teachers typically facilitate the progression of the class, yet in upper-level seminars students are expected to take a more active role.

Cultural presuppositions are internalized assumptions about language and communicative events or social situations that are culturally influenced. We gradually acquire these presuppositions through socialization, and thus they vary with the different CofPs in which we possess membership. Closely related to contextual presuppositions are contextualization cues.

"Contextualization cues" are marginal features of language such as intonation, speech rhythm, and word choice that allow one to make situated inferences (interpretations). These cues demonstrate that languages vary not only by their core grammar (i.e., syntax, phonology, and semantics) but also at a more subtle level. While contextual presuppositions are cognitive in nature, contextualization cues index them linguistically. The subtle nature of contextualization cues makes them difficult to decipher for non-members of the CofP, yet they are a crucial part of communication as they index speaker meaning. In the previous example, John's failure to retrieve the

contextualization presupposition indicated by the nonverbal cue of silence and verbal cue "that's going to be a little bit difficult" resulted in a different "situated inference" or interpretation than the one Mr. Matsuzaki had intended. John's socialization in American culture produced different contextual presuppositions which ultimately resulted in miscommunication in that particular encounter.

In another example, Gumperz discusses a situation that occurred at a British airport. Newly hired Indian and Pakistani cafeteria employees were viewed as surly and uncooperative by both customers and their supervisors. The reason was due to the intonation used when asking customers if they wanted gravy on their meals. While the employees said "gravy" using falling intonation, the British customers expected rising intonation. The British customers interpreted the employees "gravy" as "this is gravy—take it or leave it"—not as a polite request, which is what the employees intended. This example illustrates the subtle nature of contextualization cues. Both sides left this encounter feeling frustrated because the situated inferences they made were based on contextual presuppositions formed in their own cultures. This example is also noteworthy because it characterizes the kind of interactions that are becoming commonplace today. These interactions consist of speakers who have different cultural backgrounds and consequently bring entirely different sets of assumptions to the same communicative event.

While the examples up until now have focused on interethnic communication, miscommunication can also result between speakers who share the same language. Contextualization cues and the subsequent contextual presuppositions they index vary depending on the CofP.

Gumperz found this in his analysis of interracial encounters between African American and Caucasian interlocutors. Gumperz (1982a) gives an example of rising intonation functioning as a contextualization cue. In the example the teacher calls on a student to read and he answers, "I don't wanna read." The teacher interprets this as a refusal and consequently becomes quite irritated. The teacher's situated inference of this encounter was based on personal contextual presuppositions that were formed as a result of socialization in various CofPs. Presumably the teacher's various CofPs did not have many African American members. If this had been the case, the teacher may have retrieved the appropriate contextual presupposition linking the contextualization cue of rising intonation with a desire for encouragement. A related example is white teachers' negative reactions to Black students' "sharing time" stories (Michaels, 1981). The White teacher's negative reaction to their Black students' stories indicates that the discourse conventions for telling stories are different in these CofPs. The Black children organize their stories around topics; thus, they are not necessarily told in the chronological order they occur. This contrasts with the White students who tell their stories in the chronological order they took place. This resulted in the teacher not making the situated inference that the Black students were telling stories. She interpreted their stories as "rambling" and thus "off task" behavior. These two groups have different contextual presuppositions about the speech event of "story." So here we have an example of speakers that share a language, and to a certain degree culture, but their assumptions about what constitutes effective communication are very different. This further illustrates that disadvantages can begin from an early age for members of minority groups who are not able to infer meaning from the contextualization cues used by members of the dominant group.

Similarly, sociolinguist Deborah Tannen has found that people from different parts of the United States both use different contextualization cues and bring different contextual presuppositions to conversations. In her analysis of a conversation that occurred during Thanksgiving dinner (Tannen, 1984), she found striking differences in the assumptions speakers from the West Coast and East Coast have about conversation. These assumptions were so different that Tannen identified two distinct "conversational styles."

Tannen identified these styles as the "high involvement" style associated with the East Coast and the "high considerateness" style, which she links with the West Coast. High involvement style speakers generally prefer personal topics, shift topics abruptly, use a lot of overlap (simultaneous talk), and avoid pauses between speakers. High considerateness style speakers, on the other hand, tend to feel uncomfortable with personal topics, especially when they first meet someone, do not shift topics as quickly, use less overlap, and are comfortable with a certain amount of silence. Conversational styles like contextual presuppositions and contextualization cues are acquired unconsciously and vary depending on factors such as ethnicity, gender, and geographic area of residence. Tannen places these two styles at opposite ends of a continuum and is careful to point out that most speakers are located somewhere between the two. In addition, most speakers "style shift" (change the way they speak) depending on which CofP they are participating in at that moment. Even monolingual speakers do not speak the same way across all situations; conversationalists strategically change the way they speak depending on the context of the conversation.

Tannen's important work contradicts prevailing stereotypes such as "New Yorkers are pushy" and "Americans avoid silence." Involvement and considerateness are matters of degree that vary depending on one's interlocutors (speakers). For example, while a native Californian may use high considerateness when speaking with a New Yorker, the same person is high involvement when interacting with someone from the Midwest. It is important to realize that when New Yorkers, for example, get together to talk, their fast rate of speech and overlap do not signal aggression, but involvement. Thus, an interlocutor with a slower rate of speech who uses little overlap might be viewed by a New Yorker as uninterested in the conversation. Because people tend to interact in CofPs where members have similar conversational styles, we are not conscious of the contextual presuppositions and contextualization cues we bring to conversations that are realized in our conversational styles.

Gumperz's study of verbal communication locates language at the interface between the influence of the culture and society the speakers grew up in and the "real time" interaction of the "speech event." A speech event is an activity in which participants interact to achieve some outcome. An example of a speech event is a conversation held during a party. It is here that the speakers' contextual presuppositions become something concrete in the form of contextualization cues that allow other speakers to make inferences about meaning. In both intercultural interactions and interactions between interlocutors from different CofPs, parts of our group-based identities and the assumptions we hold about various speech events become apparent. Before leaving this section, I will further illustrate the culturally situated nature of contextualization cues.

As stated above, contextualization cues can signal certain speech events. In the United States, for example, there is a tendency to begin certain types of speeches with a joke. That is rooted in the contextual presupposition that one should first "break the ice" or "loosen up the audience" before beginning the actual speech. Furthermore, this is a strategic move to build solidarity with the audience since the speaker shows that he or she has a sense of humor. Another contextual presupposition held by many Americans is that of egalitarian relationships. This is very different from the Japanese who begins his or her speech with an apology. This speaker, too, is strategically using language to build solidarity with members of the audience. The audience most likely makes the situated inference that the speaker is humble because having too much pride is viewed negatively in Japanese culture (Yamada, 1997). The amount of variation in presuppositions of certain speech events is one reason why there is a tendency for interactions among interlocutors of the same CofP to proceed more smoothly.

Language and Society: Goffman

Interactional sociolinguistics was also influenced by the late sociologist Erving Goffman. Goffman (1963, 1967) studied the relationship between "self" (our sense of who we are) and society as it played out in everyday encounters. Social encounters, like speech events, are accompanied with assumptions about how to show involvement. For example, eye contact and back channels (i.e., uh-huh or yeah) indicate to a speaker that you are listening. Furthermore, different social situations come with different expectations regarding appropriate involvement. While the norms governing involvement at a religious service require the formulaic recitation of prayers, at a party (at least in many Western societies) one should be able to engage in spontaneous conversation with strangers. Maintaining involvement, then, requires both linguistic and sociocultural knowledge.

Not unlike Gumperz, Goffman maintains that our sense of self is influenced by social processes not only at the institutional level (i.e., family, school, religion, or workplace) but also at the level of the face-to-face encounter. Thus, similar to Gumperz's conceptualization of the relationship between language and culture, our socialization within various institutions affects our interactions in "real time." For example, someone who grew up in a hierarchical society such as Japan most likely has fixed ideas about relationships between superiors and subordinates. This in turn affects the way he or she interacts with people of a different age or status. These ideas are Gumperz's contextual presuppositions. This might play out in language through the use of politeness when interacting with older and younger interlocutors. Someone who grew up in a more egalitarian society such as the United States, on the other hand, would have different understandings (contextual presuppositions) about the same relationships. This is illustrated in the tendency for American college students to treat nontraditional (i.e., older) students equally, irrespective of age. These presuppositions become embedded in actual social encounters as the contextualization cues speakers use and the situated inferences they make.

Furthermore, Goffman insightfully points out that our everyday interactions give social institutions their order and stability. For example, if students did not show proper involvement in the classroom by answering teachers' questions, it would be difficult for teachers to perform their jobs and for the school ("institution") to exist. In short, while institutions do influence global assumptions about social interactions and face-to-face interactions themselves, it is the interactions themselves that give those social institutions their meaning.

"Frame" is another concept that needs defining. A frame (Bateson, 1972; Goffman, 1974) is our interpretation of a speech event or what Goffman (1963) calls a "social situation." People engaged in communication interpret or frame an interaction in a certain way. In the previous example of the American speech, the speaker's use of an utterance such as "in all seriousness" or "to get back to the topic at hand" signals the shift from the initial joke to the actual speech. These set phrases are contextualization cues indicating a frameshift from the pre-speech phase to the core of the actual speech. Frames exist at both the local level of the interaction and the global level of prototypical social situations or speech events.

Framing at the local level is related to our conceptualizations of the real-time interaction at hand. For example, a high involvement style speaker might make a situated inference such as "my story is boring my conversational partner" due to his or her lack of overlap while the high considerateness style speaker may infer that the other speaker is dominating the conversation. In both cases, the speaker's different contextual presuppositions of the speech event "conversation" lead to them framing the conversation as unsuccessful. The situated inferences made by the speakers are located at the moment of interaction, yet are simultaneously influenced by their contextual presuppositions of prototypical situations. In this case, both speakers framed the local speech event of "conversation" as unsuccessful.

Frames are at work not only at the level of face-to-face interaction, but also at the more global level of prototypical social situations and speech events. For example, in certain countries such as Korea, it is customary to ask the age of someone you meet for the first time. This is because younger speakers are expected to use honorifics when addressing older interlocutors. Thus many Koreans frame the social situation "meeting someone for the first time" as requiring the speech event "asking the interlocutor's age." Clearly this contextual presupposition or global frame influences both the speaker's and the receiver's interpretations of the real-time interaction. A speaker who did not ask the other person's age and failed to use the appropriate forms of address risks being seen as showing improper involvement. This is why in interethnic and intercultural encounters miscommunications can occur that result from different contextual presuppositions or global frames.

As these examples have suggested, frames are closely tied to both contextual presuppositions and contextualization cues. Contextual presuppositions are akin to framing at the global level. This is our expectation about certain speech events or social situations. Furthermore, contextualization cues signal the local level of framing: what is going on at that specific moment in time. A pause is a contextualization cue that often precedes a refusal. Speakers who share knowledge of contextualization cues and presuppositions are able to locate this particular pause as part of a prototypical refusal.

Both Goffman and Gumperz incorporate the influence of society and culture on people's interpretations of certain interactions. We have expectations about social situations and speech events that in turn influence how we frame particular interactions. In intercultural encounters the chances are high that these expectations will not be shared, but even interactions between members from different CofPs in the same culture can result in misunderstanding.

CONCLUSION

The rise of English as an international language is helping bridge communication gaps between people with vastly different backgrounds. In addition to native varieties such as British and American English, there are extensively used nonnative varieties. These varieties are far from deficient versions of British and American English. In fact, they are structurally sophisticated with their own distinctive features that were developed to communicate for specific purposes, which can but does not necessarily involve native speakers. Today, English is just as likely to be used as a mode of communication between speakers from China and Korea as it is between speakers from parts of North America and the United Kingdom or between someone from Japan and someone from Australia. Thus, we can no longer see the native-nonnative speaker interaction or native-native interaction as the prototype. Therefore, unlike other languages, English can no longer be viewed as the exclusive property of native speakers.

Information technology has further accelerated communication to the extent that people from different parts of the world can communicate—even in real time—without ever meeting face-to-face. Even though the developments thus far are remarkable, we have only reached the tip of the iceberg with limitless possibilities awaiting us in the future.

In this exciting time of seemingly endless ways through which to communicate with others, there is an even greater possibility for miscommunication to occur. Thus, we are living in a time where the responsibility to acquire knowledge of contextual presuppositions and contextualization cues not only falls on the shoulders of nonnative speakers.

The work of John Gumperz has made explicit ordinarily taken-for-granted features of language which are rooted in culture and can drastically and substantially affect communication. Contextualization cues are linked to contextual presuppositions that allow one to make situated inferences.

The question arises as to how one acquires knowledge of contextualization cues. This is done through extensive periods of face-to-face contact. A feature of modern societies, however, is that more and more people are interacting in a wide variety of contexts, across multiple modes of communication in brief amounts of time. Furthermore, modern societies are becoming increasingly culturally diverse and international travel is now a part of many people's professional lives. The nature of modern societies makes it very difficult for the same people to interact long enough to gain an awareness of the contextualization cues used by other speakers. A distinguishing feature between society today and Gumperz's original research is that the responsibility to learn about other cultures does not rest with ethnic minorities. If speakers aim to communicate successfully in the age of globalization, they must increase their knowledge of other cultures. Today even more so than in the past, there is an urgent need for speakers to both reflect on the cultural assumptions they bring to communicative encounters and increase their own intercultural awareness.

Knowledge of other cultures can no longer be seen as a special skill one acquires to gain a competitive edge. Quite the contrary, intercultural competence is indispensable for anyone who intends to compete in the global marketplace. Even those who never intend to leave their home countries will still be exposed to information produced by people from other cultures. Therefore, in a truly global society, regardless of language, people work together to communicate with each other.

References

Bateson, G. (1972). *Steps to an ecology of mind.* New York: Ballantine.

Goffman, E. (1959). *The presentation of self in everyday life.* New York: Anchor Books.

Goffman, E. (1963). *Behavior in public places.* New York: Free Press.

Goffman, E. (1967). *Interaction ritual.* New York: Anchor Books.

Goffman, E. (1974). *Frame analysis.* New York: Harper & Row.

Gumperz, J. (1982a). *Discourse strategies.* Cambridge, MA: Cambridge University Press.

Gumperz, J. (1982b). *Language and social identity.* Cambridge, MA: Cambridge University Press.

Hymes, D. (1974). *Foundations in sociolinguistics: An ethnographic approach.* Philadelphia: University of Pennsylvania Press.

Kakava, C. (2002). Opposition in modern Greek discourse: Cultural and contextual constraints. *Journal of Pragmatics, 34,* 1537–1568.

Lebra, T. S. (1976). *Japanese patterns of behavior.* Honolulu: University of Hawaii Press.

Michaels, S. (1981). "Sharing time": Children's narrative styles and differential access to literacy. *Language in Society, 10,* 423–442.

Schiffrin, D. (1984). Jewish argument as sociability. *Language in society, 13,* 311–335.

Scollon, R., & Scollon, S. (1981). *Narrative literacy and face in interethnic communication.* Norwood, NJ: Ablex.

Scollon, R., & Scollon S. (1996). *Intercultural communication: A discourse approach.* Oxford: Blackwell.

Tannen, D. (1984). *Conversational style: Analyzing talk among friends.* Oxford: Blackwell.

Wenger, E. (1998). *Communities of practice.* Cambridge: Cambridge University Press.

Wolfson, N. (1989). *Perspectives: Sociolinguistics and TESOL.* New York: Newbury House.

Yamada, H. (1997). *Different games, different rules: Why Americans and Japanese misunderstand each other.* Oxford: Oxford University Press.

Concepts and Questions

1. What does Charlebois mean when he uses the term "pragmatic knowledge"?

2. What does the term "speech community" mean? Can you think of some examples of those communities?

3. Why would someone from Japan, according to Charlebois, face certain communication barriers in the United States?

4. Can you think of some examples of "multilingual speech communities"?

5. What is meant by the phrase "a community of practice"? Can you think of any of these communities?

6. What is Gumperz's concept "contextual presuppositions"? Can you think of examples from the dominant culture in the United States? Do you know of any examples from other cultures?

7. Explain the following sentence: "Sociolinguist Deborah Tannen has found that conversationalists from different parts of the United States both use different contextualization and bring different contextual presuppositions to conversations."

8. How does Goffman's approach to conversation differ from that of Gumperz?

Dialogue, Argument, and Cultural Communication Codes between Israeli-Jews and Palestinians

Donald G. Ellis
Ifat Maoz

INTRODUCTION

The conflict between Palestinians and Israeli-Jews fills newspapers and television programs with images of violence and conflict. The origins of the conflict between Israeli-Jews and Palestinian-Arabs can be traced to the end of the nineteenth century with the appearance of political Zionism and the resulting waves of Jewish immigration to Palestine. Zionism sought to establish a Jewish State in Palestine. However, on the same land lived Arabs with a Palestinian national identity. This resulted in a clash between the Jewish and Palestinian communities over the ownership of the land, the right for self-determination, and statehood. Violence between the two communities first erupted in the 1920s, and has pervaded the relationship in various forms and with varying degrees of intensity ever since (Kelman, 1997; Rouhana & Bar-Tal, 1998).

The communal clash that characterized the first decades of the twentieth century escalated into a war that involved the neighboring Arab states. This war erupted after the United Nations (UN) declared in November 1947 the partition of Palestine into two

The original version of this essay first appeared in the 10th edition. This updated version appears here in print for the first time. All rights reserved. Permission to reprint must be obtained from the authors and the publisher. Dr. Donald G. Ellis teaches in the School of Communication at the University of Hartford, West Hartford, Connecticut. Dr. Ifat Maoz teaches in the Department of Communication at The Hebrew University, Mt. Scopus Campus, Jerusalem, Israel.

states—one Arab and one Jewish. The Palestinians rejected the UN partition plan and an independent Jewish state was established in 1948. Israel won the war, and the vast majority of Palestinians who lived in the portion of Palestine on which Israel was now established were dispersed to the neighboring Arab countries, partly having fled war zones and partly having been expelled by Israeli forces (Maoz, 1999).

Other historical turning points in the relationship between Israelis and Palestinians include the 1967 war between Israel on one side, and Egypt, Jordan, and Syria on the other, which brought the remainder of Palestine under Israeli control. The first intifada (1987–1993) was an uprising of the Palestinians in the West Bank and Gaza Strip territories, expressing resistance to the Israeli occupation of these lands. (Rouhana & Bar-Tal, 1998).

In 1993, peace accords were signed in Oslo, Norway, and this signaled a breakthrough in the relations between Israelis and Palestinians. This dramatic agreement included an exchange of letters of mutual recognition between representatives of the two peoples, which was followed by a declaration of principles that stipulated the establishment of a Palestinian authority in Gaza and Jericho as a first step in Palestinian self rule (Kelman, 1997). At this time—which was indeed historic—prospects for the success of the peace process seemed exceptionally good. There was hope that the peace accords would end violence and lead to reconciliation. However, a few years after signing the accords it became clear that this optimism was premature. A chain of violent incidents began in November 1995 with the assassination of the then Israeli prime minister and continued with a number of terrorist attacks in the first half of 1996. These events signaled a slowdown in the Israeli-Palestinian peace process. Increasingly, the adversaries presented obstacles and impediments to the peace process, posed problems for the implementation of the different stages of the agreements, and violated the agreements. In October 2000 the al-Aqsa intifada broke out and the relationship between the Israelis and the Palestinians again took a violent turn.

Yet, political leaders from both sides continue to try to return to peace making and peace building. Although the conflict centers on the issue of land, and who has legitimate rights to the land, an issue that has strong historical, religious, and emotional significance, it is also a cultural conflict, a conflict over identities and recognition. The political and cultural differences between Israeli-Jews and Palestinians involve negative stereotypes, mutual delegitimization, and severe miscommunication. Dialogue and group encounters are one way to cope with these difficult problems. Dialogue sessions between Israeli-Jews and Palestinians involve a process of transformative communication aimed at improving the relations between the sides (Maoz, 2000a).

TRANSFORMATIVE COMMUNICATION BETWEEN GROUPS IN CONFLICT

Intergroup dialogues are useful venues for growth, change, and conflict management. Transformative dialogue between cultural groups in conflict helps reduce prejudice and hostility and foster mutual understanding (Gergen, 1999). Such dialogue experiences have been successful at helping groups cope with conflict in Northern Ireland, South Africa, and the Middle East (Ellis, 2006).

The notion of transformative contact or dialogue, when used in the context of intergroup conflict, draws heavily from the contact hypothesis in social psychology. This theory was first presented by Allport (1954) and has been the subject of numerous studies since then (Amir, 1976; Pettigrew, 1998). The contact hypothesis states that under certain conditions contact between groups in conflict reduces prejudice and changes negative intergroup attitudes. The contact hypothesis is optimal under certain conditions. First, the two groups should be of equal status, at least within the contact situation. Contacts of unequal status, where the traditional status imbalance is maintained, can act to perpetuate existing negative stereotypes. Second, successful contact should involve personal and sustained communication between individuals from the two groups. Third, effective contact requires cooperative interdependence, where members of the two groups engage in cooperative activities and depend on one another in order to achieve mutual goals. The fourth condition of the contact hypothesis states that social norms favoring equality must be the consensus among the relevant authorities.

TRANSFORMATIVE DIALOGUES BETWEEN ISRAELIS AND PALESTINIANS

The first attempts to address the dispute between Israelis and Palestinians by means of structured communication events were in interactive problem-solving workshops developed by Herbert Kelman from Harvard University in the early 1970s and have been conducted since then by him and his colleagues (Kelman, 1997). These workshops brought together politically active and influential Israelis and Palestinians for private direct communication facilitated by unofficial third party mediators (Kelman, 1995, 1997). Since the Oslo peace agreements in 1993, numerous Israeli-Palestinian dialogue events are conducted each year that are targeted at grassroots populations from both sides (Adwan & Bar-On, 2000). These dialogue events typically last two to three days and are aimed at building peace and reconciliation through processes of constructive communication (Maoz, 2000b). The dialogues are facilitated by both Israelis and Palestinians. In some sessions all of the participants meet, and in others they are divided into smaller groups. There are also several uni-national meetings where participants meet only with members of their own group. Dialogues are conducted either in English, or in Hebrew and Arabic that is translated.

The concept of "dialogue" as discussed by scholars such as Martin Buber, Carl Rogers, and Mikhail Bakhtin is the general guiding principle of these groups. That is, the goal of the communication is to avoid "monologue," or the pressure of a single authoritative voice, and strive instead for "dialogue," which emphasizes the interplay of different perspectives where something new and unique emerges. At its best, dialogue is a search for deep differences and shared concerns. It asks participants to inquire genuinely about the other person and avoid premature judgment, debate, and questions designed to expose flaws.

The process of change and transformation during dialogue is difficult, complex, and slow. There are many issues that enter the mix of politics, psychology, culture, and communication. In our work we have found that the communication process remains central. There is simply no possibility for reconciliation and peace without sustained interaction. For this reason we direct our attention to the issues in culture and communication that characterize these groups. The remainder of this essay is devoted to explaining the cultural communication codes that typify interactions between Israeli-Jews and Palestinians, and an explanation of how these speech codes are expressed in actual dialogues when Israeli-Jews and Palestinians are arguing.

SPEECH CODES

Whenever a group of people live in a culture they have certain characteristics and behaviors in common. We know, for example, that people in cultures dress similarly, share tastes in food preparation, and have many common attitudes. But they also share orientations toward communication. Members of cultural communities share principles of language use and interpretation. This simply means that your use of language (word choice, slang, accents, syntax) and your tendencies to interpret and understand this language in a certain way are dependent on your cultural membership. For example, assume you overheard the conversation below (Ellis, 1992).

JESSE: Yea, I'm thinkin' bout getting some new ink.

GENE: Really, where you gonna put it?

JESSE: Oh, I don' know. I've still got some clean spots.

For the moment, this conversation is probably pretty confusing and odd. What does it mean to "get new ink?" Why is Gene concerned about where to put it? What do "clean spots" refer to? Who are these people and what cultural functions is this conversation serving? Is Jesse thinking about buying a new bottle of ink for his fountain pen and Gene does not think there will be room for it on his messy desk?

This is a conversation between two tattoo enthusiasts who live and work among others in a tattoo culture that has developed norms of speaking. If you were a member of the culture and understood the "speech code" then you could participate in this conversation easily and competently. You would know that "new ink" refers to a "new tattoo" and that "clean spots" were places on the body that had no tattoos. You would understand the personal identity satisfaction that members of this culture gain from their unique code of communication.

Jesse and Gene are speaking in a cultural code, and you can only understand and participate in the conversation if you understand the code. The concept of speech codes has been studied by Bernstein (1971), Ellis (1992, 1994), and Philipsen (1997). Philipsen's treatment is most thorough in communication and it is the perspective we rely on here. But first we describe two cultural communication codes termed *dugri* and *musayra* known to characterize Israeli-Jews and Arabs, respectively. This will be followed by an elaboration of the concept of speech codes and an explanation of their role in intercultural communication dialogues for peace.

Israeli-Jewish and Arab cultures have emerged from the special circumstances of their history, and different norms of communication emerge from this history. These contrasting speech codes can make for difficult and uncoordinated communication. Several researchers have described an Arab communication coded called *musayra* (e.g., Feghali, 1997; Katriel, 1986). *Musayra* means "to accommodate" or "go along with." It is a way of communicating that orients the speaker toward a harmonious relationship with the other person. *Musayra* emerges from the core values of Arab culture which have to do with honor, hospitality, and collectivism. An Arab speaker who is engaging in the code of *musayra* is being polite, indirect, courteous, and non-confrontive to the other member of a conversation.

More specifically, *musayra* is composed of four communication features. The first is **repetition** in which the communication is characterized by repetitive statements that are formulaic in nature. Repetition is used primarily for complimenting and praising others, which is an important communication activity when you are trying to be gracious and accommodating. Repetition is also used as an argumentative style where repeated phrases are used to influence beliefs rather than Western-style logic. **Indirectness** is a second feature of the *musayra* code. This is a communication strategy that reflects the cultural tendency to be interpersonally cautious and responsive to context. By being indirect, one can shift positions easier to accommodate the other person. Indirectness also facilitates politeness and face saving. **Elaboration** is a third feature and it pertains to an expressive and encompassing style. It leads to a deeper connection between speakers and affirms relationships. The final characteristic is **affectiveness** or an intuitive and emotional style. Again, this allows for identification with the other person and the maintenance of an engaged relationship.

The speech code of Israeli-Jews is a sharp contrast to *musayra*. The Israeli-Jews employ a direct, pragmatic, and assertive style. This style has been termed *dugri* by Katriel (1986). *Dugri* means "straight talk" and is a well-documented code used by Israeli-Jews. *Dugri* is the opposite of *musayra*. It is direct, explicit, and clear. *Dugri* speech is "to the point" with the communication of understanding and information as the most important communicative goals. Emotional appeals and personal niceties are of secondary importance. In *musayra* it is important to maintain the face or positive image of the other speaker. In *dugri* speech the speaker is more concerned with maintaining his or her own image of clarity and directness.

Dugri and *musayra* are excellent examples of speech codes. Philipsen (1997) describes five main ideas that characterize cultural speech codes. We can see how these are powerfully ingrained in the communication of cultural members and are often responsible for misunderstanding and problems in intercultural communication. We further elaborate on *dugri* and *musayra* by explaining them within the context of the five principles of speech codes.

Speech Codes Are Culturally Distinctive

Speech codes are identified with a specific people in a specific place. When you first listen to someone speak you often ask or wonder "where are they from?" Language is always identified with locations such as countries (e.g., American English, British English, or Australian English), regions (e.g., the South or the East), or neighborhoods. Israeli *dugri* speech is associated with native-born Israelis of Jewish heritage in the land of Israel. The code is unique to Jews primarily of European heritage, and became crystallized in the prestate period of the 1930s and 1940s (Katriel, 1986). *Musayra* is culturally distinct for speakers of Arabic and members of Arabic cultures. However, its geographic location is more complex than *dugri* because Arabic cultures are more

geographically diverse. In both cases, however, when speakers of a code change geographical locations they modify their code use.

Speech Codes Result from a Psychology and Sociology Unique to the Culture

Speech codes are intimately connected to the psychological qualities of a culture; they are related to how people see themselves. In other words, certain attitudes, values, and states of mind are more descriptive of one culture than another. For example, an Arab using a *musayra* code is maintaining consistency with his culture's expectations of honor. Honor is a controlling psychological value that legitimates a modesty code and the hospitality that one bestows. To use a *musayra* code—to be indirect, affective, and polite—is to maintain honor and express a distinct psychology of Arabs. Israeli-Jews, on the other hand, use *dugri* to express their strong native identity. This identity is rooted in the pride and strength they feel with respect to the state of Israel. Historically, Jews had been a dislocated and oppressed people but the establishment of the state of Israel altered this historical condition. *Dugri* speech is a communicative expression of this pride.

The Meaning and Significance of Messages Are Fundamentally Dependent on Codes

You may be familiar with the maxim that "meanings are in people, not words." This means that a true understanding of communication is dependent on the people speaking and the code they use. When people communicate, they are performing some type of action and that action is interpreted by others. The interpretation relies on the speech code. When an Arab speaker deploys a *musayra* code and is polite, indirect, and courteous a noncode user might interpret this as being weak, obsequious, or manipulative. This can lead to communication problems. Israeli-Jews have a reputation for being rude and aggressive. The *dugri* code contains a directness of style that includes bluntness and forthrightness. It is not uncommon to hear Israeli-Jews in a meeting say things like "you are wrong" or "not true." This kind of directness is considered rude by many, but not if you understand the code. A listener who "speaks" the *dugri* code will not come to any hasty conclusions about the dispositions of the other because they use the same code to define the communicative act. In other words, bold utterances such as "you are wrong" are understood as normal ways of speaking rather than a rude way of speaking.

Speech Codes Are Located in the Language and Communication of Native Speakers

This simply means that speech codes are on display in the language of others. These codes are not inside the heads of others or contained in the generalities about culture. They are empirically observable in the communication of cultural members. Thus, when a native Israeli speaks directly and bluntly the *dugri* code is very apparent. Speech codes are also found in the ritualized functions of communication. These are the known and repeated ways of organizing interaction, and they have code-specific symbolic forms. A greeting ritual is an example. An African American will greet another African American differently than he would a White person. They might use certain vocabulary and body movements to signal a bond or friendship. The same is true for *dugri* and *musayra*. Both have symbolic forms that project and affirm an identity. By studying these symbolic forms and communication patterns we can discover how the cultural world is orderly rather than chaotic.

Speech Codes can be Used to Understand, Predict, and Control Communication

The artful understanding and use of speech codes can be used to improve communication. People do not communicate like machines. Even if they are steeped in cultural codes they often think reflectively about the code and alter typical patterns. This means there is potential for change and opportunities to avoid the more troublesome aspects of codes. An Israeli who is being very *dugri* can learn to recognize how he is perceived by others and perhaps alter certain patterns of communication. Moreover, situations can alter speech codes. In the following section of this essay we

explain how codes are influenced by particular communication situations.

ARGUMENT BETWEEN ISRAELI-JEWS AND PALESTINIANS

Argument is a persistent characteristic of the relationship between Israeli-Jews and Palestinians. In fact, argument is very important to these groups because it is an acceptable mechanism of conflict resolution. We prefer that these two groups argue with one another rather than shoot at each other. We might expect from the previous discussion that *dugri* speech would be characteristic of Israeli-Jews and the mode of speech preferred by them during argument since Israeli-Jews have a speech code that includes an argumentative style. And, *musayra* is not argument oriented at all. Interestingly, the little research that exists on Arab argument patterns is consistent with *musayra*. Hatim (1991), in a study devoted to this issue, found that argumentation in modern Arabic is related to politeness and saving face.

Group status is one of the problems for groups in dialogue situations. When cultural groups are very different in status the arguments produced by the high status groups can carry more weight. Israeli-Jews, given their military and economic advantages, carry considerably more status into dialogues. Their speech codes, moreover, are more conducive to argument. But dialogue groups that work to promote open discussion and equal relations can help lessen status differences. They become a context that levels differences. Even though Arabs come from a cultural background where argument is considered disrespectful, there are situations where this difference can be diminished.

In our studies (Maoz & Ellis, 2001, 2002; Ellis & Maoz, 2002; Ellis & Maoz, in press), we found that the arguments during political dialogues between Israeli-Jews and Palestinians were not necessarily consistent with expectations from cultural speech codes. In other words, the Israeli-Jews do not necessarily use more assertive arguments and the Arabs are not necessarily less overtly aggressive. It appears that the dialogue context of communication does alter speech codes and provides an environment for more equal status discussion. Palestinians are more assertive during these dialogues than speech code theory would suggest. They speak more and engage in more reasoning and elaboration. This means that they do state propositions and then support them with evidence in the classic tradition of argument.

The Israeli-Jews are somewhat consistent with the *dugri* code because they are quick to object to allegations and challenge assertions made by the Palestinians. Their experience with the *dugri* code makes it easy for them to sharply deny charges and demand justifications. But these dialogues do provide an environment for transformative communication because they afford the Palestinians an opportunity to accuse the Israeli-Jews of historical injustices. This is why the Israeli-Jews are typically on the defensive with objections and challenges to various statements. But, interestingly, the Israeli-Jews are also more hesitant and submissive in these dialogues. They do things such as qualify their arguments, backtrack, and provide context. Again, they are being challenged and responding in an accommodating and yielding manner rather than in a style associated with *dugri*. It is the dialogue context, and its transformative qualities, that is probably responsible for these changes since typical roles are altered.

This dialogue context may also strengthen the sense of unity for groups with minority status. And the communication patterns reflect this. The Palestinians argue in such a way that they elaborate and provide evidence for arguments in a manner much more akin to *dugri* than their own *musayra*. They clearly use the context to transform themselves into a power coalition. The Palestinians engage in a form of "tag team" argument (Brashers & Meyers, 1989). This is where one's own group is in a repetitive elaboration of a point to produce the perception of unity. Following is an example of a tag team argument. The Palestinians are expressing their anger about being prevented from entering Jerusalem. The Israelis say it is because of security but the Palestinians "gang up" on the Israelis saying that the security measures—which are check points that the Palestinians must pass and are monitored by the Israeli military—do not work and it is just harassment.

PAL: If we go into Jerusalem not through the Machsom (Hebrew word for "checkpoint"), I can go in. They see me and they don't care. It is that they want to make it difficult for me.

PAL: There are three ways to go from Bethlehem to Jerusalem.

PAL: If I want to go to Jerusalem, I am there in five minutes.

PAL: 60,000 Palestinians every day go to Israel without permission, every day. 40,000 with permission. So it's not security, it's politics. This is the information. I am not saying this to support.

The Palestinians are emboldened. The dialogue context helps transform the indigenous code of each group. This is an important matter with respect to the power relationship between each group. It suggests that the speech codes are pliant and that situations and activities can be found that reduce the cultural strength of these codes and make change and growth more possible. Moreover, these communication experiences balance the relationship between hostile and unequal groups in such a way as to promote egalitarianism and make future interactions more productive. In some new research using Internet groups we have found that these relations remain true (Ellis & Maoz, in press).

In this essay we have explained and illustrated cultural communication patterns between Israeli-Jews and Palestinians. These two groups are in bitter conflict, experiencing tremendous pressures and tensions for reconciliation and change. Clearly, national leaders and negotiators for peace need to solve the legal and legislative issues with respect to land, sovereignty, and other legal obligations. But true peace and prosperity "on the ground" will only come when these two groups learn to work together and improve communication. We have shown in this essay that each national group has evolved a different code and orientation to communication. These codes can be bridges or barriers to communication. Although communication codes are relatively firm, they are not unyielding. We have shown that there are contexts and situations where codes do not predict communication behavior. But more importantly, a thorough understanding of codes is necessary for dialogue and negotiation. Even words that are translated the same from different languages carry additional cultural baggage that is lost in the translation. Words are not neutral. They acquire their meaning from a culturally charged set of symbols that make up a speech code. The task for the future is to continually explore the nature of speech codes and their role in dialogue and conflict management.

References

Adwan, S., & Bar-On, D. (2000). *The role of non-governmental organizations in peacebuilding between Palestinians and Israelis.* Jerusalem: PRIME (Peace Research Institute in the Middle East), with the support of the World Bank.

Allport, G. (1954). *The Nature of Prejudice.* Reading, MA: Addison-Wesley.

Amir, Y. (1976). The role of intergroup contacts in change of prejudice and ethnic relations. In. P. Kats, (Ed.), *Toward the elimination of racism* (pp. 245–308). New York: Pergamon.

Bernstein, B. (1971). *Class, codes and control.* (Vol. 1). London: Routledge & Kegan Paul.

Brashers, D. E., & Meyers, R. A. (1989). Tag-team argument and group decision making: A preliminary investigation. In B. E. Graonbeck (Ed.), *Spheres of argument: Proceedings of the sixth SCA/AFA Conference on Argumentation.* (pp. 542–550). Annandale, VA: Speech Communication Association.

Ellis, D. G. (1992). Syntactic and pragmatic codes in communication, *Communication Theory, 2,* 1–23.

Ellis, D. G. (1994). Codes and pragmatic comprehension. In S. A. Deetz (Ed.), *Communication Yearbook 17* (pp. 333–343). Thousand Oaks, CA: Sage.

Ellis, D. G. (2006). *Transforming conflict: Communication and ethnopolitical conflict.* Boulder, CO: Rowman and Littlelfield.

Ellis, D. G. & Maoz, I. (2002). "Cross-cultural argument interactions between Israeli-Jews and Palestinians. *Journal of Applied Communication Research, 30,* 181–194.

Ellis, D., & Maoz, I. (2007. Online argument between Israeli-Jews and Palestinians. *Human Communication Research.*

Feghali, E. (1997). Arab cultural communication patterns. *International Journal of Intercultural Relations, 21,* 345–378.

Hatim, B. (1991). The pragmatics of argumentation in Arabic: The rise and fall of text type. *Text, 11,* 189–199.

Gergen, K. (1999, May 27–31). *Toward transformative dialogue.* A paper presented to the 49th Annual Conference of the International Communication Association, San Francisco, CA.

Katriel, T. (1986). *Talking straight: Dugri speech in Israeli Sabra culture.* Cambridge, MA: Cambridge University Press.

Kelman, H. (1995). Contributions of an unofficial conflict resolution effort to the Israeli-Palestinian breakthrough. *Negotiation Journal, 11,* 19–27.

Kelman, H. (1997). Group processes in the resolution of international conflicts: Experiences From the Israeli-Palestinian case. *American Psychologist, 52,* 212–220.

Maoz, I. (2000a). Multiple conflicts and competing agendas: A framework for conceptualizing structured encounters between groups in conflict—the case of a coexistence project between Jews and Palestinians in Israel." *Journal of Peace Psychology, 6,* 135–156.

Maoz, I. (2000b). An experiment in peace: Processes and effects in reconciliation aimed workshops of Israeli and Palestinian youth. *Journal of Peach Research, 37,* 721–736.

Maoz, I. (1999). From conflict to peace? Israel's relations with Syria and the Palestinians. *Middle East Journal, 53,* 393–416.

Maoz, I., & Ellis, D. G. (2001). Going to ground: Argument in Israeli-Jewish and Palestinian encounter groups." *Research on Language and Social Interaction, 34,* 399–419.

Philipsen, G. (1997). A theory of speech codes. In G. Philipsen & T. L. Albrecht (Eds.), *Developing communication theories* (pp. 119–156). Albany: State University of New York Press.

Pettigrew, T. (1998). Inergroup contact theory. *Annual Review of Psychology, 49,* 65–85.

Rouhana, N., & Bar-Tal, D. (1998). Psychological dynamics of intractable ethnonational conflicts: The Israeli-Palestinian case. *American Psychologist, 53,* 761–770.

Concepts and Questions

1. What roles do land rights, religion, and cultural conflict play in defining the communicative dynamics of Israeli-Jews and Palestinian-Arabs?

2. What do Ellis and Maoz mean when they refer to "transformative communication"?

3. How does transformative communication help improve the communication between groups in conflict?

4. What conditions must be met between two groups in conflict before the contact hypothesis will help reduce prejudice and negative intergroup attitudes?

5. How does the concept of "dialogue" as discussed by Martin Buber, Carl Rogers, and Mikhail Bakhtin provide guiding principles for transformative dialogue?

6. How do cultural differences in speech codes affect communication between Israeli-Jews and Palestinian-Arabs? Provide some examples of differences in speech codes for each of these groups.

Public Speaking Patterns in Kenya

ANN NEVILLE MILLER

Culture affects every level of the public speaking process—from what constitutes a relevant example or offensive topic, to the different interpretations assigned to direct eye contact and specific gestures, to the variation in the types of evidence and argument that are most convincing to a particular audience. These differences and many others are best understood as patterns created by threads that run through the entire societal fabric. As Albert (1972) observed of Burundian speech, these practices make sense in the context of larger cultural values.

It is in the spirit of adding to knowledge about the variety of public speaking practices across the globe and to making sense of these differences in the light of overarching cultural orientations that this article examines characteristics of public speaking in the East African nation of Kenya. We will take as an organizing framework the two most frequently cited dimensions of cultural variability identified by Dutch sociologist Geert Hofstede, individualism-collectivism and power distance, as well as Edward T. Hall's concepts of monochronic and polychronic time and high- and low-context communication. But first a proviso: It is important to recognize that beyond the obvious impossibility of describing all significant influences on rhetorical practice in any single country, it is particularly difficult in Kenya (as in many other African nations) where each of the 40 to 50 indigenous cultural and linguistic groups has its own rules, values, and traditions. To complicate matters further, many of these cultures are in a state of rapid but uneven westernization. Some traditional communication patterns discussed in this essay are rapidly eroding among some, especially urban,

groups. Certain common themes that run throughout these numerous groups will be discussed here as "Kenyan culture," but any comments made must be recognized as generalizations about this diversity. The article will begin with a brief description of Kenyan value orientations and then move on to examine public speaking practices as outgrowths of these cultural patterns. Examples are based on the author's personal experience of living and working in Kenya for nine years, discussions with Kenyan colleagues and friends, and research conducted during that time on characteristics of Kenyan public speaking.

A BRIEF LOOK AT KENYAN VALUE ORIENTATIONS

Collectivism

Probably the construct most frequently used to explain similarities and differences between cultures is individualism versus collectivism (Gudykunst, 1998). African cultures as a group are considered to be collectivistic as opposed to individualistic (Hofstede, 1994; Kenyatta, 1965; Mbiti, 1970; Moemeka, 1997; Olaniran & Roach, 1994; Onwumechili, 1996). Some African scholars, in fact, have cited this as the defining quality of the African mindset (Gyekye, 1997). In collectivistic cultures, according to Hofstede (1991), "The 'we' group (or in-group) is the major source of one's identity, and the only secure protection one has against the hardships of life. Therefore one owes lifelong loyalty to one's in-groups, and breaking this loyalty is one of the worst things a person can do" (p. 50). Kenyatta (1965), writing during the colonial era, observed regarding his own traditional Kikuyu culture in central Kenya, "The personal pronoun 'I' was used very rarely in public assemblies. The spirit of collectivism was [so] much ingrained in the mind of the people" (p. 188).

The collectivistic mindset affects every aspect of life. Responsibilities toward family in Kenya extend far down the genealogical line, and are financial as well as social. Families frequently house or pay school costs for nephews, nieces, and cousins whom they may not know particularly well. Weddings, funerals, and other events, no matter how far away they take place geographically, must be attended, and usually span an entire day. In the workplace, collectivism may be manifested by the desire for job security and training over personal fulfillment (Hofstede, 1991). Employees at Kenyan businesses are rarely fired for incompetence, and as with family obligations, it is important to show solidarity with coworkers at significant times in their lives. For example, some time ago the author took part in a discussion about who would represent the university department at the funeral of a colleague's father. It was essential that the group be represented, even though the journey to and from the funeral would take three entire days.

Power Distance

Related to collectivism and also characterizing Kenyan culture is the orientation of high power distance. Power distance is defined as the extent to which less powerful members of society view the unequal distribution of power as a normal part of life (Hofstede, 1991); it is a description of the way a given society handles inequality. In low power distance societies such as the United States, egalitarianism is a primary value. People in these societies do not place much emphasis on titles, ceremony, and other outward displays of power. By contrast, most African societies are classified as high power distance (Hofstede, 1991; Olaniran & Roach 1994), and consider such practices very important.

In the family, for instance, respect and deference to parents and older relatives is a lifelong obligation. Children are not expected to make their own decisions or contradict those of their elders. In traditional Kenyan families, the power hierarchy was clearly delineated: the father is the supreme authority, followed by the mother and then frequently the oldest child. To directly question the word of the father is still unthinkable. When children begin school, their relationship to their teachers is similar to what they have with their parents. In Kenyan primary school classrooms, the teacher is an authoritative figure who displays less nurturing behavior than in a similar classroom situation in many Western nations (Maleche, 1997). In the workplace, a lower-level worker may feel uncomfortable ever directly addressing injustice by a superior unless there is a groundswell of popular dissent behind him or her. Even then the more likely method would be to approach the authority figure indirectly, either with hints or through an intermediary.

Monochronic and Polychronic Time

According to anthropologist Edward T. Hall, in cultures where the monochronic view of time predominates, people tend to run their lives by schedules in a linear fashion (Hall, 1983). They concentrate on only one thing at a time, compartmentalizing their lives—hence the term *mono*chronic. Time to such people is like a commodity; it can be bought, saved, wasted, or spent.

Most Northern Europeans and North Americans operate on monochronic time. On the other hand, the prevailing view of time in Kenya is polychronic; what is important is not schedules and efficiency, but events and people. If a workshop, dedication ceremony, fundraiser, or other event takes longer than anticipated (which it often does if speeches run long and there are more speeches than originally planned), Kenyans believe it is more important to complete the event than to rigidly adhere to schedules attendees might have for the rest of the day. Nor does being on time mean the same thing in Kenya as in the United States. It is not uncommon for weddings and other social events to begin hours late. Most people simply wait out the delays and take advantage of the opportunity to socialize. Because of increased globalization and the influence of Western media, some accommodation to the monochronic system has been made by urban Kenyans in recent years. For example, several large churches in Nairobi that are popular as wedding venues have begun to require that the ceremony begin within half an hour of the scheduled time, otherwise an extra fee is added. Overall, though, operating in monochronic time still appears to be an uncomfortable fit. The professionals who arrive at work in the morning with appointments for the day penciled in their diaries more often than not by afternoon have ordered their secretaries to make a string of calls postponing their meetings.

High- and Low-Context Communication

Although Hall's conception of high- and low-context elements in cultures is very encompassing, the focus here is on his application of these terms to interactions.

According to Hall (1981), high-context communication features "pre-programmed information that is in the receiver and in the setting, with only minimal information in the transmitted message." Low-context transactions, he explains, are the opposite: "Most of the information must be in the transmitted message in order to make up for what is missing in the context" (p. 101). Because they accommodate change easily and rapidly, low-context messages are prevalent in technologically driven societies like the United States. High-context messages are the norm in most collectivistic societies. A great amount of information is held in common among members, and so less needs to be said explicitly. Kenyan traditional culture falls toward the high-context end of the continuum. One of the marks of wisdom in the elderly is the ability to convey messages indirectly through the use of proverbs and analogies, in public as well as in private settings.

A child may not be told the error of her ways in so many words, but a carefully selected story related by the grandmother clearly communicates the correction.

PUBLIC SPEAKING PATTERNS AS OUTGROWTHS OF KENYAN VALUES

Having looked briefly at overarching Kenyan values, we now turn to examining the impact of these orientations on public speaking practice. Current research on the topic provides little guidance, as Africa is one of the least studied areas of the world in intercultural communication literature (Gudykunst, 1998; Shuter, 1997). Even in Kenya itself, there are no formal theories explaining why people speak in public today as they do. The closest approximation are descriptions in the fields of cultural anthropology and oral folklore of traditional ceremonies among specific groups. As Western-developed constructs, Hall and Hofstede's categorizations are necessarily limited in their capacity to portray communication from a truly African viewpoint, but they do provide a useful ground for comparison with more Eurocentric public speaking practice. Previous research by the author with Kenyan students and instructors of public speaking (Miller, 2002) has identified four major areas of difference between mainstream U.S. and Kenyan public speaking patterns: speaking purposes, supporting material,

credibility, and speech structure. These categories will be used as a framework for the present examination of Kenyan public speaking.

Speaking Purposes

Much public speaking in the United States is informative or persuasive in purpose; ceremonial occasions for public speaking are less common. This is due in part to the stress that mainstream U.S. culture places on informality. The average Kenyan, in contrast, will give far more ceremonial speeches in life than any other kind. These may be speeches of greeting, introduction, tribute, and thanks, among others. Life events both major and minor are marked by ceremonies, and ceremonies occasion multiple public speeches.

This means that unlike the majority of people in the United States who report that they fear speaking in public, possibly even more than they fear death (Bruskin Report, 1973; McCroskey, 1993; Richmond & McCroskey, 1995), for most Kenyans public speaking is an unavoidable responsibility. For example, when a Kenyan attends a church service or other event away from home, he or she will often be asked to stand up and give an impromptu word of greeting to the assembly. In more remote areas, where literacy rates are low and there is little access to electronic media, this word of greeting can serve an informative purpose as well, because the one who has traveled often brings news of the outside world. The "harambee," a kind of community fundraising event peculiar to Kenya, is characterized by the presence not only of a guest of honor but also of various other dignitaries of a stature appropriate to the specific occasion, all of whom are likely at some point to address the gathering. Weddings and funerals overflow with ceremonial speeches, as virtually any relative, friend, or business associate of the newly married or deceased may give advice or pay tribute. Older members of the bride's family, for example, may remind her how important it is to feed her husband well, or warn the groom that in their family men are expected never to abuse their wives but to settle marital disputes with patience. Even the woman selected to cut the cake expects to give a brief word of exhortation before performing her duty. The free dispensing of advice, a hallmark of Kenyan wedding celebrations, would be out of place at most receptions in the United States, where the focus of speeches is normally more on remembrances and well-wishing.

In fact, when it comes to marriage, speech making begins long before the actual wedding day, at bridal negotiations where up to fourty or fifty people from the two families attempt to settle on a bride price. At these negotiations especially, but in other ceremonial speeches as well, "deep" language replete with proverbs and metaphors is expected. The family of the man may explain that their son has seen a beautiful flower, or a lovely she-goat, or some other item in the compound of the family of the young lady and that they would like to obtain it for their son. In a negotiation of this type that the author recently attended, the speaker for the bride's relatives explained that the family would require twenty goats as a major portion of the bride price.

Since both parties were urban dwellers and would have no space to keep that many animals, the groom's family conferred with one another and determined that the bride's family really wanted cash. They settled on what they considered a reasonable price per goat, multiplied it by 20, and presented the total amount through their designated spokesperson to the representative of the bride. The original speaker looked at the money and observed dryly that goats in the groom's area were considerably thinner than those the bride's family was accustomed to![1] This type of indirect communication, the subtlety of which affords immense satisfaction and sometimes amusement to both speaker and listener, is a form of the high-context communication described by Hall. A full appreciation of the speech requires extensive knowledge of shared experiences and traditions.

Kenyan ceremonial speeches also display a formality that similar speeches in the United States may not exhibit. For example, it is very important at fundraisers, funerals, and other occasions for the master of ceremonies to be aware of any VIPs who are present and to ask them to give greetings in order of prominence. The unwritten rules for giving thanks at the end of such occasions are similar. The speaker must be careful to offer thanks to all persons present who have anything to do with the event. A member of parliament who speaks at many school fundraisers, for example, explained that he is careful to learn the history of the school and be sure to pay tribute to persons who have made substantial contributions to its success in the past. Even in small gatherings, a person of particular prominence should be allowed to

make opening and closing remarks and be escorted from the room at the appropriate time.

The prevalence of ceremonial speeches and the importance placed on recognition of persons of status is clearly tied to the Kenyan value of high power distance. Because differences in power are considered natural in society, it is also natural that much of public speaking should be dedicated to affirming those distinctions. Titles must be carefully mentioned and due respect given by allowing the important person to speak. Omission of requisite recognition may not be taken lightly, as when one important politician walked late into an assembly, escaping the notice of the master of ceremonies. By the end of the event, someone had called the attention of the emcee to the presence of the politician, at which point he offered him an opportunity to address the group. The politician did so, but not without first making several pointed comments about not having been asked to speak earlier.

The joining together by the community to give and receive speeches of advice for newlyweds, congratulations of colleagues, and comfort for the bereaved is also an expression of the Kenyan value of collectivism. Although this value has been modified to a degree in urban areas by the influences of Western media and globalization, it is still true that marriage, widowhood, and other major life events are community experiences. As Mbiti (1970) observes, "Whatever happens to the individual happens to the whole group, and whatever happens to the whole group happens to the individual" (p. 141). It is not surprising, then, that ceremonial speeches, frequent and formal, are a central part of the lives of most Kenyans.

Supporting Material

Traditional Kenyan speeches are not normally based on extensive formal research. Whereas in the United States statistics are often used as evidence for the assertions made, in most Kenyan speech contexts facts and figures are not especially persuasive. Kenyans think more relationally. A Kenyan pastor once told the author a story to emphasize this point. One day he stopped along the road to give a ride to a stranger. His passenger explained that he was trying to get to the hospital because his brother had just been in a bus accident. "What do you think I asked him?" the pastor prodded rhetorically as he related the tale. "I didn't ask how many people were involved. I asked him *who*. Africans don't care about numbers, we care about the relationships."

The most convincing type of supporting material for a Kenyan public speech is a narrative, and the most convincing type of narrative is the personal story. "Subjectivity is the only sensible approach to the African mind," asserts one African professor of communication who studied in the United States. "In the West an overuse of personal stories might make the speaker appear not to be objective, but not with us. We believe you only really know about something if you've experienced it." Both speakers and audiences enjoy a good story, and the accomplished speaker will develop suspense, humor, and vivid characterizations in the telling. A listener from the United States may be surprised to find that once the narrative has unfolded, the speaker may not explicitly explain the connection of the story to the main point of the speech, but simply move on to other illustrations. What is happening in such cases, though, is understandable from the standpoint of high-context communication; audience members are being given the pleasure of inferring the underlying message for themselves. Scollon and Scollon (1995) view an evidently similar practice in Athabaskan oral narrative performance as a paying of respect by the narrator to the autonomy of the listener.

Beyond narratives, several other means of supporting one's point are common in Kenyan speeches. Proverbs, which like narratives teach lessons in a subtle way, are a sign of wisdom and experience; it is the old who are normally most familiar with proverbs and maxims. That is why an older person, such as the paternal uncle, is frequently in charge of conducting marriage negotiations. Such a person has the linguistic skill necessary to perform the intricate verbal dance required in pre-wedding speeches. In the urban environment, where audiences at most events are composed of people from several language groups, proverbs from the speaker's vernacular can still be used, but the speaker usually provides translation into Swahili or English. Songs can also be supporting material. A speaker may insert a song in the middle of the speech, singing ability or lack thereof being irrelevant. For example, in a graduation speech several years ago, the academic dean of a leading private Kenyan university, in an interesting synthesis of the traditional and

contemporary, broke into strains of R. Kelly's "I Believe I Can Fly," then continued making his points.

Even audience response can be considered a type of supporting material. A speaker can leave the end of a sentence hanging and wait for the audience to fill in the blank, or lead the audience in chanting specific phrases. The latter practice has been used liberally by the nation's presidents. Founding President Jomo Kenyatta, for example, at Kenya's first Independence Day, led the audience in a crescendo of "Moto! Moto!" (Swahili for "Fire! Fire!") prior to commencing his speech. Many preachers drive home their points by allowing their audience to complete their sentences. At first glance these techniques might not appear to qualify as evidence, yet the function is exactly that of convincing the audience that the speaker's points are correct. As noted above, the use of narratives, proverbs, and songs is related to the Kenyan pattern of high-context communication, as they require shared experience for full understanding.

A close examination of these supporting materials also reveals a connection to the value of collectivism. Members of the audience at a public speech are not spectators. They are participants coming together to construct a shared communal meaning in the occasion.

Audience response is part of that process; members are convinced that the speaker's assertions are true because they have participated in creating them. In a different way, willingness to sing during a speech is related to collectivism as well. In individualistic societies like the United States, where persons must strive to prove their own worth, singing in front of an audience is a risk unless one is sure of one's abilities. Speakers in the collectivistic Kenyan culture, however, are already assured of their worth as members of the group, so level of talent is not as much of a concern. The Luganda people in neighboring Uganda express this truth in their proverb "The one who doesn't sing well sings among his own."

Credibility

The need for speaker credibility is as essential in Kenya as it is in the United States. The factors that determine credibility, however, are different. Wealth, family status, age, and ethnicity—all demographic factors—are of highest importance. Wealth, whether in terms of herds, wives, children, or money, is a strong determinant of credibility. Its effect, however, is mitigated by the extent to which that wealth has been used to help other members of society. Traditional marital status and family status have also been critical in a way that may be difficult for audiences in the United States to imagine. In many rural areas in Kenya, an unmarried man, or a married man with no sons or few children, cannot speak with authority. To participate in deliberative speaking about decisions affecting the village, he must have attained the status of elder, which often involves producing a certain number of sons or children. Traditionally, women could speak in public only on certain occasions, although in recent years this has changed. For example, a growing number of female politicians, including members of parliament, the former head of civil service, and the current minister of health, have regularly addressed large gatherings, both rural and urban. As in many collectivistic societies, age is less venerated in Kenya now than in the past. Nevertheless, even now, in certain situations the young cannot address the old in a public gathering (or in a private one either, for that matter), at least not without permission.

Finally, in a nation with fourty distinct cultural groups, ethnicity and language are important as well. Certain tribal groups have more credibility than others in addressing the nation as a whole. In culturally homogeneous gatherings, of course, to be from the same group and speak the same language is invaluable. However, language can be planned for particular effects in multiethnic gatherings as well. The immediate past president of the country, Daniel Moi, frequently divided his speeches into a more formal English section and a folksier second portion that he delivered in Swahili. It was in the second section, while using an African language, that he attempted to connect at a more emotional level with his constituents.

The Kenyan view of credibility appears to be closely tied to the value of high power distance. Similar to Albert's (1972) observations of speech behavior in Burundi, in Kenya persons with a particular status—whether due to age, wealth, or family—are automatically assured of a hearing in the public arena. Persons without these qualities understand that gaining credibility in a public speaking situation, unless they can borrow credibility through endorsement by someone who does possess these

attributes, will be a challenge. In recent years, education has become an additional factor in speaker credibility, with advanced degrees mentioned in the introduction of a speaker automatically conferring a certain amount of respect. On this issue, Mbennah (1999) notes that although an elderly speaker would generally be considered more credible, in a case where technical expertise is required the audience would consider a young person possessing this knowledge to be more credible than an elderly person who did not.

Speech Structure

Various researchers, beginning with Kaplan (1966), have suggested that the logical and organizational patterns of rhetoric are determined by culture; they are not universal. Although it is generally recognized that most mainstream U.S. speeches are organized linearly, linear patterns do not represent the only logical systems available to public speakers. The organization of many Kenyan speeches could be represented as a bicycle wheel, or what Kearney and Plax (1996) call a web organizational pattern. The spokes wander out repeatedly to the rim as the speaker gives an illustration, mentions a proverb, or tells a story, and then return back to the thesis at the center, though usually not exactly at the place from which they departed.

Often there is only one main point in such a speech, but it is developed by an abundance of supporting material. Westerners in the audience might feel bewildered and even bored because they are unable to follow the logic that ties all the points together, whereas Kenyan listeners would be absorbed in the stories and delighted with their subtle convergence back into the central theme.

It is difficult to convey this technique in print, but an introductory speech given at a large gathering at a Kenyan university recently may give an abbreviated idea of it. The master of ceremonies at the event welcomed the audience and then launched into a story about his childhood in a poor family in rural Kenya. He related that while still quite small he slept late one morning, much to his mother's irritation. Explaining this took some time as he made a number of humorous comments about how many children slept in one bed, how his mother normally disciplined him when she caught him misbehaving, how inclined he was to oversleeping at that stage of life, and so on. After the audience was thoroughly caught up in his description, the speaker brought the story to a climax. When he finally crawled out of bed, he said, his mother directed his attention outside to the garden where he was surprised to see that everything growing there had been completely flattened. "Now you see how when you are not alert you miss important things," she admonished him. "While you were sleeping, elephants were here and you never knew it." The speaker then addressed the audience directly: "We have elephants with us this morning." Amid general laughter, he invited the distinguished guests onto the stage. The implication of the story, of course, made through an amusing, much embellished personal anecdote, was that the audience should pay attention to the words of the very big people coming to address them. The point was made indirectly, and then only after the story was savored for its own sake. This might, in a Western setting, have seemed like a tangential sort of introduction, but within the Kenyan cultural environment it was extremely effective. The "bicycle wheel," or web, speech pattern that it exemplifies can be seen as an outgrowth of the collectivistic worldview, depending as it does on extensive personal narratives into which the audience enters as co-participants, and incorporating the subtle connections characteristic of high-context communication.

Under the category of speech structure we will also include the use of time in public speeches. Unlike many speeches in the United States, the majority of Kenyan speeches are not time limited. A speaker may easily wax eloquent for an hour. Even speakers given the role of delivering preliminary speeches to the main guest may speak for half an hour or more, though admittedly to the secret chagrin of their audiences who most often would prefer to hear the guest of honor. Since programs often begin long after the stated hour, the end result is that of day-long celebrations for many large public events. Not uncommon is the experience of a Kenyan colleague who got lost on the way to a wedding and arrived a full two hours late. The church compound was full of milling people which might have led an unaccustomed observer to assume that the wedding was already over. However, a quick check on the situation revealed that, in fact, the bride had not yet even arrived at the church. The tardy guest joined the rest of the crowd in waiting another forty-five minutes until the bride came. Despite the late beginning, the wedding reception was allowed to run its full course of speeches, winding up many hours later. Although some urban churches have begun to demand strict adherence to the stipulated time frame, this situation is not unusual in Kenyan weddings. Last-minute haggling over the details of the marriage negotiations may take place when the groom's family comes on the wedding day to escort his fiancée from her homestead.

This aspect of public speaking is related to both the polychronic view of time and the value of collectivism that most Kenyans hold. What is important is that the significance of the event be fully acknowledged. If that means many speakers and long speeches, so be it. Because the group is valued more highly than individual interests, it is necessary to give every relevant person the opportunity to be heard at a given occasion. Harmony is more important than whether or not an individual makes it to his or her next appointment.

CONCLUSION

Much more could be said about Kenyan public speaking practices. Even this brief discussion suggests that although the basic categories that must be considered in presenting a speech are possibly universal (Clark, 1957), what makes for effective invention, arrangement, style, memory, and delivery varies across cultures. In an increasingly global society, it is important for public speakers and audiences to understand something of the variety of culturally defined expectations regarding the form of a public speech, and that many of these differences in practice are tied to deep-seated values and traits. In collectivistic cultures like Kenya, a public speech is more than a performance by a skilled actor; it is a shared experience. It drives home its message by allowing audience members to exert the mental effort to interpret and make connections for themselves, thereby creating an even stronger bond between speaker and audience through shared comprehension. It instantiates community ties by the ritual of recurring ceremony. And with a perspective that would sound postmodern had it not been established over hundreds of years of tradition, Kenyan listeners accept the subjective experiences of the speaker with the topic as the most telling evidence possible in a public speech. As a central feature in the lives of most Kenyans, public speaking is a distinct expression and shaper of cultural identity.

Note

1. Although it is outside of the purpose of this essay to discuss the significance of the custom of African bride price, it should be noted that in most cultures the practice traditionally has not been seen as "buying" a wife, but as a means of bonding the two families together in mutual obligation and in that way strengthening the marriage of the two individuals. It also serves to show appreciation to the bride's family for the fine quality of upbringing they have given to the future daughter-in-law. The bride price is rarely paid at once, but through repeated meetings between the families that cement their relationship. Nor has it traditionally been funded solely by the parents of the groom, but rather pooled from various members of the extended family in yet another expression of collectivism.

References

Albert, E. (1972). Culture patterning of speech behavior in Burundi. In J. Gumperz & D. Hymes (Eds.), *Directions in sociolinguistics: The ethnography of communication* (pp. 72–105). New York: Holt, Rinehart and Winston.

Bruskin Report. (1973, July). *What are Americans afraid of?* (Research Rep. No. 53 C).

Clark, D. (1957). *Rhetoric in Greco-Roman education.* New York: Columbia University Press.

Gudykunst, W. (1998). Individualistic and collectivistic perspectives on communication: An introduction. *International Journal of Intercultural Relations, 22,* 107–134.

Gyekye, K. (1997). *Tradition and modernity: Philosophical reflections on the African experience.* New York: Doubleday.

Hall, E. (1981). *Beyond culture.* New York: Doubleday.

Hall, E. (1983). *The dance of life: The other dimension of time.* New York: Doubleday.

Hofstede, G. (1991). *Cultures and organizations: Software of the mind.* London: McGraw-Hill.

Kaplan, R. (1966). Cultural thought patterns in inter-cultural education. *Language Learning, 16,* 1–20.

Kearney, P., & Plax, T. (1996). *Public speaking in a diverse society.* Mountain View, CA: Mayfield.

Kenyatta, J. (1965). *Facing Mount Kenya.* New York: Vintage Books.

Maleche, H. (1997). *Interpersonal Communication in Counseling Departments in Secondary Schools in Nairobi.* Unpublished master's thesis, Daystar University, Nairobi, Kenya.

Mbennah, E. (1999). *The impact of audience worldview on speaker credibility in persuasive speaking: The case of afrocentric and eurocentric audiences.* Unpublished doctoral dissertation, Daystar University, Nairobi, Kenya.

Mbiti, J. (1970). *African religions and philosophy.* New York: Doubleday.

McCroskey, J. (1993). *An introduction to rhetorical communication* (6th ed.). Englewood Cliffs, NJ: Prentice Hall.

Miller, A. (2002). An exploration of Kenyan public speaking patterns with implications for the American introductory public speaking course. *Communication Education, 51,* 168–183.

Moemeka, A. (1997). Communalistic societies: Community and self-respect as African values. In C. G. Christians & M. Traber (Eds.), *Communication ethics and universal values* (pp. 170–193). London: Sage.

Olaniran, B., & Roach, D. (1994). Communication apprehension and classroom apprehension in Nigerian classrooms. *Communication Quarterly, 42,* 379–389.

Onwumechili, C. (1996). Organizational culture in Nigeria: An exploratory study. *Communication Research Reports, 13,* 239–249.

Richmond, V., & McCroskey, J. (1995). *Communication: Apprehension, avoidance, and effectiveness* (4th ed.). Scottsdale, AZ: Gorsuch Scarisbrick.

Scollon, R., & Scollon, S. (1995). *Intercultural communication: A discourse approach.* Cambridge: Blackwell.

Shuter, R. (1997). Revisiting the centrality of culture. In J. N. Martin, T. K. Nakayama, & L. A. Flores (Eds.), *Readings in cultural contexts* (pp. 39–47). New York: Mayfield.

Concepts and Questions

1. Why is there more ceremonial than persuasive and informative speaking in Kenya?

2. What is a major difference between people in the United States and those in Kenya with regard to their fear of public speaking?

3. How would the formality or informality found in a culture influence the perception and use of public speaking techniques?

4. Why would the notion of power distance influence public speaking? In what ways might this influence be manifested?

5. How does the concept of collectivism exhibit itself in Kenya?

6. Why do Kenyans rely on the narrative for supporting material in the public speaking context, whereas in the United States people use statistics and testimony to help accomplish their speech purpose?

7. How does the bicycle organization pattern differ from the linear method used in the United States? Does it remind you of speech organizational schemes from other cultures?

Mexican *Dichos:* Lessons through Language

CAROLYN ROY

MEXICAN CULTURE AND ITS REFLECTED IMAGES

The late Octavio Paz, one of Mexico's most renowned writers, asserts in his classic *The Labyrinth of Solitude: Life and Thought in Mexico* that the Mexican's "face is a mask" (Paz, 1961, p. 29). Paz thereby implies that knowing *the* Mexican national character might be impossible. Carlos Fuentes, another of Mexico's most esteemed men of letters, employs the imagery of dark, ancient Aztec polished hematite mirrors reflecting the soul of Mexico when he writes: "Is not the mirror both a reflection of reality and a projection of the imagination?" (Fuentes, 1992, p. 11). Despite the self-confessed inscrutable nature of Mexican national character, *dichos*—popular sayings including, but not limited to, *proverbios*/proverbs, *adagios*/adages, and *refranes*/refrains—open an avenue for exploring the attributes most esteemed and salient in Mexican popular culture. Using Fuentes' metaphor, however, our understanding of Mexican culture remains a darkly reflected image. Our understanding is further obscured by the difficulty of precise idiomatic translation of the complex Mexican language that hybridizes the Spanish brought from Europe with the intricately nuanced indigenous languages, predominantly Nahuatl, of Mexico's native peoples. Nevertheless, popular sayings heard from the northern reaches of the Chihuahuan desert to the highlands of southern Chiapas do provide insight into some commonly held values in Mexican culture.

Such popular sayings transmit "what a culture deems significant" (Samovar & Porter, 2001, p. 36).

Examination of these orally transmitted traditional values offers an excellent means of learning about another culture because these oft-repeated sayings fuse past, present, and future. These sayings focus our attention on basic principles accepted within the culture. The premise of this present exercise is that we can learn much about Mexican values through scrutiny of these distilled lessons of life transmitted through their language.

Although some of these popular sayings are uniquely Mexican, many more of them were brought to Mexico by Spaniards after 1519; therefore, they reflect the fusion of cultures, especially Castilian and Muslim, found in recently "reconquered" and unified early-sixteenth-century Spain. Because many values are universally human, similar sayings may be found just as often in cultures around the globe. For example, most cultures attribute some responsibility for a child's character or nature to the parents; hence, in the United States one might hear "like father, like son" or "a chip off the old block" while in Mexico the close approximation is *de tal palo, tal astilla* (from such a stick, such a splinter). But the proverb *Al nopal nomás lo van a ver cuando tiene tunas* (One only goes to see the cactus when it has prickly pear fruit) derives specifically from the Mexican milieu. However, one might readily overhear a parent in the United States complaining to an adult child, "You only come to see me when you want something." So the principle of the saying is universal, but the expression relates uniquely to its culture. Although some sayings are culturally unique, and others universal, our purpose here is to focus on specific Mexican sayings that reflect some of the values of that culture.

MEXICAN *DICHOS*

Popular sayings—*dichos*—reflect many of the basic values of contemporary Mexican society, although the roots of these expressions of popular culture extend far back into both European and pre-Columbian Native American civilizations. Although many of these expressions demonstrate the universality of proverbs generally, many uniquely mirror Mexican reality. Yolanda Nava writes about Latin American culture in general, but her observation applies equally well to Mexican sayings in particular. She notes, "*Dichos* feel good on the tongue . . . they are,

after all, a verbal shorthand which . . . elders used countless times to remind [one] . . . to behave wisely" (2000, p. 35). *Dichos* may be pithy condensations of wisdom gained through centuries of experience. They are one form of transmitting folk wisdom. The sayings selected here might be heard in any Mexican household.

Many of the proverbs in the following sections may be readily consulted in Sellers (1994), but caution must be exercised in reviewing Sellers' interpretations of these *dichos*. One must always maintain cognizance of the cultural context. Although a Mexican might playfully jest, saying *No hagas hoy lo que puedas hacer mañana* (Don't do today what you can put off until tomorrow), such should not be taken literally (as Sellers apparently does, p. 26). This inverted *dicho* merely jocularly reminds the listener that one should *No dejar para mañana lo que se puede hacer hoy* (Not put off until tomorrow what can be done today), a well-known adage in many cultures.

The Mexican tradition of playfulness with words, as in the previous example, or the use of double meaning (*doble sentido,* often with obscured sexual undertones—most frequently heard with such apparently innocuous words as *huevos*/eggs, *aguacates/* avocados, and so on, used as anatomical designations), or using a word for its exact opposite, has ancient roots in pre-Columbian Mexican linguistic practices. Among the Aztecs, it was proper practice to refer to an older person as "my dear young one," much as a Mexican mother today may call her toddler "my dear father" *(mi papito)*. Those expressions chosen for discussion here reflect some of the values central to Mexican popular culture. These values include cheerful acceptance of the "will of God," the need to place trust with great care, the significance of appearances, the necessity to guard one's privacy and not breach that of others, prescribed gender roles, a communal spirit, and the importance of family.

Acceptance of "God's Will"

No hay mal que por bien no venga. (There is no bad that good does not accompany.) Mexicans have often been characterized as fatalistic, but their nature seems more than merely accepting of the inevitable. Much of Mexican folk wisdom relates to acceptance of poverty and even laughing at it. Mexican folk seem to relish the challenge of finding happiness in the face of adversity.

Some of the most frequently heard proverbs reflect that optimism. This proverb might be equated to "It's an ill wind that brings nobody good," but that does not carry the same positive outlook that the Spanish phrase indicates. Closer to the Mexican concept might be "Every cloud has a silver lining."

Mejor reír que llorar. (Better to laugh than to cry.) If one laughs at adversity, whether a simple upset of plans or that which is most inevitable—death—then there is nothing that can disturb one's happiness. Much of Mexican art reflects the duality of life and death, as can be seen in art from pre-Columbian times to the present. The very popular woodcuts of José Guadalupe Posada depicting skeletons in scenes that range from the mundane to the hilariously outrageous clearly demonstrate the Mexican's friendly attitude toward death. If one can laugh, then there is no need for lament.

El hombre propone y Dios dispone. (Man proposes and God disposes.) Few Mexican women would dare to make plans, whether it be meeting for lunch tomorrow or making plans for a child's future, without adding before concluding those plans, *Si Dios quiere* (If God wills). It would be presuming much to think that one could control the future which is viewed as in God's hands alone. In the South of the United States, one hears a similar expression made popular by Southern folklorists: "If the Lord's willing and the creek don't rise," but this seems less an attitude of fatalistic acceptance than an almost humorous excuse in the event of inclement weather in the backwoods. Whereas *Si Dios quiere* is an expression used almost exclusively by Mexican women, "If the Lord's willing" may be used by males or females.

No por mucho madrugar amanece más temprano. (No matter how early one rises, the sun will not come up any sooner.) One must simply accept what one cannot change. Nothing is accomplished by unnecessary effort. Only the foolish will attempt to defy the forces of nature.

Cuando el pobre tiene para carne sea vigilia. (When the poor have [money] to buy meat, it must be Lent.) The poor must accept that when they have the good fortune to have money, then it will be a time of fasting (not eating meat). The poor must accept that they will not have good luck. This is an instance of making fun of—of laughing at—adversity.

If I am poor, I should expect to eat beans and tortillas, not meat.

Quien canta su mal espanta. (He who sings frightens away his grief.) By singing, the individual can dispel sadness and drive away gloom. Singing and other forms of music accompany most private Mexican gatherings, but can also be heard in the Metro stations and on street corners of metropolitan centers.

Sparing Bestowal of Trust

En confianza está el peligro. (There is danger in trust.) For the Mexican to place trust in another, particularly anyone who is not a blood relative, indicates that person is held in very high esteem. But when one does bestow trust, then the greatest harm possible would be to betray that trust. It is a great risk to have faith in another; therefore, trust must never be granted lightly.

La confianza también mata. (Trust also kills.) Betrayal of trust kills the spirit as surely as a bullet might kill the body. And the betrayal of trust would be the gravest ill that one friend could commit against another. Another *dicho* conveys the gravity of betrayal of trust: *Ni te fíes de amigo reconciliado, ni de manjar dos veces guisados.* (Do not trust a reconciled friend nor a dish twice cooked.) If a trust has been betrayed, the lost trust can never be recovered.

Del dicho al hecho hay mucho trecho. (From said to done, there is a great gap.) One should not trust that promises will be fulfilled. Even with the best of intentions, circumstances intervene; thus, one should always be prepared to accept less than is promised, thereby avoiding disappointment.

Músico pagado foca mal son. (The musician who has been paid plays bad music.) The most foolish act that an employer could commit would be to pay the worker before the task is completed. Such an employer would not be viewed as kind or generous, merely foolish. If a worker is paid in advance, then the foolish employer deserves to be treated with contempt. One of the first lessons to be learned when interacting within Mexican culture is that easy trust is not valued. Trust/*confianza* must be given sparingly and only after being earned. Reserving payment until the work is completed is viewed as prudent. The lesson of the saying is that paying for a job before it is completed produces bad results.

THE IMPORTANCE OF APPEARANCES

Dime con quien andas y te diré quien eres. (Tell me with whom you associate [walk, travel], and I will tell you who you are.) Whom you choose as your companions and associates reflects your quality. If you associate with "common people," then you will be judged common. It follows that one always seeks to associate with people of higher status in order to improve on one's station in life. In English one hears "Birds of a feather flock together," but that does not fully convey the idea that one can rise in status by associating with a better class of people.

Quien anda con lobos a aullar se aprenda. (One who goes around with wolves learns to howl.) In this same vein is the biblical principle in English "Evil companions corrupt good morals." If you run with the wolves, you will learn their wild ways; therefore, one should avoid such savages and associate with cultured society. One must choose associates with great care. They not only reflect one's position, but also influence one's character.

El que es buen gallo dondequiera canta. (A good rooster can crow anywhere.) Despite the previous admonitions, quality is quality no matter the circumstance. A person of true character will show that character in all circumstances, but a person of poor character will not be able to measure up in difficult circumstances.

Respect for Privacy

Agua que no has de beber, déjala correr. (Water that you do not have to drink, leave it to flow.) Aranda (1977) translates this as "Don't meddle in others' affairs; don't start trouble." If you stir up the water, then it will be undrinkable for anyone. So let everyone tend to their own problems and thus avoid spreading them to others.

Bueno aconsejar, mejor remediar. (It is good to give advice, but it is better to solve the problem.) When there is a problem, it is good to give advice when it is sought, but it would be better to solve the problem. If you cannot solve the problem, then refrain from giving advice. And there are even times when the truth is better left unsaid, as attested by the proverb *Si dices la verdad no pecas, pero no sabes los males que*

suscitas (If you tell the truth you do not sin, but you don't know the troubles you cause, so keep your own counsel).

En boca cerrada no entran moscas. (Flies do not enter a closed mouth.) If you keep your mouth shut, then you will not have to worry about "putting your foot in it." Be careful of what you say, because *Un resbalón de lengua es peor que el de los pies* (A slip of the tongue is worse than a slip of the foot). The foot will heal, but damage done by words will not. Also, *Rezarle solo a su santo* (Pray only to your saint); that is, only someone who can help you should know of your problems.

Mejor quedarse para vestir los santos que tener que desvestir un borracho. (It is better to remain single than to have to undress a drunk.) Women who do not marry are often said to "dress the saints"; that is, they spend their lives caring for the images of saints, which often involves making new garments for the images or painting and refurbishing them. Thus, single women often justify their unmarried state by suggesting that they prefer dressing the saints' images to having to undress a drunken husband.

Más vale solo que mal acompañado. (It is better to remain single than to be disagreeably accompanied.) In a society in which women are viewed as weak and vulnerable, single women must justify their unmarried state, so that women most often cite the refrain that it is better to be single than to be married to an unbearable spouse.

A la mujer ni todo el amor ni todo el dinero. (To a woman neither all your love nor all your money.) A real Mexican male must maintain control of himself and his money. Men make a certain portion of their income available to women for maintaining the household, but the rest of their earnings belong to them. One of the great enigmas of Mexican culture is the *machismo* (strong, dominant male) versus *marianismo* (longsuffering, submissive female). This concept is most readily seen in the fact that *cantinas*/bars are exclusively for males (and women of ill repute).

Triste está la casa donde la gallina canta y el gallo calla. (Sad is the house where the chicken crows and the rooster is quiet.) The proper role for a man is as the master of his house, and the woman should be silent. It is a reversal of proper roles for the Mexican woman to make the decisions and the man to allow her to do so. In English a similar refrain is "A whistling girl and a crowing hen always come to some sad end." Women are assigned their proper roles and men theirs. A sad state results when these roles are reversed.

Communalism

Mucha ayuda, poco trabajo. (Much help, little work.) When many work together, it is little work for any of them. When work is shared, it goes quickly and is not much effort for anyone. The tradition of communal work precedes European contact with the New World. Among the Aztecs, taking turns at doing community service was widely practiced.

Vida sin amigos, muerte sin testigos. (Life without friends; death without witnesses. Life without friends, no mourners when it ends.) If one does not live so as to have many friends, then death will come with no one there to mourn that death. In Mexican culture, it is extremely important that there be mourners to accompany the deceased. It has long been common practice to pay mourners so that the dead will be accompanied to the cemetery. Again, this reflects the importance of one's public persona, one's appearance to the rest of the world, even in death.

Family

¿A dónde vas que valgas más? (Where are you going that you are worth more?) Where would you be valued more than at home? The Mexican family is extended, but still very close. When an individual needs help, the family is expected to supply it. The understanding is that you are always better off at home.

Amor de padre o madre, lo demás es aire. (The love of mother or father, everything else is air.) Compared to a mother or father's love, there is nothing else of importance. Father and mother will love their children when everyone and everything else fails. It is not unusual to encounter adult children living in the home of their parents and even rearing their own children in that same home. At times this is done out of economic necessity, but just as often it is the extended family. Grandparents become the caregivers for the offspring and take a hand in their upbringing.

SUMMARY

Popular sayings reflect basic cultural values. They do not even require literacy because they transmit the values orally to all who hear them. They metaphorically condense timeless lessons into readily recalled phrases. Through *dichos* we are reminded that our experiences are not unique; others have experienced the same things in other times and other places and left messages to guide us. By reviewing a selection of Mexican *dichos,* one readily perceives some of that culture's more significant values: cheerful acceptance of one's lot in life, the need to exercise caution, the importance of appearances, the sanctity of privacy, proper gender roles, communalism, and family.

References

Aranda, C. (1977). *Dichos: Proverbs and sayings from the Spanish.* Santa Fe, NM: Swanstone Press.

Fuentes, C. (1992). *The buried mirror: Reflections on Spain and the New World.* New York: Houghton Mifflin.

Nava, Y. (2000). *It's all in the frijoles: 100 famous Latinos share real-life stories, time-tested dichos, favorite folktales, and inspiring words of wisdom.* New York: Fireside.

Paz, O. (1961). *The labyrinth of solitude: Life and thought in Mexico.* New York: Grove Press.

Samovar, L. A., & Porter, R. E. (2001). *Communication between cultures* (4th ed.). Belmont, CA: Wadsworth.

Sellers, I. M. (1994). *Folk wisdom of Mexico.* San Francisco: Chronicle Books.

Concepts and Questions

1. How does the study of familiar sayings help us understand some of the important values of a particular culture?
2. Which Mexican sayings discussed by Roy are heard in other cultures?
3. Can you think of some sayings from your own culture and relate the specific values they represent?
4. What are your favorite familiar sayings? Why have you selected these?
5. What sayings in the United States stress the value of individualism?
6. What Mexican sayings reflect the underlying religious philosophy of the culture?

Beyond Language: Nonverbal Communication Across Cultures

PETER A. ANDERSEN
HUA WANG

Language is a uniquely human form of communication, yet many of our messages lie beyond language in a communication system called body language or, more correctly, nonverbal communication (Andersen, 2004, 2007). In comparison to verbal communication, nonverbal messages are more ambiguous as they are being simultaneously signaled and interpreted through multiple channels such as facial expressions, body language, tone of voice, spatial relationships, and physical environment. In addition, although nonverbal communication can take place both intentionally and unintentionally, it often operates at a lower level of awareness than does language. People are not very conscious of their own nonverbal behavior, which is enacted mindlessly, spontaneously, and unconsciously (Andersen, 2004, 2007; Andersen & Wang, 2005). Overall, nonverbal communication is a pervasive and powerful form of human behavior, which involves a subtle, nonlinguistic, multidimensional, and spontaneous process (Andersen, 1999).

Like other forms of communication, culture often produces barriers in nonverbal communication among people from different groups. When Lars' parents first met their Italian in-laws-to-be, Giuseppe and Gina, they were shocked when they were hugged and kissed by these virtual strangers. Lars' parents, Sven and Hilda, had never been kissed or hugged by anyone like that in their native

This original essay appears here in print for the first time. All rights reserved. Permission to reprint must be obtained from the authors and the publisher. Earlier versions of this essay have appeared in previous editions. Dr. Peter A. Anderson teaches in the School of Communication at San Diego State University. Hua Wang is a doctoral student in the School for Communication at the University of Southern California.

Sweden and they naturally pulled away in shock! Giuseppe later commented to Gina that they sure seemed a bit cold and unfriendly especially since they were about to become family as a result of Lars and Nicole's upcoming marriage. Of course what they had witnessed was not intentional unfriendliness. What these warm expressive Italians had encountered is the more reserved and less expressive body language of Northern Europeans. At one time such intercultural encounters were rare; today intercultural communication is becoming increasingly common and the source of considerable confusion. With dramatically increasing numbers of people pursuing higher education, traveling for business and pleasure, and immigrating to another country, the probability of communicating with people from other cultures is greater than ever before (Brown, Kane, & Roodman, 1994; Stafford, 2005; Wellman, 1999). Understanding intercultural communication, particularly nonverbal communication for which there is no dictionary, is more important than ever before.

As the prior vignette showed, interactions between people from different cultures, especially in early stages of communication, can be confusing and frustrating. The situation gets more complicated when linguistic barriers in many intercultural transactions are compounded by differences in nonverbal behavior. Culture is "a shared system of socially transmitted behavior that describes, defines, and guides people's ways of life, communicated from one generation to the next" (Matsumoto, 2006, p. 220). Culture is mainly an unspoken, nonverbal phenomenon because most aspects of one's culture are learned through observation and imitation rather than by explicit verbal instruction or expression. The primary level of culture is communicated implicitly, without awareness, and chiefly by nonverbal means (Andersen, 1999; Hall, 1984; Sapir, 1928). Nonverbal communication has both biologically determined and cultural-specific aspects. Some factors are innate and genetic, that produce cross-cultural similarities in nonverbal behavior (Brown, 1991; Ekman, 1972), but abundant differences also exist and create miscommunication and intercultural friction and confusion.

Nonverbal messages serve a variety of functions in intercultural communication (Ting-Toomey, 1999). People rely on nonverbal cues as their identity badges through which they place themselves and others into categories (Burgoon, Buller, & Woodall, 1996). From artifacts such as clothing, jewelry, cosmetics, and accessories to use of vocalic cues such as pitch, volume, articulation, and tempo, individuals in different cultures present, enhance, and/or assert a sense of self via various nonverbal behaviors (Ting-Toomey, 1999). Not only do nonverbal messages reflect strong personal identity, they also carry and infer powerful feelings, emotions, and attitudes typically through facial, bodily, and gestural movement and use of voice (Ting-Toomey, 1999). Culture shapes the display rules of when, how, what, and with whom certain nonverbal expressions should be revealed or suppressed (Ekman & Friesen, 1975; Ekman & Oster, 1979) and dictates which displays are appropriate in which specific situations.

Prior research on intercultural communication in general and nonverbal communication in particular, has provided many useful and interesting anecdotes. This essay attempts to connect these fragmented accounts and proposes a theoretical perspective that helps to explain and understand thousands of differences in nonverbal communication across cultures. The essay will first briefly review research in cross-cultural differences that lie along eight nonverbal codes: *physical appearance, proxemics, chronemics, kinesics, haptics, oculesics, vocalics*, and *olfactics*; and then focus on six primary dimensions of cultural variation in nonverbal behavior based on the seminal work of Hall (1966a, 1976, 1984) and Hofstede (1984, 1991, 1998, 2001, 2003) in cultural dimensions, and many follow-up scholarly efforts in the field (Albert & Ah Ha, 2004; Andersen, 1988, 2000; Andersen, Hecht, Hoobler, & Smallwood, 2002; Fernandez, Carlson, Stepina, & Nicholson, 1997; Gudykunst & Nishida, 1986; Merritt, 2000; Shackleton & Ali, 1990). The six dimensions of intercultural nonverbal communication include: *context, identity, power distance, gender, uncertainty*, and *immediacy*.

NONVERBAL CODES

Nonverbal messages provide what verbal messages cannot express and usually generate more trust than verbal messages (Andersen, 1999; Ting-Toomey, 1999). A smile, a wink, a scowl, a squeaky voice,

prolonged eye contact, fingers drumming on a table top—all these expressions reveal inner feelings. Nonverbal communication runs the gamut, from easily readable threatening gestures to attitudes expressed by body posture or hidden beneath the surface of spoken words (Sheridan, 1978). The hidden differences in these various areas and masked meanings of specific nonverbal messages interweave in any intercultural encounter. Given that most discussions of nonverbal communication across cultures have been anecdotal and atheoretical, where numerous examples of intercultural differences for each nonverbal code are discussed in detail, we will discuss the basic codes of nonverbal communication only briefly.

Physical appearance is the most externally obvious nonverbal code that covers relatively stable physical features of human beings such as gender, height, weight, color of skin, and body shape, as well as the artifacts associated with one's physical appearance like clothes, jewelry, makeup, and accessories. All of these elements play an important role during initial encounters. Cultural attire is obvious and leads to ethnic stereotypes. During a field study conducted at an international airport, the senior author witnessed Tongans in multicultural ceremonial gowns, Sikhs in white turbans, Hasidic Jews in blue yarmulkes, and Africans in white dashikis—all alongside Californians in running shorts and halter tops (Andersen, 1999). Blue jeans and business suits have become increasingly accepted attire internationally, but local attire still abounds. Little formal research has been conducted on the impact of physical appearance on intercultural communication. Discussions of intercultural differences in appearance are provided by Scheflen (1974) and Samovar, Porter, and Stefani (1998). Cultural cues of physical appearance are often very subtle; for example, the level of a woman's veil in rural north India indicates her sexual or romantic interest or disinterest (Lambert & Wood, 2005). Preoccupation with physical appearance is hardly a new phenomenon. Since the dawn of culture, humans from the upper Paleolithic period (40,000 years ago) to the present have adorned their bodies in a great variety of ways (Samovar et al., 1998).

A number of studies have shown that race and culture have an effect on the recognition of faces (Meisner & Brigham, 2001; Sporer, 2001a, 2001b). We have all heard people say about people of other races: "they all look alike!" The failure to distinguish between different people of an ethnic group other than one's own, called the cross-race effect, can be the cause of embarrassing interactions where you think you recognize another person when in fact you have never seen the person before. More seriously it can even result in misidentifying a defendant in a criminal trial. The primary reason for such an effect is a lack of quality and quantity of contact with members of other ethnic groups and the human psychological tendency to stereotype, a cognitive shortcut. More intercultural contact appears to reduce that cross-race effect. But it is more than mere contact; people who have qualitatively richer intercultural interactions and spend time communicating with people of other races and ethnicities show less signs of the cross-race effect (Sporer, 2001a).

Nonverbal communication differences can be traced back to a culture's perception of the most fundamental elements—space and time. *Proxemics* generally examines communication via interpersonal space and distance. Research has documented that cultures differ substantially in their use of personal space, their regard for territory, and the meanings they assign to proxemic behavior (Albert & Ah Ha, 2004; Gudykunst & Kim, 1992; Hall, 1959, 1966a, 1966b, 1976; Scheflen, 1974). For example, people from Mediterranean and Latin cultures maintain close distance, whereas people from Northern European and Northeast Asian cultures maintain greater distances (Hall, 1966b; Beaulieu, 2004). But this behavior also is highly contextual. At rush hour in Tokyo, the normally respectful, distant Japanese are literally jammed into subways and trains.

Chronemics—or the study of meanings, usage, and communication of time—is probably the most discussed and well-researched nonverbal code in the intercultural literature (Bruneau, 1979; Gudykunst & Kim, 1992; Hall, 1959, 1976, 1984). Recent research has suggested that time orientation may actually constitute a dimension of intercultural behavior in addition to the six discussed previously (Albert & Ah Ha, 2004). Some cultures follow monochronic time schedules and use time in linear ways, whereas people in polychronic cultures tend to engage multiple activities simultaneously (Hall & Hall, 1987). The perceptions of time vary dramatically from culture to culture. In the United States, time is viewed as a commodity that can be wasted, spent, saved, and used wisely (Andersen, 1999). In the Arab and Latin American cultures, bringing in a historical time perspective is very important before addressing the current issue (Cushner & Brislin, 1996). To many Asians, time is more of a relational issue rather than a clock time issue (Tung, 1994). And in some less developed countries, life moves to the rhythms of nature: the day, the seasons, the year. Such human inventions as seconds, minutes, hours, and weeks have no real meaning.

Kinesic behavior studies include some aspects of people's facial expressions, body movements, gestures, and conversational regulators (Gudykunst & Kim, 1992; Hall, 1976; Samovar et al., 1998; Scheflen, 1974). Research has shown that subtle differences in the appearance of facial expressions of emotion across cultures can contain nonverbal "accents" that identify the expresser's nationality or culture (Marsh, Elfenbein, & Ambady, 2003). Nonetheless, there is little support for uniquely cultural facial expressions of emotion; emotional expressions are generally recognizable across culture (Beaupre & Hess, 2005; Matsumoto, 2002, 2006). Facial expressions of emotion are mostly learned from one's culture. A study of 11-month-old babies revealed that Chinese babies are less expressive than either Japanese or European American babies (Camras et al., 1998). While hereditary differences cannot be ruled out, the fact that Japanese babies behaved more like European American babies than Chinese babies suggests this is likely a difference due to socialization and enculturation. Likewise, a recent intercultural study of three-year-olds by Camras, Chen, Bakeman, Norris, and Cain (2006) found that the native Chinese children were less expressive than Chinese children who were adopted by American families, and the adopted children were less expressive than European American children. Some research suggests that Asians and other collectivistic people are less likely to recognize facial expressions, particularly negative ones, due to learned cultural display rules (Beaupre and Hess, 2005).

Gestures differ dramatically across culture in meaning, extensiveness, and intensity. Stories abound in the intercultural literature of gestures that signal endearment or warmth in one culture may be obscene or insulting in another. Scholars specifically focusing on spontaneous gestures accompanying speech claim that both the types and timing of gestures can vary with the language spoken (Goldin-Meadow, 2003). Gestures with symbolic dictionary meanings called emblems are most likely to vary across culture. One recent study shows that recognition of such cultural gestures is highest by people from the same culture and is recognized more accurately by people with more exposure to the culture and by people with greater intercultural communication competence (Molinsky, Krabbenhoft, Ambady, & Choi, 2005).

Tactile communication, called *haptics,* also shows considerable intercultural variation (Jourard, 1966; Andersen & Leibowitz, 1978; Ford & Graves, 1977; McDaniel & Andersen, 1998; Samovar et al., 1998). Research has shown vast differences in international and intercultural touch in amount, location, type, and public or private manifestation (Jones, 1994; McDaniel & Andersen, 1998). Italians, Greeks, and Latinos are more "touchy" people than the English, French, and Dutch. Touching is less common and more embarrassing and discomforting among Chinese and Japanese. And to touch an Arab Muslim with the left hand, which is reserved for toilet use, is considered a social insult (Samovar & Mills, 1998).

One important code of nonverbal communication that has attracted considerably less intercultural research attention is *oculesics,* the study of messages sent by the eyes—including eye contact, blinks, eye movements, and pupil dilation (Gudykunst & Kim, 1992; Samovar et al., 1998). Because eye contact has been called an "invitation to communicate," its cross-cultural variation is an important communication topic. In North America and Western Europe, direct eye contact communicates interest and respect, while Japanese people may look away from another's eyes almost completely to be polite (Samovar & Mills, 1998).

Vocalics, or *paralanguage,* includes all the nonverbal elements involving the use of voice. Not surprisingly, culture affects the use of vocalics (Gudykunst & Kim, 1992; LaBarre, 1985; Samovar et al., 1998; Scheflen, 1974). Members of cultures with strong oral traditions, such as African Americans and Jews, tend to speak with more passion; Italians and Greeks talk much more and louder than Asians who appreciate silence as a way of showing politeness (Samovar & Mills, 1998). However, music and singing, two universal forms of aesthetic communication, have been almost completely overlooked in intercultural research, except for an excellent series of studies (Lomax, 1968) that identified several groups of worldwide cultures through differences and similarities in their folk songs.

Finally, *olfactics,* the study of interpersonal communication via smell, has been virtually ignored in intercultural research despite its importance (Samovar et al., 1998). Americans are the most smell-aversive culture in the world (Andersen, 1998). While most people in the world emit natural body smells, the cultures in the most developed parts of the world use an array of cosmetics to eliminate body odor or to replace it with natural smells.

DIMENSIONS OF INTERCULTURAL NONVERBAL COMMUNICATION

Research has shown that cultures can be located along dimensions that help explain why people act in different ways. Most cultural differences in nonverbal behavior are a result of variations along the dimensions discussed as follows (see Table 1).

Context

The first cultural dimension of communication proposed decades ago is *context*—the degree to which communication is explicit and verbal or implicit and nonverbal. Hall (1976, 1984) has described high-context cultures in considerable detail: "A high context (HC) communication or message is one in which most of the information is either in the physical context or internalized in the person, while very little is in the coded, explicit, transmitted parts of the message"

Table 1 *Dimensions of Intercultural Nonverbal Communication*

Dimension	One Extreme	The Other Extreme
Context	Low Context	High Context
Identity	Individualism	Collectivism
Power Distance	Low Power Distance	High Power Distance
Gender	Femininity	Masculinity
Uncertainty	Uncertainty Avoidance	Uncertainty Tolerance
Immediacy	Low Contact	High Contact

(Hall, 1976, p. 91). "In a high-context culture such as that of Japan, meanings are internalized and there is a large emphasis on nonverbal codes" (Lustig & Koester, 1999, p. 108). Married couples or old friends skillfully use HC or implicit messages that are nearly impossible for an outsider to understand. The situation, a smile, or a glance provides implicit meaning that does not need to be articulated. In HC cultures, information is integrated from the environment, the context, the situation, and nonverbal cues that give the message meaning are not available in explicit verbal utterance.

Low-context (LC) messages are the opposite of HC messages; most are communicated through explicit code and usually via verbal communication (Andersen, 1999; Hall, 1976). Low-context messages must be detailed, unmistakably communicated, and highly specific. Unlike personal relationships, which are high-context message systems, institutions such as courts of law and formal systems such as mathematics and computer languages require explicit LC systems because nothing can be taken for granted (Hall, 1984).

There are huge cultural variations in the degree of context used in communication. Research suggests that the lowest-context cultures are Swiss, German, North American, and Scandinavian (Gudykunst & Kim, 1992; Hall, 1976, 1984). Low-context cultures are logical, analytical, linear, and action-oriented, and people tend to stress clearly articulated spoken or written messages (Hall, 1984). Cultures that have some characteristics of both HC and LC systems would include the French, English, and Italian (Gudykunst & Kim, 1992), which are less explicit than Northern European cultures.

The highest-context cultures are found in Asia, especially China, Japan, and Korea (Elliott et al., 1982; Hall, 1976, 1984; Lustig and Koester, 1999). Although most languages are explicit, LC communication systems, in China even the language is an implicit, HC communication system. To use a Chinese dictionary, one must understand thousands of characters that change meaning in combination with other characters along with the context. Zen Buddhism, a major influence in Asia, places a high value on silence, lack of emotional expression, and the unspoken, nonverbal parts of communication (McDaniel & Andersen, 1998). Americans often complain that the Japanese never "get to the point,"

but they fail to recognize that HC culture must provide a context and setting and let the point evolve (Hall, 1984). In a study of airport farewell episodes, McDaniel and Andersen (1998) found Asians to be the least tactile of any cultural group on earth. American Indian cultures with ancestral migratory roots in East Asia are remarkably like contemporary Asian culture in several ways, especially in their need for high context (Hall, 1984). Latin American cultures—a fusion of Iberian (Portuguese-Spanish) and Asian traditions—are also HC cultures. Likewise, Southern and Eastern Mediterranean people and people from the Persian Gulf, including Persians, Arabs, Greeks, and Turks, are HC cultures as well.

Communication is used very differently in HC and LC cultures. Andersen, Hecht, Hoobler, and Smallwood (2002) suggest that these differences between HC and LC communication can be explained by four principles.

1. *Verbal communication and other explicit codes are more prevalent in low-context cultures such as the United States and Northern Europe.* People from LC cultures are often perceived as excessively talkative, belaboring of the obvious, and redundant. People from HC cultures may be perceived as nondisclosive, sneaky, and mysterious.

2. *HC cultures do not value verbal communication the same way that LC cultures do.* Elliot et al. (1982) found that more verbal people were perceived as more attractive in the United States, but less verbal people were perceived as more attractive in Korea, which is an HC culture.

3. *HC cultures are more reliant on and tuned in to nonverbal communication.* In LC cultures, most people, particularly men, fail to perceive as much nonverbal communication as do members of HC cultures. Nonverbal communication provides the context for all communication (Watzlawick, Beavin, & Jackson, 1967), but people from HC cultures are particularly affected by these contextual cues. Thus, facial expressions, tensions, movements, speed of interaction, location of the encounters, and other subtle forms of nonverbal communication are likely to be more easily perceived by and have more meaning for people from HC cultures.

4. *Interactants expect more in HC cultures than in LC cultures* (Hall, 1976). People in HC cultures

Table 2 *Summary of Context Dimension*

Dimension 1. Context	One Extreme	The Other Extreme
The degree to which communication is explicit and verbal or implicit and nonverbal.	Low Context	High Context
Core Value	Freedom of speech, directness	Silence, indirectness
Nonverbal Traits	Literal meaning, specific details, and precise time schedules	Information in the physical context, or internalized in the person
Typical Cultures	Swiss, German, North American	China, Japan, Korea

anticipate that communicators will understand unspoken feelings, implicit gestures, and environmental clues that people from LC cultures do not process. Given that both cultural extremes fail to recognize these basic communication differences, intercultural attributions about behavior are often incorrect.

In conclusion, HC cultures rely more on nonverbal communication and less on verbal communication (see Table 2). Generally speaking, HC cultures are also somewhat more collectivistic and less individualistic than LC cultures (Gudykunst et al., 1996; Andersen et al., 2002). Given this fact, it is appropriate that the next dimension of culture to be examined is cultural identity: individualism-collectivism.

Individualism/Collectivism

A culture's degree of individualism versus collectivism is one of the most extensively researched dimensions of culture. Individualistic cultures emphasize individual-identity and value personal rights and freedom whereas collectivistic cultures advocate we-identity and are more group-oriented. Individualism/collectivism determines how people live together: alone, in families, or tribes (Hofstede, 1984), their values, and how they communicate. Americans are extreme individualists, who take individualism for granted and are usually blind to its impact until travel brings them into contact with less individualistic, more collectivistic cultures.

Individualism has been applauded as a blessing and has been elevated to the status of a national religion in the United States. Indeed, the best and worst in our culture can be attributed to individualism. Proponents of individualism have argued that it is

the basis of liberty, democracy, freedom, and economic incentive and serves as protection against tyranny. Conversely, individualism has been blamed for our alienation from one another, loneliness, selfishness, and narcissism. Indeed, Hall (1976) has claimed that as an extreme individualist, "Western man has created chaos by denying that part of his self that integrates while enshrining the part that fragments experience" (p. 9). There can be little doubt that individualism is one of the fundamental dimensions that distinguishes cultures. Western culture is individualistic, so people rely on personal judgments to a greater degree than group decisions. Eastern cultures emphasize harmony among people, between people and nature, and value collective judgments (Andersen, 1999). Tomkins (1984) demonstrated that an individual's psychological makeup is the result of this cultural dimension. Western civilization has tended toward self-celebration, positive or negative. In Asian culture, another alternative is represented, that of the balance between yin and yang.

In a landmark intercultural study of individualism in fourty noncommunist countries, Hofstede (1984) reported that the ten most individualistic nations (starting with the most) were the United States, Australia, Great Britain, Canada, the Netherlands, New Zealand, Italy, Belgium, Denmark, and Sweden, all of which primarily derive from European cultures. The least individualistic nations (starting with the least) were Venezuela, Colombia, Pakistan, Peru, Taiwan, Thailand, Singapore, Chile, and Hong Kong, all of which are Asian or South American cultures. Likewise, Sitaram and Codgell (1976) reported that individuality is a primary value in Western cultures, of secondary importance in African cultures, and of little importance in Eastern and Muslim cultures.

Table 3 *Summary of Identity Dimension*

Dimension 2. Individualism/ Collectivism	One Extreme	The Other Extreme
The degree that society reinforces individual or collective achievement and interpersonal relationships.	Individualism	Collectivism
Core Value	Individual freedom	Group harmony
Nonverbal Traits	Proximally distant, different schedules, expressive of emotions	Proximally close, coordinated facial expressions and body movements
Typical Cultures	United States, Australia, Great Britain	Venezuela, Colombia, Pakistan

Even though the United States is the most individualistic country on earth (Andersen, 1999; Hofstede, 1984), some of its regions and ethnic groups diverge in their degree of individualism. Elazar (1972) found that the central Midwest and the Mid-Atlantic states have the most individualistic political culture, whereas the Southeast is the most traditional and least individualistic; however, this relationship is all relative and, by world standards, even Alabama is an individualistic culture. As Bellah et al. (1985) stated: "Individualism lies at the very core of American culture. . . . Anything that would violate our right to think for ourselves, judge for ourselves, make our own decisions, live our lives as we see fit, is not only morally wrong, it is sacrilegious" (p. 142). Likewise, different ethnic groups may vary within a culture. African Americans, for example, greatly emphasize individualism (Hecht, Collier, & Ribeau, 1993), whereas Mexican Americans emphasize group and relational solidarity more (Albert & Ah Ha, 2004; Andersen et al., 2002). American's extreme individualism makes it difficult for them to interact with and understand people from other cultures. America is unique; all other cultures are less individualistic. As Condon and Yousef (1983) stated: "The fusion of individualism and equality is so valued and so basic that many Americans find it most difficult to relate to contrasting values in other cultures where interdependence greatly determines a person's sense of self" (p. 65).

The degree to which a culture is individualistic or collectivistic affects the nonverbal behavior of that culture in every way (see Table 3). First, people from individualistic cultures are more remote and distant proximally. Collectivistic cultures are interdependent; as a result, the members work, play, live, and sleep in proximity to one another. One study reports that people in individualistic cultures are more distant proximally than collectivists (Gudykunst et al., 1996). Hofstede (1984) cites research suggesting that, as hunters and gatherers, people lived apart in individualistic, nuclear families. When humans became agricultural, the interdependent extended family began living in proximity in large families or tribal units. Urban-industrial societies returned to a norm of individualism, nuclear families, and a lack of proximity to one's neighbors, friends, and co-workers.

Culture also sets up the way people use time. In a study of doing business with Japanese, researchers discovered that the Japanese are slow to reach a decision whereas Americans prefer to take immediate actions (Hall & Hall, 1987). The greatest distinction between the two cultures lies in the Japanese's strong dependence on groups. They base their individual identities on the groups they belong to and seek dependent relationships from larger entities, especially employers. However, such dependency would be considered a negative trait in the United States since Americans value independence.

Kinesic behavior tends to be more coordinated in collectivistic cultures, where people match one another's facial expressions, and body movements are in sync with each other. Where families work collectively, movements, schedules, and actions need to be highly coordinated (Argyle, 1975). In urban cultures, family members often do their "own thing," coming and going, working and playing, eating and sleeping on different schedules. People in individualistic cultures also smile more than do people in normatively oriented cultures (Tomkins, 1984). Individualists are responsible for their relationships and their own happiness, whereas normatively or collectively oriented people regard compliance with norms as a primary value and personal or interpersonal happiness as a secondary value (Andersen, 1999). Matsumoto (1991) reports, "collective cultures will foster emotional displays of their members that maintain and facilitate group cohesion, harmony, or cooperation, to a greater degree than individualistic cultures" (p. 132). Several scholars indicate that people in individualistic cultures display emotions more freely and diversely, particularly to out-groups, than do collectivists, who are discouraged from showing a range of positive and/or negative emotions outside of the immediate in-group (Matsumoto, 2006; Porter & Samovar, 1998). Also, as mentioned earlier, children in the more collectivistic Chinese families displayed less facial emotion than Chinese children adopted by European American parents. These adopted children displayed less facial emotion than European American children, all of which suggests that facial expressivity is a learned behavior that is encouraged in individualistic cultures and discouraged in collectivistic ones.

Lustig and Koester (1999) maintain that "people from individualistic cultures are more likely than those from collectivistic cultures to use confrontational strategies when dealing with interpersonal problems; those with a collectivistic orientation are likely to use avoidance, third-party intermediaries, or other face-saving techniques" (p. 123). In collectivistic cultures, people suppress both positive and negative emotional displays that are contrary to the mood of the group, because maintaining the group is of primary value (Andersen, 1999). Bond (1993) found the Chinese culture to be lower in frequency, intensity, and duration of emotional expression than other cultures. Bond asserts, "The expression of emotion is carefully regulated out of a concern for its capacity to disrupt group harmony and status hierarchies" (p. 245).

People in individualistic cultures are encouraged to express emotions because individual freedom is of paramount value. Research suggests that people in individualistic cultures are more nonverbally affiliative. Intuitively, the reason for this is not obvious because individualism does not require affiliation; however, Hofstede (1984) explained:

> In less individualistic countries where traditional social ties, like those with extended family members, continue to exist, people have less of a need to make specific friendships. One's friends are predetermined by the social relationships into which one is born. In the more individualistic countries, however, affective relationships are not socially predetermined but must be acquired by each individual personally. (p. 163)

In individualistic countries such as the United States, affiliativeness, dating, flirting, small talk, smiling, and initial acquaintance are more important than in collectivistic countries where the social network is more fixed and less reliant on individual initiative. Bellah et al. (1985) maintain that for centuries in the individualistic and mobile North American society, people could meet more easily and their communication was more open; however, their relationships were usually more casual and transient than those found in more collectivistic cultures.

In an impressive study of dozens of cultures, Lomax (1968) found that a country's song and dance styles were related to its level of social cohesion and collectivism. Collectivistic cultures are higher in "groupiness" and show both more cohesiveness in singing and more synchrony in their dance style (Lomax, 1968). It isn't surprising that rock dancing, which emphasizes separateness and "doing your own thing," evolved in individualistic cultures such as England and the United States. These dances may serve as a metaphor for the whole U.S. culture, where individuality is more prevalent than in any other place (Andersen, 1998).

Power Distance

Another basic dimension of intercultural communication is *power distance*—the degree to which power, prestige, and wealth are unequally distributed in a culture. Power distance has been measured in many cultures using Hofstede's (1984) Power Distance Index (PDI). Like individualism, power distance varies greatly among cultures. Cultures with high PDI scores have power concentrated in the hands of a few rather than more equally distributed throughout the population. Condon and Yousef (1983) distinguish among three cultural patterns: democratic, authority-centered, and authoritarian. The PDI is highly correlated (.80) with authoritarianism, as measured by the Fascism or authoritarianism scale (Hofstede, 1984).

High PDI countries, starting with the highest, are the Philippines, Mexico, Venezuela, India, Singapore,

Brazil, Hong Kong, France, and Colombia (Hofstede, 1984), all of which, except for France, are southern countries located near the equator. Likewise, Gudykunst and Kim (1992) report that both African and Asian cultures generally maintain hierarchical role relationships characteristic of high power distance. Asian students are expected to be modest and nonverbally deferent in the presence of their instructors. Similarly, Vietnamese people consider employers to be their mentors and will not question orders.

The lowest PDI countries are, respectively, Austria, Israel, Denmark, New Zealand, Ireland, Sweden, Norway, Finland, Switzerland, and Great Britain (Hofstede, 1984), all of which are European or of European origin, middle-class, and democratic, and located at high latitudes. The United States is slightly lower than the median in power distance, indicating smaller status differentials than in many other countries. Cultures differ in terms of how status is acquired. In many countries, such as India, class or caste determines one's status. In the United States, power and status are typically determined by money and conspicuous material displays (Andersen & Bowman, 1999).

As suggested above, the latitude of a country is an important force in the determination of power distance. Hofstede (1984) claims that latitude and climate are the major forces that shape culture. He maintains that the key intervening variable is that technology is needed for survival in a colder climate, which produces a chain of events in which children are less dependent on authority and learn from people other than authority figures. Hofstede (1984) reports a moderate-to-high (.65) correlation between PDI and latitude. In a study conducted at 40 universities throughout the United States, Andersen, Lustig, and Andersen (1990) report a −.47 correlation between latitude and intolerance for ambiguity, and a −.45 correlation between latitude and authoritarianism. This suggests that residents of the northern United States are less authoritarian and more tolerant of ambiguity. Northern cultures may have to be more tolerant and less autocratic to ensure cooperation and survival in harsher climates.

It is obvious that power distance would affect a culture's nonverbal behavior (see Table 4). Before being legislatively banned, India's rigid caste system historically limited interaction, as in the case of the "untouchables" who were at the bottom of India's five-caste system (Chinoy, 1967). Any contact with untouchables by members of other castes was forbidden and considered "polluting." Certainly, tactile communication among people of different castes was greatly curtailed in traditional Indian culture. High-PDI countries with less rigid stratification than India may still prohibit free interclass dating, marriage, and contact, all of which are taken for granted in low-PDI countries. In a recent study on status-related behavior, greater differences were discovered in the hierarchical Japanese culture than in the more egalitarian American culture (Kowner & Wiseman, 2003).

Social systems with large power discrepancies also produce unique kinesic behavior. Cultures with high power distance encourage emotions and expressions that reveal status differences. For instance, in high power distance cultures, people are expected to show only positive emotions to high-status others and only negative emotions to low-status others (Matsumoto, 1991). According to Andersen and Bowman (1999), subordinates' bodily tension is

Table 4 *Summary of Power Distance Dimension*

Dimension 3. Power Distance	One Extreme	The Other Extreme
The degree of equality or inequality between people in the country or society.	Low Power Distance	High Power Distance
Core Value	People's equality	Respect for status
Nonverbal Traits	Located at high latitudes, more tactile, relaxing and clear vocalic cues	Located near the equator, untouchable, regulated nonverbal displays
Typical Cultures	Austria, Israel, Denmark	Philippines, Mexico, Venezuela

more obvious in power-discrepant relationships. Similarly, Andersen and Bowman (1999) report that in power-discrepant circumstances, subordinates smile more in an effort to appease superiors and appear polite. The continuous smiles of many Asians are a culturally inculcated effort to appease superiors and smooth social relations—behaviors that are appropriate to a high-PDI culture.

The power distance of a culture also affects vocalic and paralinguistic cues. Citizens of low-PDI cultures are generally less aware that vocal loudness may be offensive to others. American vocal tones are often perceived as noisy, exaggerated, and childlike (Condon & Yousef, 1983). Lomax (1968) has shown that in countries where political authority is highly centralized, singing voices are tighter and the voice box is more closed, whereas more permissive societies produce more relaxed, open, and clear sounds.

Gender

Perhaps the most researched issue in social science during recent decades is gender. Nations and cultures, like humans, can be viewed as masculine or feminine. The gender orientation of culture has an impact on many aspects of nonverbal behavior (see Table 5). This includes the nonverbal expressions permitted by each sex, occupational status, nonverbal aspects of power, the ability to interact with strangers or acquaintances of the opposite sex, and all aspects of interpersonal relationships between men and women. *Gender,* as discussed in this article, refers to the rigidity of gender rules. In masculine cultures, gender rules are more rigid and traits such as strength, assertiveness, competitiveness, and ambitiousness are valued. In more feminine or androgynous cultures, attributes such as affection, compassion, nurturance, and emotionality are valued (Bem, 1974; Hofstede, 1984). In less rigid cultures, both men and women can express more diverse, less stereotyped gender-role behaviors.

Cross-cultural research shows that women are expected to be more nurturing than men, although there is considerable variation from country to country (Hall, 1984). Hofstede (1984) has measured the degree to which people of both sexes in a culture endorse masculine or feminine goals. Masculine cultures regard competition and assertiveness as important, whereas feminine cultures place more importance on nurturance and compassion. Countries with the ten highest masculinity index scores, according to Hofstede (1984), are Japan, Austria, Venezuela, Italy, Switzerland, Mexico, Ireland, Great Britain, Germany, and the Philippines. The ten countries with the lowest masculinity scores are Sweden, Norway, the Netherlands, Denmark, Finland, Chile, Portugal, Thailand, and Peru.

Not surprisingly, the masculinity of a culture is negatively correlated with the percentage of women in technical and professional jobs and positively correlated with segregation of the sexes in higher education (Hofstede, 1984). High-masculinity countries also have fewer women in the labor force, have only recently afforded voting privileges to women, and are less likely to consider wife rape a crime than are low-masculinity countries (Seager & Olson, 1986). The Scandinavian countries, with their long history of equal rights for women, are at the top of the list of feminine countries. But why would South American cultures be less masculine and not manifest the Latin pattern of machismo? Iberian countries like Spain and Portugal have relatively feminine cultures, as do

Table 5 *Summary of Gender Dimension*

Dimension 4. Gender	One Extreme	The Other Extreme
The degree of traditional gender role of achievement, control, and power.	Femininity	Masculinity
Core Value	Caring for others	Material success
Nonverbal Traits	Relaxed and coordinated vocal patterns, nurturing	High level of stress, loud, aggressive
Typical Cultures	Sweden, Norway, the Netherlands	Japan, Austria, Venezuela

their South American cultural descendents like Chile and Peru. Hofstede (1984) suggests that machismo is more present in the Caribbean region than in the remainder of South America. In fact, South America, as compared to Central America, has a much higher percentage of working women, much higher school attendance by girls, and more women in higher education (Seager & Olson, 1986).

A significant amount of research suggests that androgynous patterns of behavior (that is, both feminine and masculine) result in more self-esteem, social competence, success, and intellectual development for both males and females (Andersen, 1999). Nonverbal styles where both men and women are free to express both masculine traits (such as dominance and anger) and feminine traits (such as warmth and emotionality) are likely to be both healthier and more effective. Buck (1984) has demonstrated that males may harm their health by internalizing emotions rather than externalizing them as women usually do. Internalized emotions that are not expressed result in more stress and higher blood pressure. Not surprisingly, more masculine countries show higher levels of stress (Hofstede, 1984).

Considerable research has demonstrated significant vocal differences between egalitarian and nonegalitarian countries. Countries in which women are economically important and where sexual standards for women are permissive show more relaxed vocal patterns than do other countries (Lomax, 1968). Moreover, those egalitarian countries show less tension between the sexes, more vocal solidarity and coordination in their songs, and more synchrony in their movement (Lomax, 1968).

The United States tends to be a masculine country, according to Hofstede (1984), although it is not among the most masculine. Intercultural communicators should keep in mind that other countries may be either more or less sexually egalitarian than the United States. Most countries are more feminine than the United States (that is, nurturing and compassionate), so Americans of both sexes seem loud and aggressive by world standards. Likewise, Americans' attitude toward women may seem sexist in extremely feminine locations such as Scandinavia.

Most importantly, in relatively more feminine countries, both men and women can engage in either masculine or feminine nonverbal behaviors. In masculine countries, the nonverbal behavior of men and women is carefully prescribed and must adhere to a narrower sexual script. So, for example, in feminine countries like Sweden and Norway, women can engage in more powerful speaking styles, wear masculine clothing, and be more vocally assertive. Similarly, men in feminine countries can show emotions such as sadness or fear and engage in more nurturing and less dominant behaviors.

Uncertainty

Some cultures value change and ambiguity, whereas others value stability and certainty. Uncertainty is a cultural predisposition to value risk and ambiguity (Andersen et al., 2002; Hofstede, 1984). At the individual level, this quality is called tolerance for ambiguity (Martin & Westie, 1959). People with intolerance of ambiguity have high levels of uncertainty avoidance and seek clear, black-and-white answers. People with tolerance of ambiguity have low levels of uncertainty avoidance and tend to be more tolerant, to accept ambiguous answers, and to see many shades of gray. Similarly, Hofstede (1984) reports that a country's neuroticism or anxiety scores are strongly correlated with uncertainty avoidance. High uncertainty avoidance is negatively correlated with risk taking and positively correlated with fear of failure.

Countries vary greatly in their tolerance for uncertainty (see Table 6). In some cultures, freedom leads to uncertainty, which leads to stress and anxiety. Hofstede (1984) maintains that intolerance of ambiguity and dogmatism are primarily a function of the uncertainty-avoidance dimension rather than the power-distance dimension. The ten countries with the highest levels of uncertainty avoidance are Greece, Portugal, Belgium, Japan, Perú, France, Chile, Spain, Argentina, and Turkey (Hofstede, 1984). Countries whose culture originated in the Mediterranean region, especially southern European and South American countries, dominate the list. The ten countries lowest in uncertainty avoidance and highest in tolerance are Singapore, Denmark, Sweden, Hong Kong, Ireland, Great Britain, India, the Philippines, the United States, Canada, and New Zealand. This list is dominated by Northern European and Asian cultures, many of which were countries that were originally part of the British Empire. Not surprisingly, these low uncertainty-avoidant countries have a long history of democratic

Table 6 *Summary of Uncertainty Dimension*

Dimension 5. Uncertainty	One Extreme	The Other Extreme
The degree of avoidance or tolerance for uncertainty and ambiguity within the society.	Uncertainty Avoidance	Uncertainty Tolerance
Core Value	Certainty, what is different is dangerous	Exploration, what is different causes curiosity
Nonverbal Traits	More emotional displays higher level of anxiety	More positive and friendly to strangers
Typical Cultures	Greece, Portugal, Belgium	Singapore, Denmark, Sweden

rule that is likely to be the cause and an effect of uncertainty avoidance. Catholic and Islamic countries are higher in uncertainty avoidance, whereas Protestant, Hindu, and Buddhist countries tend to be more accepting of uncertainty (Hofstede, 1984). Eastern religions and Protestantism tend to be less "absolute," whereas Catholicism and Islam are more "absolute" than certain religions. Andersen, Lustig, and Andersen (1990) report that intolerance for ambiguity is much higher in the southern states of America than in the northern states, tending to reflect the international pattern of latitude and tolerance.

Few studies have examined nonverbal behavior associated with uncertainty. Hofstede (1984) maintains that countries high in uncertainty avoidance tend to display emotions more than do countries that are low in uncertainty avoidance. Furthermore, he reports that the emotional displays of young people are tolerated less in countries with high uncertainty avoidance. Certainly, disagreement and nonconformity are not appreciated if uncertainty avoidance is high. Nonverbal behavior is more likely to be codified and rule-governed in countries with high uncertainty avoidance. This seems to fit a country such as Japan, but the hypothesis remains to be tested. Hofstede (1984) has found that nations high in uncertainty avoidance report more stylized and ritual behavior; so we should expect that nonverbal behavior is more prescribed in these cultures. When people from the United States communicate with people from a country such as Japan or France (both high in uncertainty avoidance), the Americans may seem unruly and unconventional, whereas their Japanese or French counterparts might seem too controlled and rigid to the Americans (Lustig & Koester, 1999).

Research on uncertainty reduction and avoidance has been extended from interpersonal communication to the study of intercultural communication (Berger & Gudykunst, 1991; Gao & Gudykunst, 1990; Gudykunst, 1993, 1995; Gudykunst & Hammer, 1988), resulting in Gudykunst's Anxiety/Uncertainty Management Theory. The theory seeks to explain attitudes and behaviors toward strangers and members of other cultures (Gudykunst, 1995). Interacting with people outside of our group induces physiological arousal that is experienced as anxiety. This is consistent with the work of Hofstede (1984), who has shown that people in uncertainty-avoidant countries experience and show more anxiety than in other countries. The theory suggests that more secure, uncertainty-tolerant groups are more accepting toward people from another group or culture. Of course, much of this takes place at subtle nonverbal levels. People from cultures that embrace uncertainty are much more likely to treat strangers with positive nonverbal behaviors such as smiles and other indications of immediacy and warmth.

Immediacy

Immediacy behaviors and interpersonal warmth are actions that signal closeness, intimacy, and availability for communication rather than avoidance and greater psychological distance (Andersen, 1985, 1998). Examples of immediacy behaviors are smiling, touching, eye contact, closer distances, and more vocal animation. Some scholars have labeled these behaviors as "expressive" (Patterson, 1983). Cultures that display considerable interpersonal closeness or immediacy have been labeled "contact cultures" because people in these countries stand closer together and touch more (Hall, 1966a). People in low-contact cultures tend to stand apart and touch less. According to Patterson (1983):

> These habitual patterns of relating to the world permeate all aspects of everyday life, but their effects on social behavior define the manner in which people relate to one another. In the case of contact cultures, this general tendency is manifested in closer approaches so that tactile and olfactory information may be gained easily. (p. 145)

Interestingly, high-contact cultures are generally located in warmer countries nearer the equator and low-contact cultures are found in cooler climates farther from the equator. Explanations for these latitudinal variations have included energy level, climate, and metabolism (Andersen, Lustig, & Andersen, 1990; Hofstede, 1984). Evidently, cultures in cooler climates tend to be more task-oriented and interpersonally "cool," whereas cultures in warmer climates tend to be more people oriented and interpersonally "warm." Even within the United States, the warmer latitudes tend to be higher-contact cultures. Andersen, Lustig, and Andersen (1990) report a .31 correlation between latitude of students' university and touch avoidance. These data indicate that "students at universities located in the so-called Sunbelt are more touch-oriented." Pennebaker, Rimé, and Sproul (1994) found a correlation between latitude and expressiveness within dozens of countries. Northerners are more expressive than southerners, according to their data, in Belgium, Croatia, France, Germany, Italy, Japan, Serbia, Spain, Switzerland, and the United States, with an overall difference within the entire Northern Hemisphere. Pennebaker et al. (1994) conclude:

> Logically, climate must profoundly affect social processes. People living in cold climates devote more time to dressing, to providing warmth, to planning ahead for food provisions during the winter months. . . . In warm climates, people are more likely to see, hear, and interact with neighbors year around. Emotional expressiveness then would be more of a requirement. (pp. 15–16)

Similarly, Andersen, Lustig, and Andersen (1990) conclude:

> In Northern latitudes societies must be more structured, more ordered, more constrained, and more organized if the individuals are to survive harsh weather forces. . . . In contrast, Southern latitudes may attract or produce a culture characterized by social extravagance and flamboyance that has no strong inclination to constrain or order their world. (p. 307)

Traditionally, research has shown that high-contact cultures comprise most Arab countries, including North Africa; the Mediterranean region, including France, Greece, Italy, Portugal, and Spain; Jews from both Europe and the Middle East; Eastern Europeans and Russians; and virtually all of Latin America (Condon & Yousef, 1983; Jones, 1994; Jones & Remland, 1982; Mehrabian, 1971; Patterson, 1983; Samovar, Porter, & Jain, 1981; Scheflen, 1972). Australians are moderate in their cultural contact level, as are North Americans (Patterson, 1983). Research generally found that low-contact cultures comprise most of Northern Europe, including Scandinavia, Germany, and England; British Americans; white Anglo-Saxons (the primary culture of the United States); and virtually every Asian country, including Burma, China, Indonesia, Japan, Korea, the Philippines, Thailand, and Vietnam (Andersen, Andersen, & Lustig, 1987; Heslin & Alper, 1983; Jones, 1994; Jones & Remland, 1982; McDaniel & Andersen, 1998; Mehrabian, 1971; Patterson, 1983; Remland, 2000; Samovar, Porter, & Jain, 1981; Scheflen, 1972). Research reported by Remland (2000) indicates that people do touch significantly more in Southern Europe than in Northern Europe.

Other recent studies suggest that the biggest differences in immediacy are not between North America and Europe, both of which are probably moderate-to high-contact cultures. Compared to the rest of the world, Asian cultures are extremely noncontact (McDaniel & Andersen, 1998; Remland et al., 1991). These two studies question whether Hall's (1966a) original designation of some cultures as "low contact" is an oversimplification. Whether a generational shift or internationalization may have produced this change is unclear, but much of the Western world, including the United States, appears to be a contact culture. Indeed, McDaniel and Andersen's (1998) study of public touch suggests that the biggest difference is between Asians, who

Table 7 *Summary of Immediacy Dimension*

Dimension 6. Immediacy	One Extreme	The Other Extreme
The degree of closeness, intimacy, and availability for communication.	Low Contact	High Contact
Core Value	Certainty, what is different is dangerous	Exploration, what is different causes curiosity
Nonverbal Traits	Located in cooler climates, stand apart and touch less, stay "cool"	Located in warmer countries nearer the equator, stand closer together and touch more, expressive
Typical Cultures	Japan, China, Korea	North Africa, France, Brazil

rarely touch in public; and virtually every other culture, who manifest higher degrees of public touching. These findings are consistent with other research suggesting that China and Japan are distinctly nontactile cultures (Barnland, 1978; Jones, 1994).

Without a doubt, cultures differ in their immediacy (see Table 7). Generally, people living in northern countries, northern parts of individual countries, in traditional cultures, and in Asian cultures are the least immediate and expressive. Conversely, people living in the south, modern countries, and non-Asian cultures are the most expressive and immediate. Obviously, these findings are painted with a fairly broad brush and will await a more detailed cultural portrait.

CONCLUSION

These six dimensions of intercultural nonverbal communication aim at providing a theoretical framework that helps move studies on nonverbal communication across cultures from detailed descriptions to the realm of meanings, functions, outcomes, and relationships behind the screen. This list is neither exhaustive nor discrete. However, scholars and culture practitioners have increasingly utilized the conceptual scaffold outlined in this chapter to better understand and further explain the underlying basis of thousands of cultural differences in nonverbal behavior.

Although studying these six dimensions cannot ensure competence in intercultural communication, combining cognitive knowledge from intercultural readings and courses with actual encounters with

people from other cultures will definitely help boost one's intercultural communication competence. More importantly, these six dimensions of cultural variation in nonverbal communication have pointed out directions for future studies. As Andersen, Hecht, Hoobler, and Smallwood (2002) suggest, the rich interplay among the six dimensions, the interactions among people who differ along the same dimensions, the phenomenon that some members of a society do not seem to fully manifest the general tendencies of a particular culture, and group behavior investigated in well-situated cultural context are of great research value and potential.

References

Albert, R. D., & Ah Ha, I. (2004). Latino/Anglo-American differences in attributions to situations involving touch and silence. *International Journal of Intercultural Relations, 28,* 353–280.

Andersen, J. F., Andersen, P. A., & Lustig, M. W. (1987). Opposite-sex touch avoidance: A national replication and extension. *Journal of Nonverbal Behavior, 11,* 89–109.

Andersen, P. A. (1985). Nonverbal immediacy in interpersonal communication. In A. W. Siegman & S. Feldstein (Eds.), *Multichannel integrations of nonverbal behavior* (pp. 1–36). Hillsdale, NJ: Lawrence Erlbaum.

Andersen, P. A. (1988). Explaining intercultural differences in nonverbal communication. In L. A. Samovar & R. E. Porter (Eds.), *Intercultural communication: A reader.* Belmont, CA: Wadsworth.

Andersen, P. A. (1998). The cognitive valence theory of intimate communication. In M. T. Palmer & G. A. Barnett (Eds.), *Progress in communication sciences, Volume XIV: Mutual influence in interpersonal communication:*

Theory and research in cognition, affect, and behavior. (pp. 39–72). Stamford, CT: Ablex.

Andersen, P. A. (1999). *Nonverbal communication: Forms and functions.* Mountain View, CA: Mayfield.

Andersen, P. A. (2000). Explaining intercultural differences in nonverbal communication. In L. A. Samovar & R. E. Porter (Eds.), *Intercultural communication: A reader* (9th ed., pp. 258–279) Belmont, CA: Wadsworth.

Andersen, P. A. (2004). *The complete idiots guide to body language.* Indianapolis IN: Alpha Books.

Andersen, P. A. (2007). *Nonverbal communication: Forms and functions.* Long Grove, IL: Waveland Press.

Andersen, P. A., & Bowman, L. (1999). Positions of power: Nonverbal influence in organizational communication. In L. K. Guerrero, J. A. DeVito, & M. L. Hecht (Eds.), *The nonverbal reader* (pp. 317–334). Prospect Heights, IL: Waveland Press.

Andersen, P. A., Hecht, M. L., Hoobler, G. D., & Smallwood, M. (2002). Nonverbal communication across culture. In W. B. Gudykunst & B. Mody (Eds.), *Handbook of international and intercultural communication* (pp. 89–106). Thousand Oaks, CA: Sage.

Andersen, P. A., & Leibowitz, K. (1978). The development and nature of the construct touch avoidance. *Environmental Psychology and Nonverbal Behavior, 3,* 89–106.

Andersen, P. A., Lustig, R., & Andersen, J. F. (1990). Changes in latitude, changes in attitude: The relationship between climate and interpersonal communication predispositions. *Communication Quarterly, 38,* 291–311.

Andersen, P. A., & Wang, H. (2005). Unraveling cultural cues: Dimensions of nonverbal communication across cultures. In L. Samovar, R. Porter, & E. R. McDaniel (Eds.), *Intercultural communication: A reader* (11th ed., pp. 250–266). Belmont, CA: Wadsworth.

Argyle, M. (1975). *Bodily communication.* New York: International Universities Press.

Barnland, D. C. (1978). Communication styles in two cultures: Japan and the United States. In A. Kendon, R. M. Harris, & M. R. Key (Eds.), *Organization of behavior in face to face interaction* (pp. 427–456). The Hague: Mouton.

Beaulieu, C. M. (2004). Intercultural study of personal space: A case study. *Journal of Applied Social Psychology, 34,* 794–805.

Beaupre, M., & Hess, U. (2005). Cross-cultural emotion recognition among Canadian ethnic groups. *Journal of Cross-Cultural Psychology, 36,* 355–370.

Bellah, R. N., Madsen, R., Sullivan, W. M., Swidler, A., & Tipton, S. (1985). *Habits of the heart: Individualism and commitment in American life.* New York: Harper & Row.

Bem, S. L. (1974). The measurement of psychological androgyny. *Journal of Consulting and Clinical Psychology, 42,* 155–162.

Berger, C. R., & Gudykunst, W. B. (1991). Uncertainty and communication. In B. Dervin & M. Voigt (Eds.), *Progress in communication sciences* (Vol. 10, pp. 21–66). Norwood, NJ: Ablex.

Bond, M. H. (1993). Emotions and their expression in Chinese culture. *Journal of Nonverbal Behavior, 17,* 245–262.

Brown, D. E. (1991). *Human universals.* Philadelphia: Temple University Press.

Brown, L. R., Kane, H., & Roodman, D. M. (1994). *Vital signs 1994: The trends that are shaping our future.* New York: W. W. Norton.

Bruneau, T. (1979). The time dimension in intercultural communication. In D. Nimmo (Ed.), *Communication yearbook 3* (pp. 423–433). New Brunswick, NJ: Transaction Books.

Buck, R. (1984). *The communication of emotion.* New York: Guilford Press.

Burgoon, J., Buller, D., & Woodall, W. G. (1996). *Nonverbal communication: The unspoken dialogue* (2nd ed.). New York: McGraw-Hill.

Camras, L. A., Chen, Y., Bakeman, R., Norris, K., & Cain, T. R. (2006). Culture, ethnicity, and children's facial expressions: A study of European American, mainland Chinese, Chinese American and adopted Chinese girls. *Emotion, 6,* 103–114.

Camras, L. A., Oster, H., Campos, J., Campos, R., Ujiie, T., Miyake, K., Wang, L., & Meng, Z. (1998). Production of emotional facial expressions in European American, Japanese, and Chinese infants. *Developmental Psychology, 34,* 616–628.

Chinoy, E. (1967). *Society.* New York: Random House.

Condon, J. C., & Yousef, F. (1983). *An introduction to intercultural communication.* Indianapolis, IN: Bobbs-Merrill.

Cushner, K., & Brislin, R. (1996). *Intercultural interactions: A practical guide* (2nd ed.). Thousand Oaks, CA: Sage.

Elazar, D. J. (1972). *American federalism: A view from the states.* New York: Thomas P. Crowell.

Elliot, S., Scott, M. D., Jensen, A. D., & McDonough, M. (1982). Perceptions of reticence: A cross-cultural investigation. In M. Burgoon (Ed.), *Communication yearbook 5* (pp. 591–602). New Brunswick, NJ: Transaction Books.

Ekman, P. (1972). Universal and cultural difference in the facial expression of emotion. In J. R. Cole (Ed.), *Nebraska symposium on motivation* (pp. 207–283). Lincoln: University of Nebraska Press.

Ekman, P., & Friesen, W. (1975). *Unmasking the face.* Englewood Cliffs, NJ: Prentice-Hall.

Ekman, P., & Oster, H. (1979). Facial expression of emotion. *Annual Review of Psychology, 30,* 527–554.

Fernandez, D. R., Carlson, D. S., Stepina, L. P., & Nicholson, J. D. (1997). Hofstede's country classification 25 years later. *Journal of Social Psychology, 137,* 43–54.

Ford, J. G., & Graves, J. R. (1977). Differences between Mexican-American and white children in interpersonal distance and social touching. *Perceptual and Motor Skills, 45,* 779–785.

Gao, G., & Gudykunst, W. B. (1990). Uncertainty, anxiety, and adaptation. *International Journal of Intercultural Relations, 14,* 301–317.

Goldin-Meadow, S. (2003). *Hearing gestures.* Cambridge, MA: The Belknap Press of Harvard University Press.

Gudykunst, W. B. (1993). Toward a theory of effective interpersonal and intergroup communication: An anxiety/uncertainty management (AUM) perspective. In R. L. Wiseman & J. Koester (Eds.), *Intercultural communication competence* (pp. 33–71). Newbury Park, CA: Sage.

Gudykunst, W. B. (1995). Anxiety/Uncertainty Management (AUM) Theory: Current status. In R. L. Wiseman (Ed.), *Intercultural communication theory* (pp. 8–58). Thousand Oaks, CA: Sage.

Gudykunst, W. B., & Hammer, M. R. (1988). Strangers and hosts. In Y. Y. Kim & W. B. Gudykunst (Eds.), *Cross-cultural adaptation* (pp. 106–139). Newbury Park, CA: Sage.

Gudykunst, W. B., & Kim, Y. Y. (1992). *Communicating with strangers: An approach to intercultural communication.* New York: Random House.

Gudykunst, W. B., Matsumoto, Y., Ting-Toomey, S., Nishida, T., Kim, K., & Heyman, S. (1996). Influence of cultural individualism-collectivism, self-construals, and individual values on communication styles across cultures. *Human Communication Research, 22,* 510–543.

Gudykunst, W. B., & Nishida, T. (1986). Attributional confidence in low- and high-context cultures. *Communication Research, 12,* 525–549.

Hall, E. T. (1959). *The silent language.* New York: Doubleday.

Hall, E. T. (1966a). A system of the notation of proxemic behavior. *American Anthropologist, 65,* 1003–1026.

Hall, E. T. (1966b). *The hidden dimension* (2nd ed.). Garden City, NY: Anchor/Doubleday.

Hall, E. T. (1976). *Beyond culture.* Garden City, NY: Anchor.

Hall, E. T. (1984). *The dance of life: The other dimension of time.* Garden City, NY: Anchor.

Hall, E. T., & Hall, M. (1987). *Hidden differences: Doing business with the Japanese.* Garden City, NY: Anchor Press/Doubleday.

Hecht, M. L., Collier, M. J., & Ribeau, S. A. (1993). *African-American communication: Ethnic identity and cultural interpretation.* Newbury Park, CA. Sage.

Heslin, R., & Alper, T. (1983). "Touch: A bonding gesture." In J. M. Wiemann & R. Harrison (Eds.), *Non-verbal Interaction* (pp. 47–75). Beverly Hills, CA: Sage.

Hofstede, G. (1984). *Culture's consequences.* Beverly Hills, CA: Sage.

Hofstede, G. (1991). *Cultures and organizations: Software of the mind.* London: McGraw-Hill.

Hofstede, G. (1998). Masculinity/femininity as a dimension of culture. In G. Hofstede (Ed.), *Masculinity and femininity: The taboo dimension of national cultures* (pp. 3–28). Thousand Oaks, CA: Sage.

Hofstede, G. (2001). Culture's consequences (2nd ed.). Beverly Hills, CA: Sage.

Hofstede, G. J., Pedersen, P. B., & Hofstede G. (2003). *Exploring culture: Exercises, stories and synthetic cultures.* Yarmouth, ME: Intercultural Press.

Jones, S. E. (1994). *The right touch: Understanding and using the language of physical contact.* Cresshill, NJ: Hampton Press.

Jones, T. S., & Remland, M. S. (1982, May). *Cross-cultural differences in self-reported touch avoidance.* Paper presented at the annual convention of the Eastern Communication Association, Hartford, CT.

Jourard, S. M. (1966). An exploratory study of body-accessibility. *British Journal of Social and Clinical Psychology, 5,* 221–231.

Kowner, R., & Wiseman, R. (2003). Culture and status-related behavior: Japanese and American perceptions of interaction in asymmetric dyads. *Cross-Cultural Research, 37,* 178–201.

LaBarre, W. (1985). Paralinguistics, kinesics, and cultural anthropology. In L. A. Samovar & R. E. Porter (Eds.), *Intercultural communication: A reader* (pp. 272–279). Belmont, CA: Wadsworth.

Lambert, H. & Wood, K. (2005). A comparative analysis of communication about sex, health and sexual health in India and South Africa: Implications for HIV prevention, *Culture, Health & Sexuality, 7,* 527–541.

Lomax, A. (1968). *Folk song style and culture.* New Brunswick, NJ: Transaction Books.

Lustig, M. L., & Koester, J. (1999). *Intercultural competence: Interpersonal communication across culture.* New York: HarperCollins.

Marsh, A. A., Elfenbein, H. A., & Ambady, N. (2003). *Psychological Science, 14,* 373–376.

Martin, J. G., & Westie, F. R. (1959). The intolerant personality. *American Sociological Review, 24,* 521–528.

Matsumoto, D. (1991). Cultural influences on facial expressions of emotion. *Southern Communication Journal, 56,* 128–137.

Matsumoto, D. (2006). Culture and nonverbal behavior. In V. Manusov & M. L. Patterson (Eds.), *The Sage handbook of nonverbal communication* (pp. 219–235). Thousand Oaks, CA: Sage.

Matsumoto, D. (2002). Methodological requirements to test a possible in-group advantage in judging emotions across cultures: Comment on Elfenbein and Ambady (2002) and evidence. *Psychological Bulletin, 128,* 236–242.

Matsumoto, D. (2006). Culture and nonverbal behavior. In V. Manusov & M. L. Patterson (Eds.). *The Sage handbook of nonverbal communication* (pp. 219–235). Thousand Oaks, CA: Sage.

McDaniel, E. R., & Andersen, P. A. (1998). Intercultural variations in tactile communication. *Journal of Nonverbal Communication, 22,* 59–75.

Mehrabian, A. (1971). *Silent messages.* Belmont, CA: Wadsworth.

Meissner, C. A, & Brigham, J. C. (2001). Thirty years of investigating the own-race bias memory for faces: A meta-analytic review. *Psychology, Public Policy, and Law, 7,* 3–35.

Merritt, A. (2000). Culture in the cockpit: Do Hofstede's dimensions replicate? *Journal of Cross-cultural Psychology, 31,* 283–301.

Molinsky, A. L., Krabbenhoft, M. A., Ambady, N., & Choi, Y. S. (2005). Cracking the nonverbal code. Intercultural competence and gesture recognition across cultures. *Journal of Cross Cultural Psychology, 36,* 380–395.

Patterson, M. L. (1983). *Nonverbal behavior: A functional perspective.* New York: Springer-Verlag.

Pennebaker, J. W., Rimé, B., & Sproul, G. (1994). *Stereotype of emotional expressiveness of Northerners and Southerners: A cross-cultural test of Montesquieu's hypotheses.* Unpublished paper, Southern Methodist University, Dallas, TX.

Porter, R. E., & Samovar, L. A. (1998). Cultural influences on emotional expression: Implications for intercultural communication. In P. A. Andersen & L. K. Guerrero (Eds.) *Handbook of communication and emotion: Research theory, applications and contexts* (pp. 451–472). San Diego, CA: Academic Press.

Remland, M. S., Jones, T. S., & Brinkman, H. (1991). Proxemic and haptic behavior in three European countries. *Journal of Nonverbal Behavior, 15,* 215–232.

Remland, M. S. (2000). *Nonverbal communication in everyday life.* Boston, MA: Houghton Mifflin.

Samovar, L. A., & Mills, J. (1998). *Oral communication: Speaking across cultures.* Boston: McGraw-Hill.

Samovar, L. A., Porter, R. E., & Jain, N. C. (1981). *Understanding intercultural communication.* Belmont, CA: Wadsworth.

Samovar, P. A., Porter, R. E., & Stefani, L. A. (1998). *Communication between cultures.* Belmont, CA: Wadsworth.

Sapir, E. (1928). The unconscious patterning of behavior in society. In E. S. Drummer (Ed.), *The unconscious* (pp. 114–142). New York: Knopf.

Scheflen, A. E. (1972). *Body language and the social order.* Englewood Cliffs, NJ: Prentice-Hall.

Scheflen, A. E. (1974). *How behavior means.* Garden City, NY: Anchor.

Seager, J., & Olson, A. (1986). *Women in the world atlas.* New York: Simon & Schuster.

Shackleton, V. J., & Ali, A. H. (1990). Work-related values of managers: A test of the Hofstede model. *Journal of Cross-Cultural Psychology, 21,* 109–118.

Sheridan, J. H. (1978). Are you a victim of nonverbal "vibes"? *Industry Week, 198,* 36.

Sitaram, K. S., & Codgell, R. T. (1976). *Foundations of intercultural communication.* Columbus, OH: Charles E. Merrill.

Sporer, S. L. (2001a). Recognizing the faces of other ethnic groups: An integration of theories. *Psychology, Public Policy, and Law, 7,* 36–97.

Sporer, S. L. (2001b). The cross-race effect: Beyond recognition of faces in the laboratory. *Psychology, Public Policy, and Law, 7,* 170–200.

Stafford, L. (2005). *Maintaining long-distance and cross-residential relationships.* Mahwah, NJ: Erlbaum.

Ting-Toomey, S. (1999). *Communicating across cultures.* New York: The Guilford Press.

Tomkins, S. S. (1984). Affect theory. In K. R. Scherer & P. Ekman (Eds.), *Approaches to emotion* (pp. 163–195). Hillsdale, NJ: Lawrence Erlbaum.

Tung, R. (1994). Strategic management thought in East Asia. *Organizational Dynamics, 22,* 55–65.

Watzlawick, P., Beavin, J. H., & Jackson, D. D. (1967). *Pragmatics of human communication.* New York: W. W. Norton.

Wellman, B. (1999). The network community. In B. Wellman (Ed.), *Networks in the global village* (pp. 1–48). Boulder, CO: Westview.

Concepts and Questions

1. What does Andersen mean when he writes that "the primary level of culture is communicated implicitly, without awareness, and chiefly by nonverbal means"?

2. Do you agree with Andersen that two of the most fundamental nonverbal differences in intercultural communication involve space and time? From your experiences, what two nonverbal areas have you found most troublesome when interacting with people from different cultures?

3. From your personal experiences, can you think of different ways in which people in various cultures greet, show emotion, and beckon?

4. Do you believe that intercultural communication problems are more serious when they involve nonverbal communication or verbal communication?

5. What is kinesic behavior? How does it vary from one culture to another? What types of communication problems can be caused by cultural differences in kinesic behavior?

6. The term *haptics* refers to patterns of tactile communication. How does tactile communication differ between

cultures? Can you think of examples of how tactile communication differs among members of co-cultures? What type of communication problems might arise when people with different touching orientations interact?

7. How does physical appearance affect first impressions during interaction? How are expectations of physical appearance related to the informal-formal dimension of culture?

8. How does immediacy affect interpersonal interaction? What differences in behaviors would you expect from high- and low-contact cultures? In what way would violations of immediacy expectations affect intercultural communication?

9. How is the degree of individualism within cultures manifested in nonverbal behavior?

A Different Sense of Space

NED CROUCH

It's Sunday morning. You're up extra early so you can beat the crowds, get down to the beach, commune with nature. You want to recharge your batteries so you'll be your usual go-getter self come Monday. What could be better? The sound of the surf, a cup o' hot coffee, not a living soul in sight—nobody, that is, until a Mexican plunks down right beside you.

Crossing five hundred feet of unoccupied sand, he greets you with a polite, *"Buenos dias!"* Then he shouts excitedly to his whole family, motioning for the nursemaids and the dog to come join you.

You say, *"Buenos dias"* rather politely, but your body language betrays your displeasure. You wait a few moments so that your next action isn't too obvious. Then—knowing you're going to come off as a tight-assed gringo, but not caring—you pick up your cup and towel and head back to the hotel. You're thinking, "A half mile of beach in either direction, and they have to pick on me! What's with these people? Can't they see they're invading my personal space?"

The answer is no. No they can't. This isn't how they see it at all. Mexicans have a different sense of space. They sit down beside you because "that's where the people are." It doesn't occur to them that this is objectionable or impolite. On the contrary, it's the natural, friendly, obvious thing to do. Unlike Americans who prefer to spread out, Mexicans tend to congregate. If another gringo had come along, he would have settled about halfway toward the horizon to the south. Intuitively he would understand that both you and he want space and tranquility. If a third gringo had arrived, he would have gone halfway toward the northern horizon. According to our sense of space, we tend to seek the maximum convenient distance between one another before the inevitable crowd arrives. We draw a circle around

From Ned Crouch, *Mexicans and Americans: Cracking the Culture Code,* (2004), pp. 45–54. Used by permission of Intercultural Press, A Nicholas Brealey Publishing Company.

ourselves—a circle as big as circumstance will allow. It shrinks as conditions dictate, until we feel agitated and claustrophobic. The Mexicans look disappointed as you leave, and quietly, very quietly, the señora asks papa what happened. "I don't know. I must have done something wrong. I can't imagine what it is. Or perhaps he does not like Mexicans." Mexicans are quick to pick up on any show of irritation or impatience and assume that they have caused the displeasure. But they are also aware that some of us don't like them. They hear us complain about illegal immigrants, the oil slicks in the Gulf of Mexico, losing jobs, drugs. We blame it all on them. They have seen our police beating them on TV: They know that we can be prejudiced and they're thinking, "Maybe it's our brown skin." Somehow a moment of solitude on the beach has turned into an international racial incident. You're feeling violated; they're feeling discriminated against. While you're asking why they are so intrusive, they're wondering what it is about them that you don't like. But the real issue is not lack of manners or skin color. It's space.

BUMPER TO BUMPER

I pull into the parking lot of the Hispanic Center in Michigan with my brand new car. Wanting to avoid dings in my doors, I deliberately park three rows away from the building in an area sixty feet from any other car and ninety feet farther from the front door than the closest available parking slot. As I am getting out of my car, a woman swings through the entrance, around the median, and parks right next to me. How do I know she's not an Anglo? Could it be that she parked next to me because that's where the people are parking now?

In keeping with their sense of space, Mexicans tolerate a high compression factor. An American manager sent to Mexico was concerned because his wife had invited about thirty couples to their small apartment in Monterrey. When the guests started showing up with their children, there was hardly room to breathe. Much to his surprise, no one seemed to mind. In fact he noted that as the rooms became more crowded, his guests seemed to relax and have more fun. This is the Mexican's sense of space in action.

SOCIAL ORIENTATION

Our sense of space is directly tied to how we perceive our connection to other people. Whereas we Americans draw circles around the individual, Mexicans draw circles around the group. Most of the world is closer to the Mexicans in this regard. We— plus some western and *most* northern Europeans— are the exceptions. People from Latin America, the Middle East, Africa, and Asia tend to be more group-oriented and are less sensitive to individual space needs.

Differences in our sense of space undoubtedly contribute to the impression held by most Mexicans that Americans are somewhat cold and distant. Space becomes a big issue on trains, on planes, and in cars. Travel is definitely more uncomfortable for those of us in cultures where the sense of personal space is tighter. Our natural instinct is to feel stress when we are crowded onto a small commuter plane in Mexico, where passengers carry on a year's worth of luggage and cram themselves into smaller seats.

We Americans will always be more comfortable being separated; Mexicans will always be more comfortable being part of a group. We will always resist being crowded; they will always want to get closer. It's not personal. It's not prejudice. They don't know it, but on that Sunday morning at the beach, you would have gotten up and left if another gringo had sat next to you—only faster.

Because the Mexican and American notions of space are so deeply embedded, it is unrealistic to think that either is going to change. Nor should we expect change. Both senses of space are natural and not insensitive.

When we draw circles around ourselves, we are inside the circle looking out. Since Mexicans draw a circle around the group, they are constantly looking inward toward that group. Figuratively speaking, the Mexican family surrounded by the walls of their house look inward toward one another. We, on the other hand, are inside the house looking out through the biggest picture window we can afford, hoping that nobody will build within sight of us—a markedly different social orientation.

In the United States, our sense of space begins to develop from the moment we are brought home from the hospital in a bassinet. From that moment on, the

American child develops an expectation of privacy. He or she begins referring to "my room" and "my toys." The walls are going up. Children begin to feel more comfortable with a private space that they can crawl off to for insulation against pressure. This is quite different from the Mexican experience. We Americans become territorial about our half of the dorm room at college. We set up separate shelves in the community refrigerator. We want a den in our dream house where we can put our feet up and think about what we should have said today and mentally project what we will do tomorrow—all without interruption from the family. Not so in Mexico.

Mexicans' closer sense of space is related to the way they have been raised—living much closer together in the home and looking inward to each other for support and nurturing. Physical closeness goes along with closer families and less sibling rivalry. Each child does not get his own room. Boys and girls are not necessarily divided until a more advanced age, and then only if resources allow. There's nothing inherently better or worse about either the American or Mexican approach—although Mexican children sure do get along well, both among themselves and with others. When passing playgrounds in Mexico, I'm always struck with the pleasant sounds. No taunting, teasing, or squabbling.

There is a story about a Mexican worker who came to the United States for training. His supervisor asked a coworker to take Javier home to show him how Americans live. The American coworker took him through his house. "This is the entry hall where we take off our snowshoes. Here's the living room, but we spend more time in the den over there where the TV is. This is the dinette next to the kitchen. Here's Bertha's and my room. Here's the boys' room. Here's where little Martha sleeps, except when Grandma and Grandpa visit and she sleeps in the den." Javier was delighted with the tour and said, "You know, it's exactly the same in Mexico— except for the walls." This story is not intended to be derogatory in any way. It is instructive.

DON'T FENCE ME IN

Although Mexicans are less concerned than Americans about defining individual space, they are generally more concerned with sharply demarcating one family's living space from another family's. This usually means having a wall between houses. When Mexicans visit the United States, they often marvel at the open lawns between homes. The Mexican wonders, "How do they know where their property stops and their neighbor's begins?" Americans know. We know exactly where to mow, don't we? To construct walls between houses seems to run counter to something in the American spirit. "Something there is that doesn't love a wall," wrote Robert Frost in his quintessentially American poem, "Mending Wall." The Mexican's feelings run just as deep on the other side. For them it is important to define family space. This is because the family and its space are a final refuge from the chaos and uncertainty of life outside their walls. The home is the one place where, with all the gods playing their ungodly tricks, they can finally feel in control. Protecting the group space is paramount.

When we Americans observe Mexicans, we see them piled onto a train with families, chickens, goats, and a whole menagerie. We wonder how they can fit so many on a bus. We observe clusters of family members moving around Sears in unison. We make jokes about crowding into a pickup truck. But we are observing only the top ten percent of a cultural phenomenon that rises above the surface. What is going on underneath the surface is a clash in our opposing sense of space.

There is a strong correlation between sense of space and behavior. We Americans have a definite sense of individual space and we carry a protective shell around our individuality. Our sense of individuality goes with us wherever we go. We act independently, whereas Mexicans see themselves as part of a group. They act as a group, looking to each other for direction, approbation, and survival. When they are in their group space, they behave according to what that space is dedicated to. If they are in the receiving hall outside the mayor's office, they wait for the mayor like dutiful citizens. If they are in the polishing department, they see themselves as polishers. When they are in the home, they act like a family. As Americans, we too adjust our behavior and shift gears depending on what is required of us. We cooperate with the team and blend into the choir, but we don't shed the circle around ourselves. Typically, we see ourselves as discrete individuals operating within the group, whereas Mexicans are *the group*.

Whether working in the United States or in Mexico, Mexicans working on the factory floor of a large manufacturing entity perceive the walls of their department as enveloping their circle. In this setting, they have their backs to the wall and relate to the group. By contrast, when Americans visualize the overall operation of a plant, we see a continuous production line cutting through all departments. We draw little boxes for machines and little circles for operators performing specific tasks. Mexican workers, on the other hand, relate primarily to the inner circle of their department and secondarily to the larger space where the entire company team works together.

Another difference in our respective senses of space is that Americans feel threatened if our personal space is invaded, whereas Mexicans are alarmed if their group space is invaded. We feel as though our person is being violated. They feel that their group identity is being threatened.

HERE'S LOOKING AT YOU

What happens when you enter their space? Both Mexicans and Americans have rituals for approaching another person's or group's space. But our respective rituals are very different.

In her novel, *Stones for Ibarra* (1984), Harriet Doerr writes about a local man visiting the house where the author and her husband were living in a remote Mexican village. The local was looking for work. He didn't want to disturb the American couple needlessly, so, rather than knock on the door, he went around the house, window to window, looking in to see if they were there and if they were busy. Had they been in the kitchen sipping coffee, he would have gone to the back door and announced himself. Had they been in bed, he would have left quietly to return the next day. Within the context of his peasant Mexican culture, he was behaving perfectly properly in the way he approached the author's space. He was being polite. It was jarring to the writer, however. What if Harriet and her husband were in an intimate embrace? What if they were naked? How can someone just come up to your window and look in?

From the Mexican peasant's perspective, his actions were innocent and nonthreatening. (This may be one reason Mexican city dwellers put walls all the

way around their houses.) Had he seen anything of a personal nature, he would have averted his eyes and returned later. As for the nakedness, well, it is as natural as can be and nothing to get excited about. He would have been confused if the gringos had come out screaming and shooing him off. It would not have computed. He would not have understood why the gringos were so hostile.

BACKING OFF

You probably don't recognize that Americans routinely behave ritualistically, but we do. Imagine that you want to borrow a rake from your neighbor. First, you knock on his screen door and then quickly back up. If nobody comes, you knock again, this time yelling to the upstairs window. Did you peer in through the screen? No. Did you walk around the house looking for the rake? No. Somewhere along the line we picked up cultural cues about personal space that tell us how to approach the neighbor's house. We have learned that there is an acceptable, nonthreatening way to get the attention of a neighbor whom we consider vulnerable because his doors and windows are open.

Ritualistic practices also help us cope with confined spaces, such as crowded elevators. As we get on, we lower our eyes, turn toward the buttons, and press our floor. We face front and say nothing. If we must, we say, "Out please." or "Excuse me," with our Yankee penchant for economy of words. It's different in Mexico. They get on an elevator and say, "*Buenas tardes,*" to everybody. It is not unusual to hear chatter among the strangers. They ask permission to get off—"*Con permiso.*" The others respond, "*Propio*" (*of course*). Or they may insist that you go first.

There is a different ritual in Mexico for entering shopping spaces. We Americans go into a store and immediately put up our defense shields. If forced to speak, we say, "Just looking around." Mexicans go to a store and, recognizing that they have entered the shopkeeper's space, immediately proffer a "*Buenas tardes*" to the owner and staff. There is nothing more out of place than the woman in Bermuda shorts and Rockports who says, "*Nada mas mirando*"—a lame translation of "just looking," which to the Mexican means absolutely nothing. In Mexico the clerk will follow you around the store quietly—not uttering a word. We feel crowded by her presence. Is she checking up on us? No. She's there, close to you, in case you have any questions. Be aware that we think we're shopping, whereas they think we have come for a visit. This is their space, and we will get better service, when the time comes, if we act as though we are invitees rather than dispassionate purchasing agents.

CORRECT DISTANCE

Americans' individual space is quite well defined, though most of us don't realize it. The correct face-to-face distance between American men is one arm's length, less the hand. The distance woman-to-woman is a bit closer than man-to-man. If you are a man, the next time you're at a cocktail party or convention, try moving one half step closer to the man you're talking to. You will see him avert his eyes, shift his feet, turn sideways, and finally take a half step back. He won't be conscious of his own actions. You then take another half step closer. He will repeat his backward shuffle. Keep it up, and you could waltz him around the room and out the door.

Understanding the different boundaries of personal space is important when doing business. In the United States, if a woman were to move a little closer to a man, he may interpret the narrowing of space as an invitation to flirt, which would be taboo in the workplace. If a Mexican woman stands closer to an American male, however, it is not a come-on. In fact, it means nothing of the sort. Her circle of personal space is simply smaller, or less acutely felt than his. Men and women generally stand closer in Mexico. If you are showing a Mexican woman something on your computer screen, she will get much closer to you than an American woman would. She may stand with her legs right next to your arm or lean over your shoulder. American males should note that this is not a come-on.

In the States, the personal space between individuals remains the same, irrespective of status—whether speaking to the president of the company or the guy who sets up our AV equipment. In Mexico's more hierarchical society, there is a need to establish greater separation between the workers and the *jefe,* or "big man." The workers tend to operate together more closely than in the United States, but the president maintains more distance between himself and his accounting clerk. The Mexican boss will have an exaggeratedly large office and desk to emphasize the hierarchical distance between himself and his minions. This is his "power distance."

As an American operating with Mexicans, you want to be sensitive to the greater zone that surrounds the president of a company. But in the course of your dealings, when the president takes a step closer, puts his arms around you, and gives you an *abrazo,* or hug, he is indicating that he means to accept you as an equal. If you are a woman, the parallel behavior might be a pat on the arm and an "air kiss" (touching cheeks and smacking the void next to the woman's head), which acknowledges trust and confers respect. Whatever you do, don't pull back and blow it. In this context, the gesture signals that you have crossed into the Mexican president's circle and are trusted to work within his group. You must now maintain that relationship and build on it. I explained the *abrazo* practice to middle management at Chrysler Motors. "Hold on a minute," one man interjected. "In sensitivity training, we were told never to touch *anybody.*" I'm not suggesting you go hugging anyone unless you feel comfortable getting that close. On the other hand, be aware that men will hug men in Mexico, and it means nothing beyond friendship and acceptance.

Americans and Mexicans have been living next to each other for many years and have learned to appreciate each other's customs: I have a friend in McAllen, Texas, named Mike Heap. (There is no more Anglo-Saxon name than Mike Heap.) Mike is a laconic Texan, a cowboy, and a former bronco-buster who is now on the rodeo circuit as a clown. He loves Mexicans, his girlfriend is Mexican, and like most Anglos in the Rio Grande Valley, he speaks Spanish. When he goes to Mexico, he gives his men friends *abrazos.* I too give and receive *abrazos* when I go to Mexico. But Mike and I would never hug each other.

According to street lore, the *abrazo* came into being as a means of "patting down" the person you greet to make sure he's not armed. But, today it means, "Welcome to my space."

GROUP SPACE

How should Americans adapt our usual business practices in response to the Mexicans' sense of space? Since Mexicans draw a circle around their group and focus inward, as previously mentioned, anyone entering their space makes a big impact. So in the business setting, how you enter a Mexican group's space is important. A proper greeting, avoiding flamboyant gestures, not shouting, and general circumspection are appreciated.

Most how-to books tell you how to greet and what to wear. But remember that in addition to proper manners, violating Mexicans' group space may be perceived as a threat to how they live and work. If we go into their group space and disrupt the harmony of the group, we are signaling to the group that we do not care about them. They may assume that they are the next to be transferred, fired, or shot.

When a gringo walks into a native cantina in a remote village, suddenly everything goes quiet. When they realize you are just there to throw down tequila, they relax and start talking again. We are clearly outsiders. But once we enter the group and behave, they accept us. If we buy one of them a drink and tell a good joke, the atmosphere turns to jubilation.

In the workplace, Mexicans can favor us with cooperation and the rewards of group effort if we are sensitive to the effect we are having on their space. By minimizing disruption when we enter their space, we indicate respect for their group and earn their support. The unfortunate corollary for us is that often once we leave their space, we may no longer exist to them. We have to be in their space to get the best results. Once in their group space, we have to spend time building relationships or else we will be "out of sight, out of mind."

Concepts and Questions

1. How does Crouch link the Mexican use of space to their value toward collectivism?
2. Why does Crouch believe Americans prefer to "spread out"?
3. How does Crouch link the American attitude toward space to privacy?
4. Explain Crouch's observation that "there is a strong correlation between American sense of space and behavior."
5. What does Crouch mean when he speaks of "ritualistic practices"? How do those practices relate to the use of space?
6. Why is it important to know cultural boundaries in the use of space?
7. What is the relationship of space to power both in Mexico and in the United States?
8. Crouch asks the following question in his essay: "How should Americans adapt their use of space to the Mexican sense of space in the business setting?" How would you answer that question?
9. What specific "tips" does Crouch advance at the conclusion of his essay that might help you adapt your use of space when doing business in Mexico?

Cultural Contexts: The Influence of the Setting

6

*He who would form a correct judgment of
their tone must hear first one bell
and then the other.*

ITALIAN PROVERB

At this stage of the book, it should be clear to you that communication involves much more than the sending and receiving of verbal and nonverbal messages. Human interaction by its very nature happens within a social and physical setting—it does not occur in a social vacuum. When you are communicating, you are doing so within a specific environment or context. We now call your attention to the concept of *social context* because the setting is never neutral; it always influences how communication participants behave. Whether you are in a classroom, football stadium, night club, physician's office, business meeting, or place of worship, the social environment contains many physical and social elements that determine how you and your communication partners will produce and respond to messages while communicating. What you wear, what you talk about, to whom you talk, and even the volume of your voice is in many ways governed by the context in which you find yourself. You have learned proper patterns of communicative behavior for the various social contexts in which you find yourself. But, as with other aspects of intercultural communication, the appropriate patterns of behavior in various social contexts are culturally diverse. When you fine yourself in an unfamiliar social context without an internalized set of rules to direct you, communication problems frequently arise.

The impact and influence of context is rooted in three interrelated assumptions.

1. *Communication is rule governed* (i.e., each encounter has implicit and explicit rules that regulate your conduct). These rules tell you everything from what is appropriate attire to what topics may be discussed.
2. *The setting helps you define what "regulations" are in operation.* Reflect for a moment on your own communication behavior as you move to and from the following arenas: classroom, courtroom, church, hospital, basketball game, and movie theater. Visualize your behavior as you move from place to place.
3. *Most of the communication rules you follow have been learned as part of your cultural experiences.* Although cultures might share the same general settings, their specific notions of proper behavior for each context reflects the values and attitudes of

that culture. Concepts of turn taking, time, space, language, manners, nonverbal behavior, silence, and control of the communication flow are largely an extension of each culture.

In this chapter, we offer readings that demonstrate the crucial relationship between context, culture, and communication. What emerges from these essays is the realization that to understand communication in another culture you must know and respect the rules that govern that culture's communicative behavior in specific settings. Although intercultural communication occurs in a wide variety of contexts, we have selected three social environments where you will most likely find yourself interacting with people from diverse cultures: *business, health care,* and *education.*

As we have already indicated, the readings that follow discuss cultural diversity in communication contexts. To help you become more competent when you communicate in those contexts, we will focus on both international and domestic settings.

During the past thirty-five years, the growth of international businesses has been astonishing. Business that involved overseas transactions and generated millions of dollars annually just a few decades ago are now multibillion-dollar operations. Many former national companies have transformed themselves into global, transnational entities with offices, employees, production, and service facilities located throughout the world. This trend toward multinational companies has evolved for several reasons. One is the creation of national regulations requiring some product manufacturing to be done within a country where the product is to be marketed. An example of this is the requirement that some assembly of foreign automobiles take place in United States factories if the cars are to be sold there. A second cause has been mergers and acquisitions in which one company may buy or merge with another across national boundaries. A third impetus for this trend is a recognition that business productivity increases when work occurs in a local presence. And, finally, you can see changes that have occurred within the United States. In many geographic areas of the country, immigration has created a pluralistic, multicultural society. The result is that a multicultural workforce is now employed in most companies, whether they are local, regional, national, or international businesses.

Because of this worldwide economic growth and the internationalization of business, people no longer have the comfort of working exclusively with others who possess the same cultural background and experiences. One's associates, clients, subordinates, and even supervisors are often from different cultures and even from different countries. Many aspects of business life, such as methods of negotiation, decision making, policy formulation, socializing, gender relationships, marketing techniques, management structure, human resource management, gift giving, and patterns of communication, are now affected by cultural diversity.

What is true about the expansion of intercultural business communication also applies to the educational setting. That is to say, the forces of globalization, immigration, and population change have given large numbers of classrooms both in the United States and elsewhere a new multicultural/multinational appearance. In the United States alone, nearly one in three students now identify themselves as African American, Latino, Asian, Pacific Islander, Arab, or American Indian. Because of the cultural experiences of these groups, schools must accommodate widely diverse learning styles, interaction patterns, forms of competition or cooperation, diversity in the use and meaning of silence, as well as the status and role of the teacher.

The presence of global and multicultural populations also has major implications for health care providers. This cultural context is important for a number of reasons. First, the promotion of health and the prevention of disease is an urgent priority for any civilized culture. Second, some diseases are highly contagious and can be easily transmitted into a host culture. Third, and from a cultural perspective most important, is cultural diversity in perceptions about the causes, treatment, and prevention of illness. And finally, members of dissimilar cultures may utilize different communication patterns and styles when they interact in the health care setting. Members of one culture, for instance, may talk openly and freely to a health care provider about their medical situation whereas members of another culture may be reluctant to talk or to reveal personal information.

As we have just highlighted, your understanding of how communication operates in the multicultural business setting, the educational environment, and the health care setting becomes more important as cultural diversity continues to intensify. In order to help you communicate successfully in these arenas, we offer the following eight essays.

The first four essays focus on a setting that is found both domestically and internationally—the world of business. The concern of these selections is to demonstrate how cultural diversity touches nearly all aspects of the business context. It is obvious that all business activities involve many forms of communication, and those forms are influenced by the attitudes, values, and communication patterns unique to each culture.

Earlier in the book, you were introduced to some of the cultural differences that exist between Eastern and Western societies. One difference focused on the individualistic versus collectivistic nature of these cultures. Not realizing these differences can lead to misunderstandings if both sides do not understand the cultural dynamics involved.

The first essay in this chapter addresses some of these differences. Professor Kazuo Nishiyama provides you with an enlightened discussion of how decisions are reached in Japanese business organizations. In order for you to fully appreciate this process, Nishiyama begins with a background discussion about the corporate culture in Japan and how it fosters group-orientation. He relates how Japanese companies frequently hire new recruits selected from high school and university graduates in the month of April each year. The new recruits all receive their company orientation together at the company's training center. This process builds close bonds and interpersonal relationships that tend to last a lifetime. It is because of these close bonds and interpersonal relationships that the Japanese style of decision making is appropriate and functional.

Nishiyama shows how Japanese decision making follows a *ringi*, or group decision-making protocol. He holds that this style of decision making is rooted in the Japanese tradition of interpersonal harmony, cooperation, and consensus. In this process, plans are initiated by lower- or middle-ranking managers who are charged with drafting a proposal. However, before the proposal is written and distributed, the initiator will discuss the general idea informally with key personnel. Upon obtaining positive reactions from the appropriate people, the proposal is written along with a request for a decision. The proposal then goes through many face-to-face, informal, behind-the-scene discussions by the people who will be involved in implementing a decision. Only after informal consensus is achieved will the proposal be circulated through the management hierarchy until it receives approval. Then the document is hand delivered to the company president for his approval.

The key to the decision-making process is the *kaigi,* or a face-to-face conference. This type of discussion among Japanese business people is quite different from a business meeting in a typical Western organization. Nishiyama points out that in a Western business meeting, the proposal will be debated until a decision is made. In the Japanese system, "the Japanese business meeting is an occasion to formally confirm what has been already decided informally through intensive *nemawashi* [or informal discussions]."

Nishiyama ends his essay with detailed advice for Western business persons who are involved in negotiations or decision making with Japanese counterparts. He suggests that Westerners maintain close personal contacts, that they do not rush their Japanese counterparts, and that they do not consider *ringi* as a negative, slow process. In addition, he suggests that Westerners bring gifts for their Japanese counterparts, that they acquire a good understanding of Japanese culture and social customs, that they do not talk too much, that they be patient, and finally try to provide visual aids in Japanese.

Although the diversity found between Eastern and Western cultures looms the largest, differences between U.S. American and European business cultures can also lead to confusion and misunderstandings during intercultural communication. In the next essay, Paul Hinner presents an analysis of German and American business cultures. He begins by showing how the German and American economies are similar because they are capital based and market driven. He also indicates there are many similarities between German and American cultures due to their shared European heritage. However, he is hasty to point out that "a closer look at German and American business cultures also reveals differences."

Hinner demonstrates how Germany's position in the heart of Europe, which placed it in the center of wars and conflicts going back to antiquity, has influenced the development of many German cultural values. High uncertainty avoidance (the extent to which a member of a culture is fearful of the unknown) is a major characteristic found within the German culture. Hinner points out how this has led the Germans to create many rules and regulations that help minimize risks in advance and promote the successful accomplishment of any task at hand. Hinner also points out that Germany has a long history of regional autonomy giving the country a very different tradition than found in the United States.

As a background for further understanding German culture, Hinner describes the German legal system and how it differs from that of the United States. The major difference is that German law is code based while American law is case based. In Germany, the law seeks to anticipate illegal actions which must be listed expressly in the legal code to be deemed illegal. Law in the United States applies the principle of analogy and is able to extend existing law to cover new circumstances.

Hinner continues his essay with a description of the differences between German and American corporate organization. German companies are controlled by two different boards: a management board and a supervisory board. The management board runs the company. But, the supervisory board is charged with the task of seeing that management policies and operations are always in the best interest of shareholders. By German law, in corporations of over 500 employees, one-third of the supervisory board members must be employees. This provision is consistent with the German principles of consensus and parity. By describing the organization of American corporations and the role of their boards and CEOs, Hinner shows just how different business organizations are in Germany and the United States.

Hinner concludes his essay with a discussion of communication problems that can arise during business negotiations between Americans and their German counterparts. He explains how diversity in some cultural values influences the interactions. For instance, while both Americans and Germans tend to be monochronic in their work routines, Germans are more rigid and believe small talk to be a waste of time; meetings should commence immediately with the business at hand. Also, the German need for order and organization requires that in any business meeting the Germans will want to have an initial and comprehensive understanding of all aspects of a problem before attempting to solve it.

Mexico's proximity to the United States and the North American Free Trade Agreement (NAFTA) has dramatically increased trade negotiations between the United States and Mexico. Because of this, and the operation of U.S. businesses in Mexico, the need for a better understanding of Mexican culture and the differences in U.S.-Mexican business practices has become an essential. The importance of this relationship and the effect it is having on the cultures of both Mexico and the United States was examined in detail in a special issue of *Time* magazine in which the editors suggested that "along the U.S.-Mexican border, where hearts and minds and money and culture merge, the Century of the Americas is born" (June 11, 2001).

In their essay "U.S. Americans and Mexicans Working Together: Five Core Concepts," Sheryl Lindsley and Charles Braithwaite provide you with valuable insights into Mexican culture as it applies to the business environment. Lindsley and Braithwaite discuss five shared cultural patterns or core concepts relevant to doing business in Mexico: *confianza, simpatía, palanca, estabilidad,* and *mañana.* These are not mutually exclusive categories, but rather overlapping concepts reflecting deeply held values for many Mexicans. As these shared values make their way into the business environment, effective U.S. business managers and representatives must become aware of the influences these values have on behavior and communication.

While the previous article explored working relations between Americans and Mexicans both in the United States and in Mexico, the next article is concerned about working relationships as they exist in U.S. companies with multicultural workforces. In their article, "Beyond the Knapsack: Disrupting the Production of White Racial Privilege in Organizational Practices," Patricia Parker and Jennifer Mease explore the problems of White privilege in the U.S. workforce. Recall that John Warren's essay in Chapter 2 described many of the dynamics of White privilege and the effects it can have on those who are non-White. Parker and Mease extend this issue into the workplace by pointing out "the subtle and often unnoticed ways that the privileges of Whiteness surface in organizations . . . through the very structures and practices that we take for granted." By drawing on Peggy McIntosh's metaphor of an invisible weightless knapsack to represent special provisions or practices that protect and favor White people in society, Parker and Mease reveal the ways in which White privilege perpetuates racism and subtly and unconsciously discriminates against non-Whites. They explain how this form of racism provides "invisible White privilege, especially within intercultural spaces such as organizations, where advantage and disadvantage, access, empowerment and exploitation are determined by a White normative standard."

Parker and Mease begin with a discussion of race as a social construction with no biological basis for distinguishing human groups along lines of race. They review the ways in which the idea of race developed with the rise of a world political economy. They extend this discussion to include the idea that Whiteness is also a social construction in which "scientific" methods were used to place people in a racial hierarchy with White Europeans at the top. They follow with examples of how Whiteness and White privilege is sustained in society in general and in organizational cultures in particular.

Next, the authors provide a framework for seeing and disrupting White privilege in organizations. Drawing on the works of bell hooks, Parker and Mease outline ways in which Whiteness can be made visible by scrutinizing how words, images, and practices in everyday situations serve to protect and advantage White people and limit the life choices of non-Whites. In part of this discussion, Parker and Mease show how White privilege provides access to occupations and careers through preferences given to Whites. These preferences not only include college admissions but recruitment for entry positions of workers. They conclude their essay with a list of salient points to ponder such as the history of White privilege, the difficulty of identifying White privilege, how to interrupt White privilege in organizations, and knowing how to identify White privilege in order to point it out to others.

We devoted four essays to the business context because we believe that international business and the proper utilization of a multicultural workforce in the United States are areas where competent intercultural communication skills are very important. However, we do not want to leave you with the idea that business is the only important context. In the next two essays, we will deal with diverse cultural issues found in the health care context.

We begin with a comprehensive overview of how cultures differ in their approaches to the diagnosis, treatment, and prevention of illness. In their essay "When Cultures Collide: Alternative Medicine, Biomedicine, and the Patients in the Middle," Polly A. Begley and Debbie A. Ockey show how alternative beliefs about standard American medical practice can lead to major intercultural communication difficulties. The authors begin with a discussion about the cultural collisions that can occur when those who embrace traditional healing are faced with the biomedical culture that abounds in traditional American medicine. They then discuss how the changing global populations bring about a need for health care providers to understand diverse medical approaches.

Next, the authors relate the various belief systems related to health care by describing the biomedical belief system that is predominate in the United States and the supernatural belief system which is a traditional system that views illness as a punishment for evil deeds, an outside possession of the body, an evil spell, or a wounded soul. They also describe the holistic belief system which requires that in order for people to be well they must remain in harmony with natural laws and be able to adjust to changes in the environment. Finally, they describe alternative medical approaches that include chiropractors, massage therapists, homeopaths, and naturopaths.

Based upon the foundation they have established, Begley and Ockey discuss the challenges to providing health care that is culturally and linguistically appropriate for a diverse population. They hold that "culturally appropriate medial care includes being able to effectively treat a patient with different beliefs about the origins of illness and disease." This includes developing medical plans and recommendations that are consistent with the patient's and family's beliefs and expectations.

After discussing the issues of health literacy and the linguistic challenges inherent in a multicultural health care system, the authors provide several models for success that involve solutions and innovative programs. They call for increased knowledge and understanding of diverse health care beliefs and increasing the diversity of health care professionals. Included in their discussion are a series of questions that should be asked by health care providers to ensure that cultural diversity is taken into consideration in the development of treatment plans.

The next essay continues the discussion of the health care setting, but using a distinctive approach. In the previous essay, you learned about different approaches to healing, some of which employed treatments for the spirit or the soul. In their essay, "Three Narratives of Spiritual Healing," authors Karen Rasmussen and Jennifer Asenas explore the ways in which three culturally diverse novelists depict the process of spiritual healing through "binding up the wounds of breaking worlds." Examining texts from American Indian, African American, and Mexican American backgrounds, the authors relate tales of spiritual remediation as an antidote to individual and cultural problems. The authors use novels to accurately describe how healers in diverse cultures employ spiritual healing rituals in order to bring about cures for the ill spirit.

Rasmussen and Asenas first draw from Leslie Marmon Silko's *Ceremony*, which describes the healing journey of a World War II veteran. Next, they analyze Toni Morrison's *Beloved*, which describes the resolution of division through communal rites. Last, they draw from Ana Castillo's *So Far From God*, which dramatizes the countering of illness through spiritual healing actions. In each case, Rasmussen and Asenas provide a narrative analysis of each story. They discuss the spiritualities active in each novel and relate how each story "enacts its form of spiritual healing using a unique communication strategy." Their analysis describes the forms of communication active in each scenario and how they relate subject matter and purpose to address real-world concerns through spiritual healing.

Classrooms represent another setting that is experiencing a rapid increase in intercultural contacts. Worldwide, the children of immigrants are being educated in their new homelands. The faces of the people in these schools, and the languages they speak, are as diverse as those found in the business and health care settings. Although educational practices at any educational level of a multicultural society are affected by the cultural diversity found in each classroom, we believe that the practice of intercultural communication in the classroom is paramount. Traditional approaches to education and the use of a single communication strategy are inadequate in a multicultural context. Cultural diversity affects thinking habits and strategies, communication patterns and styles, prejudice and stereotyping, educational expectations, approaches to learning, and classroom behavior.

In her article "Culture and Communication in the Classroom," Geneva Gay introduces the semiotic relationship that exists among communication, culture, teaching, and learning. She discusses some of the critical features and pedagogical potentials for different ethnic groups of color. Her discussion of culture and communication first outlines some key assertions about culture and communication in teaching and learning in general. Gay then presents some of the major characteristics of the communicative modes of African Americans, Native Americans, Asian Americans, and European Americans. Her focus is on discourse dynamics—that is, who participates in communication, under what conditions, and how participation patterns are affected by culture.

Geneva Gay's article dealt primarily with classrooms in the United States, but, what about education in other cultures? Is it different? How different? How do cultural values affect the classroom? How is the interaction between student and teacher different from culture to culture? To what extent do the structural elements of other educational systems differ from those of the United States?

The next essay addresses some of these issues by describing how Japanese schools acculturate values through their educational practices. In their article "Enculturation of Values in the Educational Setting: Japanese Group Orientation," authors Edwin R. McDaniel and Eriko Katsumata describe and analyze the educational system prevalent in Japan and reveal how the values of the Japanese culture are not only taught in the schools but also affect the very structure of educational system.

McDaniel and Katsumata begin with a peak inside Japanese schools. They describe in detail the pre-school/kindergarten, elementary school, middle school, and high school programs as well as the university system. By reading these descriptions, you will immediately see major differences from the educational system in the United States. Throughout their detailed description you will find the common thread of collectivism that pervades the educational system. All educational experiences seem to foster the importance of the group over that of the individual. As the authors point out, "observations suggest that the Japanese educational system continues to explicitly and implicitly communicate the role of group affiliation, which remains an important aspect of Japanese social organization."

McDaniel and Katsumata conclude their article by refuting some current arguments that Japan is moving away from its collective nature. Perhaps, they suggest, change will occur; but it will come neither easily nor quickly because the value of collective effort and identity continues to be passed on to generations through the existing educational system.

Japanese Style of Decision Making in Business Organizations

Kazuo Nishiyama

Western scholars and businesspeople are still very critical of Japanese decision-making processes as being intuitive and irrational. They are often frustrated and even dismayed that seemingly ultra-modern Japanese business organizations have not adopted more objective and rational approaches to decision making as expected. The Japanese organizations may all claim that they have modernized decision-making processes with extensive use of Web sites for dissemination and e-mails for exchanges of in-house information. Except for non-traditional IT-related companies, however, almost all other companies still continue to use the traditional *ringi-seido* (group decision making) and *kaigi* (face-to-face conference). The obvious reason for this continuation is that these traditional methods of communication are not only acceptable but also feasible in the context of Japanese corporate culture. Therefore, it is important to examine specific aspects of Japanese culture that instill and perpetuate the particular type of interpersonal relationships and decision-making practices in Japanese business organizations.

EMPLOYMENT SYSTEM IN JAPAN

Japanese companies are still group-oriented organizations despite the fact that the younger Japanese generation is becoming more individualistic. The major reason for perpetuation of group orientation among Japanese salaried workers is how they are recruited and how they are trained and indoctrinated into their workplace (Nishiyama, 1995). The following

are the most common personnel recruitment practices used in Japan today:

1. Japanese companies usually recruit new employees from among new graduates of high schools and universities during the month of April. The new recruits go through induction training together at the company's training center. This training will last two or more weeks. They all live together and engage in group-oriented activities in addition to listening to lectures by senior members of the company. This "bonding" among the new recruits is considered a very important aspect of their entire career with the company. When talking about comradeship, they often say, *onaji kama no meshi wo tabeta nakama* (comrades who eat rice from the same rice cooker).

2. Japanese companies are still reluctant to hire workers who have had previous work experience with other companies. They fear that the experienced workers, called "*chuuto saiyoo sha*" (mid-career recruits), may disrupt interpersonal harmony among those who have been hired directly into the company upon completion of their education. There are, however, many exceptions today in recruitment policies. For example, IT-related companies need experienced workers who can bring with them specific, advanced skills and technical knowledge. These companies even recruit computer programmers from China, Singapore, and India because they have no time to train programmers from among new Japanese recruits, and the foreign programmers are comparatively cheaper to hire.

3. All Japanese companies use different classifications of employees in order to retain good and loyal workers and to differentiate them from other less desirable workers. There are *honyatoi* (regular employment), *rinjiyatoi* (temporary employment), *paato* (part-time employment), *keiyaku shain* (contract employee), *haken shain* (dispatched employee), etc. Those workers who are employed as regular employees usually have good educational backgrounds and personal qualifications. They comprise a group of "elite workers" who can look forward to becoming members of management and receiving lifetime employment, plus annual advancement. Temporary employees (*rinjiyatoi*) are hired when the company needs to augment its

workforce for a specific period of time. They will never be given lifetime employment, no matter how long and how hard they work for the organization. They may receive only a few basic fringe benefits, and are the first ones to be fired whenever the workload is reduced. Part-time workers (*paato*) are given hourly wages without fringe benefits. Contract employees are hired for a certain period of months or years. Computer programmers from China, for example, are contract employees hired for one or two years. Dispatched employees (*haken shain*) are recruited by a *jinji haken kaisha* (personnel dispatch company) and assigned to client companies. Many English teachers working for multinational Japanese corporations are dispatched employees. They receive their wages and fringe benefits from their personnel dispatch company, not from the corporations they work for as English teachers. Still another classification is called *friitaa* or *frii arubaitaa* (casual workers). They are young Japanese men or women who do not have any career plans or ambitions to succeed in their professions. They work whenever or wherever they decide to work as temporary workers.

Among these groups of workers, only the regular employees are bona fide employees of the company they work for. There is a distinct separation between and among these differently classified employees. These groups of employees do not interact with each other on the same level of comradeship and interpersonal trust. In fact, the regular employees sometimes discriminate other groups and cooperate with them only with a certain amount of suspicion.

BUILDING UP INTERPERSONAL RELATIONSHIPS

The above discussion clearly shows that establishing close relationships and a group-oriented mentality is reserved for regular employees. And this process begins with the induction training when they are first hired and the elaborate *nyushashiki* (entering company ceremony). During the induction training, all new employees are required to learn the "President's Teachings" (corporate missions and mottos), the "Company Song," the corporate history and philosophy, etc. All learning takes place through group

activities. Those who attend the same induction training sessions become *doohai* (the same-year comrades) and they will continue to associate with each other as such (Nishiyama, 2000).

This entering company ceremony is a major annual event just like a commencement ceremony. The president, top executives, managers, senior employees, and some parents attend the ceremony. The president welcomes the new recruits and also challenges them to work hard for the corporate goals in his inspirational speech. In response, a representative of the new recruits answers his challenge. In fact, every recruit becomes a new member of the corporate family and pledges his alliance and loyalty to the company (Rohlen, 1974). New generations of Japanese workers do not particularly like this type of induction, but they are often forced to accept these traditional practices.

Even though a Japanese company tries to establish one unified work group, it is also true that there are *habatsu*, or factions, within the company. The factions are often based on *gakubatsu*, or school cliques, *senpai-koohai kankei* (senior-junior relationship), and city or state of birth. The managers who graduated from a certain university will give personal favors to the new recruits from the same university in exchange for the latter's loyalty. If, for example, University A's graduates hold powerful executive positions in a company, the graduates of the same university will be treated better than University B's graduates. Naturally, the senior members who took good care of the new recruits will make the latter feel obligated to them, creating a mutual-dependency relationship. Obviously, relationships among these factions can become troublesome at times because of intense inter-faction rivalries and conflict.

RINGI OR GROUP DECISION MAKING

The *ringi* style of decision making is deeply rooted in Japanese culture, which emphasizes interpersonal harmony, cooperation, and consensus. Today, it is often said that modern Japanese organizations have been streamlining or rationalizing this outdated process due to wide use of in-house Web sites and e-mail networks (McDaniel, 2003). It is still true, however, that the *ringi* system, even in its modified form, is being used to satisfy a number of important sociocultural demands among the members of most

Japanese business organizations. It is almost impossible for the Japanese to abandon this process and adopt a Western decision-making style where individuals at the top management level make decisions.

Unlike their counterparts in Western business organizations, Japanese executives and managers are not real independent decision makers. A Japanese company president, for example, cannot make a quick and independent decision on his own, unless he is the founder and the majority owner of the company. And if he does so too frequently, he will be accused of being a *wanman shahoo* (dictator president). Japanese companies may use the title "Chief Executive Officer," but this Japanese C.E.O. does not have the same decision-making authority as his counterpart in Western business organizations. The position of president is oftentimes honorary given to one before his retirement or promotion to the position of a chairman. He will never, therefore, risk making any unpopular decisions on his own. His decisions are usually based on group consensus. Actually, the person in charge of decision making is *senmu torishimari yaku* (managing director) who actually runs the daily affairs of his company. But he still needs the president's seal of approval on any decisions that he may make. In addition, he still needs other executives and managers' concurrence and support.

Process of *Ringi* Decision Making

The *ringi* process begins with a *kiansha* (plan initiator), usually a lower- or middle-ranking manager (supervisor or section chief), who is in charge of drafting a *ringisho* (proposal). Before drafting this document, he discusses the general idea informally with key executives, managers, and supervisors. Only after getting fairly positive initial reactions from them will he draft the proposal document. This document includes the request for a decision, supporting data and information, detailed explanations, and justifications. This informal discussion is called *nemawashi,* which literally means "twisting the tree roots around." In practice, *nemawashi* refers to holding many face-to-face, informal, behind-the-scene discussions about a proposal among all the people who would be involved in implementing any decision to be made later.

The act of *nemawashi* is analogous to twisting a planted tree around to cut off bothersome roots or "objections" so that it can be uprooted easily. The *nemawashi* process is a sounding board for unofficially testing the responses to a proposed idea without any risk of unnecessarily causing loss of face for any one individual or group. In this process, no one individual or group can claim all the credits if it is successful, and at the same time, no one will be blamed should it fail.

Once a *ringi* proposal is completed, the initiator circulates it to every executive and manager who will be asked to approve it after careful review. The circulation is executed in reverse order of each individual's hierarchical position, beginning with the lowest-ranked supervisor, to middle management, top management, and finally to the president. The cover sheet of the proposal has many small boxes for *han* (seal of approval) to be affixed by all those who will review and approve it. The proper order of circulation is strictly adhered to because skipping any person on the hierarchical ladder will cause serious procedural and interpersonal problems. If any of the managers or executives have questions or objections, the initiator will have to answer them in person. The decision can be delayed indefinitely until the person who is objecting receives convincing justification based on new data and information. When all the seals of approval have been obtained, the document will be hand delivered to the president for his approval. This final approval from the president, called *kessai* (final approval), is the last step in the *ringi* decision-making process.

Suppose, for example, that a Japanese faculty member wants to invite an American professor to a Japanese private university as a visiting professor. The Japanese professor will begin *nemawashi* (informal consultation) among his colleagues. He needs to find out whether or not any professor in his department objects to inviting this particular U.S. professor. If he is a junior assistant professor, he will have to gain the approvals of senior professors, who may have more power. Only then can he ask his department chairperson to request that the personnel department begin the necessary paperwork for employing this foreign professor. Unlike an American university, this Japanese university chairperson needs to obtain the approval of his dean and the university president. Naturally, he has to prepare a lengthy *ringi* document and go through the process as explained above.

If one of the professors objects for any reason, the assistant professor needs to tactfully persuade this objecting professor. His reason for objection could be that he feels threatened by the visiting professor, maybe because the visitor is very famous in the same field of study. Or perhaps he received a rather negative review of his conference paper from the visitor in the past. In this case, the junior professor is required to mediate the situation. If the objecting professor grudgingly agrees to go along, he will make sure that he will receive *kashi* (credit) from the junior professor. This means that the latter owes a favor to the former, and he will have to repay this *kari* (debt) later on. During the process of *nemawashi, kashi-kari kankei* (obligatory relationship) is established quite frequently within any Japanese organization (Nishiyama, 2000).

Kaigi, or Face-to-Face Conference

Kaigi in Japanese business organizations outwardly appears to be similar to a business meeting or conference in Western business organizations. However, it is quite different from a typical Western-style meeting in its purpose, procedure, content of discussion, and participation of attendees. Generally speaking, the purpose of a Western-style business meeting is to facilitate decision making in face-to-face situations. In contrast, the Japanese business meeting is an occasion to formally confirm what has been already decided informally through intensive *nemawashi*. In many instances, Japanese participants go through the ritual of asking questions and debating certain points. But in fact, they are merely saying what has been discussed and agreed upon beforehand. And they do not want surprise questions or strong objections from any one of the participants during the actual meeting.

In the Western cultural context, it is acceptable to change one's mind about what has been informally agreed upon prior to the meeting, if a much better idea or new compelling evidence is presented. In the Japanese cultural context, however, such changing of one's mind is a serious social infraction and betrayal of interpersonal trust. Any agreement that has been reached during informal consultations is considered a firm commitment. It is different from a tentative commitment or personal opinion that Western businesspeople usually try to obtain when going through the process of "touching the bases."

The role of each Japanese participant is different from that of his Western counterpart. The Japanese chairperson's main role is not to aggressively take direct control over the decision-making process, but to mediate the consensus-building process among all participants. In fact, the second-ranking person (usually *buchoo,* or department head) will do most of the talking and direct other participants to contribute to the on-going discussion in a predetermined order. Each of the junior-ranking participants presents a brief report prepared in advance and seeks everyone's approval. The participants seldom disagree with others during face-to-face meetings because they have probably talked about his report informally and obtained everyone's concurrence beforehand. There may be a few questions for clarifications, but open arguments or heated discussions will not be permitted. In some instances when important decisions are being made, the president or the top executive may show up at the conference just for a few minutes to give the participants moral support. However, they would never stay long and participate in the actual decision-making process. *Kao wo dasu* (showing one's face) has a significant meaning in this context.

If a junior participant wishes to voice his opinion, he will preface his remarks by saying, "I may be making this comment based on my limited experience and I may be wrong, but . . ." or he may also say, "Please tell me if you think I am wrong, but . . . ." He needs to take a tentative approach and also show humility in order not to cause loss of face among any of the participants. Other participants will also hesitate to voice frank opinions or disagreement, because they fear even their constructive criticisms could be taken as personal attacks or insults. They all tend to look for subtle verbal or nonverbal cues and try to understand how the other participants feel about what is being discussed.

The above discussion seems to indicate that Japanese businesspeople would never exchange their frank, honest opinions or comments. They do so, however, by intentionally creating informal opportunities outside the conference rooms. They frequently go out together for drinking and dining where they exchange their true feelings. An unhappy participant may even complain bitterly, pretending that he has had too much to drink, but he is allowed to do so because this is one of the ways to appease the dissatisfied member. The Japanese call this method of communicating while drinking alcohol *"nomini-cation"* (drink and communicate). Even in this *nomini-cation* context, it is important for all the participants to remember their position in the organizational hierarchy. A so-called "drunk person" is expected to apologize to his senior members on the following morning for his misbehavior. He might say, "I am sorry I was so drunk last night. I don't remember what I said," even if he remembers clearly what he complained about.

Unlike the Japanese counterpart, an American chairperson controls the discussion of a conference and encourages active participation from the participants. He might even challenge every participant to openly voice his or her own opinions and comments. And the participants feel free to exchange constructive criticisms and objections based on their knowledge and experience without fear of being ostracized or alienated.

Westerners, particularly Americans, are often frustrated when they attend a so-called "decision-making conference" in Japan. They are often dismayed because they expect that the Japanese participants across the conference table would act the same way as they do. They usually find it difficult to read subtle verbal and nonverbal cues offered by the Japanese participants. For example, the Japanese would say "yes, yes" and nod their head in agreement, this is called *aizuchi* (nodding in agreement), but these verbal and nonverbal cues do not mean they are agreeing at all in most instances. They may mean "I hear what you are saying," "Please explain more," or "I will pretend I agree with you for now, but I still have objections." Another problem is that in the Japanese language, they can say, "Yes, I don't agree with you, which literally means, "Yes, you are right. I don't agree with you" (Nishiyama, 2000).

In order to accurately assess what the Japanese counterparts mean by what they say, it is often necessary for the Americans to go out drinking and dining with a few of their Japanese counterparts. Perhaps one of the Japanese participants may help them "interpret" what has transpired during the conference. He may divulge certain important information *ofureko* (off-the-record) during after-hours *nomini-cation*.

ADVICE ON OVERCOMING COMMUNICATION DIFFICULTIES

1. *Maintain close personal contacts.*
   It is extremely important to cultivate and maintain close interpersonal relationships with those who are in charge, because decisions are often made on personal preference, not merely on objective facts and data. For example, an American who makes a good impression on the initiator of a *ringi* proposal can win the latter's friendship. The Japanese representative will keep the American informed as to the progress of the decision making by the involved top executives. Sending direct e-mail reminders will not work in this context.

2. *Do not rush Japanese counterparts.*
   Western businesspeople are always working by setting deadlines for actions, because "Time is of the essence" in their culture. They must understand that Japanese deadlines are more flexible, especially when the Japanese side is the buyer in a business deal. In Japan, "A customer is king," and they expect that a seller, who has a lower status, will abide by his customer's deadline.

3. *Do not consider ringi negative because it is slow and cumbersome.*
   The *ringi* process is indeed slow and cumbersome, but implementation of the decision is swift once it is made. For example, the visiting professor in the above example does not have to worry about acquainting himself with his new Japanese colleagues because everyone in the department will already know who he is and what he has written. They may even know about his wife, children, and other personal matters. Indeed, the "Welcome Mat" will be laid out upon his arrival.

4. *Bring gifts for Japanese counterparts.*
   Gift-giving is still an important custom in establishing amicable interpersonal relationships. A gift does not have to be an expensive one, but it should be a token of friendship. For example, an American businessperson may give a bottle of Johnny Walker whiskey or a carton of American cigarettes when visiting a Japanese counterpart for the first time. This small gift is not considered as a bribe in Japan as it is a common practice among Japanese businesspeople. And the Japanese side will usually give back to the American an *okaeshi* (return gift) when he is leaving Japan.

5. *Good understanding of Japanese culture and social customs is necessary for successful participation in decision-making conference.*
   Seating should be arranged strictly according to each participant's status, not by work group or area of specialization. The order of speaking and of asking questions should also be based on the relative status of the Japanese participants. Seniority and

ranking are important. For example, a junior manager cannot speak up before his senior manager speaks. And, he must wait for a subtle signal, verbal or nonverbal, from the senior before he can speak.

6. *Do not talk too much and do not dominate discussions.* Western businesspeople have a tendency to dominate verbal exchanges when participating in a business conference with the Japanese. They believe that winning arguments or using logical persuasion will bring about good results. On the contrary, Japanese participants may be offended by an aggressive and argumentative presentation from the Western counterparts. They may win the argument, but they will lose the deal. When English is used as a medium of communication, the Japanese participants feel handicapped. They may need more time to think in Japanese first and translate their thoughts into English. During meetings and official functions, U.S. business representatives should never help a Japanese counterpart with English by trying to put words into their mouths.

7. *Be patient and disregard the "Western time orientation."* Westerners are generally "clock-oriented" whereas the Japanese are "people-oriented." This means that Japanese people are more inclined to adjust the handling of time based on who is speaking. For example, each participant could be asked to make his or her comment within five minutes, but a senior Japanese participant might take more than ten minutes and ramble along in broken English. But it would be extremely rude to stop him before he finishes what he wants to say. In this situation, who is speaking is more important than what the time restraint is.

8. *It is a good strategy to prepare visual aids in Japanese.* In order to facilitate accurate communication, visual aids such as charts, graphs, figures, or slides should be used. The Japanese usually want to have written documents that cover important data and information. This strategy will help them better understand what is being explained in English.

CONCLUSION

Despite the fact many Japanese companies claim that they are revamping the traditional decision-making practices, it seems that they are not able to make drastic changes. Clearly, they must change their personnel recruitment and training system first if they wish to create a new corporate culture amenable to more efficient digital communication. To remove the fear among managers of not knowing what is going on, the Japanese companies still continue to provide information to every level of management by the use of the *ringi* decision-making system. And in order to have amicable interpersonal relationships, Japanese managers still want to hold face-to-face conferences, even though they sometimes find it unnecessary to participate in time-consuming meetings.

During the economic boom years, prior to the burst of Japan's "Bubble Economy" in the early 1990s, there were some innovative measures to change the traditional personnel management system by doing away with permanent employment and seniority-based compensation. The subsequent recession, however, forced many Japanese companies to restructure or scale down their operations. This situation, in turn, created the fear of losing jobs among all levels of managers and they again went back to the more comfortable and nonthreatening methods of decision making that they had been used to. Those companies that claim that they streamlined decision-making practices still use *ringi* and *kaigi* in making important decisions. These traditional, culturally based methods of decision making, however modified, will continue to be used as long as Japan's corporate culture requires them.

Index of Japanese Terms

aizuchi	nodding in agreement
buchoo	department head
chuuto saiyoo sha	mid-career recruit
doohai	the same-year comrade
gakubatsu	school clique
friitaa, frii arubaitaa	casual worker
habatsu	faction
haken shain	dispatched employee
han	seal
honyatoi	regular employee
jinji haken kaisha	employee dispatch company
kaigi	face-to-face conference
kao wo dasu	showing one's face

kari	debt
kashi	credit
kashi-kari kankei	obligatory relationship
keiyaku shain	contract employee
kessai	final approval
kiansha	initiator
nemawashi	informal consultation
nyushashiki	company entering ceremony
nomini-cation	drink and communicate
ofureko	off-the-record
okaeshi	return gift
onaji kama no meshi wo tabeta nakama	comrades who ate rice from the same cooker
paato	part-time worker
ringi	group decision making
ringisho	proposal for decision
rinjiyatoi	temporary worker
senmu torishimari yaku	managing director
senpai-koohai kankei	senior-junior relationship
wanman shahoo	dictator president

References

McDaniel, E. R., (2004). Changing Japanese Organizational Communication Patterns: The Impact of Information Technology. *San Diego State University Center for International Business Education and Research* (CIBER). *Working Paper Services C04-015.*

Nishiyama, K. (1995). *Japan-U.S. Business Communication.* Dubuque, Iowa: Kendall/Hunt.

Nishiyama, K. (2000) *Doing business with Japan: Successful strategies for intercultural communication.* Honolulu: University of Hawaii.

Rohlen, T. (1974). *For harmony and strength: Japanese white-collar organization in anthropological perspective.* Berkeley, CA: University of California.

Suggested Readings

Castells, M. (2000). *End of millennium* (2nd ed.). Malden, MA: Blackwell.

Gudykunst, W.B., & Nishida, T. (1994). *Bridging Japanese/North American differences.* Thousand Oaks, CA: Sage.

Hall, I. (1998). *Cartels of the mind: Japan's Intellectual closed shop.* New York: Norton.

Japan External Trade Organization. (1992). *Japanese corporate decision-making.* Tokyo: Author.

March, R. M. (1980). *The Japanese negotiator: Subtlety and strategy beyond Western logic.* Tokyo: Kodansha International.

Quasha, S., & McDaniel, E. R. (2003). Reinterpreting Japanese business communication in the information age. In L. Samovar & R. Porter (Eds.), *Intercultural communication: A reader* (10th ed., p. 283–292). Belmont, CA: Wadsworth.

Yoshida, S. (2002). Globalization and issues of intercultural communications: Doing successful business in Asia. *Vital Speeches of the Day, 68*(22), 708–771.

Yoshimura, N., & Anderson, P. (1997). *Inside the Kaisha: Demystifying Japanese business behavior.* Boston: Harvard Business School Press.

Concepts and Questions

1. How does the employment system in Japan foster group orientation?
2. Why do Japanese employers shy away from hiring employees who have worked for other companies?
3. Why is a group-oriented mentality important to Japanese business organizations?
4. Nishiyama has indicated that although companies try to establish one unified work group, there may be factions within the company. What are the bases for these factions? How do these factions fit in with the idea of a group-oriented workforce?
5. How does the position of chief executive officer in Japanese companies differ from that position in Western business organizations?
6. Describe the process of *ringi* decision making.
7. How does the *ringi* process differ from decision-making processes in Western organizations?
8. In what ways do face-to-face conferences in Japanese business organizations differ from those in Western business organizations?
9. In a group-oriented Japanese business organization where harmonious relationships are important, how do Japanese business people exchange and express frank and honest opinions?

A Brief Comparison and Analysis of German and American Business Cultures[1]

MICHAEL B. HINNER

At first glance, German and American business cultures seem very similar. Both economies are capital based and market driven. Shares of large German and American corporations are traded in both countries. In fact, many German corporations have been active on the American market for many years now (e.g., Bayer, Mercedes Benz, T-Mobile, and Braun), as have many American corporations on the German market, (e.g., Coca Cola, Ford, McDonald's, IBM, and Microsoft). The list of German and American corporations could easily be extended. But a closer look at German and American business cultures also reveals differences. Very often such differences emerge slowly and only after a longer period of contact, cooperation, or interaction. One need only recall the problems that have been and continue to be associated with the Daimler Chrysler merger to realize the scope of the potential problems.[2] While some cultural problems might arise prior to establishing close business relationships, most tend to surface later during the day-to-day business routine after a relationship is in place (Harris & Moran, 1996; Hofstede & Hofstede, 2005; Trompenaars & Hampden-Turner, 1998).

For most people, culture is not an apparent issue if the participants appear to be fairly similar to each other (Chen & Starosta, 1998; Gudykunst & Kim, 1997; Samovar et al., 1998). It seems that people need to associate culture with something tangible and visible to realize that differences do exist. And

indeed, culture is exhibited through the visible artifacts it creates, including language (Gudykunst & Kim, 1997; Klopf, 1998; Samovar et al., 1998). So when people speak different languages or dialects, it is easier for most people to perceive a (linguistic) difference. However, in today's global economy many international business partners are fluent in English, wear similar business clothes, and often work in similar office environments so that "surface" differences tend to blend into a similar style (Harris & Moran, 1996; Hofstede & Hofstede, 2005; Samovar et al., 1998; Trompenaars & Hampden-Turner, 1998). But culture is more than external appearance and mere artifacts. Culture also includes sociofacts and mentifacts that are not always readily apparent to the observer but are expressed in the thinking process, behavior, and actions of people (Chen & Starosta, 1998; Gudykunst & Kim, 1997; Klopf, 1998; Martin & Nakayama, 1997; Samovar et al., 1998). And it is only in the day-to-day routine of constant interaction that these "hidden" differences emerge (Hofstede & Hofstede, 2005; Klopf, 1998; Samovar et al., 1998).

If, however, the external differences are striking, then the participants of an intercultural encounter will probably expect to encounter difficulties since these differences are perceivable (Chen & Starosta, 1998; Gudykunst & Kim, 1997; Klopf, 1998; Martin & Nakayama, 1997; Samovar et al., 1998). But one does not expect to encounter difficulties if there are few external differences and/or the actors appear to exhibit similar behavior. All the more surprising then if differences are encountered when least expected. Because these differences are not anticipated, they become all the more surprising due to their *unexpectness*. And this is the crux of culture: Many people associate cultural differences with exotic differences, and few expect culture to play any role in modern international business relationships (De Mooij, 2007; Harris & Moran, 1996; Hofstede & Hofstede, 2005; Trompenaars & Hampden-Turner, 1998); especially if two similar cultures are involved in an international business transaction as is the case with Germans and Americans who have a long tradition of contact and interaction.[3]

Culture is deeply rooted in history and historical developments, and it is embodied and reflected in all aspects of a society so that business culture mirrors its macroculture as well (Chen & Starosta, 1998; Gudykunst & Kim, 1997; Hofstede & Hofstede, 2005; Klopf, 1998; Martin & Nakayama, 1997; Samovar et al., 1998). German and American cultures have many similarities because they share, to some extent, a common European heritage.[4] In fact, many Americans trace their family roots back to German immigrants (German American, 2007). Conversely, the majority of Germans have been exposed to and influenced by American culture since the aftermath of World War II (*Facts about Germany,* 1996; Jankuhn et al., 1983; Zentner, 1980). This close relationship of both cultures is also illustrated by the many German loanwords in American English and the many English loanwords in contemporary German. For example, *kindergarten, kaffeeklatsch,* or *sauerkraut* in American English,[5] and *Designerbaby, Evergreen,* or *Preshave* in German.[6] Likewise, many German products have become icons in the USA (e.g., the VW beetle and Bayer aspirin), as have US products in Germany (e.g., Levi's jeans and Coke). The list of similarities and parallels could be extended easily.

But the transfer and exchange of products is not always identical because adjustments to local tastes have to be made. McDonald's, for example, includes beer in its program of beverages in Germany. And Coca Cola adapted the taste of its soft drinks to German taste buds; in particular, Fanta and Cherry Coke (Hinner, 1998). The average Bayer aspirin tablet sold in Germany has a higher dosage than in the USA, which explains why aspirin is usually only sold in pharmacies in Germany (Hinner & Rülke, 2002). And while the VW Jetta is a very popular car among young drivers in the United States, many young Germans consider it to be a car for senior citizens since the Jetta has a trunk and not a hatchback.[7]

The VW Jetta example illustrates how the same product can have different associations among consumers in different cultures. It, thus, becomes quickly apparent that classic market segmentation is insufficient in an intercultural context (De Mooij, 2007; Sandhusen, 1997). This may be illustrated by the following example. Single, female secretaries aged 20–25 years who live in the suburbs and commute to work in the city, listen to the same music, pursue the same hobbies, and have a similar disposable income might be classified as one particular segment (Homburg & Krohmer, 2003; Meffert, 2000), thus

assuming that these women exhibit similar consumer behavior if they live in similar markets. Yet, interestingly, differences do exist which could translate into missed business opportunities, differences which are not, however, found in classic segmentation categories; instead, these differences rest in cultural differences (De Mooij, 2007; Hinner, 1998, Hinner, 2004; Hinner & Rülke, 2002). If culture is not a criterion of the segmentation, then it will not be considered by marketers. So if a German shoe manufacturer were to target this particular market segment, it would probably assume that American secretaries wear footwear similar to that of German secretaries. The German manufacturer might have actually encountered American secretaries while visiting the United States on a business trip and noticed that American secretaries wear high heels in the office. But the German manufacturer might not know that American secretaries often wear sneakers during the commute to work and only change to high heels in the office. German secretaries tend to wear the same shoes during the commute and in the office. Without any knowledge of this behavioral difference, the German shoe manufacturer might miss out on an important bit of information that could also have consequences for the business. From this example it becomes apparent that direct comparisons based on classic market segmentation can miss important consumer information if cultural differences are not considered (De Mooij, 2007).

As noted above, culture is rooted in and influenced by history. Although Germany and the United States do share some cultural aspects, they are not identical cultures. Germany's location in the heart of Europe has placed it in the center of conflict for a very long time (Herrmann, 1988; Jankuhn et al., 1983; Zentner, 1980). The conflicts go back to classical antiquity and only stopped recently with the fall of the Berlin Wall in 1989 (*Facts about Germany, 1996*). These ceaseless wars and the resultant chaos are often cited as a reason for the great desire to avoid uncertainty in Germany and the need to establish order (Lord, 1998). Consequently, many rules and regulations were created in Germany so that uncertainty is reduced as much as possible (Hofstede & Hofstede, 2005). It is generally assumed in Germany that these rules and regulations have proven their worth because they help minimize risks in advance which, in turn, lead to the successful accomplishment of the task at hand (Schroll-Machl, 2002).

Germany has also a long history of regional autonomy (*Facts about Germany,* 1996; Herrmann, 1988; Jankuhn et al., 1983; Zentner, 1980). In fact, a unified country did not exist until 1871 which was divided again into two separate states for slightly more than fourty years after World War II (*Facts about Germany,* 1996, Herrmann, 1988). In other words, Germany has only been unified as country for less than a century. With such political disunion, Germany has a very different tradition than neighboring countries like France or Denmark, for example (Zentner, 1980). Over time, this strong regional diversity led to many regions being associated with specific characteristics. For example, Swabians, who live in southwestern Germany, are said to be frugal; Bavarians, who live in southeastern Germany, are said to be jovial; and North Germans are said to be taciturn. This traditional division of Germany is also expressed in linguistic differences. The German language has three principal dialect groups, namely Low German in the north, Middle German in the center, and High German in the south (König, 1989; Waterman, 1976).The primary difference between the principal dialects is expressed by the consonant shift of *p, t, k* to *f, s, ch* so that Low German *peper, water, maken* become High German *Pfeffer, Wasser, machen* (König, 1989; Waterman, 1976). The dialect difference is even more complex and includes many regionally unique words and phrases and grammatical differences which make mutual understanding very difficult (König, 1989; Waterman, 1976). For example, the word *butcher* can be *Fleischer, Fleischhacker, Metzger,* or *Schlachter* depending on where one lives and works in Germany (König, 1989). And the grammatical gender of the noun *Cola* can be feminine (i.e., *die Cola*), or neuter (i.e., *das Cola*). In fact, it is often easier for a person from North Germany to understand a native of the Netherlands than a fellow German from Swabia. Since language is a symbolic expression of culture and classified as a cultural artifact (Klopf, 1998; Samovar et al., 1998), this linguistic variety of Germany clearly expresses the degree of regional cultural diversity in Germany.

In addition to linguistic variety, German regional differences are also expressed by traditional religious differences. Germany has been divided roughly into a Protestant North and a Catholic South and West since the Reformation (Herrmann, 1988; Jankuhn et al., 1983; Zentner, 1980). And with German reunification, an atheistic East must be added—a legacy of fourty years of communism (*Facts about Germany,* 1996). While most children in West Germany celebrate either communion or confirmation, most East German children celebrate the *Jugendweihe* (i.e., a secularized ceremony to admit adolescents into adult society). Religion is an important factor in forming a culture's belief and value system because it can determine, for example, whether an individual feels obliged to help others or sees poverty as a sign of punishment (Klopf, 1998; Samovar et al., 1998).

East Germany looks back on fourty years of communism preceded by twelve years of Nazi dictatorship; this means that three generations of East Germans lived under totalitarianism. In West Germany, the twelve years of Hitler and the Holocaust were followed by sixty years of democracy and early integration into Western alliances such as NATO and the European Community (*Facts about Germany,* 1996). It is, therefore, not surprising that new regional differences evolved after World War II as well. While East Germans also point to differences among Saxons and Brandenburgers, there is also a transcending issue of East vs. West Germans (i.e., *Ossis* and *Wessis*).[8] This difference between East and West is reflected in a number of opinion polls and election results. The former communist party of East Germany still racks up about a quarter of all the votes in East Germany while in West Germany it gets less than five percent of all votes. During the last federal elections in 2005, for example, the former communist party got 25.3 percent of the votes in East Germany and only 4.9 percent of the votes in West Germany, which is 8.7 percent for all of Germany (http://www.wahl.tagesschau, 2005) since the population in West Germany is more than three times as large as in East Germany. Similarly, the majority of East Germans do not identify themselves with the Federal Republic of Germany while more than half of all West Germans do according to a recent survey (Siemon, 2007, March 22).

These strong regional differences probably also contributed to the use of so many rules and regulations in Germany because otherwise it would not have been possible to reach any consensus. In fact, Standard German can be considered an artificial dialect that combines a number of aspects from the principal dialects to achieve some degree of mutual comprehension (König, 1989; Waterman, 1976). But it also helps explain why consensus is so important to German culture because it helped establish a unified national identity. The concept of consensus and parity is even anchored in the German constitution, the *Grundgesetz* (i.e., the Basic Law, [*Facts about Germany*, 1996]. After World War II, when the Basic Law was written in West Germany, the notion of shared fiscal revenues was applied to the principle of state parity (i.e., the so-called *Länderausgleich*). This constitutional provision specifies that the rich federal states have to allocate a certain portion of their revenues to assist the poorer states. This redistribution of wealth was designed to create economic parity among all the states so that no inhabitant would be forced to live in a state that offers fewer amenities than the other states (*Facts about Germany*, 1996).[9] East Germany under communism went a step further and implemented a rigorous program of identical services and products throughout the entire country. Hence, irrespective of regional traditions, a centralized system of uniformity was introduced and enforced in East Germany, and the social class system officially abolished (*Facts about Germany*, 1996; Herrmann, 1988). After German reunification, the principle of parity was extended to the new federal states in East Germany with the introduction of the Solidarity Pact which includes a special tax to help finance the enormous costs of German reunification so that the East German infrastructure is raised to West German standards in addition to the usual *Länderausgleich* (*Facts about Germany*, 1996).

Germany is a federal republic, and regional differences play an important role in the German governmental system. The nationally elected parliament is called the *Bundestag*, and the party or parties having a parliamentary majority head the federal government under the leadership of the Federal Chancellor (*Facts about Germany*, 1996). The Chancellor, thus, automatically has a parliamentary majority in the *Bundestag*. All federal bills must be passed by a majority vote in the *Bundestag* (*Facts about Germany*, 1996). All legislation affecting the interests of the states must additionally be approved by the *Bundesrat*, the other legislative body which represents the interests of the states (*Facts about Germany*, 1996). Unlike the United States Senate, the German *Bundesrat* "does not consist of elected representatives of the people but of members of the state governments or their representatives" (*Facts about Germany*, 1996, p. 174). After a bill has passed the appropriate legislative chamber(s), it must be signed by the Federal President to become a law (*Facts about Germany*, 1996). The Federal President heads the German state but not the federal government which is headed by the Federal Chancellor as noted previously (*Facts about Germany*, 1996). Germany has, thus, two separate and distinct executive offices for state and government matters, unlike the United States which unites both executive positions in the office of the President. This division of the executive office into two separate offices with distinct duties and responsibilities is a feature that is repeated in many other German organizations such as schools and universities as well as corporations.

Not surprisingly, German and American laws are based on different legal principles. Traditionally, German law is code based, and American law case based (*Facts about Germany*, 1996; Howard, 1965). German law seeks to anticipate illegal actions which have to be listed expressly in the legal code to be deemed illegal. If an action has not been anticipated and, thus, is not included in the legal code, it is not considered to be illegal.[10] The German legal code, therefore, has to be constantly amended in order to keep abreast of changes in society or technology. This is different from United States law which applies the principle of analogy (Howard, 1965). Thus, for example, legal provisions regulating horse-drawn carriages were interpreted to also include automobiles when cars first appeared since both are road vehicles. In Germany, the traffic law had to be amended expressly to also include automobiles. German law, therefore, seeks to establish great precision which usually results in very comprehensive legal texts. Hence, the German legal principle conforms to the general concept prevalent in Germany of attempting to break everything down to the most precise subcategory possible which is designed to reduce uncertainty.[11] By breaking everything down to the smallest possible category, it is assumed that the size of the problem is also reduced and, thus, becomes more manageable.

Education is important in shaping and transmitting culture (Chen & Starosta, 1998, Gudykunst & Kim, 1997; Klopf, 1998, Samovar et al., 1998). Not surprisingly, the German educational system reflects these regional differences because education is a matter of the individual states as specified by the Basic Law

(*Facts about Germany,* 1996).[12] At the same time, there are also a number of similarities for all German states that are, to some degree, quite unique to Germany. Most German states decide during the fourth grade (i.e., when children are nine or ten years old) which type of secondary school a child is to attend. There are typically three types of secondary school in Germany: The *Hauptschule,* which is to prepare students for vocational careers; the *Realschule,* which is to prepare students for clerical positions; and the *Gymnasium,* which is to prepare students for university studies (*Facts about Germany,* 1996). Theoretically, it is possible for students of both the *Hauptschule* and *Realschule* to also attend universities (*Facts about Germany,* 1996), but in practice it does not happen very often. This effectively bars the majority of students from university studies which is one reason why the United Nations has recently criticized the German secondary education system (*Sächsische Zeitung,* 2007, March 22).

This educational segmentation is also continued in the apprenticeship and trainee programs in which adolescents are trained for a very specific, albeit highly qualified vocation (*Facts about Germany,* 1996). Even the university education is typically based on narrowly focused degrees which revolve around curricula that only contain courses on the subject in question. Thus, the German educational system—at the primary, secondary, vocational, and college levels—produces highly specialized professionals while essentially shunning a general, broader, interdisciplinary education.[13] Because German employees have been typically trained in very narrowly defined vocations and professions, it is often difficult to switch job fields since the employees do not have comparable skills and training in another occupation.[14] This, in part, explains the continued high unemployment in Germany because many of the unemployed have been trained in vocations for which there are no longer sufficient jobs available since these occupations have been superseded by new technology and/or outsourced to countries with lower wages. At the same time, Germany lacks skilled employees in other job fields—typically in newly created high-tech vocations for which the educational system has not yet been able to generate sufficient graduates.

It is, thus, not surprising that most German businesses tend to have a fairly strict division among its staff into blue and white collar employees, and also between White collar clerical positions and management posts (Hofstede & Hofstede, 2005). Trompenaars and Hampden-Turner (1998), therefore, classify German corporations as bureaucratic organizations in which personal relations play a minor role because the focus is on the tasks at hand. German corporate careers are based on professional qualifications according to Trompenaars and Hampden-Turner (1998). "Manpower planning, assessment centers, appraisal systems, training schemes and job rotation all have the function of helping to classify and produce resources to fit known roles" (Trompenaars & Hampden-Turner, 1998, p. 174). Since one of the tasks of education is to provide the right training of potential employees for the job market, this explains why the German educational system pursues a highly segmented educational approach so that these specific occupations can be filled with employees having the right qualifications.

The problem-solving methods conveyed in German schools focus not so much on finding a solution; instead, emphasis is placed on outlining and following the proper steps to a solution. Thus, the actual solution to a math problem, for example, will be awarded with only a small percentage of the points for the right answer while the majority of the points will go to the application of the right steps.[15] This explains why in a business context, so much emphasis is put on finding the right steps to a solution. Most Germans are also interested in finding long-term solutions. This may be best illustrated by the approach to house building. While many houses in the United States are built with frame construction, dry walls, and asphalt roof shingles in a relatively short period of time, most German houses are built with reinforced concrete, bricks, and cement roof tiles. Consequently, house construction typically takes much longer in Germany than in the United States. In Germany, most people still feel that a house has to be built to last for a long time so that future generations can continue to live in it as well. From a German perspective, this makes sense since the marked regional differences traditionally led many people to stay close to their home because it is there that people speak the same dialect and practice the same religion. While this has been changing, most Germans would still prefer to stay in the home region if given a choice.[16]

German corporations, not surprisingly, have a different organizational structure than U.S. corporations. Traditionally, stock markets played a minor role in the acquisition of capital in Germany. Consequently, only a small proportion of businesses in Germany are organized as a corporation (Wentges, 2002). Other reasons for the relatively small percentage of corporations in Germany include the many corporate regulations, the partial loss of control, tax disadvantages, and considerable codetermination of employees in Germany (Nassauer, 2000). Most of the capital for German businesses is provided by banks (Emmons & Schmid, 1998). It was actually the German banks which provided the capital to the growing industrial enterprises in the nineteenth century when German industrialization began. Since private citizens did not have the capital, and well-developed stock markets did not yet exist, banks were the only source of capital in Germany at that time (Nassauer, 2000). Consequently, banks often have a direct influence on German companies, which goes well beyond the typical American creditor–company relationship (Emmons & Schmid, 1998).

German corporations are controlled by two boards, the *Vorstand* (i.e., management board), which is responsible for managing the company, and the *Aufsichtsrat* (i.e., supervisory board), which exercises control over the management. According to German law, management and control of a company must be exercised separately in companies having more than 500 employees (*Facts about Germany,* 1996; Nassauer, 2000). The assumption is that management does not necessarily pursue the interests of shareholders and, therefore, requires an independent board which acts as a counterbalance to management's power (*Facts about Germany,* 1996; Nassauer, 2000).

The *Vorstand* is empowered to run the business and, thus, formulates and implements the business strategies. It also represents the company externally (Conyon & Schwalbach, 1999; *Facts about Germany,* 1996; Wentges, 2002). The *Vorstand* can consist of one or more executives. Generally, all members of the *Vorstand* are jointly responsible for decisions or actions of a corporation. In practice, though, each member of the *Vorstand* has special duties and competencies in specific business sectors (Wentges, 2002), which conforms to the German desire to segment everything according to areas of expertise. The members of the *Vorstand* are appointed by the

Aufsichtsrat for a maximum term of five years (Conyon & Schwalbach, 1999; Emmons & Schmid, 1998). Reappointments are possible (Emmons & Schmid, 1998). Once a year, the *Vorstand* has to report to the *Aufsichtsrat* on the current state and the intended business policy (Conyon & Schwalbach, 1999).

The *Aufsichtsrat* monitors the activities of the *Vorstand.* In order to match the requirements of separating the decision-making process and control, the *Aufsichtsrat* is not empowered to run a business (*Facts about Germany,* 1996; Wentges, 2002). Nevertheless, some activities by the management do require approval of the *Aufsichtsrat.* The *Aufsichtsrat* consists of three to twenty-one members, depending on the size of the corporation (*Facts about Germany,* 1996; Nassauer, 2000). While the members of the *Aufsichtsrat* are classified as non-executives, many former CEOs of the company usually chair the *Aufsichtsrat* (Emmons & Schmid, 1998).

The *Mitbestimmungsgesetz,* (i.e., the Codetermination Act of 1976) introduced the requirement to have employees in the *Aufsichtsrat.* In corporations of more than 500 employees, one third of the *Aufsichtsrat* have to be employees; in corporations of more than 2,000 employees, that number increases to half (Conyon & Schwalbach, 1999; *Facts about Germany,* 1996; Nassauer, 2000).[17] The remaining members of the *Aufsichtsrat* are elected by the shareholders at the annual shareholder's meeting. This principle of including employees in corporate governance conforms once again to the German principle of consensus and parity. The main duties of the *Aufsichtsrat* are the nomination and discharge of the members of the *Vorstand* and the appointment of the corporate auditor (Wentges, 2002). The *Aufsichtsrat* has considerable rights to receive information in order to effectively monitor the *Vorstand's* activities and fix the compensation of the corporate executives (Nassauer, 2000). Large German corporations can have up to twenty members in the *Aufsichtsrat.*

Wages and salaries of German employees are typically fixed by so-called collective tariff agreements which are negotiated between trade union representatives and the representatives of the employers' association of a particular industrial and/or service branch, for example, the metal industry which includes the automobile industry (*Facts about Germany,* 1996). These agreements regulate, for example, the wages and salaries, the working hours, holidays, minimum notice, overtime rates, and apply them to all enterprise of that particular branch in that particular region of Germany (*Facts about Germany*, 1996), thus establishing parity among all employees in the same sector. This system essentially serves to keep employees tied to a particular employer since it would make little sense to switch employers because one would continue to earn the same pay for the same job elsewhere. And since German employees are typically qualified for a specific job field, it is not easy to switch to another job field without proper qualifications as noted above. Likewise, the tariff system reduces the need for strikes, which helps reduce uncertainty for both sides. Compared to other European countries, Germany has relatively few strikes. This is usually ascribed to the collective tariff system and the principle of codetermination (*Facts about Germany*, 1996).

In the United States, corporate law is a state matter, which means that many variations exist depending on the state in which one incorporates (Witt, 2002). Equity is spread among a large number of individual share holders who usually cannot exercise much control over the corporation (Wentges, 2002; Witt, 2002). And United States corporations do not have a two-tier board system in which management and control are separated; instead, a single board of directors is responsible for running the corporation (Wentges, 2002). Of all business types, corporations make up about twenty percent in the United States, which is a much higher proportion than in Germany (Nassauer, 2000). This is primarily due to the fact that no minimum capital is needed to establish a corporation in the United States (Nassauer, 2000). In addition, it is quite common for private individuals to risk investing in businesses; consequently, banks play a smaller role in U.S. corporations than in Germany (Nassauer, 2000).

In the United States, the board of directors is responsible for running a corporation. The board is responsible for both the management of the company and the control of the management; it typically consists of eleven to thirteen members (Nassauer, 2000). The board is elected at the annual shareholders' meeting, but it is an independent entity that can reach decisions without following instructions from the shareholders (Wentges, 2002). The board is responsible for setting the corporation's strategies, controlling the executive officers, nominating the

Chief Executive Officer (CEO), and fixing the executive compensation (Wentges, 2002). The management team of a corporation is headed by the CEO who is superior to all the other managers and frequently chairs the board (Witt, 2002). The CEO is usually also the center of public attention since the CEO is usually identified with the corporation (Witt, 2002).

Thus, the CEO has a very powerful corporate position when compared to the head of a German corporation which, in turn, is a reflection of the respective general national cultures. Indeed, the national culture often serves as a model for corporate culture. So it is not surprising that German corporations are headed by two distinct governing bodies which mirror the division of power in the German executive branch while United States corporations have only one governing body which reflects the single executive branch. And, it is also not surprising that the notion of parity and consensus is incorporated into German corporate governance (i.e., the representation of the employees in the *Aufsichtsrat*), since it is a fundamental principle of the German Basic Law.

While people may take note of the differences in corporate structure and organization, few people would assume that work routines would differ dramatically and, thus, might lead to problems in working effectively and efficiently together across cultures (Hofstede & Hofstede, 2005; Trompenaars & Hampden-Turner, 1998). However, the following example will illustrate how cultural differences can influence the interaction of Germans and Americans in a typical business context, and how such subtle differences can lead to misunderstanding, frustration, and even anger.[18] In a large international electronics firm, Germans and Americans had to work closely together to solve a number of problems. Both Americans and Germans were frustrated because meetings often did not lead to any concrete results. The American participants complained that the Germans seemed to talk too much and too long while also focusing too much on individual details instead of seeing the larger picture. The Germans, in contrast, felt that the Americans were too unfocused and asked too many questions; especially after the meeting was over. The Germans accused the Americans of being too superficial because they constantly updated and changed projects and concepts. The Americans accused the German supervisors of not providing enough feedback (Schroll-Machl, 1995).

Germans, like Americans, are very task oriented. But in Germany, as noted above, the specific expertise of individuals is also considered to be very important because such expertise leads to the best possible results. Consequently, Germans will usually argue and try and convince others with facts and data (Schroll-Machl, 2002). This explains why German presentations (and applications) will contain as many facts and as much data as possible because the more facts and data one presents, the more convincing one will be. Germans do not like to make mistakes because they are expected to be experts in their field of specialization. Should, therefore, someone present the wrong facts and figures, then that person will be disrespected because that person occupies a position for which he or she does not have sufficient expertise. Consequently, most Germans do not like to admit to having made a mistake (Lord, 1998) because mistakes could result in uncertainty—something most Germans would like to avoid. Emotions are frowned upon because they are neither tangible nor objective. While Americans will also use facts and figures, they will also appeal to people's ideals and emotions; especially if they are attempting to motivate others (Lewis, 2000).

Germans tend to strictly separate business relationships from private relationships. A friendly atmosphere at work and getting along with others in a business context is considered to be a nice side effect, but it is not really essential for a successful interaction in Germany (Schroll-Machl, 2002). Indeed, it is not uncommon for German colleagues to use the formal *Sie* and the last name with title when addressing and conversing with one another even though they may have worked together for many years. The use of titles is another expression of uncertainty avoidance. If someone has a title or titles, then that person will be addressed by that/those title(s). Titles appear on bank cards, driver's licenses, and ID cards, etc. Titles identify a person's status and background, thus identifying a person's qualifications, competence, and rank within a corporate and social hierarchy.

Germans are very punctual and tend to be very monochronic in their work routine. Time is considered to be very important like in the United States, but it also leads most Germans to consider small talk to be a waste of time in a business context since it has nothing to do directly with the task at hand. Consequently, presentations and meetings will commence immediately with the business at hand

(Lewis, 2000). When Germans make appointments, they do not reconfirm them—even if the appointment is made half a year in advance; this reinforces reliability and avoids uncertainty. One usually contacts the other party only if needs to cancel or postpone the appointed meeting. Germans tend to first finish a particular task or assignment completely before commencing with another task or assignment (Lewis, 2000). This tenacious approach is often also found in product development which translates into product improvement in Germany. The aim is to achieve absolute perfection and precision in any product or product family. Hence, the reputation of German precision products and engineering is highly regarded in many parts of the world.

Another typical German characteristic is the monopolization of information. Consequently, there is little free flow of information between departments of a company (i.e., horizontal communication), and between the various hierarchical levels (i.e., vertical communication).[19] This explains why office doors are usually closed in German companies unlike American companies where employees walk down the hall to exchange information with their colleagues (Lewis, 2000). Viewed from the perspective of the perceptual process, this different "door policy" illustrates how cultural patterns influence people's thinking and behavior. When, for example, American visitors enter a typical German office building and encounter closed doors, the Americans may assume that the office doors have been closed because no one is to overhear the conversations inside the offices as might be the case in America. If those American visitors came to the German company to negotiate a deal, then the visitors may think that the Germans are deliberately trying to hide something from them. Consequently, the Americans may assume that the negotiations will be difficult, troublesome, and tricky. During the subsequent meeting, this negative predisposition of the Americans could result in a negative interpretation of everything the Germans say or seem to say and do even though that is not the intention of the Germans. This will make for a difficult meeting because the Americans will be wary and suspicious while the Germans will be wondering why the Americans are behaving so strangely. This could make the Germans wary and suspicious of the Americans' intentions.

As noted above, Germans like to be well prepared for a meeting which often translates into a lack of spontaneity. Not surprisingly, brainstorming sessions are quite rare in Germany (LeMont Schmidt, 2001). Because Germans have researched a subject and prepared themselves in great detail for a meeting, they are often inflexible in responding to unanticipated questions. When, for example, it comes to negotiating the price, most Germans are only willing to consider a divergence of ten percent from the asking price since they will have considered all aspects and determined precisely the exact price of an item in advance (Hill, 1998; Otte, 1996). This reduces the uncertainty of a bargaining session.

The following describes the different approaches typically employed by Germans and Americans when tackling a problem. Germans like to have an initial and comprehensive understanding of all aspects associated with a problem. This means that any and all details, including potential possibilities, are considered. Hence, existing approaches and solutions play an important role while new ideas are considered and evaluated critically. This evaluation process is carried out within a group. When it is assumed that all aspects have been considered and discussed, then tasks will be assigned to the team members according to their field of expertise and experience. This ends the planning phase (Schroll-Machl, 1995). Next follows the execution phase during which everyone works alone with little or no exchange of information. There is little or no need to meet and talk because everything had been discussed during the initial planning phase, including anticipated possibilities. Therefore, repetition would be a waste of valuable time. And since everyone is a specialist in their own field, there is little need to talk with others because the others would not be able to make a valuable contribution as they lack expertise outside their field of specialization. Subsequent meetings are, thus, only necessary if an intermediate meeting had been scheduled previously, or if there is an unanticipated problem. But alterations to any previously fixed details are rarely done and not liked since it indicates that the initial planning had been insufficient and, therefore, inexpert (Schroll-Machl, 1995; Gibson, 2000).

Americans, in contrast, like to focus on the goal after having been assigned a task. This is usually done in the form of brainstorming in which the team members present their thoughts and ideas. Once the goal has been determined, the team decides on a plan of action to solve the problem at hand. The team leader assigns the various tasks to the team members which ends the planning phase. The execution of the plan begins when every team member creates a detailed work plan. The experiences of the team members are applied in solving the problem. The team members often consult with one another on how to best solve the problem. This results in very active communication and a lively exchange of information among all team members while there is constant feedback on whether a solution leads to the goal or not. This exchange of information occurs also with one's superiors. The initial plan of action can be changed any time if it proves necessary and the goal becomes untenable (Gibson, 2000; Schroll-Machl, 1995).

The previous example clearly illustrates that Germans and Americans use different approaches in tackling a problem. The brainstorming session would probably cause difficulties with German team members since it is not typically applied in Germany while the detailed discussion of possible and anticipated problems would seem to be too detailed for American team members. This attitude would be frowned upon by the German team members who would consider Americans to be too superficial and imprecise. The isolated work environment with minimal or no contact with other team members and one's supervisors with little or no feedback would seem problematic to Americans because information exchange and communication are of paramount importance in solving any problem. To the Germans, this need for communication and feedback would simply signify that either the initial planning was faulty and superficial, or the American colleagues are not as expert as they claim to be; otherwise, they would be able to solve the problem at hand.

So it becomes apparent that the way things are done is not only critical in carrying out a task, but also vital in perceiving the methods others use and in evaluating their efforts. If this insight is lacking, it can result in frustration because one is unaware of why the others are behaving the way they are behaving. Viewed and evaluated from one's own perspective, another approach can be seen as inefficient and ineffective, even wrong. Understanding can be a step in the direction of respecting differences. And understanding is only possible if one is aware of the fact that differences do exist in German and American business cultures, which, in turn, influences how Germans and Americans conduct their business.

Notes

1. A number of the examples and observations contained in this text are based on the personal experiences of the author.
2. Since this paper was written, Daimler and Chrysler actually split again as Daimler sold Chrysler to the United States investment firm Cerberus. In the German media, Daimler CEO Zetsche was quoted as saying that the merger "was a bad fit."
3. It also needs to be remembered that most business partners seek contact with potential partners because each side hopes to benefit in some form from this relationship. This beneficial end goal tends to also have an impact on the interpretation and evaluation of communication between both sides (i.e., it tends to make the initial interpretation positive as long as one assumes that one is not being cheated). And, this positive association is usually also applied to the general transactional relationship.
4. For a long time, mainstream American culture traced its origins back to a distinctly European heritage which was also reflected in many school curricula.
5. These American English words were taken from *Webster's New World Dictionary* (2001), 4th edition.
6. These German words were taken from *Duden* (2006), 24th edition.
7. VW even tried to improve the lagging sales by changing the car's name in Germany from Jetta to initially Vento and later Bora, but without success.
8. Interestingly, some of the stereotypes associated with *Wessis* parallel those associated with Yankee carpetbaggers during Reconstruction in the South.
9. This principle of economic parity reaches down all the way to local municipalities in countries where richer communities have to help finance poorer communities (*Sächsische Zeitung*, March 27, 2007).
10. This can create a dilemma as a recent case of cannibalism illustrates. The German criminal code does not expressly forbid cannibalism since no one had thought this would happen in Germany. Consequently, when a person actually did commit an act of cannibalism it was not possible to convict the person of cannibalism since it had not been declared illegal. The criminal court could only rule on manslaughter.
11. Laws are, of course, a reflection of culture because laws are designed to regulate the interactions of members within a culture.
12. This regional difference is particularly noticeable at the secondary level since the states have different curricula. Consequently, it is difficult for children to overcome this gap which is why most German parents are wary of moving their families to a different state.

13. This is also expressed in the application documents. German application documents are very different from typical American application documents. A German resume contains detailed personal information including a photograph of the candidate, the date of birth and place of birth, and marital status as well as the occupation of the parents, and even the religion of the applicant. The education section describes in detail all school types starting with the elementary school while the employment section only mentions the dates of employment, the place of employment, and the occupation. A detailed job description, so typical of American resumes, is not needed because the job title suffices since German employers will know exactly what qualifications that job entails. In addition to the resume and cover letter, German applications need to also include certified copies of any and all relevant documents, certificates, degrees, letters of reference, etc.
14. German employers look for job candidates who fit precisely the job description contained in the want ads because these descriptions have been created based on the standardized occupational qualification. This is very different from the United States where it is generally assumed that not all applicants will be able to meet all specifications. Instead, it is assumed that candidates will be able to acquire the necessary skills in due time while learning on the job.
15. This information is based on what the author was told in a number of conversations with German students.
16. This information is based on information ascertained from a number of conversations with Germans in various regions. All expressed strong attachment to their home region, in part, due to linguistic and religious reasons.
17. In fact, all German companies need to have works councils (i.e., *Betriebsrat*), which are a permanent fixture in the companies. These works councils have to approve "all matters concerning personnel, such as hiring, job classifications, departmental restructuring and transfers (*Facts about Germany*, 1996, p. 393).
18. The following example is taken from Schroll-Machl, 1995.
19. Proudfoot Consulting calculated lost productivity due to improper or lack of communication in German corporations at US \$223.1 billion in 2001 which translates into 14.9% of the German GDP (see Opitz, 2003, for details).

References

Chen, G. M., & Starosta, W. J. (1998). *Foundations of intercultural communication*. Boston: Allyn and Bacon.

Conyon, M. J., & Schalbach, J. (1999). Corporate governance, executive pay and performance in Europe. In

J. Carpenter & D. Yermack (Eds.), *Executive compensation and shareholder value: Theory and evidence* (pp. 13–33). Dordrecht: Kluwer Academic Publishers.

De Mooij, M. (2007). The reflection of culture in a global business and marketing strategy. In M. B. Hinner (Ed.), *The influence of culture in the world of business* (pp. 343–356). Frankfurt am Main: Peter Lang.

Duden. (2006). Mannheim: Dudenverlag.

Emmons, W. R., & Schmid, F. A. (1998). Universal banking, control rights, and corporate finance in Germany. *Federal Reserve Bank of St. Louis Review, 80.*

Facts about Germany. (1996). Frankfurt am Main: Societäts Verlag.

German American. (2007, March 26). *Wikipedia.* Retrieved from the World Wide Web on March 29, 2007, from http://en.wikipedia.org/wiki/German-American

Gibson, R. (2000). *Intercultural business communication.* Berlin: Cornelsen & Oxford University Press.

Gudykunst, W. B., & Kim, Y. Y. (1997). *Communicating with strangers: An approach to Intercultural communication* (3rd ed.). Boston: McGraw-Hill.

Harris, P. R., & Moran, R. T. (1996). *Managing cultural differences: Leadership strategies for a new world of business* (4th ed.). Houston, TX: Gulf Publishing.

Herrmann, J., (Ed.). (1988). *Deutsche Geschichte in 10 Kapiteln.* Berlin: Akademie-Verlag.

Hill, R. (1998). *EuroManagers & Martinis.* Brussels: Europlublic SA/NV.

Hinner, M. B. (1998). The importance of intercultural communication in a globalized world. *Freiberger Arbeitspapiere der Fakultät für Wirtschaftswissenschaften 06.*

Hinner, M. B. (2004). Culture and product integration. *German American Trade 15(7),* pp. 19–21.

Hinner, M. B., & Rülke, T. (2002). Intercultural communication in business ventures illustrated by two case studies. *Freiberger Arbeitspapiere der Fakultät für Wirtschaftswissen-schaften 03.*

Hofstede, G., & Hofstede, J. G. (2005). *Cultures and organizations: Software of the mind.* New York: McGraw Hill.

Homburg, C., & Krohmer, H. (2003). *Marketing Management: Strategie, Instrument-Umsetzung-Unternehmensführung.* Wiesbaden: Gabler Verlag.

Howard, L. B. (1965). *Business law: An introduction.* Woodbury: Barron's Educational.

Jankuhn, H., Boockmann, H., & Treue, W., (Eds.). (1983). *Deutsche Geschichte in Bildern von der Urzeit bis zur Gegenwart.* Wiesbaden: Verlag für Wissenschaft und Forschung AULA GmbH.

Klopf, D. W. (1998). *Intercultural encounters: The fundamentals of intercultural communication* (4th ed.). Englewood: Morton.

König, W. (1989). *Dtv-Atlas zur deutschen Sprache* (7th ed.). Munich: Deutscher Taschenbuch Verlag.

LeMont Schmidt, P. (2001). *Die amerikanische und die deutsche Wirtschaftskultur im Vergleich: Ein Praxisbuch für Manager* (3rd ed.). Göttingen: Hainholz Verlag.

Lewis, R. D. (2000). *Handbuch internationale Kompetenz: Mehr Erfolg durch den richtigen Umgang mit Geschäftspartnern weltweit.* Frankfurt am Main: Campus Verlag.

Lord, R. (1998). *Culture shock! Germany: Guide to customs and etiquette.* Portland, OR: Graphic Arts Center Publishing.

Martin, J. N., & Nakayama, T. K. (1997). *Intercultural communication in contexts.* Mountain View, CA: Mayfield.

Meffert, H. (2000). *Marketing-Grundlagen Marktorientierter Unternehmensführung.* Wies-baden: Gabler Verlag.

Nassauer, F. (2000). *Corporate governance und die Internationalisierung von Unternehmungen* Frankfurt am Main: Peter Lang.

Opitz, I. (2003). Good internal communication increases productivity. *Freiberger Arbeitspapiere der Fakultät für Wirtschaftswissenschaften 07.*

Otte, M. (1996). *Amerika für Geschäftsleute: Das Einmaleins der ungeschriebenen Regeln.* Frankfurt am Main: Campus Verlag.

Sächsische Zeitung. (2007, March 22). Uno kritisiert das deutsche Schulsystem, 1–4.

Säschsische Zeitung. (2007, March 27). Firmen zahlen kräftig Steuern, 13.

Samovar, L. A., Porter, R. E., & Stefani, L. A. (1998). *Communication between cultures* (3rd ed.). Belmont: Wadsworth.

Sandhusen, R. L. (1997). *International marketing.* Hauppauge: Barron's Educational Series.

Schroll-Machl, S. (1995). Die Zusammenarbeit in internationalen Teams—Eine interkulturelle Herausforderung dargestellt am Beispiel USA—Deutschland. In J. M. Scholz (Ed.), *Internationales Change-Management: Internationale Praxiserfahrungen bei der Veränderung von Untenehmen und Humanressourcen* (pp. 201–222). Stuttgart: Schäffer-Poeschel Verlag.

Schroll-Machl, S. (2002). *Die Deutschen—Wir Deutsche: Fremdwahrnehmung und Selbstsicht im Berufsleben.* Göttingen: Vandenhoeck & Ruprecht.

Siemon, P. (2007, March 22). Langzeitstudie in Sachsen: Nostalgische Rückkehr zu sozialistischen Idealen. In *Dresdener Morgenpost.* Retrieved from the World Wide Web on March 26, 2007, from http://www.wiedervereinigung, de/sls/PDF/mopo 220307.pdf

Trompenaars, F., & Hampden-Turner, C. (1998). *Riding the waves of culture: Understanding diversity in global business* (2nd ed.). New York: McGraw Hill.

Bundestagswahl. (2005). Retrieved from the World Wide Web on March 23, 2007, from http://stat.tagesschau.de/wahlarchiv/wid246/index.shtml

Waterman, J. T. (1976). *A history of the German language* (Revised ed.). Seattle: University of Washington Press.

Webster's new world college dictionary (4th ed.). (2001)
Foster City, CA: IDG Books.Wentges, P. (2002).
Corporate governance und stakeholder ansatz: Implikationen für die betriebliche finanzierung. Wiesbaden: Deutscher Universitätsverlag.

Witt, P. (2002). Grundprobleme der corporate governance und international unterschiedliche Lösungsansätze. In M. Nippa, K. Petzold, & W. Kürsten (Eds.), *Corporate governance: Herausforderungen und Lösungsansätze* (pp. 41–72). Heidelberg: Physica-Verlag.

Zentner, C. (1980). *Geschichtsführer in Farbe: Weltgeschichte in Bildern, Daten, Fakten.* München: Delphin Verlag GmbH.

Concepts and Questions

1. List some of the similarities between American and German business cultures.
2. What does Hinner mean when he writes about external and hidden cultural differences?
3. How does the history of Germany affect the culture of German business organizations?
4. In what ways does the tradition of regional autonomy influence German business culture?
5. How do the bases of Amercian and German law compare? How do these differences contribute to the distinct business cultures found in each country?
6. In what ways does the German educational system differ from that of the United States? How does the German education system support German business?
7. Describe how the German culture's desire for order and hierarchy is displayed in the division of employees in business organizations.
8. What are some of the differences in the ways in which German and American corporations are organized?
9. List the advantages and disadvantages of the German corporate system of simultaneously operating under two different boards of directors. Would such a system be effective in the United States?

Beyond the Knapsack: Disrupting the Production of White Racial Privilege in Organizational Practices

PATRICIA PARKER

JENNIFER MEASE

INTRODUCTION

In one of John Grisham's most popular films, *A Time to Kill,* set in a small town in Mississippi, a White attorney, Jake Brigance (Matthew McConaughey), takes on the case of Carl Lee Hailey (Samuel L. Jackson), an African American man accused of murdering the two men who raped and beat his ten-year-old daughter as she walked home from the grocery store. Carl Lee had killed the two men in front of several witnesses after learning that they would be set free by an all-White jury. Jake set out to prove that this was a case of temporary insanity. In making his closing arguments, Jake asks the jurors to close their eyes as he recites a gripping narrative that recounts the brutality the little girl experienced. As the jurors and others in the courtroom (and in the movie audience) are entranced in imagining the little girl's fear and agony, Jake concludes with a jarring request: *"Now imagine she's White."*

At that moment eyes fly open, stunned, confused, and maybe amazed. Why the surprise? Why is Jake's request shocking? We believe part of this moment's power lies in the fact that Jake had succeeded in

This original essay appears here in print for the first time. All rights reserved. Permission to reprint must be obtained from the authors and the publisher. Dr. Patricia Parker teaches in the Department of Communication Studies, and Ms. Jennifer Mease is a doctoral student in the Department of Communication Studies at The University of North Carolina at Chapel Hill.

disrupting the silences about Whiteness that persisted throughout the racially charged court proceedings. His request points out that race not only harmed the little African American girl, but it protects little White girls. It was clear from all the usual cinematic signifiers that this film was about "race" in the Deep South—the sweltering heat, the resurgent KKK, the clashes with the NAACP. However, Jake's provocation makes present that which is often absent in the discourses about race—White privilege. His tactic seems clear: He was asking the jury to acknowledge that a temporary insanity defense would be considered "normal" if this were a White father enraged by the brutalization of his little girl who was *protected* by Whiteness rather than placed at risk by her Blackness. His statement challenges those in the court room and those watching the movie to disrupt the reproduction of Whiteness that reserves a standard of justice for White people, which would be denied to other racial groups.

We use this example to call attention to an understudied phenomenon in organizational communication: the reproduction of White privilege in everyday organizational contexts such as courtrooms, boardrooms, and school rooms, to name a few. You might be thinking that our example is "just a movie" or that it points to racial injustices of our nation's past that no longer exist. However, racism persists as socially constructed systems that privilege Whiteness. For example, similar to the storyline depicted in *A Time to Kill,* numerous studies have found that race influences the justice system at multiple stages, including arresting, detaining, diverting, and sentencing suspected offenders (for a comprehensive review of this literature see Brown et al., 2003). Indeed, one study found that as many as ninety-six percent of states studied showed evidence of bias based either on the race of the defendant or the victim (Baldus, 1998).

In this essay we respond to organizational communication scholars who have called for greater attention to the influence of race, generally, and Whiteness in particular, in organizations (Allen & Ashcraft, 2005; Grimes, 2002; Parker, 2003). Toward that end, we offer a much needed application of Peggy McIntosh's (1990) often cited essay, "White Privilege: Unpacking the Invisible Knapsack." Like McIntosh, we aim to point out the subtle and often unnoticed ways that the privileges of Whiteness surface in organizations, not just through interpersonal acts of racism, but through the very structures and practices that we take for granted.

We begin by summarizing McIntosh's concept of the invisible knapsack and then trace the origins of the privileges it contains through the social "manufacturing" process that produces it. That is, we show how concepts of race and Whiteness are socially constructed to produce and reproduce White privilege and render it invisible in intercultural spaces such as organizations. Then we present a framework—special lenses, if you will—that reveals how White privilege is operating in organizations and points to ways for disrupting its reproduction.

THE INVISIBLE KNAPSACK

"I was taught to see racism only in individual acts of meanness, not in invisible systems conferring dominance on my group" (McIntosh, 1990).

As the quote above suggests, people often think of racism as exceptional instances of rude behavior by individuals who have not learned to be polite. However, McIntosh cleverly uses the "invisible knapsack" as a metaphor to reveal how racism exists not simply in individual behavior, but as taken-for-granted societal practices. In her very personal account, McIntosh (1990) explains how she came to recognize White privilege as an invisible, weightless knapsack of special provisions (or practices) that protects and favors White people in society. She explains how, as a White person, these privileges had always seemed "normal" to her, leaving her unaware of the disadvantage these privileges created for people of other races. McIntosh came to this realization because of the frustration she felt when men had a difficult time understanding the advantages she regularly witnessed they had in society—advantages she could not participate in as a woman. As a consequence, she began to identify and question advantages she experienced in society as a White person. She was able to come up with a list of over fifty things. For example:

> When I am told about our national heritage or "civilization," I am shown that people of my color made it what it is. . . . I can swear, dress in second hand

clothes, or not answer letters, without having people attribute these choices to the bad morals, the poverty, or the illiteracy of my race. . . . I can worry about racism without being seen as self-interested or self-seeking. . . . I can choose blemish cover or bandages in "flesh" color and have them more or less match my skin.

McIntosh points out that racial advantage and disadvantage are not just a matter of blatantly held racist beliefs. They are also a matter of very subtle practices that often make navigating life in White skin an easier task than it is with other colors of skin, especially when White is assumed as normal or neutral. Even more, she points out that this advantage is sustained because we are taught not to see, or speak about, these advantages. In other words, White privilege is invisible.

McIntosh explains that not seeing White privilege (and male privilege) in society maintains the myth of meritocracy. This myth portrays democratic choice and opportunity as equally available to all when, in actuality, many doors open for certain people through no virtues of their own (Jackson, 1999). Thus, racism provides invisible White privilege, especially within intercultural spaces, such as organizations, where advantage and disadvantage, access and nonaccess, empowerment and exploitation are determined by a White normative standard. When addressing problems of race in the workplace, we often focus on how people who identify with groups in the racial minority are disadvantaged through stereotypes, prejudice, and racism. These discussions sometimes fail to recognize that the flip side of oppression is privilege. Studies of Whiteness address this failure by acknowledging that race affects all people, regardless of the color of their skin, and that the disadvantages suffered by some procure advantages for others—even if they didn't ask for it (McIntosh, 1988; Frankenberg, 1993; Roediger, 1991; Wildman, 1997).

Can unequal power systems be transformed to produce more democratic cultural spaces? Our premise is that a beginning point for such a transformation is disrupting the reproduction of White privilege. This requires understanding how the invisible knapsack was produced in the first place, and continues to be reproduced today.

MANUFACTURING THE KNAPSACK: RACE, WHITENESS, AND ORGANIZATIONS AS SOCIAL CONSTRUCTIONS

Race as a Social Construction

It is widely understood that there is no biological basis for distinguishing human groups along the lines of race (Banton & Harwood, 1975; Goldberg, 1993; Omi & Winant, 1994). The classifications that constitute references to "race"—Asian, Black, White, etc.—are social and historical constructions that have economic and political functions, but no biological determinant. While people have different physical characteristics (phenotypes) based in biology, the connection of these characteristics to racial categorization is a result of social and historical processes (Omi & Winant, 1994). Thus race can be defined as "a concept that signifies and symbolizes sociopolitical conflicts and interests in reference to different types of human bodies" (Winant, 2000, p. 172). Stated more simply, race is a product of human social and historical processes that have arbitrarily (but purposefully) created categories of people that are positioned differently in society.

An important concept in the social construction of race is *racialization*. Racialization is an ideological process that signifies the extension of racial meaning to a previously racially unclassified relationship, social practice, or group (Omi & Winant, 1994). For example, you may attach racial meanings to certain social practices, such as who makes or listens to different styles of music or who plays different sports. But the attachment of racial meanings to these practices is influenced by particular historical contexts. In fact, the process that created contemporary racial groupings, and the meanings associated with them, is a fairly recent phenomenon in human history. Winant (2000) explains:

> The idea of race began to take shape with the rise of a world political economy. The onset of global economic integration, the dawn of seaborne empire, the conquest of the Americas, and the rise of the Atlantic slave trade were all key elements in the genealogy of race . . . Though intimated throughout the world in innumerable ways, racial categorization

of human beings was a European invention. It was an outcome of the same world-historical processes that created European nation-states and empires, built the dark satanic mills of Britain (and the even more dark and satanic sugar mills of the Brazilian Reconcavo and the Caribbean), and explained it all by means of Enlightenment rationality. (p., 172)

Racialization in the United States followed a similar pattern of social and economic expedience providing social and financial benefits to certain groups. For example, the racial categories of "Black" and "White" evolved with the consolidation of racial slavery and the establishment of a color line to maintain and perpetuate this lucrative economic system (Omi & Winant, 1994). As Omi and Winant explain, "By the end of the seventeenth century, Africans whose specific identity was Ibo, Yoruba, Fulani, etc., were rendered "Black" by an ideology of exploitation based on racial logic" (p. 64). Over the same period European settlers who had initially self-identified with the common term *Christian,* shifted toward the terms *English* and *free,* and "after about 1680, taking the colonies as a whole, a new term of self-identification appeared—White" (Jordan, quoted in Omi & Winant, 1994, p. 64).

Similar racialization processes occurred in the histories of groups such as the Irish, the Italians, the Greeks, the Poles, and the Jews. As they migrated to the United States, members of these groups were often considered Black, or "off-White" well into the twentieth century . . . until political and economic processes "allowed" them to become White (Dyer, 1997; Ignatiev, 1995; Sullivan, 2006).

As you can see, race is not a neutral, biological categorization of people. Rather it is a social construction that has privileged those considered White since it originated in the era of Enlightenment (Eze, 1997; Mosse, 1978). Thus, race has always been established as relationships of domination, oppression, and privilege that position people differently in society. *Whiteness* is the primary means through which these racialized and power-laden relationships are reproduced and sustained.

Whiteness as a Social Construction

Over time, the methods of determining the "meaning" and definitions of Whiteness have changed. When race emerged during the Enlightenment, the meanings of race, and particularly Whiteness, were determined using "scientific" methods that clearly placed people in a racial hierarchy with White Europeans at the top (Eze, 1997). (This is not very surprising when you consider that White people were the ones creating these pseudo-scientific categories!) Given our current understanding that race is not a biologically given trait but socially created and assigned according to political and economic motivations, the methods for reproducing the original racial hierarchy have morphed into more subtle and elusive social practices. For example, media scholars have pointed out how films sustain White dominance through strategies of (think King Kong!) depicting White characters more positively (Projansky & Ono, 1999) or set up the "anti-racist White hero" in films that address racial struggles, such as *Mississippi Burning,* or *Dangerous Minds* (Madison, 1999).

At other times White privilege is sustained through more quotidian practices, such as daily conversation or self-labeling practices. Bonilla-Silva (2003) points out several of these conversational strategies, including minimizing the effects of racism in society through statements like "There's discrimination, but there are plenty of jobs out there" (p. 29), or naturalizing racism by suggesting "that's just the way things are." Each of these subtle acts contributes to a discourse that perpetuates racism and sustains material privileges for White people. Nakayama and Krizek (1995) point out that Whiteness is also sustained through self-labeling practices that try to deny it. One of several trends they identify among White students' self-labeling practices is the denial of racial labels by referring to themselves as "just American." While this and other similar comments may appear to promote equality through color blindness, they actually: (a) cover up the ways that Whiteness can privilege White people's lives and disadvantage others; and (b) set up White experience as "normal" and unaffected by race. These are just a few subtle practices that contribute to the complex social construction of Whiteness in society.

When we examine how Whiteness is built into society in general and organizations in particular, it is important to acknowledge that Whiteness and White people are related but not the same (Keating, 1995). Exploring Whiteness in organizations means exploring how socially constructed meanings and material realities of racial inequality are created and sustained in organizations, through practices like those identified above and by McIntosh (1990). We attempt to identify how Whiteness as a socially constructed discourse (Nakayama & Krizek, 1995) sustains certain assumptions or beliefs about organizational practices that may not espouse racism explicitly, but enable or allow racism to exist in organizations. For example, a bias in school curriculums that highlights contributions of White people, or the color of traditional Band-Aids, demonstrates that Whiteness is often socially constructed as "normal" or "neutral" through more hidden institutionalized organizational practices as much as it is through individual acts of racism.

Although White people have an important role to play in the deconstruction of racism and White privilege in society, these privileging practices of Whiteness are not exclusively sustained or maintained by White people, nor are White people inescapably bound to these practices. However, as we examine how Whiteness emerges in organizations, we see that many practices do position White people in privileged ways (although they may be disadvantaged in other ways). This privileged position often makes it difficult for them to recognize that the privilege exists. If not recognized, practices that sustain Whiteness form as "unconscious habits" of Whiteness that maintain privilege (Sullivan, 2006). By developing strategies for identifying these practices, we hope to enable the breaking of these unconscious habits and the systems of privilege they maintain. Understanding Whiteness as a set of institutionalized practices and ideas that people participate in consciously and unconsciously is an important step toward people developing the ability to interrupt subtle practices that create advantage and disadvantage. It is our hope to uncover the effects of some of these unconscious practices specifically in organizational practices.

Organizations as Cultural Spaces

We turn our attention to organizations as cultural systems that play a significant role in (re)producing understandings and practices of race in society. Culture is "a system of meaning that guides the construction of reality in a social community" (Cheney et al., 2005, p. 76). Viewing organizations as cultures means that they are not *containers* of people and their actions; rather they are emergent social arrangements that are constantly constructed through people's interactions. However, this social construction is not power-neutral

(Deetz, 1982; Mumby, 2001), nor is it race-neutral (Nkomo, 1992). Organizations are sites where White normative values and group interests are articulated and embodied in different hierarchies, practices and everyday decisions, such as who becomes CEO, who is awarded start-up funds for small businesses, and who gets hired, mentored, and promoted (Feagin, 2006).

In conceptualizing organizations as socially constructed cultural systems we can begin to see how organizations both influence, and are influenced by, racial meanings in society. Organizations of all types—especially public and private corporations—are all powerful reflections and reinforcements of the normative understandings of Whiteness in society. As Feagin (2006) aptly puts it, "U.S. corporations . . . are 'White' corporations" (p. 198). He draws this conclusion from his analysis of the racialized history of capitalism that excluded and exploited people of color, particularly in the United States but in the West in general. The particular Eurocentric, White-based racialization set in motion through capitalist practices persists in organizations and in our social consciousness as a taken-for-granted dominant ideology that favors White people (Nkomo, 1992).

Consider this illustration offered by Philomena Essed (2005) who researches and writes about racialization in professions:

> One of the guessing games we used to play at my former Dutch high school went something like this: A father and son are in a car accident. The son, who needs to be operated upon immediately, is taken to the hospital by ambulance. When the stretcher is pushed into the emergency room the only surgeon available takes one look at the patient and objects: 'I can't operate on him, he is my son.' Question: How is this possible? We would go at length, trying to explain how the father in the accident was not the real father, or the son not the real son, or something weird with the surgeon . . . Then came the 'ha-ha-got-you' moment for the storyteller: 'The surgeon was his mother!'. . . . Gender bias hit on the head, end of story back then. But is it? (p. 227)

Perhaps you've heard this brainteaser before, or you're reading it here for the first time. In any case, did you (as Essed admits she did) picture the surgeon as a White man? Once you learned that the surgeon was a woman, did you imagine that she was a Black woman? Or Native American? Or Latina? It is quite likely that you did not.

Essed uses this example to introduce what she calls *cultural cloning* or the preference for sameness in high-status professions and in corporations. She observes that candidates for professions are selected through networking, and according to their closeness to a normative (preferred) image. It is a process of systemic ordering that perpetuates Whiteness and White privilege in society and organizations. On the other hand, because organizations are social constructions they are always open to renegotiation. This means there is the possibility for producing new arrangements or power relations that disrupt White privilege. The next section outlines a framework for doing so.

A FRAMEWORK FOR SEEING AND DISRUPTING WHITE PRIVILEGE IN ORGANIZATIONS

It follows that in order to fully address systems of racial privilege and oppression in organizations we must address individual acts of prejudice *and* the perpetuation of Whiteness as privileged or "the normal standard" within specific organizational practices. To accomplish this, we propose a framework that integrates the ideas of two theorists, Diane Grimes (1999, 2002) in communication studies and Patricia Hill Collins (1998) in sociology, who challenge us to *interrogate Whiteness* and to look for practices of *containment* that keep the invisible knapsack intact. These two concepts offer tools for seeing and disrupting White privilege at work in everyday organizational practice.

Interrogating Whiteness

Drawing upon the work of cultural theorist, bell hooks (1990), Grimes (2001) introduces the concept of *interrogating Whiteness* as "an activity . . . that involves critical reflection about Whiteness and privilege and the implications of living in a race-centered society" (p. 139). She points out that not only do we need to make Whiteness visible, we need to actively scrutinize *how* words, images, and practices encountered in everyday societal situations serve to protect and advantage White people and limit the life choices of marginalized others.

To investigate how White privilege is disrupted or sustained in organizational practices, Grimes (2002) focuses on diversity management—practices that are purportedly meant to promote racial inclusion but in most cases maintain Whiteness as the status quo. Her textual analysis of trade articles written by and for diversity management practitioners in U. S. companies revealed that a few practitioners embrace an interrogating Whiteness perspective. Those who do interrogate Whiteness believe examining diversity and bias in organizations requires more than looking at the problems racial minorities confront. It requires investigating how White people protect their own "normal" status, often through unconscious behaviors and beliefs. Grimes explains that, "Writers from this perspective take seriously the perspectives of people of color and bring to light the assumptions of White privilege. This is an oppositional perspective; one that is about self-reflecting and decolonizing the mind" (p. 390). Such a perspective asks White people in particular to examine their own unconscious behaviors or beliefs that might contribute to racism, even in the absence of racist intention.

However, not all diversity practitioners take the interrogating Whiteness perspective as part of their attempts to address racial issues in the workplace. Two other perspectives more common in the literature Grimes analyzed are: *masking* and *re-centering* Whiteness. *Masking* fails to acknowledge differences sustained by Whiteness, most often by dismissing Whiteness in exchange for "American" or by using arguments of individualism, such as "I don't really consider myself White, I'm just me." These approaches emphasize how people are "all the same" in ways that often ignore the difficulties and discrimination that some people encounter due to race. Other practitioners acknowledge difference, but don't fully challenge the hierarchies associated with those differences, which Grimes calls *re-centering* Whiteness. For example, companies might boast about their affirmative action programs that demonstrate diversity as a value, but may fail to address the concerns or difficulties that marginalized people encounter once they enter the organization due to dominant organizational practices that privilege Whiteness. Such an approach maintains Whiteness as neutral and cannot acknowledge that Whiteness might pose a formidable barrier to some employees.

Although Grimes focuses her analysis on diversity management, we extend her work to examine how Whiteness is interrogated, masked, or re-centered in typical organizational practices beyond diversity efforts. We use Collins' (1998) concept of containment to integrate Grimes' strategies into a framework that reveals the forces at work in the struggle over racial meanings in organizations.

The Politics of Containment

Collins (1998) argues that systems of racial domination persist through *containment strategies* that work to silence those who speak out against or in other ways resist oppression. *Containment* and *interrogation* are opposing forces in the struggle over racial meanings in organizations. Indeed, containment strategies are often unnoticeable except through careful attention to the practices that create and sustain them—that is through interrogation. At the same time, the political outcomes of containment strategies might be quite visible. For example, Collins cites *exclusionary practices* attached to racial segregation as one of the major containment strategies operating in the United States. Although currently forbidden by law, racially segregated neighborhoods, schools, occupational categories, and access to public facilities persist through self-segregation and informal discriminatory practices in employment, housing, health, and education (Darity, 1998; Hacker, 1992).

In addition to exclusionary practices, Grimes' (2002), concepts of masking and re-centering are containment strategies because they serve to silence or deny the functioning of White privilege. For example, containment occurs through *masking* when it fails to acknowledge that notions of superiority and inferiority are present in the organization. Also, exclusionary practices might be masked through tokenism if a singular exception of racial integration is used to "prove" that exclusion does not exist. Containment also occurs through *re-centering* when it manages to "explain away" evidence of racial bias by pointing to a lack of conscious racist intention or personality differences. At other times Whiteness might be *re-centered* by informal practices such as filling jobs through informal networks of White colleagues.

To conclude this essay, we use the *interrogation-containment* framework to examine specific organizational practices where the perpetuation of Whiteness silently exists, even in situations where good intentions are present. By identifying these practices, we hope readers will be able to identify similar circumstances or practices in their organizations and interrupt unquestioned practices that might lead to racial bias in organizations.

SEEING WHITE RACIAL PRIVILEGE IN ORGANIZATIONAL PRACTICES

One way of thinking about where to see White privilege operating in organizational practices is to consider the career pathways one might take. This might include (a) having access to occupations through special training and college programs; (b) entering occupations or jobs through recruitment and hiring; (c) fitting in or finding one's place in the organizational culture; and (d) climbing the corporate ladder. We examine research on these practices to interrogate the ways in which Whiteness is privileged and to identify containment strategies—exclusion, re-centering, and masking—that would otherwise perpetuate the silencing and denial of White privilege.

White Privilege in Access to Occupations and Careers

A recent study provides convincing evidence that admission to elite colleges is one way that White privilege is maintained in organizations (Golden, 2006). In his book, *The Price of Admission: How America's Ruling Class Buys its Way into Elite Colleges—and Who Gets Left Outside the Gates,* Daniel Golden, a reporter for the *Wall Street Journal,* makes a powerful case that the number of wealthy White people given preference to highly selective colleges is much higher than that of racial minorities benefiting from affirmative action. He presents multiple case studies of the admissions practices at elite institutions including Harvard, Yale, Brown, Duke, and Stanford, showing how they favor the sons and daughters of the White-dominated upper crust of U.S. society. For example, admissions officers are provided with lists of "development cases," children whose parents have given big money to the university in the past. These preferred students are accepted regardless of their academic or character records, and many are accepted even if they rank near the bottom of their high school classes or have SAT scores 300–400 points below some rejected applicants.

This practice not only risks *re-centering* at the college by protecting White people (in this case rich White people) as the dominant social group in the university, it also extends into society at large. As Golden points out, alumni from these universities hold disproportionate sway in Congress, the judiciary, the media, Wall Street, and Fortune 500 companies—ensuring continued White dominance in these areas of concentrated power. However, *masking* is also at work as these elite colleges fail to voluntarily divulge their practices as preference for elite White students. Additionally, although people generally think that admissions preference for recruited athletes favors minority and low-income students, Golden's research debunks this idea. In fact, athletic recruitment actually tilts toward wealthy White women who are heavily recruited for patrician sports such as rowing, horseback riding, fencing, and polo. It is a practice that gives an advantage to the already advantaged.

White Privilege in Organizational Entry

Organizational entry refers to the processes through which organizational members are recruited, interviewed, and hired. One study that shows evidence of White privilege in recruitment and hiring was a 2003 study in which researchers randomly assigned traditionally White-sounding names and traditionally Black-sounding names to resumes (Bertrand & Mullainathan, 2003). The researchers found that that resumes with White-sounding names needed to send about ten resumes to get a call back, whereas Black-sounding names needed to send fifteen. Another way they phrased it was that having a White-sounding name provided the same advantage as eight years of experience! We can't know if the people who are receiving the resumes are intentionally screening for race, or if there is a subconscious bias at work here, but we can confidently conclude that Whiteness begins to influence organizational opportunity from the very beginning of the employment process. Whether conscious or not, this research shows evidence that employers consciously or subconsciously are allowing ideas of White superiority to affect their decisions. The result is *exclusion,* as people with traditionally Black-sounding names are excluded from the interview process and consequently from the organization. This could potentially *re-center Whiteness* by sustaining its status as the more common "normal" race within the organization. As mentioned earlier, if White people have not learned to interrogate Whiteness, they are likely to reproduce it.

Another instance of privileging Whiteness in recruitment and hiring relates to workers in low-skill jobs, such as day laborers and some factory workers. As current conditions of industrial restructuring have produced residential segregation by race, class, and concentration of poverty, there is increased competition for low-skill jobs from immigrants and other vulnerable groups (Browne, 1999). Some research suggests that discrimination in hiring may operate in favor of Latinos and Latinas who are viewed as belonging to the non-racialized category, "Whiteness of a different color" (Guinier & Torres, 2002, p. 7). Even within the central city, there is evidence that some employers may hire Mexican immigrants before they hire native-born African Americans residing in adjacent neighborhoods (Moore & Vigil, 1993). This is a process of racialization that hearkens back to the seventeenth century, and that *re-centers Whiteness* as the preferred image of the contemporary worker.

Fitting into the Workplace: Segmentation of "Special Interests"

It would seem that organizations that publicly promote the values of racial equality would maintain inclusive workplaces where all workers have an opportunity to feel a part of the organizational culture and have the opportunity to advance. However, many times, the project of working toward racial equality is cast as a "special interest" that is not integrated into the practices of the organization, but serves as a parallel yet separate effort. For example, in their research on diversity practices in the United States, David Thomas and his colleagues found that companies often segment diversity efforts into a patchwork of disconnected programs that are not aligned with the company's culture and values (Ely & Thomas, 2001; Thomas & Gabarro, 1999). Ely and Thomas describe one such organization in which "the firm established two committees whose mandate was to "infuse the firm's activities with a 'feminist' and 'racial' perspective, respectively; in practice, these committees had virtually no impact on the firm's work" (p. 246). In practices such as these, the presence of non-White people is desired, but there is no interrogation of practices and beliefs that enable White privilege and racism. As a consequence, many racial minorities never get a firm enough footing in the organization and the best of them leave—a phenomenon Thomas and Gabarro refer to as "squishy floors" (p. 241).

Marginalizing diversity efforts instead of integrating them into everyday organizational practices that everyone participates in can sustain White privilege in several ways. We can identify the risk for *re-centering* Whiteness, because the nonminority interests of the organization are depicted as neutral rather then being depicted as influenced by dominant forms of Whiteness and White privilege. This contrasts with "special interests" thought to serve only racial minorities. Consequently this also reinforces containment by separating the interests of people of color from the interests of White people. Depending on the extent to which these separate committees actually have the ability to affect organizational decisions, they may also serve to silence voices. If the voices of the groups designated to increase equality are systematically dismissed as "special interest" the groups actually serve to disempower rather than empower.

Climbing the Corporate Ladder: It Pays to be White!

While claims of reverse discrimination are common, statistics continue to support the claim that it literally pays to be White. Consider the following conclusions drawn in a 2004 report by the U.S. Census Bureau (DeNavas-Walt, Proctor, & Mills, 2004):

1. Black households had the lowest median income. Their 2003 median money income was about $30,000, which was sixty-two percent of the median for non-Hispanic White households (about $48,000).
2. Median money income for Hispanic households was about $33,000 in 2003, which was sixty-nine percent of the median for non-Hispanic White households.
3. Asian households had the highest median income among the race groups. Their 2003 median money income was about $55,500, 117 percent of the median for non-Hispanic White households (p. 3).

While the Asian households do have a median income that is more than that of non-Hispanic White households, this advantage disappears when you compare people of the same educational status (United States Census, 2004, Table 8). In other words the median Asian income is more because a larger percentage of that population has higher levels of education. If you compare non-Hispanic White people with Asian people of the same education, White people generally earn more. Comparing people of like education also shows that the advantage of Whiteness over other races exists at all educational levels.

It is interesting to note that the original report format re-centers Whiteness by using it as the neutral measuring stick with which other racial groups are compared, even though they could compare each racial group to the average of all racial groups. Again, do these statistics suggest that organizations consciously decide that White employees are worth more than others? Maybe. Maybe not. However, it does suggest that it literally pays to be White. Efforts to dismiss this evidence as something other than White privilege would risk *masking Whiteness* by suggesting that White people earn more, not because of unearned privilege, but because they probably deserve more.

Whiteness as the Emotional Pass Card

While we all experience emotional stress and strain within organizations, and while we all experience interpersonal tensions, Whiteness offers the privilege of the choice to "pass" on confronting potentially racist actions without worrying about how that action might disadvantage oneself or other White people in the future. In this case, it is not even the exemption from racist treatment that provides the advantage; it is the exemption from spending time and energy being vigilant and tactful in treating racism. Brenda Allen (1998) explains this privilege as it surfaces in conversations about race with those who have the privilege of passing on these emotionally demanding situations, "I do not think they understand how I feel as someone who repeatedly deals with these [potentially racist or sexist] exchanges across numerous contexts and who finds herself spending valuable mental and emotional energy trying to process them" (p. 580). Thus, even in the absence of racism, evading emotional vigilance to the threat of racism can create an emotional privilege to White people.

Stereotypes complicate this burden further, as Allen (Allen, Orbe, & Olivias, 1999) explains, "I do not always speak up when I should, partially because I do not want [my colleagues] to view me as hypersensitive or paranoid. Consequently, I'm frustrated with myself as much as I am with them" (p. 412). Thus, within organizations the burden of avoiding racial stereo-types is another emotionally demanding skill that White people are systemically exempt from. None of these means to suggest that White privilege grants a free pass from emotional strain in organizations, but it does suggest that this invisible emotion labor of dealing with race is a labor that most Whites do not have to perform, or can pick and choose when they will perform it. Furthermore, when this burden is masked or equated with other similar emotional burdens, it serves to silence the struggles and voices that would reveal this privileged position of White people.

CONCLUSION

This essay illustrates the process of interrogating Whiteness as a set of practices and ideas that privilege White people in organizations. But, as we have pointed out, both race and organizations are socially constructed. Because of this, we all have the ability to interrogate organizational practices that contain, silence, and exclude racial minorities in order to protect White privilege. These practices include, but are not limited to those we have listed here. We can challenge these practices by monitoring how race might subconsciously affect our organizational practices, even when people do not harbor bad intentions. Knowing and sharing facts about White privilege in college admissions processes, employment practices, and paid employment enables us to disprove myths that mask White privilege. Embracing multicultural and anti-racist movements as affecting all people, and consequently as something that that all people should be responsible for, is another way that we can challenge the containment that often supports White privilege. All of these things can help to create more racially just organizations, and consequently contribute to a more racially just society.

While we cannot offer an exhaustive list of containment practices or ways to challenge them, we can offer some concluding points to ponder.

- Whiteness and White privilege have a long history. While today's generation is not responsible for creating it, we are responsible for the way we deal with its legacy.
- White privilege is much more subtle and difficult to identify than bigoted racism. It is often built into organizational practices that mask it. Our ability to critically question these practices must precede our ability to defend or condemn them.
- While not a single one of us will solve the entire system of racism and White privilege, each of use can interrupt a part of that system by interrogating practices at all levels of organizations, especially those practices we participate in.
- Knowing how to identify White privilege and pointing it out to others is how each of us can help disrupt the "normal" status of White privilege. Ignoring it, even if one does not actively advocate it, is a subtle form of participation.

Armed with new knowledge and a new framework for interrogating organizational practice, you now have new choices to make. Will you interrogate or contain? Will you explain away these privileges by suggesting that something other than race is at work? Will you question others who engage in practices, even subtle practices, which mask White privilege? Or, will you (if you have one) play your emotional pass card?

References

Allen, B. J. (1998). Black womanhood and feminist standpoints. *Management Communication Quarterly, 11*(4), 575–586.

Allen, B. J., Orbe, M. P., & Olivias, M. R. (1999). The complexity of our tears: dis/enchantment and (in)difference in the academy. *Communication Theory, 9*(4), 402–429.

Ashcraft, K. L., & Allen, B. J. (2003). The racial foundation of organizational communication. *Communication Theory, 13*(1), 5–38.

Austin, R. L., & Allen, M. D. (May 2000). Racial disparity in arrest rates as an explanation of racial disparity in commitments to Pennsylvania's prisons. *Journal of Research in Crime and Delinquency, 37*, 200–220.

Banton, M., & Harwood, J. (1975). *The race concept.* London: David and Charles.

Baldus, D., et al. (1998). In The post-Furman era: An empirical and legal overview, with recent findings from Philadelphia, *Cornell Law Review, 83,* 1638.

Bertrand, M., & Mullainathan, S. (2003). *Are Emily and Greg more employable than Lakisha and Jamal?: A field experiment on labor market discrimination.* Cambridge, MA: National Bureau of Economic Research.

Bonilla-Silva, E. (2003). *Racism without racists: Color-blind racism and the persistence of racial inequality in the United States.* New York: Rowman & Littlefield.

Brown, M. K., Carnoy, M., Currie, E., Duster, T., Oppenheimer, D., Shultz., et al. (2003). *Whitewashing race:*

The myth of a color-blind society. Ewing, NJ: University of California Press.

Browne, I. (1999a). Introduction: Latinas and African American women in the U.S. labor market. In I. Browne (Ed.), *Latinas and African American women at work: Race, gender, and economic inequality* (pp. 1–31). New York: Russell Sage Foundation.

Cheney, G., Christensen, L., Zorn, T., & Ganesh, S. (2004). *Organizational communication in an age of globalization: Issues, reflections, practices.* Prospect Height, IL: Waveland Press.

Conley, D. J. (1994). Adding color to a black and white picture: Using qualitative data to explain racial disproportionality in the juvenile justice system. *Journal of Research in Crime and Delinquency, 31,* 135–48.

Crutchfield, R. D., Bridges, G. S., & Pitchford, S. R. (1994). Analytical and aggregation biases in analyses of imprisonment: Reconciling discrepancies in studies of racial disparity. *Journal of Research in Crime and Delinquency, 31,* 177–79.

Darity, W. (1998). *Persistent disparity: Race and economic inequality in the United States since 1945.* New York: Edward Elgar.

Deetz, S. (1982). Critical interpretive research in organizational communication. *Western Journal of Speech Communication, 46,* 131–149.

DeNavas-Walt, C., Bernadette, C., Proctor, D., & Mills, R. J. (2004). *Income, poverty, and health insurance coverage in the United States: 2003.* (U.S. Census Bureau, Current Population Reports, P60-226). Washington DC: U.S. Government Printing Office.

Dyer, R. (1997). *White.* New York: Routledge.

Ely, R. J., & Thomas, D. A. (2001). Cultural diversity at work: The effects of diversity perspectives on work group processes and outcomes. *Administrative Science Quarterly, 46*(2), 229–273.

Essed, P. (2005). In K. Murji & J. Solomos (Eds.), *Racialization: Studies in theory and practice* (228–247). New York: Oxford.

Eze, E. C. (1997). Introduction. In E. C. Eze (Ed.), *Race and the Enlightenment: A reader* (pp. 1–9). Cambridge, MA: Blackwell.

Feagin, J. R. (2006). Systemic racism: A theory of oppression. New York: Routledge.

Frankenberg, R. (1993). *White women, race matters: The social construction of whiteness.* Minneapolis: University of Minnesota Press.

Golden, D. (2006). *The price of admission: How America's ruling class buys its way into elite colleges—and who gets left outside the gates.* New York: Crown.

Grimes, D. S. (2001). Putting our own house in order: Whiteness, change, and organization studies. *Journal of Change Management, 14*(2), 132–149.

Grimes, D. S. (2002). Challenging the status quo?: Whiteness in the diversity management literature. *Management Communication Quarterly, 15*(3), 381–409.

Guinier, L., & Torres, G. (2002). *The miner's canary: Enlisting race, resisting power, transforming democracy.* Cambridge, MA: Harvard University Press.

Hacker, A. (1992). *Two nations: Black and White, separate, hostile, unequal.* New York: Ballantine.

Ignatiev, N. (1997). *How the Irish became white.* New York: Routledge.

Jackson, R. L. (1999). White space, white privilege: mapping discursive inquiry into the self. *Quarterly Journal of Speech, 85*(1), 38–54.

Keating, A. (1995). Interrogating "whiteness," (de)constructing "race." *College English, 57*(8), 901–918.

Madison, K. J. (1999). Legitimation crisis and containment: The "anti-racist-white-hero" film. *Critical Studies in Mass Communication, 16,* 399–416.

McIntosh, P. (1990). White privilege: Unpacking the invisible knapsack. *Independent School, 49*(2), 31–35.

Moore, J., & Vigil, J. D. (1993). Barrios in transition. In J. Moore & R. Pinderhuges (Eds.), *In the barrios: Latinos and the underclass debate* (pp. 27–49). New York: Russell Sage Foundation.

Mosse, G. L. (1978). *Toward the final solution: A history of European racism.* London: J.M. Dent & Sons.

Mumby, D. K. (2001). Power and politics. In F. M. Jablin & L. L. Putnam (Eds.), *The new handbook of organizational communication: Advances in theory, research, and methods* (pp. 585–623). Newbury Park, CA: Sage.

Nakayama, T. K., & Krizek, R. L. (1995). Whiteness: Strategic rhetoric. *Quarterly Journal of Speech, 81,* 291–309.

Nkomo, S. M. (1992). The emperor has no clothes: Rewriting race in organizations. *Academy of Management Review, 17,* 487–513.

Omi, M., & Winant, H. (1986). *Racial formation in the United States: From the 1960s to the 1980s.* New York: Routledge.

Parker, P. S. (2003). Control, power, and resistance within raced, gendered, and classed work contexts: The case of African American women. *Communication Yearbook 27,* 257–291.

Prasad, P. (1997). The Protestant ethic and the myths of the frontier: Cultural imprints, organizational structuring, and workplace diversity. In P. Prasad, A. J. Mills, M. Elmes, & A. Prasad (Eds.), *Managing the organizational melting pot: Dilemmas of workplace diversity* (129–147). Thousand Oaks, CA: Sage.

Projansky, S., & Ono, K. (1999). Strategic whiteness as cinematic racial politics. In T. K. Nakayama & J. N. Martin (Eds.), *Whiteness: The communication of social identity.* Thousand Oaks, CA: Sage.

Sullivan (2006). *Revealing whiteness: The unconscious habits of racial privilege*. In Bloomington: Indiana University Press.

U. S. Census Bureau. (2004). *Educational attainment in the United States: Table 8, Income in 2003 by educational attainment of the population 18 years and over, by age, sex, race alone, and Hispanic origin: 2004.* Retrieved March 28, 2007, from http://www.census.gov/population/www/socdemo/education/cps2004.html

Winant, H. (2000). Race and race theory. *Annual Review of Sociology, 26,* 169–185.

Concepts and Questions

1. Describe how the invisible knapsack analogy advanced by Parker and Mease applies to the problems of White privilege in organizations.

2. In what ways do Parker and Mease indicate that democratic choice and opportunity as equally available to all is a myth?

3. What do Parker and Mease mean by the idea that race is a social construction?

4. What is racialization? How has it contributed to the development of White privilege?

5. Why is Whiteness a social construction? How is it constructed?

6. What do Parker and Mease mean when they say that organizations are socially constructed cultural systems?

7. What is the process of cultural cloning? How does it manifest in organizational cultures?

8. What do Parker and Mease mean by *interrogating Whiteness?* How does this work toward promoting racial inclusion in organizations?

9. What are *containment strategies,* and how do they work to perpetuate White privilege?

10. In what ways is White privilege perpetuated through organizational entry processes?

When Cultures Collide: Alternative Medicine, Biomedicine, and the Patients in the Middle

POLLY A. BEGLEY

DEBBIE A. OCKEY

When a person is serene, the pulse of the heart flows and connects, just as pearls are joined together or like a string of red jade, then one can talk about a healthy heart.

THE YELLOW EMPEROR'S CANNON OF
INTERNAL MEDICINE, 2500 B.C.

Who or what would you consult when you begin feeling sick? If the illness was mild, would you go to your home medicine cabinet for an over-the-counter drug or your backyard herb garden? If the symptoms were more severe, would you call a doctor or a shaman? Which would you consider to be an "unconventional" remedy? Herbal medications or prescription drugs? Acupuncture or anesthetic? Qi gong or Pilates? Chiropractics or back surgery? A person's cultural background, personal values, beliefs, and attitudes influence his or her preferred medical approaches and remedies.

The collision of cultures between those who embrace traditional healing methods and those who follow the biomedical culture prevalent in American hospitals and clinics may be the most evident when we choose our approach to health and healing. Kira Salak (2006), after suffering from depression since childhood and undergoing years of therapy, eventually found relief through a shamanistic medicinal ritual deep in the Peruvian Amazon. She was given *ayahuasca,* a sacred spirit medicine. An American

This original essay appears here in print for the first time. All rights reserved. Permission to reprint must be obtained from the authors and the publisher. Polly A. Begley teaches in the Department of Communication Arts, and Debbie A. Ockey teaches English as a Second Language at Fresno City College, Fresno, California.

doctor of naprapathy, Dr. Rosetta Arvigo, sought knowledge in the rainforest of Belize and apprenticed for ten years with a famous traditional healer named Don Elijio Panti. She learned to heal with prayers, roots, vines, barks, and massage. Don Elijio Panti's healing medicine and knowledge came from the Mayan Spirits and also from years of experience and close observation of nature (Arvigo, Epstein, & Yaquinto, 1994). Dr. M. Norton, a chiropractor in Fresno, California, uses the Torque Release Technique as a gentle method of spinal/nervous system care. He believes that "the human body and mind are self-regulating and self-healing by design" and his treatment plans help people to return to "wholeness" without having to rely on drugs that mask the true cause of illness. His methods developed as a result of his training at the Life West Chiropractic College in Hayward, California, and over twenty years of professional experience helping patients deal with chronic pain (personal interview, March 23, 2006). These accounts of healing through spirit medicine, Mayan spirits, or chiropractic adjustment may be dismissed as being outside the scope of biomedicine, but in light of changing global populations, there is an urgent need for health care organizations, medical professionals, and patients to understand diverse medical approaches.

A panel of experts convened by the Institute of Medicine revealed significant health disparities among populations of different sociocultural and socioeconomic backgrounds in the United States (Smedley, Stith, & Nelson, 2003). Health providers and policymakers responded to this and other research by encouraging cultural competence training in medical schools and health organizations. Ultimately, the quality of medical services and health outcomes are directly related to whether the caregiver and patient understand each others' beliefs, values, attitudes, traditions, and practices regarding health care and are able to communicate effectively based upon this understanding. Some doctors respond to their multicultural patient loads by educating themselves about traditional medicinal approaches and cultural beliefs or developing their own models for culturally competent communication with patients. In addition, more hospitals have highly trained interpreters on staff or immediately available with a phone call.

This essay will examine influential aspects of communication between biomedical caregivers and patients from diverse cultural and linguistic backgrounds and healing traditions. It is with no small degree of trepidation that we narrowed down the topics for this essay as there are as many challenges and solutions as there are approaches to health and healing. Having provided this caveat, first, the terms culture, biomedical belief systems, supernatural belief systems, holistic belief systems, and culturally competent healthcare will be defined. Second, this review will focus on some of the communicative challenges associated with providing effective treatment and care in light of changing patient populations. Finally, some models for success and solutions for improving communicative competence in clinical encounters will be proposed.

DEFINITION OF RELEVANT TERMS

Culture

This is a broad term used to describe information passed from one generation to another within a group of people. McDaniel, Samovar, and Porter define culture as, "the rules for living and functioning in society" (2006, p. 10). In terms of health communication, Joan Luckman (2000), the author of "Transcultural Communication in Health Care," describes culture as the "specific rules for dealing with the universal events of life—birth, mating, childrearing, illness, pain, and death" (p. 21). Health organizations, such as the Healthy House Within a MATCH (Multidisciplinary Approach to Cross-Cultural Health) Coalition, are working to adopt a broader definition of culture beyond societal definitions of race and ethnicity. Marilyn Mochel, a director at the Healthy House Within a MATCH Coalition, pointed out that we should, "honor the fact that everybody is a cultural being" (personal interview, October 14, 2005). It is extremely difficult to separate our cultural values and beliefs from our ideas about appropriate and effective healing practices. They are inextricably bound up together.

Biomedical Belief System

This is the dominant medical system found in American hospitals and clinics with its own specific set of norms and values. Historically, some biomedical beliefs may be traced back to the fifth century B.C. and the Hippocratic doctors. These doctors began by "elevating themselves above root-gatherers, diviners and others whom they dismissed as ignoramuses and quacks" and established a code of physician conduct and a scientific approach that still influence modern medicine today (Porter, 2002, p. 25). The seventeenth-century philosopher, Rene Descartes, further contended that mind and body were separate from each other. This mind–body dichotomy explains that "disease is caused by physiological disturbances such as genetic disorders, biochemical imbalances, and infectious organisms" and deemphasizes psychological, emotional, or spiritual factors as sources of illness (Luckman, 2000, p. 44).

Supernatural Belief Systems

In contrast to the scientific American biomedical system, a traditional healing approach may view illness as either a punishment for evil deeds, an outside possession of the body, an evil spell, or a frightened, wandering soul. According to Amazonian shamans, "all negative thoughts . . . are dark spirits speaking to us, trying to scare us into reacting; the spirits then feed on our reactivity, growing stronger and more formidable until they finally rule over us" (Salak, 2006, p 4). A Taoist shamanistic ritual known as *shoujing* reclaims people's frightened souls and is practiced in Taipei's Hsingtien Temple. The believers will tell you there is no need to list your symptoms, because the *shoujing* ritual is a catch-all—'it cures if you're ill, and blesses if you're not'" (Hwang, 2004, p. 12–13). Hmong shamans, called *txiv neeb,* also perform ceremonies to retrieve errant souls that have been frightened away. *Txiv neeb* maintain that illness and disease are indications that a person has lost one of his or her souls (Fadiman, 1997).

Holistic Belief Systems

Holistic approaches to health assert that "a person must remain in harmony with the natural laws and be willing to continually adjust to changes in the environment" in order to restore equilibrium to the body (Luckman, 2000, p. 45). Dr. David Simon, a board-certified neurologist and the medical director and cofounder of the Chopra Center for Wellbeing, refers to this natural equilibrium or healing from

within when he explained that "the most powerful pharmacy is not the local drugstore but the human physiology. We're capable of generating the healing chemicals—antidepressants, anti-anxiety, immune strengthening" (Collie, 2007, p. 81).

Alternative Medicine

Supernatural and holistic practices are fluid to the extent that not everyone agrees to what medical approaches are included within each belief system. Thus, another term, *alternative,* is frequently used to describe any medical practice that is not validated or utilized in biomedical practices. Chiropractors, massage therapists, hypnotists, herbal therapists, homeopaths, and naturopaths are all examples of alternative medical practitioners. Today, more Americans are seeking alternative sources of cures outside the biomedical model. The National Institute of Health's National Center for Complementary and Alternative Medicine (2004) commissioned a study to determine how many adult Americans are using alternative medicine. Of a survey of 31,000 nationwide, they found thirty-six percent stated that they used some form of alternative medicine. However, if prayer is included in that list, the number increases dramatically to sixty-two percent. The most popular types of treatments were "natural" supplements including herbs, used by forty percent of the respondents, followed by deep breathing, meditation, and yoga. These patients have not rejected biomedicine. In fact, fifty-five percent said they combined alternative treatments with biomedicine (Stein, 2004, p. A01). Clearly, it is not just recent immigrants who are using traditional medicine or alternative treatments. A larger number of Americans are now turning to alternative medicine. But the term "alternative" sets up an inherent dichotomy between mainstream biomedical approaches and natural prevention and cures, so that biomedicine is perceived as the default standard for everyone. Dr. M. Norton, with Norton Chiropractic Wellness Center in Central California, argues that less invasive medical approaches and preventive care ought to be the norm while drugs and surgery should be considered *alternative* (personal interview, March 23, 2006). However, some doctors are able to bridge this gap between biomedicine and alternative care as they blend various medical approaches. One such doctor is Dr. David Simon who prefers to define his practice as *integrative* rather than alternative medicine. This approach allows for the use of "external intervention, be that pharmacology, surgery, or radiation therapy" and the use of "practices that are more about awakening a person's internal healing system" (Collie, 2007, p. 81). Dr. David Simon and the Chopra Center for Wellbeing have begun discussions with medical schools regarding an Integrative Medicine major. He is also a clinical professor at the University of California at San Diego Medical School and has third year medical students rotating in with him at the Chopra Center. Dr. Brent Bauer, Director of the Department of Internal Medicine's Complementary and Integrative Medicine Program at Mayo Clinic, Rochester, Minnesota, also states that "Even the name 'alternative'—used to describe therapies outside the scope of traditional medicine—can be misleading now. . . . As more health-care providers offer such services, it makes sense to refer to the therapies as complementary or integrative" (Oleck, 2007, p. E2).

Cultural Competency

Being aware of our own cultural values, beliefs, and attitudes and striving to understand and appreciate other cultures, the American Medical Student Association outlines the goals of culturally competent care as attaining: cultural awareness, cultural knowledge, cultural skills, and increasing cultural encounters (2005). Culturally competent communication in a health care setting relates positively to higher levels of patient satisfaction, cost efficiency, and improved health outcomes. Ultimately, the successful treatment of illness and disease hinges upon how the health care industry and patients deal with diverse approaches to health and healing while simultaneously understanding and perhaps even capitalizing on the benefits of supernatural, holistic, and alternative care.

CHALLENGES TO PROVIDING CULTURALLY AND LINGUISTICALLY APPROPRIATE HEALTH CARE IN A BIOMEDICAL SETTING

Biomedical Culture of Medicine

Health care providers are socialized during medical training into the Western *culture of medicine* which favors science and the use of the latest diagnostic technology which further separates the patient from the physician. The following section will examine some key aspects of the biomedical culture, specifically the effects of the mind–body dichotomy, cultural competency training in medical schools, patients' descriptions of their symptoms, pressure of large patient load, and values commonly reflected within hospital settings.

The major paradox of the biomedical approach is that even with an advanced and sophisticated understanding of the human body and disease, the individual patient often feels afraid, isolated, and left out of the process. The mind–body dichotomy insists that emotions for the caregiver and the patient are secondary within biomedical diagnosis and treatment plans. But studies have revealed the importance of the patient's psychological outlook in the physical healing process. Research conducted by Iwamitsu, Shimoda, Abe, Tani, Okawa, and Buck (2005) found that cancer patients who suppressed their emotions felt more "anxiety, depression, and anger" than patients who allowed themselves to express a full range of emotions (p. 202). Pain, sickness, fear, and death are the great issues of life, and more large medical facilities, such as cancer centers, are now offering various types of ongoing emotional and psychological support to help patients cope with traumatic illnesses and related treatments.

Medical schools provide training in the latest scientific research, discoveries, and technology for curing disease and illness, but are medical schools providing sufficient training for health care providers to become culturally competent communicators? A recent trend within medical schools, such as Yale, Harvard, and Stanford, has been to include a 1997 book entitled *The Spirit Catches You and You Fall Down* by Anne Fadiman as part of their curriculum. This book explores the cultural clashes and misunderstandings between Merced Community Medical Center (MCMC) in California and a Hmong refugee family from Laos with a child who had a life-threatening seizure disorder. Marilyn Mochel, director at the Healthy House Within a MATCH Coalition, works as a cultural broker for many Hmong families in Merced and other central California towns and stresses that it is important to reach students while they are in medical school with cultural competency training at a time when they are open to the information. After they begin their practice, it may be very difficult for them to accept the divergent health practices of their patients. However, many doctors and health organizations seek to remedy this situation through continued research and health promotion campaigns. For example, one large HMO, Kaiser Permanente, has a mission of "culturally, linguistically, and medically appropriate care." Susan Ryan, Kaiser Permanente C.E.O. in Fresno, California, explained that the organization plans to increase the number of languages spoken by their health care teams. They also launched a program to reach underserved families in the community in order to offer more preventive services and emphasize strategies for healthy living (Ryan, 2005). Some large medical programs are also focusing on providing linguistically appropriate care. One such example is UC Irvine College of Medicine which created a medical education program focused on Latino culture in 2004 (Association of American Medical Colleges, 2004).

Culturally appropriate medical care includes being able to effectively treat a patient with different beliefs about the origins of illness and disease. In the previously mentioned book by Anne Fadiman (1997), Lia Lee was diagnosed with a severe form of epilepsy by the MCMC. But her family recognized the signs of *qaug dab peg,* which means "the spirit catches you and you fall down," and traced her condition back to an older sister who had slammed the front door and scared three-month-old Lia's soul away. Her parents were concerned about their daughter's seizures, but also felt great pride as *qaug dab peg* marked Lia as a person of consequence in the Hmong community who could eventually be chosen as a shaman (p. 20). The vast differences between the medical teams' treatment plan and recommendations and the family's beliefs and expectations lead to inevitable misunderstandings and an ultimately tragic outcome. Carmen Arambula, the director of Health Care Policies at Metro Ministries in central California, contends that a doctor may comprehend when a person describes a squeezing sensation near the heart or explains that it "feels like an elephant is sitting on my chest." But if a patient explains that a "neighbor gave me the evil eye and infected me with his spirit," then the physician might not know that the person was describing a heart attack (personal interview, November 21, 2005). When caregivers have a deeper understanding of their patient's culture, it can help them interpret these types of descriptions or beliefs without dismissing them.

Biomedical physicians are able to "read" bodies, but these caregivers, feeling the pressure of the current cost-cutting measures of health organizations, may not be able to spend adequate time with their patients. In addition, physicians such as Dr. Linda Halderman, who practice independently, are not sufficiently compensated for "explaining, encouraging, counseling, and comforting" their patients (2007, p. B9). Dr. Halderman, who deals primarily with Medi-Cal or uninsured patients, explains that for the office visit where she must tell a frightened patient she has breast cancer Medi-Cal reimburses her only $24. Spending enough time with a patient to get to the root of the problem is an integral part of a diagnosis in alternative medicine. For example, a *txiv neeb* (Hmong shaman) routinely makes house calls and may spend an entire day with a sick person (Fadiman, 1997). In contrast, modern doctors ask that patients come to see them at hospitals and clinics no matter how weak they are, and then may only be able to spend a few minutes with them in the examination room.

Furthermore, the biomedical system reflects the values of the surrounding society, and American hospitals are set up with the values of individualism, self-reliance, and efficiency in mind. Caregivers teach patients to give themselves injections, change bandages, and take medications on their own. Hospital visiting hours are limited and most hospital rooms have only one visitor's chair. In other cultures, the importance of the extended family in the healing process is clearly recognized. Hospital rooms in Spain may be positioned around a large patio where multiple family members gather to rest and cook meals. These family members spend all day and night tending to the patient, leaving the medical staff to only provide medical care (Galanti, 2004).

Do biomedical caregivers understand and respect traditional, holistic, and alternative cures? Leoncio Vásquez Santos, an Outreach Worker with Centro Binacional para el Desarrollo Indígena Oaxaqueño Inc., translated for a woman who was trying to explain to her doctor about the *evil eye;* however, the doctor dismissed her explanation. He only wanted to hear about her symptoms and disregarded her thoughts about the source of her illness (personal interview, March 29, 2006). Marilyn Mochel, director at the Healthy House Within a MATCH Coalition, corroborated this viewpoint when she pointed out that the average doctor does not have the time or desire to hear about traditional medicine and often views it as "witchcraft" (personal interview, October 14, 2005). Dr. Matthew Norton, with Norton Chiropractic Wellness Center, described his relationship with biomedical physicians as "adversarial," and many of his patients have been told *not* to see a chiropractor by their primary care doctors. He explained the difference between biomedicine and his practice as the difference between Western versus Eastern thinking or reactive versus proactive health care (personal interview, March 23, 2006). These examples and perspectives from diverse medical approaches point to the need for medical schools to include more case studies that explore cultural viewpoints and medical practices within their curriculum.

Informed Consent and the Right to Know

Another entrenched belief of the biomedical culture is the idea of *informed consent*. Informed Consent forms precede most medical procedures in the USA and reflect the value placed on autonomy in American culture. Every patient undergoing surgery must sign a document of informed consent indicating he or she has been thoroughly briefed and understands the procedure and possible risks. These consent forms also protect the physician and hospital from malpractice suits. However, this is not a common practice in many other cultures. A sixty-five-year-old man from the Middle East expressed reluctance to sign the informed consent form before a heart catheterization because from his perspective, the doctor with all the knowledge and training should be the one to make the decision (Galanti, 2004). He may have been asking himself, "What does an untrained person know about heart catheterization?" A solution to this situation may have been to explain the historical context of informed consent and patient's rights. The importance of informed consent grew out of the tragedy of the Tuskegee syphilis study begun in 1932 in which 400 African American men were left untreated for forty years in order for scientists to research how the disease progressed. Thus, informed consent forms are important for preventing situations like the Tuskegee incident from ever happening again. However laudable the idea of informed consent may be, it still has

to be tempered with the reality that not all cultures understand or accept this idea.

Mr. Bee Yang, a professor in Social Work at California State University Fresno, is called upon frequently to act as a cultural broker in the Hmong community. He pointed out that many Hmong people have a distrust in medical systems based on their own experiences in Thailand as a minority group in refugee camps. In addition, they had no significant exposure to any type of formal medical system before coming to the United States, so hospitals and clinics were often overwhelming and confusing to them. Some concepts such as "informed consent" and "organ transplants" do not exist in the Hmong language. Therefore, patients are unaware of what they are signing or unclear about what is being interpreted for them. In addition, the Hmong culture retains oral traditions and collectivistic values. Patients need time to consider information and share it with family and community elders. They often feel pressured to agree to procedures or treatments quickly without the opportunity to discuss and weigh the choices with their extended families (personal interview, October 23, 2005).

Patient's rights are fundamental in the biomedical culture. The American Medical Association's (AMA) Principles of Medical Ethics states that a physician must "be honest in all professional interactions" (Cohen, 2006, section 6, p. 32). Even withholding information for a patient's own good which is called "therapeutic privilege" is discouraged by the AMA. However, the *right to know* is interpreted by many American physicians to mean that the information must be forced upon the patient. The Navajo people have a concept called *hozhooji* that is "consistent with the view that thought and language have the power to shape reality and control events" (Flores, Rabke-Verani, Pine, & Sabharwal, 2002, p. 272). In one case, a Navajo man refused surgery after he was told that there was a risk of not waking up in any type of operation. The doctor in this case could have followed the custom of the traditional Navajo healer and communicated the risks of surgery by referring to a hypothetical third party rather than the patient. Marilyn Mochel, director at the Health House Within a MATCH Coalition, explained that a patient also has the *right not to know*. Some cultures believe that if you predict death, you make it happen. Director Mochel explained that one alternative would be for a physician to tell a family member in the next room rather than directly informing the patient of a critical or terminal condition. In this way, the family can decide whether to break the news to the patient and in what manner (personal interview, October 14, 2005).

Health Literacy

There is another danger to a patient's health lurking within our society that has nothing to do with bacteria or viruses. This danger is the high rate of health illiteracy among the American population. Almost half of all American adults, 90 million people, have difficulty obtaining, understanding, and applying the information necessary to make effective health decisions for themselves and their families. According to the World Health Organization (1998), health literacy is defined as, "The cognitive and social skills which determine the motivation and ability of individuals to gain access to, and understand and use information in ways which promote and maintain good health ("Health Promotion Glossary").

Health literacy is related to general literacy levels, but medical jargon and health matters may be confusing even to a highly educated person. For instance, Bower and Taylor (2003) found that the customary use of medical jargon contributed to widespread inability to understand over-the-counter drug instructions. Regulations regarding the use of "plain language," such as replacing "indications," "abdominal," "pulmonary," and "persists" with "uses," "stomach," "lung," and "does not go away" were first instituted in 1999 (p. 146). When a patient does not understand, embarrassment, frustration, or lack of linguistic proficiency could prevent him or her from asking the pharmacist or caregiver for further clarification. Mr. Anthony Yamimoto, Director of Social Work Services at Children's Hospital in Fresno, described the Central California population as culturally and spiritually diverse, but some lack "medical sophistication." He described a parent who came into the hospital unable to read numbers or tell time. "Her child required routine dosages at consistent times. If the child is not given the appropriate dosage on time, the treatment is not effective and may contribute to other complications or health consequences (personal communication, October 3, 2005)."

Even when a person understands medical instructions, this does not guarantee that he or she will follow them. Wang Ming-Tao and Tang Cheng-You visit their daughter regularly in the United States from Chong-Qing City in China. Mrs. Wang, 65 years old, along with her 73-year-old husband, Mr. Tang, described her personal struggle with psoriasis. She has tried both traditional Chinese medicine and biomedicine. Both helped control the problem (not cure), but the biomedicine had very severe side effects that she could not tolerate. She noted that many Chinese will take the full dose of natural medicine prescribed by a traditional Chinese Doctor, but will not take the complete dose of drugs prescribed by a Western Doctor. The couple's daughter, Li Mann, explained that there is an underlying belief among Chinese that all medicine (natural and manufactured) is poison. Basically, a poison is being used to counter another kind of poison (disease or illness) in your body (personal interview, December 21, 2005). In contrast, the biomedical perspective contends that the benefits outweigh the side effects of prescribed medication treatment plans, especially in the case of antibiotics. Thus, one of the risks of medical illiteracy is that patients who do not finish full doses of antibiotics risk the infection returning while contributing to the problem of antibiotic-resistant diseases. Clearly, all patients need explanations in terms they understand in order to fully comprehend the consequences of not following their treatment plans. At the same time, physicians need to take into account their patient's views regarding biomedicine, prescription medications, and tolerable side effects.

Linguistic Challenges

As explained in the previous section, misunderstandings often occur between a patient and health care provider when they both speak English as their first language, but the potential for miscommunication increases when the patient's first language is not English. There are over 6,000 different languages and dialects spoken throughout the world. The inability to communicate effectively with a patient due to language barriers is one of the major challenges faced by health care professionals. The latest census statistics reflect the fact that today we need to educate health care professionals for a multicultural, multilingual world. In 2004, there were more than 49 million speakers of languages other than English in the United States. Over 22 million identified themselves as limited English proficient. This number has increased dramatically since the 1990 census when 25 million people spoke languages other than English. In addition, more than eight percent of respondents to the census survey reported that they spoke English "less than well" (Flores, 2006). Health care professionals must be able to accommodate different cultural and linguistic needs since there is no doubt that language barriers affect health care. Doctors may be using medical terms that do not have an equivalent in another language, or are too complex for the patients to understand making them feel confused and frustrated. This lack of understanding may lead to noncompliance with the doctor's instructions for treatment. In research conducted at the Medical College of Wisconsin, Dr. Glenn Flores found that twenty-six percent of the patients stated that language barriers were the major reason they did not seek treatment or deferred follow-up visits (Flores, 2006). This communication barrier is frustrating for both physicians and patients. Very often the problem is that no trained interpreter is available. One study found that no interpreter was used at all for forty-six percent of patients who spoke limited English and when an interpreter was used, thirty-nine percent had no training (Flores, Mayo, Zuckerman, Abreu, Medina, & Hardt, 2003, p. 13).

In order to communicate with a patient who does not speak English, a skilled interpreter is needed. This means someone who has been properly trained and knows enough medical terminology to correctly translate the information or treatment directions. In the United States, patients have a legal right to an interpreter, but in health care settings there are not enough well-trained interpreters available. Consequently, family members commonly interpret for each other during health care discussions. One such example involved a Laotian refugee who enlisted her 12-year-old son to interpret for her during a medical appointment. She was diagnosed as having a prolapsed uterus, but the young boy divulged, "I don't really know what a uterus is." He also had to describe to the doctor what his mother said, and he admitted that, "She tells me things I don't know how to say. Sometimes I tell the doctor something else" (Burke, 2005, p. A1). A Brandeis University report found that twenty-seven percent of patients who were not provided an interpreter did not understand how to take their medication upon leaving the hospital. In contrast, when interpreters were provided, only two percent did not understand (Brandeis University, 2002). In the previous example, the

12-year-old translator's mistranslations led to his mother taking the incorrect dose of medication and experiencing temporary dizziness and weakness. Leanne Gassaway, Vice President of Legal and Regulatory Affairs, the California Association of Health Plans, says that, "We discourage the use of children, but in an emergency they may be the only resource you have" (Burke, 2005, p. A1). Although a skilled interpreter is essential, patients must also recognize the importance of being honest with their physicians about alternative treatments or medicines they may be using. Without that information, the physician cannot develop a comprehensive treatment plan. Therefore, the physician needs to facilitate an environment where the patient feels comfortable to disclose that information.

Just being fluent in the patients' language, however, is not always sufficient. Understanding the important cultural values that facilitate communication in a particular language is also necessary. For example, many Spanish speakers will expect to be treated with *personalismo* (formal friendliness) which could be as simple as asking about the patient's family or life at each visit. In addition, showing *respeto* (respect) to the parents or oldest members of the family including using the respectful titles of *señor or señora* will make patients feel that the doctor values their concerns. Finally, demonstrating simple politeness and courtesy will ensure that patients feel the physician is *simpatico* (likeable or congenial). When the caregiver does not recognize these cultural values, the patient may perceive a lack of respect and believe that the physician does not really care about him or her (Flores, Rabke-Verani, Pine, & Sabharwal, 2002).

MODELS FOR SUCCESS: SOLUTIONS AND INNOVATIVE PROGRAMS

Knowledge and Understanding

The first step toward improving effective communication between biomedical caregivers and patients from diverse cultural and linguistic backgrounds or medical philosophies must be to increase cultural knowledge and understanding among all participants within the health care setting. *The Centro Binacional para el Desarrollo Indígena Oaxaqueño Inc.,* in Central California, works to organize and inform indigenous immigrant communities about health services available to them and offers training for health caregivers. Many indigenous immigrant groups from Mexico lived in autonomous regions, do not speak Spanish, have an elementary education, and have no knowledge of the social and political system of Mexico. Leoncio Vásquez Santos, an Outreach Worker with the *Centro,* speaks English and Mixtec in order to translate, read letters, make phone calls, or fill out paperwork for the Ñuudzahui indigenous people from northwestern Oaxaca, Mexico, now living in the Central Valley of California. Señor Santos also helped create a workshop providing information concerning prenatal care for groups of indigenous people living in Central California. Previously, many indigenous women just showed up at clinics on the day of delivery and were turned away because without a record of prenatal care, they were considered a high-risk pregnancy. Other *Centro* workshops have been developed for health care professionals to impart awareness of indigenous immigrant communities and their particular needs (personal interview, March 29, 2006).

Increasing the Diversity of Health Care Professionals

One response to health disparities in California has been to fund programs that address the shortage of diverse health care professionals. The University of California, San Francisco School of Medicine helped fund the Fresno Latino Center for Medical Education and Research in order to recruit, mentor, and tutor Latino students and other educationally disadvantaged students as they become health care professionals. Marilyn Mochel, director at the Healthy House Within a Match Coalition, recounted an instance when a bilingual nurse called her father at three o'clock in the morning to ask him how to say "gallbladder" in Spanish. Director Mochel used this example to stress that the nurse was fluent in medical English and conversational Spanish, but not in medical Spanish. Thus, the initiatives to diversify the health profession must also require medical schools to support bilingual skills, broaden cultural understanding, and teach techniques to provide cross-cultural care (personal interview, October 14, 2005).

Some studies have investigated how a caregivers' own cultural background may influence their interactions with and treatment of patients. One study of nursing students, who were mainly Caucasian, indicated low scores on a scale of cultural knowledge about African American patients. However, the scores were much higher for the senior nursing students than the freshman. The study's authors believed this could be due to the fact that the seniors had more exposure to cultural diversity through the curriculum and their training. Even sharing the same ethnicity as the patient, however, does not always guarantee that the caregiver will understand many of the important beliefs held by their patients. A study that was done at an institution which serves a large Latino population found that the family practice residents had only a limited awareness of their patients' medical beliefs. For example, ninety-four percent of the patients believed in *empacho,* (the belief food gets stuck inside the stomach and leads to vomiting, diarrhea, and fever), but seventy-seven percent of the residents knew nothing about it. Surprisingly, Flores, Rabke-Verani, Pine, & Sabharwal (2002) found that "Spanish fluency and Latino ethnicity were not associated with greater awareness of patients' beliefs" (p. 275). It is clear, therefore, that cultural competency is needed by all caregivers.

American Medical Student Association Suggestions

Medical schools and organizations strive to train a new generation of culturally competent physicians and nurses with a variety of solutions and models. One such model from the College of Medicine, Medical University of South Carolina suggests the BELIEF Instrument developed by Dobbie, Medrano, Tysinger, and Olney in 2003 (as cited in Medical University of South Carolina, n.d., p. 2):

B Health Beliefs (What caused your illness/problem?)

E Explanation (Why did it happen at this time?)

L Learn (Help me to understand your belief/opinion.)

I Impact (How is the illness/problem impacting your life?)

E Empathy (This must be very difficult for you.)

F Feelings (How are you feeling about it?)

Another interviewing tool created by Levin, Like, and Gottlieb in 2000 (as cited in Medical University of South Carolina, n.d., p. 5), the ETHNIC model, helps caregivers to find out what alternative care or remedies have been utilized by the patient in order to enhance culturally sensitive communication and avoid drug contradictions:

E Explanation (How do you explain your illness?)

T Treatment (What treatment have you tried?)

H Healers (Have you sought any advice from folk healers?)

N Negotiate (mutually acceptable options)

I (Agree on) Intervention

C Collaboration (with patient, family, and healers)

Flores, Rabke-Verani, Pine, and Sabharwal (2002) guide caregivers to listen, understand, acknowledge different beliefs, and try to negotiate a mutually acceptable treatment plan. Caregivers also have a responsibility to identify cultural values and beliefs that may affect care. Specifically, these beliefs should be accommodated in a nonjudgmental manner both in the initial clinical visit and in the treatment plan. In order to facilitate this, these researchers suggest carefully explaining the etiology of the disease and the rationale for the treatment while suggesting alternatives to any harmful home remedies the patient has been using. In the case of *empacho,* a Latino folk illness, many patients use powders which contain toxic amounts of lead. It is also pointed out that "harmless . . . alternative remedies that can be offered to families . . . include abdominal massage with warm oil and mint tea" (p. 275). Equally important are the language issues involved in patient/caregiver interactions. It is essential to use highly trained interpreters and not rely on family members or a caregiver who has limited linguistic fluency. The reliance upon untrained interpreters has resulted in serious and potentially harmful miscommunication.

Some hospitals are using advances in technology to respond to the shortage of trained interpreters. Mercy Hospital in Miami is using a new interpreting system which enables a doctor to call a translation center at any time and be instantly connected to an interpreter who appears on a video screen. One hundred and fifty languages are available including various dialects of Chinese. Other hospitals are introducing similar systems including sharing interpreters through video conferencing. The results are promising. Physicians and patients can communicate without "playing charades," and it costs significantly less than staff interpreters ("Rx for Communication," 2006, p. 14).

Identifying cultural values, accommodating home remedies or cultural practices, and carefully explaining treatment rationale can go a long way toward alleviating communication problems and building trust between the patient and caregiver. This type of clinical encounter may take a little more time, but will result in better communication, greater patient satisfaction, and less potential for misdiagnosis or harmful drug interaction.

Innovative Programs

Communication within a health care setting could be enhanced by understanding and creating practical community-based programs to lessen major cultural and linguistic challenges faced by health care providers and patients. Many HMOs, nonprofits, and community-based organizations are attempting to solve these problems with new programs and collaborations. Rev. W. Parry, the Executive Director of Fresno Metro Ministry and C. Arambula, the director of Health Care Policies, described a successful joint project called the "Navigator Program" (personal interview, November 21, 2005). The goals of most of these programs are to build cultural competence and gather more information about different healing practices in order to maximize the potential for integration. Due to space limitations, this article will only examine two such programs.

The Navigator Program

One successful solution, the Navigator Program, was developed in the Central Valley of California to help immigrant and nonnative English speakers deal with the complexities of the US health care system. This pilot program was developed jointly by Fresno Metro Ministry, Cesar Chavez Adult School, and Fresno University Medical Center. Barbara Lehman, Vice Principal of Fresno Adult School, explained that the purpose is to help adult school students learn how to "navigate" the US health care system, and then they share their knowledge with others through classroom and community presentations. Students go through a four-month-long program to study health care in a lecture format, visit hospitals and clinics, and attend practical workshops. The goal is to educate these students about the American health care system in order to help them as patients and to empower them and their communities. Lectures and workshops focus on issues such as how to get referrals, how to make appointments, the benefits of showing the doctor all the medications they are taking including home remedies and natural medicines, options if they feel they are being treated unfairly, their rights to an interpreter, and how to secure a qualified interpreter (personal communication, November 29, 2005).

New immigrants often do not realize the many services that are available to them. For example, Lupe, a student in the Navigator program, said she had not been aware that hospitals offered anything other than emergency services. She did not realize they had many clinics, or that services could be offered in your own home. Another student, Ruth, had not been aware of any procedures to complain about discrimination or how to ask for interpreters. Navigator students expressed that they gained self-esteem and learned how to assert themselves when necessary within a health care setting. They felt that despite their lack of fluency in English, they were now much more confident when accessing the health care system and being able to get the treatment or information they needed (personal communication, November 29, 2005).

Cultural Brokering

Another innovative solution to communication breakdowns between health care professionals and patients is *cultural brokering*. Brokers listen for subtle communication breakdown points and misunderstandings and mediate consensus between the parties involved. Marilyn Mochel, director at the Health House Within a MATCH Coalition, has been a nurse and a cultural broker for more than twenty years. She has witnessed the importance of cultural brokering first hand. In one situation that she was called upon to mediate, an eight-month-old Hmong infant with end-stage renal disease was almost taken away by CPS because both sides (the family and the physician) could not relate to each other's perspective and had reached an impasse. The problem was not that the family did not understand English. The problem was that the physician did not comprehend the family's urgent desire for a traditional Hmong healing ceremony. In addition, the family was unaware that at some point, the doctor no longer needs the family's consent if the situation is life-threatening. Marilyn was able to supply "the missing piece" in this dialogue and

help both sides come to a mutual acceptance of the situation and options (personal interview, October 14, 2005).

Mr. Bee Yang, from the Department of Social Work at California State University Fresno, has successfully acted as a broker many times, but he also has been involved in situations where no broker was consulted with tragic consequences. He described a case where a Hmong teenage girl had an emergency appendectomy. However, after the surgery the doctor stated that the problem was in fact a tumor on her fallopian tube. He had removed her tubes and explained she would not be able to have children. The parents who had not agreed to this were shocked and horrified. In addition, they were told she would have to have chemotherapy. The family's understanding of what the doctor told them was that she had six months to live with the chemotherapy and three without. The teenager, thinking she would die anyway, chose not to have chemotherapy. The hospital did not attempt to involve a cultural broker or another member of the community, and sent the case to Child Protective Services (CPS) as child abuse. Child Protective Services was able to get a court order and came to remove the girl from her home. Her parents tried to prevent their daughter from being removed from their home and in the ensuing chaos, both the mother and father were badly hurt by the police while their daughter was strapped screaming to a gurney; this after she had recently had surgery. The local Hmong population was understandably angry about this situation, and protested in the media. As a result of this appalling incident, Hmong community representatives were able to meet with various local officials and negotiate some changes in the way their community was being dealt with by government organizations. This involved education and understanding on both sides. As Mr. Yang pointed out, had a cultural broker been involved, they could have explained that a clan leader should have been called to mediate and a case plan negotiated with the family (personal interview, October 23, 2005).

CONCLUSION

This essay has examined some of the challenges and suggestions for effective communication between biomedical caregivers and patients from diverse cultural and linguistic backgrounds. Cultural competency is an essential part of a mutually successful encounter in a health care setting. Currently, health care professionals are beginning to research, understand, and validate the therapeutic benefits of family and community involvement, spiritual beliefs, and time-honored healing traditions. In light of today's diverse patient population, the medical field needs to explore solutions and innovative approaches to communicate effectively with the increasing number of patients who choose traditional, holistic, and alternative medical approaches to supplement biomedical treatment plans.

For many patients, it is the simple things that are missing from biomedicine. They are looking for caring, supportive, and understanding communication with their health care providers. Perhaps the best way to learn more about patients' cultures is simply by listening to and appreciating their beliefs and values. Dr. Matthew Norton, with Norton Chiropractic Wellness, contends that caregivers should see patients as "this amazing special person" instead of just "a condition" (personal interview, March 23, 2006). When biomedical professionals develop an understanding of the different cultural perspectives of their patients, they are better able to meet their needs. A physician like Dr. S. Wilson meets the needs of his patients by integrating complementary with conventional biomedical treatments at his Michigan practice and states, "Now I have a whole host of other things that I can choose from to treat them" (Oleck, 2007, p. E2). Every encounter with a patient is a valuable opportunity for understanding because both the patient and the caregiver bring different expectations and experiences into the health care setting. In today's multicultural health care environments, when physicians and other caregivers demonstrate sensitivity towards cultural differences and strive to communicate effectively with patients, and when patients take personal responsibility for their health care as they navigate the biomedical system, then the healing process can truly begin.

References

Association of American Medical Colleges. (2004, July 12). Nation's first medical education program focused on Latino culture. Retrieved October 28, 2005, from http://www.aamc.org/newsroom/bulletin/uci/040712.htm

American Medical Student Association. (2005, September 29). Cultural competency in medicine. Retrieved September 28, 2005, from http://www.amsa.org/programs/gpit/cultural.cfm

Arvigo, R., & Epstein, N. (1994). My apprenticeship with a Maya healer. San Francisco: Harper Collins.

Bower, A. B., & Taylor, V. A. (2003, March–April). Increasing intention to comply with pharmaceutical product instructions: An exploratory study investigating the roles of frame and plain language. Journal of Health Communication: International Perspectives, 8(2), 145–156.

Brandeis University, Center for Community Health Research and Action of the Heller School for Social Policy and Management. (2002, April). What a difference an interpreter can make: Health care experiences of uninsured with limited English proficiency. Retrieved January 29, 2007, from http://www.hhs.gov/ocr/lep/InterpreterDifference.pdf

Burke, G. (2005, October 24). Ban sought on child medical interpreters. The Fresno Bee, pp. A1, A16.

Collie, A. J. (2007, January). A Western doctor faces East. Hemispheres. pp. 78–83.

Cohen, R. (2006, September 17). The ethicist: Dr. Deceit. The New York Times, 6, 32.

Fadiman, A. (1997). The spirit catches you and you fall down: A Hmong child, her American doctors, and the collision of two cultures. New York: Farrar, Straus and Giroux.

Flores, G. (2006, April 27). Lost in translation: Language barriers, interpreters, communication, and quality in health care. Lecture delivered at Children's Hospital, Fresno, CA.

Flores, G., Mayo, S., Zuckerman, B., Abreu, M., Medina, L., & Hardt, E., (2003, January). Errors in medical interpretation and their potential clinical consequences in pediatric encounters. Pediatrics, 111(1), 6–14.

Flores, G., Rabke-Verani, J., Pine, W., & Sabharwal, A. (2002). The importance of cultural and linguistic issues in the emergency care of children. Pediatric Emergency Care, 18(4), 271–284.

Galanti, G. (2004). Caring for patients from different cultures (3rd ed.). Philadelphia: University of Pennsylvania Press.

Halderman, L. (2007, February 15). Some doctors don't get paid enough [Letter to the Editor]. The Fresno Bee. p. B9.

Hwang, J. (2004, August). Body and soul. Taiwan Review, pp. 12–17.

Iwamitsu, Y, Shimoda, K., Abe, H., Tani, T., Okawa, M, & Buck, R. (2005). The relation between negative emotional suppression and emotional distress in breast cancer diagnosis and treatment. Health Communication, 18(3), 201–215.

Luckman, J. (2000). Transcultural communication in health care. Albany, NY: Delmar Thomson Learning.

Medical University of South Carolina, College of Medicine. (n.d.). Cultural competency: Communication with patients. Retrieved January 14, 2007, from http://etl2.library.musc.edu/cultural/communication/index.php

McDaniel, E. R., Samovar, L. A., & Porter, R. E. (2006). Understanding intercultural communication: An overview. In L. A. Samovar, R. E. Porter, & E. R. McDaniel (Eds.), *Intercultural communication: A reader* (pp. 6–16). Belmont, CA: Thomson Wadsworth.

Oleck, C. (2007, February 17). Cutting-edge care. *The Fresno Bee*, pp. E1–E2.

Porter, R. (2002). *Blood and guts: A short history of medicine.* New York: W.W. Norton & Company.

Ryan, S. (2005, December 15). Introduction to the community: Susan Ryan, CEO, Kaiser Permanente; Lecture delivered at Community Health Care Roundtable at the Trinity Lutheran Church, Fresno, CA.

Rx for Communication (2006, November 6). *Newsweek, 14.*

Salak, K. (2006, March). Peru: Hell and back. *National Geographic Adventure.* Retrieved January 27, 2007, from http://www.nationalgeographic.com/adventure/0603/features/peru.html

Smedley, B. D., Stith, A. Y., & Nelson, A. R. (Eds.). (2003). *Unequal treatment: Confronting racial and ethnic disparities in health care.* Washington DC: The National Academies Press.

Stein, R. (2004, May 28). Alternative remedies gaining popularity: Majority in U.S. try some form, survey finds. *Washington Post, A01.*

World Health Organization. (1998). *Health promotion glossary.* Retrieved January 24, 2006, from http://www.who.int/hpr/NPH/docs/hp_glossary_en.pdf

Concepts and Questions

1. What are the three major belief systems relating to illness and healing?
2. What assumptions underlie these systems?
3. What do Begley and Ockey mean when they refer to culturally competent medicine?
4. What is the relationship between cultural values and the various belief systems about illness and healing?
5. Why is it important for biomedical caregivers to understand and respect traditional and holistic medical processes?
6. How does patient health literacy relate to effective medical treatment?
7. What problems do linguistic challenges present in the treatment of patients who do not speak or are not fluent in English?
8. Why do Begley and Ockey believe it is necessary to increase the cultural diversity of health care professionals?
9. In what ways might a health care provider's cultural background influence their interactions with patients from other cultures?
10. How does *cultural brokering* help break down communication barriers between health care professionals and patients from other cultures?

Three Narratives of Spiritual Healing

KAREN RASMUSSEN

JENNIFER ASENAS

"Religion true to its name," explains Catherine Keller "activates connection. It 'ties together,' binding up the wounds of breaking worlds. It is the bridging, bonding process at the heart of things" (47). Coping with ruptures is a constant challenge in a postmodern world marked by alienation and fragmentation (Corbin 75). This kind of coping is critical for those who straddle cultures as they live in the complexity and ambiguity of liminal spaces, in what Gloria Anzaldua, among others, calls the "borderlands." As they negotiate those spaces, individuals may succumb to fragmentation and alienation, having "so internalized the borderland conflict" so as to feel like they are "zero, nothing, no one" (Anzaldua, *Borderlands* 63). Alternatively they may embrace the richness of diversity (Anzaldua, "La Pieta" 205). This life "on the hyphen," as one of our students phrased it, requires that people merge differences while dealing with contradictions. Such an existence would appear to involve the activating of connection Keller attributes to religion, or what we label spirituality.

This essay is a study of the ways in which three culturally diverse novelists depict the process of "binding up the wounds of breaking worlds." We examine texts by women from Native American, African American, and Mexican American backgrounds, all of which feature spiritual remediation as an antidote to individual and cultural problems. The first, *Ceremony* by Leslie Marmon Silko, describes the communal healing achieved through the journey of a veteran of World War II. The second, Toni Morrison's

This original essay appears here in print for the first time. All rights reserved. Permission to reprint must be obtained from the authors and the publisher. Dr. Karen Rasmussen teaches in the Department of Communication Studies at California State University, Long Beach. Dr. Jennifer Asenas teaches in the Department of Communication Arts and Sciences at California State University, Chico.

Beloved, describes the destructiveness of division and its resolution through communal rites. The third, *So Far From God* by Ana Castillo, dramatizes the countering of patriarchal and capitalistic repression through spiritual action. The following pages discuss each work's movement from the *trauma* of rupture through its *transformation* to achieve a constructive *telos* or end.

THE NARRATIVES

Ceremony

Set in and around the Laguna Pueblo of post–World War II New Mexico, Silko's *Ceremony* embodies an exigency born of marginalization and destruction as it tells the tale of Tayo, a veteran returning from war in the Pacific. Shunned because of his half-breed status, battered by war and the forces of assimilation, he suffers from an illness resistant to Western medicine. After he gets partial relief from a Laguna shaman, he turns to a Navajo healer who guides him through a ceremony which brings him in contact with supernatural human and animal helpers. At novel's end he enters his people's sacred kiva to share what he has learned since the insights which emerge from his recovery are vital to both personal and cultural survival. The narrative that is *Ceremony,* then, defines a *trauma* rooted in destruction and marginalization for which it enacts a spiritual *transformation* through an adaptive ceremony that has the potential to promote the *telos* of survival for both Tayo and his people.

The novel details *trauma* resulting from the intersection of Native with Eurocentric cultures. Two themes are illustrative. First, *Ceremony* highlights conditions endured by those who end up in towns like Gallup, New Mexico. Made of "old tin, cardboard, and scrap wood," their homes are shabby shelters "scattered along the banks of the river" (108).[1] People "walk like survivors, with dull, vacant eyes" (115), wearing "torn old jackets" as they crouch "outside bars like cold flies stuck to the wall" (107), they work unstable jobs since "[r]eservation people . . . get laid off because" they don't "ask any questions" (115).

Second, *Ceremony* foregrounds rape of the environment and of native cultures. In the "twenties and thirties the loggers . . . cut great clearings on the plateau slopes" while their hunters killed "ten or fifteen deer each week and fifty wild turkeys in one month" (186). At New Mexico's Jackpile uranium mine, Whites took "beautiful rocks from deep within earth, . . . realizing destruction on a scale only *they* could have dreamed" (246). Silko highlights the concomitant frustration of a people who "wake up every morning of their lives to see the land which was stolen," persons forced to "watch, unable to save . . . any of the things that [are] so important to them" (126, 203). Not surprisingly, the novel boasts an array of characters beset by the "shame" and "blame that maintain the cycles of hatred and violence through the dialectic of victim and victimizer" (Arnold 77).

Tayo and *Ceremony*'s other veterans are potential conduits for the evils of assimilation which generate loss of self, culture, and voice. After he returned from the war he felt as if he were "white smoke . . . [which] had no consciousness of itself" because he "inhabited a gray winter fog on a distant elk mountain where hunters are lost indefinitely" (14, 15). Torn between old and new, he questions traditional ways (Cutchins 80). At times he sees Indian life as "pitiful and small" (127) and thus wonders "what good Indian ceremonies" could do for a "sickness" "which comes from" "wars," "bombs," and "lies" (132). And yet an upbringing rooted in reverence for his people's ways has given him a feel for ritual. And so, he understands that his cure must be "found only in something great and inclusive of everything" (125–126).

Other veterans, having abandoned their culture, exist in a world of envy, frustration, and shame as they careen from disappointment to disappointment (32, 204). They drink away "[c]ash from disability checks earned with shrapnel in the neck at Wake Island" as they sit in bars, telling stories of White women who desired them (40). Angry and confused, they experience a "paralyzing and dispiriting displacement and alienation" (Orr 74) created by a "cultural dissociation that divides oppressed people among themselves" (Lincoln 249; Cederstrom 293).

The cause of this dissolution is a witchery Silko says is a "metaphor" for the "counterforce" of "destruction and death" (Katz 193). The novel's witches want Native Americans to attribute all evil to Whites and thus "be ignorant and helpless as [they] . . . watch [their] our own destruction." Indigenous peoples can, however, "deal with White people . . . because . . . it was Indian witchery that made" Caucasians in the first place (132). *Ceremony* describes their genesis as occurring during "a witches' conference" when participants "started showing off" until "there was only one" left. This witch "presented a story" of the coming of a people with skin "like the belly of a fish" for whom the "world is a dead thing." Because such beings fear everything, even themselves, they "kill the things they fear" until they "turn on each other" (134–138). Hence, the novel argues that both cultures are victims of a force which spawns "drought, barrenness, and violent death" (129).

The antidote to this trauma is *transformation* through a spiritual ceremony directed by Navaho healer Betonie and lived by Tayo. When neither Western medicine nor a Laguna ceremony cures Tayo, his grandmother sends him to Betonie who also is of mixed race. The rite invoked is both adaptive and rooted in tradition. *Ceremony* thus employs a *mythos* in which Tayo encounters mystical helpers who shape his quest to defeat witchery. This ritual spans four nights: on the first he gains knowledge that enables him to persevere; during the second and third he experiences a restoration of balance and wholeness through an erasure of boundaries related to space and time; thus prepared, on the fourth he confronts evil as the ceremony concludes.

On the first night Tayo journeys to Betonie's hogan on a hill overlooking Gallup. He learns of three principles integral to the ceremony in which he will participate. First, the coming of Euroamericans necessitated adaptation to keep rituals "strong" because "elements in . . . [the] world began to shift." This adjusting, however, is not new, because "long ago . . . the changing began, if only in . . . the different voices . . . singing the chants" (126). Silko thus intimates that change is necessary to "revitalize Native American culture" (Cutchins 83). Second, to adapt one must negotiate transitions. Since "balances and harmonies" always are "shifting," the "becoming must be cared for closely." Third, because witchery wants Indians to believe that "all evil resides with White people" (130), thereby remaining impotent in clinging to antiquated ceremonies (126), Native peoples must take responsibility for reinventing those rites if they wish to best evil.

On the second night Tayo experiences the Navajo Ghostway, a ritual using prayer sticks, a dark flint to cut the scalp, prayers, and a sand painting of four mountains[2] accompanied by hoops through which the initiate crawls (141–142). The rite incorporates a prayer which details a person's re-union with self, "hogan," "homeland," "metaphysical world," "relatives[,] and the tribe" (Swan 321). Tayo emerges cleansed but not cured, for "it wasn't finished. . . . All kinds of evil were still on him" (144). Again, Betonie is his guide: he draws in the dirt, telling Tayo to "remember these stars. . . . I've seen them and I've seen the spotted cattle; I've seen a mountain and I've seen a woman" (152).

On the third,[3] Tayo, with the aid of mythic animals and humans, retrieves a herd of spotted cattle, creatures valuable to his people because they can withstand drought. Symbolic of a "hybridization" that "endures and survives" by honoring its traditions while adapting to change (Blumenthal ¶ 15, 24), the cattle represent what Tayo must become. When he travels to Mt. Taylor he meets Te'sh, a woman whose name links her to the deity Kochinako (Herzog 31), with whom he experiences a bonding with a feminine life force (Shaddock 115; Allen 127) that enables him to transcend his past without abandoning his roots (Rand 24). Because this stage of the ceremony enacts cultural myth, "planes of time . . . intersect . . . so that Tayo's . . . biotime merges with the single consciousness of his . . . people to become a facet of mythic time" (Swan 322).

Having transcended space and time, Tayo now is ready to face evil on the fourth night of the ceremony. Warned by Te'sh that the witches want to shape his story so they once more can be "excited" by "the violence" (231–232), he goes to the uranium mine where the ceremony is to be completed. There he finds fellow veterans who have become "[t]he destroyers, . . . [witches bent on creating] drought to sear the land, to kill the livestock, to stunt the corn plants, [thereby] . . . leaving the people more and more vulnerable to the lies" (249). He resists intervening as they torture one of their comrades, thus thwarting a witchery that wants him to bow to its power by enacting violence (253). This refusal not only "foils" the destroyers, it also lets his former friend's death "become an exorcism, an undoing of Witchery" (Slowik 116).

The *telos* of Tayo's journey is *survival*, a survival based on the "integration and wholeness" characteristic of change in which the "ordinary and mundane" intertwine "with the mysteries of living" (Morris 95). Accepting the help of two healers as well as mythical beings, he transcends place and time, an experience which enables him to shun violence to thwart evil. At novel's end he participates in three events that signal his renewal.

First, Ts'eh had charged him with transplanting a delicate plant so that it might prosper. After his victory Tayo believes himself worthy to "gather the seeds for her and plant them" so that the "plants would grow, . . . , strong and translucent as the stars" (254). This act synthesizes the need for change and the transcendence of boundaries he has experienced during the ceremony (Cotelli 180). Second, as he leaves the mine he dreams "*with his eyes open* that he . . . [is] wrapped in a blanket in the back of "his deceased uncle's wagon as relatives from his past take him "home" (254). This merger of dream and reality affirms transcendence of time and signals union with his people. Third, despite his mixed-race status, he enters the sacred kiva to tell his story, after which he is initiated into the medicine society (256–257). Thus he "reintegrate[s] . . . White and Indian," "mind and body, vision and reality." This merger coupled with his newfound acceptance affirms his ability to "negotiate dual worlds and epistemologies" (Arnold 74, 77). *Ceremony's* closing poetry pronounces witchery "dead *for now*" (261, emphasis added). Its last page reads "Sunrise,/ accept this offering,/ Sunrise" (262).

Beloved

Dedicated to the "Sixty Million and more Africans" who died in the Middle Passage and subsequent slavery, *Beloved* opens after the Civil War as Sethe and her daughter Denver cope with living in a home haunted by the ghost of Sethe's murdered child. Sethe and her four children come to Cincinnati to live with her mother-in-law, Baby Suggs. The joy Sethe experiences ends tragically: after the family invites neighbors to a celebration those persons deem excessive, agents of Sethe's former master surprise them because a displeased community gives no warning. Loathe to return to slavery, Sethe, who tries to kill her children and herself, manages to cut the throat of one daughter.[4] The child's death thus is the result of both slavery's violence and communal division.

Unable to let go of the past, too proud to ask for help, Sethe lives in isolation, an alienation augmented by the loss of her mother-in-law, sons, and lover, Paul D. Spirit broken, she has little strength to resist the torment of the strange woman called Beloved, the incarnation of her murdered child who harasses her and those she loves. *Beloved* offers readers a haunting experience that brings to the fore both issues crying to be addressed and a communal vision for the future. It does so by presenting the *trauma* of alienation and fragmentation that has its roots in the Middle Passage, resolving (at least temporarily) that trauma through a *transformative* spiritual healing which has the potential to lead to the *telos* of a communal healing founded on balance and harmony.

The work articulates the individual physical and psychic *trauma* of slavery. Each member of the Black community carries memories of physical, sexual, emotional, and spiritual abuse. Sethe, for example, was violated by a group of White men who compounded the indignity of their assault by robbing her breasts of their milk. Her lover Paul D talks of burying himself in "slop" and "jumping" into wells to avoid . . . raiders, patrollers, . . . posses and merrymakers" (70). Ella, a member of the community to which Sethe flees, was "shared" by a man and his son as a young girl. Not surprisingly, most try "to remember as close to nothing as . . . [is] safe" (6). However, they have little refuge from their collective past.

The novel's dedication "summons . . . those . . . still . . . enslaved by a past that will not die" (Marks 99). The collective legacy of the middle passage and plantation life, a heritage in which moral and social structures are out of balance, is central to the novel's conflict. When Sethe joins her children and mother-in-law, Baby Suggs, they hold a celebration that begins small but blossoms into a feast for their neighbors. The community, however, resents their generosity: "Too much, they thought. Where does she get it all" (144–145)? The next day they sit by when Sethe's master arrives to reclaim his property and then take further umbrage as she refuses to show shame when arrested, tried, jailed, and eventually released. Later, they react to Baby Suggs's death by burying a woman who had devoted all of her "freed life to harmony . . . amid a regular dance of pride, fear, condemnation and spite" coupled with the hope that Sethe would "come on difficult times" because they resent her "self-sufficiency" (179). Slavery thus has weakened the moral fiber of the community by divisive envy. Folklorists such as Biebuyck suggest that community, harmony, and restraint are common to most African cultures (Rummell 4) while other thinkers view interconnectedness as a hallmark of an African cosmology (Ryan 268). Both positions suggest that balance between the individual and the community, as well as between the living and the deceased, is central to the group's survival. The novel thus dramatizes what happens when African American communities abandon their "traditional values in favor of . . . [competitiveness characteristic] of the dominant culture" (Hinson 148).

The mysterious magic of Beloved's appearance, both as a ghost and later as a flesh-and-blood woman, calls into being the angst of a fragmented community traumatized by an unavoidable past. As ghost, she is a "spiteful," "venem[ous]" force who "shatters mirrors, puts handprints in cakes, and overturns kettles" (4). As woman she speaks the travesty of the Middle Passage. She appears inexplicably one afternoon as Sethe, Paul D, and Denver return from an outing. Taken into their family, she explains to Denver why she calls herself Beloved:

> "In the dark my name is Beloved. . . . [It's] dark. I'm small in that place. I'm like this here." She raised her head off the bed, lay down her side and curled up, . . . curled tighter. . . . "[It was] hot. Nothing to breathe down there and no room to move in. . . . A lot of people down there. Some is dead. . . . I don't know the names" (79).

Later she tells the story a second time, saying in part,

> "she took my face away . . . my dead man is not floating here his teeth are down there where the blue is and the grass so is the face I want . . . her face is mine she is not smiling . . . I am gone now I am her face my own face has left me" (223–224).

Revealing that "Sethe is the face" (225), Beloved merges the agony of separation during the Middle Passage with the pain of separation from her mother. The fragmented form of her monologue symbolizes the "isolation, chaos, and disunity" experienced on slave ships (Mbalia 101). Hence, as Beloved articulates the effects of slavery, she simultaneously presents the pain of the silence that plagues the Black community.

Redress through spiritual *transformation* occurs as two different agents stem the cycle of oppression and violence. The first is Baby Suggs, an "unchurched preacher. . . who . . . opened her great heart to those who could use it. . . . Uncalled, unrobed, unanointed, she let . . . [it] beat in their presence" (92). Baby Suggs's affirmation of self-love is a response to "self-hatred and social and spiritual death." By helping her people connect "the dismembered/unremembered parts of themselves, . . . [she] enacts a literal remembering of the dismembered African body." She thus projects "an ethos of inter-connectedness common to Afro Christianity" which "engenders an enabling vision of Black women's spiritual and sociopolitical leadership" (Ryan 281, 268).

After she dies, Baby Suggs's spirit helps Denver cope with the ravages wrought by the presence of Beloved. In quick succession, the strange but compelling woman has engrossed Denver, seduced Paul D, and almost destroyed Sethe. Denver, however, is able to act because Baby Suggs's vision inspires in her a "creative/righteous agency . . . which promote[s] healing, survival, growth" (Ryan 280). Goaded by her grandmother's spirit-visit, Denver gives voice to the pain she and her mother have been hiding.

Her story reaches Ella, a community leader who had turned her back on Sethe but goes into action when she hears of Beloved's antics. Ella reveals the importance of equilibrium between the living and the dead and an African/American spirituality. To reestablish balance requires communal action. The disharmony bred by "rampant violence" requires expulsion through "a community-sanctioned" "sacrifice . . . that reenacts the original act of violence" (Hinson 149). Hence, reestablishing balance and connection demands the expulsion of Beloved.

The second spiritual agent, then, is a group composed of Ella and thirty other women who converge on Sethe's home. They carry an array of symbols, both African and Christian, whatever "they believed would work. . . . They just started out, . . . and came together at the agreed upon time" (270–271). Their symbols reconnect them to their past as they simultaneously "use Christianity as a vehicle for their own empowerment" (Ryan 271). When they arrive at Sethe's home, they remember their envious response that fateful day so long ago. Dropping to their knees, they pray, "Yes, yes, yes, oh yes. Hear me. Hear me. Do it, maker, do it. Yes" (272). Ella hollers and the women join her to cast out the hateful spirit of Beloved. They then remember Baby Sugg's message of love, thereby integrating it into the community's "collective soul" so as to effect their own freedom. Their awareness and actions enable the community to discover "the power to rename itself, to make good its own debt, and to know itself as truly beloved" (Marks 102). They thus embrace a spirituality that insists on an "alternative perspective which grants acceptance of everyone who wants to invoke the spirit of freedom" (Daniels 5).

The exorcism which synthesizes African and Christian principles achieves a communal *telos* grounded in balance and harmony.[5] The "figure of Beloved is the difference between what ought to be saved . . . and what needs to be discarded, the limit between what can and cannot be known" (Marks 101). Slowly order returns. Denver begins her schooling, Paul D returns to Sethe, and the memory of Beloved slowly fades as she becomes "[d]isremembered and unaccounted for" (289). Having acknowledged the pain of the Middle Passage and the trauma of slavery, the community now can mend itself.

How well such healing will take hold, however, is far from certain. At novel's end, Paul D has returned to Sethe to explore the possibility of their making a life together:

> "Sethe," he says, "me and you, we got more yesterday than anybody. We need some kind of tomorrow." He leans over and takes her hand. With the other he touches her face. "You your best thing, Sethe. You are." His holding fingers are holding hers. "Me? Me?" (288).

Sethe's final questions bespeak a tentative hope that permeates Morrison's writing even as she reveals darkness and oppression, for they imply that the communal magic which drove out Beloved may bear fruit. The work's two final pages repeat the idea that the tale of Beloved "is not a story to pass on" three times (289–290). Holloway argues the repetition intimates that "this was not a story to die . . . [because] Morrision revisions 'Pass on,' inverting it to mean go on through, . . . continue, . . . tell. . . . [She] has 'passed on' this story in defiance of those who would diminish the experience she voices back into presence" (517, 521). Hence, the promise of the hope expressed by Sethe's queries is contingent on a remembrance founded on interrogation of the past followed by a passing on that embraces a painful but healing knowing.

So Far From God

Ana Castillo's *So Far From God* (SFFG) presents the lives of a family of women—mother Sofi and her four daughters Fe, Esperanza, Caridad, and La Loca Santa, the crazy saint whose "death" and "resurrection" open a work marked by parody and a pastiche of genres (Perez 62). The novel's males are weak and/or obstructionist: an irresponsible father who gambles, lovers who betray their women, and a priest insensitive to his parishioners' needs. Set in rural New Mexico during the first Iraq war, SFFG foregrounds both oppression and its spiritual remediation. Its story is a narrative moving from the *trauma* of patriarchal and capitalistic repression through *transformation* courtesy of various kinds of spirituality to the *telos* of emancipation.

The novel highlights the *trauma* perpetrated by imperialism, patriarchy, and capitalist greed. The saga of Tome, New Mexico, is the history of a people who "go on living poor and forgotten" because outsiders had taken over their land (159). The stories of the work's major characters foreground specific kinds of repression. Daughter Fe's tale, for example, indicts a materialism that destroys people and land alike. Ashamed of her family because she views them as "self-defeating and unambitious" (28), Fe shares an apartment with an Anglo with whom she works. Her life implodes when she gets a "dear *Juana*" letter from her fiancé explaining that he's not ready to get married (30). A devastated Fe goes into a year-long scream, a ruckus that permeates Sofi's house except when the shattered woman falls asleep. Healed a year later by the prayers of sister Loca, she takes a job with Acme International so she and her new husband can afford luxuries essential to the American Dream (171). Fe's employer is a munitions manufacturer who dumps toxic waste so that, as the novel says, New Mexico the "Land of Enchantment" becomes a "Land of Entrapment" littered with dead animals and populated by people stricken and dying (174). Succumbing to cancer, Fe dies painfully, for she has made a compact with a devil of capitalism, an organization that victimizes humans and the earth without conscience.

Sister Caridad represents ravaged indigenous peoples. Devastated by her own failed romance, she parties recklessly, coming home late one night "as mangled as a stray cat, having been left for dead by the side of the road" (32). She returns from the hospital hopelessly maimed to be healed miraculously by Loca's prayers. Since she refuses to describe the incident, her attacker remains a mystery to all but Loca and a local *curandera*,[6] with whom she communicates through dreams that paint her victimizer as an evil presence, a thing "made of sharp metal and splintered wood, of limestone, gold, and brittle parchment . . . [that] held the weight of a continent and was indelible as ink. . . . It . . . was darker than the dark night, and mostly . . . it was pure force" (77). Caridad's victimization thus symbolizes the impact of the conquest: metal, wood, limestone, and gold represent rape of the environment; parchment symbolizes treaties; indelibility, strength, and force reference colonization's devastating power.

Sofi's story illuminates the sins of patriarchy. The novel opens with the apparent death of her youngest daughter, Loca, followed by a funeral directed by a priest who halts the community's procession to reprimand Sofi because he considers her expression of grief excessive. When the child miraculously awakens and then flies to the top of the Church, his immediate response is to wonder whether she is "the devil's messenger or a winged angel" (22), clearly favoring the former. Castillo thus highlights an androcentric religiosity fearful of the feminine. The focus of Sofi's tale, however, is legal and familial patriarchy. After she marries the charismatic Domingo, he sells her jewelry and the land the couple got from her family as a wedding present to pay gambling debts (105). Later he disappears, leaving her to run the family's meat business. When he returns, they "pick up as husband and wife" (109). Sofi soon discovers that their "home," a house that "belonged to *her*, . . . was being transferred over to a "judge" collecting on one of Domingo's illegal bets (215) after which she kicks him out for good. Her story, then, is that of a woman who learns the hard way about legal and social male privilege.[7]

The spiritual forces of *transformation* in SFFG work on communal and individual levels to counter repression. Those forces constitute a woman-centered spirituality which contrasts sharply with the practices of the community's priest and Francisco el Penitente,

a young man who follows the way of the Penitente Brotherhood. Father Jerome's inability to meet the needs of his community is evident in his concern for funeral decorum rather than the needs of his parishioners, in his inability to connect with members of Sofi's family, and in his absence from a significant Good Friday rite (see below). His performance of faith is a "rarefied practice, divorced form the material, emotional and social world around him" (Delgallido 894). Francisco el Penitente is a *santera*, a carver of *bultos*[8] which honor the saints. Penitente societies arose in the vacuum created by a scarcity of Catholic priests in the Southwest, a vacuum exacerbated when the Church replaced Spanish clergy with their French and Anglo counterparts. His actions verge on the fanatic: working in "silence" (102), he prays as if to remove himself from the world; he denies himself comfort and pleasure; he sees his attraction to Caridad as sinful[9] (191). As a representative of an alternative to Father Jerome's conventional Catholicism, he also lives in the rarefied realm of an abstract religiosity dedicated to the hereafter, not to the exigencies of mundane living.

SFFG's counterpoint is a woman-centered, multifaceted, sometimes contradictory, set of practices centered in the home that address everyday needs. The *curandera* Dona Felicia, for example, embraces beliefs and rites based in Catholicism and indigenous cosmologies. She effects "a compromise with the religion of her people" by viewing "her god not only as Lord but as a guiding light" (60). This accommodation simultaneously reflects the "bits and pieces of the souls and knowledge of the wise teachers she [has] met" (60). She makes a Lenten pilgrimage to Chimayo, a site at which "divergent populations" define "a space for themselves" (Delgallido 896). Called New Mexico's Lourdes, its spelling, Tsimayo/Chimayo, has roots in Spanish and native languages (Delgallido 896); similarly, its holiness stems from its association with a statue of the "Black Christ" and with the "healing powers of the sacred earth" (73), the latter long venerated by native peoples of the area.

After being healed by Loca's prayers, Caridad becomes Dona Felecia's apprentice. In lieu of going to mass, she practices yoga, greeting "each day" "with a salute to the sun" (66). Learning to use "herbs, decoctions, and massages," Caridad adopts a life marked by "a rhythm of scented baths, tea remedies, rubdowns, and general good feeling" that also involves rituals centered around a home altar adorned with pictures of "saints" and "photographs of her loved ones" (63), thus retaining remnants of her Catholic upbringing. She falls in love with a woman from the Sky City of Acoma with whom she jumps from the Pueblo's cliffs to evade a stalker. As they leap, "the spirit deity Tsichtinako [calls] loudly . . ., guiding [them] . . . down deep within the soft moist dark earth where . . . [they] would . . . live forever" (211). Tsichtinako is Thought Woman, a female spirit who permeates everything, a "true creatrix" who is "thought itself" (Allen 14). This commingling of practices and beliefs is characteristic of SFFG's female characters whose spirituality resides in the home and links them to the earth as it informs their lives.

Such spirituality is potent for it supports a *telos* of emancipation which also extends to the community as a whole, as the following examples demonstrate. In the first Loca, whose powers have touched her family and who speaks regularly with female spirits, chooses to go out into the world for the first time since childhood. She lends her presence to a Good Friday Procession decked in garb symbolic of *La Virgen de Guadalupe*:

> Jesus bore His cross and a man declared that most of the Native and hispano families . . . were living below the poverty level. . . . Jesus fell, and people . . . were dying from toxic exposure in factories. . . . Jesus fell a third time [and the] air was contaminated by the pollutants coming from the factories. . . . Ayyy! Jesus died on the cross. . . . [A]nd at the hour that Jesus was laid in His tomb the sun set and . . . [t]he crow began to disperse slowly and quietly. . . . No, no one had never seen a procession like that one before (241–244).

Inexplicably stricken by AIDS, Loca dies shortly thereafter, comforted by the spirit of the Blue Nun, *aka* Sister Maria Jesus Agneda, who "bi-located" during the Inquisition to minister to Native Americans ("Blue Nun", ¶ 3).[10] As a healer who communes with female spirits and a representation of the Mexican Madonna, Loca participates in the healing power of a collective articulation of pain, thus adapting a key Catholic ritual to communal exigencies.

In the second, Sofi, who has led her community in fighting economic depression by founding cooperatives specializing in sheep-grazing, wool-weaving, and the raising of organic meat and vegetables (148), also becomes the founder of M.O.M.A.S., Mothers of Martyrs and Saints (246–247),[11] an ironic, matriarchal alternative to patriarchal Catholicism. "Saints" like Loca have to have the "potential of performing miracles while martyrs," persons sacrificed on the twin alters of capitalism and patriarchy such as Fe, are "simply revered and considered emissaries to the *santos*" (248). The Mothers hold conferences bigger than "the World Series and even the Olympics" (249) at which their "ectoplasmic" (248) children bring "all kinds of news and advice" (251) that gets passed on to appropriate agencies in support of the public good. Although M.O.M.A.S. is an ironic parody, it harkens to a time prior to the Church's "suppression of communal and female voices in the conferring of sainthood" (Sauer 72). By founding it, Sofi works "through and with the customs and culture she inherited" (Manniquez 47) in a way that reaffirms the importance of both community and the feminine. This weaving of a multifaceted, woman-centered spirituality into the fabric of a struggling community creates the possibility for the collective emancipation so crucial to individual freedom.

THE SPIRITUALITIES

Ceremony, *Beloved*, and *So Far From God* afford spiritual redress for traumas caused by racism, capitalism, and patriarchy. Those traumas activate a "major disruption" of "experience in nurturing and loving and *being*" (Holloway 516). "Instead of "surrendering to historical stasis," the writings of Silko, Morrison, and Castillo create a "gateway to a possible rebirth of imagination and sensibility" (Feng 150). Each novel enacts its form of spiritual healing using a unique communicative strategy.

The spirituality that promotes survival in *Ceremony* is the product of the *evolution* of old rites so as to "experience a web of . . . relationships" that "constantly" are "changing" (Morris 96). That both Tayo and Betonie are of mixed race is significant because that status reflects the cultural intersections faced by their peoples. Betonie can guide Tayo through the ceremony because he straddles both worlds. Hence, the principle that the ceremonies must evolve speaks to the need for a cultural revision that honors cultural roots and adapts to a world continually made new. Therefore, the spiritual evolution in *Ceremony* involves a communicative strategy Fisher labels *affirmation*, a move which yields a new beginning because it infuses "life into an idea or an identity" (132). The novel's intimation that collective "adaptation" through openness to ever-changing ceremonies is "necessary for [the] survival" of Tayo and his people grounds a communal, dynamic spirituality even as it affirms unity in difference (Blaeser 23).

To restore harmony and balance disrupted by the Middle Passage and slavery, Baby Suggs and other women in *Beloved* heal their community through a *synthesis* of the African and Eurocentric that creates an Africanized Christianity that integrates the Christian with Black cosmology as expressed through the cultural lore Morrison learned from her sisters and foremothers (Rummell 1). The novel thus uses the communicative strategy of *adaptation* in which, by making "the Gospel" their own (Akingela 263), Black people fused a West African religious heritage with a reading of Christianity consistent with that tradition, thus adjusting the Eurocentric to the African. Baby Suggs preaches a message of love with African and Christian roots; the women who exorcise Beloved take with them an assortment of symbols grounded in both orientations. Such adaptation merges aesthetics, form, and ethics (Phelan 91). Thus Morrison explains that the community's embrace of a creolized Christianity reclaims the "discredited knowledge" of "peoples of African American descent" (Feng 150).

Emancipation in *So Far From God* is the product of a *hybrid* spirituality that activates "connection between the spiritual and the material, and between the personal and the public." It involves an "acceptance of Christianity and native beliefs" that "allows for the incorporation of diverse ways of knowing." Hybridity is not synthesis because rather than moving toward a unified system, it involves the "coexistence" of diverse beliefs and practices as expressed through SFFG's array of characters (Delgallido 889–890). Dona Felecia, Caridad, Loca, and Sofi all embrace a logic of both/and as they draw on traditions that may conflict with each other. Hence, they employ *appropriation* to enact hybridity as they sample elements from Catholicism and native cosmologies, claiming the stories of others to "further" their "own ends" (Shugart 211). Donia Felecia mines the resources of the land *and* embraces Catholic rites; Caridad participates in native rituals even as she maintains a home altar before responding to the call of Thought Woman; Sofi and Loca make similar moves. Thus the novel advances a collectivity in which people draw on what's available, thereby accessing a pastiche of practices and beliefs as potential solutions to individual and communal problems.

The three novels thus employ forms of communication that relate to "reality in both subject matter and purpose," address the concerns of the "actual world of everyday experience," and provide a "guide to belief and action" (Fisher 132). The description of trauma differs in each novel and, therefore, requires a unique transformation and *telos*. This approach to spiritual regeneration resembles casuistic logic. Casuistry is a type of inquiry that merges practical reasoning with material experience. It demands a case-by-case application of moral precepts rather than a generic use of absolute principles. It is the "practical resolution of particular moral perplexities, or 'cases of conscience'" (Jonsen and Toulmin 13). By rejecting reductive Western logics that offer no solace for the oppressed, these novels "establish connective consciousness in both space and time as they illuminate the nature of relationships that comprise the web of life, linking past, present, and future in a flow of ethical action" (Morris 98). By treating complex situations as unique cases, a casuistic approach "has the advantage of casting ethics in pragmatic, concrete terms" (Miller 10). In other words, these novels remedy individual and cultural problems as well as offer modes of ethical action by grounding spiritual knowledge in life as it is actually lived.

Hence each novel can function as a case study in casuistic spirituality. *Ceremony, Beloved,* and *So Far From God* advance versions of the spiritual grounded in characters' lived experiences that foster ethical actions supportive of individual and community. In each "'spiritual isolation' is an oxymoronic construction" (Blaeser 18). Evolution which affirms continual recreation of ceremonies, synthesis which adapts the Christian and African in a dynamic system of action and belief, and hybridity which appropriates the riches of diverse traditions all speak to the complexities and contradictions of borderland living. The works of Leslie Marmon Silk, Toni Morrison, and Ana Castillo provide their readers with equipment for living (Burke 293). Through their characters the novels work through unspeakable traumas by transforming those *personae* and their communities through spiritualities that acknowledge and address multiple and contradictory identities situated within material, lived reality. Their work imagines and, therefore, makes possible life-affirming traditions that celebrate difference through acceptance.

Notes

1. References to quotations from the three novels will appear inserted parenthetically into the text of this essay.
2. The mountains are a white, blue, yellow, and dark range that represents Mt. Taylor, an especially sacred formation associated with Spider/Thought/Yellow Woman.
3. Silko's text does not designate a specific night as *the* third of the ceremony, but Swan speculates that it's "the moonlight night when he encounters the mountain lion, scared animal of cardinal *North,* while chasing the spotted cattle foretold in Betonie's prophecy" (322).
4. The work has its genesis in a newspaper account of a woman who responded to the Fugitive Slave Act by killing her daughter (Lee 571; Rushdy 572–574; Holloway 13).
5. Morrison has continually argued that her writing represents "how characters and things function in the Black cosmology" (McKay 425). The novel also incorporates Christianity, however in a revised form. There are a number of Biblical passages that Morrison revisions. Peggy Ochoa argues that Beloved is an allegorical revision of the Song of Solomon (24).
6. A *curandera* is a female healer.
7. Sofi's fourth daughter Esperanza graduates from the University of New Mexico at Albuquerque to become a journalist. To make a final break from her boyfriend Ruben, she goes to Washington to be sent to cover the war in Iraq where she dies. Her story highlights the limitations of romantic, religious, and political patriarchy.
8. Religious statues generally made of wood.
9. The relationship between El Franky and Caridad parallels that between St. Francis and St. Clare. After St. Francis's conversion to Christianity, he adopted a life of poverty. Upon hearing him preach, St. Clare left her home to become a nun. She also divested herself of worldly goods ("St Francis," ¶ 8; St. Clare, ¶ 3). Clare was a close confidant of St. Francis in life; and in death, she, like Caridad, was buried deep beneath the earth. El Franky's attraction to Caridad was platonic rather than sexual, and therefore parallel to the relationship between the two saints.
10. Sister Maria Jesus Agreda, aka the Blue Nun, dreamt that she traveled frequently to faraway lands and preached the word of God to the natives. Such claims were especially dangerous during the Spanish Inquisition. Spanish explorers unexpectedly came to her aid during her trial for witchcraft. They reported that they had met Native American tribes in New Mexico, Arizona, and Texas who were already Christians and reported being visited by a "white skinned 'Blue Lady' who appeared to many, drifting in a blue haze while she preached the word of God in their native languages" ("Blue Nun," ¶ 4).
11. The organization clearly references groups like the Mothers of the Plaza de Mayo and the Mothers of East L.A.

References

Akinyela, Makungu. "Battling the Serpent: Nat Turner, Africanized Christianity, and a Black Ethos." *Journal of Black Studies* 33 (2003): 255–280.

Allen, Paula Gunn. "The Feminine Landscape of Leslie Marmon Silko's *Ceremony.*" *American Indian Quarterly* 5.1 (1979): 7–12.

Anzaldua, Gloria. Anzaldua, Gloria. *Borderlands/La Frontera: The New Mestiza.* San Francisco: Aunt Lute, 1987.

————. "La Prieta." *This Bridge called My Back: Writings by Radical Women of Color.* Ed. Cherrie Moraga and Gloria Anzaldua. Watertown, Mass.: Persephone, 1981.

Arnold, Ellen L. "An Ear for the Story, an Eye for the Pattern: Rereading *Ceremony.*" *Modern Fiction Studies* 45.1 (1995): 69–92.

Blaeser, Kimberly M. "Pagans Rewriting the Bible: Heterodoxy and the Representation of Spirituality in Native American Literature." *ARIEL: a Review of International English Literatures.* 25 (1994): 12–31.

"The Blue Nun." 17 July 2003. http://shell.amingo.net/~tmv/Special_In4.html

Blumenthal, S. "Spotted Cattle and Deer: Spirit Guides and Symbols of Endurance and Healing in *Ceremony.*" *American Indian Quarterly* 14.4 (1990: 367–377.

Burke, Kenneth. *The Philosophy of Literary Form: Studies in Symbolic Action.* 3rd ed. 1941. Berkeley: U of California P, 1973.

Castillo, Ana. *So Far From God.* New York: Plume, 1993.

Cederstrom, Lorelei. "Myth and Ceremony in Contemporary Native American Fiction." *Canadian Journal of Native Studies* 2.2 (1982): 2–12.

Coltelli, Laura. "Re-Enacting Myths and Stories: Tradition and Renewal in *Ceremony.*" *Native American Literatures: Forum (Pisa)* 1, (1989): 173–183.

Corbin, Carol. *Rhetoric in Postmodern America: Conversations with Michael Calvin McGee.* Ed. Carol Corbin. New York: Guilford, 1998.

Cutchins, Dennis "'So That the Nations May Become Genuine Indian': Nativism and Leslie Marmon Silko's *Ceremony.*" *Journal of American Culture* 22.4 (1999): 77–89.

Daniels, Jean. "The Call of Baby Suggs in Beloved: Imagining Freedom and Resistance Through Struggle." *The Griot* 21 (2002): 1–7.

Delgadillo, Theresa. "Forms of Chicana Feminist Resistance: Hybrid Spirituality in Ana Castillo's *So Far From God.*" *Modern Fiction Studies* 44 (1998): 888–916.

Feng, Pin-Chia: Rituals of Rememory: Afro-Caribbean Religions in 'Myal' and 'It Begins with Tears.'" *MELUS* 27 (2002): 149–175.

Fisher, Walter R. "A Motive View of Communication." *Quarterly Journal of Speech.* 56 (1970): 131–139.

Herzog, Kristin. "Thinking Woman and Feeling Man: Gender in Silko's *Ceremony.*" *MELUS* 12.1 (1985): 25–36.

Hinson, Scot D. "Narrative and Community Crisis in *Beloved.*" *MELUS* 26 (2001): 147–167.

Holloway, Karla F. C. "*Beloved*: A Spiritual." *Callaloo* 13 (1990): 516–525.

Horvitz, Debroah. "Nameless Ghosts: Possession and Dispossession in *Beloved.*" *Critical Essays on Toni Morrison's* Beloved. Ed. Barbara H. Solomon. NY: G.K. Hall and Co., 1998. 93–103.

Jonsen, Albert R. and Stephen Toulmin. *The Abuse of Casuistry: A History of Moral Reasoning.* Berkeley: University of California Press, 1988.

Katz, Jane B. *This Song Remembers: Self-Portraits of Native Americans in the Arts.* Boston: Houghton-Mifflin, 1980.

Keller, Catherine. *From a Broken Web: Separation, Sexism, and Self.* Boston: Beacon, 1986.

Lee, Rachael. "Missing Peace in Toni Morrison's *Sula* and *Beloved.*" *African American Review* 28 (1994): 571–583.

Lincoln, Kenneth. *Native American Renaissance.* Berkeley: U of California P, 1983.

Manriquez, B. J. "Ana Castillo's *So Far From God*: Intimations of the Absurd." *College Literature* 29.2 (2002): 29–49.

Miller, Richard B. "Altruism, and the Limits of Casuistry." *Journal of Religious Ethics* 28 (2000): 3–35.

Mbalia, Doreatha Drummond. *Toni Morrison: Developing Class Consciousness.* London: Selingrove Susquehanna P, 1991.

Marks, Kathleen. *Toni Morrison's* Beloved *and the Apotropaic Imagination.* Colombia and London: University of Missouri Press, 2002.

Morris, Roma Heiling. "The Whole Story: Nature, Healing, and Narrative in the Native American Wisdom Tradition." *Literature and Medicine.* 15.1 (1996): 94–111.

Morrison, Toni. *Beloved.* New York: Plume, 1988.

Ochoa, Peggy. "Morrison's *Beloved*: Allegorically Othering 'White' Christianity." *MELUS* 24 (1999): 107–123.

Phelan, James. "Rhetorical Aesthetics and other Issues in the Study of Literary Narratives." *Narrative Inquiry* 16 (2006): 85–93.

Perez, Gail. "Ana Castillo as *Santera*: Reconstructing Popular Religious Praxis." *A Reader in Latina Feminist Theology: Religion and Justice.* Ed. D. L. Machado and J. Rodriguez. Austin: University of Texas Press, 2002. 143–158.

Rand, Naomi R. "Surviving What Haunts You: The Art of Invisibility in *Ceremony, The Ghost Writer,* and *Beloved.*" *MELUS* 20.3 (1995): 21–32.

Rushdy, Ashraf H. A. "Daughters Signifyin(g) History: The Example of Toni Morrison's *Beloved.*" *American Literature* 64 (1992): 567–597.

Ryan, Judylyn S. "Spirituality and/as Ideology in Black Women's Literature The Preaching of Maria W. Stewart and Baby Suggs, Holy." *Women Preachers and Prophets Through Two Millennia of Christianity.* Ed. Beverly Mayne Kienzle and Pamela J. Walker Berkeley: University of California Press, 1998. 267–287.

Rummell, Kathryn: Toni Morrison's "Beloved": Transforming the African Heroic Epic." *The Griot* 21 (2002): 1–15.

Sauer, Michelle M. "Saint-Making" in Ana Castillo's *So Far From God*: Medieval Mysticism as Precedent for an Authoritative Chicana Spirituality." *Mester* 29 (2000): 72–91.

Shaddock, Jennifer. "Mixed Blood Women: The Dynamic of Women's Relations in the Novels of Louise Erdrich and Leslie Silko." *Feminist Nightmares: Women at Odds.* Ed. Susan Ostrov Weisser and Jennifer Fleischner. New York: New York University Press, 1994. 106–121.

Shugart, Helene. "Counterhegemonic Acts: Appropriation as a Feminist Rhetorical Strategy. *Quarterly Journal of Speech* 68 (1997): 210–320.

Silko, Leslie Marmon. *Ceremony.* 1977; New York: Penguin, 1986.

Slowik, Mary. "Henry James, Meet Spider Woman: A Study of Narrative Form in Leslie Silko's *Ceremony.*" *The North Dakota Quarterly* 57.2 (1998): 104–120.

Swan, Edith. "Healing Via the Sunrise Cycle In Silko's *Ceremony.*" *American Indian Quarterly* 7.2 (1988): 313–328.

Concepts and Questions

1. How do the forms of healing described by Rasmussen and Asenas relate to the nontraditional healing belief systems discussed by Begley and Ockey?

2. In what ways do the healings described by Rasmussen and Asenas dramatize the negative social dynamics behind the illnesses?

3. What assumptions must a person hold in order to be treated successfully by a spiritual healer?

4. In the narrative *Ceremony*, what do you believe caused Tayo's dissociation and "paralyzing and dispiriting displacement and alienation"?

5. Although the novel *Beloved* took place just subsequent to the Civil War, are there influences in today's environment that could lead to the type of spiritual illness experienced by Sethe?

6. How is the history of the "conquest" of New Mexico related to the spiritual illnesses suffered by the women in the novel *So Far from God*?

7. Rasmussen and Asenas assert that each novel used a unique communicative strategy to promote spiritual healing. What strategy was used in *Ceremony*?

8. What is the communicative strategy of adaptation utilized by Baby Suggs and others in the novel *Beloved*?

9. The emancipation that occurred in *So Far from God* was brought about by what kind of communication strategy? Describe the elements of that strategy.

10. How could the communicative strategies employed in the three novels be used in contemporary attempts at spiritual healing?

Culture and Communication in the Classroom

Geneva Gay

A semiotic relationship exists among communication, culture, teaching, and learning, and it has profound implications for implementing culturally responsive teaching. This is so because "what we talk about; how we talk about it; what we see, attend to, or ignore; how we think; and what we think about are influenced by our culture . . . [and] help to shape, define, and perpetuate our culture" (Porter & Samovar, 1991, p. 21). Making essentially the same argument, Bruner (1996) states that "learning and thinking are always situated in a cultural setting and always dependent upon the utilization of cultural resources" (p. 4). Culture provides the tools to pursue the search for meaning and to convey our understanding to others. Consequently, communication cannot exist without culture, culture cannot be known without communication, and teaching and learning cannot occur without communication or culture.

INTRODUCTION

The discussions in this article explicate some of the critical features and pedagogical potentials of the culture—communication semiotics for different ethnic groups of color. The ideas and examples presented are composites of group members who strongly identify and affiliate with their ethnic group's cultural traditions. They are not intended to be descriptors of specific individuals within ethnic groups, or their behaviors in all circumstances. If, how, and when these cultural characteristics are

Reprinted by permission of the publisher from Geneva Gay, *Culturally Responsive Teaching* (New York: Teachers College Press, © 2000 by Teachers College, Columbia University. All rights reserved), 77–110.

expressed in actual behavior, and by whom, are influenced by many different factors. Therefore, the ethnic interactional and communication styles described in this article should be seen as general and traditional referents of group dynamics rather than static attributes of particular individuals.

Students of color who are most traditional in their communication styles and other aspects of culture and ethnicity are likely to encounter more obstacles to school achievement than those who think, behave, and express themselves in ways that approximate school and mainstream cultural norms. This is the case for many highly culturally and ethnically affiliated African Americans. In making this point, Dandy (1991) proposes that the language many African Americans speak "is all too often degraded or simply dismissed by individuals both inside and outside the racial group as being uneducated, illiterate, undignified or simply non-standard" (p. 2). Other groups of color are "at least given credit for having a legitimate language heritage, even if they are denied full access to American life" (p. 2). Much of educators' decision making on the potential and realized achievement of students of color is dependent on communication abilities (their own and the students'). If students are not very proficient in school communication and teachers do not understand or accept the students' cultural communication styles, then their academic performance may be misdiagnosed or trapped in communicative mismatches. Students may know much more than they are able to communicate, or they may be communicating much more than their teachers are able to discern. As Boggs (1985, p. 301) explains, "The attitudes and behavior patterns that have the most important effect upon children . . . [are] those involved in communication." This communication is multidimensional and multipurposed, including verbal and nonverbal, direct and tacit, literal and symbolic, formal and informal, grammatical and discourse components.

The discussions of culture and communication in classrooms in this article are organized into two parts. The first outlines some key assertions about culture and communication in teaching and learning in general. These help to anchor communication within culturally responsive teaching. In the second part of the article, some of the major characteristics of the communication modes of African, Native, Latino,

Asian, and European Americans are presented. The focus throughout these discussions is on discourse dynamics—that is, who participates in communicative interactions and under what conditions, how these participation patterns are affected by cultural socialization, and how they influence teaching and learning in classrooms.

RELATIONSHIP AMONG CULTURE, COMMUNICATION, AND EDUCATION

In analyzing the routine tasks teachers perform, Smith (1971) declares that "teaching is, above all, a linguistic activity" and "language is at the heart of teaching" (p. 24). Whether making assignments, giving directions, explaining events, interpreting words and expressions, proving positions, justifying decisions and actions, making promises, dispensing praise and criticism, or assessing capability, teachers must use language. And the quality of the performance of these tasks is a direct reflection of how well teachers can communicate with their students. Smith admonishes educators for not being more conscientious in recognizing the importance of language in the performance and effectiveness of their duties. He says, "It could be that when we have analyzed the language of teaching and investigated the effects of its various formulations, the art of teaching will show marked advancement" (p. 24). Dandy (1991) likewise places great faith in the power of communication in the classroom, declaring that "teachers have the power to shape the future, if they communicate with their students, but those who cannot communicate are powerless" (p. 10). These effects of communication skills are especially significant to improving the performance of underachieving ethnically different students.

Porter and Samovar's (1991) study of the nature of culture and communication, the tenacious reciprocity that exists between the two, and the importance of these aspects to intercultural interactions provides valuable information for culturally responsive teaching. They describe communication as "an intricate matrix of interacting social acts that occur in a complex social environment that reflects the way people live and how they come to interact with and get along in their world. This social environment is culture, and if we are to truly understand communication, we must also understand culture" (p. 10). Communication is dynamic, interactive, irreversible, and invariably contextual. As such, it is a continuous, ever-changing activity that takes place between people who are trying to influence each other; its effects are irretrievable once it has occurred, despite efforts to modify or counteract them.

Communication is also governed by the rules of the social and physical contexts in which it occurs (Porter & Samovar, 1991). Culture is the rule-governing system that defines the forms, functions, and content of communication. It is largely responsible for the construction of our "individual repertoires of communicative behaviors and meanings" (p. 10). Understanding connections between culture and communication is critical to improving intercultural interactions. This is so because "as cultures differ from one another, the communication practices and behaviors of individuals reared in those cultures will also be different," and "the degree of influence culture has on intercultural communication is a function of the dissimilarity between the cultures" (p. 12).

Communication entails much more than the content and structure of written and spoken language, and it serves greater purposes than the mere transmission of information. Sociocultural context and nuances, discourse logic and dynamics, delivery styles, social functions, role expectations, norms of interaction, and nonverbal features are as important as (if not more so than) vocabulary, grammar, lexicon, pronunciation, and other linguistic or structural dimensions of communication. This is so because the "form of exchange between child and adult and the conditions in which it occurs will affect not only what is said, but how involved the child will become" (Boggs, 1985, p. 301). Communication is the quintessential way in which humans make meaningful connections with each other, whether in caring, sharing, loving, teaching, or learning. Montague and Matson (1979, p. vii) suggest that it is "the ground of [human] meeting and the foundation of [human] community."

Communication is also indispensable to facilitating knowing and accessing knowledge. This is the central idea of the Sapir–Whorf hypothesis about the relationship among language, thought, and behavior.

It says that, far from being simply a means for reporting experience, language is a way of defining experience, thinking, and knowing. In this sense, language is the semantic system of meanings and modes of conveyance that people habitually use to code, analyze, categorize, and interpret experience (Carroll, 1956; Hoijer, 1991; Mandelbaum, 1968). In characterizing this relationship, Sapir (1968) explains that "language is a guide to 'social reality' . . . [and] a symbolic guide to culture. . . . It powerfully conditions all of our thinking about social problems and processes" (p. 162). People do not live alone in an "objectified world" or negotiate social realities without the use of language. Nor is language simply a "mechanical" instrumental tool for transmitting information. Instead, human beings are "very much at the mercy of the particular language which has become the medium of expression for their society" (p. 162). The languages used in different cultural systems strongly influence how people think, know, feel, and do.

Whorf (1952, 1956; Carroll, 1956), a student of Sapir, makes a similar argument that is represented by the "principle of linguistic relativity." It contends that the structures of various languages reflect different cultural patterns and values, and, in turn, affect how people understand and respond to social phenomena. In developing these ideas further, Whorf (1952) explains that "a language is not merely a reproducing instrument for voicing ideas but rather is itself the shaper of ideas, the program and guide for the individual's mental activity, for his analysis of impressions, for his synthesis of his mental stock in trade" (p. 5). Vygotsky (1962) also recognizes the reciprocal relationship among language, culture, and thought. He declares, as "indisputable fact," that "thought development is determined by language . . . and the sociocultural experience of the child" (p. 51).

Moreover, the development of logic is affected by a person's socialized speech, and intellectual growth is contingent on the mastery of social means of thought, or language. According to Byers and Byers (1985), "the organization of the processes of human communication in any culture is a template for the organization of knowledge or information in that culture" (p. 28). This line of argument is applied specifically to different ethnic groups by theorists, researchers, and school practitioners from a variety of disciplinary perspectives, including social and developmental psychology, sociolinguistics, ethnography, and multiculturalism. For example, Ascher (1992) applied this reasoning to language influences on how mathematical relationships are viewed in general. Giamati and Weiland (1997) connected it to Navajo students' learning of mathematics, concluding that the performance difficulties they encounter are "a result of cultural influences on perceptions rather than a lack of ability" (p. 27). This happens because of the reciprocal interactions among language, culture, and perceptions. Consistently, when these scholars refer to "language" or "communication," they are talking more about discourse dynamics than structural forms of speaking and writing.

Thus, languages and communication styles are systems of cultural notations and the means through which thoughts and ideas are expressively embodied. Embedded within them are cultural values and ways of knowing that strongly influence how students engage with learning tasks and demonstrate mastery of them. The absence of shared communicative frames of reference, procedural protocols, rules of etiquette, and discourse systems makes it difficult for culturally diverse students and teachers to genuinely understand each other and for students to fully convey their intellectual abilities. Teachers who do not know or value these realities will not be able to fully access, facilitate, and assess most of what these students know and can do. Communication must be understood to be more than a linguistic system.

CULTURALLY DIFFERENT DISCOURSE STRUCTURES

In conventional classroom discourse, students are expected to assume what Kochman (1985) calls a *passive-receptive* posture. They are told to listen quietly while the teacher talks. Once the teacher finishes, then the students can respond in some pre-arranged, stylized way—by asking or answering questions; validating or approving what was said; or taking individual, teacher-regulated turns at talking. Individual students gain the right to participate in the conversation by permission of the teacher. The verbal discourse is accompanied by nonverbal attending behaviors and speech-delivery mechanisms that require maintaining eye contact with the speaker and using little or no physical movement. Thus, students are expected to be silent and look at teachers when they are talking and wait to be acknowledged before they take their turn at talking. Once permission is granted, they should follow established rules of decorum, such as one person speaking at a time, being brief and to the point, and keeping emotional nuances to a minimum (Kochman, 1981; Philips, 1983).

These structural protocols governing discourse are expressed in other classroom practices as well. Among them are expecting students always to speak in complete sentences that include logical development of thought, precise information, appropriate vocabulary, and careful attention to grammatical features such as appropriate use of vocabulary and noun-verb agreement. Student participation in classroom interactions is often elicited by teachers asking questions that are directed to specific individuals and require a narrow range of information-giving, descriptive responses. It is important for individuals to distinguish themselves in the conversations, for student responses to be restricted to only the specific demands of questions asked, and for the role of speaker and audience to be clearly separated.

In contrast to the passive-receptive character of conventional classroom discourse, some ethnic groups have communication styles that Kochman (1985) describes as *participatory-interactive*. Speakers expect listeners to engage them actively through vocalized, motion, and movement responses *as they are speaking*. Speakers and listeners are action-provoking partners in the construction of the discourse. These communicative styles have been observed among African Americans, Latinos, and Native Hawaiians. As is the case with other cultural behaviors, they are likely to be more pronounced among individuals who strongly identify and affiliate with their ethnic groups and cultural heritages. For example, low-income and minimally educated members of ethnic groups are likely to manifest group cultural behaviors more thoroughly than those who are middle class and educated. This is so because they have fewer opportunities to interact with people different from themselves and to be affected by the cultural exchanges and adaptations that result from the intermingling of a wide variety of people from diverse ethnic groups and varied experiential backgrounds.

ETHNIC VARIATIONS IN COMMUNICATION STYLES

Among African Americans, the participatory-interactive style of communicating is sometimes referred to as *call-response* (Asante, 1998; Baber, 1987; Kochman, 1972, 1981, 1985; Smitherman, 1977). It involves listeners' giving encouragement, commentary, compliments, and even criticism to speakers *as they are talking*. The speaker's responsibility is to issue the "calls" (making statements), and the listeners' obligation is to respond in some expressive, and often auditory, way (e.g., smiling, vocalizing, looking about, moving around, "amening") (Dandy, 1991; Smitherman, 1977). When a speaker says something that triggers a response in them (whether positive or negative; affective or cognitive), African American listeners are likely to "talk back." This may involve a vocal or motion response, or both, sent directly to the speaker or shared with neighbors in the audience. Longstreet (1978) and Shade (1994) describe the practice as "breaking in and talking over." This mechanism is used to signal to speakers that their purposes have been accomplished or that it is time to change the direction or leadership of the conversation. Either way, there is no need for the speaker to pursue the particular discourse topic or technique further.

African Americans "gain the floor" or get participatory entry into conversations through personal assertiveness, the strength of the impulse to be involved, and the persuasive power of the point they wish to make, rather than waiting for an "authority" to grant permission. They tend to invest their participation with personality power, actions, and emotions. Consequently, African Americans are often described as verbal performers whose speech behaviors are fueled by personal advocacy, emotionalism, fluidity, and creative variety (Abrahams, 1970; Baber, 1987). These communication facilities have been attributed to the oral/aural nature of African American cultural and communal value orientations (Pasteur & Toldson, 1982; Smitherman, 1977). Many teachers view these behaviors negatively, as "rude," "inconsiderate," "disruptive," and "speaking out of turn," and they penalize students for them.

Native Hawaiian students who maintain their traditional cultural practices use a participatory-interactive communicative style similar to the call-response of African Americans. Called "talk-story" or "co-narrative," it involves several students working collaboratively, or talking together, to create an idea, tell a story, or complete a learning task (Au, 1980, 1993; Au & Kawakami, 1985, 1991, 1994; Au & Mason, 1981; Boggs, Watson-Gegeo, & McMillen, 1985). After observing these behaviors among elementary students, Au (1993) concluded that "what seems important to Hawaiian children in talk-story is not individual . . . but group performance in speaking" (p. 114). These communication preferences are consistent with the importance Native Hawaiian culture places on individuals' contributing to the well-being of family and friends instead of working only for their own betterment (Gallimore, Boggs, & Jordon, 1974; Tharp & Gallimore, 1988).

A communicative practice that has some of the same traits of call-response and talk-story has been observed among European American females. Tannen (1990) calls it "cooperative overlapping" and describes it as women "talking along with speakers to show participation and support" (p. 208). It occurs most often in situations where talk is casual and friendly. This *rapport-talk* is used to create community. It is complemented by other traditional women's ways of communicating, such as the following:

- Being "audience" more often than "speaker" in that they are recipients of information provided by males
- Deemphasizing expertise and the competitiveness it generates
- Focusing on individuals in establishing friendships, networks, intimacy, and relationships more than exhibiting power, accomplishment, or control
- Negotiating closeness in order to give and receive confirmation, support, and consensus
- Avoiding conflict and confrontation (Belensky, Clinchy, Goldberger, & Tarule, 1986; Klein, 1982; Maltz & Borker, 1983; Tannen, 1990)

While these habits of "communal communication and interaction" are normal to the users, they can be problematic to classroom teachers. On first encounter, they may be perceived as "indistinguishable noise and chaos" or unwholesome dependency. Even after the shock of the initial encounter passes, teachers may still consider these forms of communication socially deviant, not conducive to constructive intellectual engagement, rude, and insulting. They see them as obstructing individual initiative and preempting the right of each student to have a fair chance to participate in instructional discourse. These assessments can prompt attempts to rid students of the habits and replace them with the rules of individualistic, passive-receptive, and controlling communication styles predominant in classrooms.

Teachers may not realize that by doing this they could be causing irreversible damage to students' abilities or inclinations to engage fully in the instructional process. Hymes (1985) made this point when he suggested that rejecting ethnically different students' communication styles might be perceived by them as rejection of their personhood. Whether intentional or not, casting these kinds of aspersions on the identity and personal worth of students of color does not bode well for their academic achievement.

Problem Solving and Task Engagement

Many African American, Latino, Native American, and Asian American students use styles of inquiry and responding that are different from those employed most often in classrooms. The most common practice among teachers is to ask convergent (single-answer) questions and use deductive approaches to solving problems. Emphasis is given to details, to building the whole from the parts, to moving from the specific to the general. Discourse tends to be didactic, involving one student with the teacher at a time (Goodlad, 1984). In comparison, students of color who are strongly affiliated with their traditional cultures tend to be more inductive, interactive, and communal in task performance. The preference for inductive problem solving is expressed as reasoning from the whole to parts, from the general to the specific. The focus is on the "big picture," the pattern, the principle (Boggs et al., 1985; Philips, 1983; Ramirez & Castañeda, 1974; Shade 1989).

Although these general patterns of task engagement prevail across ethnic groups, variations do exist. Some teachers use inductive modes of teaching, and some students within each ethnic group of color learn deductively. Many Asian American students seem to prefer questions that require specific answers but are proposed to the class as a whole. Many Latino

students may be inclined toward learning in group contexts, but specific individuals may find these settings distracting and obstructive to their task mastery.

In traditional African American and Latino cultures, problem solving is highly contextual. One significant feature of this contextuality is creating a "stage" or "setting" prior to the performance of a task. The stage setting is invariably social in nature. It involves establishing personal connections with others who will participate as a prelude to addressing the task. In making these connections, individuals are readying themselves for "work" by cultivating a social context. They are, in effect, activating their cultural socialization concept that an individual functions better within the context of a group. Without the group as an anchor, referent, and catalyst, the individual is set adrift, having to function alone.

These cultural inclinations may be operating when Latino adults begin their task interactions with colleagues by inquiring about the families of other participants and their own personal well-being or when African American speakers inform the audience about their present psychoemotional disposition and declare the ideology, values, and assumptions underlying the positions they will be taking in the presentation (i.e., "where they are coming from"). This "preambling" is a way for the speakers to prime the audience and themselves for the subsequent performance. Students of color may be setting the stage for their engagement with learning tasks in classrooms (e.g., writing an essay, doing seatwork, taking a test) when they seem to be spending unnecessary time arranging their tests, sharpening pencils, shifting their body postures (stretching, flexing their hands, arms, and legs, etc.), or socializing with peers rather than attending to the assigned task. "Preparation before performance" for these students serves a similar purpose in learning as a theater performer doing yoga exercises before taking the stage. Both are techniques the "actors" use to focus, to get themselves in the mood and mode to perform.

Those Asian Americans who prefer to learn within the context of groups use a process of *collaborative and negotiated problem solving*. Regardless of how minor or significant an issue is, they seek out opinions and proposed solutions from all members of the constituted group. Each individual's ideas are presented and critiqued. Their merits are weighed against those suggested by every other member of the group. Discussions are animated and expansive so that all parties participate and understand the various elements of the negotiations. Eventually, a solution is reached that is a compromise of several possibilities. Then more discussions follow to ensure that everyone is in agreement with the solution and understands who is responsible for what aspects of its implementation. These discussions proceed in a context of congeniality and *consensus building* among the many, not with animosity, domination, and the imposition of the will of a few.

A compelling illustration of the positive effects of this process on student achievement occurred in Treisman's (1985; Fullilove & Treisman, 1990) Mathematics Workshop Program at the University of California, Berkeley. He observed the study habits of Chinese Americans to determine why they performed so well in high-level mathematics classes and if he could use their model with Latinos and African Americans. He found what others have observed more informally—the Chinese American students always studied in groups, and they routinely explained to each other their understanding of the problems and how they arrived at solutions to them. Treisman attributed their high achievement to the time they devoted to studying and to talking through their solutions with peers. When he simulated this process with African Americans and Latinos, their achievement improved radically. Treisman was convinced that "group study" made the difference. Given other evidence that compatibility between cultural habits and teaching/learning styles improves student performance, this is probably what occurred. Communal problem solving and the communicative impulse were evoked, thus producing the desired results.

These are powerful but challenging pedagogical lessons for all educators to learn and emulate in teaching students of color. Collective and situated performance styles require a distribution of resources (timing, collective efforts, procedures, attitudes) that can collide with school norms; for instance, much of how student achievement is assessed occurs in tightly scheduled arrangements, which do not accommodate stage setting or collective performance. Students of color have to learn different styles of performing, as well as the substantive content, to demonstrate their achievement. This places them in potential double jeopardy—that is, failing at the level of both procedure and substance. Pedagogical reform

must be cognizant of these dual needs and attend simultaneously to the content of learning and the processes for demonstrating mastery. It also must be bidirectional—that is, changing instructional practices to make them more culturally responsive to ethnic and cultural diversity while teaching students of color how to better negotiate mainstream educational structures.

Organizing Ideas in Discourse

In addition to mode, the actual process of discourse engagement is influenced by culture and, in turn, influences the performance of students in schools. Several elements of the dynamics of discourse are discussed here to illustrate this point: organizing ideas, taking positions, conveying imagery and affect through language, and gender variations in conversational styles. How ideas and thoughts are organized in written and spoken expression can be very problematic to student achievement. Two techniques are commonly identified—*topic-centered* and *topic-associative,* or *topic-chaining,* techniques. European Americans seem to prefer the first while Latinos, African Americans, Native Americans, and Native Hawaiians (Au, 1993; Heath, 1983) are inclined toward the second.

In *topic-centered* discourse, speakers focus on one issue at a time; arrange facts and ideas in logical, linear order; and make explicit relationships between facts and ideas. In this process, cognitive processing moves deductively from discrete parts to a cumulative whole with a discernible closure. Quality is determined by clarity of descriptive details, absence of unnecessary or flowery elaboration, and how well explanations remain focused on the essential features of the issue being analyzed. The structure, content, and delivery of this discourse style closely parallel the expository, descriptive writing and speaking commonly used in schools. A classic example of topic-centered discourse is journalistic writing, which concentrates on giving information about who, what, when, where, why, and how as quickly as possible. Its purpose is to convey information and to keep this separate from other speech functions, such as persuasion, commentary, and critique. Another illustration is the thinking and writing associated with empirical inquiry, or critical problem solving. Again, there is a hierarchical progression in the communication sequence—identifying the problem, collecting data, identifying alternative solutions and related consequences, and selecting and defending a solution. There is a clear attempt to separate facts from opinions, information from emotions.

A *topic-associative style* of talking and writing is episodic, anecdotal, thematic, and integrative. More than one issue is addressed at once. Related explanations unfold in overlapping, intersecting loops, with one emerging out of and building on others. Relationships among segments of the discourse are assumed or inferred rather than explicitly established (Cazden, 1988; Lee & Slaughter-Defoe, 1995). Thinking and speaking appear to be circular and seamless rather than linear and clearly demarcated. For one who is unfamiliar with it, this communication style sounds rambling, disjointed, and as if the speaker never ends a thought before going to something else.

Goodwin (1990) observed topic-chaining discourse at work in a mixed-age (4- to 14-year-olds) group of African Americans in a Philadelphia neighborhood as they told stories, shared gossip, settled arguments, and negotiated relationships. She noted the ease and finesse with which a child could switch from a contested verbal exchange to an engaging story and dramatically reshape dyadic interactions into multiparty ones. Using a single utterance, the children could evoke a broad history of events, a complex web of identities and relationships that all participants understood without having elaborate details on any of the separate segments. The talk-story discourse style among Native Hawaiians operates in a similar fashion, which explains why Au (1993) characterizes it as a "joint performance, or the cooperative production of responses by two or more speakers" (p. 113).

Two other commonplace examples are indicative of a topic-chaining or associative discourse style. One is used by many African Americans, who literarily try to attach or connect the sentences in a paragraph to each through the prolific use of conjunctive words and phrases—for example, frequently beginning sentences with "consequently," "therefore," "however," thus," "moreover," "additionally," and "likewise." These sentences are in close proximity to each other—sometimes as often as four of every five or six.

The second example illuminates the storytelling aspect of topic-chaining discourse. African Americans

(Kochman, 1981, 1985; Smitherman, 1977) and Native Hawaiians (Boggs, 1985) have been described as not responding directly to questions asked. Instead, they give narratives, or tell stories. This involves setting up and describing a series of events (and the participants) loosely connected to the questions asked. It is as if ideas and thoughts, like individuals, do not function or find meaning in isolation from context. A host of other actors and events are evoked to assist in constructing the "stage" upon which the individuals eventually interject their own performance (i.e., answer the question). This narrative-response style is also signaled by the attention given to "introductions" and preludes in writing. They are extensive enough to prompt such comments from teachers as "Get to the point" or "Is this relevant?" or "More focus needed" or "Too much extraneous stuff" or "Stick to the topic." The students simply think that these preludes are necessary to setting the stage for the substantive elements of the discourse.

Storytelling as Topic-Chaining Discourse

Speaking about the purposes and pervasiveness of storytelling among African Americans, Smitherman (1977) surmises that they allow many different things to be accomplished at once. These include relating information, persuading others to support the speaker's point of view, networking, countering opposition, exercising power, and demonstrating one's own verbal aestheticism. She elaborates further:

An ordinary inquiry [to African American cultural speakers] is likely to elicit an extended narrative response where the abstract point or general message will be couched in concrete story form. The reporting of events is never simply objectively reported, but dramatically acted out and narrated. The Black English speaker thus simultaneously conveys the facts and his or her personal sociopsychological perspective on the facts. . . . This meandering away from the "point" takes the listener on episodic journeys and over tributary rhetorical routes, but like the flow of nature's rivers and streams, stories all eventually lead back to the source. Though highly applauded by Blacks, this narrative linguistic style is exasperating to Whites who wish you'd be direct and hurry up and get to the point. (pp. 161, 148)

It takes African American topic-chaining speakers a while to get to the point—to orchestrate the cast of contributors to the action. The less time they have to develop their storylines, the more difficult it is for them to get to the substantive heart of the matter. Frequently in schools, the time allocated to learning experiences lapses while African Americans are still setting up the backdrop for "the drama"—their expected task performance—and they never get to demonstrate what they know or can do on the proposed academic task.

Posed to an African American student who routinely uses a topic-chaining discourse style, a simple, apparently straightforward question such as "What did you do during summer vacation?" might prompt a response such as the following:

> Sometimes, especially on holidays, you know, like July 4, or maybe when a friend was celebrating a birthday, we go to the amusement park. It's a long ways from where I live. And, that is always a big thing, because we have to get together and form car caravans. Jamie and Kelly are the best drivers, but I preferred to ride with Aisha because her dad's van is loaded, and we be just riding along, chilling, and listening to tapes and stuff. Going to the amusement park was a kick 'cause we had to drive a long way, and when we got there people would stare at us like we were weird or something. And we would just stare right back at them. All but Dion. He would start to act crazy, saying things like "What you lookin' at me for? I ain't no animal in no zoo. I got as much right to be here as you do." You see, Dion gets hyped real quick about this racist thing. And we be telling him, "Man, cool it. Don't start no stuff. We too far from home for that." Then, we just go on into the park and have us a good time. We try to get all the rides before everything closes down for the night. Then, there's the trip home. Everybody be tired but happy. We do this three or four times in the summer. Different people go each time. But, you know something—we always run into some kind of funny stuff, like people expecting us to make trouble. Why is that so? All we doing is out for a good time. Dion, of course, would say it's a racist thing.

The narrator does eventually answer the question, but it is embedded in a lot of other details. In fact, there are stories within stories within stories

(e.g., celebration rituals, friendships, drivers, the drive, racism, risk taking, activities at the amusement park, similarities and differences, continuity and change, etc.). These elaborate details are needed to convey the full meaning of the narrator's answer to the initial question. But to culturally uninitiated listeners or readers, such as many classroom teachers, the account sounds like rambling and unnecessarily convoluted information, or Smitherman's (1977) notion of "belabored verbosity" (p. 161).

Teachers seeking to improve the academic performance of students of color who use topic-associative discourse styles need to incorporate a storytelling motif into their instructional behaviors. This can be done without losing any of the substantive quality of academic discourses. Gee (1989) believes topic-associative talking is inherently more complex, literary, and enriching than topic-centered speech. The assertions are verified by the success of the Kamehameha Early Elementary Program, which produced remarkable improvement in the literacy achievement of Hawaiian students by employing their cultural and communication styles in classroom instruction. Boggs (1985) found that the performance of Native Hawaiian students on the reading readiness tests correlated positively with narrative abilities. The children who told longer narratives more correctly identified the picture prompts than those who responded to individually directed questions from adults.

Yet topic-associative discourse is troubling to many conventional teachers. Michaels and Cazden's (1986) research explains why. The European American teachers who participated in their study found this discourse style difficult to understand and placed little value on it. African American teachers gave equal positive value to topic-centered and topic-associative discourse. We should not assume that this will always be the case. Some African American teachers are as troubled by topic-chaining discourse among students as teachers from other ethnic groups. The ethnicity of teachers is not the most compelling factor in culturally responsive teaching for ethnically diverse students. Rather, it is teachers' knowledge base and positive attitudes about cultural diversity, and their recognition of diverse cultural contributions, experiences, and perspectives, that enhance their ability to teach ethnically diverse students effectively.

Taking Positions and Presenting Self

In addition to significant differences in the *organization* of thinking, writing, and talking, many ethnically diverse students *relate* differently to the materials, issues, and topic discussed or analyzed. Most of the information available on these patterns deals with African and European Americans. Not much research has been done on the discourse dynamics of Latinos and Native Americans. Deyhle and Swisher (1997) concluded their historical view of research conducted on Native Americans with a strong conviction that there are fundamental and significant linkages among culture, communication, and cognition that should help shape classroom instruction for ethnically diverse students. But they do not provide any descriptions of the discourse dynamics of various Native American groups. Fox (1994) examined the thinking, writing, and speaking behavior of international students from different countries in Africa, Asia, Latin America, and the Middle East studying in U.S. colleges and universities. She found that their cultural traditions valued indirect and holistic communication, wisdom of the past, and the importance of the group. Their cultural socialization profoundly affects how these students interact with professors and classmates, reading materials, problem solving, and writing assignments. How they write is especially important to their academic performance because, according to Fox (1994), "writing touches the heart of a student's identity, drawing its voice and strength and meaning from the way the student understands the world" (p. xiii).

Personalizing or Objectifying Communications

Kochman (1972, 1981, 1985), Dandy (1991), and Smitherman (1977) point out that African Americans (especially those most strongly affiliated with the ethnic identity and cultural heritage) tend to take positions of advocacy and express personal points of view in discussions. Facts, opinions, emotions, and reason are combined in presenting one's case. The worth of a particular line of reasoning is established by challenging the validity of oppositional ideas and by the level of personal ownership of the individuals making the presentations. Declaring one's personal position on issues, and demanding the same of others, is also a way of recognizing "the person" as a valid data source (Kochman, 1981). Publication is not enough to certify the authority of ideas and explanations, or the expertise of the people who author them. They must stand the test of critical scrutiny and the depth of personal endorsement.

Consequently, Kochman (1981) proposes that African Americans are more likely to challenge authority and expertise than students from other ethnic groups. He suggests the following reason for this:

> Blacks . . . consider debate to be as much a contest between individuals as a test of opposing ideas. Because it is a contest, attention is also paid to performance, for winning the contest requires that one outperform one's opponents; outthink, outtalk, and outstyle. It means being concerned with art as well as argument. . . . [B]lacks consider it essential for individuals to have personal positions on issues and assume full responsibility for arguing their validity. Otherwise, they feel that individuals would not care enough about truth or their own ideas to want to struggle for them. And without such struggle, the value of ideas cannot be ascertained. (pp. 24–25)

According to Kochman (1981), the discourse dynamics of European Americans are almost the opposite of African Americans. He says they relate to issues and materials as spokespersons, not advocates, and consider the truth or merits of an idea to be intrinsic, especially if the person presenting it has been certified as an authority or expert. How deeply individuals personally care about the idea is irrelevant. Their responsibility is to present the facts as accurately as possible. They believe that emotions interfere with one's capacity to reason and quality of reasoning. Thus, European Americans try to avoid or minimize opposition in dialogue (especially when members of ethnic minority groups are involved) because they assume it will be confrontational, divisive, and lead to intransigence or the further entrenchment of opposing viewpoints. They aim to control impulse and emotions, to be open-minded and flexible, and to engage a multiplicity of ideas. Since no person is privy to all the answers, the best way to cull the variety of possibilities is to ensure congeniality, not confrontation, in conversation. As a result of these beliefs and desires, the European American style of intellectual and discourse engagement "weakens or eliminates those aspects of character or posture that they believe keep people's minds closed and make them otherwise unyielding" (Kochman, 1981, p. 20).

Playing with and on Words

African American cultural discourse uses repetition for emphasis and to create a cadence in speech delivery that approximates other aspects of cultural expressiveness such as dramatic flair, powerful imagery, persuasive effect, and polyrhythmic patterns (Baber, 1987; Kochman, 1981; Smitherman, 1977). Some individuals are very adept at "playing on" and "playing with" words, thereby creating a "polyrhythmic character" to their speaking. It is conveyed through the use of nonparallel structures, juxtaposition of complementary opposites, inclusion of a multiplicity of "voices," manipulation of word meanings, poetic tonality, creative use of word patterns, and an overall playfulness in language usage. Although decontextualized, this statement written by a graduate student illustrates some of these tendencies: "The use of culturally consistent communicative competencies entails teachers being able to recognize the multitude of distinct methods of communication that African American students bring to the classroom." Another example of these discourse habits is the frequent use of verb pairs. Following are some samples selected from the writings of students:

- A number of public issues to be explored and represented
- Numerous factors have impacted and influenced
- Make an attempt to analyze and interpret
- No model is available to interpret and clarify
- Many ways of explaining and understanding
- A framework that will enable and facilitate
- Validity was verified and confirmed
- He will describe and give account

Two other examples are helpful in illustrating the dramatic flair and poetic flavor of playing with words that characterize African American cultural discourse. One comes from Smart-Grosvenor (1982), who describes African American cultural communication as "a metaphorical configuration of verbal nouns, exaggerated adjectives, and double descriptives" (p. 138).

She adds (and in the process demonstrates that which she explains) that "ours is an exciting, practical, elegant, dramatic, ironic, mysterious, surrealistic,

sanctified, outrageous, and creative form of verbal expression. It is a true treasure trove of vitality, profundity, rhythm—and, yes, style" (p. 138). Smitherman (1972) provides a second example of African American discourse style and aestheticism. She writes:

> The power of the word lies in its enabling us to translate vague feelings and fleeting experiences into forms that give unity, coherence, and expression to the inexpressible. The process of composing becomes a mechanism for discovery wherein we may generate illuminating revelations about a particular idea or event. (p. 91)

Ambivalence and Distancing in Communication

Classroom experiences and personal conversations with Asian international and Asian American college students and professional colleagues reveal some recurrent communication features. These individuals tend not to declare either definitive advocacy or adversarial positions in either oral or written discourse. They take moderate stances, seek out compromise positions, and look for ways to accommodate opposites. They are rather hesitant to analyze and critique but will provide factually rich descriptions of issues and events. They also use a great number of "hedges" and conciliatory markers in conversations—that is, "starts and stops," affiliative words, and apologetic nuances interspersed in speech, such as "I'm not sure," "maybe . . . ," "I don't know, but . . . ," "I may be wrong, but. . . ." These behaviors give the appearance of tentative, unfinished thinking, even though the individuals using them are very intellectually capable and thoroughly prepared academically. And many Asian and Asian American students are virtually silent in classroom discussions.

I have observed Asian and Asian American students frequently interjecting laughter into conversations with me about their academic performance. This happens in instructional and advising situations in which students are having difficulty understanding a learning task that is being explained by the teacher. Rather than reveal the full extent of their confusion, or lack of understanding, students will interject laughter into the conversations. It functions to defuse the intensity of their confusion and give the impression that the problem is not as serious as it really is. Teachers who are unaware of what is going on may interpret these behaviors to mean the students are not taking their feedback or advice seriously. Or they may assume that the students understand the issue so completely that they have reached a point in their intellectual processing where they can relax and break the mental focus (signaled by laughter). When queried about this practice, students invariably say "It's cultural" and often add an explanation for it that invokes some rule of social etiquette or interpersonal interaction that is taught in their ethnic communities. Interestingly, Japanese, Chinese, Korean, Taiwanese, and Cambodians offer similar explanations about the motivation behind and meaning of this shared behavior. These students explain that "ritualized laughter" is a means of maintaining harmonious relationships and avoiding challenging the authority or disrespecting the status of the teacher.

These communication behaviors among students of Asian origin are consistent with those reported by Fox (1994). Hers were gleaned from observations, interviews, and working with students from non-Western cultures and countries (Fox refers to them as "world majority students") on their analytical writing skills in basic writing courses at the Center for International Education at the University of Massachusetts. Data were collected over three years. Sixteen graduate students from several different disciplines participated in the formal interviews. They represented 12 countries: Korea, Japan, the People's Republic of China, Nepal, Indonesia, Brazil, India, Chile, Sri Lanka, Cote d'Ivoire, Somalia, and Cape Verde. Faculty members who worked closely with these students were also interviewed. Additional information was derived from informal conversations and interactions with other students; analysis of writing samples; the teacher's notes about how she and the students worked through writing difficulties; and students' explanations about what they were trying to say in their writing, why assignments were misunderstood, and connections among language, culture, and writing.

Among these students from different countries, several common writing habits emerged that conflict with formal writing styles of academe, known variously as academic argument, analytical or critical writing, and scholarly discourse (Fox, 1994). The characteristics and concerns included:

- Much background information and imprecise commentary
- Exaggeration for effect
- Prolific use of transitional markers, such as "moreover," "nevertheless," and "here again"
- Preference for contemplative instead of action words
- Much meandering around and digressions from the primary topic of discussion
- Emphasis on surrounding context rather than the subject itself
- Being suggestive and trying to convey feelings instead of being direct and concise and providing proof or specific illustrations, as is the expectation of academic writing in the United States
- Tendency to communicate through subtle implications
- Great detail and conversational tonality
- Elaborate and lengthy introductions
- Reticence to speak out, to declare personal positions, and to make one's own ideas prominent in writing

Although all the students shared these communication tendencies, according to Fox's (1994) study, how they were expressed in actual behaviors varied widely. Culturally different meanings of "conversational tone" illustrate this point. Fox notes:

> In Spanish or Portuguese . . . speakers and writers may be verbose, rambling, digressive, holistic, full of factual details, full of feeling, sometimes repetitious, sometimes contradictory, without much concern for literal meanings. In many Asian and African languages and cultures, metaphor, euphemism, innuendo, hints, insinuation, and all sorts of subtle nonverbal strategies— even silence—are used both to spare the listeners possible embarrassment or rejection, and to convey meanings that they are expected to grasp. (p. 22)

These descriptions of Asian American and non-Western student discourse are based on observations and conversations with a small number of people, in college classes and professional settings. How widespread they are across other educational settings, ethnic groups, generations of immigrants, and social circumstances is yet to be determined. Much more description and substantiation of these communicative inclinations are needed.

The explanation of Asian students that their discourse styles are cultural is elaborated by Chan (1991), Kitano and Daniels (1995), and Nakanishi (1994). They point to traditional values and socialization that emphasize collectivism, saving face, maintaining harmony, filial piety, interdependence, modesty in self-presentation, and restraint in taking oppositional points of view. Leung (1998) suggests some ways these values translate to behavior in learning situations, which underscore the observations made by Fox. Students socialized in this way are less likely to express individual thoughts, broadcast their individual accomplishments, and challenge or disagree with people in positions of authority, especially in public arenas. These interpretations echo the connections between Asian American culture and communicative styles provided by Kim (1978). She suggests that one of their major functions is to promote social harmony and build community. Consequently, many Asian American students may avoid confrontations as well as the expression of negative feelings or opinions in classroom discourse.

GENDER VARIATIONS IN DISCOURSE STYLES

Most of the detailed information on gender variations in classroom communication involves European Americans. Some inferences can be made about probable gender discourse styles among African, Latino, Native, and Asian Americans from their cultural values and gender socialization, since culture and communication are closely interrelated.

Females Communicate Differently from Males

Lakoff (1975) was among the first to suggest that different lexical, syntactical, pragmatic, and discourse features existed for females and males. She identified nine speech traits prolific among females that are summarized by L. Crawford (1993) as specialized vocabulary for homemaking and caregiving, mild forms of expletives, adjectives that convey emotional reactions but no substantive information, tag comments that are midway between questions and statements, exaggerated expressiveness, super

polite forms, hedges or qualifiers, hypercorrect grammar, and little use of humor.

Other research indicates that European American females use more affiliating, accommodating, and socially bonding language mechanisms, while males are more directive, managing, controlling, task focused, and action oriented in their discourse styles. Girls speak more politely and tentatively, use less forceful words, are less confrontational, and are less intrusive when they enter into conversations. By comparison, boys interrupt more; use more commands, threats, and boast of authority; and give information more often (Austin, Salem, & Lefller, 1987; M. Crawford, 1995; Grossman & Grossman, 1994; Hoyenga & Hoyenga, 1979; Maccoby, 1988; Simkins-Bullock & Wildman, 1991; Tannen, 1994). Because of these gender patterns, Maccoby (1988) concludes that "speech serves more egotistic functions among boys and more socially binding functions among girls" (p. 758).

These general trends were substantiated by Johnstone (1993) in a study of spontaneous conversational storytelling of men and women friends. The women's stories tended to be about groups of people (women and men) engaged in supportive relationships and the importance of community building. The men's stories were more about conquests (physical, social, nature) in which individuals acted alone. Invariably, the characters were nameless men who did little talking but engaged in some kind of physical action. More details were given about places, times, and things than about people. Based on these findings, Johnstone suggests that women are empowered through cooperation, interdependence, collaboration, and community. For men, power comes from individuals "conquering" and acting in opposition to others.

Research by Gray-Schlegel and Gray-Schlegel (1995–1996) on the creative writing of third- and sixth-grade students produced similar results. They examined 170 creative writing samples of eighty-seven students to determine if differences existed in how control, outcomes, relationships, and violence were used. Clear gender patterns emerged. Both boys and girls placed male characters in active roles more often than females, but this tendency increased with age only for the males. Females were more optimistic about the fate of their characters, while males were inclined to be cynical. Boys usually had their protagonists acting alone, while girls had them acting in conjunction with others. Regardless of age or the gender of the story character, boys included more crime and violence in their narratives.

Gender Communication Patterns Established Early in Life

These kinds of gender-related discourse patterns are established well before third grade, as research by Nicolopoulou, Scales, and Weintraub (1994) revealed. They examined the symbolic imagination of four-year-olds as expressed in the kinds of stories they told. The girls' stories included more order and social realism. These concepts were conveyed through the use of coherent plots with stable characters, continuous plot lines, and social and familial relationships as the primary topics of and contexts for problem solving. Their stories emphasized cyclical patterns of everyday domestic life, along with romantic and fairy tale images of kings and queens, princesses and princes. They were carefully constructed, centered, and coherent, with elaborate character and theme development, and were invariably directed toward harmonious conflict resolution.

Whenever threatening disruptive situations occurred, the girls were careful to reestablish order before concluding their stories. The boys' stories contained much more disorder and a picaresque, surrealistic aesthetic style. These traits were apparent in the absence of stable, clearly defined characters, relationships, and plots; large, powerful, and frightening characters; violence, disruption, and conflict; and a series of loosely associated dramatic images, actions, and events.

The boys were not concerned with resolving conflicts before their stories ended. Instead, action, novelty, excess, defiance, destruction, and often escalating and startling imagery drove their plots.

In summarizing differences between how boys and girls construct stories, Nicolopoulou and associates (1994) made some revealing observations that should inform instructional practices. They noted that the stories produced by girls focused on "creating, maintaining, and elaborating structure." In comparison, the stories boys told emphasized "action and excitement" and involved a restless energy that is often difficult for them to manage (p. 110). Furthermore, the boys and girls dealt with danger, disorder, and conflict very differently. The girls' strategy was *implicit avoidance* while the boys' technique was *direct confrontation*.

Another fascinating verification of theorized gender differences in communication is provided by Otnes, Kim, and Kim (1994). They analyzed 344 letters written to Santa Claus (165 from boys and 179 from girls). Although the age of the authors was not specified, they were probably eight years old or younger, since children stop believing in Santa Claus at about this time. The content of the letters was analyzed to determine the use of six kinds of semantic units, or meaning phrases: (1) polite or socially accepted forms of ingratiation, (2) context-oriented references, (3) direct requests, (4) requests accompanied by qualifiers, (5) affectionate appeals, and (6) altruistic requests of gifts for someone other than self. For the most part, results of the study confirmed the hypothesized expectations. Girls wrote longer letters, made more specific references to Christmas, were more polite, used more indirect requests, and included more expressions of affection. By comparison, boys made more direct requests. There were no differences between boys and girls in the number of toys requested or the altruistic appeals made. Findings such as these provide evidence about the extent and persistence of patterns of culturally socialized communicative behaviors.

Early gender patterns of communication may transfer to other kinds of social and educational interactions. They also can entrench disadvantages that will have long-term negative effects on student achievement. Interventions to achieve more comparable communications skills for male and female students should begin early and continue throughout the school years. Efforts should also be undertaken in both research and classroom situations to determine if or how communicative styles are differentiated by gender in ethnic groups other than European Americans. Undoubtedly some differences do exist, since discourse styles are influenced by cultural socialization, and males and females are socialized to communicate differently in various ethnic groups.

Problems with Gendered Communication Styles

The "gendered" style of communication may be more problematic than the gender of the person involved in the communication. If this is so, then a female who is adept at using discourse techniques typically associated with males will not be disadvantaged in mainstream social interactions. Conversely, males who communicate in ways usually ascribed to females will lose their privileged status. Hoyenga and Hoyenga (1979) offer some support for this premise. In their review of research on gender and communication, they report that "feminine communication styles" are associated with less intelligence, passivity, and submissiveness, while "masculine styles" evoke notions of power, authority, confidence, and leadership.

However, M. Crawford (1995) suggests that some of the claims about female–male communication differences need to be reconsidered. For example, indirectness and equivocation in communication are not inherently strategies of female subordination or dominance. They can be tools of power or powerlessness as well. Interpretations of speech behaviors may depend more on the setting, the speaker's status and communicative ability, and the relationship to listeners rather than the person's gender per se (Tannen, 1994). Sadker and Sadker (1994) propose that males may be at greater *emotional risk* than females because of their role socialization. Girls are encouraged to be caring and emotionally expressive, but boys are taught to deny their feelings and to be overly cautious about demonstrating how deeply they care. Thus, male advantages in conventional conceptions of academic discourse may be countered somewhat by the psychoemotional and social advantages that females have in interpersonal relations.

CONCLUSION

Communication is strongly culturally influenced, experientially situated, and functionally strategic. It is a dynamic set of skills and performing arts whose rich nuances and delivery styles are open to many interpretations and instructional possibilities. Ethnic discourse patterns are continually negotiated because people talk in many different ways for many different reasons. Sometimes the purpose of talking and writing is simply to convey information. It is also used to persuade and entertain; to demonstrate sharing, caring, and connections; to express contentment and discontentment; to empower and subjugate; to teach and learn; and to convey reflections and declare personal preferences. In imagining and implementing culturally responsive pedagogical reform, teachers should not merely make girls talk more like boys, or boys talk more like girls, or all individuals within and across ethnic groups talk like each other. Nor should they assume that all gender differences in communication styles are subsumed by ethnicity or think that gender, social class, and education obliterate all ethnic nuances. Instead, we must be mindful that communication styles are multidimensional and multimodal, shaped by many different influences. Although culture is paramount among these, other critical influences include ethnic affiliation, gender, social class, personality, individuality, and experiential context.

The information in this essay has described some of the patterns, dynamics, and polemics of the discourse styles of different ethnicities and groups. Since communication is essential to both teaching and learning, it is imperative that it be a central part of instructional reforms designed to improve the school performance of underachieving African, Native, Asian, and European American students. The more teachers know about the discourse styles of ethnically diverse students, the better they will be able to improve academic achievement. Change efforts should attend especially to discourse dynamics as opposed to linguistic structures. The reforms should be directed toward creating better agreement between the communication patterns of underachieving ethnically diverse students and those considered "normal" in schools.

Knowledge about general communication patterns among ethnic groups is helpful, but it alone is not enough. Teachers need to translate it to their own particular instructional situations. This contextualization might begin with some self-study exercises in which teachers examine their preferred discourse modes and dynamics, and determine how students from different ethnic groups respond to them. They should also learn to recognize the discourse habits of students from different ethnic groups. The purposes of these analyses are to identify (1) habitual discourse features of ethnically diverse students; (2) conflictual and complementary points among these discourse styles; (3) how, or if, conflictual points are negotiated by students; and (4) features of the students' discourse patterns that are problematic for the teacher. The results can be used to pinpoint and prioritize specific places to begin interventions for change.

Whether conceived narrowly or broadly, and expressed formally or informally, communication is the quintessential medium of teaching and learning. It is also inextricably linked to culture and cognition. Therefore, if teachers are to better serve the school achievement needs of ethnically diverse students by implementing culturally responsive teaching, they must learn how to communicate differently with them. To the extent they succeed in doing this, achievement problems could be reduced significantly.

References

Abrahams, R. D. (1970). *Positively Black.* Englewood Cliffs, NJ: Prentice-Hall.

Asante, M. K. (1998). *The afrocentric idea* (Rev. and exp. ed.). Philadelphia: Temple University Press.

Ascher, M. (1992). *Ethnomathematics.* New York: Freeman.

Au, K. R. (1980). Participation structures in a reading lesson with Hawaiian children: Analysis of a culturally appropriate instructional event. *Anthropology and Education Quarterly, 11,* 91–115.

Au, K. R. (1993). *Literacy instruction in multicultural settings.* New York: Harcourt Brace.

Au, K. R., & Kawakami, A. J. (1985). Research currents: Talk story and learning to read. *Language Arts, 62,* 406–411.

Au, K. R., & Kawakami, A. J. (1991). Culture and ownership: Schooling of minority students. *Childhood Education, 67,* 280–284.

Au, K. R., & Kawakami, A. J. (1994). Cultural congruence in instruction. In E. R. Rolling, J. E. King, & W. C. Hayman (Eds.), *Teaching diverse populations: Formulating a knowledge base* (pp. 5–23). Albany: State University of New York Press.

Au, K. P., & Mason, I. M. (1981). Social organizational factors in learning to read: The balance of rights hypothesis. *Reading Research Quarterly, 17,* 115–152.

Austin, A. M. B., Salem, M., & Leffler, A. (1987). Gender and developmental differences in children's conversations. *Sex Roles, 16,* 497–510.

Baber, C. R. (1987). The artistry and artifice of Black communication. In G. Gay & W. L. Baber (Eds.), *Expressively Black: The cultural basis of ethnic identity* (pp. 75–108). New York: Praeger.

Belensky, M. F., Clinchy, B. M., Goldberger, N. R., & Tarule, I. M. (1986). *Women's ways of knowing: The development of self, voice, and mind.* New York: Basic Books.

Boggs, S. T. (1985). The meaning of questions and narratives to Hawaiian children. In C. B. Cazden, V. H. John, & D. Hymes (Eds.), *Functions of language in the classroom* (pp. 299–327). Prospect Heights, IL: Waveland.

Boggs, S. T., Watson-Gegeo, K., & McMillen, G. (1985). *Speaking, relating, and learning: A Study of Hawaiian children at home and at school.* Norwood, NJ: Ablex.

Bruner, I. (1996). *The culture of education.* Cambridge, MA: Harvard University Press.

Byers, P., & Byers, H. (1985). Nonverbal communication and the education of children. In C. B. Cazden, V. P. John, & D. Hymes (Eds.), *Functions of language in the classroom* (pp. 3–31). Prospect Heights, IL: Waveland.

Carroll, J. B. (Ed.). (1956). *Language, thought, and reality: Selected writings of Benjamin Lee Whorf.* Cambridge, MA: MIT Press.

Cazden, C. B. (1988). *Classroom discourse: The language of teaching and learning.* Portsmouth, NH: Heinemann.

Chan, S. (Ed.). (1991). *Asian Americans: An interpretative history.* Boston: Twayne.

Crawford, L. W. (1993). *Language and literacy learning in multicultural classrooms.* Boston: Allyn & Bacon.

Crawford, M. (1995). *Talking difference: On gender and language.* Thousand Oaks, CA: Sage.

Dandy, E. B. (1991). *Black communications: Breaking down the barriers.* Chicago: African American Images.

Deyhle, D., & Swisher, K. (1997). Research in American Indian and Alaska native education: From assimilation to self-determinations. In M. W. Apple (Ed.), *Review of research in education* (Vol. 22, pp. 113–194). Washington, DC: American Educational Research Association.

Fox, H. (1994). *Listening to the world: Cultural issues in academic writing.* Urbana, IL: National Council of Teachers of English.

Fullilove, R. E., & Treisman, P. U. (1990). Mathematics achievement among African Americans undergraduates at the University of California, Berkeley: An evaluation of the Mathematics Workshop Program. *Journal of Negro Education, 59,* 463–478.

Gallimore, R., Boggs, J. W., & Jordon, C. (1974). *Culture, behavior and education: A study of Hawaiian Americans.* Beverly Hills, CA: Sage.

Gee, J. P. (1989). What is literacy? *Journal of Education, 171,* 18–25.

Giamati, C., & Weiland, M. (1997). An exploration of American Indian students' perceptions of patterning, symmetry, and geometry. *Journal of American Indian Education, 36,* 27–48.

Goodlad, J. I. (1984). *A place called school: Prospects for the future.* New York: McGraw-Hill.

Goodwin, M. H. (1990). *He-said she-said: Talk as social organization among Black children.* Bloomington: Indiana University Press.

Gray-Schlegel, M. A., & Gray-Schlegel, T. (1995–1996). An investigation of gender stereotypes as revealed through children's creative writing. *Reading Research and Instruction, 35,* 160–170.

Grossman, H., & Grossman, S. H. (1994). *Gender issues in education*. Boston: Allyn & Bacon.

Heath, S. B. (1983). *Ways with words: Language, life, and work in communities and classrooms*. Cambridge, England: Cambridge University Press.

Hoijer, H. (1991). The Sapir–Whorf hypothesis. In L. A. Samovar & R. E. Porter (Eds.), *Intercultural communication: A reader* (6th ed., pp. 244–251). Belmont, CA: Wadsworth.

Hoyenga, K. B., & Hoyenga, K. T. (1979). *The question of sex differences: Psychological, Cultural, and biological issues*. Boston: Little Brown.

Hymes, D. (1985). Introduction. In C. B. Cazden, V. P. John, & D. Hymes (Eds.), *Functions of language in the classroom* (pp. xi–xvii). Prospect Heights, IL: Waveland.

Johnstone, B. (1993). Community and contest: Midwestern men and women creating their worlds in conversational storytelling. In D. Tannen (Ed.), *Gender and conversational interaction* (pp. 62–80). New York: Oxford University Press.

Kim, B. L. (1978). *The Asian Americans: Changing patterns, changing needs*. Montclair, NJ: Association for Korean Christian Scholars of North America.

Kitano, H., & Daniels, R. (1995). *Asian Americans: Emerging minorities* (2nd ed.). Englewood Cliffs, NJ: Prentice-Hall.

Klein, S. S. (Ed.). (1982). *Handbook for achieving sex equity through education*. Baltimore: Johns Hopkins University Press.

Kochman, T. (Ed.). (1972). *Rappin' and stylin' out: Communication in urban Black America*. Urbana: University of Illinois Press.

Kochman, T. (1981). *Black and White styles in conflict*. Chicago: University of Chicago Press.

Kochman, T. (1985). Black American speech events and a language program for the classroom. In C. B. Cazden, V. P. John, & D. Hymes (Eds.), *Functions of language in the classroom* (pp. 211–261). Prospect Heights, IL: Waveland.

Lakoff, R. (1975). *Language and women's place*. New York: Harper & Row.

Lee, C. D., & Slaughter-Defoe, D. T. (1995). Historical and sociocultural influences on African American education. In J. A. Banks & C. A. M. Banks (Eds.), *Handbook of research on multicultural education* (pp. 348–371). New York: Macmillan.

Leung, B. P. (1998). Who are Chinese American, Japanese American, and Korean American children? In V. O. Pang & L-R. L. Cheng (Eds.), *Struggling to be heard: The unmet needs of Asian Pacific American children* (pp. 11–26). Albany: State University of New York Press.

Longstreet, W. (1978). *Aspects of ethnicity: Understanding differences in pluralistic classrooms*. New York: Teachers College Press.

Maccoby, E. E. (1988). Gender as a social category. *Developmental Psychology, 24,* 755–765.

Maltz, D. N., & Borker, R. A. (1983). A cultural approach to male-female miscommunication. In J. J. Gumperz (Ed.), *Communication, language, and social identity* (pp. 196–216). Cambridge, England: Cambridge University Press.

Mandelbaum, D. G. (Ed.). (1968). *Selected writings of Edward Sapir in language, culture and personality*. Berkeley: University of California Press.

Michaels, S., & Cazden, C. B. (1986). Teacher/child collaboration as oral preparation for literacy. In B. B. Schietfelin & P. Gilmore (Eds.), *The acquisition of literacy: Ethnographic perspectives* (pp. 132–154). Norwood, NJ: Ablex.

Montague, A., & Matson, F. (1979). *The human connection*. New York: McGraw-Hill.

Nakanishi, D. (1994). *Asian American educational experience*. New York: Routledge.

Nicolopoulou, A., Scales, B., & Weintraub, J. (1994). Gender differences and symbolic imagination in the stories of four-year-olds. In A. H. Dyson & C. Genishi (Eds.), *The need for story: cultural diversity in classroom and community* (pp. 102–123). Urbana, IL: National Council of Teachers of English.

Otnes, C., Kim, K., & Kim, Y. C. (1994). Yes, Virginia, there is a gender difference: Analyzing children's requests to Santa Claus. *Journal of Popular Culture, 28,* 17–29.

Pasteur, A. B., & Toldson, I. L. (1982). *Roots of soul: The psychology of Black expressiveness*. Garden City, NY: Anchor Press/Doubleday.

Philips, S. U. (1983). *The invisible culture: Communication in classroom and community on the Warm Springs Indian Reservation*. Prospect Heights, IL: Waveland.

Porter, R. E., & Samovar, L. A. (1991). Basic principles of intercultural communication. In L. A. Samovar & R. E. Porter (Eds.), *Intercultural communication: A reader* (6th ed., pp. 5–22). Belmont, CA: Wadsworth.

Ramirez, M., III, & Castañeda, A. (1974). *Cultural democracy, bicognitive development and education*. New York: Academic Press.

Sadker, M., & Sadker, D. (1994). *Failing at fairness: How our schools cheat girls*. New York: Touchstone.

Sapir, E. (1968). The status of linguistics as a science. In D. G. Mandelbaum (Ed.), *Selected writings of Edward Sapir in language, culture and personality* (pp. 160–166). Berkeley: University of California Press.

Shade, B. J. (Ed.). (1989). *Culture, style, and the educative process*. Springfield, IL: Thomas.

Shade, B. J. (1994). Understanding the African American learner. In E. R. Hollins, J. E. King, & W. C. Hayman (Eds.), *Teaching diverse populations* (pp. 175–189). Albany: State University of New York Press.

Simkins-Bullock, J. A., & Wildman, B. G. (1991). An investigation into the relationship between gender and language. *Sex Roles, 24,* 149–160.

Smart-Grosvenor, V. (1982). We got a way with words. *Essence, 13,* 138.

Smith, B. O. (1971). On the anatomy of teaching. In R. T. Hyman (Ed.), *Contemporary thought on teaching* (pp. 20–27). Englewood Cliffs, NJ: Prentice-Hall.

Smitherman, G. (1972). Black power is Black language. In G. M. Simmons, H. D. Hutchinson, & H. E. Summons (Eds.), *Black culture: Reading and writing Black* (pp. 85–91). New York: Holt, Rinehart & Winston.

Smitherman, G. (1977). *Talkin' and testifyin': The language of Black America.* Boston: Houghton Mifflin.

Tannen, D. (1990). *You just don't understand: Women and men in conversation.* New York: Morrow.

Tannen, D. (1994). *Gender and discourse.* New York: Oxford University Press.

Tharp, R. G., & Gallimore, R. (1988). *Rousing minds to life: Teaching, learning, and schooling in social context.* Cambridge, England: Cambridge University Press.

Treisman, P. U. (1985). *A study of the mathematics achievement of Black students at the University of California, Berkeley.* Unpublished doctoral dissertation, University of California, Berkeley.

Vygotsky, L. S. (1962). *Thought and language.* Cambridge, MA: MIT Press.

Whorf, B. L. (1952). *Collected papers on metalinguistics.* Washington, DC: Department of State, Foreign Service Institute.

Whorf, B. L. (1956). Language, mind, and reality. In J. B. Carroll (Ed.), *Language, thought and reality: Selected writings of Benjamin Lee Whorf* (pp. 246–270). Cambridge, MA: MIT Press.

Concepts and Questions

1. In what ways do students' communication abilities affect teachers' perceptions of students?
2. How important is language in the performance and effectiveness of teachers?
3. Beyond the transmission of information, what other purposes does Gay suggest that language serves?
4. What does Gay mean when she says, "languages and communication styles are systems of cultural notations and the means through which thoughts and ideas are expressively embodied"?
5. What does Gay mean when she uses the term "discourse structures"?
6. Distinguish between *passive-receptive* and *participatory-interactive* styles of discourse.
7. Describe the methods employed by many African American students to gain entry into conversations. How does this style differ from the communication styles of Native Hawaiian students?
8. Describe differences in problem-solving styles among African Americans, Latinos, Native Americans, and Asian American students.
9. Distinguish between *topic-centered, topic-associative,* and *topic-chaining* techniques in organizing ideas in discourse. Which methods are associated with which cultural groupings of students?
10. How does the African American storytelling style function as topic-chaining discourse?
11. Distinguish between female and male communication styles.

Enculturation of Values in the Educational Setting: Japanese Group Orientation

Edwin R. McDaniel

Eriko Katsumata

When I was a student, especially a junior high school student, I was always taught that everyone should place importance on harmony of their group. Therefore all students had the same bag, socks, shoes of the same color, and so on. And, for example, if one student skip a club activity or chat during a club activity, our teacher scold not only the student but also all the team members. We have collective responsibility. Even if only one student make a mistake, teacher scold all the team members with responsible for the team. Like this, Japanese always value group harmony more than individual.

UCHI[1]

INTRODUCTION

An often touted perception is that "globalization" is rapidly eroding traditional cultures and moving societies toward a "global village," modeled after Western values centering on individualism and materialism. Part of the basis for this argument arises from international exposure to Western ideals as a result of increased tourism, international economic exchanges, environmental and health issues, and the ever-expanding presence of Western media throughout the world.

One aspect of this view of globalization's influence on cultural values is that Japan is moving away from its "collectivistic" traditions toward a more "individualistic" society. Some of the more well-known arguments advocating this view have been presented by Matsumoto et al. (1996, 1997) and Takano and Osaka (1999). In what is perhaps the most widely recognized work, *The New Japan: Debunking Seven Cultural Stereotypes,* Matsumoto (2002) argues that traditional collectivism is declining among Japan's younger generations and contends that his research demonstrates "not only is the stereotype concerning Japanese collectivism not supported, but in fact the opposite may be true—the Japanese may actually be less collectivistic, that is, more individualistic than are Americans" (p. 41). These reports are used as rationale to argue that cultural changes fostered by technology, diffusion, and a basic societal reordering (i.e., globalization) are instilling younger Japanese with a stronger, growing sense of individualism.

As scholars, we were keenly aware of these reports, but as residents and teachers in Japan, personal experiences push us toward quite different conclusions. Our classroom experiences, interaction with faculty, cohorts and students, and observations of day-to-day activities raised a reasonable doubt as to the premise of a rapidly declining group orientation at any level of Japanese society. Instead of growing individualism, we were continually confronted with demonstrations of group belonging and the importance attached to group identity. From our perspective as participant-observers, we have concluded that although Japan may not be as "collectivistic" as portrayed in previous academic reports, group affiliation remains a salient component of modern Japan's social structure.

To support this view, this essay first examines literature on the role of education in communicating normative societal values and forming cultural role expectations among children. Next, we argue that every level of the current Japanese educational system continues to instill group-affiliation as a cultural value. In arguing the continuing importance of group orientation in Japanese society, we offer interpretations gained from personal observations, recurring interaction with Japanese university students, discussions with fellow faculty members, and visits to secondary schools, complemented by contemporary studies of the Japanese educational system.

RELEVANT LITERATURE

Numerous factors, such as the established social order, identity needs, and the educational system, play an important role in shaping one's cultural orientation. For example, Miller and Kanazawa (2000) contend that "social order" exerts a considerable influence on day-to-day life in Japan and is sustained through group affiliation. They define social order as:

> the degree to which people follow explicit and implicit rules of behavior. That is, a society where the great majority of citizens obey laws and conform to social norms can be described as having a high degree of social order. Japan is such a society. (p. 3)

According to their argument, the structure of Japanese society directs individuals toward group membership, which offers in return security and identity.

Acceptance of the idea that social structures and the need for identity can influence personal choices allows us to move away from the broad canvas of culture generalized and consider how societal structures can influence and govern individual attitudes and behaviors. More specifically, this essay will illustrate how daily routines in Japan's educational system implicitly and explicitly communicate the value of group perspective, thereby perpetuating a collectivistic orientation.

The role of education in the communicative transmission of cultural values and normative societal deportment cannot be overstated. According to Samovar, Porter, and McDaniel, "The formal education process prevalent in a culture is tied directly to the values and characteristics of that culture" (2006, p. 262). Miller and Kanazawa (2000) echo this view when they state that the "socialization of children in any society is done with the explicit purpose of preparing children for entry into society" (p. 25). According to Patai (2002), national character, or a society's "modal personality," is a product of people being raised in a common environment, and he reports that teachers are a primary source of children's internalization of "the moral imperatives" of their social environment (p. 18). This idea is succinctly summarized by the Chinese philosopher Tehyi Hsei, who observed, "The schools of the country are its future in miniature."

These statements aside, it is somewhat intuitive that a child's school years exert a very formative influence, one that instills values and ideals carried throughout life. As stated by Samovar, Porter, and McDaniel, education "offers every child a set of guidelines and values for living life" (2007, p. 258). Drawing on this premise, we explore each major level of the Japanese educational system, beginning with preschool and concluding with entry into the labor force. The objective is to demonstrate that enculturation of the group affiliation in Japan begins at an early age and continues throughout the school years. Personal observations and interpretations are melded with information from other reports.

Two brightly colored mini-busses stop at the entrance of the small municipal park and began ejecting a seemingly endless stream of chattering kindergarten toddlers. All wear identical bright yellow hats, with sun flaps folded down over the ears and the back of the neck. With their hair hidden, it is hard to distinguish the boys from the girls. Only on closer observation do gender distinctions become apparent. The girls are dressed in identical red shorts and a white T-shirt with red lettering. The boys sport matching dark blue shorts and blue lettering on their white T-shirts. These small distinctions in color are all that differentiate a large group of children remarkably similar in outward appearance.

INSIDE JAPANESE SCHOOLS

Pre-school/Kindergarten

In Japan, education is a required key to the door of success. In an effort to unlock this entryway, a Japanese child's student days begin early in life. Although not compulsory, pre-school is widely attended (Nemoto, 1999), and many parents spend considerable sums on tuition. The objective is to gain every possible advantage to help their child gain entrance to primary and secondary schools of ever-increasing reputation, culminating in admission to a prestigious university.

The above observations of how kindergarten students were dressed similarly for a school outing provide an illustration of early socialization to group orientation. These outward manifestations of group are a reflection of ideals imparted in preschool classrooms. In a study of twenty-seven Japanese pre-schools, Holloway (2000) found that teaching the value of group orientation was a common objective. The director of one pre-school explained it this way:

> Our basic principle is group education. The teacher does not raise individual children. Instead children learn from the group. Therefore it is essential to create a good group, and from the good group good individuals grow. (p. 68)

In summarizing her findings, Holloway reported that "the existence of individuality was not itself contested, but the opinion was strongly held that cultivation of that individuality at school was unnecessary and even harmful until the basic attributes shared by all could be firmly established" (2000, p. 110). The importance of inculcating group values in Japanese pre-schools and kindergartens is further exemplified by a 1998 Ministry of Education report which stated that an objective of kindergarten was "To encourage children to have self-realization through group activities" (Curriculum Council, 1998). The purpose of this group focus is, according to Tobin (1992), to prepare "children for the group life they will encounter in elementary school, junior high, and beyond" (p. 32).

> Each weekday morning small groups of elementary school students assemble near their homes and set out for their schoolhouse in classic military platoon formation. An older student leads the way, followed by one or two loosely arranged columns of younger students. A second older student follows at the rear. The younger children usually wear hats identical in color and shape. They also carry the ubiquitous backpack (randoseru), identifiable throughout Japan in shape and size and differing significantly in only the color—predominantly red and black, but occasionally blue. The backpacks mark the wearers as elementary students and the hats denote the school attended.

Elementary School

The weekday ritual of gathering elementary students at neighbor assembly points and walking to school under the supervision of one or two older students, usually a sixth grader, provides the children a safety net against untoward actions, such as abduction attempts (Nemoto, 1999). Concomitantly, however, the young students are instilled with a sense of belonging to a particular group and a respect for hierarchy by being

under the supervision of an older student, who is learning about group leadership and responsibility.

The practice of transiting from home to school as a group is quite in contrast to practices in the United States. There, parents usually accompany their children to a school bus stop or actually drive them to school each morning and pick them up in the afternoon.

Group affiliation takes on even greater saliency inside the Japanese elementary school classroom, where students are commonly divided into *han* groups (Nemoto, 1999; Sato, 2004; Tsuneyoshi, 2001). This organization is described by Benjamin (1997), who spent a year as a participant-observer at an elementary school near Tokyo.

> *Han* means a platoon, a squad, a working group. It has implication for being the smallest operational group in a joint endeavor and of being a group that operates with little or no hierarchy. In Japanese classrooms, each *han* includes five to eight children, depending on the size of the class, and in order to be an efficient teaching and social environment, each class should have six to eight of these groups. Both social and academic activities are carried out with *han* groups as the basic working unit. (p. 53)

Sato (2004) offers a similar picture of the elementary classroom:

> Elementary students are organized into *han,* which are groups of 4-6 students. The composition of the groups may change for different activities, such as serving lunch, cleaning the classroom, or study groups for different topics. Indeed the composition of the *han* may be subject to periodic change by the classroom teacher. However, these groupings form the basic organizational pattern for all elementary school activities. (p. 82)

Both Benjamin (1997) and Sato (2004) reported that teachers would often address the *han,* rather than a specific student, praising or admonishing the entire group instead of individuals. Student groups (*han*) assigned to serve lunch will typically wear white caps and gowns while working, which provides a form of group identity. Moreover, working in these continually changing groups helps the children develop an ability to engage in cooperative endeavors, regardless of the personnel involved. Unlike in U.S. schools, where personal relationships become primary, the

Japanese student learns that group affiliation and co-operation is the most import aspect of relationships.

Japanese primary and secondary schools also hold a variety of nonacademic events that strengthen group identity and communicate the benefits of collective effort. These frequently include an annual school-wide sports day or cultural fair, where students may perform large group dances or drill formations which require considerable cooperation. Most athletic contests pit one class, or group, against another. Individual based contests such as races are conducted, but individual winners are seldom singled out for recognition. While attending sports day at one elementary school, races among all the boys of the same year grade were observed. Each race consisted of five or six students and as one group finished, the next group started. This continued until everyone had run. There was no effort to decide an ultimate winner by holding runoff races, and all of the participants were given a small gift at the end of their race. For these boys, participation in the race was the reward; individual ability was a secondary consideration, if at all. Benjamin (1997) and Feiler (2004) report similar observations of school sports day events emphasizing group participation and cooperation.

You see them everywhere! In the subway stations, waiting at bus stops, riding bicycles, or walking in twos or threes. Weekdays, weekends, and holidays! Even during the spring and summer school breaks. All of them, boys and girls alike, wear dark colored uniforms. The boys are dressed in dark trousers and white shirt—some with a tie and jacket and others with a tight fitting, high collar military style tunic. The girls wear dark—solid or plaid—pleated skirts, white blouse, and frequently a dark jumper with a sailor motif. Outwardly, each uniform carries enough variation to indicate a specific school, but overall they mark the wearer as a middle or high school student.

Middle School and High School

Junior high school brings Japanese students into an even stronger group-oriented environment. As illustrated above, beginning with the seventh grade and continuing through high school, all students are required to wear uniforms, whether attending public or private schools. These uniforms outwardly associate the individual with a broad age group and a specific institution. Students are keenly aware that they visibly represent their school and that improper activities will reflect on the reputation of their school. In some cases, students wear small lapel pins which designate their year group, and occasionally they may be seen wearing pins that indicate their specific class (*kumi*).[2] Another means of year group designation is the use of colored neckties and "room shoes."[3] Some schools will assign different-colored ties or shoes to each year group. In other schools, clothes worn during athletic activities ("sports wear") are color coded to the student's class. These different procedures provide a nonverbal means of group identity.

Most schools place restrictions on female students wearing makeup or jewelry, and some schools go so far as designating the permissible style and length of hair (Feiler, 2004). In addition to the school dress code, which casts students into groups, the students themselves take measures to differentiate their class year. Feiler (2004), who taught at a Japanese junior high school northeast of Tokyo, reported that ninth grade students devised unwritten rules dictating how junior classes had to wear their socks, button the top button of their shirt, and similar subtleties.

In general, middle and high school students will change classmates and homerooms at the beginning of the school year. In some schools, however, students may stay with the same classmates throughout the three years of middle and high school, respectively. Unlike their U.S. counterparts, who commonly change classrooms and classmates for different subjects, Japanese students remain together and leave their homeroom only when the topic requires a laboratory or for sports activities. Usually, Japanese students even eat lunch together in their homeroom. Junior and senior high school classroom pedagogy continues to focus on small group work. Use of the *han* organization continues in middle school classes, but is less common in high school, except for cleaning groups.

Stand near the entrance of almost any U.S. high school when classes are over for the day, and you will see a steady stream of students, many driving their own cars, leaving the campus heading for home, the closest shopping mall, the nearest fast food outlet, or some other gathering place. Stand near the entrance of a Japanese school when classes are over and you will likely see only a trickle of students departing and certainly none will be driving an automobile.[4]

At the conclusion of classes, around 4:30 p.m., Japanese middle and high school students will spend fifteen to twenty minutes working in groups to clean their classroom, the hallways, and perhaps even removing litter from the campus. After janitorial chores, students usually adjourn to their school-sponsored clubs (*bukatsudou*), which can be classified into two categories—sports or culture. Generally, students may belong to only one club, but some schools allow the students to belong to two—one of each type. Clubs may meet one or two hours on school days, with activities frequently held on the weekends and throughout the summer and winter breaks.

Within the sports clubs, the students' class year also forms a group and there is typically a strict relationship between the different grades. Younger students are expected to obey the older students and perform menial tasks. This hierarchal relationship is particularly strict in sports clubs, where the entering students attend to a variety of chores, such as picking up sports gear at the conclusion of practice. Collective responsibility is assigned for these tasks, and, for example, if one or two freshmen fail to complete their part of the job, all of sport club's freshmen will be punished. This clearly demonstrates the value placed on intra-group dependency and hierarchy. It also reinforces the Japanese mentality of "I have to do my best, because I don't want to create trouble for others."

It is quite common to see high school students, still in uniform, boarding buses near their school or at subway stations as late as 5:30–6:00 p.m. on weekday evenings. Many of them are en route to a cram school (*juku*) for a few additional hours of classroom work. These institutions provide instruction targeted specifically at passing university entrance exams. When done, the student will return home to study, watch TV, listen to music, or relax in some way. Little time is available for casual interaction with people outside the student's school groups. Indeed, Johnson and Johnson (1996) reported that Japanese students enjoyed "less than half an hour in social relations with peers outside of school" (p. 4). This limited opportunity to interact with others can create a strong sense of identity with one's class and school.

Although becoming somewhat rare, a few Japanese private high schools still hold classes on Saturday. In one instance, a university freshman related that her school held classes six days a week from 8:30 in the morning until 6:00 in the evening and clubs were not allowed. When asked what she did on Sundays, the student looked briefly incredulous before replying, "Why study, of course!" Her opportunities to interact with peers other than classmates were, of course, virtually nonexistent.

While somewhat limited, Japanese junior and senior high school students are not completely restricted to their own school classmates for social interactions. They do have the opportunity to meet people outside their schools during sports club competitions, class outings to cultural sites, or at *juku* classes.

Some women come to class in stylish dresses and high heels, often complemented by a strand of pearls and a coiffure. Others wear fashionable jeans or whatever casual clothes are currently in vogue. Make up and brand name accessories are common. The men are consistently dressed in a very relaxed, casual manner. After their freshmen and sophomore years, however, the dress becomes quite casual for both men and women, with one exception. Fourth year students are often seen wearing a black suit. The men complement their white shirt with a conservative tie, and the women always wear a white blouse. These university students, in their "recruit suits," are conducting job interviews, engaged in student teaching, or otherwise attempting to find an employer.

University

Entering university is a dramatic departure from the regimented, highly structured environment of Japan's primary and secondary schools. For most, graduation from high school represents the first real opportunity to openly explore and display personal identity. This is often achieved in such small ways as having to decide for themselves what to wear each day. The opportunity for self-expression manifests itself in many forms and is clearly evident among freshmen the first few weeks of their first term.

While completion of high school provides greater personal freedom, it concurrently removes the graduate from the social support of preselected group affiliations, which have been a constant theme since preschool days. Entering college freshman, however, soon find that university life is replete with measures designed to help them form new social groups.

One such event involves a trip, modeled after a "retreat," designed to help entering students form new relationships. The "retreat" usually takes place the week before first-term classes begin and involves a department's entire freshman class going on an overnight field trip. The incoming students, accompanied by faculty, staff members, and a few upper-class students, travel to a hotel, sometimes at a hot springs spa, stopping en route at scenic or historical places. At the hotel, students listen to self-introductions by faculty members, engage in group activities, and have informal interaction with faculty members, upper-class students, and new classmates.

On the surface, everything appears somewhat impromptu but outward appearances belie an underlying organizational schema. Seating assignments on the bus and room assignments at the hotel are made sequentially using the students' university ID numbers. Freshmen are also enrolled in selected first- and second-term classes according to their ID number. Thus, students sitting next to each other on the bus, and sharing a hotel room, will also find themselves in several of the same classes. This assists incoming first-year students from different high schools and geographical locations to begin making new friends (i.e., groups).[5]

Another mechanism promoting group affiliation at the university level is the frequent absence of advance placement classes.[6] Freshmen take only first-year level classes, regardless of ability or prior experience. For example, a student that has studied English abroad will usually have greater interaction skills than someone that has not been overseas. Both students, however, will be placed in the same class without consideration for ability. Even students that have earned credits in universities in other countries will have to begin as freshman—there is usually no advance placement. Each year group advances together, as a whole, toward graduation.[7]

Another common academic practice among Japanese universities is the *zemi* (a seminar fashioned after the German model). Toward the end of their freshman or sophomore year, students will decide on a seminar topic that interests them. They may also choose a particularly *zemi* to be with their friends. The outward objective of the *zemi* is to undertake an in-depth study of a particular topic for two to three years, under the guidance of one professor, and culminate in a senior thesis. But another important aim is to help students develop interpersonal skills and relationships that can last a lifetime. According to one Japanese professor, the *zemi* is designed to help students "develop social skills and enhance interpersonal abilities . . . develop closer relationships than is possible in regular classes." To achieve this, *zemi* classmates often engage in group social events, such as dining out or sports activities; some classes even travel as a group to locations in Japan or take trips abroad.

University sports clubs provide another chance for students to join a group. Some schools host teams that engage in league competition, but often the clubs are more recreational in nature. The team members will practice before or after classes as well as on the weekend and go on outings together. Sports clubs involve demanding practice sessions and, normally, very strict rules for relations between the different class year groups. Thus, the sports club becomes both a social outlet and an important source of identity.

The importance attached to identifying with a group was discovered by an expatriate coach at a Japanese university. Finding he had enough players to form more than two complete teams, each with the necessary number of substitutes, the coach began contacting other area universities to see if a "B" team game could be arranged. But the other schools' teams reported that due to injuries they did not have enough players for a "B" game. The expatriate coach was then informed that injuries to his own players precluded a "B" team contest. Only later did he learn that players preferred to be seen as "substitutes" for the "A" team rather than as members of a "B" team!

Not only does this illustrate how university sports teams become a source of group identity, it also demonstrates the significance placed on membership in the *right* hierarchical group. For the Japanese players, it was more important to be identified as part of the "A" team group than to actually play the game. In the United States, the attitude would more likely be to use the "B" team game as an opportunity to demonstrate skills that would allow the individual to standout and vie for a promotion to the "A" team.

While university brings a degree of relief from the constraints of the rigid group organization encountered in primary and secondary schools, other collectivistic structures influence student life, as previously discussed. Even the selection of which university to attend carries a lifelong association with a group. This is because in Japan, "many companies judge and hire newcomers according to the university from which they graduate" (Nemoto, 1999, p. 189). An individual's university (group) can determine their future employer (group) and, ultimately, their socio-economic level (group).

> *An evening TV news program airs a brief segment showing young men and women, all wearing dark suits, assembled in a large auditorium. They listen passively as corporate executives expound on organizational treatises. After a few moments, the scene switches to one of uniforms being issued to the new crop of employees. The men and women then retire to locker rooms to change. When the picture returns, all are wearing identical uniforms that mark them as an employee of the company.*

Corporate Life

There is abundant literature on the role and importance of groups within Japanese corporate and governmental organizations. However, since the focus of this essay is on the educational setting, only three sources will be mentioned. Yoshimura and Anderson (1997) provide a comprehensive overview of the role of "reference groups" (p. 57) in Japanese business organizations and how they become a source of identity. Working in a Japanese industrial company between 1996 and 1999, Mehri (2005) found that groups were commonplace and often competed with each other for information and power. More recently, Abegglen (2006) argued that Japanese corporations continue to rely on a collective orientation.

> Over the past half-century of dramatic, economic, and technological change, has Japan's employment system changed? Basically, it has not. The underlying values on which it was built—the concept of community in which all fully and fairly participate as one does in family, village, and neighborhood—remain the foundation. Key practices—an emphasis on continuity, on group integrity, and on egalitarianism—remain in effect. (p. 89)

The continuation of group affiliation is exemplified by the induction ceremony rites, described above, acted out every year in early April, as companies, large and small, welcome their new employees. This opening ritual (*nyushashiki*) will be followed by weeks, or in some cases months, of classes designed to train the employees in their new responsibilities and concomitantly inculcate them with the corporate culture—into their work "group." In some cases, the corporate training can be somewhat rigorous. For example, one graduate reported that all members of her corporate entry group (*douki*) had been sent to a rural area to plant rice by hand, an extremely labor-intensive activity demanding considerable cooperative effort. This part of the training was intended to forge the members into an effective workgroup and demonstrate the benefits of collective effort.

Community Activities

Beyond corporate organization, group orientation plays a significant role in community life. For example, neighborhood and city groups are active in numerous yearly festivals. These events bring community members together to both prepare for and participate in the festivities. Participants span all generations, with elders passing down the history and tradition of the occasion to the youth. These events not only instill participants with a feeling of local area pride, the cooperative effort enculturates a group-based sense of identity. Such group participation is considered beneficial and enjoyable, as was noted by Booth's observation of a community festival where some of the people "clearly derived the main part of the pride and enjoyment they found in participation from being members of a properly organized group, not from acting spontaneously" (1995, p. 329).

Japan's group perspective can also influence such mundane activities as taking out the garbage. In Japan, each apartment complex has a specific area where garbage is placed for pickup. As discovered by the first author, who lives in Nagoya, it is unwise for a person to place garbage in any area other than their own. When leaving his apartment on a garbage pickup morning, he simply dropped off the bag at the closest collection area, which was for an apartment complex across the street. A resident of the other building saw him and insisted the bag be moved to the author's own collection point. Despite the author's protestations that all garbage would be collected that morning, the woman remained insistent. The confrontation was resolved only when he took the bag to his apartment's collection point. Your second author lives in Tokyo and is part of a 16-family group that take turns cleaning up their trash collection point each week.

> *Japanese people will do things for friends [group members] even when they don't want to. They want to keep* wa

*harmony] and not embarrass others. In class, I don't speak
English as well as I can. I don't want others to
consider me "snooty."*

SOTO[8]

WHAT DOES IT ALL MEAN?

Viewed collectively, the foregoing observations suggest that the Japanese educational system continues to explicitly and implicitly communicate the role of group affiliation, which remains an important aspect of Japanese social organization. As early as preschool, children begin learning the value of group cooperation. This instruction continues throughout primary and secondary education as students become aware of their membership in an increasing number of groups (e.g., family, school, clubs, neighborhood, city, region, nation) many of which play an important role throughout life.

In the United States, group orientation or collectivism, terms often used interchangeably, is frequently interpreted as an overt desire to belong to groups and an affinity for other reference group members. But in the Japanese educational system, as we have seen, group membership is not a personal elective. Elementary and middle school students, for example, have little choice about being assigned to a *han* or even to which *han* they belong, nor can they elect to opt out and work alone if they disagree with another group member(s). Thus, from an early age, Japanese children are taught that cooperative endeavors are the norm and personal feelings must not impede collective achievement. Additionally, the process of being assigned to an in-group lessens the necessity for an individual to develop social skills for spontaneously engaging out-group members. This may, in part, help explain the shyness often displayed by many Japanese when encountering a new social environment.

Group efforts are common in every culture as people join together to accomplish collectively what cannot be achieved individually. Even in the United States, work groups, or teams, are often formed to solve a problem or complete a project. In Japan, however, groups take on a different complexion. In relation to work groups, these differences are described by Miller and Kanazawa (2000):

> Although Japanese often work in groups, those groups have certain characteristics. They tend to be fixed and long-term, where all members share a high dependency on the group, and high visibility allows for constant monitoring and sanctioning of inappropriate behavior. Japanese are not accustomed to forming *temporary groups* composed of strangers or loose acquaintances, whose behavior cannot be controlled by the group. (p. 107)

Additionally, the Japanese practice of assigning punishment and rewards collectively, rather than individually, strengthens group cohesion and provides a means of social control as the members develop feelings of mutual obligation. This sense of obligation, coupled with the group's longevity, creates interpersonal dependencies that tend to reduce non-conformity and the frequency of "free riders." For the Japanese, group membership provides fiscal, social, and emotional support, as well as identity (Miller & Kanazawa, 2000). Moreover, the difficulty in changing groups further discourages aberrant behaviors. In Japan, job hopping, for example, is still uncommon; it is much better to remain with one organization.[9]

This is not to say that a visitor to Japan will never see displays of individuality or deviations from the norm. Small personal trinkets are usually seen dangling from the backpack of an elementary school student or even the cell phone of an adult. Junior and senior high school students find small, often imperceptible, ways to wear or modify their uniforms (Feiler, 2004). It is not unusual to see Japanese teens and young adults dressed in a manner that sets them apart from the majority of their contemporaries. However, if you encounter one person dressed strangely, you will likely see several dressed similarly—a strangely dressed *group*. Any Sunday visit to Tokyo's Harajuku Park will reveal many groups of non-conformist, but the various groups will dress and behave similarly in their non-conformity. Moreover, those assertions of non-conformity will probably be set aside on Monday, when it is time to return to their respective work groups.

Those individuals who do not wish, or cannot, conform to Japan's group-oriented social structure are left with few options. Some take residence in other countries, but this requires considerable capital or a particular skill that will gain them employment. A few even withdraw from all social life and become reclusive. Others seek employment in Japan-based foreign corporations,[10] which are not usually organized around group structures. Many simply endure the strictures of group life in order to earn income but find outlet in individual-oriented activities (e.g., reading, music, photography, travels, etc). The overwhelming majority, however, learn to successfully balance group life and personal individuality. For most Japanese, the benefits and pleasures acquired through adherence to the social structures that promote group affiliation and cooperative effort are a normal, and valued, part of social life.

> To us visitors, Japan seemed a nation where the collective good is the collective goal. This was shocking and nearly incomprehensible to those of us accustomed to the U.S. focus on the individual . . . The schools were filled with students whose collaborative sensibility and sense of responsibility stunned us.
>
> Marla Muntner[11]

PROGNOSIS

The foregoing observations of contemporary Japanese social order do not support Matsumoto's (2002) claim that Japan is becoming less group oriented. Japan's educational system inculcates group orientation and cooperation beginning in pre-school and continuing into university, ensuring that future generations will be imbued with a group perspective. Unless dramatic changes occur, these future generations will enter a workforce that is also structured to promote collective effort.

But, what about the social changes discussed by Matsumoto (2002) and others? There is no question that Japanese society is changing. Globalization is exposing almost every nation to varying beliefs and values, and Japan is no exception. Social changes in Japan range from a rising divorce rate to the adoption of a new court system, designed to introduce peer juries, and erosion of the once sacrosanct lifetime employment. There are also indications that some Japanese corporations are redefining their management practices, including basing promotion on merit rather than on seniority (Fukukawa, 2001; McDaniel, 2004). Foreign managers are becoming commonplace among Japanese professional sports teams, and foreign participants in the ancient Japanese sport of sumo are quite popular. Many of the social changes

currently underway will no doubt influence how group affiliation is approached and viewed in the future. Abegglen (2006), however, suggests that in the workplace, new innovations are actually "adaptation to changing conditions whilst leaving intact the values and practices that have characterized Japanese management and that are the key source of the system's continuing strength" (p. 89–90). Complementing this outlook, De Mente (2005) doubts that Japanese corporations will be able to adopt the merit system on a wide-scale basis "in the next decade or so, if ever, because the concept of seniority, combined with groupism and the obsession for harmony remains such a powerful part of Japanese culture" (p. 154).

There are, moreover, signs that suggest a reinforcement of the group perspective. For example, a 2001 survey suggested that "many Japanese still think a corporation exists for consumers and its employees rather than shareholders" (Fukukawa, 2001, p. 6). This indicates that some corporate employees continue to view their organization from a group affiliation perspective. More recently, Suzuki reported that corporate sports days were again becoming popular. Many organizations discontinued the practice in the early 1990s, when the bubble economy collapsed. Now companies, however, are "recognizing anew the beneficial effect" of bringing employees together, and one survey disclosed that among younger employees the desire to participate in "intra company events" rose from seventy-one percent in 1999 to eighty-three percent in 2006 (Suzuki, 2006, p. 3).

The Japanese recognize the need to restructure the educational system to "emphasize individualism and entrepreneurship" (De Mente, 2005, p. 119), and efforts are being made to effect this change. In 2002, the Ministry of Education initiated reforms with one objective being to "stimulate students to be independent and self-directed learners" (Ellington, 2005, p. 2). Soon after his election in late 2006, Prime Minister Abe announced educational reform as a top priority and formed a panel to "re-examine education from the ground up" (Nakamura, 2006, Oct 19, p. 2). But envisioned changes remain unclearly defined and there is no certainty that the pervasive emphasis on collective effort will be addressed. In fact, the New Minister of Education has announced that:

> We want to establish a constitution of education that encourages schools and communities to teach

(children) Japanese traditional social norms . . . [the] Japanese are losing certain social norms, including the notion that relying too much on others is shameful. (Nakamura, 2006, Oct 3, p. 3)

These examples from the business and education context indicate that significant change in Japan will come neither easily nor quickly. Group orientation is a form of social organization that permeates all levels of Japanese society. The value of collective effort and identity acquired through group affiliation continues to be passed on to succeeding generations through the educational process. The dilemma was summed up by the mother of two elementary school students, "The schools teach that it is OK to be different, but we don't know how to be different."

Despite exposure to Western ideals of individualism, Japan's younger generations, the existing social structure and institutional forces will inevitably channel them toward group affiliation. For the Japanese, the forces of group orientation are just as compelling, valid, beneficial, and fulfilling as individual self-promotion is in the United States. Group affiliation offers the Japanese an enduring source of identity, a high degree of certainty, and social stability, all of which are as valued as much as individuality, personal freedom, and change are in the United States.

There is, however, one factor that has not been included into the equation of cultural change. Japan's population is declining! Some twenty percent of the nation's people are over sixty-five, and in 2005 the birth rate fell to a new low of 1.25 (2.1 is needed to maintain parity). Thus, Japan's population "has the world's highest proportion of elderly people and the lowest proportion of young people" ("20% of Japan," 2006, p. 1). According to the Ministry of Health, Labor and Welfare, if these conditions continue, Japan's population could decline from its present approximate 127 million to "less than 90 million by 2055" ("Japan's population," 2006, p. 1). These circumstances will obviously have an influence on cultural change in Japan, but the type of change cannot now be determined.

CAVEAT

Throughout this essay, the concept of group orientation has been addressed from a one-dimensional perspective. This, unfortunately, may convey a misleading perception that in Japanese society group orientation works as a singular cultural force. Just as in every culture, however, in daily life the Japanese must deal with a multiplicity of cultural factors, which change as people move from one social context to another. Hierarchy, mutual obligation, and harmony have been mentioned briefly, but there is a host of other cultural dynamics that influence Japanese social life and communicative behaviors. These include such considerations as uncertainty avoidance, high-context communication, formality, face concerns, and many uniquely Japanese cultural factors like *gaman, honne/ tatemae, soto/uchi,* and others. Depending on the context and the individuals involved, these various cultural forces will exert their influence in concert, not singularly.

Notes

1. *Uchi* is a pseudonym for a third-year Japanese university student in 2006. These comments were taken verbatim from a seminar assignment report. The examples presented in italics preceding section headings were given by students or taken from personal observations and discussions with colleagues.

2. In urban areas, Japanese junior and senior high schools are quite large and usually have several "home rooms" for each class year. For example, one high school that was visited was originally built to contain 12 classes for each of the three-year groups. Students are normally assigned to a "homeroom" for at least one year, but in some cases it may be for their entire three years.

3. When entering a primary and secondary schools, students change their "street" or outside shoes for shoes or slippers worn only inside the school.

4. To obtain a drivers license in Japan, one must be 18 years of age and have completed driving school. Most of the students do not get their license until their first year in college.

5. The activities described in these two paragraphs are based on observations at a single Japanese university. Other schools use different procedures. Additionally, these trips are more common in universities that focus on the humanities. At research-oriented universities, the advanced undergraduate students are assigned to a laboratory, where they work with a professor and a small group of student cohorts.

6. Not all Japanese universities adhere to this policy. In some schools, for example, if an entering freshman scores high enough on the English placement exam, they do not have to take the first-year English course.

7. There are a couple of exceptions. One is when a student decides to spend a year abroad, typically to study a foreign language. These students will return to graduate one or two terms behind their peers. The second is with students who transfer after completing junior college. These students enter as third-year students, but may be required to make up a few selected classes (e.g., *zemi*).

8. *Soto* is a pseudonym for a first-year Japanese university student. During high school, she spent a year abroad and acquired excellent English conversation skills. In class, however, she often spoke well below the level she used in private conversation with English instructors. Her objective was to ensure she did not stand out from her classmates and disrupt class harmony.

9. There is, however, growing usage of temporary workers (*haken*) in Japanese organizations. These individuals are assigned to a company and may work for a few months or a couple of years. How they are integrated with the full-time workers is currently un-researched.

10. There are a number of other reasons why Japanese seek employment in Western subsidiary companies, not the least is higher wages than can be earned in a Japanese corporation.

11. Muntner (2003) is a U.S. elementary school teacher who, as a participant in the 2001 Japanese Fulbright Memorial Fund Teacher Program, visited elementary, junior, and senior high schools, as well as Japanese homes.

References

20% of Japan now age 65 or older. (2006, November 1). *The Japan Times*. 1.

Abegglen, J.C. (2006). *21st-century Japanese management*. NY: Palgrave-Macmillan.

Allik, J., & Realo, A. (1996). The hierarchical nature of individualism-collectivism: Comments on Matsumoto et al. (1996). *Culture and Psychology, 2*, 109–117.

Benjamin, G. R. (1997). *Japanese lessons*. NY: New York University.

Booth, A. (1995). *Looking for the lost: Journeys through a vanishing Japan*. NY: Kodansha.

The Curriculum Council. (1998, July). *National curriculum standards reform for kindergarten, elementary school, lower and upper secondary school and schools for the visually disabled, the hearing impaired and the otherwise disabled*. Ministry of Education, Culture, Sports, Science and Technology (MEXT). Retrieved October 11, 2006, from http://www.mext.go.jp/english/news/1998/07/980712.htm

De Mente, B.L. (2005). *Japan unmasked*. Tokyo: Tuttle.

Ellington, L. (2005). Japanese education. *Japan Digest*. National Clearing House for U.S.-Japan Studies. Retrieved March 10, 2007, from http://www.indiana.edu/~japan/digest5.html

Feiler, B. S. (2004). *Learning to bow*. NY: Perennial. Originally published in 1991.

Fukukawa, S. (2001, May 28). Sea change in Japan's values: Globalization, IT age prompt social diversification. *The Japan Times-on line*. Retrieved October 4, 2006, from http://search.japantimes.co.jp/print/nb20010528a2.html

Hofstede, G. (2001). *Culture's consequences* (2nd ed.). Thousand Oaks, CA: Sage. Originally published in 1980.

Holloway, S. D. (2000). *Contested childhood: Diversity and change in Japanese preschools*. NY: Routledge.

"Japan's population to fall 30% by 2055, study finds." (2006, 21 Dec). *The Japan Times*. Retrieved February 12, 2007, from http://search.japantimes.co.jp/print/nn20061221a1.html

Johnson, M. L., & Johnson, J. R. (1996, October). Daily life in Japanese high schools. *Japan Digest*. Retrieved October 14, 2006, from http://www.indiana.edu/~japan/digest9.pdf

Matsumoto, D., Kudoh, T., & Takeuchi, S. (1996). Changing patterns of individualism and collectivism in the United States and Japan. *Culture and Psychology, 2*, 77–107.

Matsumoto, D., Weissman, M. D., Preston, K., Brown, B. R., & Kupperbush, C. (1997). Context-specific measurement of individualism-collectivism on the individual level: The individualism-collectivism interpersonal assessment inventory. *Journal of Cross-Cultural Psychology, 28*(6), 743–767.

Matsumoto, D. (2002). *The new Japan: Debunking seven cultural stereotypes*. Yarmouth, ME: Intercultural Press.

McDaniel, E. R. (2004). Changing Japanese organizational communication patterns: The impact of information technology. *San Diego State University Center for International Business Education and Research* (CIBER). Working Paper Series C-04-015.

Mehri, D. (2005). *Notes from Toyota-land: An American engineer in Japan*. Ithaca, NY: Cornell University.

Miller, A. S., & Kanazawa, S. (2000). *Order by accident: The origins and consequence of conformity in contemporary Japan*. Boulder, CO: Westview.

Muntner, M. (2003). Lessons learned: A glimpse into Japanese schools and life. *Multicultural Review 12*(4), 36–38.

Nakamura, A. (2006, Oct 19). Abe, education panel get to work on reforms. *Japan Times*, p. 2.

Nakamura, A. (2006, Oct 3). Education chief wants traditional values restored. *Japan Times*, p. 3.

Nemoto, Y. (1999). *The Japanese education system*. Parkland, FL: Universal.

Patai, R. (2002). *The Arab mind* (rev. ed.). NY: Hatherleigh Press. Originally published in 1976.

Samovar, L. A., Porter, R. E., & McDaniel, E. R. (2007). *Communication between cultures*. Belmont, CA: Thompson Wadsworth.

Sato, N. E. (2004). *Inside Japanese classrooms: The heart of education*. New York: RoutledgeFalmer.

Suzuki, J. (2006, Oct. 17). Corporate Japan once again embraces sports days. *The Japan Times-On line*. Retrieved March 10, 2007, from http://search.japantimes.co.jp/member/member.html?appURL=nn20061017f2.html

Takano, Y., & Osaka, E. (1999). An unsupported common view: Comparing Japan and the U.S. on individualism/collectivism. *Asian Journal of Social Psychology*, 2, 311–341.

Tobin, J. (1992). Japanese preschools and the pedagogy of selfhood. In N. R. Rosenberger (Ed.), *Japanese sense of self* (pp. 21–30). New York: Cambridge University.

Tsuneyoshi, R. (2001). *The Japanese model of schooling: Comparisons with the United States*. New York: RoutledgeFalmer.

Yoshimura, N., & Anderson, P. (1997). *Inside the Kaisha: Demystifying Japanese business behavior*. Boston: Harvard Business School.

Concepts and Questions

1. In their article, McDaniel and Katsumata took you on a tour of the Japanese educational system. What are the differences between preschool/kindergarten education in Japan and that in the United States?

2. In what ways does the Japanese preschool/kindergarten experience promote group orientation?

3. Describe how Japanese elementary students are organized in order to promote group harmony. What role does the *han* play in this process?

4. How does the fact that teachers often address the *han* rather than individual students promote group orientation?

5. What differences in purpose are there in the wearing of uniforms by Japanese students and the wearing of uniforms by students in American public schools?

6. How does the organization and duration of the Japanese middle school or high school student differ from that of U.S. students?

7. How do students who have graduated from high school establish new group affiliations to replace the group support they had from preselected groups in their school years?

8. What conclusions can you draw about the importance of sports clubs in promoting group orientations?

9. How does the introduction of college students to corporate life in Japan differ from how it occurs in the United States?

10. Although work groups are common in all cultures to accomplish what cannot be done by individuals, what characterizes Japanese groups as being different from other groups?

Communicating Interculturally: Becoming Competent

The fish only knows that it lives in the water
after it is already on the river bank. Without
our awareness of another world out there, it
would never occur to us to change.

SOURCE UNKNOWN

We believe that the reference to "change" in this opening quotation serves as a fitting introduction to a chapter that deals with becoming a competent communicator. Part of gaining that competence requires you to examine your communication behavior and be willing to make changes that will improve the manner in which you interact with people from different cultures. We should also add as part of this introduction that while this chapter uses the term "Becoming Competent" in its title, in a sense this entire edition has been concerned with helping you become a competent intercultural communicator. Each of the preceding chapters introduced you to many diverse cultures and settings to show you how people from cultures different from your own view the world and how they interact in their world. It is our belief that by observing these cultural differences you will collect a fund of knowledge that will be helpful when you interact with people from other cultures. However, our analysis so far has been more theoretical than practical. Knowing about other cultures and people is only the first step in attempting to understand how intercultural communication works. In reality, taking part in intercultural communication requires reciprocal and complementary participation by you and your communication partner(s). This means that intercultural communication becomes an activity in which participants must make simultaneous inferences not only about their own roles but also about the role of the other(s) in the interaction. This act of mutual role taking must exist before people can achieve a level of communication that results in shared understanding. In intercultural communication, this means that you must understand both your own culture and the culture of the other person(s) as well.

The motivation for this chapter grows from our belief that communication is something *people do—a shared activity that involves action*. Regardless of how much you may understand another culture or person on an intellectual level, even if you have a clear picture of them in your head, in the final analysis communication means interaction. This means you are part of a behavioral exchange and must be prepared to adjust your communicative behaviors to the specifics of the interaction while "engaging" in communication. The series of readings in this chapter are intended to improve the way you interact by providing some of the information needed to develop and improve your intercultural communication competence.

There are two common threads that tie all the selections in this chapter together. First, they all speak of potential communication problems. Second, they also offer some solutions to those problems. It is our contention that being alert to potential problems, and knowing how to solve them, is a major step toward achieving intercultural communication competence. In short, once problems have been identified, it is easier to seek means of improvement—and improvement is at the heart of this chapter.

The first essay titled "A Model of Intercultural Communication Competence" focuses on making you a more competent communicator, which is the objective not only of this chapter but of this edition as well. In this essay, Brian H. Spitzberg offers the profile of an effective intercultural communicator. More specifically, he suggests a course of action that is likely to enhance your competence when you are in an intercultural setting. His advice is in the form of a series of ten propositions for success that have been well documented by numerous studies in communication. By letting these propositions guide your actions, Spitzberg believes you can become a more successful intercultural communicator. You are asked to (1) be motivated, (2) be knowledgeable, (3) practice using effective interpersonal skills, (4) be credible, (5) try to meet the expectations of your communication partner, (6) strike a balance between autonomy needs and intimacy needs, (7) reflect similarities, (8) manifest trust, (9) offer social support, and (10) have access to multiple relationships.

The second essay in this chapter is by Guo-Ming Chen and is titled "Intercultural Effectiveness." This selection, much like Spitzberg's, addresses the issue of how you can become a more competent intercultural communicator. Chen notes, "Only through communication competence can people from different cultures interact effectively and productively in the globalizing society." To foster that effectiveness Chen examines the area of communication competence from a host of specific features. He begins by discussing the three general components of intercultural communication competence. First, you should develop personal characteristics such as being flexible, sensitive, open-minded, and motivated. Second, you must be aware of the characteristics of your own culture and acquire knowledge of other cultures. Third, you must learn to adjust and adapt to new patterns of behavior as you come in contact with people from cultures different than your own.

Once the three universal components are identified, Chen offers a detailed summary of how these components get translated in specific behavioral skills. These actions revolve around specific behaviors that can improve your communication. The first is what Chen calls "message skills." They are the verbal and nonverbal communication skills that you need to develop as part of your training in intercultural communication. Second, Chen suggests that a competent communicator can engage in "interaction management." This is the ability to initiate, terminate, and engage in appropriate "turn-taking." Third, the successful intercultural communicator is effectively practicing "behavioral flexibility." What this means is that you can select your method of communication from a host of options, what Chen calls "selecting proper strategies." The fourth skill refers to what we presented in Chapter Two when we looked at the topic of identity. However, as Chen's essay points out, your identity, and that of your communication partner, must be managed during an interaction. More specifically, he is concerned with how you maintain your identity while also preserving someone else's. The final skill Chen discusses is called "relationship cultivation." This refers to a talent that underscores the independent and reciprocal processes of interaction we referred to in the overview of this chapter when we explained the tandem relationship existing in most communication exchanges. Chen believes it is important to establish a certain level of affiliation with your communication partner in order to satisfy his or her needs as well as yours.

A competent intercultural communicator is one who is able to adjust to and interact effectively in a culture other than his or her own. This adjustment, however, is not always a simple matter. Immersion in another culture often leads you into a condition called "culture shock" which leaves you feeling alone, alienated, confused, and disoriented. This condition may even cause you to question your ability to successfully function in the new cultural environment. Your ability to interact effectively in a host culture will depend on your ability to cope with and overcome the feelings and effects of culture shock.

A large amount of research has focused on the culture shock phenomenon, resulting in an abundant number of books and essays devoted to analyzing it and describing how to recognize and overcome its effects. Our next essay introduces you to the effects of culture shock through the personal experiences of three women. In their essay "Dialectics of Doubt and Accomplishment—Recounting What Counts in Cultural Immersions," Summer Carnett, Katherine Slauta, and Patricia Geist-Martin recount their experiences of cultural adjustment and the difficulties they faced while doing ethnographic research during a six-month immersion in Costa Rican culture.

The authors begin with a brief narrative of their arrival in San José, Costa Rica, and the difficulties they encountered just in adapting to daily routines: converting currency, ordering sandwiches in a deli, and seeking directions. They also relate that as women walking around with their *gringa* (U. S. American) faces they were easily identified as foreigners. As a result, they encountered cat calls, and more seriously an increased risk of attack by thieves and gangs who wandered the streets. Their collective reaction was that "as ethnographers, we were turned upside down." Their ability to collect data was frequently thwarted by normative Costa Rican cultural processes which produced feelings of doubt, embarrassment, and tensions from "two cultures colliding."

The authors continue their essay through individual narratives in which each author relates her personal experiences and feelings of self-doubt and incompetence during the first stages of adapting to their new cultural environment. Each author reports experiencing a sense of alienation—of not belonging, of being a tolerated outsider until they individually had encounters that made them feel a part of, and shared an identity with, the host culture. These occurrences were not instant adjustments to the culture but were small experiences that revealed the shared humanity between the authors and the people they encountered. The result of these experiences produced feelings of acceptance: Even though they did not blend in with the Costa Ricans, they were nonetheless accepted.

The authors end their essay with individual narratives that relate how they came to understand that in order for them to maintain their spiritual and psychological health in the face of culture shock, they had to learn not only how to adapt to the cultural differences, but to also embrace those differences. "Rather than fearing uncertainty, we needed to learn to enjoy it, even *relish* in it."

The final selection in this chapter by Marc D. Rich, Lucretia R. Robinson, Courtney Ahrens, and José I. Rodriguez is titled "Proactive Performance to Prevent Sexual

Assault: Understanding the Role of Masculinity in Violence Against Women." As the title indicates, the authors examine this very vital and timely topic from a somewhat unique perspective—the theater. They explain how a traveling troupe of actors, who interact with the members of their audience, seek to have their drama "reduce sexual assaults on college campuses, create empathy for women who have been assaulted, and challenge traditional gender roles." It would be a major understatement to say that the growing epidemic of assaults on women is a topic worthy of their consideration—and yours. By some estimates, twenty-seven percent of college women experience rape or attempted rape. To help reduce this serious social problem the authors share their very unique program. The traveling troupe, called interACT, visits campuses and community groups and presents a series of vignettes that depict the kind of situations that might lead to sexual assaults. All of the presentations have an emotional interactive component where members of the audience are asked to share their personal feelings regarding the skits they have observed. Part of the troupe's presentation focuses on many typical but unhealthy gender roles that can provoke, encourage, and even contribute to violence against women. Discussions center on topics such as alcohol consumption and degrading conversations about women. This give-and-take between the actors and the audience encourages a realistic examination of the problems associated with negative gender roles.

A Model of Intercultural Communication Competence

Brian H. Spitzberg

The world we live in is shrinking. Travel that once took months now takes hours. Business dealings that were once confined primarily to local economies have given way to an extensively integrated world economy. Information that once traveled through error-prone and time-consuming methods now appears in the blink of an eye across a wide range of media. People in virtually all locations of the globe are more mobile than ever and more likely to traverse into cultures different than their own. Literally and figuratively, the walls that separate us are tumbling down. Though we may not have fully become a "global village," there is no denying that the various cultures of the world are far more accessible than ever before, and that the peoples of these cultures are coming into contact at an ever-increasing rate. These contacts ultimately comprise interpersonal encounters. Whether it is the negotiation of an arms treaty, the settlement of a business contract, or merely a sojourner getting directions from a native, cultures do not interact, people do.

The purpose of this essay is to examine the concept of interactional competence in intercultural contexts. For *the purposes of this essay, intercultural communication competence is considered very broadly as an impression that behavior is appropriate and effective in a given context.* Normally, competence is considered to be an ability or a set of skilled behaviors. However, any given behavior or ability may be judged competent in one context and incompetent in another. Consequently, competence cannot be defined by the behavior or

ability itself. It must instead be viewed as a social evaluation of behavior. This social evaluation comprises the two primary criteria of appropriateness and effectiveness.

Appropriateness means that behavior is viewed as legitimate for, or fitting to, the context. To be appropriate ordinarily implies that the valued rules, norms, and expectancies of the relationship are not violated significantly. Under some circumstances, however, a person violates existing norms to establish new norms. A colleague with whom you work and almost exclusively exchange task information may one day take you aside to talk about a personal problem. This violation of norms, however, may not seem inappropriate as you come to see this person as a friend rather than just a colleague.

Effectiveness is often equated with competence (Bradford, Allen, & Beisser, 1998). Here *effectiveness* is viewed as the accomplishment of valued goals or rewards relative to costs and alternatives. Effectiveness is relative to the available options. For example, effectiveness often implies satisfaction, but there are times when all reasonable courses of action are dissatisfying or ineffective. In such a context, the most effective response may be simply the least dissatisfying. For example, many people find virtually all conflict dissatisfying. If your partner breaks up with you, you may find there is no "effective" response (i.e., something that would "win" this person back). But there are reactions that may be more or less effective in achieving other objectives (e.g., maintaining a friendship, getting your compact discs back, etc.). Effectiveness is also related to, but distinct from, efficiency. *Efficiency,* or expediency, is concerned with communication that is "direct, immediate, and to the point" (Kellerman & Shea, 1996, p. 151). Generally, more efficient communication is considered more effective because it presumes less effort. However, obviously efficient behavior is not always the most effective in obtaining preferred outcomes.

Communication in an intercultural context, therefore, is competent when it accomplishes the objectives of an actor in a manner that is appropriate to the context. *Context* here implies several levels, including culture, relationship, place, and function (Spitzberg & Brunner, 1991). The chapters of this book all illustrate the importance of culture to the use and evaluation of behavior. The competence of behavior also depends significantly on the type of relationship between the interactants. What is appropriate for spouses is not always appropriate for colleagues or friends. Competence also depends on place, or the physical environment. Behavior appropriate for fans at a sporting event will rarely be appropriate at a funeral. Finally, the competence of behavior is influenced by function, or what the communicators are attempting to do. Behavior appropriate for a conflict is often quite different than behavior appropriate for a first date.

The two standards of appropriateness and effectiveness also depend on interaction quality. Quality can be defined by these two criteria by examining the four possible communication styles that result. Communication that is inappropriate and ineffective is clearly of low quality and is referred to as *minimizing*. Communication by someone that is appropriate but ineffective suggests a social chameleon who does nothing objectionable but also accomplishes no personal objectives through interaction. This suggests a *sufficing* style, or one that is sufficient to meet the minimum demands of the situation but accomplishes nothing more. Communication that is inappropriate but effective includes such behaviors as lying, cheating, coercing, forcing, and so forth, which are messages that are ethically problematic. This *maximizing* style reflects a person who attempts to achieve everything, even if it is at the expense of others. While there may be instances in which such actions could be considered competent, they are rarely the ideal behaviors to employ in any given circumstance. Interactants who achieve their goals in a manner that is simultaneously appropriate to the context are competent in an *optimizing* way.

A MODEL OF INTERCULTURAL COMPETENCE

Most existing models of intercultural competence have been fairly fragmented (Lustig & Spitzberg, 1993; Martin, 1993). Typically, the literature is reviewed and a list of skills, abilities, and attitudes is formulated to summarize the literature (Spitzberg &

Cupach, 1989). Such lists appear on the surface to reflect useful guidelines for competent interaction and adaptation. For example, Spitzberg's (1989) review of studies reveals dozens of skills, including ability to deal with stress, understanding, awareness of culture, cautiousness, charisma, cooperation, conversational management, empathy, frankness, future orientation, flexibility, interest, managerial ability, opinion leadership, task persistence, self-actualization, self-confidence, self-disclosure, and strength of personality. Although each study portrays a reasonable list of abilities or attitudes, there is no sense of integration or coherence across lists. It is impossible to tell which skills are most important in which situations, or even how such skills relate to each other. In addition, such lists become cumbersome, as it is difficult to imagine trying to learn dozens of complex skills to become competent.

A more productive approach would be to develop an integrative model of intercultural competence that is consistent with the theoretical and empirical literatures and provides specific predictions of competent behavior. This approach is reflected in basic form in Figure 1 and elaborated by means of a series of propositions to follow. The propositions are broken down into three levels of analysis: the individual system, the episodic system, and the relational system. The *individual system* includes those characteristics of an individual that facilitate competent interaction in a normative social sense. The *episodic system* includes those features of a particular actor that facilitate competent interaction on the part of a specific co-actor in a specific episode of interaction. The *relational system* includes those components that assist a person's competence across the entire span of relationships rather than in just a given episode of interaction. Each successive system level subsumes the logic and predictions of the former. The propositions serve both to provide an outline of a theory of interpersonal competence in intercultural contexts and to offer practical advice, to the extent interactants analyze intercultural situations sufficiently, and then each proposition suggests a course of action that is likely to enhance their competence in the situation encountered.

By way of overview, the model portrays the process of dyadic interaction as a function of two individuals' *motivation* to communicate, *knowledge*

Figure 1 *An Integrative Model of Intercultural Competence*

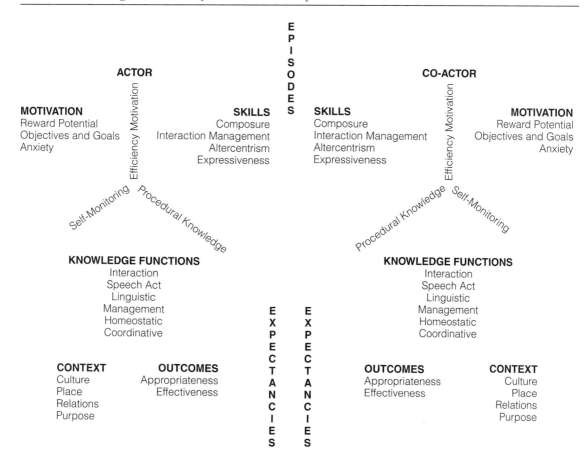

of communication in that context, and *skills* in implementing their motivation and knowledge. Over the course of the interaction both within and across episodes, behavior is matched to expectancies each person has of the other and of the interaction process. If expectancies are fulfilled in a rewarding manner, then interactants are likely to perceive both self and other as communicatively competent and feel relatively satisfied that objectives are accomplished. Interactants may be seen as incompetent because they lack motivation to perform competently, knowledge of the competent lines of action in the context concerned, or simply the communication skills to carry off a deft interaction. Also, interactants may be viewed as incompetent because their partner has unrealistic expectancies of the person or episode.

INDIVIDUAL SYSTEM

1. As Communicator Motivation Increases, Communicative Competence Increases

Put simply, the more a person wants to make a good impression and communicate effectively, the more likely it is that this person will view self, and be viewed by others, as competent. What constitutes or leads to high levels of motivation? The following propositions address this question.

1a. As Communicator Confidence Increases, Communicator Motivation Increases. Confidence results from several individual experiences. For example, a person who is nervous meeting strangers is likely to be less confident when encountering a new person from a different culture. Further, the more unfamiliar a person is with a given type of situation, the less confident that person is regarding what to do and how to do it. Finally, some situations carry more significant implications and are more difficult to manage than others. For example, getting directions to a major urban landmark is likely to permit greater confidence than negotiating a multi-million dollar contract for your company. Thus, social anxiety, familiarity with the situation, and the importance or consequences of the encounter all influence a person's confidence in a social context.

1b. As Reward-Relevant Communicator Efficacy Beliefs Increase, Communicator Motivation Increases.
Efficacy beliefs are self-perceptions of ability to perform a given set of behaviors (Bandura, 1982). Basically, the more actors believe they are able to engage in a set of valued or positive actions, the more prone they are to do so. A professional arbitrator is likely to have much higher efficacy beliefs in negotiating disputes or contracts than the average person. However, this arbitrator might not have a greater confidence than the average person in developing friendships with others in a different culture. Efficacy beliefs are therefore usually task specific and depend on familiarity with tasks and contexts.

1c. As Communicator Approach Dispositions Increase, Communicator Motivation Increases.
Approach dispositions refer to personality characteristics that prompt someone to value communicative activity. Several dispositions have been found to influence motivation. People who are higher in self-esteem, who consistently seek relatively high levels of sensory stimulation, who believe they have high levels of control over their environment, who are low in social anxiety (Neuliep & McCroskey, 1997), and who are generally well adjusted psychologically, are likely to seek out communication encounters and find them positively reinforcing. Furthermore, people who are more interculturally tolerant are more likely to engage in competent interaction across cultures (Mendleson, Bures, Champion, & Lott, 1997).

1d. As the Relative Cost–Benefit Ratio of a Situation Increases, Communicator Motivation Increases.
Put simply, every situation can be viewed as having certain potential costs and benefits. Even in no-win situations (e.g., "true" conflicts), the behavior that leads to the least costly or a painful outcome is considered the most preferable or beneficial. Likewise, in a win-win situation, the least desirable outcomes are also the most costly. As the perception of potential benefits increases relative to the potential costs of a course of action, a person becomes more motivated to pursue that particular course of action. Obviously, the weighing of costs and benefits must always be done relative to alternatives. Asking directions from someone who does not speak your language may be considered too effortful, but only relative to the alternatives of consulting a map, trial-and-error exploration, seeking someone who speaks your language and might be familiar with the locale, or getting hopelessly lost.

2. As Communicative Knowledge Increases, Communicative Competence Increases

A stage actor needs to be motivated to give a good performance to be viewed as a competent actor. However, merely wanting to perform well and being unhampered by stage fright are rarely sufficient to produce a competent performance. The actor also needs to know the script, the layout of the stage, the type of audience to expect, and so forth. Similarly, the more an interactant knows about how to communicate well, the more competent that person is likely to be.

Knowledge of interaction occurs at several microscopic levels (Greene, 1984). As identified in Figure 1, an actor needs to know the basic goals or *interaction* functions being pursued. These interaction behaviors are combined to fulfill *content* functions, which include the production of speech acts such as asking questions, asserting opinions, and making promises. To perform speech acts in turn requires knowledge of semantics, syntax, and the constituents of a meaningful sentence. In other words, grammatical sentences are formed to fulfill a *linguistic* function. Actual performance of these actions requires adaptation of this behavior to the other person. Such adaptation includes achieving coherence, continuity of topic, and relatively smooth flow of speaking turns (i.e., *management* function), a relative balance of physiological activity level (i.e., *homeostatic* function), and an individual matching of verbal and nonverbal components (i.e., *coordinative* function). Several predictions help specify the relevance of knowledge to competent interaction.

2a. As Task-Relevant Procedural Knowledge Increases, Communicator Knowledge Increases.
Procedural knowledge concerns the "how" of social interaction rather than the "what." For example, knowing the actual content of a joke would be considered the substantive knowledge of the joke. Knowing how to tell it, with all the inflections, subtle timing, and actual mannerisms, are all matters of the procedural knowledge of the joke. This knowledge is typically more "mindless" than other forms of knowledge. Many skill routines are overlearned to the point that the procedures are virtually forgotten, as in driving a familiar route home and not remembering anything about the drive upon arrival. You "know" how to drive, but you can use such knowledge with virtually no conscious attention to the process. Thus, the more a person actually knows how to perform the mannerisms and behavioral routines of a cultural milieu, the more knowledgeable this person is likely to be in communicating with others in this culture. In general, as a person's exposure to a culture increases, his or her stores of relevant subject matters, topics, language forms, as well as procedural competencies are likely to increase.

2b. As Mastery of Knowledge Acquisition Strategies Increases, Communicator Knowledge Increases.
A person who does not already know how to behave is not necessarily consigned to incompetence. People have evolved many means for finding out what to do, and how to do it, in unfamiliar contexts. The metaphor of international espionage illustrates some of the strategies by which people acquire information about others, such as interrogation (e.g., asking questions), surveillance (e.g., observing others), information exchange (e.g., disclosing information to elicit disclosure from others), posturing (e.g., violating some local custom and observing reactions to assess value of various

actions), bluffing (e.g., acting as if we know what we are doing and letting the unfolding action inform us and define our role), or engaging double agents (e.g., using the services of a native or mutual friend as informant). The more actors understand these types of strategies, the more capable they are in obtaining the knowledge needed to interact competently in the culture.

2c. As Identity and Role Diversity Increases, Communicator Knowledge Increases.
In general, the more diverse a person's exposure to distinct types of people, roles, and self-images, the more this person is able to comprehend various roles and role behaviors characteristic of a given cultural encounter. Some people live all their lives in a culture within very narrow ranges of contexts and roles. Others experience a wide variety of societal activities (e.g., jobs, tasks), roles (e.g., parent, worshiper, confidant), and groups (e.g., political party, religious affiliation, volunteer organization, cultures and co-cultures). A person who has a highly complex self-image reflecting these social identities (Hoelter, 1985) and has interacted with a diversity of different types of persons and roles (Havighurst, 1957) is better able to understand the types of actions encountered in another culture.

2d. As Knowledge Dispositions Increase, Communication Knowledge Increases.
Many personality characteristics are related to optimal information processing. Specifically, persons higher in intelligence, cognitive complexity, self-monitoring, listening skills, empathy, role-taking ability, nonverbal sensitivity, perceptual accuracy, creativity, and problem-solving ability, are more likely to know how to behave in any given encounter. In short, while mere possession of information may help, a person also needs to know how to analyze and process that information.

3. As Communicator Skills Increase, Communicator Competence Increases

Skills are repeatable, goal-oriented actions or action sequences. A person who is motivated to perform well and knows the script well still may not possess the acting skills required to give a good performance. All of us have probably encountered instances in which we knew what we wanted to say but just could not seem to say it correctly. Such issues concern the skills of performing our motivation and knowledge. Research indicates that there are four specific clusters of interpersonal skills and one more general type of skill.

Before specifying the nature of skills that facilitate intercultural communication competence, an important qualifier needs to be considered. There are probably no specific behaviors that are universally competent. Even if peoples from all cultures smile, the smile is not always a competent behavior. However, there may be skills that are consistently competent according to standards of appropriate usage within each culture. For example, probably all cultures value the smooth flow of conversation, even though they may differ in the specific behaviors and cues used to accomplish such interaction management. All cultures apparently value eye contact and the use of questions, even if they vary greatly in the *way* in which these skills are appropriately used. Any skill or ability is constrained by its own contextual rules of expression. Thus, skills are always assessed relative to their *contextual frame*. It is in this sense that the following propositions are developed regarding communication skills.

3a. As Conversational Altercentrism Increases, Communicator Skill Increases.

Altercentrism ("alter" means other, "centrism" means to focus upon) involves those behaviors that reveal concern for, interest in, and attention to another person or persons. Behaviors such as eye contact, asking questions, maintenance of others' topics, appropriate body lean and posture, and active listening all indicate responsiveness to the other person.

3b. As Conversational Coordination Increases, Communicator Skill Increases.

Conversational coordination involves all those behaviors that assist in the smooth flow of an encounter. Minimizing long response delays, providing for smooth initiation and conclusion of conversational episodes, avoiding disruptive interruptions, providing transitions between themes or activities, and providing informative feedback cues all assist in managing the interaction and maintaining appropriate pacing, rhythms, and punctuation of a conversation.

3c. As Conversational Composure Increases, Communicator Skill Increases.

To be composed in a conversation is to reflect calmness and confidence in demeanor. Composure consists of avoiding anxiety cues such as nervous twitches, tapping of feet, lack of eye contact, and breaking vocal pitch. Conversely, composure also implies behaviors such as a steady volume and pitch, relaxed posture, well-formulated verbal statements, and self-assured tones of verbal and nonverbal expression. A composed communicator tends to appear in control of his or her own behavior.

3d. As Conversational Expressiveness Increases, Communicator Skill Increases.

Expressiveness concerns those skills that provide vivacity, animation, intensity, and variability in communicative behavior. Expressiveness is revealed by such behaviors as vocal variety, facial affect, opinion expression, extensive vocabulary usage, and gestures. Expressive communication is closely associated with the ability to display culturally and contextually appropriate affect and energy level through speech and gesture.

3e. As Conversational Adaptation Increases, Communicator Skill Increases.

Adaptation is a commonly noted attribute of the competent intercultural communicator. It typically suggests several characteristics. First, rather than radical chameleon-like change, adaptation implies subtle variation of self's behavior to the behavioral style of others. Second, it implies certain homeostatic or consistency-maintaining, regulatory processes—that is, verbal actions are kept relatively consistent with nonverbal actions. Similarly, amounts of personal altercentrism, coordination, composure, and expressiveness are kept relatively consistent with personal style tendencies. Third, adaptation suggests accommodation of both the actions of the other person as well as one's own goal(s) in the encounter. Rather than implying completely alter-centric or egocentric orientations, adaptation implies altering and balancing self's goals and intentions to those of the other person. Thus, the skill of adaptation implies such behaviors as shifts of vocal style, posture, animation, and topic development, as the behaviors of the other person vary and as changes in self's goals change over the course of a conversation.

The propositions in this section have examined three basic individual components of interculturally competent communication. In general, the more motivated, knowledgeable, and skilled a person is, the more competent this person is likely to be. It is possible that a person can be viewed as highly competent if high in only one or two of these components. For example, a person who is very motivated may compensate for lack of knowledge and skill through perseverance and effort alone. Likewise, someone who is extremely familiar with a given type of encounter may be able to "drift" through an interaction with minimal access to his or her motivation. A salesperson might claim to have "written so many contracts in my life I can negotiate one in my sleep." Nevertheless, across most encounters, the more of each of these components a person possesses or demonstrates, the more competent this person's interaction is likely to be.

EPISODIC SYSTEM

The first three primary propositions represented factors that increase the likelihood of an actor to produce behaviors that are normatively competent. However, given that competence is an impression, there is no guarantee that a person who has performed behaviors that normally would be viewed as competent will be viewed as competent by a particular conversational partner in a particular relational encounter. The propositions in this section address this latter issue. These propositions are episodic in the sense that characteristics of an actor influence the impressions of the co-actor in a specific episode of interaction. The statements concern those characteristics of an actor that predict co-actor's impression of actor's competence.

4. As Actor's Communicative Status Increases, Co-Actor's Impression of Actor's Competence Increases

Communicative status is meant here to represent all those factors that enhance a person's positive evaluation. Competence is, after all, an evaluation. Generally, as a person's status goes, so goes his or her competence. There are obvious exceptions, but it is instructive to consider those status characteristics particularly relevant to communicative competence.

4a. As Actor's Motivation, Knowledge, and Skills Increase, Co-Actor's Impression of Actor's Competence Increases.

The logic of the individual system also applies to the episodic system—that is, the factors that lead a person to behave competently in a normative sense will usually lead to a competent relational performance as well (Imahori & Lanigan, 1989; Spitzberg & Cupach, 1984). This is true in two slightly different senses. In one sense, norms comprise the majority of people's views and behaviors, so a person who is normatively competent will usually be viewed as competent in any given encounter. In another sense, an actor who is motivated to interact competently with a particular co-actor, knowledgeable about this particular co-actor, and skilled in interacting with this particular co-actor also is more likely to communicate better and be viewed as competent by this co-actor in a given encounter.

Factors that facilitate motivation, knowledge, and skill in a particular episodic system are likely to be logical extensions of the individual system components. For example, motivation is likely to increase as attraction to co-actor increases and as positive reinforcement history with co-actor increases. Knowledge of co-actor is likely to increase with duration of relationship, and depth and breadth of self-disclosure between actor and co-actor increase. Skill in interacting with co-actor is likely to increase as adaptation and refinement increase over the lifetime of the relationship.

4b. As Contextual Obstruction of Actor's Performance Increase, Co-Actor's Impression of Actor's Competence Increase.

When forming an impression of an actor, a co-actor is left to determine the extent to which the actor's outcomes are due to the actor's own abilities and effort, rather than the context or other factors. For example, a physically unattractive actor who consistently makes friends and has dates is likely to be viewed as more communicatively competent than a person who is physically attractive. The reasoning is that the social context is weighted against the unattractive actor and in favor of the attractive actor. Thus, the attractive actor would achieve the same outcomes due to attractiveness rather than his or her competence, whereas the unattractive actor must overcome the contextual barriers through more competent action. In essence, all other things being equal, an actor's competence is "discounted" if there are obvious alternative explanations for the actor's good fortune. Similarly, an actor's competence is "forgiven" if there are many apparent alternative reasons for his or her failure.

4c. As Actor's Receipt of Valued Outcomes Increases, Co-actor's Impression of Actor's Competence Increases.

While the discounting effect discussed above influences impressions of competence, it is not likely to outweigh other factors entirely. If an actor is perceived as consistently achieving positive outcomes, a co-actor is likely to assume that the actor has some thing to do with this success (Kaplowitz, 1978). The negotiator who consistently presides over significant agreements is likely to be viewed as more communicatively competent as a simple result of the tangible outcomes, almost regardless of extenuating circumstances.

4d. As Actor's Extant Attributed Communicative Status Increases, Co-Actor's Impression of Actor Status Increases.

An actor who comes into an encounter with an established high level of status is more likely to be viewed as competent in subsequent interactions. In addition, an actor who has established a satisfying relationship with a particular co-actor has, in effect, established a reserve of competence in the co-actor's views. Thus, Nelson Mandela, or even Bill Gates enters any communicative situation with considerable communicative status in tow. In essence, then, the impression we initially have of an actor is likely to be the basis for our later impressions until such time that significant events

alter these impressions. Furthermore, certain cultures develop higher regard for other cultures generally. The mutual regard that Americans and Japanese Americans may share is probably quite different than that which the South African Blacks and Whites may share.

5. Co-Actor's Impression of Actor's Competence Is a Function of Actor's Fulfillment of Co-Actor's Expectancies

Over time, interactants develop expectations regarding how interpersonal interaction is likely to and should occur in particular contexts. Not surprisingly, therefore, a person's competence in a given relationship is due partly to expectancy fulfillment and violation. Research indicates that expectancies generally develop along the three fundamental EPA dimensions: *evaluation, potency,* and *activity* (Osgood, May, & Miron, 1975; Spitzberg, 1989); that is, most contexts are viewed in terms of their valence (e.g., good versus bad), power (e.g., dominant versus passive), and animation (e.g., noisy versus quiet). A traditional, noncharismatic church service typically is expected to be good (valence), with the audience passive (potency) and relatively quiet (activity). A typical party, in contrast, is expected to be good (valence), strong (potency), fast, and noisy (activity). Upon being fired, an exit interview is expected to be unpleasurable (valence), and the interviewee as weak (potency) and relatively passive (activity). The point is that experience with interpersonal encounters produces expectancies and evaluations about both anticipated and appropriate behavior. The propositions below elaborate the influence of these expectancies.

5a. As Actor's Fulfillment of Positive Co-Actor Expectancies Increases, Co-Actor's Impression of Actor's Competence Increases.

To the extent that a co-actor expects an encounter with an actor to be positive, the actor is likely to be viewed as competent to the extent that he or she fulfills these expectancies. Because the expectancies typically form a consistent system in a co-actor's mind, an actor needs to fulfill each of the EPA dimensions. If an interviewer expects interviews to

Figure 2 *A Simplified Cognitive Prototype of a Competent Communicator*

Prototype Category			The Competent Communicator			
Intermediate Inferences		Friendly	Trustworthy		Assertive	
Behavioral Indicators	Smiles	Talkative	Reliable	Honest	Gestures	Animated
		Socializes	Keeps Secrets		Expresses Opinions	

be good (E), his or her own role to be relatively powerful and the role of the interviewee to be relatively powerless (P), and the encounter to be generally quiet but quick (A), then the actor is well advised to behave according to these expectancies. Because the interviewer has developed these expectancies along all three dimensions, they tend to be "set" in relationship to each other. Thus, part of what makes the interview "well" in the interviewer's opinion is that the interviewer's role is typically powerful, and the interviews tend to go quietly and quickly.

5b. As Actor's Normative Violation of Co-Actor's Negative Expectancies Increases, Co-Actor's Impression of Actor's Competence Increases. The logic of the former proposition reverses itself when a co-actor expects an encounter to be negative. Consider the previous interview example from the interviewee's perspective. An interviewee may find interviews highly anxiety-producing, threatening, and difficult. As such, the interview context is expected to be uncomfortable, the interviewee's role as submissive, and the encounter as generally slow and inactive. So, if the interviewer wants to make a good impression, then he or she needs to violate the interviewee's expectations in an appropriate manner. Such an interviewer might change the setting to a less formal lunchroom context, dress more casually, tell some stories and initially discuss topics unrelated to the position, and generally spend time putting the interviewee in a good mood. Such an encounter violates the interviewee's expectancies, but does so in a way that is normatively acceptable and positive.

5c. As Actor's Fulfillment of Co-Actor's Competence Prototype Expectancies Increases, Co-Actor's Impression of Actor's Competence Increases. A prototype in this usage is basically a cognitive outline of concepts, analogous to a mental map of the competence territory. The prototype of a competent person is likely to consist of several levels of concepts varying in their abstraction. A simplified example of a competent communicator prototype is displayed in Figure 2 above.

At the highest level is the category label that determines what types of inferences are relevant to a given set of observed behavior. For example, observing someone changing the oil in a car is not relevant to the category of "competent communicator." At the next level are types of inferences or impressions that collectively constitute the label of competent communicator. In this hypothetical example, a competent communicator is someone who is believed to be friendly, trustworthy, and assertive. Each inference, in turn, is based on certain types of behavior. To the extent that these behaviors are observed, the inferences follow. Observed behaviors are matched or compared to those that over time have come to occupy the position of category indicators. If there is a good match, then the inferences and evaluations that make up the label of competent communicator (in this case, friendly, trustworthy, assertive) are attributed to the person observed. If only some of the behaviors match, then the inference of competence is diminished proportionately. Certain behaviors in any given encounter also may be weighted in their importance to the impression. When judging whether or not someone is being deceptive, for example, many people would rely most heavily on that person's eye contact, relative to other behaviors, in assessing his or her competence.

5d. As Actor's Normative Reciprocity of Positive Affect and Compensation of Negative Affect Increases, Co-Actor's Impression of Actor's Competence Increases.

Reciprocity implies a matching or similarity of response, whereas compensation suggests an opposite or homeostatic response. Research indicates that across most types of relationships and encounters, interactants are generally considered more competent when they reciprocate positive affect and feel more competent when they compensate for negative affect (Andersen, 1998; Spitzberg, 1989). To the extent that co-actor expresses positive affect, the actor's response in kind is likely to produce more positive impressions. When the co-actor expresses negative affect, the actor is likely to be more competent, responding with more neutral or positive affect.

5e. As Actor's Normative Compensation of Power Relations Increases, the More Co-Actor's Impression of Actor's Competence Increases.

Across most types of interpersonal relationships, complementary power relationships tend to produce higher impressions of competence. This is obviously an overstatement in many ways. For example, optimal negotiation outcomes tend to result when parties begin with a competitive and end up in a cooperative orientation. Still, this principle is useful in most types of relations.

Specifically, dominance is more competently met with passivity, and passivity with dominance, than vice versa. The validity of this proposition is best illustrated by considering its alternative. Imagine, for example, reciprocal dominance in work relationships in which every time a superior gives a subordinate orders, the superior is met with counter orders or refusal. Imagine symmetric passivity in married couples in which neither person ever actually makes a decision. In other words, relationships and encounters tend to work more smoothly and comfortably when dominant moves are responded to with complementary passive moves, and passive moves are met with more directive moves. This does not imply that people should adopt a role of passivity or dominance, but

that, in general, on a statement-by-statement basis, most interaction will be viewed as competent to the extent that its power balance is complementary rather than reciprocal.

This section has examined the episodic system of intercultural competence. Specifically, the propositions in this section have involved those characteristics of an actor that increase the likelihood that a co-actor views the actor as competent in a given episode of interaction. The following section concerns an abbreviated excursion into the relational system, in which characteristics that facilitate competence across the life span of a relationship are considered.

RELATIONAL SYSTEM

Relationships are not simply sums of episodes over time. Certainly, the more competent the average episode of interaction, the more relationally stable and satisfying the relationship is likely to be. In this sense, the logic of the individual system and episodic system also extends to the relational system. However, other factors are at work, and the following section examines some of these features. In this discussion, the phrase "relational competence" refers to the level of communicative quality in an established relationship.

6. As Mutual Fulfillment of Autonomy and Intimacy Needs Increases, Relational Competence Increases

Autonomy and intimacy are two fundamental human needs (McAdams, 1988). Typically, they exist in a form of dialectical tension: Both "struggle" for dominance over the other at any given time, but both are ever-present to some degree. The need for intimacy involves the desire for human contact, connection, belonging, inclusion, camaraderie, communal activity, and nurturance. The need for autonomy, in contrast, is a need for self-control, independence, power, privacy, and solitude. Individuals seem to fluctuate between these two needs over time. And, as with virtually all needs, as each need is fulfilled, it ceases to dominate the individual's behavior. A lonely person continuously thinks about companionship. Once companionship is found, other needs begin to influence this person's thoughts and actions. It follows that if a relationship is competent over the course of its life span, then the members need to fulfill the needs of each other as these dialectical needs fluctuate (Spitzberg, 1993).

7. As Mutual Attraction Increases, Relational Competence Increases

This highly intuitive proposition simply indicates that as partners grow more and more attracted to each other, their relationship is likely to result in and reflect mutually competent interaction over time (Eagly, Ashmore, Makhijani, & Longo, 1991). This proposition gains support from the consistent finding that attraction is closely associated, at least initially, with interpersonal similarity (Feingold, 1988). Highly similar persons provide a worldview of similar values and orientations, as well as similar communication skills that facilitate interaction (Burleson & Denton, 1992). In general, we enjoy interacting with those who are similar because they seem to "speak our language." One implication is that initial interactions with culturally dissimilar others should focus on areas of similarity that can support sufficient motivation and reinforcement for continued interaction. This is not to imply that differences are always negatively reinforcing. However, differences tend to make the *process* of communication more effortful and difficult, and thereby generally less rewarding.

8. As Mutual Trust Increases, Relational Competence Increases

Similar to the above proposition, the more partners trust one another, the more competent interaction is likely to be, and the more competent the relationship is likely to be (Canary & Spitzberg, 1989). Trust provides a context in which interaction can be more honest, spontaneous, direct, and open. Over time, such a trusting climate is likely to be mutually reinforcing and lead to a productive and satisfying communicative relationship.

9. As Access to Social Support Increases, Relational Competence Increases

Social support is anything offered by another that assists a person in coping with problematic or stressful situations. Types of support range from the tangible

(e.g., lending money) to the informational (e.g., offering advice) to the emotional (e.g., comforting words). Because stresses stimulate personal and often relational crises, anything that diminishes the effects of these stresses is likely to enhance the person's ability to manage the relationship itself. One of the common problems of sojourner couples or families is that the stresses of being in a new culture often cannot be resolved by the social support of a friendship network because it has yet to be established in the new culture.

10. As Relational Network Integration Increases, Relational Competence Increases

When discussing relationships, it is ironically easy to forget that individuals are always simultaneously members of multiple relationships. When two people come together and form a relationship, part of what determines the competence of this relationship is the extent to which each member's personal network integrates with the other person's network of social relationships. Increasingly, as businesses become multinational and move entire management teams to work with labor in other countries, the problems of social network integration become substantial. The development of common activities and goals that require cooperation or interaction across social networks, and the development of easier access to the network, are likely to facilitate this aspect of intercultural competence.

CONCLUSIONS

Before examining the implications of this essay, an important qualification needs to be considered. Specifically, most of the propositions presented here have what can be considered upper limits. Basically, too much of a good thing can be bad. For example, someone can be too motivated, be too analytical or knowledgeable, use too much expressiveness, or be too composed. Virtually any piece of advice, when carried to extremes, tends to lose its functional value. This can be viewed as a *curvilinearity principle*. In essence, as motivation, knowledge, and skill increase, so do impressions of competence, to a point after which the relationship reverses and competence impressions decrease.

Sir Karl Popper, an eminent philosopher of science, has warned that theories are only useful if they are in danger of failing. Theories that tell us what we already know must be true, tell us nothing. The point is that theories are only valuable to the extent they make risky predictions that may be disproved. It is in this sense that this essay must be viewed with caution.

Within this cautionary frame, one of the obvious, yet often ignored, lessons is the interdependence of adaptation. It is often assumed, for example, that host cultures possess a position of dominant status, and that visitors or immigrants must bear the responsibility of adapting to the host culture. Ultimately, however, competence in any encounter is contingent on all parties to the interaction. You can be highly motivated, knowledgeable, and skilled, and if the co-actors of another culture reject your legitimacy, there may be little chance of a competent interaction (Bourhis, Moise, Perreault, & Senécal, 1997). The responsibility of adaptation is best shared if competence is a preferred mode of interaction.

The predictions offered in this essay represent statements that, in the daily interplay of lives, are often in danger of being false. None of the predictions should be considered absolutely true or an infallible view of the complex canvas of intercultural relations. Nevertheless, progress in the development of knowledge results from such risky propositions, and this essay has attempted to chart a path to progress. In doing so, I have attempted to paint with broad brush strokes the outline of a theory of intercultural competence. The lines of this theory are strained by their abstraction to the point of no longer resembling the vibrant landscape they are meant to represent. Thus, like any theory or work of abstract art, the key is that the benefactor will find some significant personal meaning in it and be ever mindful that the symbol is not the thing to which it refers.

References

Andersen, P. A. (1998). The cognitive valence theory of intimate communication. In M. T. & G.A. Barnett (Eds.), *Progress in communication sciences* (Vol. 14, pp. 39–72). Stamford, CT: Ablex.

Bandura, A. (1982). Self-efficacy mechanism in human agency. *American Psychologist, 37,* 122–147.

Bourhis, R. Y., Moise, L. C., Perreault, S., & Senecal. S. (1997). Towards an interactive acculturation model: A social psychological approach. *International Journal of Psychology, 32,* 369–386.

Bradford, L., Allen, M., & Beisser, K. (1998, April). An *evaluation and meta-analysis of intercultural communication competence research.* Paper presented at the Central States Communication Association Conference, Chicago, IL.

Burleson, B. R., & Denton, W. H. (1992). A new look at similarity and attraction in marriage: Similarities in social-cognitive and communication skills as predictors of attraction and satisfaction. *Communication Monographs, 59,* 268–287.

Canary, D. J., & Spitzberg. B. H. (1989). A model of the perceived competence of conflict strategies. *Human Communication Research, 15,* 630–649.

Eagly, A. H., Ashmore, R. D., Makhijani, M. G., & Longo, L. C. (1991). What is beautiful is good. But . . . : A meta-analytic review of research on the physical attractiveness stereotype. *Psychological Bulletin, 110,* 109–128.

Feingold, A. (1988). Matching for attractiveness in romantic partners and same-sex friends: A meta-analysis and theoretical critique. *Psychological Bulletin, 104,* 226–235.

Greene, J. O. (1984). A cognitive approach to human communication: An action assembly theory. *Communication Monographs, 51,* 289–300.

Havighurst, R. J. (1957). The social competence of middle-aged people. *Genetic Psychology Monographs, 56,* 297–175.

Hoelter, J. W. (1985). A structural theory of personal consistency. *Social Psychology Quarterly, 48,* 118–129.

Imahori, T. T., & Lanigan, M. L. (1989). Relational model of intercultural communication competence. *International Journal of Intercultural Relations, 13,* 269–286.

Kaplowitz, S. A. (1978). Towards a systematic theory of power attribution. *Social Psychology, 41,* 131–148.

Kellerman, K., & Shea, B. C. (1996). Threats, suggestions, hints, and promises: Gaining compliance efficiently and politely. *Communication Quarterly, 44,* 145–165.

Lustig, M. W., & Spitzberg, B. H. (1993). Methodological issues in the study of intercultural communication competence. In R. L. Wiseman & J. Koester (Eds.), *Intercultural communication competence* (pp. 153–167). Newbury Park, CA: Sage.

McAdams, D. P. (1988). Personal needs and personal relationships. In S. Duck (Ed.), *Handbook of personal relationships: Theory, research and interventions* (pp. 7–22). New York: John Wiley & Sons.

Mendleson, J. L., Bures, A. L., Champion, D. L., & Lott, J. K. (1997). Preliminary development of the intercultural tolerance scale. *Psychological Reports, 80,* 867–876.

Neuliep, J. W., & McCroskey, J. C. (1997). The development of intercultural and interethnic communication apprehension scales. *Communication Research Reports, 14,* 145–156.

Osgood, C. E., May, W. H., & Miron, S. (1975). *Cross-cultural universals of affective meaning*. Urbana: University of Illinois Press.

Pavitt, C., & Haight, L. (1985). The "competent communicator" as a cognitive prototype. *Human Communication Research, 12,* 225–241.

Spitzberg, B. H. (1989). Issues in the development of a theory of interpersonal competence in the intercultural context. *International Journal of Intercultural Relations, 13,* 241–268.

Spitzberg, B. H. (1993). The dialectics of (in)competence. *Journal of Social and Personal Relationships, 10,* 137–158.

Spitzberg, B. H., & Brunner, C. C. (1991). Toward a theoretical integration of context and competence inference research. *Western Journal of Speech Communication, 55,* 28–46.

Spitzberg, B. H., & Cupach, W. R. (1984). *Interpersonal communication competence*. Beverly Hills, CA: Sage.

Spitzberg, B. H., & Cupach, W. R. (1989). *Handbook of interpersonal competence research*. New York: Springer-Verlag.

Concepts and Questions

1. What does Spitzberg mean when he says intercultural competence must be viewed as the social evaluation of behavior?
2. What are the individual, episodic, and relational systems of analysis?
3. What is the relationship between communicator motivation and intercultural communication competence?
4. What is communicator approach disposition, and how does it relate to intercultural communication competence?
5. What is task-relevant procedural knowledge and how does it relate to communication competence?
6. What are valued outcomes and how do they affect the entire communication encounter?
7. What is relational competence?
8. How does mutual attraction affect relational competence?
9. How can you make use of the Spitzberg model if you seek to improve the manner in which you communicate?

Intercultural Effectiveness

Guo-Ming Chen

INTRODUCTION

The trend of globalization not only encourages a closer interaction in different aspects of human society, but also provides a challenge for us to understand the magnitude and implications of such a powerful and complicated transformation of human society into a global community, in which we must learn how to collaboratively take part in shaping a better future world. The trend reflects a dilemma of the pulling and pushing between local identity and global diversity, in which people learn to integrate different cultural identities and interests and to negotiate and cocreate cultural identity through communication in order to establish a new global civic community that will decide the future of human society (Lynch, 1992). In other words, globalization has broken through the boundaries of space, time, cultural assumptions, and the scope, structure, and function of human society. It demands new forms of thought and organization, and opens up "new imperatives for investigating power linkages between thought and action, knowledge and being, structure and process" (Kofman & Youngs, 1996, p. 1).

The new imperatives of globalization require people gain the requisite knowledge and skills that account for intercultural communication competence. Only through communication competence can people from different cultures interact effectively and productively in the globalizing society (Chen & Starosta, 2005). Knowledge and skills for communication competence in the globalizing society not only help to transform individuals into multicultural

---

This original essay appears here in print for the first time. All rights reserved. Permission to reprint must be obtained from the author and the publisher. Dr. Guo-Ming Chen teaches in the Department of Communication Studies at the University of Rhode Island, Kingston, Rhode Island.

persons by fostering multiple cultural identities, but also function to nourish an awareness of these multiple identities and extend to maintain a multicultural coexistence in order to develop a global civic culture (Adler, 1988). Thus, intercultural communication competence is the key to cultivating the ability to tolerate and mutually respect cultural differences, which marks the enlightened global citizenship in different levels of future human society (Belay, 1993). Intercultural communication competence enables individuals to search for the vision, shared understanding, and sense of multiple identities that lead to the unlocking of human potential in the development of intelligence, knowledge, and creativity for a peaceful and productive society.

In order to foster the ability of intercultural communication competence in the globalizing society, the first step is to develop a global mindset. This necessitates openness to other cultures in order to facilitate intercultural interactions. Global mindset is the foundation of intercultural communication competence because a well-founded global mindset enables individuals to envision the coming of a global society and then execute intercultural communication skills appropriately and effectively. It fosters the ability to envisage changes in world trends, to engage in the process of regulating those changes, and to drive for a social context in which diversity and cultural differences are valued and balanced.

In addition to having a global mindset, intercultural communication competence in the globalizing society is comprised of three components (Chen & Starosta, 1996; Chen, 2005). First, intercultural sensitivity requires individuals to unfold and expand their personal characteristics, including flexibility, sensitivity, open-mindedness, and motivation. As the centrality of the global society, the self must be mobilized to visualize its identity for the establishment of its continuity. Through the extension of personal attributes, self-identity begins to build a bridge between the personal and social gap. A connection of I and thou creates a web of meanings shared by the global community. In other words, the ability of unfolding the self is an important way to promote creativity, learning, and innovation in the process of globalization. The inability to unfold the self, based on intercultural sensitivity to face the challenge of constant changes

and complexities of the globalizing society, often leads to an unsuccessful ride on the wave to future society.

Second, intercultural communication competence in the globalizing society requires the cognitive ability to map one's own and another's culture. It is the ability to acquire cultural knowledge. To understand ourselves as cultural beings from our own cultural perspective is the basis of knowing another's culture. It is this intercultural awareness, or mutual awareness, of cultural knowledge that makes respect and integration of cultural differences possible. Thus, the awareness of cultural knowledge is a prerequisite for reducing situational ambiguity and uncertainty in the process of intercultural or global communication. The lack of discomfort, confusion, or anxiety due to the understanding of cultural differences helps individuals adapt to situational demands of the global environment and cope with the changing environment rapidly.

Finally, intercultural communication competence requires a set of behavioral skills, or intercultural effectiveness, that are indispensable for adjusting individuals to the changes and new patterns of interaction in the globalizing society. The behavioral requirement of aligning global interaction allows individuals to negotiate multiple meanings and to manage complexity and conflicts in the global context. Hence, acting or aligning their interactions effectively in the process of intercultural or global communication enables individuals to attain their communication goals and become a global citizen.

THE CONCEPT OF INTERCULTURAL EFFECTIVENESS

The term "intercultural effectiveness" has long been used interchangeably with "intercultural communication competence," which caused much unnecessary confusion and conceptual ambiguity in the literature. A careful examination of the literature led Chen and Starosta (1996) to call for a clear conceptualization of intercultural communication competence. They found that intercultural effectiveness should be treated as a dimension of intercultural communication competence, rather than used indistinctly, because in addition to intercultural effectiveness, as mentioned above, intercultural sensitivity and intercultural awareness form the other two dimensions of the concept.

As a dimension of intercultural communication competence, *intercultural effectiveness refers to a person's ability to interact and adjust adroitly with other human beings and the environment.* As a common property of human behaviors, effectiveness can be attained through behaviors instigated by drives in one's own right. The degree of effectiveness can be measured by the extent to which a person produces an intended effect from interaction with another human and the environment. It can also be increased through socialization; thus, effectiveness relies much on the ability of personal intelligence and sensitivity (Weinstein, 1969).

Intercultural effectiveness not only refers to the individuals' ability to select among a set of communication behaviors in order to accomplish specific goals, including getting relevant information about these goals, accurately predicting the other's responses, selecting communication strategies, and correctly assessing the results of interaction in a multicultural context (Chen, 1990), but in the process of global communication, it also must consist of the element of appropriateness, which is the ability to meet the contextual requirements in the process of intercultural communication, or to recognize the different sets of rules in different situations in the globalizing society. It indicates the right quantity of message sending, the consistent quality of message delivery, the relevancy of the topical messages and situation, and the manner of expression (Chen, 1990).

In other words, intercultural effectiveness is the ability to maintain the face of one's culturally different counterparts within the constraints of the situation. This requires attention to both the verbal and nonverbal expressions so they make sense to the participants within the existing social context. It necessitates a relational context in which the structure and delivery of the messages are consonant with the particular relationship between the participants. And, finally participants must pay attention to the environmental context in which the constraints induced from the symbolic and physical environment imposed upon them are considered. Thus, intercultural effectiveness is the ability of interactants to execute communication behaviors to elicit desired responses in a global environment without violating their counterparts' norms and rules.

THE COMPONENTS OF INTERCULTURAL EFFECTIVENESS

The emphasis on the behavioral skills of intercultural effectiveness corresponds to the verbal and nonverbal communication skills that enable people to achieve their goals in intercultural interaction. Those communication behaviors of intercultural effectiveness are comprised of five components: *message skills, interaction management, behavioral flexibility, identity management,* and *relationship cultivation* (Chen, 1989, 1992; Cupach & Imahori, 1993; Hamme, 1987; Martin & Hammer, 1989; Ruben, 1977; Spitzberg, 1997; Wiseman, 2003).

Message Skills

Message skills demand the ability to exercise one's counterpart's verbal and nonverbal behaviors. Verbal skills refer to the ability to code skillfully and to create recognizable messages in the process of communication (Kim, 1994; Parks, 1994; Weber, 1994). This is the so-called "linguistic competence" or "communicative competence," which is concerned with language and messages in the interactional process, and is related to the knowledge of rules underlying the use of language (Spitzberg & Cupach, 1984).

Message skills are tempered by self-disclosure, which refers to the willingness of individuals to openly reveal information about themselves to their counterparts. In the process of communication, self-disclosure may reflect the amount, depth, intent, accuracy, and valence of the message an individual delivers (Wheeless, Erickson, & Behrens, 1986). Without self-disclosure human communication simply cannot happen. Self-disclosure, however, must be regulated by the principle of appropriateness in order to reach a successful outcome. This is especially important in intercultural communication settings, because the emphasis of self-disclosure varies among cultures, including the list of topics, the degree of intimacy, and the level of hierarchy that are all sanctioned by the culture (Chen, 1995; Nakanishi, 1987).

Similar to verbal skills, nonverbal skills refer to the ability to code skillfully and to create recognizable nonverbal messages, including those cues regarding kinesics, proxemics, paralanguage, and chronemics (Burgoon, Buller, & Woodall, 1989; Hall, 1959).

Nonverbal messages, however, are much less systematized and more ambiguous than verbal communication, and also involve those humanly and environmentally generated stimuli that convey potential nonlinguistic message values to the interactant (Samovar & Porter, 1995). To acquire nonverbal skills, as Ricard (1993) suggested, individuals need to follow five steps: assess learning needs, observe similar situations, use appropriate resources, reach tentative conclusions, and reevaluate the conclusions as necessary.

Interaction Management

Interaction management refers to the ability to initiate, terminate, and take turn in conversation "based on a reasonably accurate assessment of the needs and desires of others" (Ruben, 1976, p. 341). Ruben, for example, further stipulated that a person with low interaction management often shows the following behaviors: (1) be a part of unconcerned turn taking in conversation; (2) either dominate or refuse to interact; (3) be unresponsive or unaware towards counterparts' needs for involvement and time sharing; (4) initiate and terminate discussion without regard for the wishes of other individuals; (5) continue to talk long after obvious displays of disinterest and boredom by others; and (6) terminate discussion or withhold information when there is clear interest expressed by others for further exchange. In contrast, a person with high interaction management is extremely concerned with providing equal opportunity to all participants to contribute to discussion. In the stages of initiation and termination of discussion, he or she always indicates concern for the interests, tolerances, and orientation of others who are party to discussion.

Spitzberg and Cupach (1984) indicated that interaction management deals with one's ability to structure and maintain the procedure of a conversation. Thus, individuals with interaction management skills always know how to develop a topic smoothly during interaction and give their counterparts an opportunity to contribute to the conversation. Moreover, interaction management is also reflected in the ability of "double-emic listening" through which the interactants are able to develop a space-between and "move from their respective views to formulate an etic view of the other"

(Starosta & Chen, 2000, p. 290). Through the process of an effective interaction management, not only can one gather information to improve the quality of interaction, but he or she can also play an important role in defining how the conversation will proceed. Interaction management has been found to be a major element for being competent in intercultural communication (e.g., Chen, 1989; Olebe & Koester, 1989).

The fostering of interaction management skills is based on one's constant concern for the interests and orientations of others in interaction. This other-oriented ability or avoiding monopoly in conversation to display mutual dependency or reciprocity is embedded in the concept of "interaction involvement." According to Cegala (1981), interaction involvement is a kind of social behavior that is related to personal abilities of responsiveness, attentiveness, and perceptiveness in interaction. The three elements, i.e., *responsiveness, attentiveness,* and *perceptiveness of interaction involvement,* reflect that they are not only part of interaction or behavioral skills for effective communication, but they are also founded on the affective ability or sensitivity of the person.

Behavioral Flexibility

Behavioral flexibility is the ability to be accurate and "flexible in attending to information," and "in selecting strategies" in order to achieve personal goals in interaction (Parks, 1976, p. 16). It is the ability to select an appropriate behavior to fit different communication contexts (Bochner & Kelly, 1974). Duran (1983) used the concept of communication adaptability to explain behavioral flexibility, which shows a person's ability to feel comfortable with a variety of people in different situations. Elements of communication adaptability include being able to get along with new people, being quick to fit in with different groups of people, enjoying social gatherings where one can meet new people, and feeling relaxed in conversing with a new acquaintance.

Behavioral flexibility also refers to "environmental mobility" that requires a person to cope with different kinds of people at different levels of circumstance (Cleveland, Mangone, & Adams, 1960). From the perspective of message exchange, Argyle (1969) pointed out that behavioral flexibility denotes the ability to make the alternation and co-occurrence of specific speech choices that mark the status and affiliative relationships of interactants.

In intercultural communication behavioral flexibility is an important component for being a "multicultural person." As Adler (1998) indicated, multicultural persons are always situational in interacting with others, are always in a state of "becoming" that shows continual personal transitions, and always maintain an open boundary of the self to allow change. In other words, behavioral flexibility is found in people who are adaptive and able to integrate various communication demands in terms of culture, ethnicity, race, gender, and religion.

Finally, the development of behavioral flexibility is dependent on cognitive awareness of cultural variations and affective ability in self-monitoring. Cultural variations represent the different features of cultural context. For example, Chung and Chen (2007) summarized the differences between high-context and low-context cultures by indicating that high-context cultures are characterized by the emphasis of group value orientation, indirect communication, feeling, permanent relationship, and a spiral thinking pattern; while low-context cultures emphasize individualism, direct expression, logic, transitory relationship, and linear reasoning. Self-monitoring is an individual's ability to detect the appropriateness of their social behaviors and self-presentation in response to situational constraints and to adjust their behaviors to fit the situation (Chen & Starosta, 1997). Research has shown that persons with high self-monitoring tend to be more adaptable to diverse communication situations and more adept in the use of communication strategies (e.g., Cody, Lovette, & Canary, 1990; Spitzberg & Cupach, 1984)

Identity Management

Identity management allows individuals to maintain their counterpart's identity. Because human communication is partially prompted by a person's need to learn who he or she is, reaching a successful communication relies not only on the ability to know oneself, but also on the ability to inform one's counterparts who they are.

Although part of identity may be created by the self, it is mainly cocreated through communication with others. Through the process of negotiation, cocreation, challenge, and reinforcement between

the interactants, identity formation reflects a dynamic and multifaceted process. Thus, the salience and intensity of identity varies in different spatial and temporal situations (Collier, 1994). In addition, identity also shows diverse faces in different contexts and is presented in affective, cognitive, and behavioral levels of human interaction (Long & Chen, 2007; Lustig & Koester, 2000).

The diverse faces of identity refer to the different roles an individual plays in different contexts. In intercultural communication identity is similar to Adler's (1998) "multicultural identities" or Starosta's "dual consciousness" (2000), referring to identity as a social character that is fluid, mobile, colliding, susceptible to change, and open to variation. Moreover, identity requires the involvement of affection. In certain situations one might strongly claim one's identity to assure the psychological balance, such as in the crisis stage of intercultural adjustment. Identity also relates to one's understanding and beliefs regarding identity itself. For example, people with different cultural identity might possess a similar belief in other issues. In this situation the similar belief often outstrips one's cultural or other identities. Lastly, at the behavioral level, identity is displayed in the exchange of verbal and nonverbal messages. In other words, identity is formed through the verbal and nonverbal interaction in which participants achieve mutual understanding. Thus an individual's identity or group belonging can be identified through the analyses of verbal and nonverbal messages in the process of intracultural or intercultural communication.

The characteristics of identity show that the use of identity management skills must vary with different situations and different personal goals, and with movement from one salient identity to another (Collier, 1989; Ting-Toomey, 1989). Intercultural communication competence is then demonstrated by one's ability to effectively and appropriately enact one's counterparts' cultural identity, which manifests the match between the avowed and ascribed identity, and reinforces different identities salient in the particular situation.

Relationship Cultivation

The last component of intercultural effectiveness is relationship cultivation. The relational aspect of intercultural effectiveness emphasizes the independent and reciprocal process of interaction (Spitzberg &

Cupach, 1984). It refers to the ability to establish a certain degree of relationship with one's partner in order to satisfy each other's needs and reach a positive outcome of interaction. As an affinity-seeking behavior, relationship cultivation can be achieved through being friendly or showing concern and interest in the interaction and through such behaviors as courtesy and cooperativeness (Harris, 1973). Moreover, relationship cultivation is displayed in the degree of intimacy, relationship stability and commitment, and idiosyncratic rules created during the interaction (Imahori & Lanigan, 1989).

According to Ruben (1976), the ability of building, maintaining, or cultivating relationships is a functional flexibility in different kinds of role behaviors. In other words, individuals with the ability of relationship cultivation are able to lead the group to such outcomes as "harmonizing and mediating scraps and/or conflicts between group members, attempts to regulate evenness of contributions of group members," offer comments "relative to the group's dynamics," display "indications of a willingness to compromise own position for the sake of group consensus" (p. 350), and display interest. Although the application is in a group setting, it is generally applicable to different contexts of communication. In contrast, those individuals who are highly resistant to others' ideas or "attempt to manipulate the group by asserting authority through flattery, sarcasm, interrupting, etc.," will bring detrimental effect to relationship development. In addition, Hammer, Gudykunst, and Wiseman (1978) found that the ability to establish interpersonal relationships is a dimension of intercultural effectiveness which leads to intercultural communication competence.

APPLYING INTERCULTURAL EFFECTIVENESS

As the behavioral aspect of intercultural communication competence, the concept of intercultural effectiveness has been applied to various training programs that aim to help people or sojourners gain interactional skills in order to better communicate with those from different cultural backgrounds and to better adjust to a new culture. For example, among the five intercultural training programs proposed by

Brislin and Yoshida (1994), two of them, namely behavioral modification training and experiential learning training, fall into this category. Gudykunst, Hammer, and Wiseman (1977) also proposed an integrated model in which three approaches, including the area simulation approach, the behavioral approach, and the interaction approach, are initiated to develop the ability of intercultural effectiveness.

The behavioral and experiential approaches assume that effective communication requires individuals to have the ability to behave appropriately in a host culture. In order to achieve this goal, before entering a new culture, one should try to practice the behaviors of the host culture in a simulated host culture environment. This will reduce anxiety and fear that might happen in some situations in the host culture. BaFa baFa (Shirt, 1977) and Barnga (Thiagarajan & Steinwachs, 1990) are two common training techniques used in this approach.

The area simulation approach involves individuals in an environment that closely resembles a specific culture. In addition to learning and gathering information about the culture and increasing participants' intercultural sensitivity toward the culture, this approach aims to develop a set of new behaviors and methods of problem solving through this simulation process by interacting with members of other cultural groups. In other words, this approach emphasizes the acquisition of behavioral or problem-solving skills rather than the transmission of cultural knowledge and the creation of a similar feeling in the real cultural situation (Wright, 1970).

Finally, the interaction approach emphasizes interaction with people from the host culture before the individual sojourns to that place. Through this experiential learning process, it is assumed that participants will know the value system and appropriate behavioral system of the host culture and feel more comfortable living, working, or interacting with people there.

Nevertheless, although aiming to help participants achieve communication effectiveness through the acquisition of behavioral and interactional skills is a significant and necessary part of intercultural training program, according to Seidel (1981), to reach intercultural communication competence, an intercultural training program must integrate affective sensitivity, cognitive awareness, and behavioral skills.

CONCLUSION

The conceptual confusion and ambiguity has misled scholars to treat both intercultural communication competence and intercultural effectiveness interchangeably, which further caused the problem of inconsistency and fragmentation in the process of operationalizing the concepts. As argued in this paper, intercultural communication competence is a multidimensional concept comprising the cognitive, affective, and behavioral aspects of human interaction. Intercultural effectiveness represents only the behavioral aspect of intercultural communication competence; it is inconceivable to treat intercultural effectiveness and intercultural communication competence interchangeably.

Aiming to tackle this problem, this essay distinguished intercultural effectiveness from intercultural communication competence by conceptualizing intercultural effectiveness as the interactants' ability to execute communication behaviors to elicit desired responses in a global environment without violating their counterparts' norms and rules, and delineates message skills, interaction management, behavioral flexibility, identity management, and relationship cultivation as the five communication behaviors that form the content of intercultural effectiveness. In addition, the importance of intercultural effectiveness in the process of intercultural training was discussed as well.

Finally, it is important to take an integrated view when studying the concept of intercultural communication competence, because it is the understanding of cultural themes and the affective sensitivity of intercultural differences through acknowledgment, respect, and acceptance that help interactants act more appropriately while applying behavioral skills in intercultural communication. Future study in this line of research needs to recognize and examine the close relationship among intercultural awareness, intercultural sensitivity, and intercultural effectiveness, so that a better understanding of intercultural communication competence can be reached.

References

Adler, P. S. (1998). Beyond cultural identity: Reflections on multiculturalism. In M. J. Bennett (Ed.), *Basic concepts of intercultural communication: Selected readings* (pp. 225–245). Yarmouth, ME: Intercultural Press.

Argyle, M. (1969). *Social interaction*. London: Tavostock.

Belay, G. (1993). Toward a paradigm shift for intercultural and international communication: New research directions. In S. A. Deetz (Ed.), *Communication Yearbook, 16* (pp. 437–457). Newbury Park, CA: Sage.

Bochner, A. P., & Kelly, C. W. (1974). Interpersonal competence: Rational, philosophy, and implementation of a conceptual framework. *Speech Teacher, 23,* 279–301.

Brislin, R., & Yoshida, T. (1994). *Intercultural communication training: An introduction*. Thousand Oaks, CA: Sage.

Burgoon, J. K., Buller, D. B., & Woodall, W. G. (1989). *Nonverbal communication: The unspoken dialogue*. New York: Harper & Row.

Cegala, D. J. (1981). Interaction involvement: A cognitive dimension of communicative competence. *Communication Education, 30,* 109–121.

Chen, G. M. (1989). Relationships of the dimensions of intercultural communication competence. *Communication Quarterly, 37,* 118–133.

Chen, G. M. (1990). Intercultural communication competence: Some perspectives of research. *Howard Journal of Communications, 2,* 243–261.

Chen, G. M. (1992). A test of intercultural communication competence. *Intercultural Communication Studies, 2,* 63–82.

Chen, G. M. (1995). Differences in self-disclosure patterns among Americans versus Chinese: A comparative study. *Journal of Cross-Cultural Psychology, 26,* 84–91.

Chen, G. M. (2000). Globalization and intercultural communication competence. In *Shapes of future: Global communication in the 21st century—proceedings of the 2000 International Communication Conference* (pp. 51–64). Taipei, Taiwan.

Chen, G. M. (2005). A model of global communication competence. *China Media Research, 1,* 3–11.

Chen, G. M. (2007). A review of the concept of intercultural effectiveness. In M. Hinner (Ed.), *The influence of culture in the world of business* (pp. 97–115). Germany: Peter Lang.

Chen, G. M., & Starosta, W. J. (1996). Intercultural communication competence: A synthesis. *Communication Yearbook, 19,* 353–384.

Chen, G. M., & Starosta, W. J. (1997). A review of the concept of intercultural sensitivity. *Human Communication, 1,* 1–16.

Chen, G. M., & Starosta, W. J. (2003). A review of the concept of intercultural awareness. In L. A. Samovar and R. E. Porter (Eds.), *Intercultural communication: A reader* (pp. 344–353). Belmont, CA: Wadsworth.

Chen, G. M., & Starosta, W. J. (2005). *Foundations of Intercultural Communication*. Lanham, MD: University Press of America.

Chuang, R. (2000). Dialectics of globalization and localization. In G. M. Chen and W. J. Starosta (Eds.), *Communication and global society* (pp. 19–33). New York: Peter Lang.

Chung, J. & Chen, G. M. (2007). The relationship between cultural context and electronic-mail usage. In M. Hinner (Ed.), *The role of communication in business transactions and relationships* (pp. 279–292). Germany: Peter Lang.

Cleveland, H., Mangone, G. J., & Adams, J. C. (1960). *The overseas Americans*. NY: McGraw-Hill.

Collier, M. J. (1994). Cultural identity and intercultural communication. In L. A. Samovar & R. E. Porter (Eds.), *Intercultural communication: A reader* (pp. 36–44). Belmont, CA: Wadsworth.

Cupach, W. R., & Imahori, T. T. (1993). Identity management theory: Communication competence in intercultural episodes and relationships. In R. L. Wiseman & J. Koester (Eds.), *Intercultural communication competence* (pp. 112–131). Newbury Park: Sage.

Duran, R. L. (1983). Communicative adaptability: A measure of social communicative competence. *Communication Quarterly, 31,* 320–326.

Foote, N. N., & Cottrell, L. S. (1955). *Identity and interpersonal competence*. Chicago: Chicago University Press.

Gudykunst, W. B., Hammer, M. R., & Wiseman, R. L. (1977). An analysis of an integrated approach to cross-cultural training. *International Journal of Intercultural Relations, 2,* 99–110.

Hall, E. T. (1959). *The silent language*. Garden City, NY: Doubleday.

Hammer, M. R. (1987). Behavioral dimensions of intercultural effectiveness: A replication and extension. *International Journal of Intercultural Relations, 11,* 65–88.

Hammer, M. R., Gudykunst, W. B., & Wiseman, R. L. (1978). Dimensions of intercultural effectiveness: An exploratory study. *International Journal of Intercultural Relations, 2,* 382–392.

Harris, J. G. (1973). A science of the South Pacific: An analysis of the character structure of the Peace Corp volunteer. *American Psychologist, 28,* 232–247.

Imahari, T. T., & Lanigan, M. L. (1989). Relational model of intercultural communication competence. *International Journal of Intercultural Relations, 13,* 269–286.

Kim, M. (1994). Cross-cultural comparisons of the perceived importance of conversational constraints. *Human Communication Research, 21,* 128–151.

Kofman, E., & Youngs, G. (1996). Introduction: Globalization—the second wave. In E. Kofman and G. Youngs (Eds.), *Globalization: Theory and practice* (pp. 1–8). New York: Pinter.

Long, J., & Chen, G. M. (2007). The impact of internet usage on adolescent self-identity development. *China Media Research, 3*(2), 99–109.

Lustig, M. W., & Koester, J. (2000). The nature of cultural identity. In M. W. Lustig & J. Koester (Eds.), *Among us: Essays on identity, belonging, and intercultural competence* (pp. 3–8). New York: Longman.

Lynch, J. (1992). *Education for citizenship in a multicultural society*. London: Cassell.

Weinstein, E. A. (1969). The development of interpersonal competence. In D. A. Goslin (Ed.), *Handbook of socialization theory and research* (pp. 753–775). Chicago: Rand McNally.

Martin, J. N., & Hammer, M. R. (1989). Behavioral categories of intercultural communication competence: Everyday communicators' perceptions. *International Journal of Intercultural Relations, 13,* 303–332.

Nakanishi, M. (1987). Perceptions of self-disclosure in initial interaction: A Japanese sample. *Human Communication Research, 13,* 167–190.

Olebe, M., & Koester, J. (1989). Exploring the cross-cultural equivalence of the Behavioral Assessment Scale for intercultural communication. *International Journal of Intercultural Relations, 13,* 333–347.

Parks, M. R. (1976, December). *Communication competence*. Paper presented at the meeting of the Speech Communication Association. San Francisco, California.

Parks, M. R. (1994). Communication competence and interpersonal control. In M. L. Knapp & G. R. Miller (Eds.), *Handbook of interpersonal communication* (pp. 589–618). Thousand Oaks, CA: Sage.

Ricard, V. B. (1992). *Developing intercultural communication skills*. Malabar, FL: Krieger.

Ruben, B. D. (1976). Assessing communication competency for intercultural adaptation. *Group & Organization Studies, 1,* 334–354.

Ruben, B. D. (1977). Guidelines for cross-cultural communication effectiveness. *Group & Organization Studies, 2,* 470–479.

Samovar, L. A., & Porter, R. E. (1995). *Communication between cultures*. Belmont, CA: Wadsworth.

Seidel, G. (1981). Cross-cultural training procedures: Their theoretical framework and evaluation. In S. Bochner (Ed.). *The mediating person: Bridge between cultures*. Cambridge, MA: Schenhman.

Shirts, G. (1973). *BAFA BAFA: A cross-cultural simulation*. Delmar, CA: Simile.

Smith, S. W., Cody, M. J., Lovette, S., & Canary, D. J. (1990). Self-monitoring, gender and compliance-gaining goals. In M. J. Cody & M. L. McLaughlin (Eds.), *The psychology of tactical communication* (pp. 91–134). Clevedon, England: Multilingual Matters.

Spitzberg, B. H. (1997). A model of Intercultural communication competence. In L. A. Samovar & R. E. Porter (Eds.), *Intercultural communication: A reader* (pp. 379–391). Belmont, CA: Wadsworth.

Spitzberg, B. H., & Cupach, W. R. (1984). *Interpersonal communication competence*. Beverly Hills: Sage.

Starosta, W. J. (2000). Dual_consciousness@USAmerican. white.male. In M. W. Lustig & J. Koester (Eds.), *Among us: Essays on identity, belonging, and intercultural competence* (pp. 107–115). New York: Longman.

Starosta, W. J., & Chen, G. M. (2000). Listening across diversity in global society. In G. M. Chen & W. J. Starosta (Eds.), *Communication and global society* (pp. 279–293). New York: Peter Lang.

Thiagarajan, S. & Steinwachs, B. (1990). *Barnga: A simulation game on cultural clashes*. Yarmouth, ME: Intercultural Press.

Ting-Toomey, S. (1989). Identity and interpersonal bond. In M. K. Asante & Gudykunst (Eds.), *Handbook of international and intercultural communication* (pp. 351–373). Newbury Park, CA: Sage.

Weber, S. N. (1994). The need to be: The socio-cultural significance of black language. In L. A. Samovar & R. E. Porter (Eds.), *Intercultural communication: A reader* (pp. 221–226). Belmont, CA: Wadsworth.

Wheeless, E. W., Erickson, K. V., & Behrens, J. S. (1986). Cultural differences in disclosiveness as a function of locus of control. *Communication Monographs, 53*, 36–46.

Wiseman, R. L. (2003). Intercultural communication competence. In W. B. Gudykunst (Ed.), *Cross-cultural and intercultural communication* (pp. 191–208). Thousand Oaks, CA: Sage.

Wright, A. (1970). *Experiential cross-cultural training*. Mimeo produced by Center for Research and education. Estes Park, Colorado.

Concepts and Questions

1. What does Chen mean when he writes of a "global mindset"?
2. What is "intercultural sensitivity"? Can you think of some examples when you witnessed intercultural insensitivity?
3. Why is it difficult to "map" a culture that is different from your own?
4. What is the difference between intercultural effectiveness and intercultural competence?
5. How does self-disclosure help or hinder message skills? Can you think of some example where you observed a lack of self-disclosure impeding your interaction?
6. Why is behavioral flexibility important? Can you think of some examples when you successfully engaged in behavior flexibility? What did you do differently?
7. Why is identity management important to you and the other person?

Dialectics of Doubt and Accomplishment: Recounting What Counts in Cultural Immersion

SUMMER CARNETT

KATHERINE SLAUTA

PATRICIA GEIST-MARTIN

Back in the fall of 2004, we were making all the arrangements for our trip to conduct research in Costa Rica. Patricia's proposed research in Costa Rica was designed to investigate the holistic medicines that citizens of Costa Rica draw upon in their search for healing and health. Summer designed her project to investigate the patient–practitioner relationship, comparing communication in the context of biomedicine and holistic medicine in Costa Rica. Katherine began with an interest in exploring Nicaraguan immigrants' use of holistic medicine, but then discovered in her fieldwork the complicated forms of resistance negotiated between Nicaraguan immigrants and health care providers in Costa Rica.

Through individual narratives, we will explore the dialectics of doubting our competencies and acknowledging our accomplishments during the process of cultural immersion. Our narratives describe feelings of helplessness, embarrassment, and anger, as well as gratitude, joy, and enlightenment, demonstrating the complex range of emotions we experienced as a result of extending research outside our comfort zones. In the process of doubting our

This original essay appears here in print for the first time. All rights reserved. Permission to reprint must be obtained from the authors and the publisher. Ms. Summer Carnett is a doctoral student in the Department of Speech Communication at the University of Illinois, Urbana-Champaign. Ms. Katherine Slauta is Education Coordinator for the Fashion Institute of Design and Merchandising, San Diego, California. Dr. Patricia Geist-Martin teaches in the School of Communication at San Diego State University.

accomplishments, we learned how to develop ways of acknowledging what "counts" as doing our research. As we immersed ourselves in a new culture, we worked to remain psychologically and spiritually healthy in the midst of being constantly challenged by personal, cultural, and political complexities.

We begin this essay with a description of the *culture shock* we experienced as a result of being suddenly immersed in the culture of Costa Rica—that is, the anxiety that resulted from the loss of familiar signs and symbols of social interaction (Oberg, 1960). We describe the doubts we experienced and the discoveries we made. Then, we move to a brief discussion of the value of narrative in accounting for the debilitating doubts we experienced over the course of our fieldwork. In the third section, we offer three narratives, one from each of the authors, accounting for some aspect of doubt and discovery in our immersion in Costa Rica. By conveying ways in which culture shock promoted positive self-growth experiences in each of us, our narratives ultimately helped us to reframe our culture shock. Finally, we provide a description of some of the specific insights we gained that helped us to manage culture shock as we adapted to living in, and conducting research in, a foreign country.

DOUBTING OUR COMPETENCIES: CULTURE SHOCK ENACTED

Doubt yourself and you doubt everything you see. Judge yourself and you see judges everywhere. But if you listen to the sound of your own voice, you can rise above doubt and judgment. And you can see forever.

–Nancy Lopez (2006)

Our journey to Costa Rica was just that—a journey, an adventure, an expedition. We planned everything just right: our arrival, finding an apartment, as well as keeping a balance between travel and research. It seemed like the perfect expedition. The rainforests, the beaches, and the indigenous people fit so well with our holistic healing research. It seemed so ideal, like out of a movie. As we envisioned traveling through the rainforests of Costa Rica, observing holistic practices, and journaling daily about our experiences, our adventure grew more and more exciting. As we spoke about our future research to our colleagues,

our friends, and our families, our ideas about our journey, and more specifically, our research, became grandiose.

"We plan to come back with more data than we can handle," we said.

"Six months of nothing but research, what could be more perfect?" we asked.

Of course our excitement was met with hesitation:

"Why would you want to do that?"

"Won't it be difficult leaving your friends and family?"

"Is it worth all the hassle?"

"Why would you give up what you have at home?"

"Why Costa Rica? Can't you study that here?"

"Are you really prepared?"

Although these comments reflected some of our own doubts as we struggled with arrangements and reflected on what we would be able to accomplish in six months, our excitement eclipsed these struggles. Rather, we chose to relate and relish in the positive comments made about our upcoming adventure:

"You have such a great opportunity."

"This will be a life-altering experience."

"How many chances do you have to pick up and go?"

"You better take advantage of this while you can."

"I know you will accomplish so much."

"Imaging everything you are going to learn."

It was true. We had so much going for us. We were energetic, open-minded, and research-hungry explorers! Most importantly we were friends, embarking on a journey that we hoped would result in theses, publications, and conference papers.

* * *

In January 2005, we arrived in San José Costa Rica. As we struggled to convert dollars to the Costa Rican currency of *colones,* to communicate under seemingly simple circumstances (e.g., ordering sandwiches from a deli counter) and to navigate the Costa Rican streets (which are largely unnamed and unmarked), our grand expedition seemed far away from the reality: We were foreigners. Moreover, we were experiencing culture shock.

The term *culture shock* was coined by anthropologist Kalvero Oberg (1960) to refer to the anxiety that results from people's loss of familiar signs and symbols of social interaction. It is a psychological construct that has been utilized in describing people's psychological, emotional, behavioral, physiological, and cognitive adjustment to an unfamiliar environment (Pedersen, 1995). Although culture shock is sometimes discussed as an "exotic ailment," in fact, it "bears a remarkable resemblance to the tensions and anxieties we face whenever change threatens the stability of our lives" (Bennett, 1998, p. 215). Similarly, Storti (2001) notes that people dealing with cultural adjustment have probably been through some part of the experience (e.g., moving, changing jobs) before—but most likely not all at once in a foreign country. During cultural immersion, people are dealing with an unusually large number of unfamiliar cues, including a new climate and landscape, a change or loss of routines, a different community, and a nonnative language.

Our experience of cultural immersion was no exception. The lack of familiar cues surrounding us in Costa Rica resulted in culture shock that affected us at multiple levels. As communication scholars, we realized that writing about communication was going to be difficult when we could hardly communicate ourselves. As women, we learned that by walking around the city alone we would inevitably be subjected to cat calls, and more seriously, each time we left our homes, our "gringa" ("American") faces increased our risk of attack by thieves and gangs wandering the street. And, as ethnographers, we were turned upside down.

As ethnographers, our greatest research tools were our senses and our writing skills. Our language skills, our sense of time, our contacts, our transportation, and our spirituality all influenced how we wrote, how we researched, how we narrated communication in our new lives in Costa Rica. And, as we quickly learned, these are the most taken-for-granted tools ethnographers can bring with them to any cultural immersion experience such as ours. When we finally began to journal, take field notes, and collect data, we noticed ourselves recording the spoken words, and truly listening to what expressions went with the words spoken by the people we interviewed and observed. For example, in one interview Summer turned to Katherine and asked, "Did you see how he touched his heart when he said love? You could just tell he truly loves what he does." Not only did our field note pages began to fill with the language spoken, as they used to, but now drawings, notes concerning physical expression, and details about our surroundings began to illuminate our field notes as well.

As researchers, we collected data and planned. In fact, we had done plenty of planning before our trip. However, what we had not planned for was the Costa Rican sense of time. What would normally take a simple e-mail and phone call in order to make a contact, slowly became a month-long process of multiple visits and approvals before even one contact could be made. In addition, researching healing in Costa Rica was slow. Although rewarding, one health-related visit between patient and provider could take an hour, as opposed to the quick five-minute visits we were used to observing in the United States.

Furthermore, what was once a simple hop in the car and drive down the freeway became careful planning and an hour and a half bus or taxi ride with the *hope* of collecting data. Katherine recalls waking up at five in the morning and quickly throwing on some clothes just to get to a clinic by eight only to discover she would have to come back another day. Summer would wait hours at a clinic collecting only two questionnaires. Patricia would schedule four interviews in a day in hopes that at least one practitioner would not cancel.

Although we were slowly but surely collecting data in Costa Rica, our sense of spirit began to fade. This was *not* what we had expected. As we looked back at our planned schedules, read e-mails about the quick progress others back home were making in their research, and learned about other colleagues' publications and accolades, our handful of interviews and field notes that contained more information about facial expressions than actual verbal expressions seemed to pale in comparison.

We felt helpless. As ethnographers our tools were broken; we could not collect data as we once did. And with this sense of brokenness arrived an overwhelming sense of doubt about our competencies. The voices of our friends haunted our minds:

"Why would you want to do that?"

"Won't it be difficult leaving your friends and family?"

"Is it worth all the hassle?"

"Why would you give up what you have at home?"

"Why Costa Rica? Can't you study that here?"

"Are you really prepared?"

The doubt we felt, the embarrassment over the amount of data collected, the uncertainty in our note-taking system, and the frustration over our slow progression in learning Spanish, stemmed from our U.S. version of measuring what is considered progress, or what counts as accomplishments that could be checked off on our "to do" lists. We judged our work to the point we were never satisfied, and as a result we doubted our ability to conduct ourselves even outside the data collection process. In fact, strain, unexpected anxiety, and confusion about self-identity are among the symptoms of culture shock (Oberg, 1960) and, at times, we experienced each of these deeply.

The tensions we felt were those of two cultures colliding. Two standards pulled us back and forth, until we, as researchers and travelers, decided to stop judging ourselves and our research based on others' standards, and begin truly re-counting what counts. Although we didn't know it at the time, we were taking steps to deal with the culture shock that we were experiencing; this decision to "re-count what counts" resonates with Pedersen's (1995) description of how to deal with culture shock: "the individual needs to construct new perspectives on self, others, and the environment that 'fit' with the new situation" (p. vii). Indeed, the stories we told helped us to construct new perspectives, thereby reclaiming parts of our identities that had been lost in the chaos accompanying culture shock.

RECONSTRUCTING PERSPECTIVES: NARRATING OUR EXPERIENCES OF CULTURE IMMERSION

The word *narrative* can refer to both the process of making a story and the result of the process—the story, tale, or history (Polkinghorn, 1988). According to Richardson (1997), narrative is a mode of reasoning that we utilize to make sense of or comprehend the world and it is a mode of representation we use to tell about the world. So, when we think about narrative not just as the event recounted, but "the event that consists of someone recounting something" (Genette, 1980, p. 26), we begin to consider how narrating is a process of co-constructing together the meaning of a series of events.

All three of us have looked back at, re-read, and analyzed the products of our research—the narratives that we have written individually from our fieldwork and interaction with participants in Costa Rica. We have authored theses, colloquiums, and convention papers, and are now writing manuscripts for submission to journals. But at the same time that we were constructing narratives that represented the product of our research, we also continuously engaged in the process of narrating to others our research experience of cultural immersion. During our time in Costa Rica and since our return, friends and family have requested that we narrate our research accomplishments. Individually and together we constructed a wide array of narratives about silences, disappointments, unexpected outcomes, disruptions, constraints, and tensions (Harter, Japp, & Beck, 2005).

Over and over, we became "wounded storytellers" in the sense that there was so much more involved in our experiences in Costa Rica than any one story could tell (Frank, 1995). We were wounded in other ways as well when the story we told of a significant turning point moment was received as unimportant or curiously unrelated to our research accomplishments. Simultaneously, the validity and magnitude of our accomplishments seemed to be in question. We now fully understood what Frank meant when he said, "the truth of stories is not only what *was* experienced, but equally what *becomes* experience in the telling and its reception" (p. 22).

Our woundedness was represented in our narrative silences—"the gaps in stories, the unmentioned, or unmentionable, as well as the absence of certain stories altogether" (Harter et al., 2005, p. 13). The stories we could tell about how much time it took to accomplish any one thing were something we stifled or silenced as we searched for ways to elaborate our stories of success. As a result, our woundedness translated to "spoiled identities" (Goffman, 1963) as researchers who failed to accomplish what we had set out to accomplish.

Somewhere along the way, the three of us began to collaboratively construct a narrative of transformation. In talking with one another, we accumulated narrative emplotments that redeemed our identities as researchers, reframed key moments, and restoried our time in Costa Rica as a liberating and productive research venture (Harter et al., 2005). However, these are not stories of an imagined reality, but stories that became our experience; these are stories of what we became mindful of in remembering and reminiscing about our cultural immersion. "Life moves on," Frank (1995) points out, and "stories change with that movement, and experience changes. Stories are true to the flux of experience and the story affects the direction of that flux" (p. 22).

The flux of our experience is represented well in the story that each of us tells individually in the next section of the chapter. What follows these three stories is our own attempt to "think with" and to discover what is collaboratively constructed across the stories and what new truths are revealed in their retelling (Frank, 1995). Although earlier conceptions presented culture shock as a consistently negative experience, more recent explanations of it have described "the adjustment period as a state of growth and development which—however painful it might be—may result in positive and even essential insights" (Pedersen, 1995 p. 2). Adler (1975) views culture shock as a learning process that may eventually lead to personal growth and self-awareness. Through our narratives of transformation, the ways in which culture shock prompted each of us to grow as individuals becomes apparent.

A Puppy's Aching Cry

Patricia Geist-Martin

I have this love–hate relationship with pet shops. Basically it just seems wrong to breed puppies and put them in cages as their first experience with life away from their mothers. Some of the lucky ones are adopted within the first few days, but many spend weeks, waiting and yearning for the companionship that is instinctual.

At the same time, puppies cry out to me irresistibly. Inside or outside of cages puppies draw me to them. I can't stop myself when I see a puppy. I vocalize "How cute" they are. When I see one on the street, I ask their owner, "Can I pet your puppy?" "What is his or her name?" "How old is she?" And I depart, looking back with a bit of angst, a bit of joy.

The same thing happens at pet shops, but with less abandon. With my fingers pressed against the glass, or wiggled between the bars of the cages, all my emotions of joy, sadness, angst, and love melt together with each touch, each sound—their soft fur, rough tongue, whimper, or bark. In return, puppies direct all their energy to me, wanting to be petted,

touched, and loved. With no grudges, no judgments, and no restraint they unabashedly bask in my presence and attention.

So here I am, my first full day in Costa Rica, walking through the outlet mall in San Pedro with J.C. and Makenna, only blocks from our apartment. It is a spartan mall, many shops are empty or filled only partially. The pet shop is no different—empty cages and no other shoppers. Makenna is drawn in immediately by the beagle puppy in the cage at the window. As we walk in and turn to our right to get a closer look, the puppy looks at us and then turns away with an aching, lonely cry. Immediately I feel a soft aching in my heart and tears well up in my eyes. The beagle puppy is out of reach, but I stretch out my voice to reach her, "You are so cute!" She turns away more and howls that aching lonely cry. I turn and say "Let's go!"

Makenna looks at my tears and asks, "What's wrong, Mom?" I find it hard to speak, but say, "I just can't stand seeing the loneliness of that poor puppy. She looks like she is aching to be held.

Makenna says, "I know, I know." "Dad, Mom is sad about the puppy." And we walk, arm and arm, both knowing and feeling the sadness together.

That night, as I toss and turn searching for the position that will help me fall asleep, the cry of the beagle puppy plays over and over. I can't remove the rewind vision of the small brown and white ball of fur clinging to the corner of the metal cage.

The next morning we head out for our day's adventure crossing the soccer field adjacent to the outlet mall. I glance over at the taunting structure of the mall with no intention of going anywhere near the pet shop. I am still aching. The beagle cry still acutely pressing on my heart.

Across the field comes this mirage like vision of a beagle puppy, hopping, jumping in the tall grass, leaping after a toddler. The little boy giggles, the parents smile. A tear leaps out of my left eye. "That's the beagle!!!" I cry with a mixture of unabashed hope and thankfulness. "No way, Mom, that's can't be!" "It is, it is," I plead. I know it is. I know it can't be.

Immediately I stride toward the couple. Not even thinking how little Spanish I can speak on this second day in Costa Rica, I look to the mother's face.

"Perdón, es su perro nuevo???" (Excuse me, is your dog new?) "Si, si, lo compremos ayer" I think for a minute, "We bought it yesterday" she said.

"Si, si, ayer, alli," (yes, yes, yesterday, there) she smiles, so warmly, I feel she knows me, knows what I have struggled with the last twenty-four hours.

"Gracias, gracias," I say and turn to catch up with JC and Makenna. I whisper "gracias" one more time as the tears flow endlessly for the first time in this new adventure in Costa Rica.

In one statement of "Yes, yes, yesterday, there" my adjustment to this unfamiliar environment became less of a burden. I felt "at home" knowing the puppy had found a home. I felt the warmth of a kindred spirit in the family who seemed to know my struggle. And I felt a keen sense that with this brief encounter came a lessening of my culture shock in this foreign environment.

"QUE BLANCA ES ELLA!" ("HOW WHITE SHE IS!")

SUMMER CARNETT

March 2, 2005: I grip a stack of questionnaires in my lap as I take inventory of the waiting room of "La Clínica Alejuela," a biomedical health care clinic not far from where I live in San José, Costa Rica. Everywhere I look in this small space I see blue, blue, blue. The walls are a pretty shade of light, sky blue. The nine chairs forming an L-shaped arrangement, although constructed from hard, uninviting plastic, are a bright splash of color—a deep, almost cobalt, blue. Even the linoleum floor is blue—an appealing hue midway between the soft shade of the wall and the brilliant color of the chairs.

The room is otherwise unremarkable, except perhaps for its contrast to the waiting rooms I am accustomed to in the United States; here there are no plants, no magazines, and no art on the walls. Although the room has minimal furniture and décor, its blue chairs, floors, and especially, walls, give it a warm, calming feel. *Someone tried to make this space as inviting as possible with the resources they had,* I think to myself.

The petite, elderly woman next to me coughs loudly as she fills out the questionnaire I have given her. *That sounds painful,* I want to say, but I don't. *I think more, and speak less here in Costa Rica,* I realize. My Spanish, although improving, is far more effortful for me than my native tongue of English. Instead of speaking, I glance over at the ill woman next to me and give a small, sympathetic smile when she looks up.

My eyes then turn to the other four people present. Two men, each here alone, sit separately near the entrance. The younger of the two, a man of perhaps twenty years old, motions to me that he is done with the questionnaire. He smiles widely as I come to collect it. I thank him several times for his help: "Gracias, muchas gracias," I say. *I truly am grateful,* I think as I return to my seat; each questionnaire I collect feels like a mini-victory.

I continue my inventory of the room. The other man sitting by himself near the entrance looks to be about forty-five years old. He keeps his sunglasses on as he stares off into the other direction. I find myself wondering about his situation—what he is here for. Moments before, he declined filling out the questionnaire, telling me simply, "No, lo siento" ("No, sorry").

A young woman and her baby are the only other people seated in this small space. The woman breast-feeds her infant, cradling him to her chest with one hand, while using her other hand to mark the questionnaire, which is balanced on a clipboard on her knee. *Gracias, muchas gracias,* I say to myself as I watch her slowly circle her response to each question.

My attention shifts again as I feel a pair of eyes on me. The eyes belong to a little girl of about four years old, who has just walked in with her mother. She has a mountain of dark brown curls and huge, charcoal-colored eyes. She drops her mother's hand to run across the room to stand directly in front of where I am sitting. She stares at me unabashedly, examining my skin, my eyes, and my hair. I smile widely, unable to contain my amusement and surprise at being the object of such interest. Seeming suddenly shy, she turns away and runs back to her mother, who is putting down her purse and settling into the seat across from me.

The little girl, with her flurry of movement, has the attention of all of other people in the waiting room by now. Even the man with the sunglasses, who previously seemed to be in his own, private inner world, is watching her.

Tugging on her mother's hand, she exclaims loudly, "Qué blanca es ella!" Then, turning to face me, she yells again with excitement, this time pointing her tiny finger at me, "Qué blanca es ella!"

Suddenly all eyes are on me. I feel myself blush as I translate her proclamation in my head: "Qué blanca es ella! *How White she is!*"

I am at a loss for words as the group waits for my reaction. *How White I am,* I think, instantly hyperconscious of my light skin, blond hair, and pale blue eyes in contrast with everyone else's darker skin, hair, and eyes.

I glance again at the little girl, whose face breaks into a large smile. I relax and return to normal breathing, now aware that I was holding my breath a moment before.

Then *I* smile, at the little girl, and at the others in the room. Amazingly, each person in the room smiles back at me. Their eyes seem caring, their smiles warm and genuine.

I am realizing, *I do not blend in here, but I am accepted nonetheless.*

Being in a foreign culture and experiencing culture shock has demonstrated the truth of this simple ideal—that it is possible for a person to be different, yet completely accepted—more powerfully and beautifully than I could have imagined.

Gracias, muchas gracias, I think to myself once again, this time feeling deeply and wonderfully overwhelmed by the sentiment.

Fighting My Own Pura Vida: Transformative Awakenings in Costa Rica

Katherine M. Slauta

I stepped out of the cab onto the busy street by Parque de la Merced. "Be careful for all the Nicaraguans" yelled the cab driver as he sped off. I tensed with anger as I walked through the park to the bus stop which would take me to one of the poorest towns in the San José region, Tejarcillos. When I first started working with medical technicians that went house to house, or I should say shack to shack, providing free health care to illegal immigrant Nicaraguans, one of my primary motivations for getting up in the morning was to prove those cabbies wrong. My reasoning was selfish too. I knew as soon as another "Tico" or Costa Rican hopped in that cab, the driver would be complaining to them about the "damn Americans coming down to vacation in Costa Rica while he had a real job."

I hated the stereotype that I was a rich young woman. It tore at me that people looked at me and

thought I was a stereotypical U. S. woman in Costa Rica for travel and leisure. So, as I began my fieldwork, I did so proudly. What did those prejudiced Ticos know anyway? *I* was a poor grad student who had not a dime to her name . . . only a few dimes borrowed from the US government. I marched through the dusty dirt roads, entered homes constructed partially of wood, metal, and cardboard, and began researching as the "American investigator who was too busy caring for the Nicaraguans the discriminatory Costa Ricans didn't care about." I was too busy to worry about a stereotype. The problem in my plan was that I did worry. I hated being a cliché. I was angry. I felt helpless. What is more boring than being unoriginal? I remember being furious with my friend Manuel who continued to call me rich. "I'm not rich!" I would scream as he shook his head like I just didn't get it. The truth is . . . I didn't. The angrier I grew the more I found myself biasing my work.

One particular day as I walked through the streets of the poor Nicaraguan neighborhood, or "precario," I followed one of the technicians Viqui into the home of a young man. Earlier Viqui had mentioned he was her "special friend," and she was going to check on him because he had missed his doctor's appointment. As we entered the small, dark living room a young man greeted us. He was thin, but not in a healthy way. His hair was long but spiky. I watched him sit, timid and sad on the couch. As he greeted us he wiped lipstick off his face and slowly hid his painted finger nails away. As Viqui began to speak I learned he was a young, gay man, suffering from AIDS. Despite the fact that we attempted for half an hour to get him to go to the doctor he was not convinced. The medicine, the travel, the stigma were wearing him down. As Viqui took down the vital stats, I noticed she wrote "24" next to his age. I was shocked. "Eduardo is my age," I thought. It may sound like a strange transformation stage, but in that moment, I was different. Here was a man with so little opportunity left. A gay, Nicaraguan, illegal immigrant with AIDS, Eduardo had faced so many stereotypes and prejudices. They had worn him down . . . to the point where he didn't want to go back to the doctors. In that moment I felt selfish and realized why I was so rich.

I had attempted to humble my accomplishments, my education, and my opportunities in order to fit in. And just like Eduardo, it was killing me inside. By humbling myself, I was inevitably denying myself my gift of opportunity. As I opened my eyes around me I realized that almost everyone else was relishing in his or her opportunity. The technicians I worked with used the education they were provided to help others everyday. Most Nicaraguans played music, were happy and didn't wallow in their poor conditions. After all, by living in Costa Rica they were provided an opportunity many of their family members would have died for. My Costa Rican friends loved the fact that they had a job, even if it meant working for two dollars an hour.

Working with Eduardo opened my eyes. My thought process began to change in that moment, and in the days to come I healed. I wasn't angry, and bitter. I conducted my research because I was rich, with opportunity. The Costa Ricans always use this saying "pura vida." Everything is "pure life," or "great." My research brought me to a "pura vida," a transformation that shifted my paradigm from proving others wrong to seizing my own opportunities.

CLARIFYING THE MOMENTS: REDUCING OUR CULTURE SHOCK

Before we explore how sharing our narratives brought us to a greater understanding of our experiences in Costa Rica, it is first important that we define what we consider the "shock moments," in our narratives. As these stories are rich in examples, and provide room for interpretation, it is only fair to the reader that we clarify how we interpret these tales. That is, what the reader may interpret as shocking could have at that point in our journey become "normal," and on the contrary, what may seem "insignificant" to the reader could have been a telling moment for one of us.

Patricia's concern about puppies demonstrates many cultural differences and transitions as she attempted to define her sense of home with her family and her new surroundings. Her narrative provides various examples of cultural adaptation. In fact, through this story we are able to see Patricia's culture shock regarding mixed emotions that many experience with their transition to another culture— her emotions of "joy, sadness, angst, and love melt together" while directed toward the puppy represent the very same emotions she felt on her first day in a new country. It was her brief, but significant encounter with a Costa Rican family that helped her to feel more at home than she had felt before. This symbolic, yet very real moment of transformation allowed Patricia to reduce her culture shock and move forward to a sense of place and comfort in a foreign country.

Summer's narrative also displays multiple examples of culture shock. The narrative in which she contrasts the appearance of the clinic in Costa Rica to clinics in the United States reflects the fact that she perceived her environment as unfamiliar. Additionally, her culture shock is evident in her realization that she "think[s] more, and speak[s] less here in Costa Rica;" her ability to communicate dramatically changed as a result of being in a country where she was a nonnative speaker. Finally, physically sticking out was a main source of insecurity, and an example of culture shock. However, when a Costa Rican child joyfully pointed out her physical differences, Summer realized that it was not necessary to blend in to be accepted. The excitement of the child in pointing out the "Whiteness" of her skin was a simple yet powerful reminder that being viewed as different was not necessarily negative; in fact, the child seemed intrigued and overjoyed at the sight of such an unfamiliar face.

Katherine's account of the stereotypes she faced demonstrates her difficulty in transitioning. Despite her desire to understand the Costa Rican culture via her research, the labels placed on her acted as roadblocks in her journey. These blocks created a feeling of helplessness that many face while adapting to a new culture. However, by viewing Eduardo, a Nicaraguan immigrant also facing difficulties adapting to the Costa Rican culture, she was able to combat these blocks. Her "pura vida" revelation allowed her to realize that the roadblocks she faced were actually self-imposed. In discovering "pura vida" or "pure life," Katherine was able to reduce her culture shock by creating a new perspective on her place in Costa Rica, thus creating a state of growth and development in her research.

These specific examples of how our culture shock was reduced lead to our greatest discovery: the process of recounting what counts.

MOVING FROM DOUBT TO ACKNOWLEDGMENT: LEARNING TO "RECOUNT WHAT COUNTS"

Each of these narratives captures examples of the many instances of culture shock we encountered as we tried to understand our new surroundings and our research. It appeared that for each revelation we had about our new environment, we faced an equally telling moment of "shock," in which we learned how different we really were. For each step we took forward, it seemed we took another step back. These moments, while upsetting and shocking, were not always bad. In fact, as we shared our experiences, we realized we weren't stepping back at all. Rather, we were simply stepping a different way.

Sharing these narratives of transformative turns in our research allowed us to view our experiences with a new perspective—a process that enabled us to reframe and reduce our culture shock. Through the narratives, we recall our experiences of culture shock while simultaneously reframing them as positive growth opportunities, helping us to transform our doubt to acknowledgment. By acknowledging rather than doubting, we indeed changed our memories of research, and inevitably how we recount and narrate our journey. The following section describes this process.

* * *

"I haven't collected enough questionnaires."

"I had hoped to interview twice as many practitioners by now!"

"My Spanish isn't as good as it should be."

In order to be psychologically and spiritually healthy as we adapted to life in Costa Rica, we had to learn how to manage these self-doubts. This entailed redefining our priorities as well as our stories of "progress" and "success"—a process which we liked to refer to as "re-counting what counts." More specifically, we tried to maintain our psychological and spiritual health throughout our cultural adaptation by (a) *embracing change and uncertainty,* and (b) *recognizing accomplishments.* By utilizing these practices—discussed below—to help us "re-count what counts," we were often able to construct stories that replaced our frustration with patience, our confusion with curiosity, and our doubts with

acknowledgments—and in the process, reframe and reduce our culture shock.

Embracing Change and Uncertainty

"Change. It has the power to uplift, to heal, to stimulate, surprise, open new doors, bring fresh experience, and create excitement in life. Certainly it is worth the risk."

LEO BUSCAGLIA
(CITED IN WIEDERHOLD, 2004, P. 32)

* * *

In order to adapt to life in Costa Rica, we found that it was critical that we learned to *embrace change and uncertainty,* which required reframing culture shock as a positive, rather than a negative, experience. To explain, moving abroad changed countless aspects of our lives. Most obviously, our surroundings changed. Our new home in San José (Costa Rica's capital city) differed greatly from the suburban setting of San Diego, California, to which we were accustomed. Some of the changes in the landscape were overwhelming at first; we spent much of our first week there noticing what was "missing." We found ourselves asking a lot of questions we had not asked before about things we had taken for granted in our own country:

"Why is part of the street missing?" we wondered aloud, upon noticing the gap that exists between the sidewalk and the street on most *avenidas* in San José.

"Why are the crosswalks missing?" we asked with a mixture of curiosity and fear as we prepared to "make a run for it," dodging heavy traffic as we sprinted from one side of the street to another. Cabbies honked, annoyed—or perhaps, amused—at us, three grown women crossing the street hand-in-hand for safety, the way a parent often protectively grasps onto his or her young child.

"Why are the street signs missing?" we asked—no, *complained*—with confusion and exasperation at San José's complete absence of street signs. The Tico method of giving directions—"Detras de la iglesia catolica, 100 metros sur, y 50 metros oeste" (*"Across from the Catholic church, then 100 meters south, and 50 meters west"*)—befuddled us at first. Each set of directions we were given seemed to necessitate ten more sets of instructions:

"¿Pero, donde esta la iglesia Católica?" ("But, where is the Catholic Church?)

"Detras de la biblioteca grande y 200 metros norte." ("Across from the big library and then 200 meters north.")

"¿Pero donde esta la biblioteca grande?" ("But where is the big library?") Since we were not yet familiar with any of the popular landmarks commonly used for directions, this sort of conversation could go on for some time.

In addition to feeling overwhelmed at first by what was "missing" in our new surroundings, there were many other adjustments, including speaking a non-native language on a regular basis, meeting new people, and conducting research in a foreign context. In order to maintain our spiritual and psychological health in the face of these many changes, we had to learn not only how to *adapt* to them, but also how to *embrace* them. That is, rather than fearing uncertainty, we needed to learn to enjoy it, even *relish* in it. In this way, we reframed the unfamiliar cues surrounding us as exciting and positive, rather than threatening and negative. In other words, we reframed the culture shock we were experiencing as a positive, rather than a negative, construct. We all came to recognize this need to embrace change and uncertainty in different ways. Summer remembers the particular moment that she came to this realization:

I was taking a public bus home from a healthcare clinic that I had visited for the first time for my thesis research. Although I generally relied upon taxis (and walking) as my means of transportation within San José, I was attempting to become more familiar with the bus system. I saw buses everywhere I went in Costa Rica—it seemed that there was no destination they did not reach. Because they appeared to travel everywhere, and because they were a fraction of the cost of taxis, several weeks into my Costa Rica adventure, I decided, "I'm going to finally track down a bus schedule."

This was no easy task. The post office did not have a bus schedule, nor did the city hall, the building of tourism, or the grocery store. I was at a loss. Finally, I was able to obtain a photocopied version from a friend of my landlord (who had gotten it who-knows-where). While I was overjoyed to have a schedule in hand, I had a hard time making sense of it. Suddenly, utilizing this means of transportation seemed to me a complex series of challenges; I had to find the right bus stop, then transfer at the correct

station, and finally, recognize my intended arrival destination in time to signal to the driver to stop.

However, I had managed to make the five-mile trip from my apartment to the clinic via bus that day without incident, so I felt fairly confident as I boarded the bus to make the reverse route home. I found myself a seat and settled in for the short ride. It took me a few moments to realize that I didn't recognize any of the streets that we were traveling on. "Perhaps we are just going a different route," I thought to myself. "No need to worry."

After another five minutes passed, it became increasingly clear that we were heading in exactly the opposite direction of my apartment. I panicked for a moment, thinking, "I'm in a foreign country on a bus by myself heading who-knows-where" "Stay calm," I told myself.

Then I repeated in my head, "I'm in a foreign country on a bus by myself heading who-knows-where!"

Rather than feeling scared, I was suddenly overwhelmed by the excitement and novelty of the situation. I said to myself "It's a Thursday afternoon and rather than working away in some cubicle in the United States like so many of my friends are doing, I'm exploring a new country via the bus!"

That was an incredibly transformative moment for me. Rather than fearing uncertainty, I began to embrace and even cherish it. "Where will the bus stop next?" I wondered with excitement. Suddenly, I couldn't get enough of my new surroundings as I peered out the window. I tried to practice mindfulness (or "being in the moment"). I wanted to take it all in, fascinated by each piece of this foreign landscape: Children dressed in uniforms waved to the passing bus as they flooded out of the gates of their school. A border-collie trotted happily down the sidewalk without any signs of an owner around. A corner café invited diners in with a sign in the window reading "Bienvenidos" ("Welcome").

By embracing change and uncertainty, I was able to start noticing the wonder that Costa Rica had to offer, rather than focusing on what I perceived to be "missing." I made it back to my apartment over two hours later, when the bus finally looped back around to its original route. So then I was home again, yet it was different than before. I was different. I was finally able to embrace the change and uncertainty that living abroad presents.

For Summer, Patricia, and Katherine, learning to embrace change and uncertainty was an absolutely vital step in maintaining psychological and spiritual health while living abroad. Embracing change and uncertainty entailed acknowledging that, consistent with some conceptualizations of culture shock (e.g., Adler, 1975), encountering unfamiliar cues (i.e., experiencing culture shock) could be an exciting and positive, rather than a threatening and negative, experience. Learning to recognize accomplishments, as discussed below, was another component critical to adapting well during our cultural immersion.

Recognizing Accomplishment

"Don't take anyone else's definition of success as your own. (This is easier said than done.)"

JACQUELINE BRISKIN
(CITED IN WIEDERHOLD, 2004, P. 170)

* * *

Along with embracing change, as discussed in the section above, we realized that, in order to be psychologically and spiritually healthy while adjusting to life in Costa Rica, we needed to re-define our idea of success, and learn to *recognize accomplishments*. To explain, we came to Costa Rica with a certain framework in mind regarding what would "count" as success. In fact, within a week of arriving, the three of us held a meeting outlining what we planned for accomplishing our health communication research within a set timeframe. We jotted down phrases in our Day Timers to indicate deadlines. For example:

"February 1st: Finish establishing contacts with health-care clinics."

"April 1st: Complete data collection phase."

"May 1st: First draft of discussion due."

Our plans, although well-intended, were not always possible to adhere to. For example, despite spending well over 200 hours in health care clinics by April 1st, Summer had collected less than 100 questionnaires from patients—far fewer than she needed in order to obtain significant results. She remembers reading—with more than a little envy—an e-mail from a fellow graduate student back home at San Diego State University: "I just put the questionnaire for my thesis online yesterday, and I've already gotten 323 responses!" In only a day and a half, she had collected more than three times the number of questionnaires that Summer had gathered in two and a half months. Summer felt like she had failed.

When Summer lamented about this to Patricia and Katherine, she found that they were both incredibly empathetic, having similar complaints of their own. "I thought I would be nearly done with my data collection by now, too, but it's only recently that I've really refined my research questions," said Katherine.

"I'm upset with myself, too," said Patricia. "I've collected so many interesting stories through my research here, but I've been so exhausted at the end of the day that I haven't been writing all of these field notes down like I should be."

We talked for a few minutes more about how we had been falling short of our expectations, until we grew tired of these negative stories and decided to make a list and talk about what we *had* accomplished recently. As we each compiled our own lists, we shared some items with each other:

"How about finding our way around San José?" Katherine asked.

"Absolutely!" Summer replied. "And learning the bus schedule!" Summer added.

"What about speaking a foreign language everyday? Does that count?" asked Katherine.

"Of course it counts!" said Patricia, smiling with enthusiasm. *"We're re-counting what counts!"*

As our list continued to grow, we realized that we had accomplished more than we thought during our time in Costa Rica, in our research as well as in our personal lives. For example, although Summer had collected less than 100 questionnaires thus far, she had established enough contacts that she would soon be able to double that amount. Plus, she realized that she had collected rich qualitative data from spending so much time at the clinics. Meanwhile, Katherine had discovered a new research angle that she was passionate about, and Patricia already had hours and hours of interviews with practitioners on tape. Although we hadn't accomplished what we had initially planned to, our achievements were no less valuable. Being in a foreign context meant that we needed to shed our preconceived definitions of success. This realization helped reduce the strain, anxiety, and self-doubts that we were experiencing as a result of culture shock. By acknowledging our accomplishments and by embracing change and uncertainty, we were able to "re-count what counts," and therefore, maintain our psychological and spiritual health while living abroad.

* * * * *

We began this chapter with a description of the doubts we experienced as a result of culture shock. Then we discussed the value of narrative in managing and reframing this culture shock. Next, we offered a narrative from each of the authors, focusing upon some aspect of doubt we experienced during our cultural adaptation—and ultimately conveying how culture shock resulted in a personal growth experience for each of us. Finally, we concluded with a section on the techniques we utilized to manage our culture shock, and thereby, maintain our spiritual and psychological health while abroad. Like our experience in Costa Rica, moving from doubt to acknowledgment was a journey—difficult at times, yet ultimately, incredibly worthwhile. We learned that in order to fully appreciate our time abroad, we had to "re-count what counts."

References

Adler, P. S. (1975). The transitional experience: An alternative view of culture shock. *Journal of Humanistic Psychology, 15*(4), 13–23.

Bennett, J. M. (1998). Transition shock: Putting culture shock in perspective. In M. J. Bennett (Ed.), *Basic concepts of intercultural communication* (pp. 215–223). Yarmouth, ME: Intercultural Press.

Frank, A. W. (1995). *The wounded storyteller: Body, illness, and ethics.* Chicago: University of Chicago Press.

Genette, G. (1980). *Narrative discourse: An essay in method* (J. E. Lewin, Trans.). Ithaca, NY: Cornell University Press.

Goffman, E. (1963). *Stigma: Notes on the management of spoiled identity.* Englewood Cliffs, NJ: Prentice Hall.

Harter, L. M., Japp, P. M., & Beck, C. S. (2005). Vital problematics of narrative theorizing about health and healing. In L. M. Harter, P. M. Japp, & C. S. Beck (Eds.). *Narratives, health, and healing: Communication theory, research, and practice* (pp. 7–29). Mahwah, NJ: Erlbaum.

Lopez, N. (2006, January 6). I love the challenge. *Daily celebrations.* Retrieved February 12, 2006, from www.dailycelebrations.com/010602.htm

Oberg, K. (1960). Cultural shock: Adjustment to new cultural environments. *Practical Anthropology, 7,* 177–182.

Pedersen, P. (1995). *The five stages of culture shock: Critical incidents around the world.* Westport, CT: Greenwood Press.

Polkinghorn, D. E. (1988). *Narrative knowing and the human sciences.* Albany: State University of New York Press.

Richardson, L. (1997). *Fields of play: constructing an academic life.* New Brunswick, NJ: Rutgers University Press.

Storti, C. (2001). *The art of crossing cultures* (2nd ed.). Yarmouth, ME: Intercultural Press.

Wiederhold, B. K. (2004). *Virtual reflections.* San Diego: Interactive Medial Institute.

Concepts and Questions

1. What causes culture shock and what are some of its symptoms?
2. How can culture shock erode one's communication competencies?
3. The authors write that "there was so much more involved in our experiences in Costa Rica than any one story could tell." How does this relate to cultural immersion?
4. How did the experience with the puppy help Geist-Martin begin to overcome culture shock?
5. What is meant by Carnett's statement "I think more, and speak less here in Costa Rica"? How can this influence cultural adjustment?
6. The authors indicate that being different, or "sticking out," in another culture can produce culture shock. Do you agree with this? Why?
7. How did a visit to the Nicaraguan immigrant help Slauta begin to overcome culture shock?
8. Why can embracing change and uncertainty help with culture shock?
9. How do you think you would react if you were suddenly immersed in another culture, where your ability to communicate and function normally was removed?
10. Do you agree with the authors' contention that culture shock can cause personal growth? Why?

Proactive Performance to Prevent Sexual Assault: Understanding the Role of Masculinity in Violence Against Women

Marc D. Rich

Lucretia R. Robinson

Courtney Aherns

José I. Rodriguez

Sexual assault is not just a female problem, it's a male problem, too.

Male Audience Member

Masculinity has become a relentless test by which we prove to other men, to women, and ultimately to ourselves, that we have successfully mastered the part.

Gergen and Davis, 1997, p. 240.

Ariel is in her apartment with her friends Sonia and Jeremy. Her eyes are focused on the floor, and she is clearly upset. She attempts to explain what is wrong, but her friends are engaged in an upbeat conversation and keep talking over Ariel. Finally, she musters up the strength to speak. "Last night," she begins in a soft voice, "I think K.J. forced himself on me." The mood in the room shifts dramatically and Jeremy asks, "He did what?" Jeremy is fuming now, pacing back and forth. "That's it! I'm calling up my boys right now

and we're going to take care of this problem!" Ariel pleads with Jeremy not to leave the apartment, but he is already dialing his cell phone and making his way out the door.

The previous scene is part of the interACT troupe[1] performance on sexual assault prevention. The interACT troupe performs for approximately 2,500 audience members per year in a variety of educational and community settings throughout the United States. Using "proactive scenes," the highest level of audience involvement according to Pelias and VanOosting (1987), the goal of the interACT troupe is to reduce sexual assaults on college campuses, create empathy for women who have been assaulted, and challenge traditional male gender roles. Responding to the call from scholars to create sexual assault programs that consider the role of men in prevention, the interACT performance was designed to enroll college male students as proactive agents of change. As Berkowitz (2005) notes, "Men must take responsibility for preventing sexual assault, because most assaults are perpetuated by men against women, children, and other men. . . . Thus, effective sexual assault prevention requires that men look at their own potential for violence as well as take a stand against the violence of other men" (p. 163).

The efficacy of the interACT sexual assault prevention program has been measured by quantitative and qualitative methods, and the results have been published in books and scholarly journals (see Rodriguez and Rich, 2006; Rich and Rodriguez, 2007). In this essay, we are interested in considering how the interACT scenes illuminate traditional male gender roles, thereby enabling audience members to identify with the characters and understand the serious consequences of masculinity. Once this occurs, college men are invited on stage with the peer actor-educators to perform new gender roles that can help prevent sexual assault and provide support to women who are survivors. We base our analysis in this essay on data collected during focus groups that convened immediately after an interACT performance. In the first section of this essay we discuss the epidemic of sexual assault on college campuses. Then, we explore ways to better understand gender and masculinity. In the third section, we consider how the interACT performance provides a safe space for reconsidering masculinity and rehearsing new roles that may help prevent sexual assault.

SEXUAL ASSAULT

The interACT program was developed in response to the high incidence of sexual assault on college campuses, which has risen to near epidemic proportions (Simon, 1993). Defined as "forced sexual aggression or contact with or without penetration against a victim" (Black et al., 2000, p. 589), sexual assaults are common on college campuses due to the convergence of factors including drug and alcohol use, age of college students, independent living, and the acceptance of rape myths and norms (Holcomb et al., 1993). In addition, college women are three times more likely to be sexually assaulted than the general population, and eighty- to ninety-percent of the time, will be assaulted by someone they know (Yeater & O'Donahue, 1999). The impact of sexual assault and post-assault trauma has gained significant attention from contemporary researchers because, as Resick and Schnicke (1992) explained, "sexual assault is a major life-threatening, traumatic event from which many victims never fully recover" (p. 4).

Although statistics on sexual assault are sometimes difficult to ascertain, in one of the most cited studies Koss, Gidycz, and Wisniewski (1987) show that twenty-seven percent of college women experience rape or attempted rape, twenty-five percent of college men are involved in some form of sexual aggression, and eight percent of men raped or attempted to rape a woman since the age of fourteen. Although much of the research on sexual assault focuses on the devastating impact that these violent acts have on women, it is also important to note that ninety-three percent of perpetrators are men (National Institute of Justice Website), and that an astounding thirty-five percent of college men polled would sexually assault a woman if they knew there was no possibility of being caught (Yeater & O'Donahue, 1999). The need to address issues related to masculinity in prevention led one scholar to conclude, "I am extremely skeptical of any rape prevention work that proposes solutions to the problem of rape but leaves masculinity, as we know today, largely intact" (Capraro, 1994, p. 22). Hence, it seems clear that rape prevention programs "should focus primarily on the risks posed by male perpetrators" (National Institute of Justice Website).

The research regarding sexual assault on college campuses can surely be shocking and depressing.

Coming to an understanding of the devastating impact violent acts have on women, as well as the role that masculinity plays in the perpetuation of sexual assault, can be a difficult process for college students. However, as teacher-scholar-activists interested in the relationship between culture, gender, and performance, we strongly believe that if we take steps to uncover the male gender roles that perpetuate acts of violence against women, then we can work together to prevent sexual assault and facilitate empathic responses for survivors of assault. Before describing the interACT scene and examining how it allows for new gender enactments, we will first consider the relationship between gender, culture, and communication.

UNDERSTANDING GENDER

A burgeoning area of study in the discipline of communication studies is gender. Unlike sex, which is "determined by genetic codes that program biological features," gender is a social construction (like race) that we learn from birth (Wood & Reich, 2006, p. 178). That is, there is nothing "natural" about gender; rather, it is a learned behavior that is constructed in our interactions with others and shaped by our cultural experiences. Our gender construction begins at birth with the names we are given, the clothes we are dressed in, and the ways our rooms are decorated. In addition, even how our parents or caregivers speak to us is heavily influenced by gender and cultural norms. As Wood (2002) explains, "We are surrounded by communication that announces social images of gender and seeks to persuade us these are natural, correct ways for men and women to behave" (p. 29).

Although gender roles might appear natural, we can probably recall a time when there were consequences for not performing our gender "correctly." Perhaps as a young boy you were critiqued for crying or told that you needed to "act like a man." Growing up as a girl you might have been scolded for not "acting like a lady," or told that certain sports or toys were not for girls. As West and Zimmerman (1991) note, "to 'do' gender is not always to live up to normative conceptions of femininity or masculinity; it is to engage in behavior at the risk of gender assessment" (p. 23).

Not only do we learn about gender norms from our parents and friends, gender is also inextricably linked to culture. As Wood (2002) notes, "gender is upheld by cultural practices" (p. 29). In U.S. mainstream culture, for instance, there are clear prescriptions about how men should act. For example, during a football game it is appropriate for athletes to pat one another on the butt after a good play. However, imagine if a male classmate patted another male's butt after he did well on an exam! Furthermore, there are only certain contexts—like weddings or funerals—where men are expected to cry. As illustrated, cultural norms play a significant role in masculinity.

Although gender roles may seem rigid in the United States, Pearson and VanHorn (2004) note "Gender does not remain static over the life span" (p. 286). Hence, our ideas about femininity and masculinity are probably more fluid than we recognize on a day-to-day basis, leading some scholars to define gender as a performative act rather than a biological fact (see Augusta-Scott, 2007; Butler, 1990, 1993, 2004; Halberstam, 1998). By using performance as an explanatory metaphor to consider gender, we can begin to consider the scripts (language) we use, the costumes (clothing) we wear, and the scenes (daily interactions) we participate in that are gendered. As Bornstein (1998) explains, "Gender is interactive and relatively predictable between ourselves and another person. We know what gender to perform when relating to any given person" (p. 178). If we accept the notion that gender is not a biological fact, but rather a performative act reinforced by family, friends, and culture, we can consider the possibility that there exist alternative ways to enact gender in less rigid and more humane ways. Hence, we can begin to envision new performances of masculinity that are supportive of women and can potentially prevent sexual assault. Moreover, programs geared toward men are critical because "they are virtually always the rape perpetrator" (Rozee and Koss, 2001, p. 295). It is our belief that the interACT model provides a safe space for male college students to rehearse new gender roles.

THE interACT SCENE

The interACT scene begins with three male college students, K.J., JaCarri, and Paul, drinking and sharing stories about their night out. We portray alcohol consumption in the first scene because "the more intoxicated a man is, the greater the likelihood that he will ignore a woman's protests or be unable to interpret her words or actions as she intended them" (Bohmer & Parrot, 1993, pp. 19–20). In this scene, the men are highly energetic, and discuss the "girls" they met and phone numbers they collected. The men objectify the women, referring to the way they looked and the "skimpy" clothing that was worn. The scene quickly escalates when JaCarri notes that K.J.'s girlfriend is still out at a bar with her friends, and is probably drunk and fooling around with another guy. Paul tries to intervene, but he is shut down when JaCarri threatens him with violence, illustrating the view that "in some situations speech is appropriate in male role enactment, but in others it is not and its use casts doubt on the speaker's manliness" (Philipsen, 1975, p. 14). By the end of the scene, K.J. is in a frenzy, and ultimately explodes when his girlfriend (Ariel) comes home. The first scene ends when K.J. demands that his friends leave, and proceeds to make Ariel "sit down and shut up!" K.J. engages in a tirade, accusing Ariel of making him "look like a punk" in front of his friends. The scene ends when K.J. grabs Ariel's arm and yells, "This will never happen again!"

In the second scene, Ariel tries to explain to her friends, Sonia and Kelly, that something is wrong. We include this scene because only 3.2 percent of female college students report being raped to police or campus security, but "two-thirds of rape victims disclosed their experience to a friend" (Brown, 2005, p. 5). After Ariel states, "I think K.J. forced himself on me last night," Sonia blames her for treating K.J. poorly, drinking too much, and creating drama. Kelly is traumatized by Ariel's disclosure, and goes into a passionate monologue about calling the police and taking Ariel to the hospital before "all the evidence is lost." Ariel is unable to speak because her friends are not listening to her.

After these brief initial scenes (lasting for a total of approximately ten minutes), the remainder of the show consists of four proactive scenes that involve audience members. During the first scene, eight to ten audience members come on stage and embody the negative voices that go through a woman's head after she has been assaulted. For example, an audience member creates a frozen pose of pointing at Ariel, and then states in a demeaning voice, "You should have never gone out drinking with your friends." This first scene enables audience members to better understand how a woman might feel after surviving sexual assault. During the second proactive scene, we reenact the situation between the three men in the apartment. However, this time audience members can replace Paul and try to intervene with K.J. (the boyfriend) and JaCarri (the aggressive friend). During the third proactive scene, we recreate the situation between the three women, providing audience members with an opportunity to replace Ariel (the girlfriend) and try to get less antagonistic responses from her friends (Sonia and Kelly). During the final proactive scene Ariel comes back on stage and two audience members enact the roles of supportive friends.

RECONSTRUCTING GENDER

In their discussion of teaching gender and communication classes, Cooks and Sun (2002) note, "When students are challenged to actively seek out and perform alternatives to the binaries of male and female, they often actively resist" (p. 293). The process of questioning what we may see as traditional gender roles and examining how these roles are socially constructed can be a painful process for students. There may be additional resistance when an "expert" such as a professor presents information about gender to students who are perhaps being exposed to the literature for the first time. In the interACT scene, however, student actor-educators reenact scenes that are perceived as realistic by college students. Hence, the performances of traditional gender roles are consistent with what audience members can expect in similar situations. What starts out as a fun time between male friends quickly escalates to a violent scenario when performances of hypermasculinity are mixed with alcohol.

By creating a scene that reflects a typical night out, male audience members are able to see themselves in the characters on stage. The following comments from male students illustrate their identification with the interACT scenes:

The performance was more tangible than a lecture, it was real, and you could see the actual emotions.

That happens in real life.

I was emotionally attached to the situation because it was so real . . . it could happen to me one day, it could happen to anyone in here.

It was realistic for us, for college students, 'cause we're dealing with the same issues, out drinking with friends, the girlfriend out with her girlfriends.

Once male audience members are able to see how the scene on stage is similar to what happens in their own lives, they can become aware of the consequences of acting in traditional masculine ways. The following feedback from male audience members shows their willingness to critically assess performances of masculinity:

How easily this guy [the boyfriend] went from having fun to being a rapist. How easily things can lead to abuse. How easily it could get out of hand.

. . . everything could be fun and then one second later, poof. I thought it was a real eye opener.

You can see the build up, with the anger. I was like, aw baby, he's getting angry, he's getting angry . . . all of it's gonna happen [because] his anger is rising.

Stuff like that happens a lot with my friends. We all have girlfriends and we are always teasing. Everyone is using it to cover up, to cover up for being whipped.

It's like conversations people have, but you know, in that context, it just looks disgusting . . .

Once the men in the audience identify with the characters on stage, and recognize the pitfalls of performing masculinity in problematic ways, they are invited on stage to replace Paul's character (the third male friend) and try to intervene to prevent the sexual assault from happening in the first place. As Wood (2002) explains, "Concrete embodiments of alternatives to conventional [gender] roles create new possibilities for our own lives" (p. 25). This scene is a critical and unique aspect of the interACT program because men are enrolled as prosocial agents of change, rather than simply being blamed for women's oppression. In the following passages male students reflect on their own interventions, as well as the interventions they saw enacted by their peers on stage. They also consider additional strategies to de-escalate a violent situation:

The performance would help you resolve a situation or be able to step in if you see a friend getting emotionally charged over another person's comments, you could step in and pull him to the side and stop the situation from happening. If you were in a situation where it was getting real bad between two guys . . . I would try to break it up with comedy . . . but then I never would of thought [before viewing the performance] to just stay there, like you can easily lie and be like, dude, I'm too drunk to drive.

I wanted to go up there and say. This is it! This is exactly it! What not to do . . . Stop! I wanted to yell.

You can't let yourself become unglued . . .the guy's obviously in a very violent stage. He can be talked to, take him outside, he can be calmed down.

During the second scene in the show, when Ariel is speaking to her two female friends about the assault, the facilitator pauses the performance and asks the audience if they want to see the male version of Kelly (Ariel's friend who overreacts and demands that they go to the hospital). By bringing in a male friend we are able to demonstrate what we perceive to be realistic and heightened performances of masculinity. This scene, which is discussed in the opening of this chapter, shows how a man may quickly move to a state of violence when he believes a close friend has been sexually assaulted. The move to violence may be the first reaction a man experiences because it is a (stereo) typical masculine response, and because men may not have other less-gendered communication strategies at their disposal. Men may also believe that they are actually meeting a woman's needs by physically assaulting the perpetrator. However, after the facilitator asks for feedback, audience members consistently note that both Kelly and Jeremy are doing what they believe is best for the survivor, without actually asking Ariel what she needs. This short scene typically generates a great deal of laughter, and the audience members usually agree that this is how men would respond in a similar situation. As male audience members explain:

That's true, that's how guys react. The first thing, let's go find him, first thing is protecting my homegirl.

If a woman came up to me and told me she got raped, I would do exactly what the guy in the show did, that's the only thing I would think of before the show . . . but I never would have thought that it was for me, it's like this is for her, we're gonna kick this guy's ass, she's gonna be so happy.

Once the audience comes to the realization that physically assaulting K.J. would not alleviate the situation, the facilitator asks the audience what they believe Ariel really needs from her friends. Audience members typically respond that Ariel needs support and someone to listen to her. Then, the facilitator invites two audience members to come on stage and take on the roles of empathic friends because, according to Warshaw (1988), "The reactions of the people around her and the support she receives soon after the assault may be critical to the woman's survival and recovery" (p. 181). During the scene, however, Ariel is extremely confused about what happened, wonders if she did something to provoke the attack, and makes it very difficult for the friends to deliver their supportive messages. By coming on stage in the roll of a supportive friend, rather than a male who blames the victim or seeks to "fix the problem" by assaulting K. J., audience members come to understand that there are a variety of possible communication strategies available to men beyond the knee-jerk reactions that seem "natural" in our culture. The following statements illustrate that men are willing and able to learn new performances of masculinity:

You gotta listen to them . . . without wanting to solve the problem. Just listen to them.

. . . if she told you she is telling you for a reason, because she wants you probably there for her and not to run off and go hunt down this guy.

Before the performance I would have asked a lot of questions . . .What started it? Why didn't you stop it? I think now I would . . . ask her what her needs are and let her know I'm here just to listen to her.

After seeing different approaches to the scene it makes you kinda realize that they need you to be supportive instead of being critical and you know they need you to be more of a friend.

You learn it's not easy to just sit down and listen to someone.

CONCLUSIONS

In their essay on gender and teaching, Cooks and Sun (2002) ask, "For those critical of the pedagogy of mainstream gender research, who wish to teach outside the confining rhetoric of differences and categories, what are the possibilities?" (p. 307). Our experience with the interACT performance leads us to believe that proactive performance provides an experiential opportunity for college men to reflect on problematic aspects of traditional gender roles. Subsequently, men learn to rehearse new performances of masculinity that are both less violent and more sensitive to the needs of women who have survived sexual assault. Male gender norms can be "exposed as nonnatural and nonnecessary when they take place in a context and through a form of embodying that defies normative expectation" (Butler, 2004, p. 218). We believe that the interACT performance provides precisely the type of context that Butler is suggesting. We conclude this chapter with the words of a male audience member who underscores the importance of the interACT scenes: "You gotta remember. That victim could be your sister. That victim could be your mom. You never know. As long as this program teaches one guy, it's working."

Note

1. **interACT** is a troupe of student actor-educators housed in the Department of Communication Studies at California State University, Long Beach. Troupe members represent a variety of majors including communication studies, theater, English, psychology, film, marketing, and pre-med.

References

Augusta-Scott, T. (2007). Conversations with men about women's violence: Ending men's violence by challenging gender essentialism. In C. Brown & T. Augusta-Scott (Eds.), *Narrative therapy: Making meaning, making lives* (pp. 197–210). Thousand Oaks, CA: Sage

Berkowitz, A. D. (2005). Fostering men's responsibility for preventing sexual assault. In P. Schewe (Ed.), *Preventing violence in relationships: Interventions across the life span* (pp. 163–196). Washington, DC: American Psychological Association.

Black, B., Weisz, A., Coats, S., & Patterson, D. (2000). Evaluating a psychoeducational sexual assault prevention program incorporating theatrical presentation, peer education, and social work. *Research on Social Work Practice, 10,* 589–606.

Bohmer, C., & Parrot, A. (1993). *Sexual assault on campus: The problem and the solution.* New York: Lexington.

Bornstein, K. (1998). *My gender workbook.* New York: Routledge.

Brown, A. (2005, November 20). Increase in rape stats. *The Daily 49er,* p. 5.

Burke, P. (1996). *Gender shock.* New York: Anchor Books.

Butler, J. (1990). *Gender trouble.* New York: Routledge.

Butler, J. (1993). *Bodies that matter: On the discursive limits of "sex."* New York: Routledge.

Butler, J. (2004). *Undoing gender.* New York: Routledge.

Capraro, R. L. (1994). Disconnected lives: Men, masculinity, and rape prevention. In A. Berkowitz (Ed.), *Men and rape: Theory, research, and prevention programs in higher education* (pp. 21–34). San Francisco: Jossey-Bass.

Cooks, L., & Sun, C. (2002). Constructing gender pedagogies: Desire and resistance in the alternative classroom. *Communication Education 51*(3), 293–310.

Gergen, M. M., & Davis, S. N. (Eds.) (1997). *Toward a new psychology of gender.* New York: Routledge.

Halberstam, J. (1998). *Female masculinity.* Durham, NC: Duke University Press.

Holcomb, D. R., Sarvela, P. D., Sondag, A., & Hatton-Holcomb, L. C. (1993). An evaluation of a mixed-gender date rape prevention workshop. *Journal of American College Health, 41,* 159–164.

Koss, M. P., Gidycz, C. A., & Wisniewski, N. (1987). The scope of rape: Incidence and prevalence of sexual aggression in victimization in a national sample of higher education students. *Journal of Consulting and Clinical Psychology, 55,* 162–170.

Lippa, R. A. (2002). *Gender, nature, and nurture.* Mahwah, NJ: Lawrence Erlbaum Associates.

Lorber, J., & Farrell, S. A. (Eds.) (1991). *The social construction of gender.* Newbury Park: Sage.

National Institute of Justice. (2007, January 15). Retrieved January 15, 2007, from http://www.ncjrs.gov/pdffiles/172837.pdf

Pearson, J. C., & VanHorn, S. B. (2004). Communication and gender identity: A retrospective analysis. *Communication Quarterly, 52*(3), 284–299.

Pelias, R. J., & VanOosting, J. (1987). A paradigm for performance studies. *Quarterly Journal of Speech, 73,* 219–231.

Phillipsen, G. (1975). Speaking "like a man" in Teamsterville: Culture patterns of role enactment in an urban neighborhood. *Quarterly Journal of Speech, 61,* 13–22.

Resick, P. A., & Schnicke, M. K. (1992). Cognitive processing therapy for sexual assault victims. *Journal of Consulting and Clinical Psychology, 60,* 748–756.

Rich, M. D., & Rodriguez, J. I. (2007). A proactive approach to peer education: The efficacy of sexual assault intervention program. In L. R. Frey & K. M. Carragee (Eds.), *Communication activism.* Cresskill, NJ: Hampton Press.

Rodriguez, J., Rich, M. D., Hastings, R., & Page, J. L. (2006). Assessing the impact of Augusto Boal's "proactive performance": An embodied approach for cultivating prosocial responses to sexual assault. *Text and Performance Quarterly, 26*(3), 229–252.

Ronai, C. R., Zsembik, B. A., & Feagin, J. R. (Eds.) (1997). *Everyday sexism in the third millennium.* New York: Routledge.

Rozee, P. D., & Koss, M. P. (2001). Rape: A century of resistance. *Psychology of Women Quarterly, 25,* 295–311.

Schawartz, M. D., & DeKeseredy, W. S. (1997). *Sexual assault on the college campus: The role of male peer support.* Thousand Oaks, CA: Sage.

Simon, T. (1993). Complex issues for sexual assault peer education programs. *Journal of American College Health, 41,* 289–291.

Warshaw, R. (1988). *I never called it rape.* New York: Harper.

West, C., & Zimmerman, D. H. (1991). Doing gender. In J. Lorber & S. A. Farrell (Eds.), *The social construction of gender* (pp. 13–37). Newbury Park, CA: Sage.

Wood, J. T. (2002). *Gendered Lives: Communication, gender, and culture* (4th ed.). Belmont, CA: Wadsworth.

Wood, J. T., & Lenze, L. F. (1991) Strategies to enhance gender sensitivity in communication education. *Communication Education, 40,* 16–21.

Wood, J. T., & Reich, N. M. (2006). Gendered communication styles. In L. A. Samovar, R. E. Porter, & E. R. McDaniel (Eds.), *Intercultural communication: A reader* (pp. 177–186). United States: Wadsworth.

Yeater, E. A., & O'Donahue, W. (1999). Sexual assault prevention programs: Current issues, future directions, and the potential efficacy of interventions with women. *Clinical Psychology Review, 19*(7), 739–771.

Concepts and Questions

1. Why do the authors believe that sexual assaults on college campuses are at epidemic levels? Do you know of any such assaults on your campus?

2. Rich, Robinson, Aherns, and Rodrigueuz believe there has been a convergence of certain factors that have helped contribute to the seriousness of assaults against women. What are these factors? Do you agree with their listing?

3. What is the main goal of the interACT troupe?

4. Do you believe that "traditional male" roles contribute to violence against woman? If yes, what are these roles?

5. What is the basic content of the interACT sketches?

6. Why do the authors believe it is a good idea to involve the audience in the performances?

7. What would you suggest the content of the sketches should be so that they could capture "real-life" situations?

8. Do you believe the notion of interACT sketches followed by honest discussion between the members of the audience and the actors is a useful way to help reduce the problem of violence against women?

Ethical Considerations: Prospects for the Future

There is no single true morality. There are many different moral frameworks, none of which is more correct than the others.

GILBERT HARMAN AND JUDITH TRAVIS THOMSON

Throughout the vast majority of history, humans have lived in compact, tribal groups or small towns, where everyone knew and associated with the same people most of their lives. Contemporary civilization, however, is characterized by large, and ever increasing, urban populations which are, for the most part, a world of strangers. Generally speaking, we normally know very little about other peoples and their cultures. This lack of awareness, or ignorance of our neighbors, can lead some people to act in ways they consider to be beneficial to others but may in fact be harmful. For example, legislation subsidizing U.S. soybean farmers allows them to grow and sell their product at low prices on the world market. This helps farmers and consumers in the United States. This same legislation, however, can bring economic difficulties to, or even ruin, unsubsidized soybean farmers in a lesser developed nation because they cannot compete. Because well-intended communication can have unintended consequences, we move to questions of how to ethically treat and relate to others who see the world differently. Although these are issues that are much more speculative and harder to pin down, they are issues that all intercultural communicators must confront.

The whole purpose of this book has been to make you aware of the diversity among people and cultures—whether those cultures are across the street or across the ocean. In this chapter, we move to examine these issues in a series of essays that discuss some of the diverse variables influencing intercultural encounters. Our basic purpose now is to expose you to a number of views about the ethics of intercultural relationships so that you may develop a set of personal ethics for your intercultural interaction.

Most cultures recognize an ethical dimension of communication. This recognition exists at both the legal and the interpersonal level. In the United States, for example, legal recognition of communication ethics is manifest in libel, slander, truth-in-advertising, and political campaign practice laws. At the interpersonal level, there is an inherent need to be accountable for your communication acts. Whether the consequences of your messages are simple or profound, you cannot hide from the fact that your actions affect other people. As Shakespeare wrote in his *Comedy of Errors,* "Every why hath a where-fore." We now ask you to think about "why" and "wherefore."

Ethical considerations must be part of every intercultural encounter. For when you interact with others, your words and actions have the potential to affect their be-havior, attitudes, and beliefs. The changes might be short-term or long-term, imme-diate or delayed, but you will have an effect upon another person. The very fact that your messages have such consequences confers an ethical responsibility upon you.

This chapter examines that responsibility. In short, we now look at some of the questions you must confront as you communicate with people from cultures that are different from your own. As noted, this contact raises both ethical and philosophical issues about how people from diverse cultures can live together without destroying themselves and the planet. In short, what sort of interpersonal and intercultural ethic must we develop if we are to practice the art and science of intercultural com-munication?

To set the tone for this final chapter, we begin with two essays that examine the issue of cultural diversity and offer insight into both its importance and its limitations. One of the difficulties inherent in analyzing diversity is realizing what it is. Whether you are discussing such diverse topics as employee relations, entertainment, or edu-cation, the word "diversity" is frequently employed—but rarely defined. In the first essay, "Cultural Diversity: A World View," Thomas Sowell seeks "to separate the issue of the general importance of cultural diversity—not only in the United States but in the world at large—from the more specific, more parochial, and more ideological agendas that have become associated with that concept in recent years."

Sowell begins by speaking about the worldwide importance of cultural diversity over centuries of human development. He believes that the whole rise of humankind "has been marked by transfers of cultural advances from one group to another and from one civilization to another." He relates how many accepted parts of Western society had their origins in the Middle East or Asia. Such vital parts of Western civilization as paper and printing had their origins in China, and the worldwide numbering system in use today originated in India. Sowell also shows how aspects of some cultures are superior to those of other cultures. For instance, once paper and printing from China became the norm in Western society, the keeping of precious records, knowledge, and thought inscribed on scrolls disappeared because books were clearly superior. He holds that "a given culture may not be superior for all things in all settings, much less remain superior over time, but particular cultural features may nevertheless be clearly better for some purposes—not just different."

Sowell insists that just like civilizations, social groups differ in their effectiveness in different fields of endeavor. He then discusses the strong sociopolitical resistance to accepting the reality of different levels and kinds of skills, interests, habits, and ori-entations among different groups of people. To support his position, Sowell traces American immigration patterns and shows how various cultural groups have moved and developed in their new homes.

The second essay, by Harlan Cleveland, is titled "The Limits to Cultural Diversity." Cleveland eloquently alerts us to some of the problems associated with cultural di-versity while offering us guidance for the future. The basic problem brought about by increased cultural contact is clear for Cleveland: ethnic and religious diversity is cre-ating painful conflicts around the world. Too often these clashes turn one culture against another in ideological disputes. When this happens, according to Cleveland, "'culture' is being used . . . as an instrument of repression, exclusion, and extinction."

Cleveland fears that when people see the chaos created by different cultures, they believe that their best haven of certainty and security is a group based on ethnic similarity, common faith, economic interest, or political like-mindedness. Cleveland rejects this "single culture" hypothesis and recommends a counterforce of wider views, global perspectives, and more universal ideas. This universal view, according to Cleveland, rests in a philosophy that has civilization (universal values, ideas, and practices) as the basic core for all humanity. In this analysis, culture represents the "substance and symbols of the community," while civilization is rooted in compromise and built on "cooperation and compassion." With this orientation, people can deal with each other in ways that respect cultural differences while granting essential overarching values.

Cleveland's optimism is clearly stated in his conclusion: "For the 21st century, this 'cheerful acknowledgment of difference' is the alternative to a global spread of ethnic cleansing and religious rivalry."

Our next essay, "Toward Intercultural Personhood: An Integration of Eastern and Western Perspectives," by Young Yun Kim, is based on one of the central themes of this book—the idea that today's interconnected and fast-changing world demands that you change your assumptions about culture and your place within that culture. Recognizing these changes, Kim advances a philosophical orientation that she calls "intercultural personhood." For Kim, intercultural personhood combines the key attributes of Eastern and Western cultural traditions. She presents a model that uses these attributes and considers the basic modes of consciousness, cognitive patterns, personal and social values, and communication behavior. The notion of intercultural personhood also leads us into the concept of the multicultural person, as set forth in the next two essays.

Potentially, communication of any type can have an unintended negative effect on others. An ethical dimension must, therefore, be present in communication to minimize this possibility of harming others. In intercultural settings, where our ethnocentrism, prejudices, and lack of understanding about other cultures may influence our perceptions of others, the need for an ethical dimension in communicative interaction is paramount. The next two essays, therefore, focus directly on the complex issue of developing a personal ethic for intercultural communication.

In the first essay, "Integration in Intercultural Ethics," Richard Evanoff indicates that there have been two normative models specifying how sojourners should interact with people from their host culture. In the first, visitors adapt themselves to the norms of their hosts—sort of a "when in Rome do as the Romans do" approach. In the second, individuals maintain their own norms while respecting those of the host culture. Neither of these approaches has proven to be sufficiently satisfactory to foster effective intercultural relations. Evanoff, therefore, proposes an alternative model "in which common ground between people with different ethical norms can be actively constructed through a process of intercultural dialogue." The end goal of his proposal is the integration of ethical norms across cultures that results in a new ethic to govern relationships between individuals in cross-cultural situations.

The underlying assumption of Evanoff's integration process is that "persons who have undergone the experience of learning how other cultures perceive the world acquire an intercultural mindset." He focuses on the multiple frames of reference which are inherent in all cultures. In presenting his integration principle, Evanoff identifies three specific forms of integration: (1) the integration of multiple frames of reference into one's own thinking at the psychological level, (2) the integration of multiple frames of reference at the interpersonal/intercultural level, and (3) the conceptual integrations of specific norms at the formal level.

Evanoff begins with a discussion of integrating multiple frames of reference to develop an intercultural mindset which leads to a wider view of the world and of human possibilities. Next, he discusses the difference between integration and adaptation. He sees adaptation as the process whereby individuals adapt their personal norms to the norms of the host culture. Integration, on the other hand, concerns itself both with the psychological process by which individuals begin to incorporate values from the host culture into their own system of values as well as with the process by which the host culture may be influenced by the values of the sojourner.

Evanoff ends his essay with a discussion of integration at the formal level where critical dialogue ensues to evaluate the value system of the sojourner and the host culture. He proposes models for this form of dialogue and draws examples from Western and Asian cultures to demonstrate this form of integration.

The last essay in this chapter continues the discussion of developing a personal ethic for intercultural communication. Ninian Smart, in his article "Worldview: The Ethical Dimension," reveals the ways in which the ethical dimensions of a culture are a function of its worldview drawn from its religious experience, doctrines about the universe, and the myths and historical heroes of the cultural traditions.

Smart recognizes modern attempts such as the utilitarianism of John Stuart Mill and the scientific humanist community idea that the basis of values lies in the individual human being to build ethical systems independent of religious belief. However, he holds that such ethical systems have been inadequate because ethical systems seem to "raise questions about the worldview behind it."

Smart next conducts a discussion comparing diverse religious ethics as they apply to the Christian, Muslim, Buddhist, and Hindu ethical traditions. He points out the worldview bases for these beliefs and compares their similarities and differences. Drawing from his examples, Smart concludes that "ethics is not treated in isolation, and what is right and wrong is seen in the light of a wider cosmic vision." He ends his essay by providing what he considers to be a normative view of what constitutes right and wrong. In considering what he believes to be right and wrong, Smart reminds you that you "live in a global city in which different cultures and worldviews interact." If one group seeks to impose its views on a group that does not share those views, the result will be conflict. Second, Smart indicates that in his view the purport of religion is to stress the spiritual life, and morality has to be related to such spiritual visions.

Cultural Diversity: A World View

THOMAS SOWELL

iversity has become one of the most often used words of our time—and a word almost never defined. Diversity is invoked in discussions of everything from employment policy to curriculum reform, from entertainment to politics. Nor is the word merely a description of the long-known fact that the U.S. population is made up of people from many countries, many races, and many cultural backgrounds. All that was well known long before the word *diversity* became an insistent part of our vocabulary, an invocation, an imperative, or a bludgeon in ideological conflicts.

The very motto of the United States—*E Pluribus Unum*—recognizes the diversity of the American people. For generations, this diversity has been celebrated, whether in comedies like *Abie's Irish Rose* (the famous play featuring a Jewish boy and an Irish girl) or in patriotic speeches on the Fourth of July. Yet one senses something very different in today's crusades for "diversity"—certainly not a patriotic celebration of America and often a sweeping criticism of the United States, or even a condemnation of Western civilization as a whole.

At the very least, we need to separate the issue of the general importance of cultural diversity—not only in the United States but in the world at large—from the more specific, more parochial and more ideological agendas that have become associated with that word in recent years. I would like to talk about the worldwide importance of cultural diversity over centuries of human history before returning to the narrower issues of our time.

The entire history of the human race, the rise of man from the caves, has been marked by transfers of cultural advances from one group to another and from one civilization to another. Paper and printing, for example, are today vital parts of Western civilization—but they originated in China centuries before they made their way to Europe. So did the magnetic compass, which made possible the great ages of exploration that put the Western Hemisphere in touch with the rest of mankind. Mathematical concepts likewise migrated from one culture to another: Trigonometry came from ancient Egypt, and the whole numbering system now used throughout the world originated among the Hindus of India, though Europeans called this system Arabic numerals because the Arabs were the intermediaries through which these numbers reached medieval Europe. Indeed, much of the philosophy of ancient Greece first reached Western Europe in Arabic translations, which were then re-translated into Latin or into the vernacular languages of the Western Europeans.

Much that became part of the culture of Western civilization originated outside that civilization, often in the Middle East or Asia. The game of chess came from India, gunpowder from China, and various mathematical concepts from the Islamic world, for example. The conquest of Spain by Moslems in the eighth century A.D. made Spain a center for the diffusion into Western Europe of the more advanced knowledge of the Mediterranean world and of the Orient in astronomy, medicine, optics, and geometry. The later rise of Western Europe to world preeminence in science and technology built upon these foundations, and then the science and technology of European civilization began to spread around the world, not only to European offshoot societies such as the United States and Australia but also to non-European cultures, of which Japan is perhaps the most striking example.

The historic sharing of cultural advances until they became the common inheritance of the human race implied much more than cultural diversity. It implied that some cultural features were not only different from others but *better* than others. The very fact that people—all people, whether Europeans, Africans, Asians, or others—have repeatedly chosen to abandon some feature of their own culture in order to replace it with something from another culture implies that the replacement served their purposes more effectively: Arabic numerals are not simply different from Roman

Reprinted from *The American Enterprise*, Vol. 2, No. 3, 1991, pp. 43–55. Copyright © 1991 The American Enterprise. Reprinted by permission. Dr. Thomas Sowell is a Senior Fellow at the Hoover Institute, Stanford University, Stanford, California.

numerals; they are *better* than Roman numerals. This is shown by their replacing Roman numerals in many countries whose own cultures derived from Rome, as well as in other countries whose respective numbering systems were likewise superseded by so-called Arabic numerals.

It is virtually inconceivable today that the distances in astronomy or the complexities of higher mathematics could be expressed in Roman numerals. Merely to express the year of American independence—MDCCLXXVI—requires more than twice as many Roman numerals as Arabic numerals. Moreover, Roman numerals offer more opportunities for errors, as the same digit may be either added or subtracted, depending on its place in the sequence. Roman numerals are good for numbering kings or Super Bowls, but they cannot match the efficiency of Arabic numerals in most mathematical operations—and that is, after all, why we have numbers at all. Cultural features do not exist merely as badges of "identity" to which we have some emotional attachment. They exist to meet the necessities and forward the purposes of human life. When they are surpassed by features of other cultures, they tend to fall by the wayside or to survive only as marginal curiosities, like Roman numerals today.

Not only concepts, information, products, and technologies transfer from one culture to another. The natural produce of the Earth does the same. Malaysia is the world's leading grower of rubber trees—but those trees are indigenous to Brazil. Most of the rice grown in Africa today originated in Asia, and its tobacco originated in the Western Hemisphere. Even a great wheat-exporting nation like Argentina once imported wheat, which was not a crop indigenous to that country. Cultural diversity, viewed internationally and historically, is not a static picture of differentness but a dynamic picture of competition in which what serves human purposes more effectively survives and what does not tends to decline or disappear.

Manuscript scrolls once preserved the precious records, knowledge, and thought of European or Middle Eastern cultures. But once paper and printing from China became known in these cultures, books were clearly much faster and cheaper to produce and drove scrolls virtually into extinction. Books were not simply different from scrolls; they were *better* than

scrolls. The point that some cultural features are better than others must be insisted on today because so many among the intelligentsia either evade or deny this plain reality. The intelligentsia often use words like "perceptions" and "values" as they argue, in effect, that it is all a matter of how you choose to look at it.

They may have a point in such things as music, art, and literature from different cultures, but there are many human purposes common to peoples of all cultures. They want to live rather than die, for example. When Europeans first ventured into the arid interior of Australia, they often died of thirst or hunger in a land where the Australian aborigines had no trouble finding food or water. Within that particular setting, at least, the aboriginal culture enabled people to do what both aborigines and Europeans wanted to do—survive. A given culture may not be superior for all things in all settings, much less remain superior over time, but particular cultural features may nevertheless be clearly better for some purposes—not just different.

Why is there any such argument in the first place? Perhaps it is because we are still living in the long, grim shadow of the Nazi Holocaust and are understandably reluctant to label anything or anyone "superior" or "inferior." But we don't need to. We need only recognize that particular products, skills, technologies, agricultural crops, or intellectual concepts accomplish particular purposes better than their alternatives. It is not necessary to rank one whole culture over another in all things, much less to claim that they remain in that same ranking throughout history. They do not.

Clearly, cultural leadership in various fields has changed hands many times. China was far in advance of any country in Europe in a large number of fields for at least a thousand years and as late as the 16th century had the highest standard of living in the world. Equally clearly, China today is one of the poorer nations of the world and is having great difficulty trying to catch up to the technological level of Japan and the West, with no real hope of regaining its former world preeminence in the foreseeable future.

Similar rises and falls of nations and empires have been common over long stretches of human history. Examples include the rise and fall of the Roman Empire, the "golden age" of medieval Spain and its decline to the level of one of the poorest nations in

Europe today, and the centuries-long triumphs of the Ottoman Empire—intellectually as well as on the battlefields of Europe and the Middle East—and then its long decline to become known as "the sick man of Europe." But although cultural leadership has changed hands many times, that leadership has been real at given times, and much of what was achieved in the process has contributed enormously to our well-being and opportunities today. Cultural competition is not a zero-sum game. It is what advances the human race.

If nations and civilizations differ in their effectiveness in different fields of endeavor, so do social groups. Here there is especially strong resistance to accepting the reality of different levels and kinds of skills, interests, habits, and orientations among different groups of people. One academic writer, for example, said that 19th-century Jewish immigrants to the United States were fortunate to arrive just as the garment industry in New York began to develop. I could not help thinking that Hank Aaron was similarly fortunate—that he often came to bat just as a home run was due to be hit. It might be possible to believe that these Jewish immigrants just happened to be in the right place at the right time if you restrict yourself to their history in the United States. But, again taking a worldview, we find Jews prominent, often predominant, and usually prospering, in the apparel industry in medieval Spain, in the Ottoman Empire, in the Russian Empire, in Argentina, in Australia, and in Brazil. How surprised should we be to find them predominant in the same industry in the United States?

Other groups have also excelled in their own special occupations and industries. Indeed, virtually every group excels at something. Germans, for example, have been prominent as pioneers in the piano industry. American piano brands such as Steinway and Schnabel, not to mention the Wurlitzer organ, are signs of the long prominence in this industry of Germans, who produced the first pianos in colonial America. Germans also pioneered in piano building in czarist Russia, Australia, France, and England. Chinese immigrants have, at one period of history or another, run more than half the grocery stores in Kingston (Jamaica) and Panama City and conducted more than half of all retail trade in Malaysia, the Philippines, Vietnam, and Cambodia. Other groups have dominated retail trade in other parts of the world—the Gujaratis from India in East Africa and in Fiji and the Lebanese in parts of West Africa, for example.

Nothing has been more common than for particular groups—often a minority—to dominate particular occupations or industries. Seldom do they have any ability to keep out others—and certainly not to keep out the majority population. They are simply *better* at the particular skills required in that occupation or industry. Sometimes we can see why. When Italians have made wine in Italy for centuries, it is hardly surprising that they should become prominent among wine makers in Argentina or in California's Napa Valley. Similarly, when Germans in Germany have been for centuries renowned for their beer making, how surprised should we be that in Argentina they became as prominent among beer makers as the Italians were among wine makers? How surprised should we be that beer making in the United States arose where there were concentrations of German immigrants—in Milwaukee and St. Louis, for example? Or that the leading beer producers to this day have German names like Anheuser-Busch and Coors, among many other German names?

Just as cultural leadership in a particular field is not permanent for nations or civilizations, neither is it permanent for racial, ethnic, or religious groups. By the time the Jews were expelled from Spain in 1492, Europe had overtaken the Islamic world in medical science, so that Jewish physicians who sought refuge in the Ottoman Empire found themselves in great demand in that Moslem country. By the early 16th century, the sultan of the Ottoman Empire had on his palace medical staff forty-two Jewish physicians and twenty-one Moslem physicians. With the passage of time, however, the source of the Jews' advantage—their knowledge of Western medicine—eroded as successive generations of Ottoman Jews lost contact with the West and its further progress. Christian minorities within the Ottoman Empire began to replace the Jews, not only in medicine but also in international trade and even in the theater, once dominated by Jews. The difference was that these Christian minorities—notably Greeks and Armenians—maintained their ties in Christian Europe and often sent their sons there to be educated. It was not race or ethnicity as such that was crucial, but maintaining contacts with the ongoing progress of Western civilization. By contrast, the Ottoman Jews became a declining people in a declining empire. Many, if not most, were Sephardic Jews from Spain—once the elite of world Jewry. But by the time the state of Israel was formed in the 20th century, those Sephardic Jews who had settled for centuries in the Islamic world now lagged painfully behind the Ashkenazic Jews of the Western world—notably in income and education. To get some idea of what a historic reversal that has been in the relative positions of Sephardic and Ashkenazic Jews, one need only note that Sephardic Jews in colonial America sometimes disinherited their own children for marrying Ashkenazic Jews.

Why do some groups, subgroups, nations, or whole civilizations excel in some particular fields rather than others? All too often, the answer to that question must be: Nobody really knows. It is an unanswered question largely because it is an *unasked* question. It is an uphill struggle merely to get acceptance of the fact that large differences exist among peoples, not just in specific skills in the narrow sense (computer science, basketball, or brewing beer) but more fundamentally in different interests, orientations, and values that determine which particular skills they seek to develop and with what degree of success. Merely to suggest that these internal cultural factors play a significant role in various economic, educational, or social outcomes is to invite charges of "blaming the victim." It is much more widely acceptable to blame surrounding social conditions or institutional policies.

But if we look at cultural diversity internationally and historically, there is a more basic question whether blame is the real issue. Surely, no human being should be blamed for the way his culture evolved for centuries before he was born. Blame has nothing to do with it. Another explanation that has had varying amounts of acceptance at different times and places is the biological or genetic theory of differences among peoples. I have argued *against* this theory in many places but will not take the time to go into lengthy arguments here. A world view of cultural differences over the centuries undermines the genetic theory as well. Europeans and Chinese, for example, are clearly genetically different. Equally clearly, China was a more advanced civilization than Europe in many scientific, technological, and organizational ways for at least a thousand years. Yet over the past few centuries, Europe has moved ahead of China in many of these same ways. If those cultural differences were due to genes, how could these two races have changed positions so radically from one epoch in history to another?

All explanations of differences between groups can be broken down into heredity and environment. Yet a world view of the history of cultural diversity seems, on the surface at least, to deny both. One reason for this is that we have thought of environment too narrowly—as the immediate surrounding circumstances or differing institutional policies toward different groups. Environment in that narrow sense may explain some group differences, but the histories of many groups completely contradict that particular version of environment as an explanation. Let us take just two examples out of many that are available.

Jewish immigrants from Eastern Europe and Italian immigrants from southern Italy began arriving in the United States in large numbers at about the same time in the late 19th century, and their large-scale immigration also ended at the same time, when restrictive immigration laws were passed in the 1920s. The two groups arrived here in virtually the same economic condition—namely, destitute. They often lived in the same neighborhoods, and their children attended the same schools, sitting side by side in the same classrooms. Their environments—in the narrow sense in which the term is commonly used—were virtually identical. Yet their social histories in the United States have been very different.

Over the generations, both groups rose, but they rose at different rates, through different means, and in a very different mixture of occupations and industries. Even wealthy Jews and wealthy Italians tended to become rich in different sectors of the economy. The California wine industry, for example, is full of Italian names like Mondavi, Gallo, and Rossi, but the only prominent Jewish wine maker—Manischewitz—makes an entirely different kind of wine, and no one would compare Jewish wine makers with Italian wine makers in the United States. When we look at Jews and Italians in the very different environmental setting of Argentina, we see the same general pattern of differences between them. The same is true if we look at the differences between Jews and Italians in Australia or Canada or Western Europe.

Jews are not Italians, and Italians are not Jews. Anyone familiar with their very different histories over many centuries should not be surprised. Their fate in America was not determined solely by their surrounding social conditions in America or by how they were treated by American society. They were different before they got on the boats to cross the ocean, and those differences crossed the ocean with them.

We can take it a step further. Even among Ashkenazic Jews, those originating in Eastern Europe have had significantly different economic and social histories from those originating in Germanic Central Europe, including Austria as well as Germany itself. These differences have persisted among their descendants not only in New York and Chicago but as far away as Melbourne and Sydney. In Australia, Jews from Eastern Europe have tended to cluster in and around Melbourne, while Germanic Jews have settled in and around Sydney. They even have a saying among themselves that Melbourne is a cold city with warm Jews while Sydney is a warm city with cold Jews.

A second and very different example of persistent cultural differences involves immigrants from Japan. As everyone knows, many Japanese Americans were interned during World War II. What is less well known is that there is and has been an even larger Japanese population in Brazil than in the United States. These Japanese, incidentally, own approximately three-quarters as much land in Brazil as there is in Japan. (The Japanese almost certainly own more agricultural land in Brazil than in Japan.) In any event, very few Japanese in Brazil were interned during World War II. Moreover, the Japanese in Brazil were never subjected to the discrimination suffered by Japanese Americans in the decades before World War II. Yet, during the war, Japanese Americans overwhelmingly remained loyal to the United States, and Japanese American soldiers won more than their share of medals in combat. But in Brazil, the Japanese were overwhelmingly and even fanatically loyal *to Japan.* You cannot explain the difference by anything in the environment of the United States or the environment of Brazil. But if you know something about the history of those Japanese who settled in these two countries, you know that they were culturally different *in Japan, before* they ever got on the boats to take them across the Pacific Ocean—and they were still different decades later.

These two groups of immigrants left Japan during very different periods in the cultural evolution of Japan itself. A modern Japanese scholar has said: "If you want to see Japan of the Meiji era, go to the United States. If you want to see Japan of the Taisho era, go to Brazil." The Meiji era was a more cosmopolitan, pro-American era; the Taisho era was one of fanatical Japanese nationalism.

If the narrow concept of environment fails to explain many profound differences between groups and subgroups, it likewise fails to explain many very large differences in the economic and social performance of nations and civilizations. An 18th-century writer in Chile described that country's many natural advantages in climate, soil, and natural resources—and then asked in complete bewilderment why it was such a poverty-stricken country. That same question could be asked of many countries today. Conversely, we could ask why Japan and Switzerland are so prosperous when they are both almost totally lacking in natural resources. Both are rich in what economists call "human capital"—the skills of their people. No doubt there is a long and complicated history behind the different skill levels of different peoples and nations. The point here is that the immediate environment—whether social or geographic—is only part of the story.

Geography may well have a significant role in the history of peoples, but perhaps not simply by presenting them with more or fewer natural resources. Geography shapes or limits peoples' opportunities for cultural interactions and the mutual development that comes out of that. Small, isolated islands in the sea have seldom been sources of new scientific advances or technological breakthroughs—regardless of where such islands were located and regardless of the race of the people on these islands. There are islands on land as well. Where soil fertile enough to support human life exists only in isolated patches, widely separated, there tend to be isolated cultures (often with different languages or dialects) in a culturally fragmented region. Isolated highlands often produce insular cultures, lagging in many ways behind the cultures of the lowlanders of the same race—whether we are talking about medieval Scotland, colonial Ceylon, or the contemporary Montagnards of Vietnam.

With geographical environments as with social environments, we are talking about long-run effects, not simply the effects of immediate surroundings. When Scottish highlanders, for example, immigrated to North Carolina in colonial times, they had a very different history from that of Scottish lowlanders who settled in North Carolina. For one thing, the lowlanders spoke English while the highlanders spoke Gaelic—on into the 19th century. Obviously, speaking only Gaelic—in an English-speaking country—affects a group's whole economic and social progress. Geographical conditions vary as radically in terms of how well they facilitate or impede large-scale cultural interactions as they do in their distribution of natural resources. We are not even close to being able to explain how all these geographical influences have operated throughout history. That too is an unanswered question largely because it is an unasked question— and it is an unasked question because many are seeking answers in terms of immediate social environment or are vehemently insisting that they have already found the answer in those terms.

How radically do geographic environments differ— not just in terms of tropical versus arctic climates but also in the very configuration of the land and how that helps or hinders large-scale interactions among peoples? Consider one statistic: Africa is more than twice the size of Europe, and yet Africa has a shorter coastline than Europe. That seems almost impossible. But the reason is that Europe's coastline is far more convoluted, with many harbors and inlets being formed all around the continent. Much of the coastline of Africa is smooth—which is to say, lacking the harbors that make large-scale maritime trade possible by sheltering the ships at anchor from the rough waters of the open sea. Waterways of all sorts have played a major role in the evolution of cultures and nations around the world. Harbors on the sea are not the only waterways. Rivers are also very important. Virtually every major city on Earth is located on either a river or a harbor. Whether it is such great harbors as those in Sydney, Singapore, or San Francisco, London on the Thames, Paris on the Seine, or numerous other European cities on the Danube, waterways have been the lifeblood of urban centers for centuries. Only very recently has man-made, self-powered transportation like automobiles and airplanes made it possible to produce an exception to the rule like Los Angeles. (There is a Los Angeles River, but you don't have to be Moses to walk across it in the summertime.) New York has both a long and deep river and a huge sheltered harbor.

None of these geographical features in themselves create a great city or develop an urban culture. Human beings do that. But geography sets the limits within which people can operate—and in some places it sets those limits much wider than in others. Returning to our comparison of the continents of Europe and Africa, we find that they differ as radically in rivers as they do in harbors. There are entire nations in Africa without a single navigable river— Libya and South Africa, for example. "Navigable" is the crucial word. Some African rivers are navigable only during the rainy season. Some are navigable only between numerous cataracts and waterfalls. Even the Zaire River, which is longer than any river in North America and carries a larger volume of water, has too many waterfalls too close to the ocean for it to become a major artery of international commerce. Such commerce is facilitated in Europe not only by numerous navigable rivers but also by the fact that no spot on the continent, outside of Russia, is more than 500 miles from the sea. Many places in Africa are more than 500 miles from the sea, including the entire nation of Uganda.

Against this background, how surprised should we be to find that Europe is the most urbanized of all inhabited continents and Africa the least urbanized? Urbanization is not the be-all and end-all of life, but certainly an urban culture is bound to differ substantially from nonurban cultures, and the skills peculiar to an urban culture are far more likely to be found among groups from an urban civilization. (Conversely, an interesting history could be written about the failures of urbanized groups in agricultural settlements.)

Looking within Africa, the influence of geography seems equally clear. The most famous ancient civilization on the continent arose within a few miles on either side of Africa's longest navigable river, the Nile, and even today the two largest cities on the continent, Cairo and Alexandria, are on that river. The great West African kingdoms in the region served by the Niger River and the long-flourishing East African economy based around the great natural harbor on the island of Zanzibar are further evidence of the role of geography. Again, geography is not all-determining— the economy of Zanzibar has been ruined by government policy in recent decades—but, nevertheless, geography is an important long-run influence on the shaping of cultures as well as in narrowly economic terms.

What are the implications of a world view of cultural diversity on the narrower issues being debated under that label in the United States today? Although "diversity" is used in so many different ways in so many different contexts that it seems to mean all things to all people, a few themes appear again and again. One of these broad themes is that diversity implies organized efforts at the preservation of cultural differences, perhaps governmental efforts, perhaps government subsidies to various programs run by the advocates of "diversity."

This approach raises questions as to what the purpose of culture is. If what is important about cultures is that they are emotionally symbolic, and if differentness is cherished for the sake of differentness, then this particular version of cultural "diversity" might make some sense. But cultures exist even in isolated societies where there are no other cultures around—where there is no one else and nothing else from which to be different. Cultures exist to serve the vital, practical requirements of human life—to structure a society so as to perpetuate the species, to pass on the hard-learned knowledge and experience of generations past and centuries past to the young and inexperienced in order to spare the next generation the costly and dangerous process of learning everything all over again from scratch through trial and error— including fatal errors. Cultures exist so that people can know how to get food and put a roof over their heads, how to cure the sick, how to cope with the death of loved ones, and how to get along with the living. Cultures are not bumper stickers. They are living, changing ways of doing all the things that have to be done in life.

Every culture discards over time the things that no longer do the job or that don't do the job as well as things borrowed from other cultures. Each individual does this, consciously or not, on a day-to-day basis. Languages take words from other languages, so that Spanish as spoken in Spain includes words taken from Arabic, and Spanish as spoken in Argentina has Italian words taken from the large Italian immigrant population there. People eat Kentucky Fried Chicken in Singapore and stay in Hilton Hotels in Cairo.

This is *not* what some of the advocates of "diversity" have in mind. They seem to want to preserve cultures in their purity, almost like butterflies preserved in amber. Decisions about change, if any, seem to be regarded as collective decisions, political decisions. But that is not how any cultures have arrived where they are. Individuals have decided for themselves how much of the old they wished to retain, how

much of the new they found useful in their own lives. In this way, cultures have enriched each other in all the great civilizations of the world. In this way, great port cities and their crossroads of cultures have become centers of progress all across the planet. No culture has grown great in isolation—but a number of cultures have made historic and even astonishing advances when their isolation was ended, usually by events beyond their control.

Japan was a classic example in the 19th century, but a similar story could be told of Scotland in an earlier era, when a country where once even the nobility were illiterate became—within a short time, as history is measured—a country that produced world pioneers in field after field: David Hume in philosophy, Adam Smith in economics, Joseph Black in chemistry, Robert Adam in architecture, and James Watt, whose steam engine revolutionized modern industry and transport. In the process, the Scots lost their language but gained world preeminence in many fields. Then a whole society moved to higher standards of living than anyone had ever dreamed of in their poverty-stricken past.

There were higher standards in other ways as well. As late as the 18th century, it was considered noteworthy that pedestrians in Edinburgh no longer had to be on the alert for sewage being thrown out of the windows of people's homes or apartments. The more considerate Scots yelled a warning, but they threw out the sewage anyway. Perhaps it was worth losing a little of the indigenous culture to be rid of that problem.

Those who use the term *cultural diversity* to promote a multiplicity of segregated ethnic enclaves are doing an enormous harm to the people in those enclaves. Although they live socially, the people in those enclaves have to compete economically for a livelihood. Even if they were not disadvantaged before, they will be very disadvantaged if their competitors from the general population are free to tap the knowledge, skills, and analytical techniques that Western civilization has drawn from all the other civilizations of the world, while those in the enclaves are restricted to what exists in the subculture immediately around them.

We also need to recognize that many great thinkers of the past—whether in medicine or philosophy, science or economics—labored not simply to advance whatever particular group they happened to have come from but to advance the human race. Their legacies, whether cures for deadly diseases or dramatic increases in crop yields to fight the scourge of hunger, belong to all people—and all people need to claim that legacy, not seal themselves off in a dead-end of tribalism or in an emotional orgy of cultural vanity.

Concepts and Questions

1. How does Sowell's treatment of the notion of diversity differ from the general usage in the United States today?
2. What benefits derive from the meeting of various cultures and their inherent diversity?
3. How does cultural leadership in various fields of human endeavor change from time to time? What are the advantages and/or disadvantages of this activity?
4. Sowell asserts that some groups, subgroups, nations, or whole civilizations excel in some particular fields rather than others. What explanations does he provide to justify this assertion?
5. Sowell asserts that explanations of differences between groups can be broken down into heredity and environment. Do you agree or disagree? Why?
6. What role does geography play in developing diversity among groups?
7. Sowell differentiates between a wide view and a narrow view of diversity. What implications does he advance when people take the narrow view of diversity?
8. Do you believe, as Sowell asserts, that some people use the term *cultural diversity* to promote a multiplicity of segregated ethnic enclaves?

The Limits to Cultural Diversity

HARLAN CLEVELAND

I'm engaged just now in an effort to think through the most intellectually interesting, and morally disturbing, issue in my long experience of trying to think hard about hard subjects. I call it "The Limits to Cultural Diversity." If that seems obscure, wait a moment.

After the multiple revolutions of 1989, it began to look as if three ideas we have thought were Good Things would be getting in each other's way, which is not a Good Thing. What I have called the "triple dilemma," or "trilemma," is the mutually damaging collision of individual human rights, cultural human diversity, and global human opportunities. Today the damage from that collision is suddenly all around us.

In 1994, in the middle of Africa, ethnicity took over as an exclusive value, resulting in mass murder by machete. In ex-Yugoslavia (and too many other places), gunpowder and rape accomplish the same purpose: trampling on human rights and erasing human futures. Even on the Internet, where individuals can now join global groups that are not defined by place names or cordoned off by gender or ethnicity, people are shouting at each other in flaming, capital letters rhetoric.

Look hard at your hometown, at the nearest inner city; scan the world by radio, TV, or newspapers and magazines. What's happened is all too clear: Just when individual human rights have achieved superstar status in political philosophy, just when can-do information technologies promise what the UN Charter calls "better standards of life in larger freedom," culture and diversity have formed a big, ugly boulder in the road called Future.

"If we cannot end now our differences, at least we can help make the world safe for diversity." That was

From *The Futurist*, March–April 1995, pp. 23–26. Reprinted by permission of the World Future Society. Harlan Cleveland is a former U.S. Assistant Secretary of State, Ambassador to NATO, and President Emeritus of the University of Hawaii.

the key sentence in the most influential speech of John F. Kennedy's presidency: his commencement address at American University on June 10, 1963. That speech led directly (among other things) to the first nuclear test ban treaty. For most of the years since then, we were mesmerized by the threat of strategic nuclear war, but now a big nuclear war has become the least likely eventuality among the major threats to human civilization. And that brings us face to face with the puzzle identified in Kennedy's speech: how to make diversity safe.

But is "cultural diversity" really the new Satan in our firmament? Or does it just seem so because "culture" is being used—as *Kultur* has been used in other times and places—as an instrument of repression, exclusion, and extinction?

AN EXCESS OF CULTURAL IDENTITY

In today's disordered world, the collision of cultures with global trends is in evidence everywhere. Ethnic nations, fragmented faiths, transnational businesses, and professional groups find both their inward loyalties and their international contacts leading them to question the political structures by which the world is still, if tenuously, organized. The results are sometimes symbolic caricatures ("In Rome, can a Moslem minaret be built taller than St. Peter's dome?") and sometimes broken mosaics like the human tragedy in what used to be Yugoslavia.

More people moved in 1994 than ever before in world history, driven by fear of guns or desire for more butter and more freedom. (This was true even before a couple of million Rwandans left their homes in terror—and some were floated out of the country as cadavers.) This more mobile world multiplies the incentives for individuals to develop "multiple personalities," to become "collages" of identities, with plural loyalties to overlapping groups. Many millions of people believe that their best haven of certainty and security is a group based on ethnic similarity, common faith, economic interest, or political like-mindedness.

Societies based on fear of outsiders tend toward "totalitarian" governance. Fear pushes the culture beyond normal limits on individuals' behavior. "To say that you're ready to *die* for cultural identity," said one of my colleagues at a workshop of the World Academy of Art and Science in Romania last year, "means that you're also ready to kill for cultural identity." Said another: "The ultimate consequence of what's called 'cultural identity' is Hutus and Tutsis murdering each other."

The fear that drives people to cleave to their primordial loyalties makes it harder for them to learn to be tolerant of others who may be guided by different faiths and loyalties. But isolating oneself by clinging to one's tribe is far from a stable condition; these days, the tribe itself is highly unstable. Differences in birthrates and pressures to move will continue to mix populations together. So ethnic purity isn't going to happen, even by forcible "cleansing."

Besides, cultures keep redefining themselves by mixing with other cultures, getting to know people who look, act, and believe differently. In today's more open electronic world, cultures also expose themselves to new faiths and fashions, new lifestyles, work ways, technologies, clothing, and cuisines.

The early stage of every realization of "cultural identity," every assertion of a newfound "right" of differences, does create a distinct group marked by ethnic aspect ("Black is beautiful"), gender ("women's lib"), religion ("chosen people"), or status as a political minority. But when members of a group insisting on the group's uniqueness do succeed in establishing their own personal right to be different, something very important happens: They begin to be treated *individually* as equals and tend to integrate with more inclusive communities. Traditions of separateness and discrimination are often persistent, but they are never permanent and immutable. The recent history of South Africa bears witness.

Before the fighting in Yugoslavia, the most tolerant people in that part of the world were seen by their close neighbors to be the Serbs, Croats, and Moslems living together in Bosnia and Herzegovina, with the city of Sarajevo as a special haven of mutual tolerance.

The problem does not seem to be culture itself, but cultural overenthusiasm. Cultural loyalties, says one European, have the makings of a runaway nuclear reaction. Without the moderating influence of civil society—acting like fuel rods in a nuclear reactor—the explosive potential gets out of hand. What's needed is the counterforce of wider views, global perspectives, and more universal ideas.

Post-communist societies, says a resident of one of them, have experienced a loss of equilibrium, a culture shock from the clash of traditional cultures, nostalgia for the stability of Soviet culture, and many new influences from outside. What's needed, he thinks, is cultural richness without cultural dominance, but with the moderating effect of intercultural respect.

CULTURE AND CIVILIZATION

We have inherited a fuzzy vocabulary that sometimes treats *culture* as a synonym for *civilization*. At a World Academy workshop, my colleagues and I experimented with an alternative construct. In this construct, *civilization* is what's universal—values, ideas, and practices that are in general currency everywhere, either because they are viewed as objectively "true" or because they are accepted pragmatically as useful in the existing circumstances. These accepted "truths" offer the promise of weaving together a civitas of universal laws and rules, becoming the basis for a global civil society.

What is sometimes called "management culture" appears to be achieving this kind of universal acceptance, hence becoming part of global "civilization." But nobody has to be in charge of practices that are generally accepted. For instance, the international exchange of money—a miracle of information technologies—is remarkably efficient, daily moving more than a trillion dollars' worth of money among countries. Yet no one is in charge of the system that makes it happen. Recently, the puny efforts of governments to control monetary swings by buying and selling currencies have only demonstrated governments' incapacity to control them.

If civilization is what's universal, *culture* is the substance and symbol of the community. Culture meets the basic human need for a sense of belonging, for participating in the prides and fears that are shared with an in-group. Both culture and civilization are subject to continuous change. In our time, the most pervasive changes seem to be brought about by the spread of knowledge, the fallout of information science and information technologies.

Civil society consists of many structures and networks, cutting across cultural fault lines, brought into being by their ability to help people communicate. They are not very dependent on public authority for their charters or their funding, increasingly taking on functions that used to be considered the responsibility of national governments.

Many of these "nongovernments"—such as those concerned with business and finance, scientific inquiry, the status of women, population policy, and the global environmental common—have become effective users of modern information technologies. In consequence, they are providing more and more of the policy initiative both inside countries and in world affairs.

Civilization is rooted in compromise—between the idea of democratic state and a strong state, between a free-market economy and a caring economy, between "open" and "closed" processes, between horizontal and vertical relationships, between active and passive citizenship. The required solvent for civilization is *respect for differences*. Or, as one of my World Academy colleagues puts it, we need to learn *how to be different together.*

Civilization will be built by cooperation and compassion, in a social climate in which people in differing groups can deal with each other in ways that respect their cultural differences. "Wholeness incorporating diversity" is philosopher John W. Gardner's succinct formulation. The slogan on U.S. currency is even shorter, perhaps because it's in Latin: *E pluribus unum* ("from many, one").

LESSONS FROM AMERICAN EXPERIENCE

We Americans have learned, in our short but intensive 200-plus years of history as a nation, a first lesson about diversity: that it cannot be governed by drowning it in "integration."

I came face to face with this truth when, just a quarter century ago, I became president of the University of Hawaii. Everyone who lives in Hawaii, or even visits there, is impressed by its residents' comparative tolerance toward each other. On closer inspection, paradise seems based on paradox: Everybody's a minority. The tolerance is not despite the diversity but because of it. It is not through the disappearance of ethnic distinctions that the people of Hawaii achieved a level of racial peace that has few parallels around our discriminatory globe. Quite the contrary. The glory is that Hawaii's main ethnic groups managed to establish the right to be separate. The group separateness, in turn, helped establish the rights of individuals in each group to equality with individuals of different racial aspect, different ethnic origin, and different cultural heritage.

Hawaii's experience is not so foreign to the transatlantic migrations of the various more-or-less white Caucasians. On arrival in New York (passing that inscription on the Statue of Liberty, "Send these, the homeless, tempest-tost, to me"), the European immigrants did not melt into the open arms of the white Anglo-Saxon Protestants who preceded them. The reverse was true. The new arrivals stayed close to their own kind, shared religion and language and humor and discriminatory treatment with their soul brothers and sisters, and gravitated at first into occupations that did not too seriously threaten the earlier arrivals.

The waves of new Americans learned to tolerate each other—first as groups, only thereafter as individuals. Rubbing up against each other in an urbanizing America, they discovered not just the old Christian lesson that all men are brothers, but the hard, new, multicultural lesson that all brothers are different. Equality is not the product of similarity; it is the cheerful acknowledgment of difference.

What's so special about our experience is the assumption that people of many kinds and colors can together govern themselves without deciding in advance which kinds of people (male or female, black, brown, yellow, red, white, or any mix of these) may hold any particular public office in the pantheon of political power.

For the 21st century, this "cheerful acknowledgment of difference" is the alternative to a global spread of ethnic cleansing and religious rivalry. The challenge is great, for ethnic cleansing and religious rivalry are traditions as contemporary as Bosnia and Rwanda in the 1990s and as ancient as the Assyrians who, as Byron wrote, "came down like a wolf on the fold" but, says the biblical Book of Kings, were prevented by sword-wielding angels from taking Jerusalem.

In too many countries there is still a basic, if often unspoken, assumption that one kind of people is anointed to be in general charge. Try to imagine a Turkish chancellor of Germany, an Algerian president of France, a Pakistani prime minister of Britain, a Christian president of Egypt, an Arab prime minister of Israel, a Jewish president of Syria, a Tibetan ruler in Beijing, anyone but a Japanese in power in Tokyo.

Yet in the United States during the 20th century, we have already elected an Irish Catholic as president, chosen several Jewish Supreme Court justices, and racially integrated the armed forces right up to the chairman of the Joint Chiefs of Staff. We have not yet adjusted—as voters in India, Britain, and Turkey have done—to having a woman atop the American political heap. But early in the 21st century, that too will come. And during that same new century, which will begin with "minorities" as one in every three Americans, there is every prospect that an African American, a Latin American, and an Asian American will be elected president of the United States.

I wouldn't dream of arguing that we Americans have found the Holy Grail of cultural diversity when in fact we're still searching for it. We have to think hard about our growing pluralism. It's useful, I believe, to dissect in the open our thinking about it, to see whether the lessons we are trying to learn might stimulate some useful thinking elsewhere. We do not yet quite know how to create "wholeness incorporating diversity," but we owe it to the world, as well as to ourselves, to keep trying.

Concepts and Questions

1. What does Cleveland mean when he speaks of making diversity safe?
2. What does Cleveland imply when he refers to "an excess of cultural identity"?
3. How does loyalty to one's own cultural identity make it difficult to be tolerant of others?
4. What is meant by the term *cultural overenthusiasm*? How does it affect intercultural relations?
5. How does Cleveland differentiate between the concepts of *culture* and *civilization*?
6. What are the hallmarks of civilization? How can they be maintained?
7. What does Cleveland imply when he states that diversity cannot be governed by drowning it in integration?

Toward Intercultural Personhood: An Integration of Eastern and Western Perspectives

YOUNG YUN KIM

Millions of people cross cultural boundaries each year and partake in daily intercultural communication activities. Immigrants and refugees seek a new life away from their familiar grounds, along with various groups of temporary sojourners—from employees of multinational corporations, missionaries, diplomats, and military personnel, to professors, researchers, high school and college students, musicians and artists, and doctors and nurses. Although varied in particularities of circumstances and the levels of intensity, scope, and duration of intercultural contact, everyone who crosses cultural boundaries for a prolonged period shares the common project of new cultural learning. Indeed, one no longer has to leave home to partake in such cultural learning. With the advent of electronic communication, people around the world are increasingly exposed to the images and sounds of once distant cultures. In many urban centers, local people are routinely coming in contact with cultural strangers. Indeed, "culture" in its traditional form has become more a nostalgic concept than a reality. As Toffler (1980) observed, we find ourselves "[facing] a quantum leap forward. [We face] the deepest social upheaval and creative restructuring of all time. Without clearly recognizing it, we are engaged in building a remarkable new civilization from the ground up" (p. 44). Yet, we live in a time of clashing cultural identities. The very idea of cultural identity, coupled with xenophobic sentiments, looms over today's fractious world. Can the desire for some form of collective uniqueness be satisfied without resulting in divisions and conflicts across cultural groups? Can we aspire to live and work across cultures without losing allegiance to our own culture? Can we be open to personal growth beyond the perimeters of our own cultural upbringing?

Questions such as these underlie the presentation of *intercultural personhood* as a process in which, through extensive and prolonged intercultural communication experiences, we can gradually achieve an identity and a definition of self that integrates, rather than separates, humanity. The author prefers this concept to other similar terms such as "biculturalism" or "multicultural identity," so as to highlight an open-ended, dynamic, and evolving nature of identity adaptation and transformation, rather than to focus on additive combinations of specific cultural identities. As a way to build a case for intercultural personhood, we will first survey some of the core elements, cultural apriority, or "root ideas" in Eastern and Western cultural traditions. Certain aspects of these two traditions, often considered incompatible, are profoundly complementary and such complementary aspects can be creatively integrated into an intercultural personhood. The author's understanding of the two cultural traditions and her formulation of intercultural personhood owe much to the writings of a number of thinkers of the twentieth century who have explored ideologies larger than national and cultural interests. One such work is Northrop's *The Meeting of East and West* (1966), in which an "international cultural ideal" was presented as a way to provide intellectual and emotional foundations for what he envisioned as "partial world sovereignty." Inspiration has also been drawn from Thompson's (1973) *Passages about Earth: An Exploration of the New Planetary Culture,* which explored how Eastern mysticism was integrated with Western science and rationalism. Among other works that have influenced this author's thinking are: *Ways of Thought of Eastern People* (Nakamura, 1964); *The East and the West* (Gulick, 1963); *Communication and Culture in Ancient India and China* (Oliver, 1971); *The Tao of Physics* (Capra, 1975); *Beyond Culture* (Hall, 1976); and *Through the Moral Maze: Searching for Absolute Values in a Pluralistic World* (Kane, 1994).

This essay first appeared in the ninth edition. It has been substantially revised for this edition. All rights reserved. Permission to reprint must be obtained from the author and the publisher. Dr. Young Yun Kim teaches in the Department of Communication at the University of Oklahoma, Norman, Oklahoma.

EASTERN AND WESTERN CULTURAL TRADITIONS

Traditional cultures throughout Asia including India, Tibet, Japan, China, Korea, and those in Southeast Asia have been influenced by such religious and philosophical systems as Buddhism, Hinduism, Taoism, and Zen. On the other hand, Western Europe has mainly followed the Greek and Judeo-Christian traditions. Of course, any attempt to present the cultural assumptions of these two broadly categorized civilizations inevitably sacrifices specific details and the uniqueness of variations within each tradition. No two individuals or groups hold identical beliefs and manifest uniform behaviors, and whatever characterizations we make about one culture or cultural group must be thought of as normative tendencies that vary rather than monolithic and uniform attributes. Nevertheless, several key elements distinguish each group from the other. To specify these elements is to indicate the general interconnectedness of different societies and peoples within each of the two cultural traditions.

Universe and Nature

A fundamental way in which culture shapes human existence is through the explicit and implicit teachings about our relationships to the nature of the universe and the human and nonhuman realms of the world. Traditional Eastern and Western perspectives diverge significantly with respect to basic premises about these relationships. As Needham (1951) noted in his article, "Human Laws and the Laws of Nature in China and the West," people in the West have conceived the universe as having been initially created and, since then, externally controlled by a Divine power. As such, the Western worldview is characteristically dualistic, materialistic, and lifeless. The Judeo-Christian tradition sets "God" apart from this reality; having created it and set it into motion, God is viewed as apart from "His" creation. The fundamental material of the universe is conceived to be essentially nonliving matter, or elementary particles of matter that interact with one another in a predictable fashion. It is as though the universe is an inanimate machine wherein humankind occupies a unique and elevated position among the life-forms that exist. Assuming a relatively barren universe, it seems only rational that humans make use of the lifeless material universe (and the "lesser" life-forms of nature) on behalf of the most intensely living—humankind itself.

Comparatively, the Eastern worldview is more holistic, dynamic, and inwardly spiritual. From the Eastern perspective, the entirety of the universe is viewed as a vast, multidimensional, living organism consisting of many interdependent parts and forces. The universe is conscious and engaged in a continuous dance of creation: The cosmic pattern is viewed as self-contained and self-organizing. It unfolds itself because of its own inner necessity and not because it is "ordered" by any external volitional power. What exists in the universe are manifestations of a divine life force. Beneath the surface appearance of things, an Ultimate Reality is continuously creating, sustaining, and infusing our worldly experience. The all-sustaining life force that creates our manifest universe is not apart from humans and their worldly existence. Rather, it is viewed as dynamic and intimately involved in every aspect of the cosmos—from its most minute details to its grandest features. The traditional Eastern worldview reveres the common source out of which all things arise. As Campbell (1990) noted, "people in Eastern culture—whether they are Indians, Japanese, or Tibetan—tend to think that the real mystery is in yourself. . . . When you sit in meditation with your hands in your lap, with your head looking down, that means you've gone in and you're coming not just to a soul that is disengaged from God: you're coming to that divine mystery right there in yourself" (p. 89).

This inner-directed perspective also recognizes that everything in this world is fluid, ever-changing, and impermanent. In Hinduism, all static forms are called *maya,* that is, existing only as illusory concepts. This idea of the impermanence of all forms is the starting point of Buddhism. Buddhism teaches that "all compounded things are impermanent," and that all suffering in the world arises from our trying to cling to fixed forms—objects, people, or ideas—instead of accepting the world as it moves. This notion of impermanence of all forms and the appreciation of the aliveness of the universe in the Eastern worldview contrasts with the Western emphasis on the definitive forms of physical reality and their improvement through social and material progress.

Knowledge

Because the East and the West have different views of cosmic patterns, we can expect them to have different approaches to knowledge. In the East, because the universe is seen as a harmonious organism, there is a corresponding lack of dualism in epistemological patterns. The Eastern view emphasizes perceiving and knowing things synthetically, rather than analytically. The ultimate purpose of knowledge is to transcend the apparent contrasts and see the interconnectedness of all things. When the Eastern mystics tell us that they experience all things as manifestations of a basic oneness, they do not mean that they pronounce all things to be the same or equal. Instead, they emphasize that all differences are relative within an all-encompassing phenomenon. Indeed, the awareness that all opposites are polar and, thus, a unity is one of the highest aims of knowledge. In the words of Suzuki (1968), "The fundamental idea of Buddhism is to pass beyond the world of opposites, a world built up by intellectual distinctions and emotional defilements, and to realize the spiritual world of nondistinction, which involves achieving an absolute point of view" (p. 18).

Because all opposites are interdependent, their conflict can never result in the total victory of one side but will always be a manifestation of the interplay between the two sides. A virtuous person is not one who undertakes the impossible task of striving for the "good" and eliminating the "bad," but rather one who is able to maintain a dynamic balance between the two. Transcending the opposites, one becomes aware of the relativity and polar relationship of opposites. One realizes that good and bad, pleasure and pain, life and death, winning and losing, light and dark, are not absolute experiences belonging to different categories, but merely two sides of the same reality—extreme parts of a single continuum. The Chinese sages in their symbolism of the archetypal poles, *yin* and *yang,* have emphasized this point. And the idea that opposites cease to be opposites is the very essence of *Tao.* To know the Tao, the illustrious way of the universe, is the highest aim of human learning.

This holistic approach to knowledge in the East is pursued by means of "concepts by intuition," a sense of the aesthetic components of things. A concept by intuition is something immediately experienced, apprehended, and contemplated. Northrop (1966) described it as the "differentiated aesthetic continuum" within which there is no distinction between subjective and objective. The aesthetic continuum is a single all-embracing continuity. The aesthetic part of the self is also an essential part of the aesthetic object, whether the object is a flower or a person. Taoism, for example, pursues an undifferentiated aesthetic continuum as it is manifested in the differentiated, sensed aesthetic qualities in nature. The Taoist claim is that only if we take the aesthetic continuity in its all-inclusiveness as ultimate and irreducible, will we properly understand the meaning of the universe and nature. Similarly, Confucianism stresses the all-embracing aesthetic continuum with respect to its manifestations in human nature and its moral implications for human society: Only if we recognize the all-embracing aesthetic manifold to be an irreducible part of human nature will we have compassion for human beings other than ourselves.

Whereas the Eastern knowledge tradition has concentrated its mental processes on the holistic, intuitive, aesthetic continuum, the Western pursuit of knowledge has been based on a more dualistic worldview. In this view, because the world and its various components came into existence through the individual creative acts of a god, the fundamental question is, "How can I reach out to the external inanimate world or to other people?" In this question, there is a basic dichotomy between the knower and the things to be known. Accompanying this epistemological dualism is the emphasis on rationality in the pursuit of knowledge. Since the Greek philosopher Plato "discovered" reason, virtually all subsequent Western thought—its themes, questions, and terms—relies on an essential rational basis. This is an indication that, while the East has tended to emphasize the direct experience of oneness via intuitive concepts and contemplation, the West has viewed the faculty of the intellect the primary instrument of worldly mastery. Compared with Eastern thought that tends to conclude in more or less vague, imprecise statements, consistent with its existential flexibility, Western thought emphasizes clear and distinct categorization and the linear, analytic logic of syllogism. Whereas the Eastern cultural drive for human development is aimed at spiritual attainment of oneness with the universe, the Western cultural drive finds its expression in its drive for material and social progress.

Time

Closely parallel to differences between the two cultural traditions regarding the nature of knowledge are differences in the perception and experience of time. Along with the immediate, undifferentiated experiencing of here and now, the Eastern time orientation can be portrayed as a placid, silent pool within which ripples come and go. Historically, the East has tended to view worldly existence as cyclic and has often depicted it with metaphors of movement such as a wheel or an ocean: The "wheel of existence" or the "ocean of waves" appears to be in a continual movement but is "not really going anywhere." Although individuals living in the world may experience a rise or fall in their personal fortunes, the lot of the whole is felt to be fundamentally unchanging. As Northrop (1966) observed, "the aesthetic continuum is the greater mother of creation, giving birth to the ineffable beauty of the golden yellows on the mountain landscape as the sun drops low in the late afternoon, only a moment later to receive that differentiation back into itself and to put another in its place without any effort" (p. 343).

Because worldly time is not experienced as going anywhere and because in spiritual time there is nowhere to go but the eternity within the now, the future is expected to be virtually the same as the past. Recurrence in both cosmic and psychological realms is very much a part of the Eastern thought. Thus, the individual's aim is not to escape from the circular movement into linear time, but to become a part of the eternal through the aesthetic experience of the here and now and the conscious evolution of spirituality to "know" the all-embracing, undifferentiated wholeness. In contrast, the West has represented time either with an arrow or as a moving river that comes out of a distant place and past (which are not here and now) and that goes into an equally distant place and future (which also are not here and now). In this view of time, history is conceived of as goal-directed and gradually progressing in a certain direction (toward the universal salvation and second coming of Christ or, in secular terms, toward an ideal state such as boundless freedom or a classless society).

Closely corresponding to the above comparison is Hall's (1976) characterization of Asian cultures as "polychronic" and Western cultures as "monochronic" in their respective time orientations. Hall explained that individuals in a polychronic system are less inclined to adhere rigidly to time as a tangible, discrete, and linear entity; instead, they emphasize completion of transactions in the here and now, often carrying out more than one activity simultaneously. Comparatively, according to Hall, a monochronic system emphasizes schedules, segmentation, promptness, and standardization of activities. We may say that the Eastern polychronic time orientation is rooted in the synchronization of human behavior with the rhythms of nature, whereas the Western time orientation is driven by the synchronization of human behavior with the rhythms of the clock or machine.

Communication

The traditional Eastern and Western perspectives on the universe, nature, knowledge, and time are reflected in many of the specific activities of individuals as they relate themselves to fellow human beings—how individuals view self and the group, and how they use verbal and nonverbal symbols in communication.

The view of self and identity cultivated in the Eastern tradition is embedded within an immutable social order. People tend to acquire their sense of identity from an affiliation with, and participation in, a virtually unchanging social order. As has been pointed out in many of the contemporary anthropological studies, the self that emerges from this tradition is not the clearly differentiated existential ego of the West, but a less distinct and relatively unchanging *social ego*. Individual members of the family tend to be more willing to submit their own self-interest for the good of the family. Individuals and families are often expected to subordinate their views to those of the community or the state. The Eastern tradition also accepts hierarchy in social order. In a hierarchical structure, individuals are viewed as differing in status, although all are considered to be equally essential for the total system and its processes. A natural result of this orientation is the emphasis on authority—the authority of the parents over the children; of the grandparents over their descendants; of the official head of the community, the clan, and the state over all its members. Authoritarianism is an outstanding feature of Eastern life, not only in government, business, and family, but also in education and in beliefs. The more ancient a tradition, the greater is its authority.

Comparatively, the Western view, in which God, nature, and humans are more distinctly differentiated, fosters the development of autonomous individuals with strong ego identification. The dualistic worldview is manifested in an individual's view of his or her relationship to other persons and nature. Interpersonal relationships are essentially egalitarian-cooperative arrangements between two equal partners in which the personal needs and interests of each party are more or less equally respected, negotiated, or resolved by compromise. Whereas the East encourages submission (or conformity) of the individual to the group, the West celebrates individuality and individual needs to drive the group. If the group no longer serves the individual needs, then it (not the individual) must be changed. The meaning of an interpersonal relationship is decided primarily by the functions that each party performs in satisfying the needs of the other. A relationship is regarded as healthy to the extent that it serves the expected function for all parties involved. As extensively documented in anthropology and cross-cultural psychology (e.g., Triandis, 1995), individualism is the central theme of the Western personality distinguishing the Western world from the collectivistic non-Western world.

This pragmatic interpersonal orientation of the West can be contrasted with the Eastern tradition, in which group membership is taken as given and therefore unchallenged, and in which individuals must conform to the group in case of conflicting interest. Members of the group are encouraged to maintain harmony and minimize competition. Individuality is discouraged, while moderation, modesty, and the bending of one's ego are praised. In some cases, both individual and group achievement (in a material sense) must be forsaken to maintain group harmony. In this context, the primary source of interpersonal understanding is the unwritten and often unspoken norms, values, and ritualized mannerisms pertinent to a particular situation. Rather than relying heavily

on explicit and logical verbal expressions, the Eastern communicator grasps the aesthetic essence of the communication dynamic by observing subtleties in nonverbal and circumstantial cues. Intuition, rather than rational thinking, plays a central role in the understanding of how one talks, how one addresses the other, under what circumstances, on what topic, in which of various styles, with what intent, and with what effect.

These implicit communication patterns are reflected in the Eastern fondness for verbal hesitance and ambiguity out of fear of disturbing or offending others (Cathcart & Cathcart, 1982; Kincaid, 1987). Even silence is sometimes preferred to eloquent verbalization in expressing strong compliments or affection. Easterners are often suspicious of the genuineness of excessive verbal praises or compliments because, according to their view, the truest feelings must be intuitively apparent and therefore do not need to be, and cannot be, articulated. As a result, the burden of communicating effectively is shared by both the speaker and the listener who is expected to "hear" the implicit messages through empathic attentiveness. In contrast, the Western communicative mode is primarily direct, explicit, and verbal, relying on logic and rational thinking. Participants in communication are viewed as distinctly different individuals, and their individuality has to be expressed through accurate verbal articulation. Inner feelings are not to be intuitively understood but to be honestly and assertively verbalized and discussed. Here, the burden of communicating effectively lies primarily with the speaker.

The preceding characterization of Eastern and Western communication patterns is largely consistent with observations made by other scholars such as Robinson (2003) and Yum (1994). Hall, in particular, has depicted Asian cultures as "high-context" in comparison with the "low-context" cultures of the West. The focal point of Hall's cross-cultural comparison is "contexting," that is, the act of taking into account information that is either embedded in physical or social context (which includes nonverbal behaviors) or internalized in the communicator. In this scheme, low-context communication, which is more prevalent in the West, is observed when most interpersonal information is expressed by explicit, verbalized codes.

BEYOND CULTURAL DIFFERENCES

The above-described cultural premises of the East and the West suggest the areas of vitality, as well as the areas of weakness, that are characteristic of each civilization. The Western mechanistic and dualistic worldview has helped to advance scientific efforts to describe systematically and explain physical phenomena, leading to extremely successful technological advancements. The West has learned, however, that the mechanistic worldview and the corresponding communication patterns may not adequately help illuminate the rich, complex, and often paradoxical nature of life and human relationships and that such an epistemological constraint can cause alienation from self and others. The West has seen that its dualistic distinction between humanity and nature brings about alienation from the natural world. Even as the analytical mind of the West has led to modern science and technology, it also has brought about knowledge that is often fragmented and detached from the totality of reality.

In comparison, the East has not experienced the level of alienation that the West has. At the same time, however, the East has not seen as much material and social development. Its holistic and aesthetic worldview has not been conducive to the development of science or technology. Its hierarchical social order and binding social relationships have not fostered the civic-mindedness, worldly activism, humanitarianism, and volunteerism that flourish in the West. Many of the Asian societies continue to struggle to bring about democratic political systems that are based on the rights and responsibilities of individuals.

Clearly, the range of sophistication of Western contributions to the socio-material domain far exceeds that of contributions from the East. However, the Eastern emphasis on aesthetic and holistic self-mastery offers a system of life philosophy that touches on the depth of human experience vis-à-vis other humans, the natural world, and the universe. Indeed, many have expressed increasing realization of limitations in the Western worldview. Using the term "extension transference," for instance, Hall (1976) pointed out the danger of the common intellectual maneuver in which technological "extensions" including language, logic, technology, institutions, and scheduling are confused with or take the place of the process extended. We observe the tendency in the West to assume that the remedy for problems arising from technology should be sought not in the attempt to rely on an ideal minimum of technology, but in the development of even more technology. Burke (1974) called this tendency "technologism": "[There] lie the developments whereby 'technologism' confronts its inner contradictions, a whole new realm in which the heights of human rationality, as expressed in industrialism, readily become 'solutions' that are but the source of new and aggravated problems" (p. 148).

Self-criticisms in the West have been also directed to the rigid scientific dogmatism that insists on the discovery of truth based on the mechanistic, linear causality, and objectivity. In this regard, Thayer (1983) commented:

> What the scientific mentality attempts to emulate, mainly, is the presumed method of laboratory science. But laboratory science predicts nothing that it does not control or that is not otherwise fully determined. . . . One cannot successfully study relatively open systems with methods that are appropriate only for closed systems. Is it possible that this is the kind of mentality that precludes its own success?" (p. 88)

Similarly, Hall (1976) has pointed out that the Western emphasis on logic as synonymous with the "truth" denies that part of human self that integrates. Hall sees that logical thinking is only a small fraction of our mental capabilities and that there are many different and legitimate ways of thinking that have tended to be less emphasized in Western cultures (p. 9).

The concerns raised by these and other critics of scientific epistemology do not deny the value of the rational, inferential knowledge. Rather, they are directed to the proclivity to regard concepts that do not adhere to its mode as invalid. They suggest the possibly erroneous belief that scientific knowledge is the only way to discover truth, when, in reality, the very process of doing science requires an immediate, aesthetic experience of the phenomenon under investigation. Without the immediately apprehended component, the theoretical hypotheses proposed could not be tested empirically with respect to their truth or falsity and would lack the relevance to the corresponding reality. As Einstein once commented, "Science is the attempt to make the chaotic diversity of our sense-experience correspond to a logically uniform system of thought" (Quoted in Northrop, 1966, p. 443). Likewise, the wide spectrum of our everyday life activities demands both scientific and aesthetic modes of apprehension: abstraction as well as concreteness; perception of the general and regular as well as the individual and unique; the literalism of technical terms as well as the power and richness of poetic language, silence, and art. If we limit ourselves to the dominant scientific mode of apprehension and do not value the aesthetic mode, then we would be limiting the essential human to only a part of the full span of life activities.

Incorporation of the Eastern view might bring the West to a greater awareness of the aliveness and wholeness of the universe we inhabit and the life we live. The universe is engaged in a continuous dance of creation in each instant of time. Everything is alive, brimming with a silent energy that creates, sustains, and infuses all that exists. In this regard, Maslow (1971) referred to Taoist receptivity or "let-be" as an important attribute of self-actualizing persons:

> We may speak of this respectful attention to the matter-in-paradigm as a kind of courtesy or deference (without intrusion of the controlling will) which is akin to "taking it seriously." This amounts to treating it as an end, something per se, with its own right to be, rather than as a means to some end other than itself, such as a tool for some extrinsic purpose. (p. 68)

Such aesthetic perception is an instrument of intimate human meeting, a way to bridge the gap between individuals and groups. In dealing with each other aesthetically, we do not subject ourselves to a rigid scheme, but do our best in each new situation, listening to the silence as well as the words, and experiencing the other person as a whole living entity with less infusion of our own egocentric and ethnocentric demands. A similar attitude can be developed toward the physical world, as is witnessed in the rising interest in the West in ecological integrity and holistic medicine (e.g., Brody, 1997; Wallis, 1996).

INTERCULTURAL COMMUNICATION AND PERSONAL TRANSFORMATION

The preceding considerations suggest that many Eastern and Western philosophical premises offer views of reality that are not necessarily competitive, but can be complementary. Of course, the entire values, norms, and institutions of the West cannot, and should not, be substituted for their Eastern counterparts, and vice versa. The West may no more adopt the worldviews of the East than the East may adopt the worldviews of the West. Rather, we recognize that a combination of rational and intuitive modes of experiencing life leads to a life that is real. From this understanding may arise an affirmation of the interrelatedness of cultures and a reconciliation synthesis of the two seemingly incompatible perspectives.

Our task, then, is to reach for the unity in human experiences and simultaneously to express diversity. The purpose of evolution is not to create a homogeneous mass, but to continuously unfold an ever diverse and yet organic whole. In this regard, knowledge of differing cultural traditions can help societies and individuals move toward greater self-understanding, especially by revealing blind spots that can be illuminated only by adopting a vastly different way of seeing. The task of synthesizing elements of Eastern and Western cultural traditions is taken not merely to satisfy an esoteric academic curiosity, but also out of keen relevance to the everyday realities of numerous individuals whose life experiences extend beyond their primary cultural world. Through extensive and prolonged experiences of interfacing with other cultures, many people have already embarked on a personal evolution, creating a new culture of their own, fusing diverse cultural elements into a single personality. As Toffler (1980) noted, they have created a new personal culture that is "oriented to change and growing diversity" that attempts "to integrate the new view of nature, of evolution and progress, the new, richer conceptions of time and space, and the fusion of reductionism and holism, with a new causality" (p. 309).

The growing tendency of individuals to move beyond a particular cultural tradition is a direct function of dramatically increasing intercultural communication activities—from the personal experiences of diverse people and events through direct encounters to observations via various communication media such as books, magazines, television programs, movies, magazines, art museums, music tapes, and electronic mail. Communicating across cultural identity boundaries is often challenging because it provokes questions about our presumed cultural premises and habits, as well as our natural tendency of intergroup

Figure 1 *The Stress-Adaptation-Growth Dynamic*

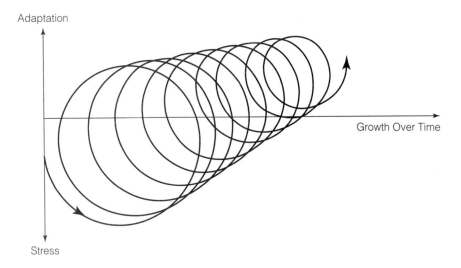

Adaptation

Growth Over Time

Stress

posturing, the "us-and-them" categorical differentiation. Yet it is precisely such challenges that offer us openings for new cultural learning, self-awareness, and personal growth. The greater the severity of intercultural challenges, the greater the potential for reinvention of an inner self that goes beyond the boundaries of the original cultural program.

The author (Kim, 1988, 2001, 2005) has theorized about this interplay of intercultural challenges and potential personal transformation as an unfolding of the *stress-adaptation-growth dynamic*. As shown in Figure 1, the stress-adaptation-growth dynamic plays out not in a smooth, arrow-like linear progression, but in a cyclic and continual "draw-back-to-leap" movement. As a newcomer strives to meet the challenges of the host environment, some aspects of the host culture are internalized. A "crisis," once managed, presents an opportunity for new learning and self-renewal. To the extent that stress is responsible for frustration and anxiety, it is also credited as a necessary impetus for new learning and growth. As the fluctuations of stress and adaptation diminish over time, a calming of the overall life experiences takes hold. In this process, our identity is transformed gradually and imperceptibly from an ascribed or assigned identity to an achieved or adopted identity, that is, an *intercultural personhood* at a higher level of integration (Grotevant, 1993). Such an identity transformation takes place in a progression of stages. In each stage, new concepts, attitudes, and behaviors are incorporated

into an individual's inner constitution. As previously unknown life patterns are etched into our nervous systems, they become part of our new psyches. The evolution of our identity from cultural to intercultural is far from smooth or easy. Moments of intense stress can reverse the process at any time because individuals may, indeed, regress toward reidentifying with their origins, having found the alienation and malaise involved in maintaining a new identity too much of a strain (De Vos & Suarez-Orozco, 1990). Such strain may take various forms of an identity crisis (Erickson, 1968) and cultural marginality (Stonequist, 1964; Taft, 1977). Yet the stress experience also challenges individuals to accommodate new cultural elements and become more capable of making deliberate and appropriate choices about action as situations demand.

The concept, *intercultural personhood* (Kim, 1988, 2001, 2005) projects a special kind of mindset that promises greater fitness in our increasingly intercultural world. Intercultural personhood represents a continuous struggle of searching for the authenticity in self and others within and across cultural groups. It is a way of existence that transcends the perimeters of a particular cultural tradition, and one that is capable of embracing and incorporating seemingly divergent cultural elements into one's own unique worldview. The process of becoming intercultural affirms the creative courage and resourcefulness of humans because it requires discovering new symbols and new patterns of life. This creative process of identity development speaks to a uniquely human plasticity, "our relative freedom from programmed reflexive patterns . . . the very capacity to use culture to construct our identities" (Slavin & Kriegman, 1992, p. 6). It is the expression of normal, ordinary people in the act of stretching themselves out of their habitual perceptual and social categories.

DATA AND CASE ILLUSTRATIONS

A broad body of social science research findings render direct or indirect empirical support for the above-described theoretical interrelationship of intercultural stress, adaptation, and subsequent growth, leading to a gradual identity transformation toward an increasingly intercultural personhood. Research data have been generated in more than half a century of social scientific studies of sojourners and immigrants in the United States and more recently in a variety of European and Asian countries. (See Kim, 2001, for a detailed literature review.) In a study of multiple immigrant groups, for instance, Eaton and Lasry (1978) reported that the stress level of more upwardly mobile immigrants was greater than those who were less upwardly mobile. Among Japanese Americans (Marmot & Syme, 1976) and Mexican American women (Miranda & Castro, 1977), the better adapted immigrants had initially experienced a somewhat greater frequency of stress-related symptoms (such as anxiety and a need for psychotherapy) than the less adapted group. Similarly, findings from Ruben and Kealey's (1979) study of Canadian technical advisors in Nigeria revealed that those who were the most effective in their new environment underwent the most intense culture shock during the initial transition period. More recently, Milstein (2003) reported that the sojourn experience in Japan among exchange students from the United States and a number of other countries has resulted in increased levels of "self-efficacy." The study also showed that the increase in self-efficacy is linked positively to the self-reported level of challenge the students experience as well as to the self-reported success of sojourn. Intercultural transformation of long-term settlers have been confirmed in numerous immigrant studies. Dasgupta (1983), for instance, reported that Asian Indian immigrants were able to resolve the conflict

between their traditional value of holism and ascription and the American values of individualism, achievement, and competition by dichotomizing and attaining a healthy balance between primary in-group relationships and achievement in their occupational lives in the larger society. A similar progressive convergence of the "subjective meaning system" of Puerto Ricans in New York toward that of Anglo Americans was found by Szalay and Inn (1988). Murphy-Shigematsu (1987) reports that Amerasians with first-generation Japanese mothers and White American fathers have struggled with their mixed racial and cultural conditions and have succeeded in forming their authentic identity in society. Likewise, Suro (1998) reports that long-term Hispanics showed diminished Hispanic "cultural scripts" in their judgments and increased social interactions with non-Hispanics.

In addition to research findings pointing to the process of personal transformation, there are many publicly available first-hand accounts of individuals whose life stories bear witness to concrete realities of intercultural personhood. Such accounts have appeared in case studies, memoirs, biographical stories, and essays of self-reflection. Many of these accounts present vivid insights into the emotional ebb and flow of the progress toward intercultural personhood. Perhaps one of the most succinct testimonials to the present conception of intercultural personhood was offered by *Muneo Yoshikawa* (1978). As someone who had lived in Japan and in the United States, Yoshikawa offered the following insight into his own psychic development—an insight that captures the very essence of what it means to be an intercultural person:

> I am now able to look at both cultures with objectivity as well as subjectivity; I am able to move in both cultures, back and forth without any apparent conflict. . . . I think that something beyond the sum of each [cultural] identification took place, and that it became something akin to the concept of "synergy"— when one adds 1 and 1, one gets three, or a little more. This something extra is not culture-specific but something unique of its own, probably the emergence of a new attribute or a new self-awareness, born out of an awareness of the relative nature of values and of the universal aspect of human nature. . . . I really am not concerned whether others take me as a Japanese or an

American; I can accept myself as I am. I feel I am much freer than ever before, not only in the cognitive domain (perception, thoughts, etc.), but also in the affective (feeling, attitudes, etc.) and behavioral domains. (p. 220)

An illustration of intercultural personhood is offered by *Duane Elgin,* who was born and raised in the United States as a Christian and studied Buddhism in Tibet and Japan for many years. In his book, *Voluntary Simplicity* (1981), Elgin integrated the philosophical ideas of Eastern and Western worldviews into his concept of "voluntary simplicity." He presented this idea as "global common sense" and as a practical lifestyle to reconcile the willful, rational approach to life of the West and the holistic, spiritual orientation of the East. Examining historical trends, cycles of civilizations, and related ecological concerns, Elgin proposed voluntary simplicity as a goal for all of humanity. The main issue Elgin addresses is how humans can find ways to remove, as much as possible, the non-essential "clutters" of life. He suggests, for example, that one own or buy things based on real needs and consider the impact of one's consumption patterns on other people and on the earth. Before purchasing nonessential items, one should ask oneself if these items promote or compromise the quality of one's non-material life. One could also consciously simplify communications by making them clearer, more direct, and more honest, eliminating idle, wasteful, and manipulative speech. One should also respect the value of silence and nonverbal actions.

Intercultural personhood is further illustrated in the writings of the Nobel Literature Prize winning author *Salman Rushdie.* His writings have been the process of self-discovery as he has been experiencing it in his own life as an immigrant. First as a Muslim in predominantly Hindu India, next as an Indian migrant to Pakistan, and then as an Indian-Pakistani living in Britain, Rushdie faced first hand some of the most drastic and all-encompassing intercultural experiences. In *Imaginary Homelands,* Rushdie (1992) specifically addressed the creative inspiration that he personally draws from the tug between the old and the new, the familiar comfort of home and the freedom of the unknown. In his own words,

[our] identity is at once plural and partial. Sometimes we fall between two stools. But however ambiguous and shifting this ground may be, it is not an infertile

territory for a writer to occupy. If literature is in part the business of finding new angles at which to enter reality, then once again our distance, our long geographical perspective, may provide us with such angles. (p. 15)

The creative insights rooted in the life of intercultural personhood are also what has been the driving passion for the 2006 winner of the Nobel Prize in Literature, the Turkish novelist *Orhan Pamuk.* Pamuk, who has defended Salman Rushdie after the publication in 1988 of *The Satanic Verses,* is renowned for his delicate explorations of East-West relations. Like Rushdie, Pamuk is widely admired for having captured in his writings new symbols for the interlacing of cultures. In an interview with the National Public Radio following the Nobel Prize announcement (National Public Radio, October 12, 2006), Pamuk affirmed the centrality of intercultural interests in his work and further articulated his own inclusive intercultural identity orientation.

My whole book, my whole life, is a testimony to the fact that East and West actually combine, come together gracefully, and produce something new. That is what I have been trying to do all my life, trying to prove. . . . I don't believe in clashes of civilization. I think that was a fanciful idea which, unfortunately, is sometimes coming to be true. But no, I think that East and West meet. I think that my whole work is a testimony to the fact that we should find ways of looking, combining East and West without any clash, but with harmony, with grace, and produce something new for humanity.

Revealed in these and other personal stories are some common patterns associated with the development of intercultural personhood. One such pattern is a mind-set that is less parochial and more open to different perspectives. Each story is tangible proof for this author's notion that we can rise above the hidden grips of our childhood culture and discover that there are many ways to be "good," "true," and "beautiful." In this process, we can attain a *wider circle of identification,* approaching the limits of many cultures and, ultimately, of humanity itself. This process is analogous to climbing a mountain. As we reach the mountaintop, we see that all paths below lead to the same summit and that each path offers unique scenery. Likewise, the process of becoming intercultural leads to an awareness of ourselves as being part of a larger, more inclusive whole and gives us a greater empathic capacity to "step into and imaginatively participate in the other's world view" (Bennett, 1977, p. 49).

Such a development, in turn, will endow us with a special kind of *freedom* and *creativity,* with which we can make deliberate choices about action in specific situations rather than to have these choices simply be dictated by habitual conventions of thought and action. This personal evolution presents the potential for achieving what Harris (1979) defined as "optimal communication competence." An optimally competent communicator, according to Harris, has a refined "meta system" for critiquing his or her own managing system and interpersonal system. The very existence of the meta system makes the difference between the optimal level and the other two levels of competence a qualitative one.

In the end, it is through the experiences of intercultural communication and through the process of becoming intercultural that we can better serve as cross-links of our intercultural world. Intercultural persons can help provide an infrastructure of moral cement that holds together the human community and discourages excessive identity claims at the exclusion of other identities. They are among the ones who can best meet the enormous challenge that confronts us all—"to give not only yourself but your culture to the planetary view" (Campbell, 1990, p. 114).

References

Bennett, J. (1977, December). Transition shock: Putting culture shock in perspective. In N. Jain (Ed.), *International intercultural communication annual* (Vol. 4, pp. 45–52). Falls Church, VA: Speech Communication Association.

Brody, J. (1997, November 6). U.S. panel on acupuncture calls for wider acceptance. *The New York Times,* p. A10.

Burke, K. (1974). Communication and the human condition. *Communication, 1,* 135–152.

Campbell, J. (1990). *An open life* (in conversation with M. Toms). New York: Harper & Row.

Capra, F. (1975). *The Tao of physics.* Boulder, CO: Shambhala.

Cathcart, D., & Cathcart, R. (1982). Japanese social experience and concept of groups. In L. Samovar & R. Porter (Eds.), *Intercultural communication: A reader,* (3rd ed., pp. 120–127). Belmont, CA: Wadsworth.

Dasgupta, S. (1983). *Indian immigrants: The evolution of an ethnic group.* Unpublished doctoral dissertation, University of Delaware, Newark.

De Vos, G., & Suarez-Orozco, M. (1990). *Status inequality: The self in culture.* Newbury Park, CA: Sage.

Eaton, W., & Lasry, J. (1978). Mental health and occupational mobility in a group of immigrants. *Science and Medicine, 12,* 53–58.

Elgin, D. (1981). *Voluntary simplicity.* New York: Bantam Books.

Erickson, E. (1968). *Identity, youth, and crisis.* New York: Norton.

Grotevant, H. (1993). The integrative nature of identity: Bridging the soloists to sing in the choir. In J. Kroger (Ed.), *Discussions on ego identity* (pp. 121–146). Hillsdale, NJ: Lawrence Erlbaum.

Gulick, S. (1963). *The East and the West.* Rutland, VT: Charles E. Tuttle.

Hall, E. (1976). *Beyond culture.* Garden City, NY: Anchor Books.

Harris, L. (1979, May). *Communication competence: An argument for a systemic view.* Paper presented at the annual meeting of the International Communication Association, Philadelphia, PA.

Kane, R. (1994). *Through the moral maze: Searching for absolute values in a pluralistic world.* New York: Paragon House.

Kim, Y. Y. (1988). *Communication and cross-cultural adaptation: An integrative theory.* Clevedon, United Kingdom: Multilingual Matters.

Kim, Y. Y. (2001). *Becoming intercultural: An integrative theory of communication and cross-cultural adaptation.* Thousand Oaks, CA: Sage.

Kim, Y. Y. (2005). Adapting to a new culture: An integrative communication theory. In W. Gudykunst (Ed.), *Theorizing about intercultural communication* (pp. 375–400). Thousand Oaks, CA: Sage.

Kincaid, L. (1987). Communication East and West: Points of departure. In L. Kincaid (Ed.), *Communication theory: Eastern and Western perspectives* (pp. 331–340). San Diego, CA: Academic Press.

Marmot, M., & Syme, S. (1976). Acculturation and coronary heart disease in Japanese-Americans. *American Journal of Epidemiology, 104*(3), 225–247.

Maslow, A. (1971). *The farther reaches of human nature.* New York: Viking.

Milstein, T. J. (2005, March). Transformation abroad: Sojourning and the perceived enhancement of self-efficacy. *International Journal of Intercultural Relations, 29,* 217–238.

Miranda, M., & Castro, F. (1977). Culture distance and success in psychotherapy with Spanish speaking clients. In J. Martinez, Jr. (Ed.), *Chicano psychology* (pp. 249–262). New York: Academic Press.

Nakamura, H. (1964). *Ways of thought of Eastern peoples.* Honolulu: University of Hawaii Press.

Needham, J. (1951). Human laws and laws of nature in China and the West. *Journal of the History of Ideas,* XII.

Northrop, F. (1966/1946). *The meeting of the East and the West.* New York: Collier Books.

Oliver, R. (1971). *Communication and culture in ancient India and China.* New York: Syracuse University Press.

Robinson, J. (2003). Communication in Korea: Playing things by eye. In L. Samovar & R. Porter (Eds.), *Intercultural communication: A reader* (10th ed., pp. 57–64). Belmont, CA: Wadsworth.

Ruben, B., & Kealey, D. (1979). Behavioral assessment of communication competency and the prediction of cross-cultural adaptation. *International Journal of Intercultural Relations, 3*(1), 15–27.

Rushdie, S. (1992). *Imaginary homelands: Essays and criticism 1981–1991.* New York: Penguin.

Slavin, M., & Kriegman, D. (1992). *The adaptive design of the human psyche.* New York: Guilford.

Stonequist, E. (1964). The marginal man: A study in personality and culture conflict. In E. Burgess & D. Bogue (Eds.), *Contributions to urban sociology* (pp. 327–345). Chicago: University of Chicago Press.

Suro, R. (1998). *Strangers among us: How Latino immigration is transforming America.* New York: Alfred A. Knoff.

Suzuki, D. (1968). *The essence of Buddhism.* Kyoto, Japan: Hozokan.

Szalay, L., & Inn, A. (1988). Cross-cultural adaptation and diversity: Hispanic Americans. In Y. Y. Kim & W. B. Gudykunst (Eds.), *Cross-cultural adaptation: Current approaches* (pp. 212–232). Newbury Park, CA: Sage.

Taft, R. (1977). Coping with unfamiliar culture. In N. Warren (Ed.), *Studies in cross-cultural psychology* (Vol. 2, pp. 121–153). London: Academic Press.

Thayer, L. (1983). On "doing" research and "explaining" things. *Journal of Communication, 33*(3), 80–91.

Thompson, W. (1973). *Passages about earth: An exploration of the new planetary culture.* New York: Harper & Row.

Toffler, A. (1980). *The third wave.* New York: Bantam Books.

Triandis, H. (1995). *Individualism and collectivism.* Boulder, CO: Westview Press.

Wallis, C. (1996, June 24). Healing. *Time,* 58–64.

Yoshikawa, M. (1978). Some Japanese and American cultural characteristics. In M. Prossor (Ed.), *The cultural dialogue: An introduction to intercultural communication* (pp. 220–239). Boston, MA: Houghton Mifflin.

Yum, J. (1994). The impact of Confucianism on interpersonal relationships and communication patterns in East Asia. In L. Samovar & R. Porter (Eds.), *Intercultural communication: A reader,* (7th ed., pp. 75–86). Belmont, CA: Wadsworth.

Concepts and Questions

1. What is meant by the term *intercultural personhood?*
2. How do Eastern and Western teachings about humankind's relationship to the nature of the universe differ?
3. In what major ways do Eastern and Western approaches to knowledge differ?
4. How do Eastern time orientations differ from those found in the West?
5. How do differences in Eastern and Western views of self and identity affect intercultural communication?
6. What are the major differences between Eastern and Western modes of communication?
7. What strengths and weaknesses are found in Eastern and Western worldviews?
8. How could an integration of Eastern and Western perspectives benefit both Eastern and Western cultural life?
9. What conditions are required for the emergence of intercultural personhood?
10. List and discuss what you would personally have to do to achieve interpersonal personhood.

Integration in Intercultural Ethics

Richard Evanoff

INTRODUCTION

Normative approaches to how sojourners should inter-act with people from their host cultures typically suggest that individuals should either adapt themselves to the norms of their host culture ("when in Rome do as the Romans do") or maintain their own norms while respecting those of the host culture. Recent work which attempts to apply "third culture" theory to intercultural dialogue on ethics (Casmir, 1997, Evanoff, 2000) suggests an alternative model in which common ground between people with different ethical norms can be actively constructed through a process of intercultural dialogue in which existing norms are critiqued and new norms are formulated. The end goal of such a process is an integration of norms across cultures which serve to govern relationships between individuals in cross-cultural situations. The following sections consider three specific forms of integration: (1) how multiple frames of reference can be integrated into one's own thinking at the individual/psychological level; (2) how multiple frames of reference can be integrated at the interpersonal/intercultural level; and (3) how specific norms can be conceptually integrated at the formal level.

INTEGRATING MULTIPLE FRAMES OF REFERENCE

Integration and "Third Cultures"

Persons who have undergone the experience of learning how other cultures perceive the world acquire an intercultural mind-set (Adler, 1977; Fisher, 1988),

From Richard Evanoff, "Integration in Intercultural Ethics," *Journal of Intercultural Relations, 20,* 421–437, Copyright Elsevier (2006). Richard Evanoff teaches environmental ethics and intercultural communication in the School of International Politics, Economics, and Businesds at Aoyama Gakuin Unitersity, Tokyo, Japan.

which enables them to make judgments by the standards of more than one culture (i.e., from multiple frames of reference). The process of developing an intercultural mind-set leads to a wider view both of the world and of human possibilities. By empathetically engaging ourselves with the viewpoints of other cultures we also gain a more objective view than it would be possible for us to have by merely looking at the world through the lens of our own culture.

The same process can work in the reverse, of course. People from other cultures may be able to learn from our experiences and, in the process, dialogue based on an empathetic cross-cultural understanding of different traditions becomes possible. A willingness to learn from other cultures does not mean the outright abandoning of one's own cultural traditions and values, although in the process of exposing ourselves to different ways of thinking we will inevitably be led to a penetrating reexamination of our own culture and values. Out of such reflection we gain a wider and more highly differentiated view of the world which can nonetheless be integrated into a wider and more comprehensive worldview.

M. Bennett's (1993) well-known developmental model of intercultural sensitivity delineates six stages individuals typically go through in the process of acquiring an integrated perspective. In the earlier "ethnocentric" stages difference is either simply not recognized (denial); difference is acknowledged but one culture is believed to be superior to another (defense); or difference is minimized by adopting a facile universalism (minimalization). In the later "ethnorelative" stages, differences are accepted in a simplistic, relativist way (acceptance); individuals become capable of adopting the frame of reference of another culture (adaptation); or individuals adopt a bi-cultural perspective which utilizes multiple cultural frames of reference (integration).

Each of these stages represents a more highly differentiated framework for dealing with cross-cultural differences. The tendency to think in terms of universals and absolutes typically occurs only at relatively unreflective stages. As reflection increases and the awareness of differences expands, individuals begin to think in more relativistic terms. Relativism itself is transcended, however, once individuals begin to consciously evaluate the norms and values of both their own and the other culture. It is recognized that while a variety of (possibly viable) options for thought and action are open to the individual, some must be chosen over others simply in order to get on with one's life. At the final stage, which roughly corresponds to Perry's (1999) "commitment in relativism," individuals acquire a bicultural perspective by integrating at least some of the ideas and values of the other culture into their own way of thinking. Thus, the process of developing intercultural sensitivity has the potential to transform sojourners in significant ways.

Levels similar to Bennett's "integrated" stage have been described by other authors in the field of intercultural communication. Useem, for example, uses the term "third cultures," to refer to "cultural patterns inherited and created, learned and shared by the members of two or more different societies who are personally involved in relating their society, or segments thereof, to each other" (Useem, 1971, p. 14; see also Useem, Useem, & Donoghue, 1963). Yoshikawa's concept of "dynamic inbetweenness" holds that a "third perspective" can be created in cross-cultural exchanges between Asians and Westerners which "does not represent exclusively either the Eastern perspective or the Western perspective" (Yoshikawa, 1987, p. 329). Adler, citing Tillich, suggests that the formation of a multicultural personality involves creating "a third area beyond the bounded territories, an area where one can stand for a time without being enclosed in something tightly bounded" (Adler, 1977, p. 26). Postcolonial cultural studies in the UK have also advanced the concept of "hybridity" (Werbner & Modood, 1997). Bhabha (1994) specifically contends that it is possible for immigrants to create a "third space," in which various aspects of both the dominant and the immigrant culture are hybridized in ways which transform each.

Not all individuals successfully make the transition to a multicultural perspective, of course. J. Bennett (1993) distinguishes between "constructive marginality," which achieves higher levels of self-differentiation and integration, and "encapsulated marginality," which results in psychological disintegration. Both the constructive and the encapsulated marginals have stepped outside of their original cultures into a cultural "void" (Durkheim's anomie), a place beyond conventional social practices where no norms exist. The constructive marginal sees this emptiness as space for individual creativity; in the absence of clearly defined rules opportunities arise for creating new ways of doing things. The encapsulated marginal, on the other hand, experiences this emptiness as loss and disorientation; since all standards are culturally constructed, nothing is true and nothing is worth doing. Moving beyond culturally prescribed norms means either that the individual will begin to decisively construct his or her own identity or that there will be a loss of identity, difficulty in decision making, alienation, excessive self-absorption, multiplicity, and a "never-at-home" feeling. Constructive marginals are in a good position to act as go-betweens in intercultural negotiations because they are capable not just of understanding the basic outlooks of two (or more) cultures but also of integrating perspectives which on the surface may seem "incommensurable."

Integration vs. Adaptation

Integration is a fundamentally different concept from adaptation, which has long been a central organizing principle in the field of intercultural communication (see Ellingsworth, 1988; Kim, 1989, 1991a, 2001; Kim & Gudykunst, 1988; Searle & Ward, 1990; Ward, 1996; Ward & Rana-Deuba, 1999). Whereas adaptation may be conceived as the process by which sojourners adapt their personal norms to the norms of the host culture, integration concerns itself both with the psychological process by which individuals begin to incorporate values from the host culture into their own system of values and with the process by which the host culture may also be influenced by the values of sojourners. Transformation should be seen not simply in terms of individuals changing themselves to fit into their host cultures but also as the process by which host cultures transform themselves to accommodate the presence of sojourners. In the same way that evolutionary biology (Levins & Lewontin, 1985) has replaced its original conception of adaptation (organisms adapt themselves to preexisting niches in the natural environments they inhabit) with a more dialectical view (organisms co-adapt with their natural environments through mutual transformations), so too can the concept of adaptation in intercultural communication be modified to show both how sojourners adjust themselves to their host cultures and how host cultures adjust themselves to the presence of sojourners in their midst. Exactly what adjustments need to be made on both sides itself becomes one of the primary concerns of intercultural dialogue on ethics. In the process of engaging in such dialogue, both sojourners and their host cultures may be transformed and a measure of integration achieved.

Berry's model of acculturation (Berry, 1992, 1997, 2004; Berry, Kim, Power, Young, & Bujaki, 1989; see also Piontkowski, Florack, Hoelker, & Obdrza lek, 2000) delineates four basic ways in which sojourners can adjust themselves to their host cultures: (1) assimilation, in which sojourners consider it valuable to maintain relationships with other groups but not to maintain their own cultural identity; (2) separation, in which sojourners consider it valuable to maintain their own cultural identity but not to maintain relationships with other groups; (3) marginalization, in which sojourners fail to maintain both their own cultural identity and relationships with other groups; and (4) integration, in which sojourners try to maintain both their own cultural identity and relationships with other groups. This model can also be applied reflexively to members of the host culture, who may correspondingly think that sojourners should either: (1) be assimilated into the host culture and not maintain their original cultural identity; (2) be separated from the host culture but allowed to maintain their own identity; (3) be marginalized from both the host culture and their own identity; or (4) be integrated into the host culture and allowed to maintain their own identity. In the integrative mode sojourners may be able to integrate values from both their original and their host cultures in original ways, while members of the host culture may also be able to integrate some of the values of sojourners into their own value systems.

Berry indicates that the integrative mode "is associated with the least acculturative stress and the most positive psychological and sociocultural adaptations" (2004, p. 181), although he admits that integration may only be achievable in societies that are consciously multicultural. Integration aims at a "mutual accommodation." and requires immigrants to adopt the basic values of the receiving society and the receiving society to adapt national institutions (e.g., education, health, justice, labor) to better meet the needs of all groups now living together in the larger plural society," (2004, p. 177).

Berry sees integration as being a preferable option both for long-term sojourners and for host countries rather than assimilation, separation, or marginalization. The normative implication of this conclusion is that sojourners can profitably integrate aspects of both their own culture and the host cultures in their own psychological outlooks, while host countries can profitably pursue policies that promote multiculturalism within their own societies. At its worst, adaptation means that sojourners simply resign themselves to acting in accordance with the norms of their host culture, a strategy which may appeal to some precisely because it avoids open confrontation. Missing from this "when-in-Rome-do-as the-Romans-do" account of adaptation, however, is the possibility that at least some of the norms the sojourner starts out with, may, upon reflection, prove to be more desirable than the norms of the culture they are expected to adapt themselves to. There is no reason to assume that sojourners should simply assimilate by giving up their own cultural values and conforming to the values of their host culture. The converse is also true, of course. There is no reason to assume that sojourners should simply be accepted "as they are" into the host culture. Rather, cross-cultural contact allows sojourners and members of the host culture to actively negotiate the norms which will govern relationships between them.

Such considerations raise the possibility of both sides engaging in constructive criticism of the values and norms of both cultures. It is often claimed that such criticism should not be engaged in because it shows a lack of "respect" for the other culture. This may be true of uninformed or vituperative criticism and of attempts to forcefully impose one culture's set of values on another. The goal of constructive criticism, however, is to discover strengths and weaknesses in each of the respective positions and then to see if it may be possible either to reconcile positive aspects of each into a new conceptual framework or to imagine entirely new sets of norms that can be applied to interactions between people from the respective cultures.

Integration, then, is not simply a matter of sojourners adapting themselves to the norms of the host culture, but rather a process of coadaptation in which the sojourner and host culture mutually adapt themselves to each other. Casmir describes the creation of ethical norms to govern such situations as "third culture building," in which "human beings from more widely differing cultural backgrounds achieve their adaptation-tasks together" (1997, p. 100). Many cross-cultural encounters are by their very nature anomic. There may be no precedents for the participants to follow and no mutually agreed-upon customs or norms to give guidance to action. Since the norms to govern the relationship between the participants may not yet exist, these norms must be created through the dialogue process itself. It is evident, however, that many of the norms one culture or the other takes as valid will simply have no credibility with people from the other culture. Moreover, when commonalities of the "least-common-denominator" variety are found, they are frequently unsuitable for the more complex situations the participants find themselves in. Such problems are not insurmountable, but they are indeed problems which virtually anyone who engages in extended cross-cultural dialogue on ethics will be obliged to face. The attempt to create new norms to govern new cross-cultural situations often involves considerable frustration, but also offers the possibility of a mutual learning process for both sojourners and members of the host culture.

While culture shock can be a debilitating experience for some, for others it can involve a dynamic and creative process of transformation. Furnham (1988; see also Ward, Bochner, & Furnham, 2001) suggests that although many researchers in the field of intercultural communication have focused on the negative aspects of cultural adjustment, there may also be positive aspects. Adler has proposed thinking of culture shock as a profound learning experience that leads to a high degree of self-awareness and personal growth. Rather than being only a disease for which adaptation is the cure, culture shock is likewise at the very heart of the cross-cultural learning experience. It is an experience in self-understanding and change (Adler, 1987, p. 29).

Kim and Ruben propose a model for "intercultural transformation," defined as a process of internal change in which the "individuals' cognitive, affective, and behavioral patterns are viewed to develop beyond their original culturally conditioned psychological parameters" (Kim & Ruben, 1988, p. 299). The transformation follows a "stress-adaptation-growth" pattern. In monocultural situations individuals exist in

a state of homeostasis in which their socialized view of reality remains unchallenged. Cross-cultural encounters introduce a perturbation into the system which may stimulate various adaptive strategies as a response. In the process of working out these strategies the individuals experience internal growth. Such growth, it should be noted, can occur both in sojourners and in members of their host cultures.

In Piagetian (Piaget, 1982) terms, cross-cultural encounters present fresh perspectives which cannot simply be assimilated into existing schemas (i.e., frames of reference), but rather must be accommodated through the construction of larger, more highly differentiated and integrated schemas. The ability to employ a variety of different conceptual schemes undoubtedly gives a wider understanding of any given phenomenon, without, however, exhausting it. By comparing these various frames of reference and subjecting them to critical examination, we may be able to dialectically integrate aspects of each of them into even more highly differentiated conceptual schemes. Integration is neither a process of taking over the ideas and values of another culture whole nor a process of simply setting two cultures side by side and syncretizing them. Rather, it represents the stage at which individuals are able to fully transcend their own cultures and internalize perspectives gained from a different culture. The process involves a critique of one's own original cultural values and norms. With increased intercultural experience and reflection some of these values and norms may be deemed worth retaining while others are discarded.

The process also involves, however, a critique of the adopted culture's values and norms. One need not adopt the other culture "whole"; rather there can also be a measure of selectivity in which some values are deemed worthy of emulation while others are not. In this process our existing cognitive and moral schemas begin to break down and to be reconfigured on a wider scale. While elements of our previous way of thinking may be purged, new ideas and values may also be accommodated. The new schema is not simply a pastiche of incongruous ideas and values drawn from a variety of cultural sources (as postmodernists might think) but rather a fairly integrated and "synergetic" whole (cf. Hampden-Turner, 1970). Further development is possible if the process is repeated, that is, if greater differentiation is initiated and new forms of integration are sought out.

At this point we might begin to speak of a seventh stage, beyond M. Bennett's original six, namely, a "generative" stage in which entirely new forms of culture are creatively produced. The generative stage would transcend both Bennett's ethnocentric and ethnorelative stages. The goal is not simply to say which of the existing cultural pies is best (ethnocentricism) nor to simply say that each of the pies is equally delicious on its own terms (ethnorelativism), but to make a different and better pie. The generative stage provides for the possibility of both personal and social transformation. Not all of the new options we are able to generate will be of equal value (some may be flops, others unworkable), but there is nonetheless a need for ongoing experimentation.

INTEGRATION ACROSS CULTURES

Integration and Value Pluralism

Since it cannot be assumed that individuals from different cultures will automatically arrive at a shared perspective on the basis of existing similarities and since, in any event, existing norms may be entirely inadequate to address challenges presented by newly emergent problems, there is thus the need to construct new norms across cultural lines that are able to effectively deal with shared problems. A constructivist approach to cross-cultural dialogue on ethics (cf. Evanoff, 1999, 2004) sees increased contact between people from various cultures as creating an opportunity for entirely new forms of social interaction to emerge. Cross-cultural dialogue can work toward the effective integration of ideas that on the surface appear incommensurable and, moreover, toward the generation of entirely new concepts and norms appropriate to newly emergent problems.

Cross-cultural dialogue on ethics is possible precisely because ethical principles, as with all other forms of culture, are humanly produced and culturally transmitted. Ethical dialogue does not founder simply because ethical principles are neither innate nor written into the metaphysical scheme of things. If ethical norms are cultural creations, then they can also be revised in response both to newly emergent problems and to new perspectives gained through cross-cultural contact. Cross-cultural encounters create an entirely new context in which the norms that will govern interactions between the participants do not yet exist and hence must be created. Given the anomic nature of cross-cultural interactions, there is very little, if anything, that can be assumed about the particular beliefs and values the participants will initially bring with them to the dialogue process.

Nonetheless, it is doubtful that there are ever any cross-cultural encounters in which the participants share absolutely nothing in common; the participants in cross-cultural dialogue can and should make good use of whatever preexisting common ground they can draw on. In fact, the types of conflicts one finds between moral conceptions of the good *between* societies are probably no greater than the types of conflicts one finds between moral conceptions of the good *within* pluralistic societies. In some cases there may even be more agreement across cultures among certain groups than within cultures. Secularists in the West and in Islamic countries, for example, may have more in common with each other than they do with fundamentalists in their respective cultures.

Within any given culture there can be a variety of competing value systems. We should not look at cultures as maintaining a completely monolithic system of values which all members accept or are expected to accept. Even at the individual level consistency is rarely the case; a plurality of values and a plurality of ways of thinking about values are empirical facts (cf. Kekes, 1993, p. 11). The same individual can hold to a variety of values, some of which may conflict with each other; working out a measure of consistency (coherence, reflective equilibrium) is one of the goals of ethical reflection at the individual level.

How values are ranked may depend, in part, on the various roles the individual assumes in society. Certain types of behavior are expected from individuals who occupy certain roles; in different roles other types of behavior will be expected. How an individual deals with others in business relationships may be governed by a different set of norms than how one deals with family members. Another factor that can influence the values an individual holds are the various groups one belongs to. The relationship between the individual and the group is often reciprocal. Individuals bring certain values with them to the group, which may transform the overall values of the group. At the same time, however, the group exercises a measure of influence over the values the individual holds.

Singer (1987, p. 24) argues that each individual is in a sense always "culturally unique" because there is never complete agreement with regard to the value-rankings of the various individuals which make up any group. Members of a given group rarely accept all the values of the group and even the values they do accept may be ranked differently. To the degree that an individual shares the values of a given group the individual will tend to identify with that group; if the difference between the values held by the individual and those held by the group are too disparate, the individual will cease to identify with that group.

Further compounding the problem, as Singer points out, is the fact that at any given time an individual may, and in fact usually does, belong to a number of different groups, each with a different value structure. While some values may overlap, others may not. Since, in most cases it is unlikely that two individuals will belong to exactly the same groups, it is unlikely that they will ever share exactly the same values. Even if they do belong to exactly the same groups and share the same basic set of values, they may rank these values differently. The conclusion that we reach at the purely empirical level is that the value systems of two individuals will rarely, if ever, converge.

At the normative level, it seems equally futile to look for a single set of values which could compel agreement on all points. First, such agreement would effectively create a monolithic social system in which all individuality was destroyed. Second, in destroying individuality all bases for criticizing the system would also be destroyed. Without criticism, innovation is impossible and without innovation it is impossible for our ethical systems to keep pace with changing external circumstances.

Constructivism vs. Essentialism

Essentialism can be defined as the view that there are certain, "essential," values which are shared by all members of a culture or by all humans by virtue of being human. The idea that there is a "common core" of cultural values shared by everyone within a given culture, however, is as fragile as the argument that there is a "common core" of values shared between cultures. For any given cultural value, no matter how widely held, there will almost always be dissent. Nonetheless, certain values may come to be widely shared by the people of a given society and can therefore be regarded as dominant. Dominant values are those which achieve a relatively high degree of intersubjective agreement in a given culture, but they can nonetheless shift as old values are challenged and new values arise.

Variation in values both within and between cultures can be empirically registered by adopting a statistical rather than an essentialist approach to cultural values. Hofstede (1984, p. 31; see also Bennett, 1998, p. 7) has demonstrated how empirical comparisons can be made between the values held by different cultures by plotting the relative distributions of a given value in two or more societies. The distributions typically form a bell curve for each of the societies with the dominant value represented at the peak of the curve and marginal values represented at the bottoms of the slopes. Cross-cultural comparisons can be made both by comparing modal values (represented by the peaks) and by comparing extreme values (areas where there is no overlap between them). There is nearly always some overlap, however, in the values held by particular individuals in different cultures.

This approach has the advantage of going beyond an impressionistic (and essentialist) study of "national characters." The implication for cross-cultural dialogue on ethics is that there are likely to be intra-cultural differences with respect to any given value. "Dominant" values cannot be reified into cultural absolutes but are rather subject to statistical variation. For example, while individualism may be a dominant value in the United States and collectivism a dominant value in Japan, some Americans may be more oriented toward collectivism while some Japanese may be more oriented toward individualism (cf. Hofstede, 1984; Kim, Triandis, Kagitcibasi, Choi, & Yoon, 1994; Singelis, Triandis, Bhawuk, & Gelfand, 1995; Triandis, 1995). Moreover, the distributions are subject to change over time. Japanese society could become more oriented toward individualistic values (which in fact is the direction Japan seems to be heading in) or America could become more oriented toward collectivist values (which Western communitarians would urge us toward). Cultures, as much as evolving species (see Mayr, 1994), are better described not in essentialist terms ("collectivism is a Japanese value") but rather in constructivist terms ("a high percentage of Japanese presently hold collectivist values"). Constructivism embraces the existentialist slogan "existence precedes essence." If a group of people begin to act in a way that is entirely different from how they have acted in the past, they simply redefine their culture. What is "typical" is simply a statistical average at a given point in time. Values and ethical norms are not fixed but can change as the values of the individuals in a given culture shift.

Simply recognizing that values can be as variable within cultures as they are between cultures, opens up considerable possibilities for cross-cultural dialogue because it no longer becomes necessary for individuals to be "cheerleaders" for the particular set of values which happen to be dominant in their own cultures. Values can be defended not because they are "a part of our culture." but because they are worth defending; if they are not worth defending they should be changed. Values become reified not only when they are taken as being an unchangeable part of "human nature," but also when they are taken as being an unchangeable part of one's culture. The result is a form of false consciousness which can be neither empirically grounded nor philosophically justified. Reified values cannot be empirically grounded because of the fact of intracultural variability; there is no one value or set of values which is completely shared by every member of a given society. Reified values cannot be philosophically justified because individuals are always in a position to question the dominant values of their culture. From a constructivist perspective, dialogue can only proceed by looking at the merits of the arguments which are used to support various positions; they can never be justified on the grounds that a given idea or value is an essential (i.e., uncontestable, nonnegotiable) aspect of a given culture.

INTEGRATION AT THE FORMAL LEVEL

Integrative Agreements

The purpose of cross-cultural dialogue, in the view developed above, is not to arrive at "universal" ways of behaving but rather to arrive at a measure of agreement that enables people to successfully interact with each other across cultural boundaries and to solve problems of mutual concern. Cross-cultural dialogue recognizes that all ways of thinking and behaving are contingent, none are absolute, and therefore alternative ways of thinking and behaving are always available. If the practices of a given culture are called into question, such practices can only be justified if persuasive reasons can be given for why a given set of alternatives has been chosen to the exclusion of others. The argument that "cultural differences must be respected" is not in itself a justification. Cross-cultural dialogue must go beyond simply "respecting cultural differences" by engaging in the potentially subversive act of asking cultures to justify why they do things the way they do.

Our discussion thus far has centered on integration at the psychological and social levels. We turn now to a consideration of integration at the formal level between ideas and plans for action which, on the surface, appear initially to be contradictory. A dialectical approach to intercultural dialogue refuses, in ethnocentric fashion, to take any existing culture as a final model. Rather it subjects all existing cultural traditions to reflective criticism, recognizing both that no one culture has a monopoly on good ideas and that no culture is immune to legitimate criticism. By setting two or more cultural traditions in juxtaposition with each other and engaging in dialogue, new ideas can emerge which will be different from the ideas already present within either one of them.

Traditional approaches to dialogue emphasize finding preexisting "common ground" between the disputants and a willingness on the part of the disputants to accept compromise on points which cannot be agreed upon. An alternative possibility, however, is to work towards what Pruitt calls "integrative agreements," defined as "those that reconcile (i.e., integrate) the parties' interests and hence yield high joint benefit" (Pruitt, 1994, p. 487). Integrative agreements rely on a fundamentally dialectical approach which takes neither the initial conditions of the dispute nor the initial positions of the negotiators as fixed. The basic idea can be illustrated with an example offered by Pruitt: two sisters who were quarreling over an orange finally decided to compromise by splitting the orange in half. The first sister used the pulp from her half to make juice and threw away the rind; the second sister used the rind from her half to make cake and threw away the pulp. An integrative agreement would have given all the pulp to the first sister and all the rind to the second.

It is clear that integrative agreements may not be able to solve all types of conflicts—cases in which both the first and second sisters want to make orange juice, for example—and at times compromise may be the best that can be hoped for. Nonetheless, integrative agreements are especially interesting from a constructivist perspective because they involve reconstruing the problem (instead of simply taking the original positions as they are, they give a more highly differentiated account of the possibilities) as well as dialectical integration (instead of seeing the two positions as "incommensurable," they look for ways in which certain aspects of the original positions can be dropped and others combined). The sort of creative brainstorming found in integrative agreements involves moving beyond making rational decisions within a narrow conceptual framework toward making decisions that take other conceptual frameworks into account and critically synthesizes them into a larger framework. Rationality of this latter sort involves going beyond one's present understanding of a situation and seeking out a more objective and holistic view. It involves, that is, a wider understanding of both the situation itself and the perception of that situation held by the person one is engaging in dialogue with.

In the dialectical view, if all schemas are partial, then they cannot be judged on the basis of whether or not they are "true" in an apodeictic sense, but rather must be assessed on the basis of their comprehensiveness. Schemas that account for more of our experience and organize that experience in more coherent fashion are preferable to those which leave significant data out of account and are incoherently organized or conflict with other schemas we also think are worth adhering to. Taylor (1993) contends that it is possible on the basis of practical reason alone to evaluate the adequacy of competing moral claims even when common ground is lacking (as in cross-cultural disputes). He offers three argument forms which do not appeal to foundational criteria. Position B is superior to position A if: (1) B accounts for more facts than A and thus represents a gain in understanding; (2) A cannot account for why there was a need for B to arise as an alternative; or (3) B reduces errors by pointing out contradictions, clearing up confusions, or drawing attention to significant considerations which

A neglected. Cast in constructivist terms, B can be said to be superior to A if the schemas it employs are more highly differentiated and integrated.

A similar process in which lower-order schemas are replaced by higher-order schemas can be employed in reaching integrative agreements. Whereas the original perception of a problem may be fairly narrow in scope and simplistic in its analysis, the new perception is both more comprehensive and more complex. While it is not necessary to assimilate everything that one's dialogue partner believes into this higher-order schema, it may nonetheless be possible to assimilate those features which can be positively evaluated. The partner as well is capable of moving from lower-level to higher-level schemas and a more highly differentiated understanding of the situation. The perspective that emerges is in essence an entirely new one, which critically incorporates elements of each of the original perspectives but also transcends them. Suedfeld and Tetlock (1977) refer to the end result as a state of "integrative complexity." Integrative complexity involves a more highly differentiated conception of the problem at hand and a more highly integrated view of how the problem can best be solved.

Models of Cross-Cultural Criticism

An integrative approach to cross-cultural dialogue can be analyzed in terms of four distinct types of criticism. The first is a purely ethnocentric form of criticism which is based primarily on cultural stereotypes and simply pits one culture against another to see which is "superior." For example, Asians and Westerners debating collectivism vs. individualism might cast the debate in a purely bivalent form of logic: either collectivism is right and individualism is wrong, or vice versa. At the ethnocentric stage Asians might contend that collectivism is superior to Western individualism, while Westerners might contend that individualism is superior to Asian collectivism.

The second form of criticism is intracultural criticism, in which individuals engage in a reflective critique of their own cultural norms and traditions in an effort to identify both their positive and negative aspects. At the stage of intracultural criticism it may be agreed that Asian collectivism can be broken down into both a positive side ("cooperation") and a negative side ("conformity") and that Western individualism similarly has a positive side ("self-reliance") and a negative side ("self-indulgence"). We thus arrive at a more highly differentiated understanding of what is usually referred to as collectivism and individualism. At this stage a more dialectical form of reasoning is employed which takes the statements "collectivism is good" or "individualism is bad" as being true in some respects but false in others.

The third form of criticism is intercultural criticism in which what are regarded as the positive features of one culture are compared with the negative features of the other culture. At this stage it may be concluded that the value of "cooperation" is indeed superior to the value of "self-indulgence," while the value of "self-reliance" is superior to the value of "conformity."

The fourth form of criticism is integrative criticism in which an effort is made to create an entirely new framework, or schema, which integrates positive aspects of both traditions, while discarding their negative aspects. At the integrative stage the Western value of "self-reliance," regarded at the previous stage as superior to Asian "conformity," might be combined with the Asian value of "cooperation," regarded at the previous stage as superior to Western "self-indulgence."

The four modes are diagrammatically summarized in Figure 1. Whereas the original opposition between Asian collectivism and American individualism was cast in dichotomous terms (i.e., the two perspectives are "incommensurable"), a constructivist approach shows how the two concepts can be effectively integrated at the formal level. It should be noted that the account given here describes merely the dialectical logic that underlies constructive dialogue and not the process by which initial evaluative judgments are arrived at (i.e., what is to be regarded as "positive" and "negative"). Arguments must still be presented to show why "self-reliance" and "cooperation" are superior to "self-indulgence" and "conformity," for example. The merit of this approach, however, lies in the fact that it shifts the debate away from a debate about "incommensurable" cultural differences to a debate about the viability of particular values which can, in principle, be adopted by any culture.

Integrative criticism involves a dialectical reconciliation of concepts that, in their initial formulation, may appear as polarities. Hampden-Turner refers to integration of this sort as "synergy," which he defines as "the optimal integration of that which was formerly differentiated" (1970, p. 190). "Synergy" can be used to refer to any sort of integration which simultaneously allows for high degrees of differentiation to be maintained. Hampden-Turner offers as examples a list of polar concepts drawn from personality theory, which includes (among others) dependency vs. autonomy, extraversion vs. introversion, and tender-minded vs. tough-minded. More recent work by Hampden-Turner and Trompenaars (2000) develops and applies a theory of value reconciliation in which such seemingly conflicting values as universalism-particularism, individualism-communitarianism, specificity-diffuseness, achieved-ascribed status, inner direction-outer direction, and sequential and synchronous time can be reconciled in business and other settings.

Figure 1 *Models of Cross-Cultural Criticism*

Collectivism (Asia) vs. Individualism (the West)	
I. Ethnocentric criticism	
ASIA	THE WEST
(+) Collectivism is good	(+) Individualism is good
II. Intracultural criticism	
ASIA	THE WEST
(+) Cooperation is good	(+) Self-reliance is good
(−) Conformity is bad	(−) Self-indulgence is bad
III. Cross-cultural criticism	
ASIA	THE WEST
(+) Cooperation is better than self-indulgence	(+) Self-reliance is better than conformity
IV. Integrative criticism	
ASIA	THE WEST
(+) Cooperation and self-reliance are good	(−) Conformity and self-indulgence are bad

Kim (1991b) similarly thinks that cross-cultural differences between the West and the East can be seen in complementary rather than in contradictory terms. The emphasis on rationality in the West, for example, complements rather than contradicts the emphasis on intuition in East Asian cultures. Moreover, it would be wrong to simply stereotype the West as "rational" and the East as "intuitive"—the West has developed intuitive modes of thinking just as the East has developed rational modes of thinking, even though neither of these modes have historically been dominant parts of their respective cultures. The goal of an integrative approach is to find ways of combining seemingly opposite cultural tendencies into a wider framework which, in the end, will hopefully help to resolve cross-cultural conflicts and also offer a fuller and more holistic view of human possibilities.

MacIntyre (1988) further argues that while no existing tradition presents us with a universal conception of ethics, dialogue between various traditions can enlarge our views of how ethics (and many other areas of human experience) can be conceived. MacIntyre outlines three stages which traditions pass through in the process of developing a wider perspective:

> a first in which the relevant beliefs, texts, and authorities have not yet been put in question; a second in which inadequacies of various types have been identified, but not yet remedied; and a third in which response to those inadequacies has resulted in a set of reformulations, reevaluations, and new formulations and evaluations designed to remedy inadequacies and overcome limitations. (1988, p. 355)

Once the inadequacies have been recognized a tradition finds itself in an "epistemological crisis" (1988, p. 362), which can only be overcome by formulating new theoretical frameworks which meet three requirements: (1) they must be able to satisfactorily solve the recognized inadequacies in a way that (2) explains why the tradition was previously unable to deal with them and (3) preserves a fundamental continuity with that tradition.

There are obvious similarities here both with Taylor's account of practical reason and with Piaget's concept of accommodation: when anomalous experiences or data cannot be assimilated into existing schemas, the schemas themselves must be enlarged to accommodate them. While MacIntyre confines himself to a consideration of how a particular tradition can enlarge itself through a process of "imaginative conceptual innovation" (1988, p. 362), our contention is that in situations where two or more cultures are engaged in creative dialogue with one another, entirely new "traditions" may emerge in which competing views are able to dialectically converge. While there will undoubtedly be some continuity with the original traditions, the extent to which such continuity must be "fundamental" in McIntyre's sense is not clear. From a constructivist view "fundamental" cannot be understood in an essentialist sense (a view which McIntyre's Aristotelianism might tend toward) to mean the preservation of some "core" aspects of a given culture, but rather must be taken in an evolutionary sense to refer to the need for a measure of continuity rather than purely disruptive, irrational, and perhaps maladaptive change. In this view, then, the issue is not so much maintaining continuity with past traditions, as MacIntrye holds, but rather having the ability to let go of one tradition and to actively participate in the creation of an entirely new one. The "new tradition" may not maintain continuity with any one tradition but perhaps with several.

It is clear that the results of the dialectical process we have been describing cannot be taken as "universal," but they are rather the product of specific cross-cultural interactions arising out of a need to reach a measure of convergence on the norms that will govern the relations between particular cultures and enable them to work together effectively on common problems. Such convergence is not rendered possible on the basis of some absolute point of view which transcends the existing traditions, but rather emerges out of the dialogue itself. Thus, the dialogue may begin with particular concepts and particular forms of rationality, but in the process of exchange those concepts and forms of rationality can themselves be transformed. In other words, an entirely new point of view is possible, one that is forged out of material already present within the contending traditions, yet designed to produce a measure of agreement between them.

The result would not be a universal account of human experience, but it would be a wider and more adequate account than that obtained previously within any of the original traditions. We do not achieve a more holistic perspective by attempting to step outside of all cultures and positing a set of historical principles valid for all cultures but rather by comparing and integrating a variety of different particular perspectives into a more comprehensive framework. The only way to arrive at a truly "universal" conception would be to attempt to integrate all possible cultural perspectives into a single comprehensive system. Such a move, however, is probably impossible on purely logistic grounds, unnecessary because we do not need a framework for "everything" but simply a framework for being able to resolve particular problems faced by particular groups of people, and undesirable because such a high level of convergence would act as a restraint on the ability of new, creative, divergent forms of thinking to emerge.

CONCLUSION

While it is doubtful that the integrative method proposed here can be applied to all cross-cultural differences with respect to values and norms, there are undoubtedly a large number of areas in which it could be successfully employed, not only at the interpersonal level of communication, but also at the intergroup and international levels. Empirical research reveals a wide variety of values and norms held by different cultures with respect to such areas of human interaction as friendship, marriage, education, business, politics, and so forth, indicating that the relativity of values and norms across cultures can be registered as a simple empirical fact. However, cultural relativity (the empirical observation that cultures have different norms and values) is not the same as cultural relativism (the normative judgment that such differences must simply be accepted). There is a need, therefore, to supplement descriptive, empirical approaches to the study of cross-cultural interactions with a normative consideration of how differences in cultural values and norms can be actively negotiated across cultures.

While this paper has endeavored to offer a cross-disciplinary approach to intercultural ethics by combining both theoretical work in the field of intercultural communication and normative philosophical analysis, undoubtedly there is a need for further research into how an integrative approach to intercultural ethics might illuminate specific ethical problems which arise in the "real world," both as encountered experientially and as revealed in empirical studies. The process of integration offers an alternative to perspectives on

ethics based on either adaptation or respect. The concept of integration is primarily normative, however, rather than empirical. That is, it presents a method for resolving cross-cultural conflicts which can be consciously adopted by the participants in intercultural dialogue. While there may in fact be norms held by different cultures which are truly incommensurable, and therefore not susceptible to integration, it is nonetheless possible that new norms can be created in cross-cultural encounters which integrate values from the respective cultures and enable the participants to deal more effectively with problems of mutual concern.

References

Adler, P. S. (1977). Beyond cultural identity: Reflections upon cultural and multicultural man. In R. W. Brislin (Ed.), *Topics in culture learning: Concepts, applications, and research* (pp. 24–41). Honolulu: University of Hawaii Press.

Adler, P. S. (1987). Culture shock and the cross-cultural learning experience. In L. F. Luce & E. C. Smith (Eds.), *Toward internationalism: Readings in cross-cultural communication,* (2nd ed., pp. 24–35). Cambridge: Newbury.

Bennett, J. (1993). Cultural marginality: Identity issues in intercultural training. In R. M. Paige (Ed.), *Education for the intercultural experience* (pp. 109–135). Yarmouth, ME: Intercultural Press.

Bennett, M. (1993). Towards ethnorelativism: A developmental model of intercultural sensitivity. In R. M. Paige (Ed.), *Education for the intercultural experience* (pp. 21–71). Yarmouth, ME: Intercultural Press.

Bennett, M. (Ed.). (1998). *Intercultural communication: A current perspective. Basic concepts of intercultural communication:* Selected readings (pp. 1–34). Yarmouth, ME: Intercultural Press.

Berry, J. (1992). Acculturation and adaptation in a new society. *International Migration, 30,* 69–84.

Berry, J. (1997). Immigration, acculturation, and adaptation. *Applied Psychology: An International Review, 46,* 5–68.

Berry, J. (2004). Fundamental psychological processes in intercultural relations. In D. Landis, I. M. Bennett, & M. I. Bennett (Eds.), *Handbook of intercultural training,* (3rd ed., pp. 166–184). Thousand Oaks, CA: Sage.

Berry, J., Kim, U., Power, S., Young, M., & Bujaki, M. (1989). Acculturation attitudes in plural societies. *Applied Psychology: An International Review, 38,* 185–206.

Bhabha, H. (1994). *The location of culture.* London: Routledge.

Casmir, F. L. (1997). Ethics, culture, and communication: An application of the third-culture building model to international and intercultural communication. In

F. L. Casmir (Ed.), *Ethics intercultural and international communication* (pp. 89–118). London: Lawrence Erlbaum.

Ellingsworth, H. w. (1988). A theory of adaptation in intercultural dyads. In Y. Y. Kim & W. B. Gudykunst (Eds.), *Theories in intercultural communication* (pp. 259–279). Newbury Park, CA: Sage.

Evanoff, R. (1999). Towards a constructivist theory of intercultural dialogue. In N. Honna, & Y. Kano (Eds.), *International communication in the 21st century* (pp. 109–153). Tokyo: Sanseido.

Evanoff, R. (2000). The concept of "third cultures" in intercultural ethics. *Eubois Journal of Asian and International Bioethics, 10,* 126–129

Evanoff, R. (2004). Universalist, relativist, and constructivist approaches to intercultural ethics. *International Journal of Intercultural Relations, 28,* 439–458.

Fisher, G. (1988). *Mindsets: The role of culture and perception in international relations.* Yarmouth, ME: Intercultural Press.

Furnham, A. (1988). The adjustment of sojourners. In Y. Y. Kim & W. B. Gudykunst (Eds.), *Cross-cultural adaptation: Current approaches* (pp. 42–61). Newbury Park, CA: Sage.

Hampden-Turner, C. (1970). Synergy as the optimization of differentiation and integration by the human personality. In I. W. Lorsch & P. R. Lawrence (Eds.), *Studies in organization design* (pp. 187–196). Homewood: R. D. Irwin.

Hampden-Turner, C., & Trompenaars, F. (2000). *Building cross-cultural competence: How to create wealth from conflicting values.* New Haven, CT: Yale University Press.

Hofstede, G. (1984). *Cultures consequences: International differences in work-related values.* Newbury Park, CA: Sage.

Kekes, I. (1993). *The morality of pluralism.* Princeton, NJ: Princeton University Press.

Kim, Y. Y. (1989). Intercultural adaptation. In M. K. Asante & W. B. Gudykunst (Eds.), *Handbook of international and intercultural communication* (pp. 279–294). Newbury Park, CA: Sage.

Kim, Y. Y. (1991a). Communication and cross-cultural adaptation. In L. A. Samovar & R. E. Porter (Eds.) *Intercultural communication: A reader* (6th ed., pp. 383–390). Belmont, CA: Wadsworth.

Kim, Y. Y. (1991b). Intercultural personhood: An integration of Eastern and Western perspectives. In L. A. Samovar & R. E. Porter (Eds.), *Intercultural communication: A reader* (6th ed., pp. 401–411). Belmont, CA: Wadsworth.

Kim, Y. Y. (2001). *Becoming intercultural: An integrative theory of communication and cross-cultural adaptation.* Thousand Oaks, CA: Sage.

Kim, Y. Y., & Gudykunst, W. B. (Eds.). (1988). *Cross-cultural adaptation.* Newbury Park, CA: Sage.

Kim, Y. Y., & Ruben, B. D. (1988). Intercultural transformation: A systems theory. In Y. Y. Kim & W. B. Gudykunst (Eds.), *Theories in intercultural communication* (pp. 299–321). Newbury Park, CA: Sage.

Kim, U., Triandis, H. C., Kagitcibasi, C., Choi, S. C., & Yoon, G. (Eds.). (1994). *Individualism and collectivism: Theory, method, and applications.* Newbury Park, CA: Sage.

Levins, R., & Lewontin, R. (1985). *The dialectical biologist.* Cambridge, MA: Harvard University Press.

MacIntyre, A. (1988). *Whose justice? Which rationality?* London: Duckworth.

Mayr, E. (1994). Typological versus population thinking. In E. Sober (Ed.), *Conceptual issues in evolutionary biology,* (2nd ed.) (pp. 157–160). Cambridge, MA: MIT Press.

Perry, W. G. (1999). *Forms of ethical and intellectual development in the college years: A scheme.* San Francisco, CA: Jossey-Bass.

Piaget, I. (1982). Functions and structures of adaptation. In H. C. Plotkin (Ed.), *Learning, development, and culture* (pp. 145–150). Chickchester [West Sussex, England]; New York: Wiley.

Piontkowski, U., Florack, A., Hoelker, P., & Obdrzalek, P. (2000). Predicting acculturation attitudes of dominant and non-dominant groups. *International Journal of Intercultural Relations, 24,* 1–26.

Pruitt, D. G. (1994). Achieving integrative agreements in negotiation. In G. R. Weaver (Ed.), *Culture, communication and conflict: Readings in intercultural relations* (pp. 487–497). Needham Heights, MA: Simon & Schuster.

Searle, W., & Ward, C. (1990). The prediction of psychological and sociocultural adjustment during cross-cultural transitions. *International Journal of Intercultural Relations, 14,* 449–464.

Singelis, T. M., Triandis, H. C., Bhawuk, D. S., & Gelfand, M. (1995). Horizontal and vertical dimensions of individualism and collectivism: A theoretical and measurement refinement. *Cross-Cultural Research, 29,* 240–275.

Singer, M. R. (1987). *Intercultural communication: A perceptual approach.* Englewood Cliffs, NJ: Prentice-Hall.

Suedfeld, P., & Tetlock, P. E. (1977). Integrative complexity of communications in international crises. *Journal of Conflict Resolution, 21,* 169–184.

Taylor, C. (1993). Explanation and practical reason. In M. Nussbaum & A. Sen (Eds.), *The quality of life* (pp. 208–231). Oxford: Clarendon.

Triandis, H. (1995). *Individualism and collectivism: New directions in social psychology.* Boulder, CO: Westview.

Useem, J. (1971). *The study of cultures. Studies of third cultures: A continuing series* (No.6, pp. 1–27). East Lansing: Institute for International Studies in Education, Michigan State University.

Useem, J., Useem, R. H., & Donoghue, J. (1963). Men in the middle of the third culture: The roles of American and non-Western people in cross-cultural administration. *Human Organization, 22,* 169–179.

Ward, C. (1996). Acculturation. In D. Landis, & R. S. Bhagat (Eds.), *Handbook of intercultural training,* (2nd ed., pp. 124–147). Thousand Oaks, CA: Sage.

Ward, C., Bochner, S., & Furnham, A. (2001). *The psychology of culture shock* (2nd ed.). East Sussex: Routledge.

Ward, C., & Rana-Deuba, A. (1999). Acculturation and adaptation revisited. *Journal of Cross-cultural Psychology, 30,* 372–392.

Werbner, P., & Modood, T. (Eds.). (1997). *Debating cultural hybridity.* London: Zed Books.

Yoshikawa, M. J. (1987). The double-swing model of intercultural communication between the East and the West. In L. D. Kincaid (Ed.), *Communication theory: Eastern and Western perspectives* (pp. 319–329). San Diego, CA: Academic Press.

Concepts and Questions

1. Describe the two types of normative approaches to intercultural interaction discussed by Evanoff. How do they differ? Give an indication of the effectiveness of each normative approach.

2. What does Evanoff mean by frames of reference?

3. Describe what Evanoff means when he talks about integrating multiple frames of reference.

4. How does integration of multiple frames of reference lead to a better approach to intercultural communication?

5. Evanoff believes that integration and adaptation are different concepts. What is meant by integration? What is adaptation, and how does it differ from integration?

6. What does Evanoff mean by the process of transformation? How does it affect the sojourner and the host culture?

7. Why does Evanoff believe that cross-cultural dialogue on ethics is possible?

8. In the area of ethics, what does Evanoff mean by the term "essentialism"?

9. If the goal of Evanoff's thoughts is to attain the ability to construct a cross-cultural ethic, how might essentialism help or hinder that activity?

10. If you were to find yourself in a position where your employment required you to relocate to a foreign culture for a prolonged time, how easy or difficult would it be for you to construct an appropriate cross-cultural ethic?

Worldview: The Ethical Dimension

Ninian Smart

INTRODUCTION

The ethical dimension of a religion or worldview is shaped by the other dimensions, but *it also* helps to shape them. If the numinous experience revealed to early Israel and to the prophets a mysterious and dynamic deity, their moral insights suggested that this God was a good God. He demanded not just sacrifices but also contrition, not just observance of the Sabbath but also uprightness in conduct. If the mystical experience revealed to early Buddhism a realm of peace and pure consciousness, moral insight also showed that this peace was to be shared with others. and that ultimately no inner illumination not accompanied by compassion for the suffering of other living beings was worth having.

Buddhists, Hindus, and Jains have a special attitude toward moral action because they believe in reincarnation. Since one may be reborn in animal or insect form, one must have a sense of solidarity with other living beings. In the religions of the West, however, the dominant view has been that human beings have souls but animals do not. In theory at any rate, Indian traditions have a greater moral obligation toward animals and other living forms than has been the case in the West. But in recent times in the West a greater concern with our living environment, together with the influence of the East on our culture, has led to changes in attitudes. We see campaigns to save whales and leopards, for example. Whatever our specific attitudes, there is no doubt that the scope of morality is affected by our general worldview.

Morality is affected also by our picture of the ideal human being. The Christian looks to Christ and to the saints and heroes of the tradition. The Buddhist

From *Ninian Smart, Worldviews: Crosscultural Explorations of Human Beliefs,* 3rd ed., pp. 104–117, © 2000. Reprinted by permission of Pearson Education, Inc., Upper Saddle River, NJ.

looks to the Buddha, the Muslim to Muhammad, the Hindu to Rama and Krishna and others, the Taoist to Lao-tse, and the Confucianist to Confucius.

So we can already see that there are ways in which the ethical dimension relates to religious experience, to doctrines about the cosmos, and to the myths and historical heroes of the traditions.

In modern times an attempt has been made to try in one way or another to set up ethics on an independent basis—that is independent of traditional religious belief. But as we shall see such an attempt cannot be completely successful, because every ethical system seems to raise questions about the worldview behind it.

Thus, probably the most powerful and influential ethical system—or set of systems—in modern times has been utilitarianism, which had its chief expression in the nineteenth century through the writings of John Stuart Mill (1806–1873). Its importance lies in trying to see moral action in terms of its utility, and utility in terms of whether something helps produce human happiness or reduce human suffering. It thus shapes much of modern politics and economics in the democratic West. In the West we tend to think in utilitarian terms: to think of whether a given aspect of our institutions, such as divorce law, will bring the greatest happiness to the greatest number and the least suffering to the least number. We conduct economic policy on the basis that we should prosper in such a way that everyone can realize a reasonable degree of happiness and freedom from poverty. The American constitution speaks of the pursuit of happiness, and socialism is often based on the idea that it will banish poverty and free people for better things. In such ways our whole Western culture is drenched with utilitarian thoughts.

This utilitarianism is often coupled with the idea, celebrated by the scientific humanist, that the basis of all values in the individual human being, and that which is most important is how individuals relate to one another. In his book *I and Thou*, the Jewish writer Martin Buber looks, as we have seen, to the deeper human relationships as the center of the meaning of life.

Somewhat opposed to the individualism of much of the West's thinking is the collectivism of the Marxist tradition. Here human behavior and economics are so closely woven together that ethics is also seen as collective: Actions are good insofar as they bring about a revolution that will consolidate socialism, or insofar as they preserve the revolution and help in the march toward an ideal society in which human beings live in harmony.

Either the study of religious ethics can deal with the facts about morality and structures of moral thinking, or else it can reflect on what is right and wrong from a normative stance. Our prime concern here is with the former approach, but I shall say something briefly about the normative questions in due course; that is, about what ethical values we might adopt.

COMPARATIVE RELIGIOUS ETHICS

The cross-cultural study of religious ethics is sometimes called "comparative religious ethics." This is quite a recent coinage, and only in the last few years has a really systematic attempt been made to open up the field. However, there were some notable previous enterprises that dealt with ethics in a comparative way. Perhaps most important among these was the *Encyclopedia of Religion and Ethics,* edited by James Hastings before, during, and just after World War I. The *Encyclopedia,* in many enormous volumes, gave liberal and learned treatment to a host of vital themes in the study of religion and, as its title implies, included much on moral views and practices everywhere in the world.

At one level, comparative religious ethics is aimed simply at delineating the various moral systems found in societies all over the world. Sometimes it is necessary to distinguish between what are called the great and the little traditions. For instance, one can view the ethical beliefs of the Sri Lankans from the angle of the great tradition, namely, official Buddhist belief as expressed through the scriptures and the preaching of the monks. But one can also see what the actual beliefs are in the villages of the highlands (for example), where elements other than "official Buddhism" come into play. Or, one could look to what the actual moral outlook is, say, of the average Italian as compared with the official teachings of the Catholic Church. Probably it is enough for us to say that just as there are many Buddhisms and many Christianities, so there are many Buddhist moralities and many Christian moralities.

When we find that there are, in fact, likenesses and differences among cultures in regard to right and wrong, we begin to ask wider questions. What accounts for these likenesses and differences? One thing we might begin to do is correlate moral values with kinds of doctrines, myths, and experiences.

But the major faiths have much in common as far as moral conduct goes. Not to steal, not to lie, not to kill, not to have certain kinds of sexual relations—such prescriptions are found across the world because such rules are necessary if there is to be a society at all. The widespread breaking of these rules would lead to chaos. Society can exist only where such wrong acts are in the minority.

However, what they mean in greater detail may vary quite a lot. In matters of sex, for example, there are varying systems. A Christian generally has only one wife, divorce notwithstanding—and for a long time in much of the Christian tradition even divorce was ruled out. A Muslim male, in contrast, may have up to four wives at one time, and divorce is built into the original legal system. As for killing, some societies allow the right of self-defense, and in war the killing of the enemy may be deemed a duty. Some religions are cautious about war or exclude it altogether, as do the Quakers; for others war is a natural means of spreading the domain in which the faith is exercised. This is notably so in the Islamic idea of the *Jihad*, or holy struggle.

The way in which the rules themselves are viewed often differs, and this means that there are different models of virtue. For the Jew and the Muslim, for instance, the rules are part of the fabric of divinely instituted law—Torah and Shari'a, respectively. Obedience to the rules is obedience to God. In Judaism, obedience is qualified by the belief that the commandments are part of a contract or covenant between God and his people. In Buddhism the rules of morality are part of the "eightfold path" that leads to ultimate liberation. It is not that God has to be obeyed, but rather that, as part of the general effort at self-purification, it is wise to be good. The model for the monotheist is the obedient person of faith, such as Abraham. The model Buddhist is the person of superior insight.

Although Hinduism often involves belief in one divine Being, it shares with Buddhism a sense that the law or dharma is not so much something that is commanded by God, but rather that it is part of the nature of the world. The law is part of the fabric of the cosmos, so that to follow it is to follow the natural bent of things. Thus, Hinduism makes the caste system (itself controlled by dharma) an aspect of cosmic order. Moreover, the order of the world includes the way the moral fabric of things is expressed through karma. My moral acts will bear fruits both in this life and in subsequent existences. So even if ultimately—as some believe—karma is controlled by God, there is still a natural mechanism that rewards good and punishes evil. This comes to be tied in with the idea of merit: The wise person acquires merit through his or her good deeds so that he or she may be reborn in more propitious circumstances.

In order to see in more detail how belief and spiritual practice affect ethics, it may be useful to sketch the dynamics of a number of systems.

I have already alluded to the way in which in the Buddhism of the Theravada ethical conduct is woven into the eightfold path and so becomes part of the means of attaining liberation. This helps explain why one of the five precepts of Buddhism forbids taking "drugs and intoxicants" (the word covers liquor and other things) because liquor clouds the mind and also arouses anger. The clouding of the mind must be avoided because the task of the saintly person is to cultivate clarity of consciousness and self-awareness. It is through this clarity that detached insight can be gained; such insight is liberating and can bring about ultimate decease and escape from the round of rebirth. Further, anger and allied emotions are the opposite of the peace that liberation should bring. So far, then, we can see the ban on drugs and liquor as fitting into the way a person should train himself or herself.

But not everyone is at all close to gaining nirvana. Monks and nuns are sometimes thought to be closer to attaining nirvana, but ordinary lay people may have their chance in some future life. The teaching of karma and rebirth binds together the differing layers of Buddhist society by projecting a person's career into the future beyond the grave. The ordinary person gains merit by virtuous acts in this life and hopes for some better state in the next. Indeed, the person who gives generously to the Order and follows the moral path may be reborn in a heaven. This heaven, though, is not everlasting. It is not the final goal. Here is a major difference between Buddhism and traditional Christianity. In Christianity the final judgment consigns people to heaven or hell. But in Buddhism, a person's merit is in due course exhausted, and he or she is obliged to disappear from paradise and be reborn in some other state—perhaps as a nun close to gaining nirvana. This is in accord with the Buddhist idea that all existence, including heavenly (and for that matter hellish) existence, is impermanent: Only nirvana is the Permanent, and it lies beyond existence, beyond this world and the next.

In brief, Theravada Buddhism has traditionally seen morality as part of the path that leads to nirvana, and as something that operates within a universe controlled by karma. Karma is the law of reward and penalty within the framework of rebirth, in which my status as human or animal or whatever results from my acts in previous lives. In Theravada Buddhism, morality is seen as partly a matter of being prudent—either because it helps achieve the state of final freedom and true happiness, or because at least it helps to give you a better life next time around. Morality also involves peace and, to some degree, withdrawal from the bustle of the world. This Buddhist moral code has two tiers: There is a higher, more severe, level of personal conduct for monks and nuns, and a less rigorous ethic for the laity and the mass of the people.

The ethic of Islam, in contrast, has quite a different atmosphere. For one thing, it does not (until we get to the mystical movement of inner quest known as Sufism) have two levels. It is a religion that applies equally to all men under Allah. The duality between the numinous Allah and his humble worshipers gives the latter a sense of equality and humility. Thus Islam (the word literally means "submission to God") contains a strong sense of brotherhood. It is true that, from a modern Western point of view, there is inequality for women. Islamic law and custom, stemming from the Qur'an and from the developing tradition, impose restrictions on women. Men can have up to four wives at once, but polyandry (that is, a woman having several husbands) is ruled out. Although it is not laid down in revelation, the custom of wearing the veil is widespread for women in Muslim countries. Even if women have property rights, and are protected by what in the time of the Prophet was essentially a reforming movement, some might think women's status inferior. But this is not the way orthodox Muslims view things. For them, Islamic law treats women and men as being separate and equal, because they have separate natures and functions.

The Otherness of Allah, which flows from the numinous character of the Prophet's revelations, means that all that is created is seen as coming from him; the laws by which people are supposed to live flow from him too. Thus the pattern of religious experience that was so central in the rise of Islam is consistent with, and indeed favors, the belief that there is a divinely instituted law. It happened also that early Islam saw itself as related to other revelations: So, too, in Islam there was Law, but Law with its own special features, for this was a new revelation to Muhammad that would set its seal upon the other traditions.

The emphasis on law also sprang from the strong sense of community in early Islam. Not only are all men under Allah brothers, but there is a particular community that has his blessing. The community was brought into being under the leadership of the Prophet, and before his death he succeeded in uniting a large part of the Arabs of his immediate region. The Islamic community was just embarking on those spectacular victories that stretched the new imperial power from Afghanistan to Morocco and from Spain to Iran. So the Law became the way the details of community life were defined. It covers much more than morals in the narrow sense: It embraces questions of finance, slavery, ritual, and so on.

Along with their moral teachings, religions tend to demand certain religious duties, such as keeping the Sabbath, going on pilgrimage, giving alms to the monastic order, and so on. They are religious duties rather than ethical ones in the sense that the latter directly concern people's dealings with other people. Religious duties deal especially with duties to God or duties to those who in some special way manifest religious truth. The idea behind such duties is often that they simply arise from the nature of faith: The person who loves God worships him, and this is a religious duty as well as being a result of such love. Sometimes they are seen as duties because they help bring about that kind of feeling that makes them a joy as well as an obligation. Sometimes they can be seen as a kind of exchange: The Buddhist who gives food to monks or nuns gets from them teachings that help him or her on the path toward perfection.

The importance of brotherhood and the community in Islam is seen in the requirement to give alms. The poor brother or sister is helped. The duty when called on to fight a *jihad;* or holy war, on behalf of Islam reflects the fact that Islam does not make a sharp division between Church and State. The aim is to build a society that is Islamic, and this may mean using all the levers of power, including war, against the enemies of Islam. Since Allah is, in essence, power—however much Allah may also be compassionate and merciful—it is not surprising that earthly power should be seen as a way of expressing and strengthening Allah's dominion. By contrast, Buddhism centers not on power but peace, even emptiness, and tends to have an "otherworldly" outlook. The problem of Buddhist kingship is the issue of how power can be used at all, for power may mean trampling on the lives of people, thus corrupting our consciousness and storing up bad forces of karma.

The contrast between the Islamic and Buddhist traditions comes out also in the figures of the great founders. Muhammad was not just a man of God; he was the skillful diplomat, statesman, and general. The Buddha, according to predictions at his birth, was either to become a political world-conqueror or a spiritual one. In leaving his princely palace and setting out on the quest for truth through poverty and homelessness, he gave up all worldly power. In return he gained enlightenment, and in fact helped shape the world that came after him. But there he was—the lone sage, lean from fasts, his eyes unmoving beneath the tree as he attained purity of consciousness and that inner light that for him lit up the nature of all the world and became the source of his teaching. He was diplomatic in his preaching skills, and kingly in his noble demeanor. But he was not literally either a diplomat or a politician, still less a general. Three centuries or so afterward, the Indian emperor Ashoka destroyed a neighboring people in his pursuit of wider imperial power, but he was so tormented by his aggressive actions that henceforth he tried to rule as a king of peace. At the heart of Buddhism lies a dilemma about power.

Christianity presents a third face. (And Buddhism, too, evolved a somewhat different emphasis in its later forms.) Christianity's face is that of Christ's, and he unites in himself motifs that help shape Christian ethics. Through much of Christian history, Christ basically has come in two guises: as the God who, becoming human, met death upon the Cross, and as the God who, risen into the heavens, comes to judge the living and the dead, at the dreadful and glorious end of human history. The first Christ is empty of power, in the worldly sense; the second is the essence of majesty. The one is the suffering Servant, the other the fearful Judge. All of this reflects the fact that Christians have seen Christ as both human and divine. He lives in two worlds: In our earthly world he bears the marks of humility and love, and in the other, the numinous power that belongs to the divine Being.

To some extent this ambiguity is found in the way the New and Old Testaments relate to each other. Christianity inherited much of the early Jewish tradition, but looked at it in a different way. It kept some of the old Law, notably the Ten Commandments, but it thought that Christ himself was now the pattern for living, and so his life, death, and resurrection brought in a new covenant; although Christians thought of the old covenant as part of the way God revealed himself to people—and to the people of Israel in particular—there was no need to follow the Law in the old way.

The two faces of Christ have given Christian morality a tendency toward inner struggle, thus, for the early Church, participation in warfare was wrong, as Christians sought to live a harmless and upright life. Yet the Church was the extension of God's power and had responsibility to the world God had created. When the Church came to dominate the Roman Empire, emphasis began to shift to theory of the "just" war. A war might justly be fought in self-defense; later also religious wars, known as the Crusades, became duties. Christ as judge came to be seen as the embodiment of power in the service of justice.

But at the heart of Christian morality is the ideal of *agape*, or reverential love: the love of God and neighbor. This love for other human beings extends to one's enemies, following the example of Christ, who said "Father, forgive them" from his Cross. This reverential love stems partly from the perception that every person is made in the image of the Creator and thus in the image of Christ himself.

Christian views of ethics are also much affected by the doctrine of the Fall. Judaism has not made of Genesis what the Christian tradition has. For Christianity, Adam's acts implicate the whole human race in a disaster, as a result of which human nature is corrupted. Humans are not able to be virtuous by themselves but need the help of God, through grace. The great emphasis on Original sin arises from the conviction that Christ's death made a critical difference to the relationship between God and the human race. So it was clear that the greatness of Christ as "second Adam" must be reflected in the vast significance of the first Adam's act, whereby he and Eve and all of us became separated from God. The salvation in Christ presupposed the Adamic disaster. Thus, Christianity has seen human nature as unable to perfect itself by human action—only by tapping the power or grace of Christ can the Christian grow in moral stature. A major thought of the early reformers, Luther in particular, was that the Roman Catholic Church suggested that people could (and should) improve their spiritual status by going on pilgrimages, giving to the Church and the poor, attending Mass, and so on. All of this suggested that people could gain something by performing good works, when it is only through God's grace (said Luther) that we can do anything good.

This position holds that much depends on the means of grace, that is, the way through which the Christian is supposed to receive the power of Christ. In much of mainstream Christianity, Catholic, and Orthodox, that power comes primarily through the sacraments, above all the Mass or divine Liturgy. For much of later Protestantism, the chief sacrament is the Word—Christ as found in the Bible and in preaching, stirring people to holy living. The sacraments stress the divine side of Christ; preaching often brings out the human side. In the one case we receive power through the action of God in ritual; in the other case we gain power through inspiration and the example of the man Jesus.

Many of the later disputes about details of morality spring from some of these ideas and practices. The Catholic Church's defense of marriage as a lifelong union and its opposition to divorce owe a lot to the notion that marriage is a divinely created sacrament. The sacrament of marriage confers God's inner grace and power on a couple and a family through the physical and social acts of living together. The

Christian debate with others over abortion stems from the question of the sanctity of human life, which in turn has to do with the doctrine that the individual is made in the image of God. And Christian social action, such as that of Mother Teresa of Calcutta, stems from this same sense of reverence for others, which is part of true love, following Jesus' example.

If Christian attitudes demonstrate a tension between this world and the other, so there is a tension in Buddhism between liberation and compassion. As we have seen, there is a certain prudence about right behavior: Being good helps toward the attainment of final release, or at least toward getting a better life next time around. But compassion for the suffering of others should mean sacrificing oneself, even one's own welfare. Even nirvana may have to be put off if one is to serve their suffering fellow beings. Out of this self-sacrifice there came to be—as we have seen—a strong emphasis in Greater Vehicle Buddhism on the figure of the Bodhisattva, the being destined for Buddhahood who nevertheless puts off his own salvation in order to stay in the world to help others. There were various figures of Bodhisattvas who came to be revered and worshipped, such as the great Bodhisattva Avalokitesvara who, as his name implies, "looks down" with compassion upon those who suffer in the world. The Bodhisattva was thought to have attained such a vast store of merit through his many lives of self-sacrifice (given that he had gained enough already to be "due" for nirvana) that he could distribute this immense surplus to others to help them on their way. Thus, the otherwise unworthy faithful person could, by calling on the Bodhisattva, gain extra merit bringing him or her closer to final release from suffering. So in many ways the Greater Vehicle idea runs parallel to Christianity. But instead of the idea of love or *agape*, in Buddhism compassion is central.

Just as in Christianity "living in the world," rather than withdrawals from the world, was emphasized, so in the Greater Vehicle the sharp cleft between nirvana over there (so to speak) and worldly life here, was called into question. It is possible for the Buddhist to pursue his or her ideal of imitating the Bodhisattva (indeed of *becoming* a Buddha-to-be) through living the good life in this world. Sometimes this had strange results. In medieval Japan the warrior class came to see techniques like archery and swordplay as methods which, if suitably adapted, could teach selflessness. In this manner even warfare would be a means of gaining higher insight. On the whole, however, Buddhist ethics have been eager to minimize violence.

THE NATURE OF MORALITY

In all these examples we can see that ethics is not treated in isolation, and what is right and wrong is seen in the light of a wider cosmic vision. Yet in modern philosophy, especially since Kant in the late-eighteenth century, there has been a quest to establish what Kant called the "autonomy," or independence, of morals.

Philosophers have tried to show that right and wrong can be defined independently of some wider superstructure of belief. What is right and wrong is right and wrong not because God or the Buddha says so: God or the Buddha says so because he sees what is right and wrong. What is right is right because it is right on its own account, not because God says so. Kant thought the test of what is right and wrong is the so-called categorical imperative, to which he gave various formulations.

In essence, the categorical imperative amounted to a two-sided demand. One side holds that anything moral beings will must, to be right, be capable of being a universal law, that is, a law that all can follow. The other side holds that one should treat another human being always as an end in himself or herself and never merely as a means. Kant thought these principles were categorical, not hypothetical. A categorical imperative is absolute; it applies unconditionally. A hypothetical imperative is, by contrast, one that applies only if some condition is met. For instance, the imperative, "If you want to avoid lung cancer, give up smoking" is hypothetical, because it depends on a condition, namely that you want to avoid lung cancer. You might not care. But (according to Kant), "Do not steal" is unconditional. It applies whatever your desires are. Indeed, typically, moral imperatives run contrary to what you want. A moral demand is one that one can will to become a universal law. Thus, stealing cannot become universal without a contradiction. If people did not refrain from stealing there would be, could be, no private property; without property there would be nothing to steal. Likewise, it would be self-contradictory to imagine universal lying. If

everyone lied, there could be no orderly system of communication, and language would collapse. So the very use of language presupposes truth-telling.

Kant thought also that the categorical imperative as a test of what is right and wrong is not something imposed on the individual from outside. To act morally one has to revere the moral law and apply it to oneself. So each moral person is a legislator and, in a sense, the source of morality. It is presupposed that all people, as the source of morality, are to be given reverence. Hence, the second formulation of the categorical imperative requires us to treat another person never merely as a means but also always as an end in him- or herself. So treating a person, say a prostitute, merely as a means for producing pleasure, is an offense against the moral law.

All this implies that we can by reason establish what is right and wrong; morality does not have any external source, not even God. It derives, as I have said, from each person as his or her own moral legislator.

But although Kant argued for the independence of morality, and so was the forerunner of many other Western thinkers who believe that you can have "morals without religion," he thought that from a practical perspective God was presupposed by the moral law. It seems incongruous that virtue should not be matched by happiness. But in this world it is not possible for the virtuous person to gain the bliss that he or she deserves. Moreover, it is not even possible in our brief lives to achieve absolute goodness or moral perfection. We can only attain an approximation. Yet, in principle, the moral law makes absolute demands on us. Kant thought that the demands of the moral law in practice indicate that we should live on after death, and that God should in the end match our virtue with full happiness. So God and immortality are practical outcomes of the demands of the moral law. Although morality does not derive from God, we can infer a God from the moral law.

Instead of immortality, Kant could no doubt have thought of reincarnation as an alternative model of the upward striving for ultimate perfection. Had he been an Indian he might have come to very different conclusions about the presuppositions of the moral law, and karma might have taken the place of God. What appear to us as reasonable conclusions from within the perspective of our own culture may in fact look different from another cultural perspective. There are other problems with Kant's position. Not all moral rules conform to his test. Although he may rightly think that stealing and lying contain, if universalized, an inner contradiction, this does not so obviously apply (for example) to incest. We could imagine a society that does not have a strict rule against incest. Perhaps it would not break down, although it might be inferior to ours. There are also problems with the exceptions that inevitably seem to have to be made to any rule. Wouldn't stealing bread to feed a starving child be justified if there were no other way to get food? Kant's doctrines have been subject to much debate. Refinements of his approach—what might be called the logical approach—to morality have been made in modern times. But partly because of difficulties in his position, many modern philosophers have looked to consequences as holding the key to right and wrong.

In this view, known as utilitarianism, the test of a rule, an institution, or an action is whether it brings the greatest happiness to the greatest number of people and/or the least suffering to the least number. Stealing becomes wrong not only because it harms individuals, but also because it encourages people who militate against society. There are problems with the utilitarian view as well. What if sacrificing a small minority led to greater happiness for the majority? We might justify treating people merely as means if all we were interested in was worldwide happiness or suffering. Kill a person for some crime, in order to keep society orderly and make people safer and happier: Is this not treating the criminal just as a means? The next thing we know, we might treat noncriminals in the same way.

A NORMATIVE VIEW

Already we are sliding into questions of what is normative. What is actually right or wrong? Up to now we have been trying to look at patterns of ethical thought in relation to the religious ideas and practices that shape them. What I now venture to say on what I think to be right and wrong is only one opinion (I have no special authority), and there can be many others. But it might be interesting for you to think about some of the ideas that occur to someone, like myself, who has immersed himself in the comparative study of religion and of comparative religious ethics.

The first thing to examine is that we live in a global city in which different cultures and worldviews interact. When one group seeks to impose its standards on a group that does not share the same values, conflict arises. So it seems to me that there is a great case for religious toleration, and for a form of society in which there can be genuine plurality of beliefs and values. This toleration should breed an ethic of what might be called social personalism: I respect the social values of the other person because I respect the person in question—what another loves I love (in a way) because I love that person.

But second, it seems to me that the purport of religion is to stress the spiritual life—worship of God, a vision of the goodness of the world, the practice of meditation, a perception of the impermanence of things, and so on. Morality has to be related to such spiritual vision and life. It is true that the religions do not agree by any means and their atmospheres often greatly differ; but they still are like fingers pointing at the moon: they point to what lies beyond. This pointing to what lies beyond challenges the "worldly" notions of happiness and welfare that often enter into the calculations of modern folk, in the utilitarian tradition. True peace of spirit can (I would suggest, from a religious angle) be achieved only if one is in relationship to what lies Beyond. What is needed is *transcendental* humanism: prizing human welfare but seeing it in the light of a vision of what is eternal.

We can learn something from the tension in religion between the dynamic power of the numinous experience and the tranquility of the mystical. There is a tension, too, between the divine and human sides of Christ, and between the other worldly and this-worldly sides of insight and compassion in Buddhism. The religious person should not shrink from action in the world, and we should welcome the turbulence of human creativity and drive. But it has to have a balancing sense of peace. Thus it would seem to me that at times we cannot shrink from the use of force; society needs it to maintain order, and nations and classes may need protection from genocide and slavery. But the true aim should always be to minimize violence. As we sometimes cause pain to minimize pain, as in surgery, so we may use force to minimize violence. This attitude is often not reflected in the machismo of police forces or the nationalist hatreds of the military, although they often say that their true aim is order and peace. Force and violence are distasteful, and because they are minimally needed their excessive and common use should not be condoned.

Ultimately we need the sense of the Beyond in order to see anew the sacredness of the person. In a sense, each person is a world, a cosmos in itself. The world is alive when the cosmos and human consciousness interact, and the fields are lit up with green, the sky with blue, the birds with fluttering motion, the rain with wetness, and the sun with warmth. From my cosmos I should revere the world of others. Persons are in this way like gods: they should be treated with reverence in their creativity and joy, and with compassion in their lonely suffering. Religions give differing expressions to the overarching meaning attached to each individual. Faith helps us see the immortal dignity of each person.

Religions have often used force on people and have often been intolerant. In our own day, secular worldviews have engaged in force and practiced intolerance of human values. But perhaps because of this, the religious and secular worldviews can learn from mutual criticism.

Concepts and Questions

1. What does Smart mean when he says "the ethical dimension of a religion or worldview is shaped by the other dimensions, but it also helps to shape them"?
2. Give some examples of why Smart believes that ethical systems based on nonreligious principles such as utilitarianism or secular humanism fail to adequately meet the needs of an ethical system.
3. Give examples of the commonalities among major faiths regarding moral conduct.
4. How does Smart differentiate between religious duties and ethical or moral duties?
5. From Smart's perspective, how does living in a global city affect the development of an ethic for intercultural communication?
6. What are some of the conditions that would have to exist in order to develop such an ethic?
7. According to Smart, how does a sense of the Beyond relate to the development of an ethical system?
8. What lesson do you believe can be learned from having knowledge about both religious and secular worldviews?
9. How easy or difficult would you find the task of building a cross-cultural ethic based on Smart's discussion of religious and secular worldviews?
10. If you were assigned to work in a foreign culture for an extended period, how easy or difficult would it be for you to construct an appropriate cross-cultural ethic?

Index

social order in, 438–439
worldviews in, 30, 31–34
Ebonics, 195, 204
Economic issues
collectivism and, 25
Egyptian worldview and, 166
geography and, 429
globalization's influence on, 7
indigenous worldview and, 58n36
Western mind-set and, 60
Education
about Islam, 168–169
of African American students, 348
discourse structures in, 350
diversity of communication styles in, 351–362
in German culture, 305–306, 311n12
increased diversity and, 288, 293
in Japanese culture, 294, 366–375
in Jewish American culture, 77
in Kenyan culture, 252, 256
median incomes and, 321
of U.S. immigrants, 194–195
U.S. pluralism and, 189
Effectiveness, 381
Efficacy beliefs, 384
Efficiency, 381
Ego, 41–42, 94–95
Egypt, 132, 244
Egyptian culture, 24, 132, 163–170
Elementary school education, 367–368
Ellis, Donald G., 234, 244–250
Emblems, 267
Emotional expression, 21–22, 43, 266
in classrooms, 356
of girls versus boys, 361
in Indian business communications, 159–160
in individualistic versus collectivist cultures, 271
stereotypes and, 321–322
Whiteness and, 321–322
Emotional sensitivity, 42, 137–138
Employment transients, 119–121
Encapsulated marginality, 448
English language, 20, 238, 242, 330–331

Enlightenment mentality, 39, 40
Environment
conservation issues related to, 7, 34, 41
cultural diversity and, 428–429
definition of, 9
Environmental mobility, 396–397
Episodic system, of analysis, 382, 387–390
Equality, 187, 188–190, 320–321
Erabi, 130, 142
Essentialism, 452–453
Ethics, 32
Asiacentric worldview and, 44, 45
integration and, 447–457
religious worldviews and, 459–467
Ethnic conflicts
cognitive syndromes and, 22, 24–25
context versus content in, 18
current issues with, 16
dynamics of culture and, 12
See also Warfare
Ethnic groups
argument and, 248
cultural diffusion and, 12
cultural diversity within, 427–428
domination of, 426–427
function of culture and, 11
Jews as, 70
as model minorities, 72
U.S. assimilation of, 187–188
in U.S. workforce, 320–321
See also specific groups
Ethnic identity
of Chinese Americans, 97–102
definition of, 93
of Korean adoptees, 106–114
theoretical foundations of, 94–96
See also Identity
Ethnic jokes, 75–76
ETHNIC model, 332–333
Ethnic nationalist groups, 192
Ethnocentrism
in Chinese culture, 61–62
learning about cultures and, 38
out-groups and, 25
overview of, 12–13, 25
in Western culture, 60, 61–62
Etiquette, 60–61, 299–300, 331

Euro-American culture
educational experiences in, 354–357
emotional expression in, 266, 271
eye contact in, 15
Mexican combination with, 235
narratives in, 240
origins of, 424
racialization and, 316
speech communities of, 238
worldviews of, 4
Eurocentrism, 38, 39–40
Europe, 429
European culture
genetic differences in, 427
immediacy in, 276
language in, 20
student/teacher perspective of, 40
uncertainty in, 274
Evanoff, Richard, 422–423, 447–459
Evil eye, 328
Exclusion Act, 94
Exclusionary practices, 319, 320
Expectancy fulfillment, 388–389
Experiential approach, 398
Expressive cultures, 21
Expressiveness, 386
Extension transference, 440
Extremist views, 192–193, 194
Eye contact, 15, 158, 267

Face, 141, 157–158, 174–175
Face negotiation theory, 133, 172–177
Face recognition, 265–266
Facial expressions, 266
False consensus, 18
Family interpreters, 331
Family structures
of Chinese Americans, 97–99, 101
and cultural distance, 18
in Eastern versus Western cultures, 137–138
in Jewish American culture, 77
in Kenya, 175–176, 251–252
Korean adoptees in, 105–114
lesbian/gay disclosure and, 224
Mexican dichos and, 262–263
personal space in, 283
in U.S. interethnic families, 195

Whiteness (Contd.)
  research history of, 80–81
  as social structure, 84, 316–317
  unconscious habits of, 317
  U.S. workforce and, 291–292
Wilde, Oscar, 226
Wipro Technologies, 159
Wisdom, 37
Wittgenstein, Ludwig, 61
Women
  classroom communication style
    of, 351, 359–361
  in feminine versus masculine
    cultures, 273–274
  in Kenya, 176
  in Muslim faith, 167–168
  religious ethics and, 462
  sexual assault of, 413–418
  in U.S. versus German
    businesses, 303
Workforce
  access to jobs in, 319–320
  in Germany, 307–311, 311n13

  in Japan, 295–301
  in United States, 291–292
World Bank, 60
World War II, 94, 303, 304, 428
Worldviews
  change process and, 34–35
  definition of, 14, 29, 38
  elements of, 29–30
  environmental issues and, 34, 41
  ethical dimension of, 459–467
  examples of, 14
  formation of, 30–31
  hierarchies and, 37–39
  importance of, 28–29
  learning about/from cultures
    and, 38–40
  overview of, 3–4
  religion and, 30, 31–34, 49–54
  structures of, 4, 48–49
  types of, 31
  See also specific worldviews
Writing, 356, 357, 358
Wu wei, 148

Yellow Emperor's Cannon of Internal
    Medicine, 324
Yiddish, 75
Yin/yang, 131, 148, 149, 437
Yugoslavia, 431, 432

Zaire River, 429
Zanzibar, 429
Zarathustra, 50, 51
Zemi, 370
Zen Buddhism, 42, 43, 268
Zero doctrine, 147
Zhong, Mei, 67, 93–104
Zimbabwe, 59
Zimmerman, A. L., 67, 87–92
Zionism, 244
Zoroastrianism, 50, 56n12